Lecture Notes in Computer Science 1292

Edited by G. Goos, J. Hartmanis and J. van Leeuwen

Advisory Board: W. Brauer   D. Gries   J. Stoer

T0223721

Springer
Berlin
Heidelberg
New York
Barcelona
Budapest
Hong Kong
London
Milan
Paris
Santa Clara
Singapore
Tokyo

Hugh Glaser   Pieter Hartel
Herbert Kuchen (Eds.)

Programming Languages: Implementations, Logics, and Programs

9th International Symposium, PLILP'97
Including a Special Track on Declarative
Programming Languages in Education
Southampton, UK, September 3-5, 1997
Proceedings

 Springer

Series Editors

Gerhard Goos, Karlsruhe University, Germany

Juris Hartmanis, Cornell University, NY, USA

Jan van Leeuwen, Utrecht University, The Netherlands

Volume Editors

Hugh Glaser
Pieter Hartel
University of Southampton, Department of Electronics and Computer Science
Southampton SO17 1BJ, UK
E-mail: (hg,phh)@ecs.soton.ac.uk

Herbert Kuchen
Westfälische Wilhelms-Universität Münster, Institut für Wirtschaftsinformatik
Grevener Str. 91, D-48149 Münster, Germany
E-mail: herbert@helios.uni-muenster.de

Cataloging-in-Publication data applied for

Die Deutsche Bibliothek - CIP-Einheitsaufnahme

Programming languages : implementations, logics and programs ;
9th international symposium ; proceedings / PLILP '97, Southampton,
UK, September 1 - 3, 1997 ; including a special track on declarative
programming languages in education / Hugh Glaser ... (ed.). - Berlin ;
Heidelberg ; New York ; Barcelona ; Budapest ; Hong Kong ;
London ; Milan ; Paris ; Santa Clara ; Singapore ; Tokyo : Springer,
1997
  (Lecture notes in computer science ; Vol. 1292)
  ISBN 3-540-63398-7

CR Subject Classification (1991): D.1.1, D.1.6, D.3.1, D.3.4,F.3.1, F.3.3,
F.4.1-3, K.3.2, I.1.3, I.2.1

ISSN 0302-9743
ISBN 3-540-63398-7 Springer-Verlag Berlin Heidelberg New York

© Springer-Verlag Berlin Heidelberg 1997
Printed in Germany

Typesetting: Camera-ready by author
SPIN 10546391   06/3142 – 5 4 3 2 1 0   Printed on acid-free paper

Preface

This volume contains the proceedings of the *Ninth International Symposium on Programming Languages, Implementations, Logics, and Programs*, PLILP'97. It was held in Southampton, UK, in conjunction with the *Sixth International Conference on Algebraic and Logic Programming*, ALP'97, and the *Third International Workshop on Higher-Order Algebra, Logic and Term Rewriting*, HOA'97. The previous PLILP meetings took place in Orléans, France (1988), Linköping, Sweden (1990), Passau, Germany (1991), Leuven, Belgium (1992), Tallinn, Estonia (1993), Madrid, Spain (1994), Utrecht, The Netherlands (1995), and Aachen, Germany (1996). All proceedings have been published by Springer-Verlag as Lecture Notes in Computer Science volumes 348, 456, 528, 631, 714, 844, 982 and 1140.

The PLILP symposium aims at stimulating research on declarative programming languages, and seeks to disseminate insights in the relation between implementation techniques, the logics of those languages, and the use of these languages in constructing real programs. Topics of interest include implementation of declarative concepts, integration of paradigms, compiler specification and construction, program analysis and transformation, programming environments, executable specifications, reasoning about language constructs, experiences in constructing applications, and typing and structuring systems.

The cooperation with ALP and HOA, together with a special track on declarative programming languages in education, has strengthened the attractiveness of the overall event and – as a consequence – the quality of the presentations. The quality and number of submitted papers serves as an indication of the success of this approach. Out of 68 submissions, 25 papers (37%) were selected, as well as some poster and system demonstrations. In addition to the selected contributions, invited talks were given by Neil Jones and Guy Cousineau.

The special track on declarative programming languages in education represents the state of the art in teaching methods using functional and logic languages. It followed the successful Symposium on *Functional Programming Languages in Education*, held in Nijmegen, The Netherlands, in 1995, and which appeared as Springer-Verlag LNCS volume 1022. These papers on education were selected by a separate programme committee chaired by Krzysztof Apt, Paul Klint, and Pieter Hartel.

All communication in organising the symposium was done electronically: submitting papers, distributing papers to reviewers, transmitting and discussing reviews among the program committee members, and giving feedback to the authors. This helped both to reduce the cost of organising the symposium and to keep the time between the deadline for submissions and the conference short.

On behalf of the two programme committees we thank all those who submitted papers. We thank the referees for their careful work in the reviewing and selection process.

Hugh Glaser and Pieter Hartel, Southampton
Herbert Kuchen, Münster   June 1997

Programme Committee

Programme Committee of the Special Track on Education

Referees

B. Aarts, Lex Augusteijn, Maria Garcia de la Banda, Frank van den Beuken, Paul Blampied, George Horatiu Botorog, Francisco Bueno Carrillo, Manuel Chakravarty, Olaf Chitil, Justin Cormack, Agostino Cortesi, M. Danelutto, Anthony Daniels, Bart Demoen, Thierry Despeyroux, Roberto Di Cosmo, Remi Douence, Dirk Dussart, Moreno Falaschi, Pascal Fradet, Maurizio Gabbrielli , Benedict R. Gaster, Roberto Giacobazzi, Ana Gil-Luezas, Hugh Glaser, J.C. Gonzalez-Moreno, P. Gorissen, Steve Gregory, Yike Guo, John Hannan, Fritz Henglein, Pascal Van Hentenryck, Graham Hutton, Tetsuo Ida, Suresh Jagannathan, Paul Jansen, Gerda Janssens, David Jeffery, Thomas Jensen, Mark P. Jones, Peter Kacsuk, Andy King, F.E.J. Kruseman Aretz, Herbert Kuchen, Konstantin Laufer, Julia Lawall, Daniel Le Métayer, Javier Leach, Martin Leucker, John Lloyd, Rita Loogen, Francisco Lopez Fraguas, Salvador Lucas, Andrew Macdonald, Dale Miller, M. Mohnen, Juan José Moreno-Navarro, Angelo Montanari, Luc Moreau, Martin Müller, Tobias Müller, Peter Moller Neergaard, Zsolt Nemeth, Joachim Niehren, Hanne Riis Nielson, Susana Nieva., Henning Niss, Javier Oliver, Wouter van Oortmerssen, Jukka Paakki, Norbert Podhorszki, German Puebla, Zsolt Puskas, Christian Queinnec, Mario Rodriguez-Artalejo, Mads Rosendahl, Konstantinos Sagonas, Vladimiro Sassone, Mitsuhisa Sato, Christian Schulte, Jens Peter Secher, Kish Shen, Etsuya Shibayama, Yuka Shimajiri, Gert Smolka, Zoltan Somogyi, Harald Sondergaard, Morten Heine Sorensen, Michael Sperber, Paul Steckler, Mario Suedholt, Taro Suzuki, Kazuko Takahashi, Yukihide Takayama, Jorma Tarhio, Colin J. Taylor, Peter Thiemann, Germán Vidal, Hing Wing To, Jörg Würtz

Referees for the Special Track on Education

Krzysztof Apt, Silvia Breitinger, Maurice Bruynooghe, Pierre Deransart, Marko van Eekelen, Matthias Felleisen, Daniel Friedman, Alfons Geser, Bob Harper, Pieter Hartel, Pascal van Hentenryck, Manuel Hermenegildo, Angel Herranz-Nieva, Paul Hudak, John Hughes, Juan José Moreno-Navarro, Paul Klint, Jacques Loeckx, Rita Loogen, Julio Mario, John O'Donnell, Rinus Plasmeijer, Jacques Riche, Karel de Vlaeminck, David Warren

The PLILP '97 conference was organised in cooperation with the British Computer Society, the Association of Logic Programming, the European Association for Programming Languages and Systems and Compulog Net (the ESPRIT Network of Excellence in Computational Logic).

Table of Contents

Compilation

Evaluation

Education: Invited Paper

Education: Methodologies

Education: Tools and Themes

Poster Presentations

Narrowing the Narrowing Space[*]

Sergio Antoy[1] and Zena M. Ariola[2]

[1] Portland State University
[2] University of Oregon

Abstract. We introduce a framework for managing as a whole the space of a narrowing computation. The aim of our framework is to find a finite representation of an infinite narrowing space. This, in turn, allows us to replace an infinite enumeration of computed answers with an equivalent finite representation. We provide a semidecidable condition for this result. Our framework is intended to be used by implementations of functional logic programming languages. Our approach borrows from the memoization technique used in the implementation of functional languages. Since narrowing adds non-determinism and unifiers to functional evaluation, we develop a new approach based on graphs to memoize the outcome of a goal.

Keywords Functional logic programming, Narrowing, Narrowing space, Computed expression, Regular computed expression, Finite representation.

1 Introduction

A fundamental problem in the integration of functional and logic programming is how to deal with the fact that the execution of a program may lead to the evaluation of a functional expression containing uninstantiated logic variables. Both narrowing and residuation have been proposed for this problem. Residuation delays the evaluation of functional expressions that contain uninstantiated logic variables. It is conceptually simple and relatively efficient, but incomplete, i.e., unable to compute the results of a computation in some cases. By contrast, narrowing is complete if an appropriate strategy is chosen but has the propensity to generate infinite search spaces. When this situation arises, narrowing becomes incomplete in practice in the sense that it cannot compute, with finite resources, the complete solution of a goal. This paper partially fixes this problem.

The last decade has seen the discovery of many narrowing strategies, e.g., [2,4,6,8–11,13,14,16,17,20–24,26,27]. Recent optimality results [2,3] seem to suggest that the contribution of narrowing strategies alone to the efficient execution of functional logic computations has reached its theoretical limit. Yet, we will explain with some examples that the application of these strategies leaves much

---

[*] This work has been supported in part by the National Science Foundation under grants CCR-9406751, CCR-9410237, CCR-9624711.

to desire in practice. The focus of this paper is in "managing" a narrowing strategy by aiming at a finite representation, in the form of a possibly cyclic graph, of the narrowing space of a goal. While there is no guarantee that we will succeed, if we do we are able to provide a simple finite representation of the set of the goal's computed expressions.

Section 3 describes our framework. We discuss how to finitely represent the possibly infinite narrowing space of a goal, and prove soundness and completeness of our representation. We investigate known and new techniques for increasing the chances of obtaining a finite representation of a narrowing space. We show how to obtain a finite representation of an infinite set of computed expressions from a finite representation of a narrowing space.

2 Preliminaries

Rewriting, see [7,19] for tutorials, is a computational paradigm convenient for studying functional and functional logic computations. A rewrite program is a set of rewrite rules or oriented equations, pairs of terms denoted by $l = r$, where l is a pattern and all the variables of r are in l. Rewriting a term t into u, written as $t \rightarrow u$, is the operation of obtaining u by replacing in t an instance of some rule left-hand side l with the corresponding instance of the right-hand side r. For example, consider the program that defines addition on the natural numbers represented in unary notation,

```
0 + y   = y
s x + y = s (x + y)
```

and term t defined as $s\ (s\ 0) + 0$. According to the second rule, instantiated by $\{x \mapsto s\ 0, y \mapsto 0\}$, term t rewrites into $s\ (s\ 0 + 0)$. Additional rewrite steps eventually yield $s\ (s\ 0)$ which is a normal form, i.e., it cannot be rewritten and is understood to be the result of the computation.

Narrowing differs from rewriting by using unification instead of pattern matching, but is identical to rewriting in most other aspects. For example, term t defined as $u + 0$ is narrowed into 0, written as $u + 0 \leadsto_{\{u \mapsto 0\}} 0$, as follows. Term t is first instantiated to $0 + 0$ by $\{u \mapsto 0\}$. Then, $0 + 0$ is rewritten as usual. Choosing instantiations and rewrites is the task of a narrowing strategy. Narrowing is often used in functional logic programming for its ability to solve equations, i.e., computing unifiers with respect to an equational theory [10]. For example, consider the equation $u + s\ 0 == s\ (s\ 0)$, where "$==$" denotes the equality predicate. The second rule is applied to the equation by instantiating u to $s\ w$ obtaining $s\ (w + s\ 0) == s\ (s\ 0)$. Then, the first rule is applied by instantiating w to 0. The resulting equation, $s\ (s\ 0) == s\ (s\ 0)$, is trivially (syntactically) true. The composition of $\{u \mapsto s\ w\}$ with $\{w \mapsto 0\}$ contains $\{u \mapsto s\ 0\}$ which is the equation's solution.

The functional expressions narrowed in the examples presented in this paper are boolean expressions and are referred to as *goals*. Considering only goals is not a limitation. To evaluate a functional expression t, regardless of its type, we solve the equation (goal) $t == x$, where x is a new variable. The equality symbol

"==" is an overloaded operator defined by a few rules for each type. Below we show these rules for the natural numbers.

```
0 == 0      = true
s _ == 0    = false
0 == s _    = false
s x == s y  = x == y
```

This definition, known as *strict equality*, is more appropriate than syntactic equality when computations may not terminate. It is easy to generalize the rules above to other types.

Our framework is largely independent of the narrowing strategy. In all our examples we employ the strategy presented in [2].

3 The Framework

Memoization [25] is a technique aimed at improving the performance of functional languages. A memoized function remembers the arguments to which it has been applied together with the results it generates on them. If it is applied to the same argument again it returns the stored result rather than repeating the computation. Although memoization entails an overhead, it may provide substantial benefits. For example, consider the program that defines the Fibonacci function:

```
fib 0         = 0
fib (s 0)     = s 0
fib (s (s x)) = fib (s x) + fib x
```

It is easy to see that the computational complexity of *fib* is exponential in its argument. The culprit is the third rule, since for any $n > 1$ it requires twice the computation of *fib* $(n-2)$. Memoization has a dramatic effect on the complexity of *fib*. Once either one of the two addends originating from the right-hand side of the third rule is computed, the other addend is computed in constant time. Thus, the computational complexity of *fib* changes from exponential to linear.

Extending memoization to narrowing is not straightforward, since the result of a narrowing computation can be an infinite collection of substitutions or computed expressions. This situation creates new problems, but also the opportunity for benefits greater than those arising in purely functional computations.

We introduce our framework with an example. Let us extend the definition of addition given earlier with the rules defining the usual "less than or equal to" relational operator.

```
0 <= y      = true
s x <= 0    = false
s x <= s y  = x <= y
```

Consider the goal $u \leq u+v$, where u is an uninstantiated variable. The narrowing computation of this goal non-deterministically takes either of two paths:

$$u \leq u + v \overset{+}{\leadsto}_{\{u \mapsto 0\}} true \qquad \text{or} \qquad u \leq u + v \overset{+}{\leadsto}_{\{u \mapsto s\ w\}} w \leq w + v$$

(the superscript + stands for one or more narrowing steps). The second path yields a goal equal to the original one, except for a renaming of w, hence the goal's narrowing space is infinite. It is easy to verify that a complete narrowing strategy computes on $u \leq u + v$ the infinite set of substitutions $\{\{u \mapsto 0\}, \{u \mapsto s\ 0\}, \{u \mapsto s\ (s\ 0)\}, \ldots\}$. If, during this computation, we recognize that $w \leq w + v$ is (a variant of) a problem that has been already tackled, we achieve two major advantages: We save a good deal of computation, and we obtain a finite representation of the narrowing space. This representation, shown in the left part of Figure 1, is a graph whose edges are narrowing steps composed with permutations, i.e., renaming of variables. The label of an edge shows the substitution of its starting node's variables.

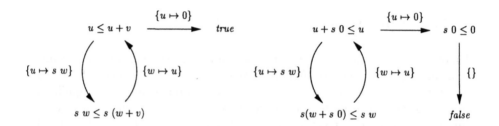

Fig. 1. Graph representation of the narrowing space of two goals.

A finite representation of the narrowing space has the potential of replacing an infinite computation with a finite one. By analyzing the finite representation of the narrowing space we infer that our goal is satisfied for all u. This allows us to replace an infinite enumeration of the goal's solutions with a single, simpler, more general solution. Equally important, we may discover that a goal has no solutions. For example, if we apply the same reasoning to the goal $u + s\ 0 \leq u$, we obtain the finite representation shown in the right part of Figure 1. From it we infer that the goal has no solutions. In contrast, the direct application of a narrowing strategy to this goal keeps looking forever for a solution that does not exist.

3.1 Space Representation

There are two differences between the functional evaluation of an expression and narrowing which affect how to memoize functional logic computations. The first difference concerns the outcome of a narrowing computation. In functional logic programming one is interested in narrowing computations of the form $t_0 \leadsto_{\sigma_1} t_1 \leadsto_{\sigma_2} \cdots \leadsto_{\sigma_n} t_n$, where t_n is a constructor term. The result of this computation is the *computed expression* $\sigma_1 \circ \cdots \circ \sigma_n \llbracket t_n$, i.e., t_n is the normal form of $\sigma_n(\cdots \sigma_1(t_0) \cdots)$.

The second relevant difference concerns non-determinism. Functional computations are *don't care* non-deterministic, i.e., for a complete evaluation strategy, all reduction choices lead to the same result. Functional logic computations are *don't know* non-deterministic, i.e., different narrowing choices lead to possibly different results as shown in Figure 2. Narrowing computations are not linear sequences of steps, but rather trees of steps whose branches often cannot be joined together. Non-determinism leads to a large, possibly infinite, set of results that is inconvenient or impossible to store directly.

This consideration suggests a strategy of initially memoizing the results of a single narrowing step of a goal, rather than trying to accumulate the entire set of its computed expressions. We choose to store this information as a graph. The vertices of the graphs are goals, i.e., terms being narrowed, and the edges are narrowing steps between these goals. Generally, we are interested only in the substitution of a narrowing step. Thus, we discard the rule and the position of the step and we label an edge with the step's substitution. Terms that differ only by a renaming of variables are considered to be the same vertex. This decision, of course, raises some concerns that we will address shortly.

Definition 1. Let g be a goal. A *graph representation* of the narrowing space of g computed by a strategy S is a finite rooted directed labeled graph G such that g is the root vertex of G, and if t is a vertex of G, $t \rightsquigarrow_\sigma t'$ according to strategy S iff for some permutation μ, $\mu(t')$ is a vertex of G and there is an edge in G from t to $\mu(t')$ with label $\sigma \circ \mu$.

There may exist many graph representations of the narrowing space of a goal. Representations with a smaller number of vertices are more desirable in our framework. A procedure that from a goal g attempts to construct a graph representation of the narrowing space of g is straightforward to implement from Definition 1.

We wish to reason about the narrowing derivations of a goal g by unfolding (traversing paths of) a graph representation, when it exists, of g's narrowing space. Since a graph may identify terms that differ by a renaming of variables, it could happen that the "derivations" that we unfold from the graph do not belong to the narrowing space of g. In fact, this indeed happens in general. Consider a program that computes the leftmost decoration of a binary tree.

```
leftmost (leaf x)     = x
leftmost (branch l _) = leftmost l
```

A graph representation of the narrowing space of the goal *leftmost t == c*, where t is an uninstantiated variable and c is a normal form of the decoration type, has an edge beginning and ending at the goal itself with label $\{t \mapsto branch\ t\ \_\}$. This edge does not correspond to a narrowing step, since it is well-known that the unifier of a narrowing step is an idempotent substitution. However, this is not a problem for derivations ending in a constructor term, which are the only derivations that we care about.

The *narrowing space* of a goal g computed by a strategy S is the set of the narrowing derivations starting from g whose steps are computed by S. Since every time that we use a rule R in a step we consider a variant of R with new variables, narrowing derivations that differ only for a renaming of these variables compute *equivalent* substitutions, i.e., substitutions differing only by permutations. If G is a labeled graph whose edges are labeled by substitutions, the substitution *computed* by a path P of G is the composition of the labels of P's edges.

Proposition 2. *Let G be a graph representation of a goal's g narrowing space computed by a strategy S.*

- *If P is a non-empty path of G that connects g to a constructor term g' and computes δ, then $g \overset{+}{\leadsto}_{\delta'} g'$, for some δ' equivalent to δ. (Soundness)*
- *If $g \overset{+}{\leadsto}_{\delta} g'$, where g' is a constructor term, is a narrowing derivation computed by S, then there exists a path P in G that connects g to g' and computes a substitution equivalent to δ. (Completeness)*

Proof. (Soundness) The proof is by induction on the length of P. Base case: P consists of a single edge. Since g and g' are distinct vertices of G and g' is either *true* or *false*, the claim is immediate. Ind. case: Let P consist of an initial edge (g, t) with label ρ followed by a non-empty path P' that computes substitution ρ'. By definition of graph representation, there exists a permutation μ such that $\rho = \sigma \circ \mu$ and $g \leadsto_\sigma \mu^{-1}(t)$ is a narrowing step. By the induction hypothesis, there exists a substitution $\bar\rho'$ equivalent to ρ' such that $t \overset{+}{\leadsto}_{\bar\rho'} g'$. $t \overset{+}{\leadsto}_{\bar\rho'} g'$ implies that $\mu^{-1}(t) \overset{+}{\leadsto}_{\mu \circ \rho''} g'$, for some substitution ρ'' equivalent to $\bar\rho'$. Since the equivalence of substitutions is a transitive relation, ρ' and ρ'' are equivalent as well and there exists a permutation τ such that $\rho' = \rho'' \circ \tau$. Thus there exists a narrowing derivation of g to g' that computes the substitution $\sigma \circ \mu \circ \rho''$. Since $\sigma = \rho \circ \mu^{-1}$, this is $\rho \circ \rho''$, i.e., $\rho \circ \rho' \circ \tau$ which is equivalent to the substitution computed by P. (Completeness) By definition of graph representation, for each step of $g \overset{+}{\leadsto}_{\delta} g'$ computed by S there is a corresponding edge in G, hence there is a path P, connecting g to g', associated to the entire derivation. Using a technique similar to that used in the proof of soundness, it can be verified that P computes a substitution equivalent to δ. □

There are a number of options to consider when building the narrowing space of a goal. One is whether to look for a single computed expression or for an enumeration of computed expressions. Another is whether to construct the narrowing space depth-first (for efficiency) or breadth-first (for completeness). Some of these options could be left to the programmer via annotations in a program or could be decided from program analysis. A third option deserving further investigation is iterative deepening, which compromises between depth- and breadth-first. We will discuss later how iterative deepening allows us to find all the solutions of a goal for some goals that do not have a graph representation.

3.2   Space Analysis

The graph representation of the narrowing space of a computation may allow us to infer properties of the entire computation. Every path from a goal to a constructor term gives us a computed expression. Cycles in the graph representation of a narrowing space are particularly interesting, since they finitely represent infinite sets of computed expressions. For example, let G denote the graph representation of the narrowing space of $u \leq u + v$ which is shown in the left part of Figure 1. Any path of G consists of zero or more traversals of the loop followed by the final edge reaching *true*. The substitution computed by this path is $\{u \mapsto s^n \; 0\}$, where n is the number of loop traversals. In the above notation, following a common practice, if f is a function from a type T into T, then $f^n \; x$, $n > 0$ stands for $f^{n-1} \; (f \; x)$ and $f^0 \; x = x$, for all $x \in T$. Thus, we conclude that goal $u \leq u + v$ is solved for any natural number u, or in other words that the goal's computed expression is $\{\} \llbracket \textit{true}$. By contrast, plain narrowing enumerates an infinite set of ground computed expressions of this goal.

Unfortunately, it does not always seem possible to simplify an infinite set of substitutions to a single, more general substitution. For example, consider the following program

```
double 0     = 0
double (s x) = s (s (double x))

half 0       = 0
half (s 0)   = 0
half (s (s x)) = s (half x)
```

and the goal *double (half u)* $==$ *u*, where u is an uninstantiated variable. The narrowing space of this goal is shown in Figure 2. Using the notation discussed earlier, we finitely represent the set of computed expressions of this goal with the following two computed expression-like formulas $\{u \mapsto s^{2n} \; 0\} \llbracket \textit{true}$ and $\{u \mapsto s^{2n+1} \; 0\} \llbracket \textit{false}$, where n ranges over $\mathbb{N}$. These formulas are clear and intuitive, but ad hoc to this example.

To obtain a finite representation of the set of computed expressions of a goal g, when g's narrowing space has a graph representation, we introduce a new concept. We regard a graph representation of a narrowing space as a finite state machine—both are finite rooted directed labeled graphs. If we apply to a graph representation of a narrowing space a standard algorithm for the construction of a regular expression associated to a finite state machine, we obtain expressions, which by analogy with regular expressions, we call *regular substitutions*. Regular substitutions represent possibly infinite sets of substitutions. If we use regular substitutions instead of plain ones in computed expressions, we get *regular computed expressions*, which represent possibly infinite sets of computed expressions. The notation is familiar and fairly intuitive. For example, the infinite set of computed expressions of the goal of Figure 2 is entirely represented by the two regular computed expressions $\{u \mapsto s \; (s \; u)\}^* \circ \{u \mapsto 0\} \llbracket \textit{true}$ and $\{u \mapsto s \; (s \; u)\}^* \circ \{u \mapsto s \; 0\} \llbracket \textit{false}$.

Definition 3. *Regular substitutions*, rs for short, are expressions defining sets of substitutions as follows: If σ is a substitution, then the regular substitution σ denotes the set of substitutions $\{\sigma\}$. It will be clear from the context whether we talk about σ as a regular substitution or as a substitution. If σ and η are

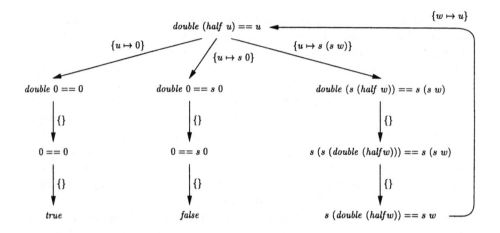

Fig. 2. Graph representation of the narrowing space of *double (half u) == u*.

regular substitutions, then

$$(\sigma)\,|\,(\eta) \qquad \text{is an rs denoting the set } \sigma \cup \eta$$
$$(\sigma)(\eta) \text{ or } (\sigma)\circ(\eta) \text{ is an rs denoting the set } \{\sigma'\circ\eta' \mid \sigma'\in\sigma, \eta'\in\eta\}$$
$$(\sigma)^* \qquad \text{is an rs denoting the set } \{\{\}\}\cup\sigma\cup\sigma\circ\sigma\cup\cdots$$

A *regular computed expression*, *RCE* for short, of a goal g is a pair $\sigma\,[\![\,t$, where σ is a regular substitution and, for all $\sigma'\in\sigma$, $\sigma'\,[\![\,t$ is a computed expression of g. The use of parentheses can be reduced using standard conventions on precedence and associativity of regular expression operators.

Proposition 4. *If the narrowing space of a goal g has a graph representation, then the set S of computed expressions of g has a finite representation.*

Proof. Regard the graph representation of the narrowing space of g as a finite state machine M where the states are goals, the initial state is g, the final states are constructor normal forms, the moves are narrowing steps between the goals (modulo renaming), and the inputs are the substitutions of the above narrowing steps. The elements of S are all and only the pairs $\sigma\,[\![\,n$, where n is a final state and σ is a regular expression defining the inputs accepted by M that terminate in n. Since the number of final states of M is finite, the set S is finite as well. □

A semidecision procedure for the existence of a finite representation of the set S of computed expressions of a goal g is trivial. First, attempt to construct a graph representation G of g's narrowing space. If this construction terminates, compute the set S of regular computed expressions accepted by G. Propositions 2 and 4 are the basis for the correctness of this procedure.

3.3 Memoization

Representing the narrowing space of a goal as a graph and regarding this graph as a finite state machine allows us to obtain a finite representation of the goal's computed expressions. This is crucial to memoization in functional logic programming. If we have to solve a goal a second time, it would be unnecessarily wasteful to analyze the graph again to retrieve the goal's computed expressions. To obtain a performance similar to that of memoization in functional languages, we use the graph representation of a goal's narrowing space to compute a table-like structure in which each vertex of the graph is mapped to its set of computed expressions. These expressions are computed by a straightforward application of Proposition 4. From the graph of Figure 2 we obtain the following table. As in the previous section, we use the intuitive notation of RCEs.

$double\ (half\ w) == w$ $double\ (s\ (half\ w) == s\ (s\ w)$ $s\ (s\ (double\ (half\,w))) == s\ (s\ w)$ $s\ (double\ (half\,w)) == s\ w$	$\{\{w \mapsto s^{2n}\ 0\} \mathbin{[\!]} true,$ $\{w \mapsto s^{2n+1}\ 0\} \mathbin{[\!]} false\}$ for $n \in \mathbb{N}$
$double\ 0 == 0$ $0 == 0$	$\{\{\} \mathbin{[\!]} true\}$
$double\ 0 == s\ 0$ $0 == s\ 0$	$\{\{\} \mathbin{[\!]} false\}$

Fig. 3. Memoization of the goals occurring in the narrowing space of Figure 2.

We could memoize functional logic computations also without our framework. However, without our framework some difficulties arise. If narrowing a goal yields a sequence of computed expressions that are not all computed at the same time, then the association between a goal and its computed expressions is dynamic. Creating and maintaining a dynamic association is computationally more complicated and expensive. Retrieving the association at different times might produce different results. Later results could be more informative than earlier results, since more computed expressions may become known, a situation that we think is undesirable in a declarative environment.

3.4 Simplification

It is well known that simplification rules reduce the size of the narrowing space of certain goals [15]. A simplification rule is a rewrite rule used to perform deterministic steps during a narrowing derivation. For example, referring to the program of Section 2, we can extend the definition of the addition operator with the following simplification rules.

```
y + 0     = y
y + (s x) = s (y + x)
```

Simplification rules are beneficial to reduce the size of a goal's narrowing space only when, in a narrowing step, they are used in place of, rather than in addition to, standard rules. To preserve the completeness of narrowing when simplification rules are used in this fashion, no term can have an infinite derivation in which only simplification rules are applied, a condition not always easy to ensure in practice. Not surprisingly, it turns out that simplification rules are also useful in our approach.

For example, the narrowing space of the goal $u + v == v + u$ is infinite and does not have a finite representation in our framework. The reason is that goals of the form $s^n u == u + s^n 0$, for increasing values of n, keep being created. However, if we use the above simplification rules, we obtain a (finite) graph representation of the narrowing space. This graph is small and simple, and it allows us to infer the computed expression $\{\} [\!] true$.

Since our framework thrives on cycles, it is interesting to explore the effects of non-terminating simplification rules. Take for example the rule

$$x+y = y+x \tag{1}$$

that subsumes both the simplification rules for addition proposed earlier, but cannot be used in the classic approach [15]. If we use this rule *in place* of the defining rules of "+" we immediately get a cycle, but nothing else. If we use this rule *in addition* to the defining rules of "+" we increase the out-degree of many vertices when we attempt to compute the graph representation of the narrowing space. Neither alternative seems profitable. To benefit from using the above rule, it is necessary to perform a more sophisticated analysis of the narrowing space. This will be discussed at the end of the next section.

3.5 Fertilization

It is clear from the previous section that techniques which prune the narrowing space are doubly beneficial in our framework, since they may prune portions of space that have no finite representation. Pruning all these portions makes the difference between a finite and an infinite representation of a goal's narrowing space. A powerful technique to this end has its roots in induction. To introduce this technique, consider again our first goal, $u \leq u + v$. We can prove it by induction on u as follows. There are two cases. Base case: Prove the goal for $u = 0$. Ind. case: Prove the goal for $u = s\ w$ assuming $w \leq w + v$. Both cases are proved directly by rewriting. The analogy with a narrowing computation is striking. During the construction of a graph representation, we use an induction hypothesis when we find in the graph being constructed a variant of the current goal. In the following we show that when the goal is an equation, it is possible to do better.

A *recursive* constructor is a data constructor of a type T that has an argument of type T. For example, *successor* and *cons* are recursive constructors of natural numbers and lists, respectively. Automated theorem provers, e.g., [5,12], recognize recursive constructors and create induction hypotheses. When the goal is an equation, theorem provers apply an induction hypothesis by replacing in the current goal an instance of the equation's left-hand side with the corresponding instance of the right-hand side or vice versa. This operation is called "fertilization" in [5]. We show, in Figure 4, how fertilization allows us to finitely

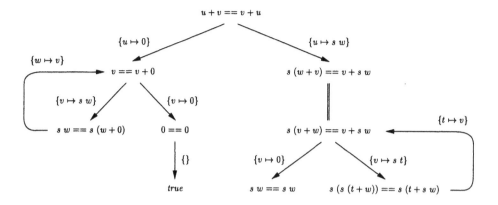

Fig. 4. Partial graph representation of the narrowing space of $u + v == v + u$. The narrowing space of $s\ w == s\ w$, omitted from the figure, has a graph representation and computed expression $\{\}\,[\!]\,true$. To contain the size of the figure, some steps are performed in parallel. The double vertical line denotes the fertilization step.

represent the narrowing space of $u + v == v + u$. Fertilization involves the terms connected by a double vertical line. The equation $s\ (w + v) == v + s\ w$ can be considered the reduct of the inductive case of a proof that $w + v == v + w$. Hence, the latter is an inductive hypothesis. Consequently, we can replace $w + v$ with $v + w$ and we obtain $s\ (v + w) == v + s\ w$, which turns out to be easier to solve. Note that in the replacement of terms originating from fertilization, variables must be intended as Skolem constants, thus their names matter.

The practicality of fertilization for the execution of functional logic programs will have to be assessed. However, fertilization has some immediately apparent potential advantages with respect to simplification. Simplification rules must be coded by the programmer, whereas fertilization rules originate spontaneously during the execution of a program. When a goal is being narrowed, we expect that only a small number of fertilization rules will originate, a number definitely smaller than the cardinality of a useful set of simplification rules. Furthermore, each simplification rule must be tried on every subgoal, whereas fertilization rules are applied more selectively. In [5] a fertilization rule is used only once and then discarded, a policy that further speeds up a computation. Finally, simplification rules must be terminating, whereas fertilization rules have no such a requirement.

Earlier we considered $x + y == y + x$ as a simplification rule. Using this rule, in addition to the defining rules of "+", to solve $u + v == v + u$ yields a representation, not necessarily a finite one, of the goal's narrowing space that obviously embeds the graph of Figure 4. By analyzing a large enough portion of this representation, we discover, as we did earlier, that $\{\}\,[\!]\,true$ is a computed expression. Clearly, this entirely solves the goal, since it is its most general solution. Consequently, we have found a finite representation of the set of the goal's computed expressions, even if the goal's narrowing space has no finite representation in our framework. Here is where iterative deepening pays off. We work on the construction of a graph representation of a goal's narrowing space until a predetermined amount of resources has been consumed. Then we analyze the possibly incomplete graph representation of the narrowing space. If we determine that all the goal's computed expressions have been found, e.g., using the RCE calculus presented in the next section, there is no need to complete the construction of the graph. In this way, we succeed in finding a finite representation of a goal's set of computed expressions even for some goals that do not have graph representations of their narrowing spaces. For example, this situation happens for $u + v == v + u$ when we use the non-terminating simplification rule of display (1). Note that according to the rules defining "$==$", the goal $u + v == u + v$ is not solved, though the sides of the equation are syntactically equal.

3.6 RCE Calculus

Up to this point, for the sake of intuition and readability, we adopted a cavalier attitude toward the computation and presentation of the finite representation of an infinite set of computed expressions. Presenting to the user precise and easy to read RCEs is a challenging problem.

From a graph representation of a goal's narrowing space, we obtain a finite representation of the goal's set of computed expressions with any algorithm that computes the regular expression accepted by a finite state machine. The major difference with respect to standard regular expressions is that the alphabet symbols are replaced by substitutions and the concatenation of symbols is replaced by the composition of substitutions. Regular expressions can be simplified to be more readable. These simplifications improve the readability of RCEs as well. In addition, substitutions are objects much richer than alphabet symbols and their composition gives rise to a whole new class of simplification rules. We discuss some of these rules and show how their application allows us to determine, mechanically and rather easily, that the computed expression of $u + v == v + u$, the goal of Figure 4, is $\{\} \parallel true$.

Figure 1 shows a common pattern for recursive types such as natural numbers, lists, and trees. This pattern consists of a loop with an exit. While many goals may have complicated graph representations of their narrowing spaces, often these graphs embed a loop with an exit. For example, this situation occurs twice in Figure 4 and once more in its omitted portion. We generalize these loops with exits as follows. Let T be a recursive type. Partition the constructors of T into a set $\{r_1, \dots r_i\}$ of recursive constructors, a notion discussed in Section 3.5, and a set $\{n_1, \dots, n_j\}$ of non-recursive constructors. If c is a constructor of T, let $\bar{c}$ denote the *linear* term $c(v_1, \dots, v_n)$ where n is the arity of c and $v_1, \dots, v_n$ are distinct variables. It can be verified by induction that the *regular substitution*

$$(\{u \mapsto \bar{r}_1\} \mid \dots \mid \{u \mapsto \bar{r}_i\})^* \circ (\{u \mapsto \bar{n}_1\} \mid \dots \mid \{u \mapsto \bar{n}_j\}) \qquad (2)$$

defines all the instances of type T and consequently can be simplified to the identity substitution. Referring to the left part of Figure 1, we simplify $(\{u \mapsto s\ w\} \circ \{w \mapsto u\})^* \circ \{u \mapsto 0\}$ to the identity after explicitly composing the two substitutions in parentheses.

A second useful simplification rule, which we use to simplify the RCE computed for the goal of Figure 4, is the following. Let T be a type and u a variable of type T. Consider the regular substitution

$$\{u \mapsto t_1\} \mid \ldots \mid \{u \mapsto t_n\} \tag{3}$$

If the set of terms $\{t_1, \ldots, t_n\}$ is complete for (the constructors of) T in the sense of [18], then the regular substitution of display (3) defines all the instances of type T [18, Lemma 3], and consequently can be simplified to the identity substitution. Referring to Figure 4, we first simplify the substitution of the goal's RCE by repeatedly applying the simplification rule of display (2) thus obtaining $\{u \mapsto 0\} \mid \{u \mapsto s\ w\}$. Since the set $\{0, s\ w\}$ is complete for the type of u, using the simplification rule of display (3) we reduce this regular substitution to the identity.

While finding "the simplest" presentation of an RCE may be impossible or impractical, we obtain good improvements with the above simplification rules.

4 Conclusions

We have presented a framework for narrowing akin to memoization in functional programming. The key feature of our framework is its ability, in some cases, to provide a finite representation of an infinite narrowing space. This, in turn, allows us to finitely represent the set of a goal's computed expressions and to associate this set to the goal. This association plays the same role of the association of a computation with its result present in the memoization of functional languages.

A major advantage of our framework is its potential to find computed expressions more efficiently than plain narrowing alone and/or to find computed expressions that are more general than those obtained by plain narrowing alone. These two features are closely interrelated. Referring to the first example of Figure 1, consider the goal

$$u \leq u + v\ \wedge\ member(u, l)$$

where u is an uninstantiated variable, "$\wedge$" is the conjunction operator, and *member* is a predicate that checks whether its first argument, an element, occurs in its second argument, a list of elements. If l is a long list of big numbers, plain narrowing solves this goal inefficiently, regardless of which goal is selected first, since a large number of narrowing steps are needed in each case. Our framework speeds up this computation tremendously, since only a handful narrowing steps are needed. This speed up is achieved without asking the programmer to supply evaluation annotations or mode declarations or other similar devices that may make a program less general and/or less declarative and/or more difficult to understand and code.

Equally important, our framework may quickly find that a goal cannot be solved (its computed expression is $\{\} \mathbin{[\![} false)$ where plain narrowing alone searches forever. The right part of Figure 1 contains an example that proves this point.

Our framework accommodates techniques, or even extends them and promotes new ones, intended to reduce the size of the narrowing space. We limited our detailed discussion to simplification and fertilization. *Generalization* [5], similar to fertilization, turns out to be useful in some situations. *Inductive inference* [1] allows us to detect situations in which simply performing further narrowing steps to find a graph representation of the narrowing space is useless. For example, in the space of $u + v == v + u$ computed without using simplification and/or fertilization rules, it is possible to infer the infinite sets of subgoals $s^n\ u == u + s^n\ 0$, for $n \in \mathbb{N}$.

An interesting aspect of our framework is the language, substantially identical to that of regular expressions, used to finitely represent possibly infinite sets of substitutions. This language, in addition to the well-know simplification rules of regular expressions, allows new simplification rules specific to substitutions. We have only superficially discussed how to present RCEs to the user. This appears to be mostly a syntactic, though non trivial, issue. A more substantial problem is how to use RCEs internally when their substitutions cannot be simplified to usual ones, but contain the "or" or the Kleene closure operators. This could be solved by extending the notion of a term. The implications of this extension on unification and other components of a functional logic language require further study.

References

1. D. Angluin and C. Smith. Inductive inference: Theory and methods. *Computing Surveys*, 15(3):237–269, 1983.
2. S. Antoy, R. Echahed, and M. Hanus. A needed narrowing strategy. In *Proc. 21st ACM Symposium on Principles of Programming Languages*, pages 268–279, Portland, 1994. URL www.cs.pdx.edu/~antoy/publications.html.
3. S. Antoy, R. Echahed, and M. Hanus. A parallel narrowing strategy. In *14th Int'l Conference on Logic Programming*, Leuven, Belgium, July 1997. (to appear) URL www.cs.pdx.edu/~antoy/publications.html.
4. A. Bockmayr, S. Krischer, and A. Werner. An optimal narrowing strategy for general canonical systems. In *Proc. of the 3rd Intern. Workshop on Conditional Term Rewriting Systems*, pages 483–497. Springer LNCS 656, 1992.
5. R.S. Boyer and J.S. Moore. Proving theorems about LISP functions. *JACM*, 22(1):129–144, Jan. 1975.
6. J. Darlington and Y. Guo. Narrowing and unification in functional programming - an evaluation mechanism for absolute set abstraction. In *Proc. of the Conference on Rewriting Techniques and Applications*, pages 92–108. Springer LNCS 355, 1989.
7. N. Dershowitz and J. Jouannaud. Rewrite systems. In J. van Leeuwen, editor, *Handbook of Theoretical Computer Science B: Formal Methods and Semantics*, chapter 6, pages 243–320. North Holland, Amsterdam, 1990.
8. R. Echahed. On completeness of narrowing strategies. In *Proc. CAAP'88*, pages 89–101. Springer LNCS 299, 1988.
9. R. Echahed. Uniform narrowing strategies. In *Proceedings of the Third International Conference on Algebraic and Logic Programming*, pages 259–275, Volterra, Italy, September 1992.

10. M. J. Fay. First-order unification in an equational theory. In *Proc. 4th Workshop on Automated Deduction*, pages 161–167, Austin (Texas), 1979. Academic Press.

11. L. Fribourg. SLOG: A logic programming language interpreter based on clausal superposition and rewriting. In *Proc. IEEE Internat. Symposium on Logic Programming*, pages 172–184, Boston, 1985.

12. S.J. Garland and J.V. Guttag. Inductive methods for reasoning about abstract data types. In *ACM SIGACT-SIGPLAN Symposium of Principles of Programming Languages*, pages 219–228, 1988.

13. E. Giovannetti, G. Levi, C. Moiso, and C. Palamidessi. Kernel LEAF: a logic plus functional language. *The Journal of Computer and System Sciences*, 42:139–185, 1991.

14. W. Hans, R. Loogen, and S. Winkler. On the interaction of lazy evaluation and backtracking. In *Proc. of the 4th International Symposium on Programming Language Implementation and Logic Programming*, pages 355–369. Springer LNCS 631, 1992.

15. M. Hanus. Lazy narrowing with simplification. *Computer Languages (to appear)*, 1997.

16. A. Herold. Narrowing techniques applied to idempotent unification. Technical Report SR-86-16, SEKI, 1986.

17. S. Hölldobler. *Foundations of Equational Logic Programming*. Springer LNCS 353, 1989.

18. G. Huet and J.-M. Hullot. Proofs by induction in equational theories with constructors. *JCSS*, 25:239–266, 1982.

19. J. W. Klop. Term Rewriting Systems. In S. Abramsky, D. Gabbay, and T. Maibaum, editors, *Handbook of Logic in Computer Science, Vol. II*, pages 1–112. Oxford University Press, 1992.

20. S. Krischer and A. Bockmayr. Detecting redundant narrowing derivations by the LSE-SL reducibility test. In *Proc. RTA'91*. Springer LNCS 488, 1991.

21. A. Middeldorp and E. Hamoen. Counterexamples to completeness results for basic narrowing (extended abstract). In *Proceedings of the Third International Conference on Algebraic and Logic Programming*, pages 244–258, Volterra, Italy, September 1992.

22. J. J. Moreno-Navarro, H. Kuchen, R. Loogen, and M. Rodríguez-Artalejo. Lazy narrowing in a graph machine. In *Proc. Second International Conference on Algebraic and Logic Programming*, pages 298–317. Springer LNCS 463, 1990.

23. J. J. Moreno-Navarro and M. Rodríguez-Artalejo. Logic programming with functions and predicates: The language BABEL. *Journal of Logic Programming*, 12:191–223, 1992.

24. W. Nutt, P. Réty, and G. Smolka. Basic narrowing revisited. *Journal of Symbolic Computation*, 7:295–317, 1989.

25. S. L. Peyton Jones. *The implementation of Functional Programming Languages*. Prentice-Hall International, Englewood Cliffs, N.J., 1987.

26. U. S. Reddy. Narrowing as the operational semantics of functional languages. In *Proc. IEEE Internat. Symposium on Logic Programming*, pages 138–151, Boston, 1985.

27. J.-H. You. Unification modulo an equality theory for equational logic programming. *The Journal of Computer and System Sciences*, 42(1):54–75, 1991.

An Object Calculus with Algebraic Rewriting

Adriana Compagnoni
University of Edinburgh
Department of Computer Science,
Edinburgh EH9 3JZ, U. K.
abc@dcs.ed.ac.uk

Maribel Fernández
LIENS (CNRS URA 1327)
École Normale Supérieure
45 Rue d'Ulm, 75005 Paris, France
maribel@dmi.ens.fr

Abstract. In trying to use Abadi and Cardelli's object calculi as a foundation for a programming language the addition of algebraic data types arises naturally. This paper defines such an extension, shows a motivating example, and explores the new calculi by establishing properties such as Church-Rosser, subject reduction and uniqueness of types.

Keywords: Object calculi; Rewriting; Combined calculi; Type systems.

1 Introduction

Abadi and Cardelli [2] presented a simple object calculus, *the ς-calculus*, which can be used to model object oriented languages in the same way as functional languages are modelled by the λ-calculus. The untyped ς-calculus supports *method update*. The first-order (typed) version of the calculus, extended with a subtyping relation, models also object subsumption.

The ς-calculus is computationally complete (the λ-calculus can be encoded as shown in [2]). However, it lacks expressiveness for the representation of data types: data types can be encoded (e.g. through encodings in the λ-calculus), but this kind of encoding is inefficient and unnatural. To overcome this, Abadi and Cardelli [1] introduced in the typed ς-calculus free algebras that can be thought of as built-in data structures. In this paper we go one step further, by extending the untyped calculus with constants and object rewrite rules. In this way we can also model other computational features that are not present in the ς-calculus, such as non-determinism (choice operators).

More precisely, we define an extension of the ς-calculus where algebraic operators can be used to build objects. Objects can have algebraic expressions as fields or methods, and conversely algebraic operations or constructors can take objects as arguments. For example, a list can be a field of an object and we can also form lists or trees of objects. Formally, the calculus is defined by extending the syntax of the ς-calculus with a set of *algebraic symbols* which are used to build objects, and with *algebraic rewrite rules on objects*. To illustrate the expressiveness of the calculus, we give an example of a text editor using lists of characters. Alternative choices of syntax are discussed in the conclusions.

The Church-Rosser property of the ς-calculus is not preserved in this extension even if the algebraic rules are confluent (we give a counterexample). But we show that with suitable restrictions on the form of the rewrite rules (namely by requiring linear left-hand sides), it is possible to restore this important property.

We present also a typed version of our extended calculus, which satisfies uniqueness of types and subject reduction. The subtyping rules of [2] can be added in a straightforward way to model subsumption of objects. The extension of this calculus with subtyping rules on algebraic types is beyond the scope of this paper and is under development. Also the recursive types of [2] can be added to give more informative typings for objects whose methods return *self* or an updated version of *self*. With these extensions, the calculus of Gordon and Rees [5], which was used to study the correspondence between operational semantics and equivalence in the equational theory of Abadi and Cardelli, can be seen as a particular case: it corresponds to the typed ς-calculus with recursive types and subtyping, extended with a type Bool, constructors True and False, and a conditional defined by two rewrite rules.

Fisher, Honsell and Mitchell [9] have developed an alternative object calculus: a λ-calculus of extensible objects. We expect that the same ideas can be applied to their calculus as well.

2 The Calculus

In this section we define an untyped object calculus which is an algebraic extension of the pure object calculus of Abadi and Cardelli [2]. This extended calculus will serve as a basis for the definition of a typed algebraic object calculus in the following sections.

2.1 Syntax

Definition 1. The set $O(\mathcal{L}, \mathcal{F}, \mathcal{X})$ of *objects* is defined inductively from denumerable pairwise disjoint sets $\mathcal{L}$ (*labels*), $\mathcal{X}$ (*variables*), and $\mathcal{F}$ (*algebraic symbols with fixed arities*), as follows:

1. $\mathcal{X} \subseteq O(\mathcal{L}, \mathcal{F}, \mathcal{X})$;
2. if $f \in \mathcal{F}$ has arity n, and $a_1, \ldots, a_n$ are objects, then $f(a_1, \ldots, a_n)$ is an object;
3. if $l_1, \ldots, l_n$ are different labels and $b_1, \ldots, b_n$ objects, then $[l_i = \varsigma(x_i) b_i{}^{1 \leq i \leq n}]$ is an object with *method names* $l_1, \ldots, l_n$ and *methods* $\varsigma(x_i) b_i$ $(1 \leq i \leq n)$, where the order of these components does not matter;
4. if a is an object with method name l then $a.l$ is an object;
5. if a is an object with method name l then $a.l \Leftarrow \varsigma(x) b$ is an object.

In a method $\varsigma(x) b$, x is the *self variable* and b the *body*. A method that does not use its self parameter (i.e. x does not appear in b) is called a *field*. The last two object constructors in the previous definition are called *field selection* and *field update* respectively, or *method invocation* and *method update* respectively, depending on whether we speak of a field or a proper method. Objects that are built using only symbols in $\mathcal{F}$ and $\mathcal{X}$ will be called *algebraic objects*.

The symbol ς is a binder. The definitions of free and bound variable, as well as substitution, are standard. We refer the reader to [2] for additional details of these issues. Substitutions will be denoted by $\{x_1 \mapsto o_1, \ldots, x_n \mapsto o_n\}$ where $x_1, \ldots, x_n$ are different variables. We work modulo α-conversion, identifying $\varsigma(x) b$ with $\varsigma(y) b\{x \mapsto y\}$ when y is not free in b. We will use the following standard abbreviations: O instead of $O(\mathcal{L}, \mathcal{F}, \mathcal{X})$ when $\mathcal{L}$, $\mathcal{F}$, and $\mathcal{X}$ are clear from the context, $a.l := b$ for $a.l \Leftarrow \varsigma(y) b$ when y does not appear in b, and $[\ldots, l_i = b_i, \ldots]$ for $[\ldots, l_i = \varsigma(x_i) b_i, \ldots]$ when x_i does not occur in b_i.

2.2 Reduction Rules

The reduction relation of our calculus combines *algebraic reductions* and *pure object reductions* (corresponding to method invocation and update). The algebraic reductions are induced by a set R of *object rewrite rules*, which are written $l \to r$ where l and r are algebraic objects in O, $l \notin \mathcal{X}$, and the variables that appear in r appear also in l. We define first the one-step reduction relation. We use $\equiv$ to denote syntactic equality, and $-$ as a distinguished variable in contexts. A *context* is an object e with an occurrence of the free variable $-$. If e is a context and a an object, we write $e[a]$ for the result of replacing $-$ by a in e.

Definition 2. We write $a \to b$, for $a, b \in O$, if there is some object o such that $o \equiv [l_i = \varsigma(x_i) b_i \ ^{1 \leq i \leq n}]$, and either

1. $a \equiv o.l_j$ for some $1 \leq j \leq n$, and $b \equiv b_j\{x_j \mapsto o\}$, or
2. $a \equiv o.l_j \Leftarrow \varsigma(x) c$ and $b \equiv [l_j = \varsigma(x) c, l_i = \varsigma(x_i) b_i \ ^{1 \leq i \leq n, i \neq j}]$, or
3. $a \equiv l\sigma$ for some substitution σ and object rewrite rule $l \to r$, and $b \equiv r\sigma$.

The reduction relation on objects is closed under contexts: $a \to b$ implies that $C[a] \to C[b]$ for any context C. We denote by $\to^*$ the transitive reflexive closure of $\to$.

Parts 1 and 2 of the previous definition give the operational semantics of method invocation and update. A method invocation $o.l$ reduces to the result of the substitution of the object o for the self parameter in the body of the method named l. A method update $o.l_j \Leftarrow \varsigma(x) c$ replaces the method l_j with $\varsigma(x) c$ (it is an atomic operation). Note that this is a "functional" operation: an update produces a modified copy of the object. These reductions (parts 1 and 2 of the previous definition) coincide with the pure object reductions of the ς-calculus [2], and will be denoted by $\to_\varsigma$. Part 3 defines the algebraic reductions of our calculus, which will be denoted by $\to_R$. Then $\to = \to_\varsigma \cup \to_R$.

Abadi and Cardelli originally defined a particular strategy of rewriting for their calculus: no reductions under binders (this corresponds roughly to weak head reduction in λ-calculus), but in [2] they lift the restriction. We do not fix any strategy, since the properties we are going to show for the extended calculus hold for any strategy.

2.3 An Example

Here we give an example of a text editor where we use the recursive nature of objects that allows methods to refer to each other, and algebraic expressions to represent the text with lists.

$$
\begin{aligned}
Editor \equiv [\, &text = [\; before = l_1, \\
&\qquad\qquad after = l_2, \\
&\qquad\qquad cursor = \varsigma(s)hd(s.after)\;], \\
&input = \varsigma(s)\lambda x.s.text := (s.text.before := s.text.before@[x]), \\
&find = \varsigma(s)\lambda x.\text{if } s.text.cursor = x \\
&\qquad\qquad \text{then } s.message := \text{``found''} \\
&\qquad\qquad \text{else if } s.text.cursor \neq \star \\
&\qquad\qquad\qquad \text{then } s.forward.find(x) \\
&\qquad\qquad\qquad\quad \text{else } s.message := \text{``not found''}, \\
&init = \varsigma(s)s.text := ((s.text.before := nil).after := [\star]), \\
&forward = \varsigma(s) \text{ if } s.text.cursor \neq \star \\
&\qquad\qquad \text{then } s.text := ((s.text.before := \\
&\qquad\qquad s.text.before@[s.text.cursor]).after := tl(s.text.after)) \\
&\qquad\qquad \text{else } s.message := \text{``end of text''}, \\
&backwards = \varsigma(s) \text{ if } s.text.before \neq nil \\
&\qquad\qquad \text{then } s.text := ((s.text.after := \\
&\qquad\qquad last(s.text.before)::(s.text.after)).before := \\
&\qquad\qquad no\text{-}last(s.text.before)) \\
&\qquad\qquad \text{else } s.message := \text{``beginning of text''}, \\
&message = \text{`` ''} \;]
\end{aligned}
$$

The text is divided by the *cursor* into two parts: *before* and *after*, and the *cursor* is the first character of the *after* list. The initial values of *before* and *after*, l_1 and l_2, are irrelevant. An empty line is a list with the distinguished character $\star$ only. We write $[\star]$ for $\star::nil$, and $[x]$ for $x::nil$. Lists have the constructors *nil* and $::$ as usual, and *hd, tl, @, no-last,* and *last* are defined with the following rules.

$$
\begin{array}{ll}
hd(x::l) \to x & tl(x::l) \to l \\
nil@y \to y & (x::l)@y \to x::(l@y) \\
no\text{-}last(x::nil) \to nil & no\text{-}last(x::(y::l)) \to x::no\text{-}last(y::l) \\
last(x::nil) \to x & last(x::(y::l)) \to last(y::l)
\end{array}
$$

Similarly, we introduce booleans by defining *true, false,* and *if then else.* In the tests, equality ($=$) means syntactic equality. The lambda abstraction is defined as in [2], by encoding it in the ς-calculus.

There is a choice to represent lists (and booleans). Instead of defining algebraic objects with their rewriting rules, we can write them as objects with methods as follows:

$$
\begin{aligned}
before &= [val = ..., hd = ..., tl = ..., @ = ..., last = ..., no\text{-}last = ...] \\
after &= [val = ..., hd = ..., tl = ..., @ = ..., last = ..., no\text{-}last = ...]
\end{aligned}
$$

the disadvantage being that the definitions for the different constructors are repeated in each list. The term rewriting option avoids such repetitions.

Abadi and Cardelli [2] presented an example of a calculator which can also benefit from using term rewriting to define the arithmetic operations instead of encoding them.

3 Properties

The ς-calculus is confluent [2], i.e. if $o \to_\varsigma^* o_1$ and $o \to_\varsigma^* o_2$, then $o_1 \to_\varsigma^* o_3$ and $o_2 \to_\varsigma^* o_3$ for some o_3. But we cannot expect to have the same property in our extension, since the algebraic rules are arbitrary. In order to obtain a confluent calculus we need to impose some restrictions on the algebraic rewrite rules.

Even if we consider only algebraic reductions that are confluent we cannot ensure confluence of the combined calculus. The following is a simple counterexample (a similar problem appears in combinations of λ-calculus and algebraic rewriting, see e.g. [4] which inspired our counterexample). Assume we are working with a set $\mathcal{F}$ of symbols that contains the object constants 0 and 1, the unary symbol S, and the binary symbol f. The rewrite rules $\{f(x, x) \to 0, \ f(x, S(x)) \to 1\}$ induce a reduction relation that is confluent for the set of algebraic objects built from $\mathcal{F}$ and a set $\mathcal{X}$ of variables. However, if we consider the whole set O of objects and the full reduction relation $\to_R \cup \to_\varsigma$, the calculus is not confluent: the problem is that the object $o.l$, where $o \equiv [l = \varsigma(x) \ S(x.l)]$, reduces in the object calculus to $S(o.l)$, then the object $f(o.l, o.l)$ can be reduced in two ways, either to 0 or to 1.

To ensure confluence in combinations of λ-calculus and algebraic rewriting the standard solution is to restrict the set of algebraic rules to left-linear rules, or to introduce types to avoid infinite reductions. We will take the first alternative. Using proof techniques similar to the ones used for λ-calculus (see e.g. [10]), we will show that the extended ς-calculus is confluent with respect to $\to_R \cup \to_\varsigma$ when R is left-linear and confluent for algebraic objects. The second alternative, restricting the set of objects to those that are strongly normalizing, will be explored in future work.

We will use two lemmas, the first one shows that the confluence of R extends to the whole set $O(\mathcal{L}, \mathcal{F}, \mathcal{X})$ of objects, and the second one establishes the commutation of $\to_R$ and $\to_\varsigma$ when R is left-linear.

Lemma 3. *If R is left-linear and confluent for algebraic objects, then R is confluent for $O(\mathcal{L}, \mathcal{F}, \mathcal{X})$.*

Proof. Assume $o_1 {}_R^* \leftarrow o \to_R^* o_2$. We will show by structural induction that there exists o_3 such that $o_1 \to_R^* o_3$, $o_2 \to_R^* o_3$. We distinguish the cases:

1. $o \equiv [l_i = \varsigma(x_i) b_i^{\ 1 \le i \le n}]$. Then the reductions $\to_R$ take place inside the objects b_i, that is, $o_1 \equiv [l_i = \varsigma(x_i) b_i'^{\ 1 \le i \le n}]$, $o_2 \equiv [l_i = \varsigma(x_i) b_i''^{\ 1 \le i \le n}]$, and $b_i \to_R^* b_i'$, $b_i \to_R^* b_i''$ ($1 \le i \le n$). By induction, there exists b_i''' such that $b_i' \to_R^* b_i'''$ and $b_i'' \to_R^* b_i'''$. Hence we can take $o_3 \equiv [l_i = \varsigma(x_i) b_i'''^{\ 1 \le i \le n}]$.

2. $o \equiv a.l_j$. We proceed as in the previous case.

3. $o \equiv (a.l_j \Leftarrow \varsigma(x)\, b)$. We proceed as in the previous cases.

4. $o \equiv f(a_1, \ldots, a_n)$. Let u_k, $1 \leq k \leq m$, be the maximal subexpressions of the form $[l_i = \varsigma(x_i)b_i \,^{1 \leq i \leq n}]$, $a.l_j$, or $(a.l_j \Leftarrow \varsigma(x)\, b)$ in $a_1, \ldots, a_n$. We will replace them by different new variables $w_1, \ldots, w_m$, obtaining in this way an algebraic object o' (since no occurrences of non-algebraic constructors are left). Since R is algebraic and left-linear, the reductions $\rightarrow_R^*$ made in the u_k are independent from those in o', hence:

- $o'_1 \,_R^* \leftarrow o' \rightarrow_R^* o'_2$,
- $o_1 = o'_1\{w_1 \mapsto v_1, \ldots, w_m \mapsto v_m\}$ where $u_k \rightarrow_R^* v_k$, $1 \leq k \leq m$, and
- $o_2 = o'_2\{w_1 \mapsto v'_1, \ldots, w_m \mapsto v'_m\}$ where $u_k \rightarrow_R^* v'_k$, $1 \leq k \leq m$.

Since o', o'_1, and o'_2 are algebraic objects, and R is confluent, there exists o'_3 such that $o'_1 \rightarrow_R^* o'_3 \,_R^* \leftarrow o'_2$. By induction, u_k is confluent, hence, there exists v''_k such that $v_k \rightarrow_R^* v''_k$ and $v'_k \rightarrow_R^* v''_k$, for $1 \leq k \leq m$. Then we take $o_3 = o'_3\{w_1 \mapsto v''_1, \ldots, w_m \mapsto v''_m\}$.

The assumption of left-linearity is not necessary in the previous lemma, it just makes the proof easier. However, the hypothesis of algebraic rules in R is crucial.

Lemma 4. *If R is left-linear, and confluent for algebraic objects, then*

$$b \,_\varsigma^* \leftarrow o \rightarrow_R^* a \;\Rightarrow\; \exists c : b \rightarrow_R^* c \,_\varsigma^* \leftarrow a.$$

Proof. We will use a reduction relation $\Rightarrow_\varsigma$ that makes parallel $\rightarrow_\varsigma$-reductions in one step. It is defined inductively:

1. $o \Rightarrow_\varsigma o$,
2. if $o \equiv [l_i = \varsigma(x_i)b_i \,^{1 \leq i \leq n}]$, then $o.l_j \Rightarrow_\varsigma b_j\{x_j \mapsto o\}$,
3. if $o \equiv [l_i = \varsigma(x_i)\, b_i \,^{1 \leq i \leq n}]$, then $(o.l_j \Leftarrow \varsigma(x)\, c) \Rightarrow_\varsigma [l_j = \varsigma(x)\, c, l_i = \varsigma(x_i)\, b_i \,^{1 \leq i \leq n, i \neq j}]$,
4. $[l_i = \varsigma(x_i)b_i \,^{1 \leq i \leq n}] \Rightarrow_\varsigma [l_i = \varsigma(x_i)b'_i \,^{1 \leq i \leq n}]$, if $b_i \Rightarrow_\varsigma b'_i$ $(1 \leq i \leq n)$.
5. $o.l \Rightarrow_\varsigma o'.l$, if $o \Rightarrow_\varsigma o'$,
6. $(o.l_j \Leftarrow \varsigma(x)\, c) \Rightarrow_\varsigma (o'.l_j \Leftarrow \varsigma(x)\, c')$, if $o \Rightarrow_\varsigma o'$, $c \Rightarrow_\varsigma c'$,
7. $f(a_1, \ldots, a_n) \Rightarrow_\varsigma f(a'_1, \ldots, a'_n)$, if $a_i \Rightarrow_\varsigma a'_i$ $(1 \leq i \leq n)$.

We will prove that $o_2 \,_\varsigma \Leftarrow o \rightarrow_R o_1$ implies $o_2 \rightarrow_R^* o_3 \,_\varsigma \Leftarrow o_1$, for some o_3. This allows us to close the diagram $b \,_\varsigma^* \Leftarrow o \rightarrow_R^* a$ (by induction on the lengths of the derivations $o \rightarrow_R^* a$ and $o \Rightarrow_\varsigma^* b$). Note that $\Rightarrow_\varsigma^* \equiv \rightarrow_\varsigma^*$, which completes the proof.

We proceed by induction on the structure of o, distinguishing cases according to the definition of $o \Rightarrow_\varsigma o_2$.

1. $o \equiv o_2$. Then we take $o_3 \equiv o_1$.
2. $o \equiv [l_i = \varsigma(x_i)b_i \,^{1 \leq i \leq n}].l_j$ and $o_2 \equiv b_j\{x_j \mapsto [l_i = \varsigma(x_i)b_i \,^{1 \leq i \leq n}]\}$. Since R is algebraic, no rewrite rule applies at the root of o, then $b_k \rightarrow_R b'_k$ for some $1 \leq k \leq n$, and $o \rightarrow_R o_1 \equiv [l_i = \varsigma(x_i)b_i \,^{1 \leq i \leq n, i \neq k}, l_k = b'_k].l_j$. Let b'_j denote either b_j if $j \neq k$, or b'_k if $j = k$. Then $o_1 \Rightarrow_\varsigma o_3 \equiv b'_j\{x_j \mapsto [l_i = \varsigma(x_i)b_i \,^{1 \leq i \leq n, i \neq k}, l_k = b'_k]\}$, and $o_2 \rightarrow_R b'_j\{x_j \mapsto [l_i = \varsigma(x_i)b_i \,^{1 \leq i \leq n}]\} \rightarrow_R^* b'_j\{x_j \mapsto [l_i = \varsigma(x_i)b_i \,^{1 \leq i \leq n, i \neq k}, l_k = b'_k]\}$ as well, because $o \rightarrow_R o_1$.

3. $o \equiv ([l_i = \varsigma(x_i)b_i{}^{1 \leq i \leq n}].l_j \Leftarrow \varsigma(x)c)$ and $o_2 \equiv [l_j = \varsigma(x)c, l_i = \varsigma(x_i)b_i{}^{1 \leq i \leq n, i \neq j}]$. Since R is algebraic, no rewrite rule applies at the root of o, then either $b_k \rightarrow_R b_k'$ for some $1 \leq k \leq n$, or $c \rightarrow_R c'$. We take $o_3 \equiv [l_j = \varsigma(x) c'', l_i = \varsigma(x_i) b_i''{}^{1 \leq i \leq n, i \neq j}]$, where $c'' = c'$ or $c'' = c$, depending on whether there was a reduction on c, and similarly for b_i''. Then $o_2 \rightarrow_R o_3$, and $o_1 \Rrightarrow_\varsigma o_3$.

4. $o \equiv [l_i = \varsigma(x_i)b_i{}^{1 \leq i \leq n}]$ where $b_i \Rrightarrow_\varsigma b_i'$ $(1 \leq i \leq n)$, and $o_2 \equiv [l_i = \varsigma(x_i)b_i'{}^{1 \leq i \leq n}]$. Since R is algebraic, $o_1 \equiv [l_i = \varsigma(x_i)b_i''{}^{1 \leq i \leq n}]$ where $b_i \rightarrow_R b_i''$ for some i. By induction, there exists b_i''' such that $b_i' \rightarrow_R^* b_i'''{}_\varsigma \Leftarrow b_i''$. Then we can take $o_3 \equiv [l_i = \varsigma(x_i)b_i'''{}^{1 \leq i \leq n}]$.

5. $o \equiv a.l$, where $a \Rrightarrow_\varsigma a'$, and $o_2 \equiv a'.l$. Since R is algebraic, $o_1 \equiv a''.l$, where $a \rightarrow_R a''$. By induction, there exists a''' such that $a' \rightarrow_R^* a'''{}_\varsigma \Leftarrow a''$. Then we can take $o_3 \equiv a'''.l$.

6. $o \equiv (a.l_j \Leftarrow \varsigma(x) c)$, where $a \Rrightarrow_\varsigma a'$ and $c \Rrightarrow_\varsigma c'$, then $o_2 \equiv (a'.l_j \Leftarrow \varsigma(x) c')$. Since no algebraic reduction applies at the root of o, there are two cases:

   - $a \rightarrow_R a_1$ and then $o_1 \equiv (a_1.l_j \Leftarrow \varsigma(x) c)$. By induction there exists a_3 such that $a' \rightarrow_R^* a_3 {}_\varsigma\Leftarrow a_1$, then we can take $o_3 \equiv (a_3.l_j \Leftarrow \varsigma(x) c')$.
   - $c \rightarrow_R c_1$ and then $o_1 \equiv (a.l_j \Leftarrow \varsigma(x) c_1)$. By induction there exists c_3 such that $c' \rightarrow_R^* c_3 {}_\varsigma\Leftarrow c_1$, then we can take $o_3 \equiv (a'.l_j \Leftarrow \varsigma(x) c_3)$.

7. $o \equiv f(a_1, \ldots, a_n)$, where $a_i \Rrightarrow_\varsigma a_i'$ $(1 \leq i \leq n)$, and $o_2 \equiv f(a_1', \ldots, a_n')$. There are two cases:

   - If the algebraic reduction does not take place at the root, then $o_1 \equiv f(a_1'', \ldots, a_n'')$, where for one i, say j, $a_j \rightarrow_R a_j''$, and for the others $a_i \equiv a_i''$. By induction, there exists a_j''' such that $a_j' \rightarrow_R^* a_j'''{}_\varsigma \Leftarrow a_j''$. Hence, we take $o_3 \equiv f(a_1''', \ldots, a_n''')$, where $a_i''' = a_i'$ for $i \neq j$.
   - If the algebraic reduction takes place at the root, then $o \equiv l\sigma$, for some rewrite rule $l \rightarrow r$, and $o_1 \equiv r\sigma$. The redexes u_i which are reduced in the step $o \Rrightarrow_\varsigma o_2$ must occur under variables x_i in l. These variables are uniquely identified, because l is left-linear. Then we can define a substitution σ' such that $o_2 \equiv l\sigma'$, and $\sigma \Rrightarrow_\varsigma \sigma'$. Then $o_2 \rightarrow_R r\sigma' {}_\varsigma\Leftarrow o_1$.

Note the essential use of left-linearity in the last part of the proof.

Theorem 5. *The extended object calculus defined by a set R of left-linear and confluent algebraic rewrite rules is confluent with respect to $\rightarrow_R \cup \rightarrow_\varsigma$.*

Proof. First of all, note that since $\rightarrow_\varsigma$ is confluent for pure objects, it remains confluent in the extension with algebraic symbols (the standard technique of Tait and Martin-Löf can be used). Also, $\rightarrow_R$ is confluent for $O(\mathcal{L}, \mathcal{F}, \mathcal{X})$, by Lemma 3.

By Lemma 4, $\rightarrow_R$ and $\rightarrow_\varsigma$ commute with each other. Hence, using the lemma of Hindley and Rosen [12] which says that if two reduction relations are confluent and commute with each other then their union is confluent, we deduce the confluence of $\rightarrow_R \cup \rightarrow_\varsigma$.

4 Typed Calculus

Abadi and Cardelli defined a typed version of the ς-calculus, developing a first-order type system with object types. In the syntax the main change is that objects come with annotated types, as in $o \equiv [l_i = \varsigma(x_i : A)\, b_i\ ^{1 \le i \le n}]$, where the associated type is $A \equiv [l_i : B_i\ ^{1 \le i \le n}]$. We refer to [2] for details. In this section we add to the first-order typed ς-calculus an account for typed algebraic objects.

So far the untyped ς-calculus has been extended with algebraic symbols such as *true, false, zero, succ, nil*, etc. The next step is to type them, and to this aim we extend the object types with parametric type constants. With the same philosophy of only considering objects of the calculus to be those algebraic symbols which were applied to all their arguments (see Definition 1), we only want to type algebraic symbols when applied to all their arguments, and only consider types those constants which are given all their parameters. The types are defined with the following syntax

$$
\begin{aligned}
A ::= &\ [l_i : A\,^{1 \le i \le n}] && \text{an object type} \\
\mid &\ C_{A, \cdots, A} && \text{a type indexed constant}
\end{aligned}
$$

with $\mathcal{K}$ a set of type constants and $C \in \mathcal{K}$. The set $\mathcal{K}$ contains type constructors, such as a constant *Bool* to type *true* and *false*, and *Nat* to type *zero* and *succ(zero)*, or *Char* to type the letter *a*. In our example of the editor we used lists of characters to represent the text. The situation is slightly more complicated with lists. We would like to have polymorphic lists and yet remain in a first-order calculus. We then declare a parametric constant

$$List :: 1$$

that given a type yields another type. So *List* by itself is not a type, but a type constructor, while $List_{Char}$ is. Then *nil*, which was a constant symbol in the untyped calculus, now needs a type to form a list, in other words, an object that can be typed. Thus, in our environment (which we shall later call Σ) we declare

$$nil :: [1](List_1)$$

indicating that it takes one parameter type as argument and forms a list of that type. Our notation resembles that of command declarations in LaTeX where the number of arguments is declared between square brackets and an ordinal is used to indicate where to use each argument, but we omit the #. Then we can type $nil_{Char} : List_{Char}$. $List_{Char}$ is obtained by $List_1[Char]$ which denotes the substitution of 1 by *Char* in $List_1$.

Similarly, for cartesian products we declare a constructor $\times :: 2$ for which we shall use infix notation. The symbol *pair* is declared as follows:

$$pair :: [2](1, 2 \triangleright 1 \times 2)$$

meaning that *pair* takes two types, an element of the first type, and an element of the second type, and produces an element of the cartesian product of the first and second type. Then, $pair_{A,B}(a,b)$ has type $A \times B$, if a has type A and b has type B, where $A \times B$ is the result of $1 \times 2[A,B]$. Note that in $[2](1, 2 \triangleright 1 \times 2)$ the first 2 is a cardinal while the other numbers are ordinals.

Notation: The expression $A[B_1, \cdots, B_n]$ denotes the simultaneous substitution of $1, \cdots, n$ by $B_1, \cdots, B_n$ in A. We write A for $A_1, \cdots, A_n \triangleright A$ when $n = 0$.

The reader has probably noticed that $[2](1, 2 \triangleright 1 \times 2)$ could be interpreted as $\Lambda X.\Lambda Y.X \to Y \to X \times Y$ in System F, but note that we do not need the full power of β-reduction since we only use syntactic substitution (numbers are replaced by expressions containing no numbers).

The calculus we are about to define should be able to detect that $nil.l$ is ill typed. The way it enforces that is by preventing algebraic symbol specifications from containing object types. Hence a declaration

$$nil :: [1][l : B, l_i : B_i {}^{1 \leq i \leq n}]$$

is not legal. But that doesn't mean that the function hd cannot manipulate lists of objects, for example. This will become clearer once the rules are presented. Take the expression $hd(o::l)$ which rewrites to the object o. All we need to do to type it is declare

$$hd :: [1](List_1 \triangleright 1)$$

and instantiate 1 with the corresponding object type in the typing rule for algebraic values (VALALG) defined below.

The algebraic symbols and the type constructors are declared with a specification in an environment Σ. The environment is reminiscent of that of LF [6].

To formalize declarations in Σ we introduce the notion of *algebraic pre-types*. Intuitively, algebraic pre-types are types, other than object types, which can have natural numbers in them. These numbers behave as place holders and shall be used for syntactic substitution only. For example $List_1$ and 1×2 are pre-types.

We define a set of *algebraic pre-types* with the following grammar:

$$P ::= \mathbb{N} \qquad \text{a natural number}$$
$$| \quad C_{\mathbb{N}, \cdots, \mathbb{N}} \quad \text{a parameterised constant}$$

Constants (types or algebraic symbols) are declared in Σ with a *specification* of the form:

$$S ::= \mathbb{N} \qquad\qquad \text{a constructor arity}$$
$$| \quad [\mathbb{N}](P, \cdots, P \triangleright P) \quad \text{an algebraic symbol specification}$$

The sets $\mathcal{K}$ (of type constants), $\mathbb{N}$ (of the natural numbers), $\mathcal{X}$ (of object variables), $\mathcal{L}$ (of object labels), and $\mathcal{F}$ (of algebraic symbols) are pairwise disjoint. Note that $[1](List_1)$ is a specification and not a pre-type.

A type constructor is declared in Σ with specification (or arity) n, written $C :: n$, indicating how many types it needs to be saturated. For example $Bool$ has arity 0 and $List$ has arity 1. An algebraic symbol in $\mathcal{F}$ is declared with a specification $f :: [n](P, \cdots, P \triangleright P)$ indicating its functionality.

4.1 Rules

Typing assumptions for object variables (x:A) will be given in a context Γ. The expression $\Gamma \vdash_\Sigma \diamond$ means that Γ and Σ are well formed, $\Gamma \vdash_\Sigma A$ means A is a type with respect to Γ and Σ, and $\Gamma \vdash_\Sigma a : A$ means that object a has type A with respect to Γ and Σ. The typing rules are as follows, where we use the notation "$\Gamma \vdash_\Sigma B_i$ for all $1 \le i \le n$" as an abbreviation for n antecedents of the same shape if $n > 0$, and if $n = 0$ for $\Gamma \vdash_\Sigma \diamond$.

$$\frac{\Gamma \vdash_\Sigma B_i \ \text{ for all } 1 \le i \le n}{\Gamma \vdash_\Sigma [l_i : B_i^{1 \le i \le n}]} \qquad (\textsc{TypeObj})$$

$$\frac{\Gamma \vdash_\Sigma A_i \text{ for all } 1 \le i \le n \quad (C :: n) \in \Sigma}{\Gamma \vdash_\Sigma C_{A_1, \cdots, A_n}} \qquad (\textsc{TypeCons})$$

$$\emptyset \vdash_\emptyset \diamond \qquad (\textsc{EnvCtxEmpty})$$

$$\frac{\Gamma \vdash_\Sigma \diamond \quad C \notin dom(\Sigma)}{\Gamma \vdash_{\Sigma, C :: n} \diamond} \qquad (\textsc{EnvParType})$$

$$\frac{\begin{array}{c}\Gamma \vdash_\Sigma B_j \text{ for all } 1 \le j \le m \\ \Gamma \vdash_\Sigma P_i[B_1, \cdots, B_m] \text{ for all } 1 \le i \le n \quad f \notin dom(\Sigma)\end{array}}{\Gamma \vdash_{\Sigma, f :: [m](P_1, \cdots, P_{n-1} \,\triangleright\, P_n)} \diamond} \qquad (\textsc{EnvAlg})$$

$$\frac{\Gamma \vdash_\Sigma A \quad x \notin dom(\Gamma)}{\Gamma, x : A \vdash_\Sigma \diamond} \qquad (\textsc{CtxVar})$$

$$\frac{\Gamma \vdash_\Sigma \diamond \quad x{:}A \in \Gamma}{\Gamma \vdash_\Sigma x : A} \qquad (\textsc{ValVar})$$

$$\frac{\Gamma, x_i : A \vdash_\Sigma b_i : B_i \ \text{ for all } 1 \le i \le n \quad \left(\text{where } A \equiv [l_i : B_i^{1 \le i \le n}]\right)}{\Gamma \vdash_\Sigma [l_i = \varsigma(x_i : A)\,b_i^{1 \le i \le n}] : A} \qquad (\textsc{ValObj})$$

$$\frac{\Gamma \vdash_\Sigma a : [l_i : B_i^{1 \le i \le n}] \quad 1 \le j \le n}{\Gamma \vdash_\Sigma a.l_j : B_j} \qquad (\textsc{ValSel})$$

$$\frac{\Gamma \vdash_\Sigma a : A \quad \Gamma, x : A \vdash_\Sigma b : B_j \quad 1 \le j \le n \quad \left(\text{where } A \equiv [l_i : B_i^{1 \le i \le n}]\right)}{\Gamma \vdash_\Sigma (a.l_j \Leftarrow \varsigma(x : A)b) : A} \qquad (\textsc{ValOv})$$

$$\frac{\begin{array}{c}\Gamma \vdash_\Sigma B_j \text{ for all } 1 \le j \le m \\ \Gamma \vdash_\Sigma a_i : P_i[B_1, \cdots, B_m] \text{ for all } 1 \le i \le n \\ (f :: [m](P_1, \cdots, P_n \triangleright P)) \in \Sigma\end{array}}{\Gamma \vdash_\Sigma f_{B_1, \cdots, B_m}(a_1, \cdots, a_n) : P[B_1, \cdots, B_m]} \qquad (\textsc{ValAlg})$$

In the rule ENVALG, $B_1, \cdots, B_m$ are arbitrary types (they may be the empty object type, for example), their role is to ensure that if any of the P_i is parametric (i.e. it contains natural numbers), it is well formed in the sense that it yields a proper type when instantiated (See lemma 8.). Observe that natural numbers can only appear in Σ.

4.2 Properties of the Typed Calculus

In this section we highlight some properties of the typed calculus. The omitted proofs are standard and straightforward. We use J to denote arbitrary statements. $\Gamma \subseteq \Delta$ means that if $x{:}A$ is in Γ then it is in Δ.

Lemma 6 Determinism. *Any provable statement, other than $\Diamond$, uniquely determines the last rule of its derivation.*

Lemma 7. *If $\Gamma \vdash_\Sigma A$ then A doesn't contain any natural numbers.*

Lemma 8 Substitution. *Given $\Gamma \vdash_\Sigma P[B_1, \cdots, B_n]$ it follows that for all $C_1, \cdots, C_n$ if $\Gamma \vdash_\Sigma C_i$ for every $i \in \{1 \cdots n\}$ then $\Gamma \vdash_\Sigma P[C_1, \cdots, C_n]$.*

Proof. If P has no natural numbers in it, the result is immediate. Otherwise, the proof follows by induction on the derivation of $\Gamma \vdash_\Sigma P[B_1, \cdots, B_n]$, using Determinism 6 and Lemma 7.

Definition 9. An object rewrite rule $l \rightarrow r$ is *type preserving* if for every substitution σ, $\Gamma \vdash_\Sigma l\sigma : A$ implies $\Gamma \vdash_\Sigma r\sigma : A$.

The system satisfies the uniqueness of types property (which follows by Determinism 6), the type annotations on constants such as *nil* are needed for this property to hold. Provided the algebraic rewrite rules are type preserving, the system satisfies the subject reduction property as well.

Proposition 10 Uniqueness of Types. *If $\Gamma \vdash_\Sigma a : A$ and $\Gamma \vdash_\Sigma a : A'$, then $A \equiv A'$.*

Lemma 11 Context Lemma. *1. If $\Gamma \vdash_\Sigma \Diamond$ then all variables in Γ are different.*
  2. If $\Gamma \vdash_\Sigma J$ then $\Gamma' \vdash_\Sigma \Diamond$ for every prefix Γ' of Γ.
  3. If $\Gamma_1, x{:}A, \Gamma_2 \vdash_\Sigma J$ then $\Gamma_1 \vdash_\Sigma A$ with a shorter subderivation.

Lemma 12 Strengthening. *If $\Gamma_1, x{:}A, \Gamma_2 \vdash_\Sigma J$ and x is not free in J then $\Gamma_1, \Gamma_2 \vdash_\Sigma J$.*

If one tries to prove Weakening (Corollary 15) directly by induction on derivations the induction hypothesis is too weak in the case of VALOBJ. An analogous problem occurs in the lambda calculus for the abstraction rule, and was identified by McKinna and Pollack. We use their idea of *renaming* [8].

Definition 13. Let $\Gamma \vdash_\Sigma \Diamond$ and $\Delta \vdash_\Sigma \Diamond$. A *renaming* for Γ in Δ is a parallel substitution γ from variables to variables such that for every $x{:}A$ in Γ, $\gamma(x){:}A$ is in Δ. We write $J[\gamma]$ for the result of performing the substitution γ in J. The renaming $\gamma\{x \mapsto y\}$ maps x to y and behaves like γ elsewhere.

Proposition 14 Renaming. *If $\Gamma \vdash_\Sigma J$ and γ is a renaming for Γ in Δ then $\Delta \vdash_\Sigma J[\gamma]$.*

Proof. By induction on the derivation of $\Gamma \vdash_\Sigma J$. Let γ be a renaming for Γ in Δ. Most cases follow easily using the induction hypothesis or the definition of renaming. We consider here the case of VALOBJ being the last applied rule. Let $z_1, \cdots, z_n \notin dom(\Delta)$. Define n renamings, one for each i, $\gamma_i = \gamma\{x_i \mapsto z_i\}$. To prove that γ_i is a renaming for $\Gamma, x_i{:}A$ in $\Delta, z_i{:}A$ we need to prove that $\Delta, z_i{:}A \vdash_\Sigma \diamond$. By Context Lemma 11(3), there is a subderivation of $\Gamma \vdash_\Sigma A$. Then, by the induction hypothesis, $\Delta \vdash_\Sigma A$, and by CTXVAR $\Delta, z_i{:}A \vdash_\Sigma \diamond$. We can now apply the induction hypothesis to obtain $\Delta, z_i{:}A \vdash_\Sigma b_i[\gamma\{x_i \mapsto z_i\}] : B_i$ for all $i \in \{1..n\}$. Then by VALOBJ $\Gamma \vdash_\Sigma [l_i = \varsigma(z_i : A) \, b_i[\gamma\{x_i \mapsto z_i\}]^{1 \le i \le n}] : A$, and, by the definition of substitution, $\Gamma \vdash_\Sigma [l_i = \varsigma(x_i : A) \, b_i^{1 \le i \le n}][\gamma] : A$.

Weakening now follows as a corollary of renaming taking γ to be the identity substitution.

Corollary 15 Weakening. *If $\Gamma \vdash_\Sigma J$ and $\Gamma \subseteq \Delta$, with $\Delta \vdash_\Sigma \diamond$, then $\Delta \vdash_\Sigma J$.*

Lemma 16 Term Substitution. *If $\Gamma_1, x{:}A, \Gamma_2 \vdash_\Sigma b : B$ and $\Gamma_1 \vdash_\Sigma a : A$ then $\Gamma_1, \Gamma_2 \vdash_\Sigma b\{x \mapsto a\} : B$.*

Proof. By induction on the derivation of $\Gamma_1, x{:}A, \Gamma_2 \vdash_\Sigma b : B$, using Strengthening Lemma 12, Weakening (Corollary 15), and Context Lemma 11(1).

Proposition 17 One-Step Subject Reduction. *Let R be a set of type preserving algebraic rewrite rules. Then if $a \to b$, $\Gamma \vdash_\Sigma a : A$ implies $\Gamma \vdash_\Sigma b : A$*

Proof. By induction on the derivation of $\Gamma \vdash_\Sigma a : A$. We show here two representative cases only.

VALSEL Let $a \equiv o.l_j$. We consider the case of an outermost redex first, with $o \equiv [l_i = \varsigma(x_i) \, b_i^{\ 1 \le i \le n}]$, $b \equiv b_j\{x_j \mapsto o\}$, and $A \equiv B_j$. By assumption, $\Gamma \vdash_\Sigma o : [l_i : B_i^{1 \le i \le n}]$ and $1 \le j \le n$. By Determinism, $\Gamma, x_j : [l_i : B_i^{1 \le i \le n}] \vdash_\Sigma b_j : B_j$. By Substitution Lemma 16, $\Gamma \vdash_\Sigma b_j\{x_j \mapsto o\} : B_j$. Otherwise, the reduction is inside o, and the result follows by the induction hypothesis and the rule VALSEL.

VALALG Let $a \equiv f_{B_1, \cdots, B_m}(a_1, \cdots, a_n)$ and $A \equiv P[B_1, \cdots, B_m]$. If there exists a rule $l \to r$ in R and a substitution σ such that $f_{B_1, \cdots, B_m}(a_1, \cdots, a_n) \equiv l\sigma$ and $b \equiv r\sigma$, then because R is type preserving $\Gamma \vdash_\Sigma r\sigma : A$. Otherwise, the reduction is inside some a_i and, by the induction hypothesis and the rule VALALG, $\Gamma \vdash_\Sigma b : A$.

Proposition 18 Subject Reduction. *Let R be a set of type preserving algebraic rewrite rules. Then if $a \to^* b$, $\Gamma \vdash_\Sigma a : A$ implies $\Gamma \vdash_\Sigma b : A$*

Proof. The proof is by induction on the definition of $\to^*$. The reflexivity case is immediate; the one step reduction case follows from Proposition 17, and the transitivity case follows by the induction hypothesis.

Under the assumption of subject reduction we can also prove the confluence of the typed calculus, provided that R is left-linear and confluent for algebraic objects. The proof is a straightforward adaptation of the one given in Section 3.

4.3 Example: Types for the Editor

The editor presented in Section 2.3 can also be defined in the typed calculus. Assuming that the constant type $Char$ is in Σ, and that we also have a parametric constant $List :: 1$ in Σ, we can define an object type:

$$B \equiv [before : List_{Char}, after : List_{Char}, cursor : Char].$$

The type of the editor, according to the previous rules, and assuming the constant type $String$ is also in Σ, would have the form:

$$E \equiv [text : B, input : A_1, find : A_2, init : A_3,$$
$$forward : A_4, backwards : A_5, message : String]$$

We can derive the types $A_1, \ldots, A_5$ in E using the typing rules given in the previous section, together with the standard rules for lambda abstraction. We use an environment Σ containing also the constant type $Bool$, the symbol *if then else* with specification $[1](Bool, 1, 1 \triangleright 1)$, and @ $:: [1](List_1, List_1 \triangleright List_1)$, hd $:: [1](List_1 \triangleright 1)$, tl $:: [1](List_1 \triangleright List_1)$, last $:: [1](List_1 \triangleright 1)$, no-last $:: [1](List_1 \triangleright List_1)$. Γ is a set of assumptions for variables containing $l_1 : List_{Char}$, $l_2 : List_{Char}$.

It is easy to check that the field *text* has type B, and that the types of the other methods are $A_1 \equiv Char \triangleright E$, $A_2 \equiv Char \triangleright E$, $A_3 \equiv E$, $A_4 \equiv E$, $A_5 \equiv E$. Hence we get

$$E = [text : B, input : Char \triangleright E, find : Char \triangleright E, init : E,$$
$$forward : E, backwards : E, message : String].$$

But this is a recursive equation; to solve it, we need recursive types. This is actually the case each time we want to type objects whose methods return self or an updated self. A *recursive type* $\mu(X)B\{X\}$ where X is a type variable and the notation $B\{X\}$ indicates that X may occur free in B, is the unique solution of the equation $X = B\{X\}$ up to isomorphism. We refer to [2] for a detailed account of recursive types in the ς-calculus. Adding the rules for recursive types to our calculus and the necessary type annotations and folds to the self variables in the editor, we obtain the following type:

$$E \equiv \mu(X) [text : B, input : Char \triangleright X, find : Char \triangleright X, init : X,$$
$$forward : X, backwards : X, message : String].$$

The addition of the fragments Δ_X and Δ_μ, from Abadi and Cardelli's first order object calculus with recursion, and the reduction rules $fold(A, unfold(a)) \rightarrow a$ and $unfold(fold(A, b)) \rightarrow b$ to our calculus preserves all the properties from Section 4.2.

5 Conclusions

To our knowledge this is the first attempt to combine object calculi with algebraic rewriting. It is well-known that algebraic rewrite rules provide flexibility in the definition of data types. For example, they have been successfully used in combination with the λ-calculus to obtain a uniform system where one can model higher-order functions and data types [3, 7]. Combining the three calculi we inherit the expressiveness of the λ-calculus to manipulate higher-order functions, the versatility of algebraic rewriting to define first-order data types, and the power of the primitives of the ς-calculus to model objects. The λ-calculus can be encoded in the ς-calculus, so we can simply use its encoding; however, the object rewrite rules cannot be encoded and hence the combination presented in this paper is a proper extension of the ς-calculus.

There is another way to add algebraic objects to the calculus, suggested by Martín Abadi in private communication. Instead of adding the set $\mathcal{F}$ of algebraic symbols one could add a set $\mathcal{O}$ of object symbols. An object symbol would just be like a constant added to the grammar, and we would have expressions like $o.l$, where o is an object constant.

In some sense, the two approaches are equally expressive, since we can always translate back and forth:

for f in $\mathcal{F}$, of arity n, invent a symbol o in $\mathcal{O}$, and translate:

$$f(t_1, ..., t_n) = ((...(o.arg_1 := t_1)...).arg_n := t_n).val$$

For example we would need to ensure that if f has arity 4 then $((o.arg_1 := t_1).arg_3 := t_3).val$ translated as $f(t_1 - t_3-)$ is an illegal expression; also the updating of the val field should be protected. We would also need to add equations or rewrite rules reflecting the behaviour of the constant o as an object, extending $\rightarrow_\varsigma$ so that $(...o.arg_i := t_i...).arg_i = t_i$.

In our approach, we see the algebraic symbols as "constructors of objects", in the same way as the square brackets for instance are constructors of objects in the pure calculus. For example, the natural number 0 is an object, and so is $+(0,0)$. In this sense, any $f \in \mathcal{F}$ is a constructor of objects, and when the right number of arguments are given, it produces an object. These algebraic objects are like "black boxes", in contrast with the square brackets that build "white boxes" where we can see the contents of the fields. In a language based on our calculus the compiler can make the translation from the algebraic syntax to the one with square brackets and object constants.

There are other possibilities for a type system for our calculus. We can write a type system in Barendregt's cube style where a parametric type is a constant in the context with appropriate arity. For example $LIST : \star \rightarrow \star$. But then we need a rule $(\square, \square)$ to be able to show the well-formation of $\star \rightarrow \star$. Although this approach allows us to do what we want, it still allows for more than we intend. For example we can not only form parametric constants, but also abstractions from types to types, in other words the full power of F^ω. Alternatively, we can define the language of kinds with the following grammar: $K ::= \star \mid K \rightarrow K$. But this again allows for more than what we need. For example the kind $(\star \rightarrow \star) \rightarrow \star$ will allow a parametric type to take another parametric type as argument, but we only want a calculus of ground types. Moreover both alternatives allow parametric types and algebraic constants to be partially applied. We then took a third option in which we define the term constructors with specifications in such a way that they can only be typed when applied to all their arguments.

The calculus is extended straightforwardly with the subtyping rules of [2] and the usual subsumption rule for typing. At this stage we do not add subtyping on parametric types, this is a subject of current study and beyond the scope of this paper. We believe that subtyping on constants does not pose any problem provided the set of subtyping axioms on types is transitively closed. Since the subtyping of objects is invariant in its components, the subtyping for parametric types is somewhat orthogonal to the object subtyping. In the example of the lists, if A is a subtype of B one might want to consider $List_A$ a subtype of $List_B$. It remains to be seen if a type inference algorithm in the style of [11] can be defined.

Acknowledgements
We thank Healfdene Goguen for his help in refining earlier versions of the type system, David Aspinall for useful discussions, and Martín Abadi, Ian Mackie, James McKinna, Stefan Kahrs, and three anonymous referees for comments on earlier versions of this paper.

References

1. M. Abadi and L. Cardelli. A theory of primitive objects. Untyped and first-order systems. In *Theoretical Aspects of Computer Software*, pages 296–320. Springer-Verlag, 1994.
2. M. Abadi and L. Cardelli. A theory of primitive objects. Untyped and first-order systems. *Information and Computation*, 125(2):78–102, 1996.
3. Val Breazu-Tannen and Jean Gallier. Polymorphic rewriting conserves algebraic strong normalization. *Theoretical Computer Science*, 83(1), 1991.
4. Val Breazu-Tannen and Jean Gallier. Polymorphic rewriting conserves algebraic confluence. *Information and Computation*, 82:3–28, 1992.
5. A. Gordon and G. Rees. Bisimilarity for a first-order calculus of objects with subtyping. In *Proc. 23rd ACM Symposium on Principles of Programming Languages*, St. Petersburg Beach, Florida, 1996.
6. R. Harper, F. Honsell, and G. Plotkin. A framework for defining logics. *Journal of the ACM*, 40(1):143–184, 1993.
7. J.-P. Jouannaud and M. Okada. Executable higher-order algebraic specification languages. In *Proc. 6th Annual IEEE Symposium on Logic in Computer Science*, pages 350–361, 1991.
8. J. McKinna and R. Pollack. Pure type systems formalized. In J-F Groote and M Bezem, editors, *Proc. of the International Conference on Typed Lambda Calculi and Applications*, volume 664 of *Lecture Notes in Computer Science*. Springer-Verlag, 1993.
9. J. Mitchell, F. Honsell, and K. Fisher. A lambda calculus of objects and method specialization. *Nordic Journal of Computing*, 1(1):3–37, 1994.
10. F. Müller. Confluence of the lambda-calculus with left-linear algebraic rewriting. *Information Processing Letters*, 41:293–299, 1992.
11. J. Palsberg. Efficient inference of object types. In *Proc. 9th Annual IEEE Symposium on Logic in Computer Science*, Paris, France, 1994.
12. B. K. Rosen. Tree-manipulating systems and Church-Rosser theorems. *Journal of the ACM*, 20:160–187, 1973.

Inheritance and Selective Method Dispatching in Concurrent Haskell

José E. Gallardo, Francisco Gutiérrez and Blas C. Ruiz

Dpto. de Lenguajes y Ciencias de la Computación
E.T.S.I. Informática. Campus Teatinos, 29071–Málaga, Spain
e–mail:{pepeg,pacog,blas}@lcc.uma.es
fax: +34–5–2131397   phone number: +34–5–2132795

Abstract. We incorporate object oriented features into the functional language *Haskell*: inheritance and methods with *super* and *self* references. Parametric polymorphism is retained in object classes. Interfaces are used to describe protocols (as a set of overloaded functional methods) and methods can be defined by default. Object classes implement (or inherit) interface methods. These classes and interfaces are organised in a hierarchical structure. We have integrated our model with *Concurrent Haskell*. The integrity of object attributes can be guaranteed via a guarded construct, which can also be used to selectively accept messages, depending on the object state and message arguments. The synchronisation mechanism is shown by examples. Our model offers a way out from the inheritance anomaly problem in most cases by incorporating synchronisation constraints into the inheritance hierarchy.

Keywords : *Concurrent objects, functional programming, guarded methods, inheritance anomaly, Haskell.*

1   Introduction

Object oriented languages are widely used because the generated code can be easily reused. Some of the most powerful features of these kinds of languages are polymorphism and class inheritance. The *inheritance anomaly* is a well known phenomenon that appears when adding concurrency to an object oriented language (this is broadly described in [MatYon93]): the *synchronisation constraints* on a method of a parent class need to be changed as a result of extending that class (synchronisation constraints determine if a concurrent object may accept a subset of messages in order to maintain its internal integrity). The occurrence of the inheritance anomaly depends on the synchronisation scheme of the language and the possibility of redefining the synchronisation code without non-trivial class redefinitions (maybe using inheritance).

Concurrence is usually incorporated using either *active objects* (with autonomous bodies/threads) or *passive objects*: messages may be processed concurrently and can be accepted using some form of guarded mechanism (*declarative model* using [MitWel94] terminology). In the former model, each object must have a *body* (an internal method owning a thread of control). Some researchers have pointed out the difficulty of integrating inheritance with this model because the definition of the subclass requires total redefinition of the body, and also complete knowledge and access to the synchronisation constraints code of the ancestor class. Due to this, we have considered the declarative model. [MatYon93] have studied the inheritance anomaly problems when guards are boolean expressions whose terms are either constants or instance variables. To avoid these problems, our model also allows sending operations inside the guards. In this way, modifications of synchronisation constraints are redefined using inheritance.

We introduce an extension to the language *Haskell 1.3* [MooHam96] that deals with *Object Oriented features*. Our extended language implements inheritance, and references to the special names *self* and *super* can be used in methods. This feature makes it possible to model *late binding*: sending a message to *self* within a method currently defined can invoke a method in a subclass that is not defined already. The type checking system guarantees safe message passing (i.e., a message sent to an object will always be dispatched). Polymorphism is described in the same fashion as *Haskell*.

Objects are essentially mutable so the state of an object is represented using mutable references [LauPey96]. In our model, side-effecting methods update the state of the object in place instead of returning a new object as in [HugSpa95]. Moreover, objects can make input/output operations over the real world through an *IOC* monad, defined on top of the *Haskell 1.3 IO monad* that provides named concurrent threads, while preserving the *referential transparency* of pure functional languages. This *IOC* monad will be used to solve synchronisation problems due to *self* references. We also achieve the implementation of a model for *selective method dispatching*. Our model offers a way out from the inheritance anomaly problem in most cases by incorporating synchronisation constraints into the inheritance hierarchy.

The main aim of this paper is to show that the *Haskell* type system may be used to model object oriented features without further extensions.

The rest of the paper is organized as follows. In section 2 we review some concepts related to monadic programming and introduce the *IOC* monad. In section 3 we summarise our proposal by means of examples. Some guidelines to translate our language into *Haskell* are presented in section 4. Finally in section 5 we review related work and conclude the article.

2   The IOC Monad

Monads [Moggi89] are algebraic structures, taken from category theory, that may be used to structure functional programs [Wadler92]. From the point of view of a *Haskell* programmer, a *monad* is an instance of the **Monad** class:

```
data M a = ...
class Monad m where
    (>>=)  :: m a -> (a -> m b) -> m b
```

```
(>>)    :: m a -> m b -> m b
return :: a -> m a

p >> q  = p >>= \_ -> q
```

```
instance Monad M where ...
```

The idea is that a computation delivering a value of type a is represented through a value of type M a, where M is an instance of the class above. The return function embeds a value into a monad. The (>>=) operator may be used to sequence two monadic computations passing the result from the first computation to the second. The (>>) operator ignores the result of its first argument.

Input and output operations may be integrated in a pure functional language using monads without sacrificing *referential transparency* [LauPey96]. This idea has been taken into *Haskell 1.3*. A value of type IO a stands for an input/output operation that returns a value of type a. The following program reads a character from the keyboard and displays it on the screen:

```
main :: IO ()
main = getChar   >>= \c ->
       putChar c >>
       return ()
```

In [PGF96] the language is extended with explicit concurrency, mutable variable references (MutVars) and synchronising mutable variables (MVars), using the following functions :

```
newMutVar    ::                    IO (MutVar a)
writeMutVar :: MutVar a -> a -> IO ()
readMutVar  :: MutVar a ->        IO a

newMVar      ::                    IO (MVar a)
putMVar      :: MVar a -> a ->    IO ()
takeMVar     :: MVar a ->         IO a
```

In addition, the forkIO function (with type IO () -> IO ()) is used to introduce a new action that will be reduced concurrently.

In order to implement the features we present in this paper we need named processes, so the following monad is defined:

```
type ProcessId = Int
data ProcState = State ProcessId (MVar ProcessId)
newtype IOC a  = IOC (ProcState -> IO (a, ProcState))

instance Monad IOC where
  return x    = IOC (\s -> return (x,s))
  IOC m >>= f = IOC (\s -> m s >>= \(x,s') ->
                           let IOC f' = f x
                           in f' s')
```

The `MVar` in `ProcState` is a shared reference to a global counter used to generate new process identifiers.

These identifiers will later be used to resolve non suspension of messages sent to the *self*. In order to use the *Concurrent Haskell* primitives we define two functions over `IO` and `IOC` computations:

```
lift :: IO a -> IOC a
lift ac = IOC (\s -> ac >>= \x -> return (x,s))


liftDown :: ProcState -> IOC a -> IO a
liftDown st (IOC t) = t st >>= \(x,_) -> return x
```

From these functions it is easy to implement a `forkIO` version for the `IOC` monad:

```
forkIOC :: IOC () -> IOC ()
forkIOC m = nextProcessSt >>= \nextSt ->
     (lift . forkIO . liftDown nextSt) m
 where
  nextProcessSt :: IOC ProcState
  nextProcessSt =
       readState                     >>= \(State _ maxIdMVar) ->
       takeMVar maxIdMVar            >>= \maxId                ->
       putMVar maxIdMVar (maxId+1) >>
       return (State (maxId+1) maxIdMVar)
```

Each time a process is scheduled through a `forkIOC` action a new identifier is assigned to it.

3 The language

In the following new keywords are written in bold type, examples in the new language are typed using italics and standard *Haskell* code is in typewriter font.

3.1 Classes and Interfaces

An interface is a collection of abstract functions (*methods*) and is defined using an **interface** declaration. We indicate, for each method within the interface, the type of its possible arguments and always, the type of its response (this must be an *IOC* type). A response is produced when a method is received and is returned as an *IOC* type. Here is a basic interface for object collections:

interface *ICollection*
 where
   isEmpty   :: *IOC Bool*
   notEmpty   :: *IOC Bool*
   isFull   :: *IOC Bool*
   notFull   :: *IOC Bool*

$$len \qquad :: \ IOC \ Int$$

$$
\begin{aligned}
isEmpty & = \mathbf{self} \ ! \ notEmpty >>= \ \backslash b \rightarrow return \ (not \ b) \\
notEmpty & = \mathbf{self} \ ! \ isEmpty >>= \ \backslash b \rightarrow return \ (not \ b) \\
isFull & = return \ False \\
notFull & = \mathbf{self} \ ! \ isFull >>= \ \backslash b \rightarrow return \ (not \ b)
\end{aligned}
$$

A *default definition* for a method may be given in an interface. If a method is neither defined nor inherited in a class, the default method is used. Most of the methods in the *ICollection* interface are defined by default. The first two definitions are cyclic, so at least one of them must be defined. The word **self** within a method denotes the receiver of the message which invoked the method and may be used by an object to send a message to itself. The (!) operator is used to send messages to an object. In the implementation of a default method, messages are typically sent to **self**, so we must ensure that **self** can receive these messages.

An interface can be *extended* by another interface. In this way, methods defined in the former can be sent to **self** objects used in methods defined in the latter. Interface extension is transitive and defines a multiple inheritance hierarchy on the interfaces. For example, the *IBuffer* interface:

interface *IBuffer a* **extends** *ICollection*
> *where*
> | | | |
> |---|---|---|
> | put | :: $a \rightarrow$ | $IOC \ ()$ |
> | get | :: | $IOC \ a$ |
> | move | :: **Self** $\rightarrow$ | $IOC \ ()$ |
>
> *move buff =* *buff* ! *isEmpty* $>>=$ \\b $\rightarrow$
> *if b then return()*
> *else buff* ! *get* $>>=$ *item* $\rightarrow$ (**self** ! *put) item* $>>$
> (**self** ! *move) buff*

declares three different methods and defines one of them by default. The meaning of *get* and *put* methods is the usual one. The third method can be used to move the contents of its buffer argument to the receiver object.

The method *isEmpty* from the interface *ICollection* is used in the default definition of *move*. If a class implements the interface *IBuffer* it must also implement the interface *ICollection*, i.e. the interface *IBuffer* extends the interface *ICollection*. The type **Self** used in the declaration of *move* denotes the type of **self**.

A class is a template to create objects and is defined via an **object class** declaration. Interfaces used by the object are declared, announcing whether it is inherited or implemented for each method. Instance variables and their types along with the implementation of non-inherited methods are shown after the *where* clause. Functions that implement object methods are able to access the object instance variables.

Generic classes are used to define objects that are polymorphic in their instance variables. Afterwards, we can create instances with different actual types. Typical examples of generic classes are *buffers*. Let us define a *Buffer* class whose base type is polymorphic:

object class *Buffer a*
    use *ICollection* **implement** *isEmpty, len*
    use *IBuffer*   **implement** *put, get*
   where
   instanceVars *xs::[a] size::Int*
   methods
     put x   = **become** *(Buffer (xs++[x]) (size+1))*
     get   = **when** *(***self** *! notEmpty) >>*
                 let (y:ys) = xs in
                 become *(Buffer ys (size-1)) >> return y*
     isEmpty   = *return (size == 0)*
     len   = *return size*

newBuffer = **new** *(Buffer [] 0)*

The word **become** is used to change the state of the receiving object, while **new** is used to create new objects. The **when** *(* **self** *! notEmpty)* action is used to suspend execution of the *get* method if the response to the *(***self** *! notEmpty)* message is false (see next section).

As the example above shows, an object class may implement several interfaces (this is a well-known idea and it is also incorporated in modern object oriented languages like *Java* [ArnGos96]). An object belonging to this class may receive any of the messages in these interfaces.

3.2 Selective method dispatching

Several processes may send messages to the same object, so the **become** operation (that updates the state of the object) is atomic. However, it is not guaranteed that the whole body of the method will be reduced in *mutual exclusion*. Due to this, we have also enriched our model through *guards* (or *synchronisation constraints*) in the methods. Guarded methods are executed in *mutual exclusion* with respect to receiver object: a single process may execute a guarded command or a **become** operation over an object at the same time. This restriction is needed to ensure consistency among parts of the object state appearing in the guards and **become** operations. As the following example shows

    newBuffer >>= \buf1 →...
    newBuffer >>= \buf2 →...
    forkIOC ((buf1 ! move) buf2 >> ...) >>
    forkIOC (buf2 ! get >>= \item →...)

the *move* method does not guarantee that the entire contents of the *buf2* buffer is moved to the receiver object (*buf1*) nor that the state of the receiver is unchanged by a third object during the reduction of the *move* method. In order to solve these problems, the execution of a method may be protected by *synchronisation conditions* through a **when** construction. This function is overloaded so that we can use as a synchronisation condition a boolean expression or a sequence of actions that returns a boolean value. The meaning of the **when** construction is standard: a guarded command may be selected if its synchronisation condition holds.

A synchronisation condition may depend on the message arguments and the object state. A method may have several guards. The following example implements an *Agent* object that manages a shared resource. Maximal uses of resources are taken into account. If the requested amount of resources is not available, the requesting process will be suspended:

```
interface IAgent
    where
        free         :: Int → IOC ()
        acquire      :: Int → IOC ()
        timesEmpty:: IOC Int

object class Agent
    use IAgent     implement     free, acquire, timesEmpty
    where
    instanceVars resources::Int tEmpty::Int
    methods
    free n        = become (Agent (resources+n) tEmpty)
    acquire n     = when (n < resources) >>
                    become (Agent (resources-n) tEmpty)
                    alt
                    when (n == resources) >>
                    become (Agent 0 (tEmpty+1))
    timesEmpty = return tEmpty
```

The *acquire* method has two guarded sequences of actions separated by using the reserved word **alt**. No functions are defined for these guards so they cannot be inherited. If several guards are true, only the guarded action corresponding to one of them will be reduced. If none of them holds, the evaluation of the method is suspended until the receipt of a new message. At that moment, the former process will be repeated. Note that the actions appearing inside a **when** construction may be executed several times (in mutual exclusion) while the corresponding methods may finally not be selected (the programmer must be aware of these situations).

The implementation of a class could be hidden, but to use an object the synchronisation constraint associated with a method may be needed. For this purpose synchronisation constraints can optionally be expressed within curly brackets after each method name in the **use** clause (this information is useful in solving the inheritance anomaly):

    use *IBuffer*   **implement** *put, get{notEmpty}*

3.3 Inheritance

Our language implements *single inheritance* object classes, and interfaces can be used to simulate a restricted *multiple inheritance* form. A subclass may inherit methods defined in other classes or define methods that are declared in another interface. The following example refines the *Buffer* class. An extra instance variable (the buffer maximum size) is needed at the *BoundedBuffer* class. The *put* method is redefined while the *isFull* method is implemented.

object class *BoundedBuffer* **extends** *Buffer*
    use *IBuffer*   **inherit**   *get*
                                    implement *put{notFull}*
    use *ICollection*   **inherit**   *isEmpty, len*
                                    implement *isFull*
  where
  instanceVars *maxLen::Int*
  methods
    isFull $=$ **self** ! *len* $>>= \setminus l \rightarrow return(l >= maxLen)$
    put n $=$ **when** *(self* ! *notFull)* $>>$
                            *(***super** ! *put) n* $>>$
                            become *(BoundedBuffer maxLen)*

The attributes of the *superclass* are not visible in the subclass. In order to access them messages must be used. The word **extends** indicates that *BoundedBuffer* is a subclass of *Buffer*. The meaning of **super** is well-known in object oriented programming: the expression **super** ! *put* means that the receiver of that message is the object itself, but acting as an instance of the superclass. Therefore, the search for the right method starts at the parent of the class where the method that uses **super** is defined. On the other hand, when a *BoundedBuffer* object receives a *get* message the method in the superclass is used (because it is inherited):

    get $=$ **when** *(self* ! *notEmpty)* $>>$
                let (y:ys) $=$ *xs in*
                become *(Buffer ys (size-1))* $>>$ *return y*

While evaluating the code corresponding to *get*, the message **self** ! *notEmpty* is sent to the original object, i.e. the *BoundedBuffer* object. On this occasion, the default definition for the *notEmpty* method is used

    notEmpty $=$ **self** ! *isEmpty* $>>= \setminus b \rightarrow return$ *(not b)* and finally the *isEmpty* code inherited from the superclass is invoked. If the method was redefined at the subclass, this redefinition would be used. In order to create a new *BoundedBuffer*, a *Buffer* must be created and extended:

$newBoundedBuffer\ maxLen =$
  $newBuffer >>= \backslash buf \rightarrow$
  new *(BoundedBuffer maxLen)* **extends** *buf*

3.4 Inheritance anomaly

If the *inheritance anomaly* is not considered in the language, code reuse is drastically limited. The solution we present consists of including synchronisation constraints in the inheritance hierarchy. A subclass may inherit or redefine the method corresponding to a constraint. In this fashion, a superclass method may be reused in a subclass while changing its synchronisation constraint. The following example shows a new kind of buffer where an item can be obtained only when the buffer is not going to become empty. A new method that retrieves two consecutive items from the buffer is added too. Note that this cannot be achieved by just sending two *get* messages to the buffer:

interface *IBuffer2 a* **extends** *IBuffer a*
  where
  get2   ::   *IOC (a,a)*
  canGet2   ::   *IOC Bool*

  canGet2   = **self** ! *len* >>= $\backslash l \rightarrow return(l >= 2)$

object class *Buffer2* **extends** *Buffer*
  use *IBuffer*   **inherit**   *put, get*
  use *ICollection* **inherit**   *isFull, len*
                         implement *isEmpty*
  use *IBuffer2*   **implement** *get2{canGet2}*
  where
  methods
  get2   = **when** *(self* ! *canGet2)* >> **self** ! *get* >>= $\backslash i1 \rightarrow$
                     self ! *get* >>= $\backslash i2 \rightarrow return(i1,i2)$
  notEmpty   = **self** ! *len* >>= $\backslash l \rightarrow return(l>=2)$

$newBuffer2 = newBuffer >>= \backslash buf \rightarrow$ **new** *Buffer2* **extends** *buf*

In order to redefine the semantics of *get* only its synchronisation constraint has to be changed by redefining *notEmpty*. By separating the synchronisation code from other parts of method definition, the number of redefinitions is minimised. This is possible because the synchronisation constraint corresponding to each method is shown after its declaration.

4 Implementation

We are writing a pre-processor to translate our language into *Concurrent Haskell* [PGF96] and now present the foundations of our model, based on [PieTur94] and [HugSpa95]. We translate each **interface** into a *Haskell* class and each **object class** into one or several *Haskell* instances. Interface hierarchy is implemented using *Haskell* class contexts. The object hierarchy is composed of data structures that are successively refined: an instance of a class always contains an instance of its *superclass*. This is an essential concept, because when a method is inherited, it is dispatched in the *superclass*.

If we consider *non-mutable objects* (as in [PieTur94]), a side effecting method must return a new copy of the object with the state updated. An inherited method must send the same message to its *super* and compose the final object through a reconstruction function (**recons**) using the *super* response. In [HugSpa95] this reconstruction function is an additional parameter in the *Haskell* code implementing each method :

```
class InterfaceId obj where
  m :: InterfaceId  self => (obj -> self) -> obj -> self
instance InterfaceId  ClassData where
  -- the method implementation
  m recons obj = recons (g obj)      -- g computes the response
instance InterfaceId  SubclassData where
  -- in a subclass an inherited method is sent to the super
  m recons obj = m (recons . immerse obj) (super_of obj)
```

The last instance defines a version of the method when *self* type is `SubclassData`. Using the above model the implementation of the sending operator is

```
(!) self m = m (\x -> x) self
```

Our approach considers *mutable objects* that are implemented using references [LauPey96]. The side effecting methods update the state of the object in place, so we do not need the reconstruction of the object. Consequently, our implementation of methods do not have the extra argument representing the reconstruction function. Instead the argument representing *self* is needed:

```
class InterfaceId obj where
  m :: InterfaceId self => self -> obj -> IOC r
instance InterfaceId ClassData  where
  -- method implementation
  m self obj  = return (g obj)
instance InterfaceId SubclassData where
  -- a method inherited in a subclass
  m self obj  = m self (super_of obj)
```

This translation implements *late binding*. In short, we declare a *Haskell* class for each *OOP* interface and a *Haskell* instance for each interface used by the *OOP* class. The implementation of the sending operator is

```
(!) :: self -> (self -> self -> response) -> response
(!) self m = m self self
```

So, a method always begins to execute from the expression m **self self** and
if it is inherited causes successive evaluation of the form m **self super**, in such
a way that the *super* type goes on changing. Thus, it is necessary to guarantee
the correct type of function corresponding to the method.

For example, the resulting classes for the *ICollection* and *IBuffer* interfaces
are:

```
class ICollection obj where
 isEmpty     :: ICollection self => self a -> obj a -> IOC Bool
 ...
 isEmpty self obj = self ! notEmpty >>= \b -> return(not b)
 ...
class ICollection obj => IBuffer obj where
 put  :: IBuffer self => self a -> obj a -> a       -> IOC ()
 move :: IBuffer self => self a -> obj a -> self a -> IOC ()
 ...
 move self obj buff = ...
                      -- the same code defined in the interface
```

Let us observe that the full power of constructor classes [Jones95] is needed in
order to implement the polymorphic interfaces. The translation corresponding
to an object class consists of a new datatype definition (containing a reference
to the *super* state or () if the defined object is on top of the hierarchy) and
one instance for each used interface (synchronisation variables are omitted for
simplicity):

```
data Buffer' a = Buffer () [a] Int
data Buffer a = BufferRef (MutVar (Buffer' a))

instance ICollection Buffer where
 isEmpty self (BufferRef ref) =
     readMutVar ref >>= \(Buffer super xs size) ->
     return (size==0)
 ...
instance IBuffer Buffer where
 get self (BufferRef ref)   =
     readMutVar ref >>= \(Buffer super xs size) ->
     ... -- the translation code for "when (self ! notFull)" >>
     let (y:ys) = xs in
     writeMutVar ref (Buffer super ys (size-1)) >>
     return y
 ...
```

If we derive a subclass that extends an existing class, we obtain a new datatype
definition and its corresponding instances:

```
data BoundedBuffer' a = BoundedBuffer (Buffer a) Int
data BoundedBuffer a  =
         BoundedBufferRef (MutVar (BoundedBuffer' a))

instance ICollection BoundedBuffer where
 isEmpty self (BoundedBufferRef ref) =
     readMutVar ref >>= \(BoundedBuffer super maxLen) ->
     super ! isEmpty
 isFull self (BoundedBufferRef ref) =
     readMutVar ref >>= \(BoundedBuffer super maxLen) ->
     self ! len      >>= \l ->
     return (l >= maxLen)
 ...
instance IBuffer BoundedBuffer where
 get self (BoundedBufferRef ref) =
     readMutVar ref >>= \(BoundedBuffer super maxLen) ->
     super ! get
 ...
```

Note that the code corresponding to inherited methods has automatically been generated.

5 Related work and conclusions

There are many proposals that integrate inheritance in a functional framework. [RGGG96,Wallac95] use constructor classes [Jones95] to overload the message-sending operator. [Odersk91,ThoTof94] model inheritance using subtyping. The lack of subtypes in overloaded languages may be overcome using the second order typed λ-calculus. Existential types [Laufer96,PieTur94] may be used to achieve data hiding and dynamic binding (the Chalmers implementation of *Haskell* already includes these kinds of types). On the other hand, [Castag95] describes a language called $\lambda - object$ based on an object calculus ($\lambda\& - calculus$). A special $\beta - rule$ is used to model overloading and late binding. The main drawback in this approach is that the resulting language is not lazy. Inheritance can also be modelled using Barendregt's *GTS* (*Generalised Type Systems*) [Baren92]. In [Barthe95] *GTS* are extended to incorporate inheritance. *Coercions* are included in the type system environment (a coercion represents a subclass relation). However, this work does not model *self* references. In static typed object–oriented languages, like ours, it is necessary to guarantee the correct type of the function solving the message. As we have shown, this is achieved by the Haskell class system extended with the use of constructors. Other approaches such as [Bruce94] solve the previous problem with a type system that assigns a special type to *self*.

Our proposal shows the possibility of modelling concurrent object-oriented features in a functional framework (particularly in *Haskell*) without needing high-order extensions. By incorporating synchronisation constraints into the inheritance mechanism, we achieve a homogeneous model: *late binding* is extended by allowing polymorphic messages in synchronisation constraints. This idea is not original. [MitWel94] uses a *deontic logic* for the expression of synchronisation constraints. Private methods for *guarded objects* are deontic operators but we think that the resulting code is hard to read. [Shibay90] proposes a model based on inheritance of synchronisation schemes, using a classification of methods. This is not needed in our approach because methods can be classified using interfaces. In this way, we also resolve the restriction of the [SHBM96] proposal as behaviour and synchronisation can be separated. [Frølun92] proposes a design in which synchronisation constraints become increasingly restrictive in subclasses. This idea can be incorporated into our model by defining operators to compose synchronisation constraints.

Acknowledgements

We would like to thank the referees for some valuable comments and corrections.

References

[ArnGos96] Ken Arnold and James Gosling. *The Java Programming Language.* Addison Wesley Longman, 1996.

[Baren92]   Henk Barendregt. *Lambda calculi with types.* Handbook of Logic in Computer Science (Abramsky et a. o., Editors.), Vol 2, Oxford Publ., p. 117-309, 1992.

[Barthe95] Gilles Barthe. *Inheritance in type theory.* Research Report, Nijmegen University, September'1995.

[Bruce94]   Kim B. Bruce. *A paradigmatic object–oriented programming languaje: Design, static typing and semantics.* Journal of Functional Programming, 4(2), p. 127–206, April'1994.

[Castag95] Giuseppe Castagna. *A meta-language for typed object-oriented languages.* Theoretical Computer Science, 151(2), p. 297-352, November'1995.

[Frølun92] Svend Frølund. *Inheritance of synchronization constraints in concurrent object-oriented programming languages.* In Proceedings of ECOOP'92, LNCS 615, Springer Verlag 1992.

[HugSpa95] J. Hughes and J. Sparud. *Haskell ++: An Object-Oriented Extension of Haskell.* Dep. of Comp. Science, Chalmers University, April'1995.

[Jones95]   Mark P. Jones. *A System of Constructor Classes: overloading and implicit higher–order polymorphism.* Journal of Functional Programming, 5(1), p.1-35, January'1995.

[Laufer96] K. Laufer. *Type Classes with Existential Types.* Journal of Functional Programming, 6(3), p. 485–517, May'1996.

[LauPey96] J. Launchbury and S.L. Peyton Jones. *State in Haskell.* Lisp and Symbolic Computation, 8(4), p. 293–341, 1996.

[MatYon93] S. Matsuoka and A. Yonezawa *Analysis of Inheritance Anomaly in Object-Oriented Concurrent Programming Languages.* Research Directions in Concurrent Object-Oriented Programming (Agha and al., editors), MIT-Press, 1993.

[MitWel94]   S.E. Mitchell and A.J. Wellings. *Synchronisation, Concurrent Object-Oriented Programming and the Inheritance Anomaly*. Tech.Rep., Dep. Comp. Sc., York University, June'1994.

[Moggi89]   Eugenio Moggi. *Computational lambda–calculus and monads*. In Proceedings of IEEE Symposium on Logic in Computer Science, California, June'1989.

[MooHam96]   B.J. Moose and K. Hammond (editors). *Report on the Programming Language Haskell, A Non-Strict Purely Functional Language, Version 1.3*. Research Report YALE/DCS/RR–1106, Yale University, March'1996.

[Odersk91]   Martin Odersky. *Objects and Subtyping in a Functional Perspective*. IBM Research Report RC 16423, January'1991

[PieTur94]   B. Pierce and D. Turner. *Simple type-theoretic foundations for object-oriented programming*. Journal of Functional Programming, 4(2), p. 207-247, April'1994.

[PGF96]   S.P. Jones, A. Gordon and S. Finne. *Concurrent Haskell*. Proceedings of the 23rd ACM Symposium on POPL, Florida, January'1996.

[RGGG96]   B.C. Ruiz, J.E. Gallardo, P. Guerrero and F.Gutiérrez. *Clasificación de objetos funcionales en entornos concurrentes*. In Proceeding of APPIA–GULP–PRODE'96 (M. Navarro, editor), p. 581-584, San Sebastián (Spain), 1996.

[Shibay90]   Etsuya Shibayama. *Reuse of concurrent object descriptions*. In Proceeding of TOOLS 3 (Meyer et al., eds), p. 254–266, 1990.

[SHBM96]   F. Sánchez, J. Hernández, M. Barrena and J.M. Murillo. *Composición de restricciones de Sincronización en Lenguajes Concurrentes Orientados a Objetos*. In Proceeding of II Jornadas de Informática (B. Clares, editor), Almuñecar (Spain), July'1996.

[ThoTof94]   Lars Thorup and Mads Tofte. *Object–Oriented Programming and Standard ML*. ACM Workshop on ML and its Applications, Orlando, June'1994.

[Wadler92]   Philip Wadler. *The essence of functional programming*. In Proceeding of 19'th ACM Symposium on Principles of Programming Languages, Santa Fe, January'1992.

[Wallac95]   Malcolm Wallace. *Functional Programming and Embedded Systems*. PhD Thesis; York University, Dp. of Computer Science, January'1995.

Overriding Operators in a Mixin-Based Framework*

Davide Ancona and Elena Zucca

DISI - Università di Genova
Via Dodecaneso, 35, 16146 Genova (Italy)
email: {davide,zucca}@disi.unige.it

Abstract. We show that many different overriding operators present in programming languages can be expressed, adopting a mixin-based framework, in terms of three basic operators. In particular we propose two orthogonal classifications: *strong* (the overridden definition is canceled) or *weak* (the overridden definition still remains significant, as in Smalltalk's *super* feature), and *preferential* (priority to one of the two arguments) or *general*. We formalize the relation between all these versions. Our analysis and results are not bound to a particular language, since they are formulated within an algebraic framework for mixin modules which can be instantiated over different core languages.

Keywords: Reasoning about Language Constructs, Modularity, Object Oriented Languages.

Introduction

The name *mixin* (*mixin class*, *abstract class*) has been introduced in the object oriented community to denote a class where some methods are not defined (*deferred*), which can be effectively used for instantiation only when combined with some other class. The importance of this notion has been subsequently stressed by many authors [4, 3, 5, 10, 7] w.r.t. different aspects.

In particular, it has been recognized that the mixin notion is independent from the object oriented nature of the language and can be formulated in the more general context of module composition [3], as follows. A *mixin module* is a module in the usual sense (a collection of definitions of components of different nature, e.g. types, functions, procedures, exceptions and so on), but where the definition of some components can be deferred to another mixin (even in a mutually recursive way). Thus the typical operator for composing mixins is a binary *merge* operator. In some preceding work [2] (whose short preliminary version has appeared in [1]), we have provided formal foundations for the mixin notion: more precisely, we have defined an algebraic model of mixins and three basic operators (*merge*, *reduct* and *freeze*) whose semantics is given w.r.t. to this model. These operators constitute a kernel language both syntactically and semantically independent from the language used for defining module components, i.e. the *core* language following the terminology introduced with Standard ML [13]. In other words, our semantic model is parameterized by the semantic model used for the core language.

---

* This work has been partially supported by Murst 40% - Modelli della computazione e dei linguaggi di programmazione and CNR - Formalismi per la specifica e la descrizione di sistemi ad oggetti.

In this paper, our aim is to analyze, on the formal basis provided by the model mentioned above, various forms of inheritance mechanisms present in object oriented languages. We adopt the generic name of *overriding* for a binary operator on mixins which allows both the two arguments to provide a definition for the same component (differently from merge which assumes no conflicting definitions). We propose a first classification of overriding operators based on the way the rejected (overridden) definition is handled: *strong* overriding means that this definition is simply ignored, while *weak* overriding means that this definition can still be accessed in some special way, as it happens e.g. in Smalltalk with the *super* feature. Moreover, for each class of overriding operators, we consider a preferential form, where the priority in conflicts is given to one of the two arguments (e.g. the right), and a *general* version which allows to take a different choice for each conflict. This flexibility in solving conflicts is very useful for tackling problems related to multiple inheritance, as extensively illustrated in [10], where the possibility of taking a different choice for each conflict is achieved by *hiding* the definitions one wants to reject.

We show how to express each one of these operator by means of our basic mixin operators. For strong overriding, we show that the preferential version can be obtained as a particular case of the general version, and that, anyway, this general version "adds no expressive power". For weak overriding, we show that the analogue does not hold: general weak overriding is "more expressive" than combination of left and right weak overriding. Moreover, our analysis clarifies that the *super* feature of Smalltalk incorporates two different possibilities: the "standard" use (the invocation *super m* occurs within a class which (re)defines *m*) and a "spurious" use (the invocation *super m* occurs within a class which does not provide an own definition for *m*) which turns out to be a way for allowing a static binding of this invocation to a (subsequently provided) definition. Since our general weak overriding operator corresponds to a generalization of the standard use only, its preferential version turns out to be different from Smalltalk overriding. As a side result, we obtain a formalized version of the result of [4] (the inheritance mechanisms of Smalltalk and Beta are essentially the same).

The paper is organized as follows: in Sect.1 we briefly present our formal model and the basic mixin operators. In Sect.2 and Sect.3 we analyze the strong and the weak overriding operator, respectively. In the Conclusion we summarize the results of our work.

1 Mixins and Their Basic Operators

In this section we present the intuitive notion of *mixin*, by means of some examples written in a toy object oriented language, and the formal model we propose for this notion. Then, we define three basic operators for manipulating mixins and one derived operator. Since in this paper the aim is the analysis of overriding operators, we keep the presentation as simple as possible; the reader can refer to [1, 2] for an extended presentation.

Consider the following example. In a bookshop, clients may have some facilities if they own a card. A card contains some information, like its price and the discount rate on books, and can be modeled by the following class:

```
Card = class
        card_price = 20
        book_discount = 0.9
       end
```

Assume now that we want to add a new feature to a card: for each purchased book, the owner of the card receives a bonus whose amount depends on the (discounted) price of the book.

That corresponds to define the following *mixin*:

```
Bonus = mixin
          bonus(book_price) = (book_price * self.book_discount) div 10
        end
```

As shown by the example, a mixin is like an ordinary class, with the difference that it may contain invocations of *deferred* methods (like **book_discount** in the example), which have to be provided by another mixin. Note that an usual class, like **Card** above, can be seen as a mixin with no deferred methods (*concrete mixin*).

The basic operator for combining mixins is merge (+). For instance, **Card** and **Bonus** can be combined together giving the new class **BonusCard**.

In this example, the mixin **Bonus** depends on the class **Card**, but the converse does not hold; hence **BonusCard** could be also expressed as the result of applying the "parametric" class **Bonus** to the argument **Card**. Anyway, in the general case **Card** could in turn contain invocations of methods defined in **Bonus**, justifying the use of a binary operator resembling sum. The merge operation is commutative and is well-defined only if there there are no conflicting definitions in the two mixins (as in the example).

A natural semantic view of a mixin is as a function from *input* components into *output* components: the output components are the defined components; the input components are the deferred components plus the defined components whose redefinition can change other components (*virtual* components following C++ terminology for methods). This way of modeling self-dependence has been introduced by W. Cook [6].

We give a model based on the above idea, but abstract enough to include a variety of modular languages. To this end, functions modeling mixins do no longer have as argument and result just records of components, but arbitrary semantic structures, whose definition is depending on the (semantic framework modeling the) underlying language, which we call *core framework*. Formally, we take the approach of *institutions* [8], and assume a category of *signatures* **Sig** and a *model* functor $Mod: Sig^{op} \rightarrow \mathbf{Cat}$; moreover, we assume to be defined over signatures an inclusion relation, a constant $\emptyset$ (the empty signature) and the operations of union, intersection and difference.

The interested reader can refer to [2] for the precise formal definition of core framework, including all the assumptions we need over signatures and models for the following technical treatment. In the examples, we assume uni-sorted partial algebras as simple concrete instance of core framework.

We give now the formal definition of mixin signatures and models.

Definition 1. A *mixin signature* is a pair of signatures $<\Sigma^{in}, \Sigma^{out}>$, called the *input* and the *output* signature, respectively. A *mixin model* over a mixin signature $<\Sigma^{in}, \Sigma^{out}>$ is a (total) function $F: Mod(\Sigma^{in}) \rightarrow Mod(\Sigma^{out})$.

Intuitively, a mixin signature models the syntactic interface of a mixin module. The input signature gives all the components definitions in the module may depend from (components which possibly appear "on the right side" of definitions). The output signature gives all the components which are defined in the module (components which appear "on the left side" of definitions).

For instance, the mixin **Bonus** defined above denotes a mixin model F_{Bonus} over the mixin signature

$<\Sigma_{Bonus}^{in}, \Sigma_{Bonus}^{out}>$, where
$(\Sigma_{Bonus}^{in})_0 = \{book\_discount\}$, $(\Sigma_{Bonus}^{in})_1 = \{bonus\}$, $(\Sigma_{Bonus}^{in})_i = \emptyset, \forall i > 1$,
$(\Sigma_{Bonus}^{out})_1 = \{bonus\}$, $(\Sigma_{Bonus}^{out})_i = \emptyset, \forall i \neq 1$.

The function F_{Bonus}, taken an algebra A over Σ_{Bonus}^{in}, returns an algebra B over Σ_{Bonus}^{out} s.t. for each $v \in V$, $bonus^B(v) = (v * book\_discount^A)$ div 10.

We give now the formal definitions of the three basic operators for composing mixin modules (merge, reduct and freeze), plus a derived hiding operator. For each operator, we give in Fig.1 a typing rule specifying compatibility conditions between the types (interfaces) of the arguments, and the type of the result. See [2] for the semantic rules of these operators.

In the typing rules, $M: \Sigma^{in} \to \Sigma^{out}$ means that M is a mixin module over the mixin signature $<\Sigma^{in}, \Sigma^{out}>$.

(M-ty)
$$\frac{M_i: \Sigma_i^{in} \to \Sigma_i^{out} \qquad i = 1, 2}{M_1 + M_2: \Sigma_1^{in} \cup \Sigma_2^{in} \to \Sigma_1^{out} \cup \Sigma_2^{out}} \qquad \Sigma_1^{out} \cap \Sigma_2^{out} = \emptyset$$

(R-ty)
$$\frac{M: \Sigma^{in} \to \Sigma^{out}}{\sigma^{in}|M|_{\sigma^{out}}: \Sigma'^{in} \to \Sigma'^{out}} \qquad \begin{array}{l} \sigma^{in}: \Sigma^{in} \to \Sigma'^{in} \\ \sigma^{out}: \Sigma'^{out} \to \Sigma^{out} \end{array}$$

(Fr-ty)
$$\frac{M: \Sigma^{in} \to \Sigma^{out}}{\textbf{freeze } \Sigma^{fr} \textbf{ in } M: \Sigma^{in} \setminus \Sigma^{fr} \to \Sigma^{out}} \qquad \Sigma^{fr} \subseteq \Sigma^{out}$$

(H-ty)
$$\frac{M: \Sigma^{in} \to \Sigma^{out}}{\textbf{hide } \Sigma^{hd} \textbf{ in } M: \Sigma^{in} \setminus \Sigma^{hd} \to \Sigma^{out} \setminus \Sigma^{hd}} \qquad \Sigma^{hd} \subseteq \Sigma^{out}$$

Fig. 1.

The merge operation allows to "sum" two mixin modules, say M_1 and M_2, obtaining a new module where some deferred component of M_1 is made concrete by the definition given in M_2 and conversely. Intuitively, the definitions in $M_1 + M_2$ are obtained taking the union of the definitions of M_1 and M_2; no conflict can arise since no components can be defined simultaneously in the two modules.

The reduct operation allows to change both the input and the output signature of a mixin module, in a very flexible way. Intuitively, σ^{in} corresponds to replace every name appearing on the right side of definitions (Σ^{in}) by a new name (Σ'^{in}), while σ^{out} corresponds to choose new names at the left side of definitions and to associate with each new name the definition which was associated with its image via σ^{out}.

Consider again the mixin BonusCard defined by BonusCard=Card+Bonus; let σ^{in} be the signature morphism mapping book_discount to total_discount and let σ^{out} be the signature morphism mapping bonus and bonus_copy to bonus. Then, the mixin $\sigma^{in}|$BonusCard$|_{\sigma^{out}}$ is equivalent to the following:

```
mixin
  bonus(book_price) = (book_price * self.total_discount) div 10
  bonus_copy(book_price) = (book_price * self.total_discount) div 10
end
```

As an abbreviation, when $\sigma^{in} = id_{\Sigma^{in}}$ [resp., $\sigma^{out} = id_{\Sigma^{out}}$] we simply write $M_{|\sigma^{out}}$ [resp., $_{\sigma^{in}|}M$]. Moreover, when σ^{in} is an inclusion, we write $_{\Sigma'^{in}|}M_{|\sigma^{out}}$ and when σ^{out} is an inclusion we write $_{\sigma^{in}|}M_{|\Sigma'^{out}}$.

The freeze operator allows to make a module independent from the redefinition of some defined components, say Σ^{fr}. Referring again to the preceding example, **freeze book_discount in BonusCard** is equivalent to the following mixin definition:

```
mixin
 card_price = 20
 book_discount = 0.9
 bonus(book_price) = (book_price * 0.9) div 10
end
```

The semantics of a mixin where the Σ^{fr}-components have been frozen is a function which does no longer depend on these components.

In addition to the three basic operators, we define an hiding operator which will be used in the following for expressing weak overriding operators. The hiding operation allows to hide some defined components from the outside. Note that hiding a component is different from forgetting its definition by means of the reduct operation.

The hiding operator can be defined in terms of the three basic operators as follows.

(H-sem) **hide** Σ^{hd} **in** $M = ($**freeze** Σ^{hd} **in** $M)_{|\Sigma^{out}\setminus\Sigma^{hd}}$

Hiding components requires first freezing them, in such a way that all the other definitions will refer from now on to their current definitions.

2 Strong Overriding

In this section we introduce a *general strong* overriding operator on mixins. Differently from merge, this operator allows to deal with clashes of method definitions, by specifying for each pair of conflicting definitions which one takes the precedence. Classical left or right preferential overriding can be obtained as particular instances of this operator.

Consider the following two mixins designed as extensions of a class **MotorVehicle**:

```
Public =
mixin
 servicing(vehicle_age) = if vehicle_age ≤ 6 then 2 else 1
 max_speed(road_type) = if road_type = "high-way" then 80 else 60
end

Long =
mixin
 servicing(vehicle_age) = if vehicle_age ≤ 9 then 3 else 2
 max_speed(road_type) = if road_type = "high-way" then 70 else 50
end
```

The two mixins **Public** and **Long** define for a public and a long vehicle, respectively, how often it must be serviced (**servicing** method) and which is its maximum allowed speed (**max_speed** method).

Assume now to combine these two mixins together in order to obtain a public long vehicle. Since they both define the same methods, we must use an overriding operator instead of merge. Note that `Public` imposes a stronger restriction on servicing, while `Long` on the maximum speed. Therefore, we need to take the definition for `servicing` and `max_speed` from `Public` and `Long`, respectively. In other words, we need an overriding operator which allows to specify the precedence at the level of single methods. We denote this operator as follows:

$$\texttt{PublicAndLong} = \texttt{Public} \xLeftarrow[\texttt{servicing max\_speed}]{} \texttt{Long}$$

Preferential overriding will be denoted by $\leftarrow$, with the convention that the overridden mixin is pointed by the arrow.

Note that the mixin `PublicAndLong` is equivalent to $(\texttt{Public} \to \texttt{Long})_{|\texttt{servicing}} + (\texttt{Public} \leftarrow \texttt{Long})_{|\texttt{max\_speed}}$. This fact holds in general, as formally stated in the following.

The typing rule for general strong overriding requires that for each pair of conflicting definitions one (second side condition) and only one (first side condition) is taken.

$$(\text{GSO-ty}) \quad \frac{M_i : \Sigma_i^{in} \to \Sigma_i^{out}, i = 1, 2}{M_1 \xleftrightarrow[\Sigma_1\ \Sigma_2]{} M_2 : \Sigma_1^{in} \cup \Sigma_2^{in} \to \Sigma_1^{out} \cup \Sigma_2^{out}} \qquad \begin{array}{l} \Sigma_1 \cap \Sigma_2 = \emptyset \\ \Sigma_1 \cup \Sigma_2 = \Sigma_1^{out} \cap \Sigma_2^{out} \end{array}$$

The semantics of general strong overriding is easily expressed via the basic operators:

$$(\text{GSO-sem}) \quad M_1 \xleftrightarrow[\Sigma_1\ \Sigma_2]{} M_2 = M_{1|\Sigma_1 \cup (\Sigma_1^{out} \setminus \Sigma_2^{out})} + M_{2|\Sigma_2 \cup (\Sigma_2^{out} \setminus \Sigma_1^{out})}$$

Preferential strong overriding is obtained as a special case of general strong overriding:

$$(\text{PSO-ty}) \quad \frac{M_i : \Sigma_i^{in} \to \Sigma_i^{out}, i = 1, 2}{M_1 \leftarrow M_2 : \Sigma_1^{in} \cup \Sigma_2^{in} \to \Sigma_1^{out} \cup \Sigma_2^{out}}$$

$$(\text{PSO-sem}) \quad M_1 \leftarrow M_2 = M_1 \xleftrightarrow[\emptyset\ \Sigma_1^{out} \cap \Sigma_2^{out}]{} M_2 =$$
$$M_{1|\emptyset \cup (\Sigma_1^{out} \setminus \Sigma_2^{out})} + M_{2|(\Sigma_1^{out} \cap \Sigma_2^{out}) \cup (\Sigma_2^{out} \setminus \Sigma_1^{out})} =$$
$$M_{1|\Sigma_1^{out} \setminus \Sigma_2^{out}} + M_{2|\Sigma_2^{out}} = M_{1|\Sigma_1^{out} \setminus \Sigma_2^{out}} + M_2$$

The following proposition states the well-definedness of the strong overriding and some relations between merge, general and preferential strong overriding.

Proposition 2. *Let $M_i : \Sigma_i^{in} \to \Sigma_i^{out}$, $i = 1, 2$ be two mixins satisfying the side conditions of typing rule (GSO-ty). Then*

1. *the semantics of $M_1 \xleftrightarrow[\Sigma_1\ \Sigma_2]{} M_2$ is well-defined;*
2. *if $\Sigma_1^{out} \cap \Sigma_2^{out} = \emptyset$ then $M_1 \xleftrightarrow[\emptyset\ \emptyset]{} M_2 = M_1 + M_2$;*
3. *$M_1 \xleftrightarrow[\Sigma_1\ \Sigma_2]{} M_2 = (M_1 \to M_2)_{|\Sigma_1 \cup (\Sigma_1^{out} \setminus \Sigma_2^{out})} + (M_1 \leftarrow M_2)_{|\Sigma_2 \cup (\Sigma_2^{out} \setminus \Sigma_1^{out})}$.*

We have shown that preferential strong overriding is a particular instance of general strong overriding; now, we state that however general strong overriding can always be obtained by a suitable combination (via merge) of preferential overriding.

Intuitively, (3) shows that the way of computing $M_1 \xrightarrow[\Sigma_1 \ \Sigma_2]{} M_2$ and $M_1 \leftarrow M_2$ is essentially the same: the resulting mixin is obtained by selecting, for each pair of conflicting definitions, the mixin which takes the precedence. In terms of operational semantics, the *look-up* semantics defined in [6] for preferential overriding also applies to the general case: the only difference is the starting point of the method look-up, that now depends on the particular method which is invoked.

In the next section we will see that this relation between the preferential and the general version does not hold for weak overriding.

3   Weak Overriding

By *weak* overriding we mean a mechanism similar to that of *super* and *inner* provided by Smalltalk [9] and Beta [11], respectively, i.e. a binary operator which allows to choose one of the two alternatives for each pair of conflicting definitions in the two mixin arguments, like strong overriding, but leaving the possibility of referring to the rejected definition too, by means of an ad-hoc linguistic mechanism.

We start by presenting a preferential version of the operator, corresponding to Smalltalk and Beta inheritance; then we define a "weak version" of the general strong overriding of Sect.2.

Examples. Consider a variant of the example of cards used in Sect.1. Assume now that, in a card with bonus, the bonus amount depends on the full price of the purchased book, ignoring the discount.

```
BonusCard = mixin
                card_price = 20
                book_discount = 0.9
                bonus(book_price) = book_price div 10
            end
```

For each kind of card with bonus, a student may have a "student version" of that card, with some additional facilities, such as a lower price of the card and a higher discount on books. However, the bonus for students must be applied to the discounted price. Formally, we define the following mixin:

```
Student =
mixin
 card_price = 0.8 * other.card_price
 book_discount = 0.9 * other.book_discount
 bonus(book_price) = other.bonus(book_price * self.book_discount)
end
```

The *other* prefix is used for referring to overridden definitions; we have adopted this name, instead of either *super* or *inner*, to stress the fact that the operator is the same whichever is the inheritance relation between the two arguments.

Let $\overset{st}{\leftarrow}$ denotes the preferential weak overriding operator corresponding to inheritance of Smalltalk and Beta. Then, the mixin **StudentBonusCard = BonusCard** $\overset{st}{\leftarrow}$ **Student** is equivalent to the following:

```
mixin
  card_price = 16
  book_discount = 0.81
  bonus(book_price) = (book_price * self.book_discount) div 10
end
```

The invocations via *other* inside **Student** have been replaced by the corresponding definitions in **BonusCard**.

We consider now an example in which the left argument too contains invocations via *other*. Assume to introduce another specialization of the notion of card, i.e. a card for regular clients, implemented by the following mixin:

```
Regular =
mixin
  card_price = 10 + other.card_price
  bonus(book_price) = (book_price * other.book_discount) div 5
end
```

Intuitively, the "regular version" of a card is 10 units more expensive, but allows to obtain a greater bonus (depending on the discounted price of books).

The mixin **RegularStudent** $= $ **Student** $\overset{st}{\leftarrow}$ **Regular** is equivalent to the following:

```
mixin
  card_price = 10 + (0.8 * other.card_price)
  book_discount = 0.9 * other.book_discount
  bonus(book_price) = (book_price * 0.9 * other.book_discount) div 5
end
```

The invocations via *other* inside **Student** have been left unbound, corresponding to the intuition that the mixin **RegularStudent** must still be composed with another mixin (e.g. **BonusCard**) in order to become concrete.

This example illustrates, moreover, a different use of the *other* mechanism: in the definition of **bonus** in **Regular** there is an invocation **other.book_discount** even though no new definition for **book_discount** is provided in the mixin[2].

This invocation looks at first sight equivalent to **self.book_discount**; anyway, the two invocations have a different behavior once that a definition has been actually provided (for instance, composing **Regular** with **Student**). Indeed, both are associated with this definition, but **other.book_discount** is permanently associated with it (static binding), while **book_discount** could be redefined later (late binding).

As a consequence, in **RegularStudent** the invocation **other.book_discount** has been replaced by the definition of **book_discount** in **Student**, while, in the case of an invocation **self.book_discount** at the same place, we would have obtained the following definition for **bonus**:

```
bonus(book_price) = (book_price * self.book_discount) div 5
```

In summary, when composing two mixins M_1 and M_2 by means of the $\overset{st}{\leftarrow}$ operator, an *other.m* invocation in, say, M_1 is:

— left unbound in $M_1 \overset{st}{\leftarrow} M_2$;

---

[2] That possibility corresponds to what actually happens in Smalltalk.

- statically bound to (replaced by) the definition provided by M_2, if any, in $M_2 \overset{st}{\leftarrow} M_1$, otherwise left unbound.

The situation is summarized in Table 1.

	$M_1 \overset{st}{\leftarrow} M_2$	$M_2 \overset{st}{\leftarrow} M_1$ $m = expr$ in M_2	$M_2 \overset{st}{\leftarrow} M_1$ m not defined in M_2
$other.m$ in M_1	unbound	bound to $expr$	unbound

Table 1. Smalltalk weak overriding

Assume that we need a combination of **Student** and **Regular** where the definitions for the methods **card_price** and **bonus** are taken from **Student** and **Regular**, respectively. This combination is denoted as follows:

StudentAndRegular = Student $\xleftarrow{\quad}$ $\xrightarrow[\text{card\_price bonus}]{\quad}$ Regular

We analyze what should happen to $other.m$ invocations in this case. Note that the solution summarized in Table 1 makes no sense in this case, since there is no fixed preference relation between M_1 and M_2. Anyway, in the case in which m is defined in both the mixins, as e.g. **bonus** in the example, the operator gives preference to one of them (**Regular**), hence the schema of Table 1 can still be applied. In the case in which m is defined only in the mixin where the $other.m$ invocation occurs, there is no other possibility than leaving the invocation unbound. The only ambiguous situation is when m is not defined in the mixin containing the $other.m$ invocation (as for the **other.book_discount** invocation in **Regular**). Indeed, in this case the two alternatives (leaving the invocation unbound or replacing the invocation by the definition in the other mixin, if any) are both possible.

In the following, we present a definition of weak overriding operator which always chooses, in this situation, the first solution. Hence, with this operator the *other* mechanism exclusively allows to refer to overridden definitions, rejecting the "spurious" use allowed in Smalltalk. For instance, the mixin **StudentAndRegular** turns out to be equivalent to the following:

```
mixin
  card_price = 0.8 * (10 + other.card_price)
  book_discount = 0.9 * other.book_discount
  bonus(book_price) = (book_price * other.book_discount) div 5
end
```

As a consequence, the preferential weak overriding defined as particular case of this general weak overriding, i.e.

$$M_1 \leftarrow M_2 = \xleftarrow{\quad} \xrightarrow[\emptyset \ \Sigma_1^{out} \cap \Sigma_2^{out}]{\quad},$$

where $M_i : \Sigma_i^{in} \to \Sigma_i^{out}$, $i = 1, 2$, is different from $\overset{st}{\leftarrow}$.

Note that $\mathtt{StudentAndRegular} = (\mathtt{Student} \dashrightarrow \mathtt{Regular})_{|\mathtt{card\_price}} + (\mathtt{Student} \leftarrow \mathtt{Regular})_{|\mathtt{bonus}}$; moreover in the following we will see that this is not always the case; differently from the case of strong overriding, Prop. 2(3) does not hold for weak overriding.

Finally, the reader could wonder whether it is possible to define a version of general weak overriding which is the true generalization of Smalltalk overriding, i.e. allowing the spurious use of the *other* mechanism. Actually, two different versions could be defined. The first version "goes to the opposite" w.r.t. the operator we have presented above, i.e. chooses always to replace *other.m* invocations in one argument by the definition provided by the other argument, if any. The second version is "general" w.r.t. the spurious use too, and corresponds to choose, for each case of *other.m* invocation without a corresponding redefinition, whether this invocation should be left unbound or bound.

To give an example, the instance of the operator $\xleftarrow{\hspace{1cm}}\xrightarrow[\mathtt{card\_price}\ \mathtt{bonus,book\_discount}]{}$ specifies that an invocation $\mathtt{other.book\_discount}$ in the right argument must be replaced by the definition provided by the left argument, if any, while an invocation $\mathtt{other.book\_discount}$ in the left argument must be left unbound.

Anyway, both these versions of the operator have a complicate semantics and look of difficult intuitive understanding, hence we do not give their formal definitions in the paper.

Semantics. We give now the semantics of Smalltalk weak overriding and general weak overriding, expressed via the basic operators defined in Sect.1. In this way we show that the *other* feature can be considered as an implicit renaming/hiding mechanism (indeed, in Eiffel [12] the possibility of referring to overridden components is achieved via explicit renaming).

Assumption 3 *Let* $\mathbf{Sig}^{self}$, $\mathbf{Sig}^{other}$ *be two isomorphic subcategories of* $\mathbf{Sig}$, *with* $\Sigma_1 \cap \Sigma_2 = \emptyset$ *for any* $\Sigma_1 \in \mathbf{Sig}^{self}$, $\Sigma_2 \in \mathbf{Sig}^{other}$. *We denote by* $o.\Sigma$ *the isomorphic image of* Σ *in* $\mathbf{Sig}^{other}$, *for any* $\Sigma \in \mathbf{Sig}^{self}$; *moreover, we assume an isomorphism[3]* $s_\Sigma : \Sigma \to o.\Sigma$.

In the following, we assume that, for any mixin $M : \Sigma^{in} \to \Sigma^{out}$, the input signature Σ^{in} is the union of two (disjoint) signatures, one in $\mathbf{Sig}^{self}$ and the other in $\mathbf{Sig}^{other}$, while the output signature Σ^{out} is in $\mathbf{Sig}^{self}$. That models the fact that a mixin may contain method invocations of the form *other.m*, but cannot define methods of this form.

The typing rule for Smalltalk weak overriding has no side conditions, as it was for preferential strong overriding. The signature $\Sigma_2^{in} \cap o.\Sigma_1^{out}$ represents the methods invoked via *other* in M_2 which have a corresponding definition in M_1 and, hence, are bound to this definition in the resulting mixin and disappear from its input signature.

(stWO-ty)
$$\frac{M_i : \Sigma_i^{in} \to \Sigma_i^{out}, i = 1, 2}{M_1 \overset{st}{\leftarrow} M_2 : \Sigma_1^{in} \cup (\Sigma_2^{in} \setminus o.\Sigma_1^{out}) \to \Sigma_1^{out} \cup \Sigma_2^{out}}$$

The formal definition of Smalltalk weak overriding as derived operator is as follows.

---

[3] In categorical terms, s is a natural isomorphism from the embedding of categories $i_{\mathbf{Sig}^{other}, \mathbf{Sig}}$ to $i_{\mathbf{Sig}^{self}, \mathbf{Sig}} \circ s._{-}$.

(stWO-sem) $M_1 \overset{st}{\leftarrow} M_2 = \text{hide } \Sigma^{hd} \text{ in } (M_{1|\sigma_1} + {}_{\sigma_2|}M_2)$
where

$\sigma_1 \colon (\Sigma_1^{out} \setminus \Sigma_2^{out}) \cup \Sigma^{hd} \to \Sigma_1^{out}$, $\sigma_1 = \epsilon + (s_{\Sigma_2^{in} \cap o.\Sigma_1^{out}} \circ \sigma^{hd-1})$
  with $\epsilon \colon \Sigma_1^{out} \setminus \Sigma_2^{out} \hookrightarrow \Sigma_1^{out}$
$\sigma_2 \colon \Sigma_2^{in} \to (\Sigma_2^{in} \setminus o.\Sigma_1^{out}) \cup \Sigma^{hd}$, $\sigma_2 = id + \sigma^{hd}$
  with id the identity over $\Sigma_2^{in} \setminus o.\Sigma_1^{out}$
for some $\sigma^{hd} \colon \Sigma_2^{in} \cap o.\Sigma_1^{out} \to \Sigma^{hd}$ isomorphism
  with $\Sigma^{hd} \cap (\Sigma_1^{in} \cup (\Sigma_1^{out} \setminus \Sigma_2^{out}) \cup (\Sigma_2^{in} \setminus o.\Sigma_1^{out}) \cup \Sigma_2^{out}) = \emptyset$

Each method symbol $other.m$ in $\Sigma_2^{in} \cap o.\Sigma_1^{out}$ must be bound to the corresponding overridden definition of m in M_1 and hidden; to this end we rename both by the same name in a signature Σ^{hd} of fresh names (in order to avoid name clashes). The existence of σ^{hd} is guaranteed by our assumptions on the core framework. The output interface of M_1 is transformed via σ_1 in such a way that two kinds of output components are visible:

- the output components which are not overridden by M_2, which do not change name $(\Sigma_1^{out} \setminus \Sigma_2^{out})$;
- the output components which correspond to some $other.m$ component of M_2, which are renamed by fresh names (Σ^{hd}).

Note that some output component could stay in both the categories above and in this case would be "duplicated".
The input interface of M_2 is transformed via σ_2 in such a way that $other.m$ components are renamed by fresh names (Σ^{hd}), while all the other input components do not change name $(\Sigma_2^{in} \setminus o.\Sigma_1^{out})$.
In the definition of σ_i, $i = 1, 2$, we have used the operation $+$ on signature morphisms (see [2]).
The typing rule for general weak overriding has the same side conditions (with the same meaning) of the typing rule for general strong overriding and is, like that, symmetric.

(GWO-ty)
$$\frac{M_i \colon \Sigma_i^{in} \to \Sigma_i^{out}, i = 1, 2}{M_1 \overset{}{\underset{\Sigma_1 \ \Sigma_2}{\longleftrightarrow}} M_2 \colon (\Sigma_1^{in} \setminus o.\Sigma_1) \cup (\Sigma_2^{in} \setminus o.\Sigma_2) \to \Sigma_1^{out} \cup \Sigma_2^{out}}$$

$\Sigma_1 \cap \Sigma_2 = \emptyset$, $\Sigma_1 \cup \Sigma_2 = \Sigma_1^{out} \cap \Sigma_2^{out}$

The only input components which become hidden are those in $\Sigma_i^{in} \cap o.\Sigma_i$, representing the invocations via $other$ in M_i of methods overridden by M_i, $i = 1, 2$. The semantics of general weak overriding is derived in a similar way as for Smalltalk weak overriding, with the difference that now, by symmetry, the signature morphisms involved are four, two for the input and output signatures of M_1 and two for the input and output signatures of M_2.

(GWO-sem) $M_1 \overset{}{\underset{\Sigma_1 \ \Sigma_2}{\longleftrightarrow}} M_2 = \text{hide } \Sigma_1^{hd} \cup \Sigma_2^{hd} \text{ in } ({}_{\sigma_1^{in}|}M_{1|\sigma_1^{out}} + {}_{\sigma_2^{in}|}M_{2|\sigma_2^{out}})$
where

$\sigma_1^{out} \colon \Sigma_1 \cup (\Sigma_1^{out} \setminus \Sigma_2^{out}) \cup \Sigma_2^{hd} \to \Sigma_1^{out}$, $\sigma_1^{out} = \epsilon_1 + (s_{\Sigma_2^{in} \cap o.\Sigma_2} \circ \sigma_2^{hd-1})$
$\sigma_2^{out} \colon \Sigma_2 \cup (\Sigma_2^{out} \setminus \Sigma_1^{out}) \cup \Sigma_1^{hd} \to \Sigma_2^{out}$, $\sigma_2^{out} = \epsilon_2 + (s_{\Sigma_1^{in} \cap o.\Sigma_1} \circ \sigma_1^{hd-1})$
  with $\epsilon_1 \colon \Sigma_1 \cup (\Sigma_1^{out} \setminus \Sigma_2^{out}) \hookrightarrow \Sigma_1^{out}$, $\epsilon_2 \colon \Sigma_2 \cup (\Sigma_2^{out} \setminus \Sigma_1^{out}) \hookrightarrow \Sigma_2^{out}$,
$\sigma_i^{in} \colon \Sigma_i^{in} \to (\Sigma_i^{in} \setminus o.\Sigma_i) \cup \Sigma_i^{hd}$, $\sigma_i^{in} = id_i + \sigma_i^{hd}$, $i = 1, 2$
  with id_i the identity over $\Sigma_i^{in} \setminus o.\Sigma_i$, $i = 1, 2$

for some $\sigma_i^{hd}: \Sigma_i^{in} \cap o.\Sigma_i \to \Sigma_i^{hd}$ isomorphism, $i = 1, 2$
where Σ_1^{hd}, Σ_2^{hd} disjoint signatures s.t.
$$\Sigma_i^{hd} \cap (\Sigma_1 \cup (\Sigma_1^{out} \setminus \Sigma_2^{out}) \cup (\Sigma_1^{in} \setminus o.\Sigma_1) \cup \Sigma_2 \cup$$
$$(\Sigma_2^{out} \setminus \Sigma_1^{out}) \cup (\Sigma_2^{in} \setminus o.\Sigma_2)) = \emptyset, \ i = 1, 2$$

Proposition 4. *The semantics of* $\overset{st}{\leftarrow}$ *and* $\xleftrightarrow[\Sigma_1 \ \Sigma_2]{}$ *(where* Σ_1, Σ_2 *satisfy the side conditions of typing rule (GWO-ty)) is well-defined.*

As for strong overriding, we can define the preferential version, denoted by $\leftarrow$, as a particular instance of the general operator.

(PWO-ty) $\qquad \dfrac{M_i: \Sigma_i^{in} \to \Sigma_i^{out}, i = 1, 2}{M_1 \leftarrow M_2: \Sigma_1^{in} \cup (\Sigma_2^{in} \setminus o.(\Sigma_1^{out} \cap \Sigma_2^{out})) \to \Sigma_1^{out} \cup \Sigma_2^{out}}$

(PWO-sem) $\quad M_1 \leftarrow M_2 = M_1 \xleftrightarrow[\emptyset \ \ \Sigma_1^{out} \cap \Sigma_2^{out}]{} M_2$

Since in this particular case we can choose $\Sigma_1^{hd} = \emptyset$ with σ_1^{hd} the identity, we can derive the following independent definition for $\leftarrow$:

(PWO-sem*) $\ M_1 \leftarrow M_2 = \text{hide } \Sigma_2^{hd} \text{ in } (M_{1|\sigma_1^{out}} + \sigma_2^{in}|M_2)$
  where
  $\sigma_1^{out}: (\Sigma_1^{out} \setminus \Sigma_2^{out}) \cup \Sigma_2^{hd} \to \Sigma_1^{out}, \ \sigma_1^{out} = \epsilon_1 + (s_{\Sigma_2^{in} \cap o.(\Sigma_1^{out} \cap \Sigma_2^{out})} \circ \sigma_2^{hd-1})$
    with $\epsilon_1: \Sigma_1^{out} \setminus \Sigma_2^{out} \hookrightarrow \Sigma_1^{out}$
  $\sigma_2^{in}: \Sigma_2^{in} \to (\Sigma_2^{in} \setminus o.(\Sigma_1^{out} \cap \Sigma_2^{out})) \cup \Sigma_2^{hd}, \ \sigma_2^{in} = id_2 + \sigma_2^{hd}$
    with id_2 the identity over $\Sigma_2^{in} \setminus o.(\Sigma_1^{out} \cap \Sigma_2^{out})$
  for some $\sigma_2^{hd}: \Sigma_2^{in} \cap o.(\Sigma_1^{out} \cap \Sigma_2^{out}) \to \Sigma_2^{hd}$ isomorphism
  where $\Sigma_2^{hd} \cap ((\Sigma_1^{out} \setminus \Sigma_2^{out}) \cup \Sigma_1^{in} \cup \Sigma_2^{out} \cup (\Sigma_2^{in} \setminus o.(\Sigma_1^{out} \cap \Sigma_2^{out}))) = \emptyset$

Note the different typing and semantic rules for $\overset{st}{\leftarrow}$ and $\leftarrow$. This corresponds to the fact that, as explained before, in $\leftarrow$ (and more generally in $\xleftrightarrow[\Sigma_1 \ \Sigma_2]{}$), *other* invocations in one argument are bound to definitions in the other only if these definitions are actually overridden, while in Smalltalk it is also possible in a subclass to refer via *super* to a method of the superclass which has not been overridden in the subclass. Recalling the example of Sect. 3, we have that **Student** $\leftarrow$ **Regular** is equivalent to the following mixin:

```
mixin
 card_price = 10 + (0.8 * other.card_price)
 book_discount = 0.9 * other.book_discount
 bonus(price) = (book_price * other.book_discount) div 5
end
```

which is not equivalent to **Student** $\overset{st}{\leftarrow}$ **Regular**.
We prove now that the analogue of Prop. 2(3) does not hold for weak overriding, i.e., general weak overriding cannot be obtained by a combination of left and right weak overriding. Formally,

$$M_1 \xleftrightarrow[\Sigma_1 \ \Sigma_2]{} M_2 \neq (M_1 \rightarrow M_2)_{|\Sigma_1 \cup (\Sigma_1^{out} \setminus \Sigma_2^{out})} + (M_1 \leftarrow M_2)_{|\Sigma_2 \cup (\Sigma_2^{out} \setminus \Sigma_1^{out})}.$$

Actually, the two sides of the inequality above do not even have the same type; indeed, the left side has input signature $(\Sigma_1^{in} \setminus o.\Sigma_1) \cup (\Sigma_2^{in} \setminus o.\Sigma_2)$, while the right side has signature $\Sigma_1^{in} \cup \Sigma_2^{in}$; indeed, if there is in, e.g., M_1 an *other.m* invocation with m in Σ_1, then in $M_1 \xleftarrow{\;\;\Sigma_1\;\;\Sigma_2\;\;} M_2$ this invocation is bound (hence canceled from the input signature), while in $M_1 \leftarrow M_2$ this invocation is left unbound, hence in the whole right side.

This type mismatch can be eliminated by applying to the left side a suitable reduct operator adding dummy components; anyway, we still get two mixins which are not equivalent, i.e.

$$\Sigma_1^{in} \cup \Sigma_2^{in} \,|\, (M_1 \xleftarrow{\;\;\Sigma_1\;\;\Sigma_2\;\;} M_2) \neq (M_1 \to M_2)_{|\Sigma_1 \cup (\Sigma_2^{out} \setminus \Sigma_1^{out})} + (M_1 \leftarrow M_2)_{|\Sigma_2 \cup (\Sigma_1^{out} \setminus \Sigma_2^{out})}.$$

To see that, consider the following two mixin definitions:

```
Card1 =                                  Card2 =
mixin                                    mixin
  card_price = other.book_discount *       card_price = 10 + other.card_price
              other.card_price             book_discount = 0.85
  book_discount = 0.8                    end
end
```

Then, Card1 $\xleftarrow{\text{book\_discount}\;\;\text{card\_price}}$ Card2 is equivalent to the following mixin:

```
mixin
  card_price = 10 + (0.85 * other.card_price)
  book_discount = 0.8
end
```

while Card1 $\to$ Card2 and Card1 $\leftarrow$ Card2 are equivalent, respectively, to the following mixins:

```
mixin
  card_price = 0.85 * (10 + other.card_price)
  book_discount = 0.8
end
```

```
mixin
  card_price = 10 + (other.book_discount * other.card_price)
  book_discount = 0.85
end
```

Therefore, the mixin Card1 $\xleftarrow{\text{book\_discount}\;\;\text{card\_price}}$ Card2 is different from (Card1 $\to$ Card2)$_{|\text{book\_discount}}$ + (Card1 $\leftarrow$ Card2)$_{|\text{card\_price}}$.

Note that this counter-example works since the definition of card_price in Card1 refers via *other* both to card_price and book_discount. Indeed, if we adopt the restriction taken in [10], which forbids a method definition to refer via *other* to overridden versions of other methods, then this counter-example is no longer valid. Note also that under this restriction, it is not possible for a mixin M to refer via *other* to a method which M does not define, therefore $\overset{st}{\leftarrow}$ should be equivalent to $\leftarrow$.

This restriction cannot be expressed in our framework by a type constraint, since the type information associated with mixins only say which are the invocations allowed in the whole set of definitions: a more sophisticated type system would be required, keeping trace of the input components corresponding to any subset of definitions. Anyway, we can express an analogous restriction at the semantic level, requiring that any method definition does not actually depend on *other* invocations of other methods, i.e. these components are dummy components. This is formalized by the following assumption.

Assumption 5 *For any mixin* $M: \Sigma^{in} \to \Sigma^{out}$, *with* Σ^{in} *disjoint union of* Σ_{self}^{in} *signature in* $\mathbf{Sig}^{self}$ *and* Σ_{other}^{in} *signature in* $\mathbf{Sig}^{other}$,

for any $\Sigma \subseteq \Sigma^{out}$, *there exists* $M_\Sigma: \Sigma_{self}^{in} \cup (o.\Sigma \cap \Sigma_{other}^{in}) \to \Sigma$ *s.t.*
$M_{|\Sigma} = {}_{\Sigma^{in}|}M_\Sigma$.

This assumption requires that, for each subset Σ of the output components, their definitions can be equivalently expressed by using either invocations via *self* (Σ_{self}^{in}) or invocations via *other* of the components in the subset. Hence, in particular, the definition of a single component, say m, can be equivalently expressed by using only either invocations via *self* or invocations *other.m*.

The following theorem states that, under the semantic version of the restriction in [10] formalized by Assumption 5, Smalltalk overriding and preferential weak overriding are the same and general weak overriding can be expressed by a combination of left and right weak overriding; both the results hold modulo a type conversion which intuitively means that one of the two sides of the equality has some more input components which are dummy.

Proposition 6. *Under the assumption 5 the following facts hold:*

1. *For any pair of mixins* M_i, $i = 1, 2$, ${}_{\Sigma_1^{in} \cup (\Sigma_2^{in} \setminus (\Sigma_1^{out} \cap \Sigma_2^{out}))|}(M_1 \overset{st}{\leftarrow} M_2) = M_1 \leftarrow M_2$

2. *For any pair of mixins* M_i *and pair of signatures* Σ_i, $i = 1, 2$, *satisfying the side conditions of typing rule (GWO-ty),*

$${}_{\Sigma_1^{in} \cup \Sigma_2^{in}|}(M_1 \xleftrightarrow[\Sigma_1 \; \Sigma_2]{} M_2) =$$
$$(M_1 \rightarrow M_2)_{|\Sigma_1 \cup (\Sigma_1^{out} \setminus \Sigma_2^{out})} + (M_1 \leftarrow M_2)_{|\Sigma_2 \cup (\Sigma_2^{out} \setminus \Sigma_1^{out})}$$

4   Conclusion

We have shown that, adopting the general framework for mixin modules proposed in [1, 2], it is possible to express a large variety of overriding mechanisms in terms of a restricted set of primitives; this approach allows to compare the expressive power of these overriding operators and to formulate some results about their behavior on a formal basis.

In particular, we have proposed two orthogonal classifications for overriding: either *strong* or *weak* depending whether it offers the possibility of referring to overridden definitions; either *preferential* or *general* depending whether the precedence between methods is specified at mixin-level or at the level of single methods. General overriding turns out to be useful for dealing with multiple inheritance.

As a concrete case, we have considered Smalltalk inheritance, which corresponds to a particular version of preferential weak overriding.

We have proved that general strong overriding does not add expressive power to the corresponding preferential version. On the contrary, general weak overriding turns out to be more expressive than preferential weak overriding.

Moreover, the preferential weak overriding operator we propose, since it rejects the spurious use of the *super* mechanism, is different from Smalltalk overriding. Finally, we have considered the restriction proposed in [10], which allows to refer to an overridden method m only in the definition which overrides m and we have shown that, under this restriction, the expressive power of general and preferential weak overriding becomes the same and Smalltalk overriding coincides with preferential weak overriding.

This analysis has shown three facts concerning methodological aspects.

First, the pseudo-variable *super* in Smalltalk offers two orthogonal features: possibility of referring to overridden methods and method invocation with static binding. This leads to a rather unclean overriding operation, whose extension to the general version turns out to be very complex.

Second, general weak overriding is a too flexible operation and in some cases it is difficult to predict the behavior of the resulting mixin.

Third, the restriction proposed in [10] actually enhances software reliability: it eliminates the spurious behavior of Smalltalk inheritance and the cases which make general overriding too complex.

References

1. D. Ancona and E. Zucca. An algebraic approach to mixins and modularity. In M. Hanus and M. Rodríguez Artalejo, editors, *ALP '96 - 5th Intl. Conf. on Algebraic and Logic Programming*, number 1139 in Lecture Notes in Computer Science, pages 179–193, Berlin, 1996. Springer Verlag.
2. D. Ancona and E. Zucca. A theory of mixin modules: basic and derived operators. Technical Report DISI-TR-96-24, DISI, University of Genova, 1996. Submitted for publication.
3. G. Bracha. *The Programming Language JIGSAW: Mixins, Modularity and Multiple Inheritance*. PhD thesis, Department of Comp. Sci., Univ. of Utah, 1992.
4. G. Bracha and W. Cook. Mixin-based inheritance. In *Proc. of the Joint ACM Conf. on Object-Oriented Programming, Systems, Languages and Applications and the European Conference on Object-Oriented Programming*, October 1990.
5. G. Bracha and G. Lindstrom. Modularity meets inheritance. In *Proc. International Conference on Computer Languages*, pages 282–290, San Francisco, April 1992. IEEE Computer Society.
6. W.R. Cook. *A Denotational Semantics of Inheritance*. PhD thesis, Dept. of Computer Science, Brown University, 1989.
7. D. Duggan and C. Sourelis. Mixin modules. In *Intl. Conf. on Functional Programming*, Philadelphia, May 1996. ACM Press.
8. J. A. Goguen and R. Burstall. Institutions: abstract model theory for specification and programming. *Journ. ACM*, 39(1):95–146, 1992.
9. A. Goldberg and D. Robson. *Smalltalk-80: the Language and Its Implementation*. Addison-Wesley, 1983.
10. M. Van Limberghen and T. Mens. Encapsulation and composition as orthogonal operators on mixins: a solution to multiple inheritance problems. *Object Oriented Systems*, 3:1–30, 1996.
11. O. L. Madsen, B. Møller-Pedersen, and K. Nygaard. *Object-oriented programming in the Beta programming language*. Addison-Wesley, 1993.
12. B. Meyer. *Object-oriented Software Construction*. Computer Science series. Prentice Hall, 1988.
13. R. Milner, M. Tofte, and R. Harper. *The Definition of Standard ML*. The MIT Press, Cambridge, Massachussetts, 1990.

Resolution for Logic Programming with Universal Quantifiers

Antony F. Bowers[1] and Patricia M. Hill[2] and Francisco Ibañez[3]⋆

[1] University of Bristol, BS8 1UB, UK (bowers@cs.bris.ac.uk. +44 117 9545152)
[2] University of Leeds, LS2 9JT, UK (hill@scs.leeds.ac.uk. +44 113 2336807)
[3] Universidad Nacional de San Juan, Argentina (fibanez@iinfo.unsj.edu.ar)

Abstract. It is clearly desirable that logical specifications and the programs that implement them should be as close as possible. Such a claim is often made in support of the logic programming paradigm. However, SLD-resolution, the basic procedural semantics for logic programming, is only defined for programs whose statements are Horn clauses. Most research for extending the Horn clause framework has been concerned with allowing negative literals in the bodies of the statements where SLD-resolution is extended with negation-as-failure. However, one of the main components of first order logic not allowed in clauses is (explicit) quantification. This paper addresses this problem by showing how SLD-resolution can be extended to allow for universally quantified implication formulas as conjuncts in the body of the statements. It will be shown that this technique includes negation-as-failure as a degenerate case.

Keywords: Universal quantifiers, implication, logic programming, resolution, programming languages, specification

1 Introduction

A logic program is composed of statements which in their simplest form are Horn clauses with exactly one positive literal. However, it has always been recognised that Horn clauses have inadequate expressiveness for programming declaratively and considerable research has been done in extending the Horn clause framework to allow for more than one positive literal in the clause. Much less attention has been given to developing an extension that allows the use of logical quantifiers in the statements. Moreover, since, in logic programming, Horn clauses are usually written as (implicitly universally quantified) implication formulas it is reasonable to consider nesting the Horn clause construct within the clause itself. As a negative formula can be directly expressed as an implication formula, this framework includes the normal clause as a special case.

To motivate the ideas in this paper, consider the definition of ⊆ given below. The specification for ⊆ is that it must be true if all the elements of the set in the first argument are elements of the set in the second. Using first order logic

---

⋆ P.M. Hill and F. Ibañez were supported by EPSRC grant GR/H/79862 (and assuming the Clark completion [8]) this is expressed:

$x \subseteq y \leftarrow \forall a(a \in x \rightarrow a \in y)$.

The same predicate can also be defined using only Horn clauses:

$x \subseteq y \leftarrow x = \emptyset$

$x \subseteq y \leftarrow a \in x \wedge a \in y \wedge x1 = x \backslash \{a\} \wedge x1 \subseteq y$.

Unlike the first version, this has no obvious relationship with the specification.

The main contribution of this paper is to provide a sound procedure, called *quantifier evaluation*, for directly evaluating quantified expressions such as that used in the first definition of $\subseteq$. This quantifier evaluation procedure has a simpler formulation than that of negation-as-failure and SLDNF yet includes these as degenerate cases. Although completeness results are not proved here, it is shown that the procedure can solve many problems not solvable using the well-known Lloyd-Topor transformation method [10] and compares favourably with that proposed by Sato and Tamaki [15]. For arbitrary programs which may not be in a suitable form for quantifier evaluation, it is shown how the Lloyd-Topor transformations can be adapted to transform programs to an appropriate form for evaluation. Finally, we describe a straightforward implementation, demonstrated in Gödel, with clear possibilities for parallelism. It should be noted that this quantifier evaluation method evolved from an earlier study of bounded quantifications and their implementation [4, 17]. Section 7 contains further discussions concerning the connection with this and other related work.

Gödel [9] is used to illustrate the use of quantifiers and their implementation as it already allows the use of arbitrary first order formulas (including quantifiers) in the bodies of statements and goals. For example, using Gödel, we could write the specification and definition for $\subseteq$:

```
SubsetEq(x,y) <- ALL [a] (Element(a,x) -> Element(a,y)).
```

However, as described here in Section 6, the current Gödel implementation of this procedure is in Prolog. Thus the extension can be easily added to any logic programming language including Prolog itself.

In the next section, we provide the necessary background for the paper, introducing examples of programs that are used in the rest of the paper. In Section 3, q-normal programs and similar concepts are defined. In Section 4, we give the quantifier evaluation method for processing the universal quantifier. In Section 5 we show how the Lloyd-Topor transformations can be adapted to provide a procedure for mapping arbitrary programs to a form suitable for the quantifier evaluation method. An outline of the actual Gödel implementation of statements with quantified expressions is given in Section 6. We conclude in Section 7.

2 Basic Concepts and Notation

2.1 Notation

The set of free variables in a formula F is denoted by fvar(F). The notation $\overline{x}$ denotes the sequence or set (depending on context) of variables $x_1, \ldots, x_n$

for some n. $\forall \overline{x}F$ (resp., $\exists \overline{x}F$) means that all the variables in $\overline{x}$ are universally (resp., existentially) quantified in F. If $\overline{x}$ is empty, then $\forall \overline{x}F$ and $\exists \overline{x}F$ are both equivalent to F. Also, $\forall F$ (resp., $\exists F$) is short for $\forall \overline{x}F$ (resp., $\exists \overline{x}F$) where $\overline{x} = \text{fvar}(F)$. A *substitution*, denoted by θ or ϕ (possibly subscripted), is defined to be an idempotent mapping from a finite set of variables to terms. $\theta \restriction V$ denotes the restriction of θ to the variables in V.

To reduce the number of cases and simplify the notation, we often denote a formula F as $X \wedge W \wedge Y$ where W, X or Y can be any formula including *True*, *False* or another conjunction[4]. Thus a formula is sometimes regarded as a conjunction of a number of subformulas, the empty conjunction denoted by *True*. Similarly for disjunction although the empty disjunction is *False*.

2.2 A program and its completion

Definition 2.1 A *statement* is a formula of the form $\forall(H \leftarrow B)$ where the *head* H is an atom. It is a *normal* if the *body* B is a conjunction of literals[5]. Normally, the quantifier is omitted. A *(normal) program* P is a set of (normal) statements. $S \ll_V P$ denotes a variant S of a statement in P with $\text{fvar}(S) \cap V = \emptyset$.

A *goal statement* for a program P, which is a statement, is used instead of the usual notation $\leftarrow T$ for a goal for P. In particular, a goal $\leftarrow T$ can be written $q(\overline{x}) \leftarrow T$ where $\overline{x} = \text{fvar}(T)$ and q is a new predicate.

The soundness of our quantifier evaluation rule is demonstrated within the context of the completion of a program [8]. We repeat the definition here (based on that in [11]) as it is used directly in the proof of soundness in Section 4.

Definition 2.2 Suppose the definition of an n-ary predicate p in a program is: $\{H_1 \leftarrow B_1, \cdots, H_k \leftarrow B_k\}$. Then the *completed definition* of p is the formula

$$\forall \overline{x}(p(\overline{x}) \leftrightarrow E_1 \vee \cdots \vee E_k)$$

where, for each $i \in \{1, \ldots, k\}$, E_i is $\exists \overline{y_i}((\overline{x} = \overline{t_i}) \wedge B_i)$, H_i is $p(\overline{t_i})$, $\overline{y_i} = \text{fvar}(H_i \leftarrow B_i)$, and $\overline{x} \cap \overline{y_i} = \emptyset$.

The *completion* comp(P) of a program P is the set of completed definitions of predicates in P together with the equality theory CET [8] for the functions[6] and predicates of P. If G is the goal statement $U \leftarrow T$, and θ a substitution for the variables in U then θ is a *correct answer* for P and G if comp$(P) \models \forall(U \leftarrow T) \rightarrow \forall U\theta$.

A normal program is evaluated using SLDNF-resolution. At each step of this procedure, a *computation rule* is used to determine which literal is selected for processing. One that only selects atoms or ground negative literals (called *safe*) is sufficient for the soundness of SLDNF-derivations. If, in a derivation, the body of the final goal statement is a formula other than *True* and there are no selectable literals, then the derivation *flounders*.

---

[4] We ignore the syntactic distinction between $(X \wedge W) \wedge Y$ and $X \wedge (W \wedge Y)$.
[5] A literal is a positive or negative atom.
[6] Constants are regarded as functions of arity 0.

2.3 Gödel

The language Gödel has an expressive syntax[7] which can be used both as a data base query language and as a language for (possibly) runnable specifications. We illustrate both applications here.

As an example of the Gödel syntax and use of Gödel as a data base query language, consider the following geographic data base.

City(Amsterdam, Holland).   City(Brussels, Belgium).
City(Cologne, Germany).   City(Essen, Germany).
City(Paris, France).   City(Rotterdam, Holland).
Distance(Amsterdam,Brussels,185). Distance(Cologne,Brussels,190).
Distance(Essen, Brussels, 200).   Distance(Paris, Brussels, 270).
Distance(Rotterdam,Brussels,125). Distance(Brussels, Brussels, 0).

Then to ask if all cities within a certain distance (say 199 km) of Brussels (other than Brussels itself) are in the same country, we might write the goal statement:

```
Test <- SOME [country]
    ALL [city] (SOME [d] (Distance(city,Brussels,d) & 0<d & d=<199)
                -> City(city, country)).
```

To illustrate Gödel as a specification language, consider the binary predicate ReverseList where both arguments are lists and each is the reverse of the other. With ReversePos, the ith element of the first list must be the same as the element in the ith position from the end of the second list (where i is the third argument).

```
ReverseList(x1,x2) <-
    Length(x1,1) & Length(x2,1) &
    ALL[i] (1 =< i =< 1 -> ReversePos(x1,x2,i,1)).
ReversePos(x1,x2,i,1) <- Element(x1,i,a) & Element(x2,1-i+1,a).
Element([a|_],1,a).
Element([_|x],i,a) <- i > 1 & Element(x,i-1,a).
```

Length is a predicate provided by the Gödel system module Lists. The notation a =< i =< b is syntactic sugar for the atom Interval(a,i,b) and is used to generate values for i (or check that the values of i lie) between the bounds a and b.

Without explicit use of the implication symbol, any intended implication may be hard to identify. For example, if the statement defining ReverseList was:

```
ReverseList(x1,x2) <-
    Length(x1,1) & Length(x2,1) &
    ALL[i] ((1 > i) \/ (i > 1) \/ ReversePos(x1,x2,i,1)).
```

the subformula restricting the domain of i would be less easy to identify although, no doubt, algorithms for finding such formulas could be constructed.

---

[7] Note that in Gödel, variables begin with lower case letters while functions and predicates begin with upper case letters. The connectives conjunction, disjunction, negation, and left and right implication are denoted by &, \/, ~, <-, ->, respectively. The universal and existential quantifiers are denoted by ALL [..] and SOME [..].

2.4 Transformations to eliminate quantifiers

If the program is not normal, then it can be transformed to a normal program using the Lloyd-Topor transformations [10]. Below, we present a slightly modified form of these transformations, where V and W are formulas other than $True$, Σ is the set of predicates in the program, and $q \notin \Sigma$ a new predicate. The statement $A \leftarrow X \wedge U \wedge Y$, where U is not a conjunction of literals, is selected from the program. Depending on the formula U and assuming $\bar{u} = \mathrm{fvar}(U)$, one of the actions given in the table below is performed[8].

$$
\begin{array}{lll}
1 & A \leftarrow X \wedge \neg(V \wedge W) \wedge Y, \quad \Sigma \mapsto \left\{ \begin{array}{l} A \leftarrow X \wedge \neg V \wedge Y \\ A \leftarrow X \wedge \neg W \wedge Y \end{array} \right\}, & \Sigma \\
2 & A \leftarrow X \wedge \neg(V \vee W) \wedge Y, \quad \Sigma \mapsto A \leftarrow X \wedge \neg V \wedge \neg W \wedge Y, & \Sigma \\
3 & A \leftarrow X \wedge \neg(V \rightarrow W) \wedge Y, \quad \Sigma \mapsto A \leftarrow X \wedge V \wedge \neg W \wedge Y, & \Sigma \\
4 & A \leftarrow X \wedge \neg\neg V \wedge Y, \qquad\qquad \Sigma \mapsto A \leftarrow X \wedge V \wedge Y, & \Sigma \\
5 & A \leftarrow X \wedge \neg\exists \bar{x} V \wedge Y, \quad \Sigma \mapsto \left\{ \begin{array}{l} A \leftarrow X \wedge \neg q(\bar{u}) \wedge Y \\ q(\bar{u}) \leftarrow V \end{array} \right\}, & \Sigma \cup \{q\} \\
6 & A \leftarrow X \wedge \neg\forall \bar{x} V \wedge Y, \quad \Sigma \mapsto A \leftarrow X \wedge \neg V \wedge Y, & \Sigma \\
7 & A \leftarrow X \wedge (V \vee W) \wedge Y, \quad \Sigma \mapsto \left\{ \begin{array}{l} A \leftarrow X \wedge V \wedge Y \\ A \leftarrow X \wedge W \wedge Y \end{array} \right\}, & \Sigma \\
8 & A \leftarrow X \wedge (V \rightarrow W) \wedge Y, \quad \Sigma \mapsto \left\{ \begin{array}{l} A \leftarrow X \wedge \neg V \wedge Y \\ A \leftarrow X \wedge W \wedge Y \end{array} \right\}, & \Sigma \\
9 & A \leftarrow X \wedge \exists \bar{x} V \wedge Y, \qquad \Sigma \mapsto A \leftarrow X \wedge V \wedge Y, & \Sigma \\
10 & A \leftarrow X \wedge \forall \bar{x} V \wedge Y, \qquad \Sigma \mapsto \left\{ \begin{array}{l} A \leftarrow X \wedge \neg q(\bar{u}) \wedge Y \\ q(\bar{u}) \leftarrow \neg V \end{array} \right\}, & \Sigma \cup \{q\}
\end{array}
$$

Given any initial program P with predicates Σ, a sequence of these transformations must terminate and the resulting program P' (called the *normal form of P*) is normal [11]. Moreover, if U is a logical consequence of $\mathrm{comp}(P')$ and all predicates in U are in Σ, then U is a logical consequence of $\mathrm{comp}(P)$. For instance, the original definition for $\subseteq$ with set of predicates $\{\subseteq, \in\}$ would be transformed using steps 10 and 8 as follows:

$$
\begin{array}{l}
x \subseteq y \leftarrow \forall a(a \in x \rightarrow a \in y), \{\subseteq, \in\} \mapsto \left\{ \begin{array}{l} x \subseteq y \leftarrow \neg q(x,y) \\ q(x,y) \leftarrow \neg(a \in x \rightarrow a \in y) \end{array} \right\}, \{\subseteq, \in, q\} \\
\qquad\qquad\qquad\qquad\qquad\qquad \mapsto \left\{ \begin{array}{l} x \subseteq y \leftarrow \neg q(x,y) \\ q(x,y) \leftarrow a \in x \wedge \neg a \in y \end{array} \right\}, \{\subseteq, \in, q\}
\end{array}
$$

Note that, with this program, the goal statement $r(x) \leftarrow \{1,2\} \subseteq \{9,1,6,5,2,x\}$ would flounder using SLDNF-resolution.

Applying these transformations to the definition of ReverseList gives:

```
ReverseList(x1,x2) <-
    Length(x1,l) & Length(x2,l)  & ~ NotReversed(x1,x2,l).
NotReversed(x1,x2,l) <-
    1 =< i =< l & ~ Match(x1,x2,i,l).
Match(x1,x2,i,l) <- ReversePos(x1,x2,i,l).
```

---

[8] It is assumed that all quantified variables are already renamed uniquely.

where `NotReversed` and `Match` are new predicates and `ReversePos` is defined as before. With this transformed program, `ReverseList` can only be used to check that one list is the reverse of the other. In particular, the goal statements

```
Test(z) <- ReverseList([1,2,3,4],z).
Test(z) <- ReverseList(z,[1,2,3,4]).
```

will both flounder. To explain this, consider the first of these goals. The call to `Length(x1,1)` will succeed with 1 bound to 4 and the call to `Length(x2,1)` will then bind x2 to a list of length 4 with all elements unique variables. Thus, with a safe computation rule, since x2 is not ground, the call to `~NotReversed(x1,x2,1)` will flounder. The behaviour will be similar for the second goal, although since in Gödel a call to any `Length` atom delays if both arguments are variables, `Length(x2,1)` will be evaluated before `Length(x1,1)`.

3 Restricted Quantifications

In the examples in Section 2, formulas with universal quantifiers are implication formulas of the form $V \to W$. This is a natural way to use a universal quantifier, since V restricts the domain of the quantified variables, while W gives the condition that must be satisfied by all the values in the restricted domain.

Definition 3.1 A *restricted quantification* is a formula of the form $\forall \overline{x}(V \to W)$. It is *atomic* if V and W are atoms. W is called the *head* and V the *body*.

Note that, by reversing the implication part of the formula and adding a universal quantifier for the free variables, a restricted quantification with an atomic head becomes a statement. Also note that a negative literal $\neg A$ is a special case of a restricted quantification since it can be expressed as $\forall \overline{x}(A \to \textit{False})$ where $\overline{x}$ is empty.

Definition 3.2 A *quantified-normal (q-normal) formula* F is of the form $F_1 \wedge \cdots \wedge F_n$ where each F_i is either

- an atom (called an *atomic conjunct of F*) or
- an atomic restricted quantification.

An atom A occurs *positively* in F if, for some i, either $A = F_i$, or F_i is an atomic restricted quantification whose head is A. An atom A occurs *negatively* in F if, for some i, A is the body of the atomic restricted quantification F_i. A variable $x \in \text{fvar}(F)$ occurs *positively* (resp., *negatively*) in F if it occurs in an atom that occurs positively (resp., negatively) in F.

A *q-normal statement* is a statement whose body is q-normal. A *q-normal program* is a program whose statements are all q-normal.

Definition 3.3 A *computation rule* $\mathcal{C}$ is a function from a set of q-normal formulas to the set of atoms and atomic restricted quantifications occurring in them such that if $\mathcal{C}$ is defined for the q-normal formula F, $\mathcal{C}(\mathcal{F}) = \mathcal{L}$ for some conjunct L of F. L is called the *selected formula*.

Since a negative literal is equivalent to an atomic restricted quantification, the definition of a q-normal program includes a normal program as a special case. The specification of $\subseteq$ in Section 1 and the ReverseList program in Section 2 are already in q-normal form. However, the goal statement for the European database in Subsection 2.3 is not. We show later how this can be transformed to q-normal form.

4 Quantifier Evaluation

4.1 SLDQE-derivations

An SLDQE-derivation (and tree) for a goal statement and a program is an extension of an SLD-derivation (and tree) for processing the restricted quantifications. The definitions for SLDQE follow closely those for SLDNF in [11] although, here, goal statements are used in place of goals[9]. This facilitates a more elegant formulation of the procedure for the restricted quantifications. Note that the use of goal statements is in line with earlier observations in [12] that a resultant[10] encapsulates most of the information about a derivation.

If the body of a goal statement is of the form

$$X \wedge \forall \overline{x}(V \to W) \wedge Y$$

where $\forall \overline{x}(V \to W)$ is the selected formula and $\overline{x}$ is a subset of the free variables in V, the *quantifier evaluation* step replaces the body by

$$X \wedge W \phi_1 \wedge \cdots \wedge W \phi_m \wedge Y$$

where $\{\phi_1, \ldots, \phi_m\}$ is a finite set of all computed answers for $W \leftarrow V$ with the given program using an SLDQE-derivation. The basic theoretical requirement is that if $x \in \overline{x}$, $x\phi_i$ is ground and if $y \in \text{fvar}(V)\backslash\overline{x}$, $y\phi_i = y$ for $1 \le i \le m$. The precise definition of an SLDQE-derivation needs to be inductive. If the selected formula is a restricted quantification $V \to W$, then the answer set for $W \leftarrow V$ has to be obtained using a subsidiary SLDQE-tree. Similarly, SLDQE-trees may require subsidiary SLDQE-derivations. The depth of nesting of subsidiary SLDQE-derivations or trees is called the *rank* of the computation. For lack of space, we give a shortened version of the definition where the base cases ($k = 0$) are implicitly included with the inductive ones. In the following definitions, P is a q-normal program and G is a q-normal goal statement of the form $U \leftarrow T$.

Definition 4.1 An *SLDQE-refutation of rank k* for P and G consists of sequences $G = G_0, G_1, \ldots, G_n$ and $C_1, \ldots, C_n$ of statements such that $G_n = U\theta_n \leftarrow \text{True}$ and, for each $i \in \{0, \ldots, n-1\}$ either:

---

[9] We have based our definition on that of [11]. However, this definition is known to have problems and it has now been superseded by that in [2]. There appears no technical reason why the abbreviated form of the definition of SLDQE given here should not be expanded to one that corresponds to this improved version.

[10] A resultant is a generalisation of a statement where the head can be any formula.

1. $G_i = U\theta_i \leftarrow X \wedge A \wedge Y$, A is the selected atom, $H \leftarrow B \ll_{\text{fvar}(G_i)} P$, $\text{mgu}(\{A, H\}) = \theta'_i$, $C_{i+1} = H \leftarrow B$, $\theta_{i+1} = \theta_i \theta'_i$ and $G_{i+1} = U\theta_{i+1} \leftarrow X\theta'_i \wedge B\theta'_i \wedge Y\theta'_i$; or

2. $k > 0$, $G_i = U\theta_i \leftarrow X \wedge \forall \overline{x}(V \rightarrow W) \wedge Y$, the selected formula in the body of G_i is $\forall \overline{x}(V \rightarrow W)$, and $\{\phi_1, \ldots, \phi_m\}$ is a ground answer-set with domain $\overline{x}$ for an SLDQE-tree of rank $k - 1$ for P and $W \leftarrow V$. In this case, $C_{i+1} = W \leftarrow V$, $\theta_{i+1} = \theta_i$ and $G_{i+1} = U\theta_{i+1} \leftarrow X \wedge W\phi_1 \wedge \cdots \wedge W\phi_m \wedge Y$.

In both cases, G_{i+1} is said to be *derived* from G_i and C_{i+1}.

The substitution $\theta_n \restriction U$ is a *computed answer* for P and G.

Definition 4.2 A *completed SLDQE-tree of rank k* for P and G is a finite tree satisfying:

1. each node of the tree is a q-normal goal statement;
2. the root node is G;
3. Suppose $G' = U\theta \leftarrow X \wedge S \wedge Y$ is a non-leaf node in the tree and that S is the selected formula, then either
   (a) S is an atom and, for each statement $H \leftarrow B \ll_{\text{fvar}(G')} P$ where there exists $\text{mgu}(\{S, H\}) = \theta'$, the node has a child $U\theta\theta' \leftarrow X\theta' \wedge B\theta' \wedge Y\theta'$;
   (b) $k > 0$ and S is of the form $\forall \overline{x}(V \rightarrow W)$, $\{\phi_1, \ldots, \phi_m\}$ is a ground answer-set with domain $\overline{x}$ for an SLDQE-tree of rank $k - 1$ for P and $W \leftarrow V$, and there is a single child $U\theta \leftarrow X \wedge W\phi_1 \wedge \cdots \wedge W\phi_m \wedge Y$;
4. Suppose $G' = U\theta \leftarrow X \wedge S \wedge Y$ is a leaf node in the tree and that S (distinct from *True*) is the selected formula, then S is an atom and there does not exist $H \leftarrow B \ll_{\text{fvar}(G')} P$ so that $\{H, S\}$ unifies;
5. $U\theta \leftarrow$ *True* is a *successful* leaf node with answer $\theta \restriction \text{fvar}(U)$.

The set of answers at successful leaf nodes is an *answer-set* for P and G. If each answer is ground, then the answer-set is *ground*.

An *SLDQE-refutation* (*completed SLDQE-tree*) for P and G is an SLDQE-refutation (completed SLDQE-tree) of rank k for P and G for some k.

SLDQE-derivations and trees are not defined here but can be defined similarly to SLDNF-derivations and trees [11].

4.2 Soundness of SLDQE-resolution

There are two main results, both proved similarly to the corresponding results for SLDNF-resolution [11, Theorems 15.4, 15.6]. Remarkably, the proofs are in fact slightly simpler due to the more uniform way in which the variables and sets of computed answers are handled in the quantifier evaluation step. The following lemma in [11, Lemma 15.3] is similar to one by Clark [8] and needed in the first proof below.

Lemma 1. *Let P be a q-normal program and G a q-normal goal statement of the form $U \leftarrow T$. Suppose the selected formula in T is an atom. Then, if $\{G_1, \ldots, G_r\}$ is the set of derived goal statements, $\text{comp}(P) \models G \leftrightarrow G_1 \wedge \cdots \wedge G_r$.*

Theorem 2. *Let P be a q-normal program and $\forall \bar{y}(T \to U)$ an atomic restricted quantification. If $\{\theta_1, \ldots, \theta_l\}$ is a ground answer-set with domain $\bar{y}$ for P and $U \leftarrow T$, then $\mathrm{comp}(P) \models \forall(\forall \bar{y}(T \to U) \leftarrow U\theta_1 \wedge \cdots \wedge U\theta_l)$.*

Proof. The proof is by induction on the rank of the completed SLDQE-tree used to obtain the answer-set $\{\theta_1, \ldots, \theta_l\}$. Suppose $k = 0$. Then the result follows by induction on the depth of the tree using Lemma 1.

Next, suppose the result holds for SLDQE-trees of rank k. Consider an SLDQE-tree of rank $k+1$ for P and $U \leftarrow T$ with ground answer-set $\{\theta_1, \ldots, \theta_l\}$. We establish the result by a secondary induction on the depth d of this tree.

If $d = 1$, $T = \forall \bar{x}(V \to W)$ and the answer set for $W \leftarrow V$ is empty. Thus, by the primary induction hypothesis, $\mathrm{comp}(P) \models \forall(V \to W)$ so that the answer set for $U \leftarrow T$ consist of just the identity substitution. The result then follows.

Now suppose that an SLDQE-tree for P and G has depth $d + 1$. If an atom is selected, the result follows from Lemma 1 and the secondary induction hypothesis. Suppose $T = X \wedge \forall \bar{x}(V \to W) \wedge Y$ where $\forall \bar{x}(V \to W)$ is selected and that $\{\phi_1, \ldots, \phi_m\}$ is a ground answer-set with domain $\bar{x}$ for an SLDQE-tree of rank k for P and $W \leftarrow V$. By the primary induction hypothesis $\mathrm{comp}(P) \models \forall(\forall \bar{x}(V \to W) \leftarrow W\phi_1 \wedge \cdots \wedge W\phi_m)$. As $x\phi_i$ is ground for each $x \in \bar{x}$, $fvar(X \wedge W\phi_1 \wedge \cdots \wedge W\phi_m \wedge Y) = fvar(T)$. So, by the secondary induction hypothesis, $\mathrm{comp}(P) \models \forall(\forall \bar{y}(U \leftarrow X \wedge W\phi_1 \wedge \cdots \wedge W\phi_m \wedge Y) \leftarrow U\theta_1 \wedge \cdots \wedge U\theta_l)$ and hence $\mathrm{comp}(P) \models \forall(\forall \bar{y}(U \leftarrow T) \leftarrow U\theta_1 \wedge \cdots \wedge U\theta_l)$.

Theorem 3. *Let P be a q-normal program and G a q-normal goal statement. Then every computed answer for P and G is a correct answer for $\mathrm{comp}(P) \cup \{G\}$.*

Proof. Let G be the q-normal goal statement $U \leftarrow T$ and θ a computed answer of P and G. We have to show $\mathrm{comp}(P) \models \forall(U \leftarrow T) \to \forall U\theta$ and hence that $\mathrm{comp}(P) \models \forall T\theta$. The result is proved by induction on the length of the SLDQE-refutation. Suppose $n = 1$. Then T is *True* and θ is trivial. It follows that $\forall U\theta$ is a logical consequence of $P \cup \{G\}$ and hence of $\mathrm{comp}(P) \cup \{G\}$.

Next suppose the result holds for computed answers obtained using SLDQE-refutations of length $n - 1$. Let $T = X \wedge S \wedge Y$ and S the selected formula. Suppose S is an atom. Let $H \leftarrow B \ll_{fvar(U \leftarrow T)} P$ and $\mathrm{mgu}(\{H, S\}) = \theta$. By the induction hypothesis, $\mathrm{comp}(P) \models \forall(X \wedge B \wedge Y)\theta$. Therefore $\mathrm{comp}(P) \models \forall B\theta$. Consequently $\mathrm{comp}(P) \models \forall S\theta$. Hence $\mathrm{comp}(P) \models \forall T\theta$.

Secondly, suppose $S = \forall \bar{x}(V \to W)$. Then there is a ground answer set $\{\phi_1, \ldots, \phi_m\}$ with domain $\bar{x}$ for P and $W \leftarrow V$. Theorem 2 shows that $\mathrm{comp}(P) \models \forall(S \leftarrow W\phi_1 \wedge \cdots \wedge W\phi_m)$. Using the induction hypothesis, $\mathrm{comp}(P) \models \forall(X \wedge W\phi_1 \wedge \cdots \wedge W\phi_m \wedge Y)$ and hence $\mathrm{comp}(P) \models \forall(T\theta)$.

4.3 Completeness of SLDQE-resolution

In the case of SLDNF-derivations, the computation rule must not select non-ground negative literals. The more general procedure defined here allows for any computation rule but may still flounder if there is no applicable step.

Definition 4.3 For an SLDQE-derivation, the computation will *flounder* if either there is no selected formula or the selected formula is $\forall \bar{x}(V \to W)$ and either there is no completed SLDQE-tree for $W \leftarrow V$ or the answer-set for $W \leftarrow V$ is not ground with domain $\bar{x}$.

To explain these conditions, consider the following program P:

```
S(A,B). S(A,D).
Q(A,B). Q(A,C).
R(u).
```

and goal statements

```
T(y) <- ALL [x] (S(x,y) -> Q(x,y)).
T(y) <- ALL [x] (R(x) -> Q(x,y)).
```

With the first goal, we can compute directly the answer `y = B`. However, this does not represent the complete solution since any substitution binding `y` to t such that `<- S(`t`,y)` finitely fails is also a correct answer for this goal with comp(P). For instance, `y = C` and `y = A` are also correct answers[11]. With the second goal, note that `ALL [x] (R(x) -> Q(x,_))` is not a logical consequence of comp(P) although without the groundness condition, this goal would succeed.

Note that the implementation described in Section 6 assumes, for the restricted quantification $\forall \bar{x}(V \to W)$ to be selected that fvar(V) = $\bar{x}$.

As for SLDNF-resolution, we can define a condition under which, for some computation rule, an SLDQE-derivation will not flounder.

Definition 4.4 A q-normal statement $H \leftarrow B$ is *q-admissible*[12] if every variable that occurs negatively in B is either in H or an atomic conjunct of B. $H \leftarrow B$ is *q-allowed* if every variable that occurs in H or negatively in B is in an atomic conjunct of B. A q-normal program P is *q-allowed* if every statement in P is q-admissible and every statement defining a predicate that is in an atom that occurs positively in the body of a statement in P is q-allowed. (Thus, if $H \leftarrow$ *True* is q-allowed, then H must be ground.)

Theorem 4. *Let P be a q-normal program and G a q-normal goal statement of the form $U \leftarrow T$. Suppose $P \cup \{G\}$ and G are q-allowed. Then:*

1. *Every computed answer for P and G is ground for all variables in U.*
2. *There is an SLDQE-derivation for P and G that does not flounder.*

Proof. First note that, since P and G are q-allowed, every goal statement in an SLDQE-derivation (including subsidiary computations for the restricted quantifications) is q-allowed.

Part 1 then follows, since, if the final goal is $U\theta \leftarrow$ *True*, $U\theta$ must be ground.

Part 2 also follows since a q-allowed goal statement will always contain either an atom or a restricted quantification of the form $\forall \bar{x}(V \to W)$ where

---

[11] The solution is best represented by the disequation `y ~= D`.

[12] We prefix the concepts "allowed" and "admissible" with "q" to distinguish them from the similar concepts defined for normal programs and goals.

$\mathrm{fvar}(\forall \bar{x} V) = \emptyset$ and, by Part 1, every answer-set for any subsidiary computations for the restricted quantifiers will always be ground. Thus, if atoms are selected first, the derivation will not flounder.

Consider again the program and goal statements for `ReverseList` given in Subsections 2.3 and 2.4. These are q-allowed. Using SLDQE-resolution, neither of the goals flounder and both have the computed answer `z = [4,3,2,1]`.

Completeness results for SLDQE-resolution, similar to the those for SLDNF-resolution as given in [11], can be stated and proved using Theorem 4.

5 Transforming Programs to q-normal Programs

SLDQE is defined for q-normal programs and goal statements only. If the program is not q-normal, then it can be transformed to a q-normal program using a modified form of the transformations in Subsection 2.4. Let Σ be the set of predicates in the program and $q, r \notin \Sigma$ new predicates. The statement $A \leftarrow X \wedge U \wedge Y$, where U is not a conjunction of atoms, negated atoms and atomic restricted quantifications, is selected from the program. Depending on the formula U, and assuming $\bar{u} = \mathrm{fvar}(U)$, one of the actions in the table below is performed[13].

1	$A \leftarrow X \wedge \neg(V \wedge W) \wedge Y,$	$\Sigma \mapsto \left\{ \begin{array}{l} A \leftarrow X \wedge q(\bar{u}) \wedge Y \\ q(\bar{u}) \leftarrow \neg V \\ q(\bar{u}) \leftarrow \neg W \end{array} \right\},$	$\Sigma \cup \{q\}$
2	$A \leftarrow X \wedge \neg(V \vee W) \wedge Y,$	$\Sigma \mapsto A \leftarrow X \wedge \neg V \wedge \neg W \wedge Y,$	$\Sigma.$
3	$A \leftarrow X \wedge \neg(V \rightarrow W) \wedge Y,$	$\Sigma \mapsto A \leftarrow X \wedge V \wedge \neg W \wedge Y,$	$\Sigma.$
4	$A \leftarrow X \wedge \neg\neg V \wedge Y,$	$\Sigma \mapsto A \leftarrow X \wedge V \wedge Y,$	$\Sigma.$
5	$A \leftarrow X \wedge \neg\exists \bar{x} V \wedge Y,$	$\Sigma \mapsto A \leftarrow X \wedge \forall \bar{x}(V \rightarrow \mathit{False}) \wedge Y,$	$\Sigma.$
6	$A \leftarrow X \wedge \neg\forall \bar{x} V \wedge Y,$	$\Sigma \mapsto A \leftarrow X \wedge \neg V \wedge Y,$	$\Sigma.$
7	$A \leftarrow X \wedge (V \vee W) \wedge Y,$	$\Sigma \mapsto \left\{ \begin{array}{l} A \leftarrow X \wedge q(\bar{u}) \wedge Y \\ q(\bar{u}) \leftarrow V \\ q(\bar{u}) \leftarrow W \end{array} \right\},$	$\Sigma \cup \{q\}$
8	$A \leftarrow X \wedge (V \rightarrow W) \wedge Y,$	$\Sigma \mapsto \left\{ \begin{array}{l} A \leftarrow X \wedge q(\bar{u}) \wedge Y \\ q(\bar{u}) \leftarrow \neg V \\ q(\bar{u}) \leftarrow W \end{array} \right\},$	$\Sigma \cup \{q\}$
9	$A \leftarrow X \wedge \exists \bar{x} V \wedge Y,$	$\Sigma \mapsto A \leftarrow X \wedge V \wedge Y,$	$\Sigma.$

10a $A \leftarrow X \wedge \forall \bar{x} V \wedge Y$
$\quad V \neq V_1 \rightarrow V_2,$

$\Sigma \mapsto \left\{ \begin{array}{l} A \leftarrow X \wedge \forall \bar{x}(q(\bar{v}) \rightarrow \mathit{False}) \wedge Y \\ q(\bar{v}) \leftarrow \neg V \end{array} \right\}, \; \Sigma \cup \{q\}$
$\bar{v} = \mathrm{fvar}(V)$

10b $A \leftarrow X \wedge \forall \bar{x}(V \rightarrow W) \wedge Y$
$\quad V$ or W is not atomic.

$\Sigma \mapsto \left\{ \begin{array}{l} A \leftarrow X \wedge \forall \bar{x}(q(\bar{v}) \rightarrow r(\bar{w})) \wedge Y \\ q(\bar{v}) \leftarrow V \\ r(\bar{w}) \leftarrow W \end{array} \right\}, \; \Sigma \cup \{q, r\}$
$\bar{v} = \mathrm{fvar}(V), \bar{w} = \mathrm{fvar}(W).$

It is useful to compare these with those in Section 2. First note that transformations 2, 3, 4, 6 and 9 are identical. Secondly, note that disjunction has been treated differently. This is because in any implementation, it is best to avoid re-computing other parts of the formula in the body of the statement. By creating a

---

[13] As before, we assume here that all quantified variables are already renamed uniquely.

new predicate for each disjunct, this can be avoided. This change affects 1, 7 and 8. Transformation 5 has been altered to exploit the improved implementation of the universal quantifier. Finally, 10 is replaced by two; 10a which only applies when the quantified formula is not an implication and 10b which applies when it is an implication but it is not atomic. It should be noted, that the effect of 10a is the same as 10 followed by 5 using the Lloyd-Topor transformations.

Theorem 5. *Let P be a program with predicates Σ. Then a sequence of these transformations must terminate and the resulting program P', called the* q-normal *form of P, is* q-normal.

Proof. We define a termination function μ from programs to the non-negative integers. First, we define the mapping μ from a formula to a non-negative integer inductively as follows:

$$
\begin{aligned}
\mu(\text{atom}) &= 0 & \mu(\neg V) &= 2\mu(V) + 1 \\
\mu(V \wedge W) &= \mu(V) + \mu(W) + 1 & \mu(V \vee W) &= \mu(V) + \mu(W) + 2 \\
\mu(V \rightarrow W) &= 2\mu(V) + 2\mu(W) + 2 & \mu(\exists \bar{x} V) &= \mu(V) + 1 \\
\mu(\forall \bar{x} V) &= 2\mu(V) + 2,\ V \neq V_1 \rightarrow V_2 & \mu(\forall \bar{x}(V \rightarrow W)) &= 2\mu(V) + 2\mu(W)
\end{aligned}
$$

Let
$$
\mu(P) = \sum_{H \leftarrow B \in P} \mu(B)
$$

Then each transformation 1-10b maps P to a program P_1 where, if $\mu(P) = t$ and $\mu(P_1) = t_1$, then $t_1 < t$. Hence the process terminates. P' must be q-normal since if it was not q-normal, one of the transformations 1-10b would apply.

Lemma 6. *let P be a program with predicates Σ and P' a q-normal form of P. If the closed formula U contains only predicates in Σ and $\mathrm{comp}(P') \models U$, then $\mathrm{comp}(P) \models U$.*

Proof. If P' is obtained from P by one of the transformations 2, 3, 4, 5, 6 or 9, the completions of programs P and P' are logically equivalent and the result is trivial. Consider transformation 1. Then the completed definition of q
$$
q(\bar{z}) \leftrightarrow \exists \bar{u}(\bar{z} = \bar{u} \wedge \neg V) \vee \exists \bar{u}(\bar{z} = \bar{u} \wedge \neg W)
$$
is in $\mathrm{comp}(P')$. Since $\mathrm{comp}(P)$ includes the equality theory CET, this formula is equivalent to $q(\bar{u}) \leftrightarrow \neg V \vee \neg W$ which is equivalent to $q(\bar{u}) \leftrightarrow \neg(V \wedge W)$ The result now follows. The proofs for transformations 7, 8, 10a, and 10b are similar.

Definition 5.1 Let P be a program, G a goal statement $U \leftarrow T$, $\mathrm{fvar}(T) = \bar{y}$ and q a predicate not in P. A *computed answer* for P and G is the computed answer for a q-normal form of $P \cup \{q(\bar{y}) \leftarrow T\}$ with goal $U \leftarrow q(\bar{y})$.

Theorem 7. *Let P be a program and G a goal statement. Then every computed answer for P and G is a correct answer for $\mathrm{comp}(P) \cup \{G\}$.*

The proof of this corresponds almost exactly to that of the equivalent result for the Lloyd-Topor transformations [11, Theorem 18.7], but uses Lemma 6 to justify the transformations.

To illustrate the transformations and advantages of using SLDQE-resolution, we reconsider the European program given in Subsection 2.3. The goal

```
Test <- SOME [country]
    ALL [city] (SOME [d] (Distance(city, Brussels, d) & 0<d=<200)
          -> City(city, country)).
```

is not q-normal but can be transformed by the sequence of transformations $\{9, 10a, 9\}$ to the q-normal form:

```
Test <- ALL [city] (NearBrussels(city) -> City(city, country)).
NearBrussels(city) <- Distance(city, Brussels, d) & 0 < d =< 199.
```

which will succeed using SLDQE-resolution.

6   Implementation

The implementation of SLDQE-resolution described here is used in the Gödel system produced at Bristol University, which compiles the source programs into Prolog. SICStus Prolog [7] was used as the target language.

A q-normal statement with no restricted quantification is a definite clause, and so maps directly into Prolog. Therefore, we only consider the treatment of an atomic restricted quantification $F =$ ALL [Xs] $(V \rightarrow W)$ which is a sub-formula of the body of a goal statement. Note that we present a simplified view of the code since, being part of a larger system, it also has to keep track of the free and bound variables and perform other routine tasks. In the Gödel implementation we require all variables in fvar(ALL [Xs] V) to be bound to ground terms before the restricted quantification ALL [Xs] $(V \rightarrow W)$ can be selected. This is more restrictive than the theoretical requirements given in Section 4, but enables more co-routining and hence reduces the risk of floundering.

Assuming V and W are bound to the Prolog equivalents for the Gödel expressions V and W, we substitute for F the Prolog code:

```
gsetof(Xs, V, Ys), gfreeze(Us, try(Ys, Xs, W, Es))
```

Here, Us is the list of variables in $fvar(V)\backslash Xs$ and Es the list of variables in $fvar(W)\backslash(Xs \cup fvar(V))$. The predicate try/4 is a part of the Gödel run-time library, and its Prolog implementation is as follows:

```
try([Values|Rest], QuantVars, Goal, FreeVars) :-
   copy_term(c(QuantVars, Goal, FreeVars),
             c(QuantVarsCopy, GoalCopy, FreeVarsCopy)),
   QuantVarsCopy = Values, FreeVarsCopy = FreeVars,
   call(GoalCopy), try(Rest, QuantVars, Goal, FreeVars).
try([], _, _, _).
```

The Prolog predicate gsetof/3 is part of the implementation for set processing in Gödel and built on top of Prolog's setof/3. gsetof(Xs, V, Ys) differs from setof(Xs, V, Ys) in that it delays until there are no variables in V that do not also appear in Xs. The predicate gfreeze/2 is built on top of SICStus Prolog's freeze/2. gfreeze(Us, G) takes the list of variables Us, and delays the call to G until all variables in the list have been bound to ground terms. Thus neither of the calls to gsetof and gfreeze will proceed until fvar(V)\Xs $= \emptyset$. Suppose fvar(V)\Xs $= \emptyset$. The call to gsetof will compute Ys, the list of lists of the domain values representing the computed answers $\phi_1, \ldots, \phi_m$ for W <- V. Moreover, it will generate a run-time error if any values in Ys are non-ground. The call to copy_term/2 (in the definition of try) makes a copy of W with fresh variables, while keeping track of which of those new variables represent variables in Xs, and which represent variables in Es. The two equalities then instantiate the copy of W appropriately.

7 Discussion

One reason for the lack of research on the design of execution procedures for programs with quantifiers is that such a program can be transformed by means of the Lloyd-Topor transformations to an equivalent normal program [10]. As explained in Subsection 2.4, this method causes floundering problems when the transformed program is executed via SLDNF-resolution.

An alternative transformation technique using unfold/fold transformations to synthesise Horn clause programs from q-normal ones is described by Tamaki and Sato in [15]. The precise conditions when the technique works are not explicitly given, making comparisons difficult. However, the theoretical framework for SLDQE-resolution is at least as powerful as the techniques of [15]. We have implemented each of the examples given in [15] in Gödel. In Example 3, there is an implicit assumption about the program's types without which the transformation would not work. If this information is included explicitly, then the same queries can be evaluated using the Gödel implementation. Of the other examples, we have either translated the code directly to Gödel and obtained the same results (Example 2) or, where there are free variables occurring in the range formula (as in Example 1), made simple changes to the program to eliminate this problem. Note that in this latter case, the SLDQE procedures can, in theory, directly evaluate such programs, but this is not supported in the current Gödel implementations. We believe that quantifier evaluation has the distinct advantage over both the Lloyd-Topor and Tamaki-Sato approaches in that it is not a series of transformations but provides a procedure for directly evaluating universally quantified formulas.

A completely different strategy for extending the Horn clause framework with quantifiers and implications has been adopted by λProlog [14]. This uses the logic of heriditary Harrop formulas with a procedural semantics based on intuitionistic provability. Our approach differs fundamentally with regard to both the intended logical meaning of a program and in the procedure for deriving answers. The logic of a program as defined in Section 3 is based on classical logic whereas a λProlog program is defined to be a theory in intuitionistic logic. The execution procedure defined in Section 1 does not separate the universal quantifier from the implication formula and we have defined a method that just builds on resolution without any changes to unification. In λProlog, an implication formula in a goal is evaluated by adding the body formula as a clause to the program and then trying to solve the head; a universally quantified formula is interpreted as an instruction to generate a new constant and use it in place of the quantified variable when solving the formula which is in the scope of the quantifier.

The integrated functional and logic language Escher [13], which is based on multiple rewrite rules, also provides a mechanism for dealing with quantifiers and implications that is more powerful than Lloyd-Topor. However, implementation techniques for this language are still under development.

The quantifier evaluation technique described here was derived from work on bounded quantifications. A *bounded quantification* [4, 17] is a quantification that ranges over a finite domain [16]. These were introduced to logic programming to enhance expressiveness [4] and enable repetitive computations to be implemented more efficiently by using iteration rather than recursion [5, 1]. It has also been shown that parallel implementations of bounded quantifications can obtain good speed-ups over sequential processing [3, 6]. Thus further work must be done to clarify the potential gains for parallel implementations of SLDQE-resolution.

References

1. K.R. Apt. Arrays, bounded quantification and iteration in logic and constraint programming. In *Proc. of GULP-PRODE'95* Salerno, Italy, 1995.
2. K.R. Apt and H.C. Doets. A new definition of SLDNF-resolution. *Journal of Logic Programming*, 18(2):177–190, 1992.
3. H. Arro, J. Barklund, and J. Bevemyr. Parallel bounded quantification—preliminary results. *ACM SIGPLAN Notices*, 28(5):117–124, August 1993.
4. J. Barklund. Bounded quantifications for iterations and concurrency in logic programming. *New Generation Computing*, 12(2), 1994.
5. J. Barklund and J. Bevemyr. Prolog with arrays and bounded quantification. In *Logic Programming and Automated Reasoning (LPAR'93)*. Springer-Verlag, 1993.
6. J. Barklund and J. Bevemyr. Executing bounded quantifications on shared memory multiprocessors. *PLILP*, LNCS 714, pages 302–317, 1993. Springer-Verlag.
7. M. Carlsson and J. Widén. SICStus Prolog user's manual. Technical Report 6R88007C, Swedish Institute of Computer Science, 1991.
8. K.L. Clark. Negation as failure. In H. Gallaire and J. Minker, editors, *Logic and Data Bases*, pages 293–322. Plenum Press, 1978.
9. P.M. Hill and J.W. Lloyd. *The Gödel Programming Language*. MIT Press, 1994.
10. J.W. Lloyd and R.W. Topor. Making Prolog more expressive. *Journal of Logic Programming*, 1(3):225–240, 1984.
11. J.W. Lloyd. *Foundations of Logic Programming*. Springer-Verlag, 2nd ed., 1987.
12. J.W. Lloyd and J.C. Shepherdson. Partial evaluation in logic programming. *The Journal of Logic Programming*, 11(3&4):217–242, 1991.
13. J.W. Lloyd. Programming in an integrated functional and logic language. *Journal of Functional and Logic Programming*, 1997. To appear.
14. G. Nadathur. A proof procedure for the logic of hereditary harrop formulas. *Journal of Automated Reasoning*, 11:115–145, 1993.
15. T. Sato and H. Tamaki. First order compiler : A deterministic logic program synthesis algorithm. *Journal of Symbolic Computation*, 8:605–627, 1988.
16. R. D. Tennent. *Semantics of Programming Languages*. Prentice-Hall, 1991.
17. A. Voronkov. Logic programming with bounded quantifiers. In A. Voronkov, editor, *Logic Programming – 2nd Russian Conf. on Logic Programming*, pages 486–514. Springer-Verlag, 1992.

A Declarative Approach to Concurrent Programming

Steve Gregory

Department of Computer Science
University of Bristol
Bristol BS8 1UB, England

steve@cs.bris.ac.uk

Abstract

Tempo is a language based on classical first-order logic, which can be used for both specifying and implementing concurrent systems. As a declarative programming language, it is unique in that a program explicitly specifies the safety properties that it satisfies. Unlike most specification languages, a Tempo specification of a concurrent system can be executed, also concurrently.

An earlier paper presented a subset of Tempo, in which simple synchronization problems could be expressed by precedence relations between events. In this paper we describe a major extension to the language which greatly increases its expressive power. In particular, the language now includes facilities to perform computation — data values, operations on them, and control features — as well as synchronization.

1 Introduction

1.1 Background

Concurrent and distributed software systems are becoming increasingly familiar, with the widespread use of computer networks and multiprocessor architectures. However, concurrent (reactive) programming remains a more difficult task than writing sequential (transformational) programs. One reason is the extra programming effort required for interprocess synchronization and communication; another is that the sequence of actions executed by a concurrent program is inherently non-deterministic, depending on the relative speeds of processes, and the program must behave correctly in *any* possible execution. A further complication is that numerous different concurrent programming paradigms exist. To solve a problem efficiently for a new paradigm may require a different algorithm; at best, the same algorithm may need to be expressed in a different way.

We believe that it is important to find ways to ease the task of constructing correct and reliable concurrent software. The approach that we advocate is to provide a high-level programming language in which there is a clear connection between a concurrent program and the properties that the program satisfies. This can not only make it easier to write a program that satisfies its specification, but can also expose the relationship between programs written for different paradigms. Before describing the language that we propose, we briefly discuss the background to this research.

Specifications and Programs. One method of improving the reliability of programs is by proving that a program satisfies a specification, or systematically deriving a program from such a specification. The design of languages for specifying concurrent systems is an active research area (Section 4.2). They can usually express the *safety* properties (those that always hold) and *progress* properties (those that eventually hold) of concurrent algorithms. Unfortunately, no known specification language has been able to bridge the gap between specifications and programs written in real, widely used programming languages: proving or deriving such programs remains a manual process, with no guarantee of correctness.

Declarative Programming. A declarative program can, ideally, be viewed as both an executable program and a specification of the program's behaviour. We believe that declarative languages have an important role to play in program design. In many circumstances (e.g., for pedagogical and prototyping purposes) it is impractical to maintain two separate representations (program and specification) of an algorithm. Then an executable specification can offer the "best of both worlds".

In practice, declarative languages have tended to be used more for the features that they provide than because they are declarative. For example, concurrent logic programming languages such as Parlog (Gregory, 1987) and KL1 (Ueda and Chikayama, 1990) are symbolic concurrent programming languages which can be implemented quite efficiently. However, they are declarative only in that a program explicitly describes the final result that it computes (not a very important property in most concurrent programs). All other safety and progress properties are *implicit*, relying on the proper use of control features, so they are therefore not necessarily preserved by program transformation or parallel execution.

1.2 Tempo

Tempo is a concurrent programming language which has much in common with Parlog, KL1, etc., but is significantly more declarative: a Tempo program explicitly describes *all safety properties* that it satisfies, not just the final result that it computes, so these properties are preserved by transformation, parallel execution, etc.

Like some other formalisms (Pratt, 1986; Kowalski and Sergot, 1986), Tempo describes concurrent systems as partially ordered sets of atomic *events*. Tempo differs from those languages by possessing a procedural interpretation that allows these descriptions to be executed. For example, a semaphore could be represented in Tempo by a relation between P and V (sequences of events representing decrementing and incrementing the semaphore, respectively) and N, the semaphore's initial value. The *temporal constraint* semaphore(P,V,N) simply states that, at any time, the number of P events executed less the number of V events executed cannot exceed N:

```
semaphore(P, V, N)  ← V « P, semaphore(P, V#1, N+1);
                      P « V,  N >= 1, semaphore(P#1, V, N-1).
```

Tempo was originally presented in (Gregory and Ramirez, 1995). That version of the language could express the synchronization aspects of a limited range of examples, but could not perform computation. The new language presented here is a major extension to, and a superset of, the original language: it is able to represent and manipulate data values (numbers, data structures, etc.), as required in a general purpose programming language. This has been achieved in a declarative framework and without modifying the original subset of the language.

1.3 This Paper

Section 2 describes the design of Tempo. The language features are presented incrementally, beginning with the original subset of Tempo and successively relaxing restrictions on the syntax. For each extension, the syntax and operational semantics are stated, justified, and illustrated. The Tempo language itself is simple and based on a familiar logical syntax, but the procedural interpretation is new, so the emphasis is on explaining how the language can be implemented. We assume an implementation comprising a "compiler", which adds constraints to the source program, and an interpreter. The paper presents a simple interpreter and lists the compilation rules. Section 3 demonstrates the expressive power of Tempo by showing how a few typical concurrent problems can be solved. Section 4 summarizes Tempo, compares it with other concurrent languages, and outlines future research.

2   The Tempo Language

2.1 Events and Precedence

The key feature of Tempo is the *temporal constraint*, which describes a relation between *events*. Events are atomic (they have no duration), so their main attribute is their *execution time*. A temporal constraint is an atomic formula $p(t_1,...,t_j)$, where p is a *temporal relation*, either primitive or defined by a Tempo program.

The primitive temporal relation '$\ll$' (see Figure 1) constrains the order in which two events are executed: $X \ll Y$ is read "X precedes Y" and indicates that the execution time of event X is earlier than that of event Y. Mutually unconstrained events may occur in any order, or even simultaneously. The absolute execution time of an event cannot be specified, with one exception: if $X \ll X$, the execution time of X is the special value *eternity*; in this case, X is an *eternity event*. Eternity events are *never* executed. The '$\ll$' predicate is transitive and no event precedes itself except an eternity event, which is preceded by *every* event.

$$\forall X \forall Y \forall Z \ (X \ll Y \ \wedge \ Y \ll Z \ \rightarrow \ X \ll Z)$$
$$\forall X \forall Y \ (time(Y, eternity) \ \rightarrow \ X \ll Y)$$
$$\forall X \ (X \ll X \ \rightarrow \ time(X, eternity))$$
$$\forall X \forall Y \ (time(Y, eternity) \ \wedge \ Y \ll X \ \rightarrow \ time(X, eternity))$$
$$p(s_1, ..., s_i, X\#N, t_1, ..., t_j) \ \leftrightarrow \ (\exists Y \ offs(X, N, Y) \wedge X \ll Y \wedge p(s_1, ..., s_i, Y, t_1, ..., t_j))$$
$$Y = X\#N \ \wedge \ Z = X\#N \ \rightarrow \ Y = Z$$
$offs(X, N, Y)$: event Y is the Nth offspring of event X.

Figure 1: Properties of '$\ll$' and '#'

Tempo programs define each temporal relation r by a single definite clause whose head arguments are distinct variables $V_1, ..., V_k$:

$$r(V_1, ..., V_k) \leftarrow C_1, ..., C_m.$$

This is logically equivalent to

$$r(V_1, ..., V_k) \leftrightarrow \exists V_B \ C_1 \wedge ... \wedge C_m.$$

where V_B denotes the clause's *body variables*: those appearing in $C_1, ..., C_m$ but not in $V_1, ..., V_k$. Each C_i is a temporal constraint (or any other type of constraint introduced below). Note that the order of constraints in a conjunction is irrelevant.

Each event E has (conceptually) an infinite number of *offspring* events, named E#1, E#2, etc., which are implicitly preceded by E itself. Events of the form E#N may appear in queries and in bodies, but not heads, of relation definitions. E#N is treated exactly like a body variable F such that E$\ll$F, except that E#N can be constrained by other constraints that refer to E. The '#' notation is defined in Figure 1. For example, the following query defines two sequences of events A, A#1, A#1#1, ..., B, B#1, B#1#1, ... such that A«B, A#1«B#1, etc.:

    ← A «* B.

    E «* F ← E « F, E#1 «* F#1.

Execution. Logically, the solution to a Tempo query is an answer substitution giving an execution time *t* for each event *E*. In practice, Tempo computes this implicitly, by actually *executing* an event *E* at time *t*. That is, events are executed in the specified order. Events with an execution time of *eternity* are never executed. Each event is executed as soon as its predecessors have been executed, without waiting for a complete solution.

A Tempo interpreter works as follows. It *tries* each event E in the query, checking whether a constraint X«E exists (E is *disabled*) or not (E is *enabled*). Once E is enabled it can be *executed*: all constraints of the form E«F are deleted and each event F (previously preceded by E) is tried. If E is not disabled but appears as an argument of a user-defined temporal constraint, that constraint is *expanded* (replaced by the body of its defining clause) until E becomes either enabled or disabled. When a constraint is expanded, its body variables are tried. Events of the form E#N are treated in the same way as body variables, but Compilation Rule 1 is applied first, to make explicit the precedence constraints; for example, the '«*' definition above is translated as follows:

    E «* F ← E « F, E#1 «* F#1, E « E#1, F « F#1.

Figure 2 outlines the interpreter algorithm, while Figure 3 shows a trace of the interpreter for the query A«*B.

Compilation Rule 1. For each event E#N appearing in a relation definition or query, add the constraint E«E#N.

2.2 Values and Functions

The language outlined above, and in (Gregory and Ramirez, 1995), cannot express computation because there is no way to represent or manipulate data. To remedy this, we now allow temporal constraints to include *data values* as well as events, distinguished by the argument positions in which they appear. A temporal relation definition may be accompanied by a declaration:

    type $r(type_1, ..., type_k)$.

where each $type_i$ indicates the type of the *i*th argument of *r*: e (event) or d (data). Every temporal relation must have at least one event argument; if the type declaration is omitted, *all* arguments are events. Both arguments of the '«' primitive are events.

The types of variables in a relation definition are determined at compile time. *V* is a *data variable* if it appears in data argument positions in head and/or body constraints, or an *event variable* if it appears in event argument positions; it is not allowed in both. Event variables must appear in event argument positions of body constraints, while each data argument position must contain a *data value*, defined as a data variable, a constant, or a structured term $k(t_1,...,t_j)$, where $t_1, ..., t_j$ are data values.

Data values can be manipulated by *function constraints*: $f(t_1,...,t_j)$ where *f* is a *function relation*. All arguments of function constraints are data values, and are classified into input arguments and (at least one) output arguments, which must be variables. Each data variable in a relation definition must appear exactly once in a

place query constraints in constraint set CS; place query variables in try list TL;
while TL is not empty:
  delete first member E of TL;
  while E is con(C) in CS:
    replace C in CS by the body of its defining clause;
    add body variables (if any) to rear of TL;
  if E is enabled in CS then execute E.

if E appears on right of a '«' constraint in CS then E is disabled in CS
else if E appears in a user-defined temporal constraint C in CS then E is con(C) in CS
else E is enabled in CS.

execute E: for each precedence constraint in CS with E on left (E«R):
          delete E«R;
          add R to rear of TL if not in TL.

Figure 2: A simple Tempo interpreter

CS	TL	
{A«*B}	[B,A]	B is con(A«*B)
{A«B, A#1«*B#1, A«A#1, B«B#1}	[B,A,B#1,A#1]	B is disabled
	[A,B#1,A#1]	A is enabled: execute A
{A#1«*B#1, B«B#1}	[B#1,A#1,B]	B#1 is disabled
	[A#1,B]	A#1 is con(A#1«*B#1)
{A#1«B#1, A#1#1«*B#1#1,		
A#1«A#1#1,		
B#1«B#1#1, B«B#1}	[A#1,B,B#1#1,A#1#1]	A#1 is enabled: execute A#1
{A#1#1«*B#1#1,		
B#1«B#1#1, B«B#1}	[B,B#1#1,A#1#1,B#1]	B is enabled: execute B
{A#1#1«*B#1#1, B#1«B#1#1}	[B#1#1,A#1#1,B#1]	B#1#1 is disabled
	[A#1#1,B#1]	A#1#1 is con(...)
...	...	...

Figure 3: Execution of query A«*B

position where it is given a value (a head argument or an output argument of a function constraint); no cycles are allowed.

Although we only use familiar primitives ('+', '*', etc.) in this paper, functions can in general be defined by the user. We do not prescribe a language in which to define function relations. Any reasonable functional or logic programming language could be used for this purpose, provided that

Each function constraint can be evaluated when all of its input arguments are ground (variable free) and, after evaluation, will produce ground values for all of its output arguments.

The following example defines clock, representing a clock that maintains the time in hours and minutes, and increments it by one minute with each tick:

```
← clock(T, 0, 0).

type clock(e, d, d).
clock(Tick, H, M) ← +(M, 1, M1), mod(M1, 60, M2),
    //(M1, 60, H1), +(H, H1, H2), mod(H2, 24, H3),
    clock(Tick#1, H3, M2).
```

If the final argument position of a function relation f is its only output argument, we can omit the constraint $f(t_1,...,t_{j-1},V)$ and replace all occurrences of V by $f(t_1,...,t_{j-1})$. The `clock` relation can be defined using this functional syntax as follows:

```
type clock(e, d, d).
clock(Tick, H, M) ← clock(Tick#1, (H+(M+1)//60) mod 24, (M+1) mod 60).
```

Execution. All functional and logic programming languages feature something like our function constraints, but it is not obvious how these should be implemented in Tempo: the aim of a Tempo program is to execute events, not to compute values.

A simple method would be to *eagerly* evaluate function constraints as soon as they are created. Because there is no control flow in Tempo, a function that produces a value for a variable must be evaluated before its consumers. A drawback of this eager approach is that a function constraint would be evaluated even if its output is not needed. More seriously, if a function includes event values (Section 2.3), it may be impossible to evaluate it immediately. Many (concurrent or lazy) languages *suspend* functions until their input arguments are available. We rejected this option in Tempo because it would introduce implicit synchronization between the evaluation of function constraints; this would duplicate much of the functionality that Tempo provides explicitly via events, and may be complex to implement.

Our chosen strategy avoids the disadvantages of both eager and lazy evaluation. Just before expanding a temporal constraint that contains output variables of a function constraint C, we evaluate C. If the input arguments of C contain data variables output from other function constraints, those are evaluated first, and so on. This guarantees that all data arguments of a temporal constraint C are ground terms by the time that it is expanded, which in turn ensures that all function constraints created when C is expanded have ground inputs, so they can be evaluated when their outputs are required. Unlike lazy evaluation, our compiler can determine which functions need to be evaluated before expanding each temporal constraint.

2.3 Events with Values

In many cases, the relative execution time is not the only important attribute of an event. For example, an act of interprocess communication in a concurrent program can be modelled as an event that has data associated with it.

We now allow an event E to (optionally) have a data value, named $E^\wedge$. If an event has a data value, it must be a ground term and must be attached to the event *before* it is executed. The value can be accessed only *after* the event is executed, by which time its value (if any) is fixed. In this way, the execution of event E provides the necessary synchronization between the producer and consumer of the value $E^\wedge$.

An event E can be given a value t by using an assignment $E^\wedge := t$. Assignment is a new primitive temporal relation, read logically as equality. The data value of event E can be accessed by placing $E^\wedge$ in a data argument of a temporal constraint, an input argument of a function constraint, or on the right of an assignment.

Figure 4 shows a concurrent algorithm for incrementally computing factorials: one process generates a stream of consecutive integers (1, 2, ...); another process receives these integers, multiplies each by the last factorial computed, and outputs the resulting factorials (1!, 2!, ...). The two processes are represented by the constraints `ints(I,1)` and `fact(I,F,1)`, and the message streams are events I and F, depicted in Figure 5 (circles represent events, numbers in them show the events' values, and an arrow from E to F shows the precedence E≪F). The optional F≪*I#1 constraint in the query prevents integers from being generated faster than they are consumed.

```
← ints(I, 1), fact(I, F, 1), F«* I#1.

type ints(e, d).
ints(I, N) ← I^:= N, ints(I#1, N+1).

type fact(e, e, d).
fact(I, F, NF) ← F^:= NF*I^, fact(I#1, F#1, NF*I^).
```

Figure 4: Concurrent factorials program

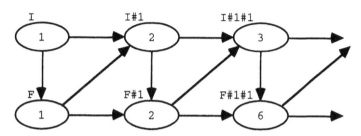

Figure 5: Events I and F in factorials program

Execution. The implementation must ensure that (a) values are given to events before they are executed and (b) accessed after they are executed.

The first requirement can be satisfied by performing an assignment $E^:=V$ before E is executed. However, it cannot be done arbitrarily early, in case the value of V is not available. Our solution is to do the assignment *before* executing E, but *after* E is enabled. The second requirement is to ensure that the value $D^$ is not accessed until D has been executed. Since $D^$ may appear either in a user-defined temporal constraint or on the right of an assignment, there are two cases to consider:

1. An assignment $E^:=t$ must be delayed until the events on which t depend have been executed, to avoid assigning a non-ground value to an event. This is achieved by Compilation Rule 2, which exploits the fact that an assignment to E is not performed while E is disabled. For example, in the fact clause of Figure 4, the constraint I«F is automatically added, delaying the assignment F^:=NF*I^ until I is executed and therefore has a value.

   Definition. Term t *depends on* event D if t is $D^$, or t is a structured term containing a value that depends on D, or t is an output variable of a function constraint with an input argument that depends on D.

   Compilation Rule 2. For each assignment $E^:=t$ in a conjunction Cs, and for each event D on which t depends, add the constraint $D«E$ to Cs.

2. A user-defined temporal constraint C must not be expanded until all of its data arguments are ground, i.e., until the events on which they depend have been executed. This is achieved by Compilation Rule 3, which exploits the fact that C will not be expanded while all of its event arguments are disabled. For example, in the fact clause of Figure 4, the constraints I«I#1 and I«F#1 are added, delaying the expansion of fact(I#1,F#1,NF*I^) until I is executed.

   Compilation Rule 3. For each user-defined temporal constraint C in a conjunction Cs, and for each event D in $DATA_C$ and E in $EVENT_C$, add the constraint $D«E$ to Cs. $DATA_C$ is the set of events on which the data arguments of C depend; $EVENT_C$ is the set of C's event arguments.

2.4 Disjunction

As well as atomic constraints, a constraint may be a disjunction $(Cs_1; \ldots; Cs_n)$, where each Cs_i is a conjunction of constraints (called an *alternative*, to distinguish it from the *top-level conjunction*). The order of alternatives in a disjunction is not significant. Constraints inside disjunctions must be atomic (disjunctions cannot be nested) and, to avoid problems with variable scope, cannot be function constraints. Disjunction has two roles in Tempo: to test data values and to allow non-determinism in the order of events, which is essential in specifying concurrent phenomena. We describe each of these in the next two subsections.

Conditionals

Disjunction can be used to test data values, like conditionals in conventional languages, using a new kind of constraint: a *test constraint* $t(t_1,...,t_j)$ where t is a *test relation*. Like a function constraint, all arguments are data values, but a test constraint has no output arguments and may fail. We only use familiar primitives ('==', '<', '>=', etc.) in this paper, but test relations may also be defined by the user in any suitable functional or logic programming language.

For example, suppose that we wish to generate all factorials up to (say) 10000. The infinite generator of Figure 4 could be changed into a finite program by redefining the `ints` and `fact` relations with an additional "counter" argument. However, a much more elegant method is possible: simply add to the query an extra constraint `upto(10000,F)`, constraining all descendants of the first descendant of `F` whose data value is greater than 10000 to be eternity events. The following query will terminate after generating the first factorial greater than this limit:

```
← ints(I, 1), fact(I, F, 1), F«* I#1, upto(10000, F).

type upto(d,e).
upto(X, F)  ←  X < F^, F#1 « F#1;
               X >= F^, upto(X, F#1).
```

Execution. If any test constraint fails, the alternative containing it is deleted from the disjunction. When the disjunction alternatives contain mutually exclusive tests, as in the examples above, the disjunction becomes "flat" and is handled in the normal way. The main implementation issue is to ensure that tests are not evaluated before their arguments are ground (i.e., all events on which their arguments depend have been executed). This is achieved by the following:

Compilation Rule 4. For each disjunction J, add (at the top level) constraints T«U for each T in $TESTED_J$ and U in $USED_J$. $USED_J$ is the set of events that appear in J on the right of '«' constraints or in user-defined temporal constraints; $TESTED_J$ is the set of events on which arguments of tests in J depend.

Restriction 1. For each disjunction J, $USED_J$ and $TESTED_J$ must be disjoint.

Disjunction Rule. While checking whether event E is enabled, a disjunction J such that E is in $USED_J$ is tried only if E is not disabled at the top level; i.e., disjunctions are tried after '«' constraints and user-defined temporal constraints.

For example, for the disjunction in the `upto` definition, *TESTED* is {F} and *USED* is {F#1}, so the compiler adds the (redundant) constraint F«F#1.

Non-determinism

Disjunctions do not necessarily include test constraints and, even if they do, they need not be mutually exclusive. Then the role of the disjunction is to express non-determinism in the order of events. For example, Figure 6 defines a stack: the temporal constraint stack(Push,Pop) describes the relation between a sequence of *push* events and a sequence of *pop* events; the data value of each event is the value to be *push*ed or *pop*ped. The disjunction reflects non-determinism: at any time, if the stack is non-empty (list(L)), the next transaction may be either a *push* or a *pop*.

```
← producer(Push), stack(Push, Pop), consumer(Pop).

stack(Push, Pop) ← stack1(Push, Pop, []).

type stack1(e, e, d).
stack1(Push, Pop, L) ←
   Pop « Push, list(L), Pop^:=head(L), stack1(Push, Pop#1, tail(L));
   Push « Pop, stack1(Push#1, Pop, [Push^|L]).
```

Figure 6: Stack

Execution. If the alternatives of a disjunction contain mutually inconsistent temporal constraints, as in Figure 6 (Pop«Push and Push«Pop), the interpreter must select an alternative to use. The way in which this choice is made is a key aspect of the design of Tempo.

While checking whether an event E is enabled and the constraint set contains a disjunction J such that E is in $USED_J$, all tests in J are first evaluated (as explained above). If the result is still a disjunction, each alternative is checked: If E is enabled in at least one alternative but not all (E is *conditionally enabled*), J is *reduced* by deleting all alternatives in which E is disabled. Since disjunctions are tried only if E is not disabled at the top level (by the Disjunction Rule), E can now be enabled and progress can be made. The programmer can control when a disjunction is reduced by using sufficient precedence constraints at the top level. For example, in the query of Figure 6, Push will not be enabled by the stack(Push,Pop) constraint until producer(Push) unconditionally enables it.

To simplify implementation, temporal constraints can be expanded, and assignments done, only at the top level. For this reason the programmer must observe the following:

Restriction 2. If event E appears in a disjunction in a user-defined temporal constraint, but is not disabled in the same alternative, E must be disabled at the top level.

Restriction 3. If event E is enabled in a disjunction alternative that has an assignment to E, but E is not disabled in all other alternatives, E must be disabled at the top level.

2.5 Concurrency

The above language can specify concurrent systems, and these specifications can be executed by our sequential interpreter. However, as a concurrent programming language, Tempo also allows a query to be *solved* concurrently. If any group of constraints in a conjunction is enclosed in braces (not affecting the logical reading), it will be executed as a separate process. For example, a query may take the form

$\leftarrow \{Cs_1\}, \ldots, \{Cs_m\}$.

Each process solves its own constraints independently, except where it shares events with other processes; a shared event is executed when it has been enabled by *all* processes that share it. Shared events provide the communication medium between Tempo processes.

Execution. A constraint of the form $\{Cs_i\}$ spawns a new invocation of the Tempo interpreter to solve Cs_i. Each interpreter works in the way that we have described, except that an event cannot be executed as soon as it is found to be enabled. Instead, when a process P finds that event E is enabled by the constraints in P, it informs all other processes that share event E, and passes them the value (if any) that P has given to E. When all processes have done this, E's value is communicated to all of them, which then treat the event as executed.

The Disjunction Rule of Section 2.4 is hard to implement in a concurrent interpreter because no single process has access to all constraints. We therefore modify it so that a process must wait for all other processes to enable an event before checking it against a disjunction:

Disjunction Rule'. While checking whether event E is enabled, a disjunction J such that E is in $USED_J$ is tried only if E is not disabled at the top level *and* E has been (unconditionally) enabled by all other processes.

Restriction 5. Two disjunctions J and K must appear in the same process unless $USED_J$ and $USED_K$ are disjoint.

Also, Compilation Rules 1–4 must be modified so that their explicit '«' constraints are added to *every* process where they are needed.

For example, the stack query of Figure 6 can be executed as three processes: two clients, sending "messages" on Push and Pop, and a server that receives messages from each client:

$\leftarrow$ {producer(Push)}, {stack(Push, Pop)}, {consumer(Pop)}.

The server process {stack(Push, Pop)} initially waits for either Push or Pop to be enabled by its respective sender, because of the new Disjunction Rule. If Push is then enabled by the {producer(Push)} process, the server will conditionally enable Push and commit to the second alternative of its disjunction. Alternatively, if {consumer(Pop)} enables Pop, the server will test that L is non-empty and, if so, will conditionally enable Pop and commit to the first alternative of its disjunction.

3 Programming in Tempo

3.1 Example: Bounded Buffer

In Figure 4, the F«*I#1 constraint has the effect of placing a buffer of size 1 on the I channel. This can be generalized to a bounded buffer of any specified size N that can be placed between any producer and consumer process, as shown in Figure 7. A different way to implement a buffer of size N is as a chain of N processes, each containing a buffer of size 1; Figure 8 shows this algorithm written in Tempo.

To show that these two algorithms are equivalent (in respect of their safety properties), it is only necessary to prove that

bounded_buffer(R, S, N) $\leftrightarrow$ bounded_buffer_m(R, S, N)

and this can be done quite simply using standard logic program transformation techniques. Space limitations prevent the inclusion of the proof here, but similar proofs were presented in (Gregory, 1996), in the original subset of Tempo.

```
← {producer(R)}, {bounded_buffer(R, S, N)}, {consumer(S)}.

type bounded_buffer(e, e, d).
bounded_buffer(R, S, N) ← buffer(R, S), bounded(R, S, N).

buffer(R, S) ← S^:=R^, buffer(R#1, S#1).

type bounded(e, e, d).
bounded(R, S, N) ← N >= 2, bounded(R#1, S, N-1);
                   N == 1, S «* R#1.
```

Figure 7: Single-process bounded buffer program

```
← {producer(R)}, {bounded_buffer_m (R, S, N)}, {consumer(S)}.

type bounded_buffer_m(e, e, d).
bounded_buffer_m(R, S, N) ←
   N >= 2, buffer1(R, M), bounded_buffer_m(M, S, N-1);
   N == 1, buffer1(R, S).

buffer1(R, S) ← {buffer(R, S), S «* R#1}.          % *Spawn* buffer *process*
```

Figure 8: Multi-process bounded buffer program

3.2 Servers

Many-to-One Communication. A *server* is a process that provides a service to a variable number of *client* processes. To implement servers in Tempo we use a technique similar to that used in concurrent logic programming languages: message streams (linear event structures) from all clients are combined, using a merge constraint, into a single stream which is passed to the server. For example, the stack program of Figure 6 can be rewritten for two producers as follows (this can easily be extended to allow a larger, dynamically varying, number of clients):

```
← {producer(Push1)}, {producer(Push2)}, {consumer(Pop)},
  {merge(Push1,Push2,Push), stack(Push, Pop)}.

merge(M1, M2, M) ← M1 « M2, M^:=M1^, merge(M1#1, M2, M#1);
                   M2 « M1, M^:=M2^, merge(M1, M2#1, M#1).
```

Bidirectional Communication. Servers usually return a response to requests received from clients. One way to arrange this in Tempo is by providing one event structure to carry requests from client to server and another to convey replies back to the client; whenever a new client is created, a merge constraint must be introduced in the request stream and a split constraint in the reply stream. The problem with this technique is that it works only if replies are generated by the server in the same order as requests are received. This is not generally true: for example, an FTP server may answer a request for a small file before sending a larger file requested earlier.

A better way to handle bidirectional communication in Tempo is by using *request/reply structures*: binary event trees of the form shown in Figure 9. Here, the value of event E is a request, the value of E#2 is the reply, while E#1 is (as usual) the next request in the sequence. Each request event precedes both the corresponding reply and the next request, but the replies may be sent in any order. These structures can be combined almost as easily as linear event structures. Instead of merge, we use the merge2 relation, defined as follows:

merge2(M1, M2, M) ← merge(M1, M2, M), mergeb(M1, M2, M).

mergeb(M1, M2, M) ← M1 « M2, M1#2^:=M#2^, mergeb(M1#1, M2, M#1);
                    M2 « M1, M2#2^:=M#2^, mergeb(M1, M2#1, M#1).

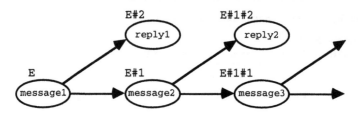

Figure 9: Request/reply event structures

Example: Disk Scheduler

Consider an operating system in which user processes perform disk I/O operations by sending requests to a disk driver process. This can be represented by a Tempo query

← {clients(D)}, {disk(D)}.

where D is a request/reply structure with D, D#1, etc. labelled by disk I/O operations (*read* or *write* from/to a given disk address); D#2, D#1#2, etc. are labelled with the replies. clients(D) defines the combined output D (produced by merge2) of all clients. disk(D) is the disk driver, which replies to I/O requests in order of arrival.

A disk scheduler tries to minimize disk head movement by rearranging pending I/O requests by cylinder number before passing them to the disk driver. This is expressed in Tempo as a constraint scheduler(C,D) between two request/reply structures:

← {clients(C)}, {scheduler(C, D), disk(D)}.

Figure 10 shows a definition of scheduler(C,D) which implements the C-SCAN scheduling algorithm (Andrews, 1991). It has a state comprising a list, initially empty, of pending I/O requests and the current cylinder position Pos of the disk head. When an request is received on C (C«D), it is stored in the pending requests list together with a unique identifier. A match constraint searches for the request with a matching identifier among D and its descendants, and copies its reply to C#2. When the disk is ready (D«C) and there are pending requests (list(Buff)), the best of them, according to the current disk position, is removed from the buffer and passed to the disk driver. The function select(Pos,Buff,Best,Rest), not defined here, searches Buff for the entry Best with the smallest cylinder number no less than Pos, if one exists, else the smallest cylinder number of all; Rest is the remainder of Buff.

4   Conclusions

4.1 Summary

Tempo is declarative in that the order of events, and their values, is determined only by the constraints in a program, *not* by (e.g.) the order of items in conjunctions and disjunctions, the use of braces, or the difference between ':=' and '=='. This makes it

```
scheduler(C, D) ← sched(C, D, T, [], 0, 1), D «* T.

type sched(e, e, e, d, d, d).
sched(C, D, T, Buff, Pos, Id) ←
   select(Pos, Buff, Best, Rest),
   ( C « D,
         match(C#2, D, T, Id),
         sched(C#1, D, T, [(C^, Id) | Buff], Pos, Id+1);
      D « C, list(Buff),
         D^:= arg(1, Best), T^:= arg(2, Best),
         sched(C, D#1, T#1, Rest, D^, Id)   ).

type match(e, e, e, d).
match(Cr, D, T, Id) ←  T^ == Id, Cr^:= D#2^ ;
                       T^ \== Id, match(Cr, D#1, T#1, Id).
```

Figure 10: C-SCAN disk scheduler

easy to develop concurrent algorithms: the constraints are defined first and then they can be grouped into parallel components using braces. Standard techniques can be used to prove programs equivalent and to derive programs from specifications, all expressed in Tempo (Gregory, 1996). (It is not possible to prove progress properties — that a given event will eventually be executed — without recourse to the operational semantics. For this, the language provides an implicit fairness guarantee: every unconditionally enabled event will eventually be executed.)

Tempo embodies a novel, unconventional programming paradigm: *events* are first-class objects in the language while *state* is implicit, being represented by data arguments of constraints. A major advantage of this is that it makes possible Tempo's constraint-oriented style of specifying events: the execution time, and the number of offsprings, of E are described by the conjunction of a number of constraints on E. This in turn allows programs to be composed by conjunction (as in the upto example of Section 2.4 and the merge2 example of Section 3.2).

A prototype implementation of Tempo has been used to test all examples in this paper; it is available from http://star.cs.bris.ac.uk/software/tempo.html. Although high-performance implementations have not yet been developed, we believe that Tempo can be implemented efficiently. Computation, performed by function constraints on data variables, is separated from synchronization and communication, which involves events, so Tempo can be considered a coordination language, which adds concurrency to any computation language, declarative or otherwise. Ramirez (1996) proposes a language, Tempo++, that combines Tempo (for synchronization) with a computation language such as Prolog in an object-oriented framework.

4.2 Comparison

Tempo as a Specification Language. As a specification language for concurrent systems, Tempo is closer to languages based on temporal logic, e.g., Unity (Chandy and Misra, 1988; Misra, 1995) and TLA (Lamport, 1994), than process algebras (Hoare, 1985; Milner, 1989). Unity and TLA specifications can express progress properties of algorithms, as well as safety properties, but are not executable. Like Tempo, TLA uses classical logic as far as possible, restricting the use of temporal logic to specify progress. In Tempo, as in Unity and TLA, a specification of an algorithm's properties can be refined to a lower-level form that represents the algorithm itself: an algorithm is correct if it logically implies the specification (Gregory, 1996). Unity and TLA both model concurrent systems by sequences of actions that modify a single shared state. This is adequate for specifying and reasoning about systems, but the shared state might be a bottleneck if the specifications were to be executed. In contrast, Tempo's event sequences are independent unless explicitly constrained; this allows a specification of a distributed system to be executed in an equally distributed manner.

Tempo as a Programming Language. We have already mentioned how Tempo replaces the extralogical control features (e.g., modes and sequential operators) of concurrent logic programming by declarative equivalents. From a programming viewpoint, the main difference between the two types of language is the use of the logical variable. In concurrent logic programming languages, a variable can be included in a data structure and, at the same time, act as a communication channel. This allows for some elegant programming techniques; for example, the disk scheduler of Section 3.2 can be implemented elegantly by including reply variables in request messages. On the other hand, implementation can be expensive because every variable is potentially shared, so suspension, locking, etc., are necessary. In contrast, Tempo follows a principle advocated by the designers of Linda (Carriero and Gelernter, 1989): to separate computation from coordination. Tempo events can have data values, but events cannot appear in data structures.

Logical variables effectively provide a global address space: any two processes that receive a message containing a variable can use it to communicate directly. Global communication, of a very different form, is also provided by the Linda model. Tempo has more in common with message passing languages: processes can communicate directly only if they share events. This is much more efficient to implement in a distributed system.

Concurrent constraint programming (Saraswat, 1993) generalizes concurrent logic programming to allow the values of variables to be defined by a conjunction of constraints imposed incrementally and concurrently. Another family of declarative languages is based on executable temporal logic (Moszkowski, 1986; Abadi and Manna, 1987; Fisher, 1993; Cleary and Smith, 1996). Although, in principle, temporal logic can express safety and progress properties of concurrent programs, we are not aware of a concurrent programming language entirely based on temporal logic.

4.3 Future Work

We are currently introducing the concept of real time into Tempo, to allow real-time applications to be tackled. Real-time extensions have been made to many concurrent languages, including Parlog and concurrent constraint languages (Saraswat *et al.*, 1994; De Boer and Gabbrielli, 1995), but it is a particularly natural development of Tempo, since the execution time of events is already a first-class concept in the language. Although Tempo provides a novel constraint-oriented way to specify events, their *data values* are simply assigned; these too might usefully be defined by constraints, along the lines of existing constraint programming languages (Van Hentenryck, 1989; Saraswat, 1993). Several other extensions could be made to the language: event offsprings could be given meaningful names (e.g., M#reply instead of M#2); events might have duration instead of being atomic; and so on.

As well as the language design, we plan to apply Tempo to large-scale concurrent applications, develop an efficient implementation of Tempo (probably by building on an existing declarative language implementation and using that language to define

Tempo's function and test constraints), and to make detailed comparisons with other concurrent programming and specification languages.

References

Abadi, M. and Manna, Z. 1987. Temporal logic programming. *Proc. of the Symp. on Logic Programming*, S. Haridi (Ed.). IEEE Computer Society Press, pp. 4–16.

Andrews, G.R. 1991. *Concurrent Programming: Principles and Practice.* Benjamin/Cummings.

Carriero, N. and Gelernter, D. 1989. How to write parallel programs: a guide to the perplexed. *ACM Computing Surveys 21*, 3, pp. 323–357.

Chandy, K.M. and Misra, J. 1988. *Parallel Program Design.* Addison-Wesley.

Cleary, J.G. and Smith, D.A. 1996. Declarative I/O, assignment and concurrency. Technical report. Dept. of Computer Science, Univ. of Waikato.

De Boer, F.S. and Gabbrielli, M. 1995. Modelling real-time in concurrent constraint programming. In *Proc. of the Intl. Logic Programming Symp.*, J.W. Lloyd (Ed.). MIT Press, pp. 528–542.

Fisher, M. 1993. Concurrent Metatem: a language for modelling reactive systems. *Proc. of Parallel Architectures and Languages Europe.*

Gregory, S. 1987. *Parallel Logic Programming in PARLOG.* Addison-Wesley.

Gregory, S. 1996. Derivation of concurrent algorithms in Tempo. In *Proc. of the 5th Intl. Workshop on Logic Program Synthesis and Transformation*, M. Proietti (Ed.). Springer-Verlag, pp. 46–60.

Gregory, S. and Ramirez, R. 1995. Tempo: a declarative concurrent programming language. In *Proc. of the 12th Intl. Logic Programming Conf.*, L. Sterling (Ed.). MIT Press, pp. 515–529.

Hoare, C.A.R. 1985. *Communicating Sequential Processes.* Prentice Hall.

Kowalski, R.A. and Sergot, M.J. 1986. A logic-based calculus of events. *New Generation Computing 4*, pp. 67–95.

Lamport, L. 1994. The temporal logic of actions. *ACM Trans. on Programming Languages and Systems 16*, 3, pp. 872–923.

Milner, R. 1989. *Communication and Concurrency.* Prentice Hall.

Misra, J. 1995. A logic for concurrent programming. *J. of Computer and Software Engineering 3*, 2, pp. 239–300.

Moszkowski, B. 1986. *Executing Temporal Logic Programs.* Cambridge Univ. Press.

Pratt, V. 1986. Modeling concurrency with partial orders. *Intl. J. of Parallel Programming 15*, 1, pp. 33–71.

Ramirez, R. 1996. *A Logic-Based Concurrent Object-Oriented Programming Language.* PhD thesis. Univ. of Bristol.

Saraswat, V.A. 1993. *Concurrent Constraint Programming.* MIT Press.

Saraswat, V.A., Jagadeesan, R., and Gupta, V. 1994. Foundations of timed concurrent constraint programming. In *Proc. of the 9th IEEE Symp. on Logic in Computer Science*, S. Abramsky (Ed.). IEEE Computer Society Press.

Ueda, K. and Chikayama, T. 1990. Design of the kernel language for the Parallel Inference Machine. *Computer J. 33*, 6, pp. 494–500.

Van Hentenryck, P. 1989. *Constraint Satisfaction in Logic Programming.* MIT Press.

Transformation of Divide & Conquer to Nested Parallel Loops

Christoph A. Herrmann and Christian Lengauer

Fakultät für Mathematik und Informatik,
Universität Passau, Germany

{herrmann,lengauer}@fmi.uni-passau.de
http://www.fmi.uni-passau.de/~lengauer

Abstract. We propose a sequence of equational transformations and specializations which turns a divide-and-conquer skeleton in Haskell into a parallel loop nest in C. Our initial skeleton is often viewed as general divide-and-conquer. The specializations impose a balanced call tree, a fixed degree of the problem division, and elementwise operations. Our goal is to select parallel implementations of divide-and-conquer via a space-time mapping, which can be determined at compile time. The correctness of our transformations is proved by equational reasoning in Haskell; recursion and iteration are handled by induction. Finally, we demonstrate the practicality of the skeleton by expressing Strassen's matrix multiplication in it.

Keywords: divide-and-conquer, equational reasoning, Haskell, parallelization, skeleton, space-time mapping.

1 Introduction

Divide-and-conquer ($\mathcal{DC}$) is an important programming paradigm. It describes the solution of a problem by dividing it into a number of subproblems, which are solved recursively until a basic case is reached, and then combining the solutions of the subproblems to get the solution of the original problem. Because of the wide applicability of $\mathcal{DC}$ it has often been formulated as an *algorithmic skeleton* [4,5], which can be used as a basic building block for programming. One purpose of the skeleton concept is to provide the user with efficient implementations of popular paradigms. In this approach, the algorithmic skeleton for a paradigm corresponds to an executable but unintuitive *architectural skeleton* [13]. To make the correspondence between the algorithmic and the architectural skeleton formally precise, we work in the domain of functional programming, in which skeletons are predefined higher-order polymorphic functions.

The fact that the subproblems are independent makes $\mathcal{DC}$ particularly attractive for parallelization. That is, one major purpose of an architectural skeleton for $\mathcal{DC}$ is to provide an efficient implementation for a given parallel computer. However, in order for a corresponding efficient architectural skeleton to exist, the algorithmic skeleton has to satisfy certain conditions.

The aim of this paper is to specialize an algorithmic skeleton for $\mathcal{DC}$ to a form for which there is an efficient parallel implementation. Each specialization step imposes a new restriction to that end, e.g., a fixed division degree of data or of work, etc. We present only a single path in the tree of possible specializations of $\mathcal{DC}$; other specializations are also possible. Some specialized skeletons (we call them *sources*) can be transformed into *functional target* skeletons, which have an obvious correspondence with nested parallel loop programs. Our so-called "call-balanced fixed-degree $\mathcal{DC}$" skeleton and all of its specializations can be compiled into an intermediate code consisting of sequential and parallel loops, which can be translated easily to different parallel machines. The loop nest can be viewed as our architectural skeleton. In the absence of resource constraints, it will provide the fastest possible execution given the data dependences imposed by divide-and-conquer.

The abstract computational model in which we justify and describe our specializations is the *call tree*. The root of the call tree represents the entire problem instance, the ith son of a node N represents the ith subproblem instance of the problem instance which N represents.

One property we require in our specializations is the balance of the call tree. We distinguish two kinds of balance. In *call balance*, all leaves of the call tree have the same distance from the root. In *data balance*, all sons of a node of the tree carry approximately the same amount of data. Our mapping techniques are static, i.e., we cannot enforce either form of balance on the call tree at run time.

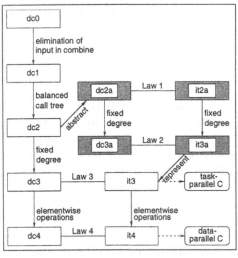

Fig. 1. Specializations of $\mathcal{DC}$

Fig. 1 depicts the skeletons we present in this paper, and their dependences. Downward arrows denote specializations, undirected edges equivalences, dashed arrows a switch in language (from Haskell to C).

The paper is structured as follows. In Sect. 2, the skeletons dc0 to dc3 are defined. In Sect. 3, we transform the call-balanced fixed-degree $\mathcal{DC}$ skeleton dc3, which is recursive, into skeleton it3, which is iterative (in the sense that it uses list comprehensions). Then we provide rules for translating it3, which is as close to loops as we can get in Haskell, to a parallel loop nest in C. In Sect. 4, we specialize skeleton dc3 further, with elementwise operations on balanced data partitions, and present a corresponding C loop program. In Sect. 5, we specify Strassen's matrix multiplication with the instantiated skeleton dc4 to demonstrate an application. The last section summarizes our results and discusses related work. Implementational and proof details omitted due to lack of space can be found in [10].

2   Specializing $\mathcal{DC}$

In this section, we propose a sequence of specializations of a skeleton for general divide-and-conquer. We write our skeletons in the language Haskell [19].

First, we present a form of $\mathcal{DC}$, which we think of as most general. Essentially, the only restriction we make at this point is that subproblems be solvable independently. This property seems to us at the heart of the notion of $\mathcal{DC}$.

This most general form is then specialized to enforce a balanced call tree, and subsequently further to enforce a fixed degree of the problem division.

2.1   General $\mathcal{DC}$ (dc0)

Under the premise that the subproblems can be solved independently, the general $\mathcal{DC}$ skeleton can be specified as follows:

```
dc0 :: (a->Bool)->(a->b)->(a->[a])->((a,[b])->b)->a->b
dc0 p b d c x = r x
   where r x = if p x then b x
                      else c (x, map r (d x))
```

As composite data structure, we have chosen the list arbitrarily; other choices can be envisioned. The skeleton is parametrized by four *customizing functions*: the predicate p, which recognizes the basic case, the basic function b, which is applied in this case, and the functions d for dividing a problem into a list of independent subproblems and c for combining the input data and the list of subproblem solutions to the solution of the original problem. The customizing functions are parameters which must be fixed at *compile time*, i.e., *before* we parallelize. Only the last parameter x, the data, is a run-time parameter.

Our justification of presenting dc0 is that it is the only one in our sequence of skeletons in which important $\mathcal{DC}$ algorithms like the quicksort are expressed naturally. In the quicksort, the input data is used by the combine function.

```
quicksort :: Ord a => [a]->[a]
quicksort xs = dc0 p b d c xs
   where p xs              = length xs < 2
         b xs              = xs
         d (x:xs)          = [filter (<x) xs, filter (>x) xs]
         c ((x:xs),[l,g]) = l ++ x:(filter (==x) xs) ++ g
```

2.2 $\mathcal{DC}$ without combining the input data (dc1)

Our first specialization is to eliminate the use of the input data x in the combine function and achieve a more regular form dc1. This skeleton has the same expressive power as dc0 [10].

```
dc1 :: (a->Bool)->(a->b)->(a->[a])->([b]->b)->a->b
dc1 p b d c x = r x
    where r x = if p x then b x
                      else (c . map r . d) x
```

2.3 Call-balanced $\mathcal{DC}$ (dc2)

Whether skeleton dc1 will terminate cannot be decided before run time. As a consequence, a schedule cannot be determined at compile time. Thus, we propose a skeleton dc2, which is dc1 with the additional property of *call balance*, which is that all leaves are located at the same level of the call tree, say level n. The effect of balance is discussed in Sect. 3.5. We can choose parameter n in dependence of the number of available processors. We have to adapt the customizing functions a bit [10]. The basic function has to be replaced by the application of dc1. The divide and combine function have to be extended to handle the case in which the basic case is reached after fewer than n recursive calls.

```
type Nat = Int
```

```
dc2 :: (a->b)->(a->[a])->([b]->b)->Nat->a->b
dc2 b d c n x = r n x
    where r n x = if n==0 then b x
                        else (c . map (r (n-1)) . d) x
```

2.4 Call-balanced fixed-degree $\mathcal{DC}$ (dc3)

In skeleton dc2, the existence of a potential son of a node in the call tree depends on run-time data, which makes it impossible to compute a static allocation of the nodes at a level of the call tree.

For an efficient static parallelization, it is convenient to bound the number of subproblem instances by a constant. In this case, subtrees of the call tree can be assigned to partitions of the topology at compile time and administration overhead at run time is avoided. In most cases, the degree of the problem division is 2. Examples of higher degrees are, e.g., Karatsuba's polynomial product [2, Sect. 2.6] with a degree of 3 and Strassen's matrix multiplication [18,11] with a degree of 7. For some algorithms, the degree is not fixed. One example is the multiplication of large integers by Schönhage and Strassen using Fermat's numbers [16], where the division degree is approximately the square root of the input vector size.

Whereas, for a particular division degree, a $\mathcal{DC}$ skeleton can be defined in Haskell (using tuples) and checked at compile time, this cannot be done for the entire class of fixed-degree $\mathcal{DC}$, due to the limitations of the type system of Haskell. Therefore, skeleton dc3 is defined to be dc2 with an additional constraint on function d. This constraint is written as a list comprehension:

```
dc3 :: Nat->(a->b)->(a->[a])->([b]->b)->Nat->a->b
dc3 k b d c n x = dc2 b dd c n x
    where dd x = [(d x)!!i | i<-[0..k-1]]
```

3 Transforming call-balanced fixed-degree $\mathcal{DC}$ into loops

In this section, we show how the recursive call-balanced fixed-degree $\mathcal{DC}$ skeleton (dc3) can be transformed into an intermediate iterative program, which can be implemented easily on many parallel systems.

In Subsect. 3.2, we state as Law 1 that the abstract version dc2a (see Fig. 1) of the call-balanced skeleton dc2 is equivalent to the linearly recursive skeleton it2a which enumerates the levels of the call graph. In Subsect. 3.3, we use this equivalence to prove the equivalence of dc3a and it3a, stated as Law 2. Subsect. 3.4 contains the functional target skeleton it3 whose equivalence with dc3 is stated in Law 3. In Subsect. 3.6, we transform it3 into a C program with annotations for parallelism.

But, first, we define a few Haskell functions, which are used in the remainder of this paper.

3.1 Definition of auxiliary Haskell functions

Our goal is a linearly recursive program which iterates through the levels of the call tree. Consider the collection of input data at different levels. At level 0, the input data is a single object (the input data of the problem). At level 1, it is a list (of input data of the subproblems). At level 2, it is a list of lists (of input data of the subproblems of the subproblems), etc. In Haskell, a list and a list of lists are of different type, i.e., a function which can deal with all levels, taking the level as a parameter, is not well-typed. Therefore, we use instead the algebraic data type PS (for "powerstructure"), which defines a superset of what we intend to define. A single element is defined with the constructor Sgt, a list of powerstructures is made a powerstructure using the constructor Com.

```
data PS a = Sgt a | Com [PS a] deriving (Eq,Show)
```

We use the following functions to work with data type PS:

```
sgt   :: a->PS a        ;   sgt a = Sgt a
unsgt :: PS a->a        ;   unsgt (Sgt a)  = a
com   :: [PS a]->PS a   ;   com as = Com as
uncom :: PS a->[PS a]   ;   uncom (Com as) = as

dmap :: (PS a->PS b)->Nat->(PS a->PS b)
dmap f 0      = f
dmap f n | n>0 = com . map (dmap f (n-1)) . uncom

comp :: [a->a]->a->a
comp [] = id             ;   comp (f:fs) = f . comp fs

down :: (Nat->a->a)->Nat->a->a
down f n = comp [f i | i<-[0..n-1]]
```

```
up :: (Nat->a->a)->Nat->a->a
up f n   = comp [f i | i<-[n-1,n-2..0]]

partition :: Nat->Nat->[a]->[[a]]
partition k n xs = [ [xs !! (i*k+j) | j<-[0..k-1]]
                     | i <- [0..k^n-1]]

unpartition :: Nat->Nat->[[a]]->[a]
unpartition k n xs = [ xs !! i !! j | i<-[0..k^n-1], j<-[0..k-1]]

singleton :: a->[a]     ;    singleton x = [x]
```

sgt, unsgt, com and uncom are wrappings resp. unwrappings of data type PS.
dmap f n applies a function to the nth level of a powerstructure. comp takes a
list of functions and composes them. The functions down and up take a function
and a number n and compose this function n times with itself, while counting
the number down resp. up. The function partition takes parameters k and n,
and maps a list of length k^{n+1} bijectively to k^n lists of length k taking successive
elements. unpartition k n is the inverse of partition k n. singleton creates
a singleton list.

3.2   Transforming dc2 into linear recursion

Here is the new Haskell definition for dc2, which works on powerstructures instead of lists; we name it dc2a (a is for *abstract*):

```
dc2a :: (PS a->PS b)->(PS a->PS a)->(PS b->PS b)->Nat->PS a->PS b
dc2a bb dd cc n =
   if n==0 then bb
            else cc . dmap (dc2a bb dd cc (n-1)) 1 . dd
```

Let us show how to express dc2 in terms of dc2a:

```
dc2_by_dc2a :: (a->b)->(a->[a])->([b]->b)->Nat->a->b
dc2_by_dc2a b d c n = unsgt . dc2a bb dd cc n . sgt
   where bb = sgt . b . unsgt
         dd = com . map sgt . d . unsgt
         cc = sgt . c . map unsgt . uncom
```

We observe that the linearly recursive function it2a equals dc2a, and state
this as Law 1.

```
it2a :: (PS a->PS b)->(PS a->PS a)->(PS b->PS b)->Nat->PS a->PS b
it2a bb dd cc n = down (dmap cc) n . dmap bb n . up (dmap dd) n
```

Imagine function up to build *up* the call tree, and function down to tear it
down.

LAW 1   dc2a = it2a

3.3 The abstract version of dc3

Skeleton dc3a is the abstract version of dc3 (see Fig. 1), and skeleton it3a is its iterative counterpart.

```
dc3a :: Nat->(PS a->PS b)->(PS a->PS a)->(PS b->PS b)->Nat->PS a->PS b
dc3a k b d c n = dc2a b dd c n
   where dd x = com [uncom (d x) !! i | i<-[0..k-1]]

it3a :: Nat->(PS a->PS b)->(PS a->PS a)->(PS b->PS b)->Nat->PS a->PS b
it3a k b d c n = it2a b dd c n
   where dd x = com [uncom (d x) !! i | i<-[0..k-1]]
```

LAW 2   dc3a = it3a

3.4 The functional target skeleton it3

In the previous subsection, the function dmap is used for distributing a function call to all nodes at a fixed level of the call tree.

In order to express this application easily by a single linear recursion, the nodes at the mentioned level have to be represented by a one-dimensional data structure; we use a list. The structural information that is contained in the tree is used to derive functions which manipulate the linear structure. Fig. 2 shows on the left the application on the abstract side (using trees) and on the right the concrete side (using lists) obtained from the left by the representation mapping. We obtain the functional target skeleton, it3, after the following sequence of transformations: we express dc3 in terms of dc2a, exploit the equivalence of recursion and iteration on the abstract side, i.e., express dc3 in terms of it2a, and replace all abstract operations by their representation.

```
it3 :: Nat->(a->b)->(a->[a])->([b]->b)->Nat->a->b
it3 k b d c n x =
  let a0 = singleton x
      a1 = (let h = a0:[ [d (h !! (m-1) !! (l'div'k)) !! (l'mod'k)
                            | l <- [0..k^m-1]]
                         | m<-[1..n]] in h) !! n
      a2 = [b (a1!!i) | i<-[0..k^n-1]]
      a3 = (let g = a2:[ [ c (let args = [g !! (m-1) !! (k*i+j)
                                            | j <- [0..k-1]]
                              in args)
                            | i <- [0..k^(n-m)-1]]
                         | m<-[1..n]] in g) !! n
      a4 = head a3
  in a4
```

LAW 3   dc3 = it3

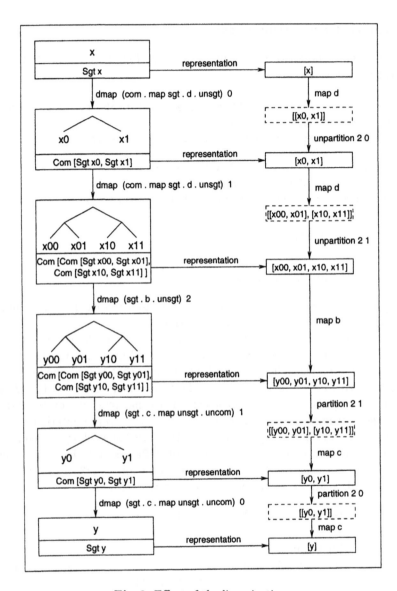

Fig. 2. Effect of the linearization

3.5 Implementational issues introduced by dc2

With dc2, we have obtained a schedule for the parallel implementation:

for t = 0 to n-1
    perform divide operations at level t in parallel ;
solve the subproblems at level n in parallel ;
for t = n+1 to 2*n
    perform combine operations at level 2*n-t in parallel

Algorithms on sparse data structures (e.g., the product of sparse matrices), which are represented by trees of logarithmic depth, can be given a schedule at compile time by expressing them in dc2, whereas the allocation remains an issue for run time.

3.6 Transformation into C

Let us present the main rules we used in our transformation from Haskell into C.

We do not provide a formal proof of their semantic correctness; this would require a formal semantics for both Haskell and C. The correspondences of data structures resp. control structures between Haskell and C should be obvious.

1. (Int,+,-,*,'div','mod',^) in Haskell and (int,+,-,*,/,%,pow(.,.)) in C correspond.
2. The run-time argument of the Haskell function is referred to as input in the C code, the result of the function is assigned to the variable output.
3. The body of a non-recursive let expression with equations sorted in the direction of the data dependences is transformed into a sequence of C assignments.
4. Lists in Haskell are represented in C as arrays. This correspondence is sound with respect to the structure, because in C different elements of an array can represent arrays of different sizes (like in Haskell lists can contain lists of different lengths).
5. Due to the correspondence (4), the application of the transformed singleton function to a[0] has to be a and the one of (!!i) to a has to be a[i] (especially the application of head to a has to correspond to a[0]).
6. List comprehensions in Haskell have a correspondence to loops in C, which iterate through an array. Whether a loop can be implemented in parallel, depends on lack of data dependences between array elements.

These rules do not form a complete translation system from Haskell to C:

1. The laziness of Haskell is not preserved.
2. Partial application is not possible in the C programs. This does not hurt here because we have only one run-time argument.
3. At present, nested skeleton definitions have to be expanded in the transformation by hand.
4. Higher-order functions not eliminated in the transformation are not handled, since there is no interface for passing functions between Haskell and C.
5. Polymorphic types have to be instantiated at compile time.

Our transformation scheme is sufficient for our purposes, since our foremost goal is to derive efficient parallel schedules at compile time.

4 Further specializations and their implementation

The specializations made so far consider only parallelism introduced by solving independent subproblems. To exploit parallelism in the application of the divide and combine function, the skeleton has to be specialized further for data-parallel operations.

4.1 Specialization with balanced data division and elementwise operations

First, we impose a balance on the data division, in order to achieve a balanced load of distributed data and parallel operations.

Balancing the data division means splitting the data into a fixed number of partitions of the same size. This is always possible by filling partitions with empty elements. Each partition is assigned to the part of the topology which handles the according problem instance. We choose the same degree for the data division as is given for the problem division. This has the advantage that communications are avoided in cases where each partition makes up the input of a separate subproblem.

The specialization with a balanced data division does not lead to a loss of expressive power. The only difference is that the access to a data element is now indirect: first one selects the partition which contains the element and then the position of the element in the partition.

The second specialization restricts the expressive power of the skeleton to elementwise operations on the zip of the partitions, i.e., only elements which have the same index within their partition can be combined. Because the partitions all have the same size, due to the preceding specialization, zipping is always possible without additional restrictions. As a result, each partition contains the zip of its own data with the data of the other partitions. Then, all partitions contain the same data, but the function they apply to it is different. The advantage is that communications become much more regular and the customizing functions can be viewed as vectorized operations.

Other, more liberal specializations could be considered as well but are not discussed here. For a particular implementation of the scan function, it could be useful to broadcast an element of one data partition to all elements of another data partition. Even more flexibility could be achieved, if the communication operations were defined in a small language, which is not too powerful in order to assure a space-time mapping at compile time.

The definition of the skeleton with elementwise operations, which we call dc4, is given in terms of the skeleton with a balanced data division, which is itself expressed in terms of dc3:

```
dc4 :: Nat->(a->b)->([a]->[a])->([b]->[b])->Nat->[a]->[b]
dc4 k b d c n x = ...
```

We omit the body due to lack of space; see [10]. The type differs slightly from dc3. Here, divide function d and combine function c are supposed to take a list of length k as input and output. The input elements of divide and the output elements of combine correspond to the data elements with the same index in different partitions, the output elements of divide and the input elements of combine correspond to the data elements with the same index in different subproblems resp. subproblem solutions.

4.2 The intermediate C code for dc4

Skeleton it4 [10], the functional target skeleton of the transformation of dc4, can be translated to the C code below using the rules we proposed in Subsect. 3.6.

LAW 4   dc4 = it4

In the process of equational reasoning, nested list comprehensions appear. These correspond to nested parallel loops at the imperative side. The number of iterations of the two inner-most loops differ dependent on the context, but their product does not. Therefore, we flatten the two nested comprehensions to obtain a single parallel loop. The program we obtain is data-parallel: the outer iterations are sequential, the inner ones parallel. Therefore, the program can be implemented easily on SIMD or, after conversion into an SPMD program, on MIMD machines. We show only the most interesting parts of the program, i.e., the loops that implement the skeleton. Instead of d, b, and c, we use divide, basic, and combine, respectively. These functions expect an additional parameter that indicates which element of the result list is desired. The function pow(b,m) determines b to the power of m. The input data after algorithm-specific adaptations is located in h[0], the output data before adaptations is delivered in g[old(m)]. digpos(k,d,v) delivers the dth least significant digit of the natural number v denoted in radix k, and digchange(k,d,v,i) replaces this digit by i. The innermost for loops collect only a constant number of pointers and can be resolved at compile time.

```
seqfor(m=1;m<=n;m++)
   parfor(q=0;q<pow(k,n);q++) {
      for(i=0;i<k;i++)
         arg_d[q][i] = h[old(m)][digchange(k,n-m,q,i)];
      divide(h[new(m)][q],arg_d[q],digpos(k,n-m,q));   }

parfor(q=0;q<pow(k,n);q++)
   basic(g[0][q],h[old(m)][q]);

seqfor(m=1;m<=n;m++)
   parfor(q=0;q<pow(k,n);q++) {
      for(i=0;i<k;i++)
         arg_c[q][i] = g[old(m)][digchange(k,m-1,q,i)];
      combine(g[new(m)][q],arg_c[q],digpos(k,m-1,q));   }
```

5 Strassen's matrix multiplication

Strassen's matrix multiplication [18] computes the product of two matrices of size $m \times m$ sequentially in time of $O(m^{\log_2 7})$ ($\log_2 7 \approx 2.81$) instead of $O(m^3)$ of the trivial algorithm. For a parallel computation, the gain is in the savings of processors. Where, e.g., for the trivial algorithm, 512 ($= 8^3$) processors are necessary to reduce a problem of size $2^{n+3} \times 2^{n+3}$ to problems of size $2^n \times 2^n$, which can be solved in parallel, our modification of Strassen's algorithm requires only 343 ($= 7^3$) processors. Minor disadvantages are the overhead in parallel dividing and combining, and a more complicated data dependence pattern which may lead to more communications on some machines. In principle, one can achieve a faster execution time with the same number of processors using Strassen's algorithm in place of the conventional one. Multiprocessors often come in sizes of powers of 2, but Strassen's algorithm is expressed for virtual machines with sizes of powers of 7. This requires a mapping from virtual space to a cartesian product of real space and real time, which motivates the need for advanced space-time mapping techniques.

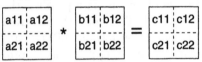

Fig. 3. Matrix partitions

In the following program, strassen, matrices are represented by lists of rows, where each row is represented by a list of column elements. Program strassen takes a parameter n and two matrices xss and yss of size $2^n \times 2^n$, and returns the product of xss and yss. Fig. 3 shows one step of the recursive decomposition of the matrices. How the cs are computed from the as and bs can be taken from the where clause of program strassen.

```
strassen :: Num a => Nat->[[a]]->[[a]]->[[a]]
strassen n xss yss =
    (   d1d2 n
        . from_quadtree n
            . project 4 7 n
                . dc4 7 b d c n
            . embed 4 7 n (0,0)
        . to_quadtree n
    . d2d1 n )
    (zipWith zip xss yss)
    where b (a,b) = a*b
        d [(a11,b11),(a12,b12),(a21,b21),(a22,b22),_,_,_] =
            [(a11+a22,b11+b22),
             (a21+a22,b11),
             (a11,b12-b22),
             (a22,-b11+b21),
             (a11+a12,b22),
             (-a11+a21,b11+b12),
             (a12-a22,b21+b22)]
```

```
c [m1,m2,m3,m4,m5,m6,m7]
  = let c11 = m1+m4-m5+m7
        c12 = m3+m5
        c21 = m2+m4
        c22 = m1+m3-m2+m6
    in [c11,c12,c21,c22,0,0,0]
```

strassen is based on skeleton dc4 and implemented using the C code presented in Subsect. 4.2. If one assumes matrices stored in row major order, as we do, some permutations have to be applied before and after. To express Strassen's algorithm with the parallel C skeleton presented in Subsect. 4.2, one has to compile the customizing functions from Haskell to C. We are working on a compiler which translates a tiny subset of Haskell to C for this purpose.

6 Results and related work

Starting with a general specification of $\mathcal{DC}$ we have obtained a sequence of skeletons, corresponding to different classes of $\mathcal{DC}$.

Quicksort fits well into skeleton dc0, because it uses the input data in combining. Problems like adaptive integration, evaluation of expressions, and satisfiability of boolean expressions can be solved by dc1, because only the results of the subproblem solutions are needed. dc2 is ideal for $\mathcal{DC}$ operations on sparse structures represented by trees. The class of dc3 covers algorithms by which information can be computed from a dense structure in a balanced way, e.g., reductions, list homomorphisms, the maximum segment sum problem, the convex hull problem, etc. The benefit of dc4 is that it enforces a balanced division of output data as well, as is important for the scan algorithm, the fast Fourier transform, bitonic sort, Karatsuba's polynomial product, and Strassen's matrix multiplication.

For the less specialized skeletons, efficient implementations will need to exploit load information at run time whereas, for the more specialized skeletons, a space-time mapping determined at compile time is better.

Huang et al. [12] have presented a derivation of a parallel implementation of Strassen's matrix multiplication algorithm using tensor product formulas. The result is a loop program similar to ours.

The strength of our method is in that an algorithm, which is well structured (i.e., fits into a skeleton after adaptations) but hard to implement by hand without recursion (like Strassen's), can be compiled from a functional specification to a low-level target program, whose structure is so simple that every operation can be given a point in time and space at compile time.

Our skeletons are given in the functional language Haskell, i.e., they have a syntax, a type, and a semantics which is referentially transparent. This enables reasoning about the correctness of an implementation. Furthermore, because Haskell is executable and has a C interface, one might use our fast, parallel C program for the skeleton and still keep its parameters, the customizing functions, in Haskell.

Aside from [12], there is other work related to ours. Misra [14], and Achatz and Schulte [1] restrict themselves to a binary division of data and problems. Mou's [15] approach allows an arbitrary division of problems and a division of multi-dimensional data into two parts per dimension, but does not say anything about a higher division degree. Cole [4] does not consider input and output data which are distributed among the processors. None of these papers presents explicitly a nested loop program, and Mou's approach is the only one that is powerful enough to handle Strassen's matrix multiplication with distributed input and output data, aside from ours.

There has also been related work in our own group. First, there is work on the parallelization of the *homomorphism* [3], a basic DC skeleton somewhat more restrictive than ours. There exists a theory for the transformational parallelization of homomorphisms [17,7]. The class of *distributable homomorphisms* (DH) [6] corresponds to the combine phase of our skeleton dc4 with a binary divide function (this class is called C-algorithms in [8]). For all functions of the DH class, a common hypercube implementation can be derived by transformation in the Bird-Meertens formalism [6].

The class of "static DC" [8] is an analog of our dc3 skeleton, however, with the capability of applying different divide (combine) functions at different descendants (ascendants) in the call tree. The analog of our Law 1 in [8] is Theorem 2.

In our own earlier work [9], we have obtained loop programs similar to the one presented here by parallelization in a space-time mapping model related to the hypercube. There, we have been informal; here we have focussed on a more precise, top-down development in the framework of equational reasoning.

Acknowledgements

Thanks to John O'Donnell for many fruitful discussions in which he convinced us to base our approach on equational reasoning in Haskell. Thanks also to Sergei Gorlatch for discussions. Two PLILP reviews contained very valuable feedback on the presentation. Financial support was provided by the DFG through project RecuR2 and by the DAAD through an ARC exchange grant.

References

1. K. Achatz and W. Schulte. Architecture independent massive parallelization of divide-and-conquer algorithms. In *Mathematics of Program Construction*, Lecture Notes in Computer Science 947, pages 97–127. Springer-Verlag, 1995.
2. A. V. Aho, J. E. Hopcroft, and J. D. Ullman. *The Design and Analysis of Computer Algorithms*. Series in Computer Science and Information Processing. Addison-Wesley, 1974.
3. R. S. Bird. Lectures on constructive functional programming. In M. Broy, editor, *Constructive Methods in Computing Science*, NATO ASI Series F: Computer and Systems Sciences, Vol. 55, pages 151–216. Springer-Verlag, 1988.
4. M. I. Cole. *Algorithmic Skeletons: Structured Management of Parallel Computation*. Research Monographs in Parallel and Distributed Computing. Pitman, 1989.

5. J. Darlington, A. Field, P. Harrison, P. Kelly, D. Sharp, Q. Wu, and R. While. Parallel programming using skeleton functions. In A. Bode, M. Reeve, and G. Wolf, editors, *Parallel Architectures and Languages Europe (PARLE '93)*, Lecture Notes in Computer Science 694, pages 146–160. Springer-Verlag, 1993.

6. S. Gorlatch. Systematic efficient parallelization of scan and other list homomorphisms. In L. Bougé, P. Fraigniaud, A. Mignotte, and Y. Robert, editors, *Euro-Par'96*, Lecture Notes in Computer Science 1124, pages 401–408. Springer-Verlag, 1996.

7. S. Gorlatch. Systematic extraction and implementation of divide-and-conquer parallelism. In H. Kuchen and D. Swierstra, editors, *Programming Languages: Implementation, Logics and Programs*, Lecture Notes in Computer Science 1140, pages 274–288. Springer-Verlag, 1996.

8. S. Gorlatch and H. Bischof. Formal derivation of divide-and-conquer programs: A case study in the multidimensional FFT's. In D. Mery, editor, *Formal Methods for Parallel Programming: Theory and Applications*, pages 80–94. IEEE Computer Society Press, 1997.

9. C. A. Herrmann and C. Lengauer. On the space-time mapping of a class of divide-and-conquer recursions. *Parallel Processing Letters*, 6(4):525–537, 1996.

10. C. A. Herrmann and C. Lengauer. Parallelization of divide-and-conquer by translation to nested loops. Technical Report MIP-9705, Fakultät für Mathematik und Informatik, Universität Passau, March 1997.

11. E. Horowitz and S. Sahni. *Fundamentals of Computer Algorithms.* Computer Software Engineering Series. Computer Science Press, 1984.

12. C.-H. Huang, J.R. Johnson, and R.W. Johnson. Generating parallel programs from tensor product formulas: A case study of Strassens's matrix multiplication algorithm. In *Proc. Int. Conf. on Parallel Processing*, volume III, pages 104–108, 1992.

13. S. Kindermann. Flexible program and architecture specification for massively parallel systems. In B. Buchberger and J. Volkert, editors, *Parallel Processing: CON-PAR 94 - VAPP VI*, Lecture Notes in Computer Science 854, pages 160–171. Springer-Verlag, 1994.

14. J. Misra. Powerlist: A structure for parallel recursion. *ACM Trans. on Programming Languages and Systems*, 16(6):1737–1767, November 1994.

15. Z. G. Mou. Divacon: A parallel language for scientific computing based on divide-and-conquer. In *Proc. 3rd Symp. Frontiers of Massively Parallel Computation*, pages 451–461. IEEE Computer Society Press, October 1990.

16. A. Schönhage and V. Strassen. Schnelle Multiplikation grosser Zahlen. *Computing*, 7:281–292, 1971.

17. D. B. Skillicorn. *Foundations of Parallel Programming.* Cambridge International Series on Parallel Computation. Cambridge University Press, 1994.

18. V. Strassen. Gaussian elimination is not optimal. *Numerische Mathematik*, 13:354–356, 1969.

19. S. Thompson. *Haskell - The Craft of Functional Programming.* International Computer Science Series. Addison-Wesley, 1996.

Transforming Lazy Functions
Using Comportment Properties

Ross Paterson

University of North London

Abstract. This paper develops a source-to-source transformation that seeks to delay the creation of thunks as much as possible, often eliminating them altogether. The generated programs make use of simpler representations, including types in which all expressions terminate. The transformation is guided by an abstract interpretation, with the abstract values of basic comportment analysis concretized as representation types related by injections.

The transformation of functions is polyvariant, with functions mapped to natural transformations. This leads to a clean treatment of higher order functions.

Keywords: static analysis, abstract interpretation, automatic program transformation

1 Introduction

If a function is lazy, its argument must be passed as a suspended computation, or *thunk*. This object is typically created on the heap, or *boxed*, and the function using it must inspect the thunk to determine whether it has been evaluated. It has long been recognized that these thunks are a major obstacle to the application of conventional compiler technology to lazy functional languages. They have been attacked using strictness analysis [9], which determines that certain sub-expressions must be evaluated in order to produce the final output. Instead of being suspended, such expressions may be safely evaluated early, and their values passed in an unboxed form on the stack.

There is also a dual approach, known as termination analysis, which determines that certain sub-expressions will have been evaluated by a certain point. If we know that an argument of a function will have been evaluated by the time the function is called, we can pass the argument in unboxed form to a call-by-value variant of the function (even if the function is not strict).

A typical functional language incorporates lazy data structures, and strictness analysis techniques have been developed that produce information about latent demand [14]. Similarly termination analysis may be extended to produce statements about latent termination: though an expression might not terminate, it may be that if it does then its components will also have been evaluated.

The information supplied by these analyses has been used to improve compiler performance, but the changes to the code generator are seldom formally verified. Exceptions include the work of Danvy and Hatcliffe [3] and of Burn and Le Métayer [1], who describe modifications of the continuation-passing transform to incorporate simple strictness information. Paterson [11] defines a transformation based on projection-based strictness analysis. The transformation moves backwards to perform evaluation as early as possible, and as a side-benefit discovers unused components of data structures. The transformation of this paper is dual to that one; it moves forward, delaying boxing as much as possible, and as a side-benefit discovers unused alternatives.

We shall confine our attention to forwards analyses, which may infer that the value of an expression lies within a subset of values, called a *comportment property* [2]. It is customary to render the analysis tractable by using a finite set of properties, indexed by an abstract domain. For the purposes of simple strictness analysis, it suffices to use properties that are ideals, but in order to encompass other properties, including termination, totality and constancy, this restriction must be dropped.

This paper is concerned with exploiting the results of comportment analysis to transform programs into forms operating on reduced types. For this we require a source language whose type system allows us to express such distinctions as whether or not a type includes the bottom element $\perp$. This is routine in denotational semantics; we need only model our source language on the denotational meta-language [8]. An appropriately modified typed λ-calculus is discussed in Sect. 2.

Next we develop concrete representations of basic comportment properties over each type as subtypes, each with an embedding into the original type. As defined by Cousot and Cousot [2], the qualification "basic" indicates that the properties we use are not closed under disjunction (union). Thus we use an approximation of union in the analysis of conditionals, losing some information in comparison with the full-flown comportment analysis. Section 3 presents the easy case of non-functional types. The principal difficulty is with function types, discussed in Sect. 4. Since a function will be specialized in different ways for different input subtypes, we can represent it as a family of related functions, i.e. a natural transformation. The class of natural transformations is sufficiently constrained that it may be embedded in the original function type.

In Sect. 5 we define an abstract interpretation and accompanying source-to-source transformation, which transforms an expression to one of the reduced type. The abstract interpretation is a fairly standard comportment analysis (except for the treatment of fixed points). The novelty is the translation into forms exploiting the subtype representations to achieve greater efficiency. In particular, the creation of closures is delayed as long as possible, and often eliminated.

Our transformation exploits termination properties directly, producing improved representations of values known to terminate, and permitting eager evaluation where it does not harm termination. Strictness properties may be used indirectly, as sketched in Ex. 2 in the next section.

There are some similarities between our work and binding time analysis, which identifies subexpressions whose values will be statically known, given that part of the input will be static. Our abstract interpretation is particularly close to that of Hunt and Sands [7]. However, the transformations we consider are much less ambitious than those performed by specializers using binding time information. On the other hand we use an extended definition of staticness, using static values within dynamic structures. We are also able to transform the program without knowing the values of the static inputs.

2 A Source Language with Explicit Lifting

The denotational semantics of lazy functional programs often refers to a lifting domain constructor $A_\perp$, which adds an additional bottom element to the domain A. For example, a numeric type might be modelled as $N_\perp$ for some set N, and a sum type as $(A + B)_\perp$, where $+$ denotes disjoint union. The addition of the bottom element is required to model the possibility of nontermination. The key to thunk removal is a source language modelled on the meta-language, in which this lifting is explicit, and therefore susceptible to transformation [8]. Such a language might serve as a core language, to which a more comfortable source language is translated as a first step in compilation.

We assume a collection of base types A, B, etc, which correspond to flat sets, without a bottom element. Then the types of our language are described by the following grammar:

$$t ::= B \mid \varnothing \mid t \times t \mid t + t \mid t_\perp \mid t \to t$$

Here $\varnothing$ represents the empty type, and $\times$, $+$ and $\to$ are unlifted. Note that many types, including base types and sum types, have no bottom element. Any expression of such a type must terminate, and can thus be safely evaluated early instead of being suspended in a thunk. The aim then becomes to transform programs to equivalent programs using types with fewer liftings.

On the other hand, we may not define values by general recursion unless the type concerned is known to have a least element $\perp$ and thus support the Kleene definition of fixed points. We define a class of *pointed* types by stating that $t_\perp$ is always pointed, $s \times t$ is pointed if both s and t are, and $s \to t$ is pointed if t is.[1]

Our source language is a simply typed λ-calculus, similar to those of [6,8]. We assume the families of constants c^t listed in Fig. 1. We also assume a fixed set of constants $c^{B_1 \to \cdots B_n \to B}$ for base types $B_1, \ldots, B_n$ and B. Variables x^t are also typed, but we will routinely omit the type superscripts on variables and constants where they are irrelevant or may be deduced from the context.

Most of these constants are familiar, as long as one remembers that sums are unlifted. The main novelty lies in the constants *lift*, *fail* and *ext*, which manipulate lifted types, and satisfy the axioms

$$ext\ f\ fail = \perp \tag{1}$$

$$ext\ f\ (lift\ x) = f\ x \tag{2}$$

---

[1] If t is pointed, then $t + \varnothing$ and $\varnothing + t$ also have least elements, but we will not be using them here.

$$empty^{\emptyset \to t}$$

$$fst^{s \times t \to s} \qquad inl^{s \to s+t} \qquad\qquad fix^{(t \to t) \to t} \text{ for pointed } t$$

$$snd^{s \times t \to t} \qquad inr^{t \to s+t} \qquad\qquad fail^{t} \bot$$

$$pair^{s \to t \to s \times t} \qquad choose^{(s \to u) \to (t \to u) \to s+t \to u} \qquad lift^{t \to t_\bot}$$

$$ext^{(s \to t) \to s_\bot \to t} \text{ for pointed } t$$

Fig. 1. Constants

Operationally, *ext f x* forces the evaluation of x to weak head normal form, and if this terminates then (tail-) calls f with the result as argument.

We aim to delay the application of *lift* as long as possible, hoping to cancel it with a subsequent *ext*. There is some similarity to deforestation [4,13], but here we preserve the structure of the source program.

As the standard interpretation of our language is trivial, we shall proceed by proving equalities in the logic associated with our language. This logic comprises axioms including those above (see [6,8] for details), β- and η-equivalence and Scott induction.

Example 1. Suppose the familiar type Int is expanded as $\mathbb{Z}_\bot$, for the primitive flat type $\mathbb{Z}$ representing the integers or some finite approximation. The familiar constants **1**, **2**, etc. are similarly expanded as *lift*(1), *lift*(2) etc. for $1, 2, \ldots : \mathbb{Z}$. Similarly, functions like $* : \text{Int} \to \text{Int} \to \text{Int}$ are expanded as

$$x * y \triangleq ext \ (\lambda u.\ ext \ (\lambda v.\ lift \ (u \star v)) \ y) \ x$$

using a primitive function $\star : \mathbb{Z} \to \mathbb{Z} \to \mathbb{Z}$, corresponding to a machine instruction. Similarly, the function $\lambda \mathbf{x}.\ \mathbf{2} * \mathbf{x}$ might be transformed to

$$\lambda \mathbf{x}.\mathbf{2} * \mathbf{x} = \lambda x.\ ext \ (\lambda u.\ ext \ (\lambda v.\ lift \ (u \star v)) \ x) \ (lift \ 2)$$
$$= ext \ (\lambda v.\ lift \ (2 \star v))$$

Example 2. Suppose a function $f : s_\bot \to t$ is discovered to be strict by the analysis discussed here or any other. Then any occurrence of f may be replaced by the term $ext \ (f \circ lift)$. Then the transformation of Sect. 5 will promote the *lift* through f, producing an improved translation. In this way we achieve similar effects to previous approaches in which strictness information had been used to enable local optimizations to remove thunks [5,12].

3 Embeddings of Non-functional Types

In this section and the next we define for each type t a lattice of subtypes of t. In the analysis, this lattice is represented by an abstract domain $\mathcal{D}_t^{\#}$, which is a finite lattice under the ordering $\subseteq^{\#}$. A concretion mapping $C_t[\cdot]$ relates the two lattices. Types that do not contain $\to$ are easier to handle, and will be treated first.

Example 3. For the type $\mathbb{Z}_\perp$, the relevant subtypes are

$\varnothing_\perp$, which can be used for expressions that are known not to terminate,
$\mathbb{Z}$, which can be used for expressions that are known to terminate, and
$\mathbb{Z}_\perp$, which can be used for any expression.

To complete the lattice, we add the type $\varnothing$. These types may be arranged in a lattice, with the inclusions made explicit as embedding functions between subtypes, as on the right side of Fig. 2. The figure also shows the corresponding abstract domain $\mathcal{D}_{\mathbb{Z}_\perp}^\#$ and the concretion map.

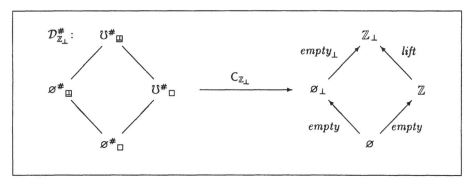

Fig. 2. Abstract domain $\mathcal{D}_{\mathbb{Z}_\perp}^\#$ and lattice of subtypes of $\mathbb{Z}_\perp$

The rather curious names of the abstract values on the left are explained by the definition of the abstract domains $\mathcal{D}_t^\#$ by induction over t:

- For a base type B (for example $\mathbb{Z}$), $\mathcal{D}_B^\#$ consists of the two values $\varnothing_B^\#$ and $\mho_B^\#$, with $\varnothing^\# \sqsubseteq^\# \mho^\#$.
- The domain $\mathcal{D}_\varnothing^\#$ consists of a single value $\varnothing_\varnothing^\#$.
- For any type t, the abstract domain $\mathcal{D}_{t_\perp}^\#$ consists of values $\alpha_{\boxplus}$ and $\alpha_{\square}$, for $\alpha \in \mathcal{D}_t^\#$. (The significance of the notation is that the subtype denoted by $\alpha_{\boxplus}$ includes the bottom element of $t_\perp$, while the subtype denoted by $\alpha_{\square}$ does not.) The constructors $\cdot_{\boxplus}$ and $\cdot_{\square}$ are monotonic, and $\alpha_{\square} \sqsubseteq^\# \alpha_{\boxplus}$ for each α.
- For types s and t, the abstract domain $\mathcal{D}_{s\times t}^\#$ consists of pairs $\alpha \boxtimes \beta$ for $\alpha \in \mathcal{D}_s^\#$ and $\beta \in \mathcal{D}_t^\#$, such that either both α and β are the least elements of their respective lattices, or neither is (i.e. a smash product). The pairs are ordered pointwise.
- For types s and t, the abstract domain $\mathcal{D}_{s+t}^\#$ consists of pairs $\alpha \boxplus \beta$ for $\alpha \in \mathcal{D}_s^\#$ and $\beta \in \mathcal{D}_t^\#$, ordered pointwise.

The concretion maps are also defined by induction on the structure of t, as follows:

$$C_B[\mho_B^\#] = B \qquad\qquad C_{t_\perp}[\alpha_\boxminus] = (C_t[\alpha])_\perp$$
$$C_B[\varnothing_B^\#] = \varnothing \qquad\qquad C_{t_\perp}[\alpha_\square] = C_t[\alpha]$$
$$C_\varnothing[\varnothing_\varnothing^\#] = \varnothing \qquad\qquad C_{s \times t}[(\alpha \boxtimes \beta)] = C_s[\alpha] \times C_t[\beta]$$
$$C_{s+t}[(\alpha \boxplus \beta)] = C_s[\alpha] + C_t[\beta]$$

Each abstract domain $\mathcal{D}_t^\#$ has a least element $\varnothing_t^\#$, indicating no values, whose concrete value is a type that is equivalent to $\varnothing$. At first glance that this might seem useless, since the abstract interpretation can hardly assign this value to any expression. However $\varnothing_t^\#$ is useful in compound abstract values. For example, *inl* produces only values in the left part of a sum type, so the type of its result could be simplified to $s + \varnothing$. Similarly, *fail* produces only the bottom element of a lifted type; the type of its result could be simplified to $\varnothing_\perp$, and the type being lifted could be simplified to $\varnothing$. The abstract version of the product domain is formed using the smash product because we do not wish to have distinct points representing $\varnothing \times \varnothing$ and $\varnothing \times t$.

Each abstract domain $\mathcal{D}_t^\#$ also has a greatest element $\mho_t^\#$. It is easy to establish that if t does not include $\to$, then $C_t[\mho_t^\#] = t$, though this will not hold for types including $\to$. For each type t, the concretion map C_t maps the abstract domain $\mathcal{D}_t^\#$ to a lattice of subtypes of this type $C_t[\mho_t^\#]$. To make this lattice explicit, we define for each $\alpha \subseteq^\# \alpha'$ in $\mathcal{D}_t^\#$, a function $C_t[\alpha \subseteq^\# \alpha'] : C_t[\alpha] \to C_t[\alpha']$. These functions are also defined by induction over t, as in Fig. 3.

$$C_t[\alpha \subseteq^\# \alpha'] \,:\, C_t[\alpha] \to C_t[\alpha']$$

$$C_B[\varnothing_B^\# \subseteq^\# \varnothing_B^\#] = empty$$
$$C_B[\mho_B^\# \subseteq^\# \mho_B^\#] = id$$
$$C_B[\varnothing_B^\# \subseteq^\# \mho_B^\#] = empty$$

$$C_\varnothing[\varnothing_\varnothing^\# \subseteq^\# \varnothing_\varnothing^\#] = empty$$

$$C_{s \times t}[\alpha \boxtimes \beta \subseteq^\# \alpha' \boxtimes \beta'] = C_s[\alpha \subseteq^\# \alpha'] \times C_t[\beta \subseteq^\# \beta']$$

$$C_{s+t}[\alpha \boxplus \beta \subseteq^\# \alpha' \boxplus \beta'] = C_s[\alpha \subseteq^\# \alpha'] + C_t[\beta \subseteq^\# \beta']$$

$$C_{t_\perp}[\alpha_\boxminus \subseteq^\# \alpha'_\boxminus] = (C_t[\alpha \subseteq^\# \alpha'])_\perp$$
$$C_{t_\perp}[\alpha_\square \subseteq^\# \alpha'_\boxminus] = lift \circ C_t[\alpha \subseteq^\# \alpha']$$
$$C_{t_\perp}[\alpha_\square \subseteq^\# \alpha'_\square] = C_t[\alpha \subseteq^\# \alpha']$$

Fig. 3. Injections between types $C_t[\alpha]$

Proposition 4. *For each type t and $\alpha \subseteq^\# \beta \in \mathcal{D}_t^\#$, the function $C_t[\alpha \subseteq^\# \beta]$ is bimonotone.*[2]

That is, these functions are subspace injections.

Proposition 5. *For each type t and $\alpha \subseteq^\# \beta \subseteq^\# \gamma \in \mathcal{D}_t^\#$,*

$$C_t[\alpha \subseteq^\# \alpha] = id_{C_t[\alpha]} \tag{3}$$
$$C_t[\beta \subseteq^\# \gamma] \circ C_t[\alpha \subseteq^\# \beta] = C_t[\alpha \subseteq^\# \gamma] \tag{4}$$

That is, C_t is a functor from $\mathcal{D}_t^\#$ to the category of our source language.

3.1 A Note on the Computational Pre-order

In addition to the set-based inclusion ordering (our $\subseteq^\#$), previous accounts of comportment analysis [2,10] make use of the computational or Egli-Milner ordering for the calculation of fixed points. The requirement that functions also preserve this ordering has the additional benefit of reducing the size of the abstract function domains, making the analysis more tractable.

There is a complication, however: the computational relation between properties is not anti-symmetric. To turn it into an ordering, one must deal with equivalence classes of properties, eliminating the distinction between a property and its convex closure. However we require this distinction for the description of the latent termination properties mentioned in Sect. 1. For example, it may be that we are not sure whether a list-valued expression will terminate, but we know that if it does then the head will not be $\perp$. The use of the computational ordering would identify this property with the set of all lists. Hence we require a different definition of fixed points; we shall use the inclusion ordering.

We can however define a computational *pre-order* $\sqsubseteq^\#$, using it to restrict the size of the abstract function domains. Since this pre-order has such a minor role, we only sketch it here. In each abstract domain $\mathcal{D}_t^\#$, the point $\varnothing^\#$ is isolated in the $\sqsubseteq^\#$ pre-order. The domains $\mathcal{D}_{s \times t}^\#$ and $\mathcal{D}_{s+t}^\#$ inherit the pre-order pointwise. The pre-order $\sqsubseteq^\#$ on $\mathcal{D}_{t_\perp}^\#$ is defined by the following rules:

$$\alpha \neq \varnothing^\# \Rightarrow \alpha_\boxdot \sqsubseteq^\# \alpha_\square$$
$$\alpha \sqsubseteq^\# \beta \Rightarrow \alpha_\square \sqsubseteq^\# \beta_\square$$
$$\alpha \sqsubseteq^\# \beta \Rightarrow \alpha_\boxdot \sqsubseteq^\# \beta_\boxdot$$
$$\alpha \subseteq^\# \beta \Rightarrow \alpha_\boxdot \sqsubseteq^\# \beta_\boxdot$$

4 Embeddings of Higher Types

So far, our abstract values describe the sets of values that an expression might produce. This cannot be directly extended to functions: while strict functions

---

[2] A function f is bimonotone if $x \leq y \Leftrightarrow f\,x \leq f\,y$.

$\mathbb{Z}_\perp \to \mathbb{Z}_\perp$ are in one-to-one correspondence with elements of the type $\mathbb{Z} \to \mathbb{Z}_\perp$, and strict total functions may be represented by $\mathbb{Z} \to \mathbb{Z}$, no simple representation is available for functions that are merely known to be total.

In analysing a function, we want to know what set of outputs can be produced from a given set of inputs. In all cases the empty set of inputs should produce the empty set of outputs. We also expect that larger sets of inputs will produce larger sets of outputs, and that more defined inputs will produce more defined outputs. Hence we define $\mathcal{D}^{\#}_{s \to t}$ as the set of functions $\mathcal{D}^{\#}_s \to \mathcal{D}^{\#}_t$ that preserve $\varnothing^{\#}$ and are monotonic with respect to both $\subseteq^{\#}$ and $\sqsubseteq^{\#}$. Both the order $\subseteq^{\#}$ and the pre-order $\sqsubseteq^{\#}$ are extended pointwise to functions.

Example 6. The domain $\mathcal{D}^{\#}_{\mathbb{Z}_\perp \to \mathbb{Z}_\perp}$ has 7 elements, exactly those listed as basic comportments by Cousot and Cousot [2]. We define the abstract functions by their actions on non-$\varnothing^{\#}$ elements:

$\lambda \alpha.\, \mho^{\#}_{\boxplus}$	representing all functions
$\lambda \alpha.\, \mho^{\#}_{\square}$	constant, total functions
$\lambda \alpha.\, \varnothing^{\#}_{\boxplus}$	divergent functions
$\lambda \alpha.\, \alpha$	strict, total functions
$\lambda \alpha.\, \alpha \cup^{\#} \mho^{\#}_{\square}$	total functions
$\lambda \alpha.\, \alpha \cup^{\#} \varnothing^{\#}_{\boxplus}$	strict functions
$\lambda \alpha.\, \varnothing^{\#}_{\square}$	empty

The orderings are exactly as in [2].

Suppose that the abstract interpretation of a function $f : s \to t$ yields a function $\varphi \in \mathcal{D}^{\#}_s \to \mathcal{D}^{\#}_t$. For each abstract input α, there will be a version $f_\alpha : C_s[\alpha] \to C_t[\varphi\,\alpha]$. That is, the transformation is polyvariant.

Example 7. Abstract interpretation of $ext\,(\lambda\,u.\,lift\,(2 \star u)) : \mathbb{Z}_\perp \to \mathbb{Z}_\perp$ yields the identity function on $\mathcal{D}^{\#}_{\mathbb{Z}_\perp}$, indicating that the function is both strict and total. Transformation yields four versions mapping between corresponding subtypes, as shown in Fig. 4. In this case, the transformed functions connect corresponding types in the two lattices because the abstract function was the identity. Other abstract functions will produce different patterns.

The commuting diagram of Fig. 4 is typical of the general situation, for the families of versions will be natural transformations:

$$C_{s \to t}[\varphi] = C_s \dot{\to} C_t \circ \varphi$$

That is, the type $C_{s \to t}[\varphi]$ consists of families of functions $f_\alpha : C_s[\alpha] \to C_t[\varphi\,\alpha]$ for each $\alpha \in \mathcal{D}^{\#}_s$, satisfying

$$f_{\alpha'} \circ C_s[\alpha \subseteq^{\#} \alpha'] = C_t[\varphi\,\alpha \subseteq^{\#} \varphi\,\alpha'] \circ f_\alpha \tag{5}$$

However, we stipulate that $C_{s \to t}[\varnothing^{\#}_{s \to t}]$ is empty.

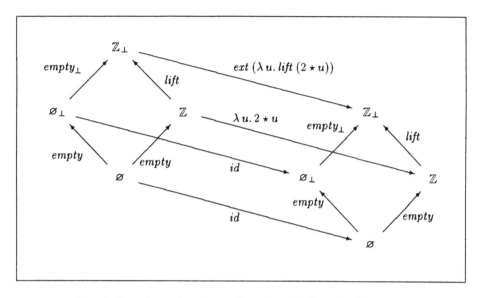

Fig. 4. Transformed versions of $ext\,(\lambda\,u.\,lift\,(2 \star u)) : \mathbb{Z}_\perp \to \mathbb{Z}_\perp$

When such a natural transformation f exists, the instance $f_{\mathcal{U}\#}$ determines all the others, because each function $C_t[\varphi\,\alpha \subseteq^\# \varphi\,\alpha']$ is injective. However the existence of $f_{\mathcal{U}\#}$ does not guarantee the existence of the natural transformation; our algorithm will construct the whole transformation.

These families will be implemented by iterated products of function types. It is important to note that the abstract domains $\mathcal{D}_t^\#$ will not appear in the transformed program. Selection of a component f_α will be represented by extraction of a known position in the tuple of functions. Unless f is a variable, this extraction can be done statically.

If $\varphi \subseteq^\# \varphi'$ in the pointwise ordering, then there is a corresponding injection $C_{s \to t}[\varphi \subseteq^\# \varphi']$ between the natural transformations, defined by:

$$(C_{s \to t}[\varphi \subseteq^\# \varphi']\,f)_\alpha = C_t[\varphi\,\alpha \subseteq^\# \varphi'\,\alpha] \circ f_\alpha$$

It is straightforward to verify that

- $C_{s \to t}[\varphi \subseteq^\# \varphi']\,f$ is natural,
- $C_{s \to t}[\varphi \subseteq^\# \varphi']$ is bimonotone, and
- $C_{s \to t}$ is a functor.

With the introduction of function types, the type $C_t[\mathcal{U}_t^\#]$ is no longer identical to t. However, it is isomorphic to t.

Proposition 8. *For each type t, there is an isomorphism $i_t : C_t[\mathcal{U}_t^\#] \cong t$.*

Proof. The required isomorphism is defined by induction over t. This is straightforward except for the case $s \to t$, for which we define

$$i_{s \to t}\,g = i_t \circ g_{\mathcal{U}\#} \circ i_s^{-1}$$

$$(i_{s\to t}^{-1} f)_\alpha = \begin{cases} empty_{s\to t} & \text{if } \alpha = \varnothing_s^\# \\ i_t^{-1} \circ f \circ i_s \circ C_s[\alpha \subseteq^\# \mho_s^\#] & \text{otherwise} \end{cases}$$

where $empty_{s\to t}$ is the unique element of $C_s[\varnothing_s^\#] \to C_t[\varnothing_t^\#]$.

Then for $g : C_{s\to t}[\mho_{s\to t}^\#]$ and $\alpha \neq \varnothing^\#$ (the empty case is trivial),

$$
\begin{aligned}
(i_{s\to t}^{-1} (i_{s\to t} g))_\alpha &= i_t^{-1} \circ i_t \circ g_{\mho^\#} \circ C_s[\alpha \subseteq^\# \mho_s^\#] \circ i_s^{-1} \circ i_s \\
&= g_{\mho^\#} \circ C_s[\alpha \subseteq^\# \mho_s^\#] && \text{by assumption} \\
&= C_t[\mho_{s\to t}^\# \; \alpha \subseteq^\# \mho_{s\to t}^\# \; \mho_s^\#] \circ g_\alpha && \text{by (5)} \\
&= C_t[\mho_t^\# \subseteq^\# \mho_t^\#] \circ g_\alpha \\
&= g_\alpha
\end{aligned}
$$

The reverse equality is demonstrated by instantiation. □

Thus for each abstract value $\alpha \in \mathcal{D}_t^\#$ there is an embedding $\alpha^{\mathbb{E}} : C_t[\alpha] \to t$ defined by $\alpha^{\mathbb{E}} = i_t \circ C_t[\alpha \subseteq^\# \mho_t^\#]$. The image of this function $\alpha^{\mathbb{E}}$ is the property used in the conventional interpretation.

5 Abstract Interpretation and Transformation

Abstract interpretation of a closed expression $e : t$ will yield a value $e^\# \in \mathcal{D}_t^\#$, representing the type of the transformed expression. Transformation of e will yield an expression $e^\star : C_t[e^\#]$. The transformation will be considered correct if

$$e = (e^\#)^{\mathbb{E}} (e^\star) \tag{6}$$

so that the behaviour of the original expression e can be recovered from the transformed version. The correctness condition is extended to expressions with free variables in Sect. 5.2.

The following lemma is used frequently in the proofs.

Lemma 9. *The condition* $f = \varphi^{\mathbb{B}} f'$ *is equivalent to*

$$\forall \alpha \in \mathcal{D}_s^\#. \; f \circ \alpha^{\mathbb{B}} = (\varphi \; \alpha)^{\mathbb{B}} \circ f'_\alpha$$

The forward implication is established by expanding the definitions and simplifying. The reverse direction follows by instantiating α to $\mho_s^\#$.

We consider first the abstract interpretation and transformation of the constants.

5.1 Translation of Constants

For each constant $c : t$, we shall define an abstract constant $c^\# \in \mathcal{D}_t^\#$ and a translated constant $c^\star : C_t[c^\#]$ satisfying

$$c = (c^\#)^{\mathbb{E}} (c^\star) \tag{7}$$

In most cases this property is easily verified.

The definitions of the abstract constants $c^\# \in \mathcal{D}_t^\#$ are mostly standard (e.g. in [7]). The constant *empty* is new, but its transformation is straightforward:

$$empty^\# \; \alpha = \varnothing_t^\#$$
$$empty_\alpha^\star = empty$$

The product constants are translated to themselves:

$$
\begin{array}{lclclcl}
fst^\# (\alpha \boxtimes \beta) & = & \alpha & snd^\# (\alpha \boxtimes \beta) & = & \beta & pair^\# \; \alpha \; \beta & = & \alpha \boxtimes \beta \\
fst_{\alpha \boxtimes \beta}^\star & = & fst & snd_{\alpha \boxtimes \beta}^\star & = & snd & (pair_\alpha^\star \; x)_\beta \; y & = & pair \; x \; y
\end{array}
$$

Injections into sums can only produce values in one arm of the sum:

$$
\begin{array}{lclclcl}
inl^\# \; \alpha & = & \alpha \boxplus \varnothing^\# & & inr^\# \; \beta & = & \varnothing^\# \boxplus \beta \\
inl_\alpha^\star & = & inl & & inr_\beta^\star & = & inr
\end{array}
$$

We must combine the results of the two arms of a *choose*:

$$choose^\# \; \varphi \; \psi \; (\alpha \boxplus \beta) = \varphi \; \alpha \cup^\# \psi \; \beta$$
$$((choose_\varphi^\star \; f)_\psi \; g)_{\alpha \boxplus \beta} = choose \; (C_t[\varphi \; \alpha \subseteq^\# \gamma] \circ f_\alpha) \; (C_t[\psi \; \beta \subseteq^\# \gamma] \circ g_\beta)$$
$$\text{where } \gamma = \varphi \; \alpha \cup^\# \psi \; \beta$$

Note that if α is $\varnothing^\#$, then since φ is strict $\gamma = \psi \; \beta$ and the left branch is transformed to $\lambda x^\varnothing . e = empty$. The program will then contain types $\varnothing + t$. We assume that a subsequent pass will reduce these, eliminating associated injections and *chooses*.

Failure can only produce the bottom element of lifting:

$$fail^\# \; \alpha = \varnothing^\#{}_\square$$
$$fail_\alpha^\star = empty_\perp$$

Applications of *lift* are delayed:

$$lift^\# \; \alpha = \alpha_\square$$
$$lift_\alpha^\star = id$$

For evaluation, there are two possibilities. If the expression to be evaluated is already unboxed, no evaluation is required:

$$ext^\# \; \varphi \; \alpha_\square = \varphi \; \alpha$$
$$(ext_\varphi^\star \; f)_{\alpha_\square} = f_\alpha$$

If the argument is boxed, the evaluation remains, and we must ensure that its result type is pointed:

$$ext^\# \; \varphi \; \alpha_\square = \varphi \; \alpha \cup^\# \perp^\#$$
$$(ext_\varphi^\star \; f)_{\alpha_\square} = ext \; (C_t[\varphi \; \alpha \subseteq^\# \gamma] \circ f_\alpha) \text{ where } \gamma = \varphi \; \alpha \cup^\# \perp^\#$$

where for each pointed type t, $\perp_t^{\#}$ is the least element of $\mathcal{D}_t^{\#}$ such that the image of $\perp_t^{\#^{\mathrm{E}}}$ contains the bottom element of t. We can define $\perp_t^{\#}$ by the following rules:

$$\perp_{s \times t}^{\#} = \perp_s^{\#} \boxtimes \perp_t^{\#}$$

$$\perp_{t_{\perp}}^{\#} = \varnothing^{\#}{}_{\boxdot}$$

$$\perp_{s \to t}^{\#} \, \alpha = \perp_t^{\#} \text{ for } \alpha \neq \varnothing_s^{\#}$$

For example, $\perp_{\mathbb{Z}_{\perp}}^{\#} = \varnothing^{\#}{}_{\boxdot}$, whose concretion is the one point type $\varnothing_{\perp}$. In general, for any pointed type t, $\perp_t^{\#} \in \mathcal{D}_t^{\#}$ abstracts a one point type, that point being mapped by $\perp_t^{\#^{\mathrm{E}}}$ to the bottom element of t.

Recursion also requires a pointed type:

$$fix^{\#} \, \varphi = \bigcup_{n \in \omega}^{\#} \varphi'^n (\varnothing^{\#}) \text{ where } \varphi' \, \alpha = \varphi \, \alpha \cup^{\#} \perp^{\#}$$

$$fix_{\varphi}^{\star} \, f = fix \, (C_t [\varphi \, \gamma \subseteq^{\#} \gamma] \circ f_{\gamma}) \text{ where } \gamma = fix^{\#} \varphi$$

By Lemma 9, the instance of (7) for fix is equivalent to

$$\forall \varphi \in \mathcal{D}_{t \to t}^{\#}. \forall f : C_{t \to t}[\varphi]. \, fix \, (\varphi^{\mathrm{E}} \, f) = (fix^{\#} \, \varphi)^{\mathrm{E}} \, (fix_{\varphi}^{\star} \, f) \qquad (8)$$
$$= \gamma^{\mathrm{E}} \, (fix \, (C_t [\varphi \, \gamma \subseteq^{\#} \gamma] \circ f_{\gamma}))$$

Since $\perp^{\#} \subseteq^{\#} \gamma$, we know that γ^{E} is strict, and hence (8) follows from

$$f \circ \gamma^{\mathrm{E}} = (\varphi \, \gamma)^{\mathrm{E}} \circ f'_{\gamma} = \gamma^{\mathrm{E}} \circ C_t [\varphi \, \gamma \subseteq^{\#} \gamma] \circ f'_{\gamma}$$

As noted in Sect. 3.1, our definition of $fix^{\#}$ differs from that of the Cousots [2], who use the sequence $\varphi^n (\perp^{\#})$, which is a chain under the computational ordering. In contrast, we seek the smallest strict property for recursive functions.

The translation of a base constant $c^{B_1 \to \cdots B_n \to B}$ is

$$(c^{B_1 \to \cdots B_n \to B})^{\#} \, \alpha_1 \, \ldots \, \alpha_n = \mho_{B_1 \to \cdots B_n \to B}^{\#}$$

$$(\ldots ((c^{B_1 \to \cdots B_n \to B})_{\alpha_1}^{\star} \, x_1) \, \ldots)_{\alpha_n} \, x_n = c^{B_1 \to \cdots B_n \to B} \, (\alpha_1{}^{\mathrm{E}} \, x_1) \, \ldots \, (\alpha_n{}^{\mathrm{E}} \, x_n)$$

Here each α_i is either $\mho_{B_i}^{\#}$, representing B_i, or $\varnothing_{B_i}^{\#}$, representing $\varnothing$. Hence each $\alpha_i{}^{\mathrm{E}}$ is either id or $empty$. The application of the constant will only produce a result if all of its arguments exist.

5.2 Transformation of Expressions

An expression $e : t$ with free variables $x^{t_1}, \ldots, x^{t_n}$ may be considered as a function of type $t_1 \times \cdots \times t_n \to t$. Hence we define the set $\mathrm{Env}^{\#}$ of abstract environments as the domain of mappings of variables x^t to abstract values from $\mathcal{D}_t^{\#}$, such that if any variable is mapped to $\varnothing^{\#}$, they all are.

For any variable x^t, let $x^{\star}$ denote a family of variables indexed by $\mathrm{Env}^{\#}$, such that for each $\eta \in \mathrm{Env}^{\#}$, $x^{\star}$ has type $C_t [\eta \, x^t]$.

Definition 10. If $e : t$, we write $e \overset{e^{\#}}{\Longrightarrow} e^{\star}$ to mean

1. $e^{\#} : \mathsf{Env}^{\#} \to \mathcal{D}_t^{\#}$ maps the empty environment to $\varnothing^{\#}$ and is monotonic with respect to both $\subseteq^{\#}$ and $\sqsubseteq^{\#}$. (That is, $e^{\#}$ is an abstract interpretation of e.)
2. $e^{\star}$ is a family of expressions $e_{\eta}^{\star} : C_t[e^{\#} \eta]$ indexed by environments $\eta \in \mathsf{Env}^{\#}$, such that if $\eta \subseteq^{\#} \eta' \in \mathsf{Env}^{\#}$, then

$$\bigwedge_{x^s} (x_{\eta'}^{\star} = C_s[\eta_x \subseteq^{\#} \eta'_x](x_{\eta}^{\star})) \Rightarrow e_{\eta'}^{\star} = C_t[e^{\#}\eta \subseteq^{\#} e^{\#}\eta'] (e_{\eta}^{\star})$$

(That is, $e^{\star}$ is a natural transformation.)
3. For each $\eta \in \mathsf{Env}^{\#}$,

$$\bigwedge_{x^s} (x = \eta_x^{\mathrm{E}} (x_{\eta}^{\star})) \Rightarrow e = (e^{\#} \eta)^{\mathrm{E}} (e_{\eta}^{\star})$$

(That is, the combination of abstract interpretation and transformation is correct.)

From these definitions it is easy to prove the following result, which enables us to transform any λ-expression.

Theorem 11.

1. *If a constant c satisfies $c = (c^{\#})^B (c^{\star})$, then $c \overset{\overline{c^{\#}}}{\Longrightarrow} \overline{c^{\star}}$ where $\overline{c^{\#}} \, \eta = c^{\#}$ and $\overline{c^{\star}}_{\eta} = c^{\star}$.*
2. *$x \overset{x^{\#}}{\Longrightarrow} x^{\star}$ where $x^{\#} \, \eta = \eta_x$*
3. *If $e \overset{e^{\#}}{\Longrightarrow} e^{\star}$, then $\lambda x . e \overset{f^{\#}}{\Longrightarrow} f^{\star}$, where*

$$f^{\#} \, \eta \, \alpha = e^{\#} \, \eta[x \mapsto \alpha]$$
$$(f_{\eta}^{\star})_{\alpha} = \lambda x_{\eta}^{\star} . e_{\eta[x \mapsto \alpha]}^{\star}$$

4. *If $e_1 : s \to t$, $e_2 : s$, $e_1 \overset{e_1^{\#}}{\Longrightarrow} e_1^{\star}$ and $e_2 \overset{e_2^{\#}}{\Longrightarrow} e_2^{\star}$, then $e_1 \, e_2 \overset{e^{\#}}{\Longrightarrow} e^{\star}$, where*

$$e^{\#} \, \eta = (e_1^{\#} \, \eta) (e_2^{\#} \, \eta)$$
$$e_{\eta}^{\star} = (e_{1\eta}^{\star})_{e_1^{\#}\eta} (e_{2\eta}^{\star})$$

Example 12. For the function

$$thrice : (t \to t) \to t \to t$$
$$thrice \; f \; x \overset{\triangle}{=} f \, (f \, (f \, x))$$

the transformed version is

$$thrice^{\#} \; \varphi \; \alpha \; = \varphi \, (\varphi \, (\varphi \, \alpha))$$
$$(thrice_{\varphi}^{\star} \; f)_{\alpha} \; x \overset{\triangle}{=} f_{\varphi(\varphi \; \alpha)} (f_{\varphi} \; \alpha \, (f_{\alpha} \; x))$$

Note the use of three (possibly) different transformations of f.

Sometimes we will prefer weaker translations than those defined above. For example, if the above translation is applied to the term $(\lambda x.(x,x)) \circ lift$, the *lift* will be duplicated. If these *lifts* are not subsequently consumed by the transformation, the resulting program might generate two thunks where formerly there was one. The detection of such situations requires a linearity analysis (as with deforestation in similar situations [13]). Such an analysis is beyond the scope of this paper, but we can offer the following result, which guarantees the correctness of such weakenings.

Proposition 13. *If $e : t$, $e \overset{e^{\#}}{\Longrightarrow} e^{\star}$ and $e^{\#} \subseteq^{\#} e^{\#\prime} \in \mathsf{Env}^{\#} \to \mathcal{D}_t^{\#}$, then $e \overset{e^{\#\prime}}{\Longrightarrow} e^{\star\prime}$, where*

$$(e^{\star\prime})_{\eta} = \mathsf{C}_t[e^{\#} \ \eta \subseteq^{\#} e^{\#\prime} \ \eta] \ (e_{\eta}^{\star})$$

Example 14. Suppose $e : s_{\perp} \times t$ and we wish to force the transformed version to use a lifted type for the first component. Then we can use this proposition with

$$e^{\#\prime} \ \eta = e^{\#} \ \eta \cup^{\#} \perp^{\#} \boxtimes \mho^{\#}$$

6   Conclusion

We have proved the correctness of a source-to-source transformation intended to remove thunks from the source program. The transformation of functions is polyvariant, with functions mapped to natural transformations, and is able to deal with higher order functions in a clean way. Such transformations are made possible by a source language in which lifting is explicit, and not all types need have a bottom element [8].

There are several areas in which this work could be extended.

Polymorphism. Our transformation assumed a monotyped language. It appears that many polymorphic functions, such as *thrice* above, could be handled by applying our rules to symbolic expressions representing abstract values.

Efficiency of the analysis. The abstract domains of even basic comportment analysis are rather large, but many of the points they contain contribute little to the quality of the transformation. It would be useful to identify useful subdomains. Similarly, one might like to cut down the sizes of the families of function variants used.

Quality of the generated program. We have said nothing about pragmatic issues, not even a guarantee that the transformation will improve the program. However we have given a framework (Prop. 13) within which such choices may be made while maintaining the correctness of the resulting transformation.

Recursive types. It is relatively straightforward to extend this work to (purely positive) retractive types, like the type of finite, partial and infinite lists. Adding initial types, like finite lists, would provide opportunities for further optimizations. However some care would be required: sometimes evaluating the large data structure early (rather than on demand) may be wasteful of space.

References

1. Geoffrey L. Burn and Daniel Le Métayer. Proving the correctness of compiler optimisations based on a global program analysis. In *Fifth International Symposium on Programming Language Implementation and Logic Programming*, volume 714 of *Lecture Notes in Computer Science*, pages 346–364, Tallinn, Estonia, August 1993. Springer.
2. Patrick Cousot and Radhia Cousot. Higher-order abstract interpretation (and application to comportment analysis generalizing strictness, termination, projection and PER analysis of functional languages). In *International Conference on Computer Languages*, pages 95–112. IEEE Computer Society Press, 1994.
3. Olivier Danvy and John Hatcliff. CPS-transformation after strictness analysis. *ACM Letters on Programming Languages and Systems*, 1(3):195–212, 1992.
4. G.W. Hamilton. Higher order deforestation. In *Programming Languages: Implementations, Logics and Programs*, volume 1140 of *Lecture Notes in Computer Science*, pages 213–227. Springer, 1996.
5. A. Reza Haydarlou and Pieter H. Hartel. Thunk lifting: Reducing heap usage in an implementation of a lazy functional language. *Journal of Functional and Logic Programming*, 1995.
6. Brian T. Howard. Inductive, projective, and pointed types. In *ACM International Conference on Functional Programming*, pages 102–109, Philadelphia, May 1996.
7. Sebastian Hunt and David Sands. Binding time analysis: A new PERspective. In *ACM Symposium on Partial Evaluation and Semantics-based Program Manipulation*, pages 154–165. ACM SIGPLAN Notices 26(9), September 1991.
8. John Launchbury and Ross Paterson. Parametricity and unboxing with unpointed types. In *European Symposium on Programming*, volume 1058 of *Lecture Notes in Computer Science*, pages 204–218, Linköping, Sweden, April 1996. Springer.
9. Alan Mycroft. The theory and practice of transforming call-by-need into call-by-value. In B. Robinet, editor, *International Symposium on Programming*, volume 83 of *Lecture Notes in Computer Science*, pages 270–281. Springer, 1980.
10. Alan Mycroft and Kirsten Lackner Solberg. Uniform pers and comportment analysis. In *Programming Languages: Implementations, Logics and Programs*, volume 982 of *Lecture Notes in Computer Science*, pages 169–187. Springer, 1995.
11. Ross Paterson. Compiling laziness using projections. In *Static Analysis Symposium*, volume 1145 of *Lecture Notes in Computer Science*, pages 255–269, Aachen, Germany, September 1996. Springer.
12. Simon L. Peyton Jones and John Launchbury. Unboxed values as first class citizens in a non-strict functional language. In *Conference on Functional Programming Languages and Computer Architecture*, pages 636–666, Cambridge, MA, 1991.
13. Philip Wadler. Deforestation: Transforming programs to eliminate trees. *Theoretical Computer Science*, 73:231–248, 1990.
14. Philip Wadler and John Hughes. Projections for strictness analysis. In *Conference on Functional Programming Languages and Computer Architecture*, volume 274 of *Lecture Notes in Computer Science*, pages 385–407, Portland, OR, 1987. Springer.

Transformations for Efficient Evaluations in Functional Programming[*]

Salvador Lucas

Departamento de Sistemas Informáticos y Computación
Universidad Politécnica de Valencia
Camino de Vera s/n, E-46071 Valencia, Spain.
e.mail: slucas@dsic.upv.es
URL: http://www.dsic.upv.es/users/elp/slucas.html

Abstract. Rewriting is a suitable mechanism to implement functional programming languages. The definition of efficient evaluation strategies is a natural concern in this setting. Recently we have shown that, by imposing some simple restrictions on the replacements which are allowed for the arguments of functions, we can obtain efficient head-evaluations of terms in a certain class of programs. We are also able to completely evaluate terms, but in this case, the efficiency of computation can be compromised. This paper concerns the definition of program transformations that enable efficient but still complete evaluation of function calls.

Keywords: evaluation, functional programming, program transformation, term rewriting.

1 Introduction

Functional languages which allow the definition of functions by means of patterns (e.g. Haskell, Hope or Miranda), are well suited to use term rewriting [4] as execution principle. Computing involves reduction of (input) terms to a normal form [9]. Any effective execution procedure must include a normalizing rewriting strategy able to compute the normal form of the input term if it exists. Such a reduction strategy is expected to be efficient both in performing only useful reductions and in its implementation [8]. For orthogonal term rewriting systems (TRSs), the Huet and Levy's notion of *needed reduction* [2] formalizes what we mean by a *useful reduction*. Needed reduction is any strategy which only selects needed redexes. A redex of a term t is needed if it is reduced (itself or some of its residuals) in every reduction sequence leading t to a normal form. Reduction of needed redexes is normalizing and, moreover, each step do actually contributes to normalization. Computing such needed redexes is not possible in the general case, but some approximations have been defined in the literature [2, 8].

Using *strongly replacing-independent* TRSs [7], it is possible to define a needed reduction strategy by only considering syntactic replacement restrictions: a mapping $\mu : \Sigma \rightarrow \mathcal{P}(\mathbb{N})$ (called the *replacement map*) indicates the fixed argument

---

[*] This work has been partially supported by CICYT under grant TIC 95-0433-C03-03.

positions $\mu(f) \subseteq \{1, \ldots, k\}$ of each k-ary function f for which we enable replacements. The restrictions on arguments are lifted to occurrences and the resulting restriction on rewriting is said context-sensitive rewriting (*csr*) [5, 6]. Given an orthogonal TRS $\mathcal{R}$, we are able to define a *canonical* replacement map $\mu_{\mathcal{R}}^{com}$ under which *csr* is able to compute head-normal forms [5]. An orthogonal, strongly replacing-independent TRS makes this by only reducing needed redexes [7]. The computation of such redexes is very easy, since we can take *any* replacing redex occurrence. This is to say that the replacement restrictions themselves are able to capture only needed redexes. Therefore, the implementation of a head-normalizing strategy for orthogonal strongly replacing-independent TRSs is nicely simple. For this reason, in this paper we analyze the problem of transforming an arbitrary TRS into an equivalent strongly replacing-independent TRS. This is always possible. However, orthogonality is not always preserved. Therefore, we have some limits in obtaining the desired benefits.

Computing head-normal forms is not completely satisfactory in functional programming. Our final goal is to *evaluate* a term t, i.e., to obtain the constructor term δ (the value of t) which expresses the meaning of t. *csr* is also able to compute values by using a less restrictive replacement map $\mu_{\mathcal{R}}^{\mathcal{B}}$ [5]. However, when dealing with orthogonal strongly replacing-independent TRSs, if we use $\mu_{\mathcal{R}}^{\mathcal{B}}$ instead of $\mu_{\mathcal{R}}^{com}$ (and $\mu_{\mathcal{R}}^{com} \neq \mu_{\mathcal{R}}^{\mathcal{B}}$) we loose the nice correspondence between replacing redexes and needed redexes. Now we have replacing redexes which are *not* needed. To solve this problem, we introduce a new transformation which is able to combine the requirement of achieving complete evaluations by only reducing the needed redexes which can be computed by means of replacement restrictions.

In Section 2, we give some preliminary definitions. In Section 3, we recall the main definitions concerning *csr*. Section 4 gives the transformations to obtain a strongly replacing-independent TRS from a given TRS. In Section 5, we define a program transformation which raises the good properties of *csr* concerning head-evaluations to complete evaluations. Section 6 compares with some related work and concludes.

2 Preliminaries

Let us first introduce the main notations used in the paper [1, 4]. V denotes a countable set of variables and Σ denotes a set of function symbols $\{\mathbf{f}, \mathbf{g}, \ldots\}$, each of which has a fixed arity given by a function $ar : \Sigma \to \mathbb{N}$. By $\mathcal{T}(\Sigma, V)$ we denote the set of terms. $\tilde{t}$ denotes a k-tuple $t_1, \ldots, t_k$ of terms, where k will be clarified from the context. $Var(t)$ is the set of variables in a term t. Terms are viewed as labelled trees in the usual way. Occurrences $u, v, \ldots$ are chains of positive natural numbers used to address subterms of t. If W is a set of occurrences, $u.W$ is the set $\{u.v \mid v \in W\}$. Occurrences are ordered by the standard prefix ordering: $u \leq v$ iff $\exists w \ v = u.w$. $O(t)$ denotes the set of occurrences of a term t. Given a subset $U \subseteq O(t)$, $U{\downarrow}$ is the set $U{\downarrow} = \{v \in O(t) \mid u \in U \wedge v \leq u\}$. $t|_u$ is the subterm at occurrence u of t. $t[s]_u$ is the term t with the subterm at the occurrence u replaced with s. $root(t)$ is the symbol labelling the root of t. $\Sigma(t) =$

$\{f \in \Sigma \mid \exists u \in O(t).root(t|_u) = f\}$ is the set of symbols from Σ appearing in t. Given a $T \subseteq \mathcal{T}(\Sigma, V)$, $\Sigma(T) = \cup_{t \in T} \Sigma(t)$. $O_\Sigma(t) = \{u \in O(t) \mid root(t|_u) \in \Sigma\}$ is the set of nonvariable occurrences in a term t. $O_V(t) = O(t) \backslash O_\Sigma(t)$ is the set of variable occurrences. We refer to any term C, which is the same as t everywhere except below u, i.e., $\exists s. C[s]_u = t$, as the *context* within the replacement occurs.

A rewrite rule is an ordered pair (l, r), written $l \to r$, with $l, r \in \mathcal{T}(\Sigma, V)$, $l \notin V$ and $Var(r) \subseteq Var(l)$. l is the left-hand side (*lhs*) of the rule and r is the right-hand side (*rhs*). A TRS is a pair $\mathcal{R} = (\Sigma, R)$ where R is a set of rewrite rules. $L(\mathcal{R})$ is the set of *lhs*'s of $\mathcal{R}$. An instance $\sigma(l)$ of a *lhs* $l \in L(R)$ is a redex. $O_\mathcal{R}(t) = \{u \in O(t) \mid \exists l \in L(\mathcal{R}) : t|_u = \sigma(l)\}$ is the set of redex occurrences in a term t. Given a TRS $\mathcal{R} = (\Sigma, R)$, we consider Σ as the disjoint union $\Sigma = \mathcal{C} \uplus \mathcal{F}$ of symbols $c \in \mathcal{C}$, called *constructors*, having no associated rule and symbols $f \in \mathcal{F}$, called *defined functions* or *operations*, which are defined by some program rule $f(\tilde{l}) \to r \in R$: $\mathcal{F} = \{f \in \Sigma \mid f(\tilde{l}) \to r \in R\}$ and $\mathcal{C} = \Sigma \backslash \mathcal{F}$. Constructor terms (i.e., *values*) are denoted $\delta \in \mathcal{T}(\mathcal{C}, V)$.

For a given TRS $\mathcal{R} = (\Sigma, R)$, a term t rewrites to a term s (at the occurrence u), written $t \xrightarrow{u}_\mathcal{R} s$ (or just $t \to s$), if $t|_u = \sigma(l)$ and $s = t[\sigma(r)]_u$, for some rule $l \to r$ in R, occurrence u in t and substitution σ. $\to_\mathcal{R}$ is the one-step rewrite relation for $\mathcal{R}$. A term t is in head-normal form if there is no derivation $t = t_1 \to t_2 \to \cdots$ starting from t which reduces the root of a term t_i, $i \geq 1$.

$\mathbb{N}_k^+$ is an initial segment $\{1, 2, \ldots k\}$ of the set of positive natural numbers $\mathbb{N}^+$, where $\mathbb{N}_0^+ = \emptyset$. $\mathcal{P}(\mathbb{N})$ is the powerset of natural numbers.

3 Context-sensitive rewriting

A mapping $\mu : \Sigma \to \mathcal{P}(\mathbb{N})$ is a *replacement map* (or Σ-map) for the signature Σ iff for all $f \in \Sigma$. $\mu(f) \subseteq \mathbb{N}_{ar(f)}^+$. A Σ-map μ determines the *argument* positions which can be reduced for each symbol in Σ [5, 6]. If we assume an arbitrary ordering in the signature[2] $\Sigma = \{f_1, \ldots, f_n\}$, then we express a Σ-map as $\mu = \langle I_1, \ldots, I_n \rangle$, where $I_j = \mu(f_j)$ for $1 \leq j \leq n$. Given $\Delta \subseteq \Sigma$, $\mu \downarrow_\Delta$ is the Δ-map given by: $\mu \downarrow_\Delta (f) = \mu(f)$ for all $f \in \Delta$.

The ordering $\subseteq$ on $\mathcal{P}(\mathbb{N})$ extends pointwise to an ordering $\sqsubseteq$ on M_Σ, the set of all Σ-maps: $\mu \sqsubseteq \mu'$ if for all $f \in \Sigma$, $\mu(f) \subseteq \mu'(f)$. $(M_\Sigma, \sqsubseteq, \mu_\perp, \mu_\top, \sqcup, \sqcap)$ is a complete lattice: for all $f \in \Sigma$, $\mu_\perp(f) = \emptyset$, $\mu_\top(f) = \mathbb{N}_{ar(f)}^+$, $(\mu \sqcup \mu')(f) = \mu(f) \cup \mu'(f)$ and $(\mu \sqcap \mu')(f) = \mu(f) \cap \mu'(f)$. Thus, $\mu \sqsubseteq \mu'$ means that μ considers less positions than μ' for reduction.

The set of μ-*replacing* occurrences is given by: $O^\mu(x) = \{\epsilon\}$ if $x \in V$, $O^\mu(f(t_1, \ldots, t_k)) = \{\epsilon\} \cup \bigcup_{i \in \mu(f)} i.O^\mu(t_i)$. In csr, we only rewrite on *replacing* occurrences: t μ-rewrites to s, written $t \hookrightarrow_{\mathcal{R}(\mu)} s$, if $t \xrightarrow{u}_\mathcal{R} s$ and $u \in O^\mu(t)$. The set of *replacing redexes* is $O_\mathcal{R}^\mu(t) = O_\mathcal{R}(t) \cap O^\mu(t)$. The set of *non-replacing* occurrences is $\widetilde{O^\mu}(t) = O(t) \backslash O^\mu(t)$. We also have $O_\Sigma^\mu(t) = O_\Sigma(t) \cap O^\mu(t)$ and $O_V^\mu(t) = O_V(t) \cap O^\mu(t)$.

A term t is μ-*compatible* ($\text{comp}_\mu(t)$) if its non-replacing occurrences are variables: $\text{comp}_\mu(t)$ iff $\widetilde{O^\mu}(t) \subseteq O_V(t)$. Equivalently, $\text{comp}_\mu(t)$ holds iff $O_\Sigma(t) \subseteq$

---

[2] Usually, the order in which the symbols are written.

$O^\mu(t)$. There exists a *minimum* $\Sigma(t)$-map μ_t ensuring compatibility: if $t = x$, then $\mu_t(f) = \emptyset$ for all $f \in \Sigma$. If $t = f(t_1, \ldots, t_k)$, then $\mu_t = \mu_t^\epsilon \sqcup \mu_{t_1} \sqcup \cdots \sqcup \mu_{t_k}$, where μ_t^ϵ is $\mu_t^\epsilon(f) = \{i \mid t_i \notin V\}$ and $\mu_t^\epsilon(g) = \emptyset$ for all $g \neq f$.

Example 3.1 *Given* $t = \text{first}(0, x)$, $\Sigma(t) = \{0, \text{first}\}$, *and we have:*
$$\mu_{\text{first}(0,x)} = \mu_{\text{first}(0,x)}^\epsilon \sqcup \mu_0 \sqcup \mu_x = \langle \emptyset, \{1\} \rangle \sqcup \langle \emptyset, \emptyset \rangle \sqcup \langle \emptyset, \emptyset \rangle = \langle \emptyset, \{1\} \rangle.$$
For $t' = \text{first}(s(x), y :: z)$, $\Sigma(t') = \{s, ::, \text{first}\}$, *and we get* $\mu_{\text{first}(s(x),y::z)} = \mu_{\text{first}(s(x),y::z)}^\epsilon \sqcup \mu_{s(x)} \sqcup \mu_{y::z} = \langle \emptyset, \emptyset, \{1,2\} \rangle \sqcup \langle \emptyset, \emptyset, \emptyset \rangle \sqcup \langle \emptyset, \emptyset, \emptyset \rangle = \langle \emptyset, \emptyset, \{1,2\} \rangle.$

Analogously, for a set of terms T, we define $\mu_T = \sqcup_{t \in T} \mu_t$. These replacement maps characterize compatibility: $\text{comp}_\mu(t) \Leftrightarrow \mu_t \sqsubseteq \mu$ and $\text{comp}_\mu(T) \Leftrightarrow \mu_T \sqsubseteq \mu$.

Given a TRS $\mathcal{R} = (\Sigma, R)$, its *canonical replacement map* $\mu_\mathcal{R}^{com}$ is $\mu_\mathcal{R}^{com} = \sqcup_{l \in L(\mathcal{R})} \mu_l$, where $L(\mathcal{R})$ is the set of *lhs*'s of the TRS. $\mu_\mathcal{R}^{com}$ is the minimum replacement map which makes the *lhs*'s of the TRS compatible terms.

Example 3.2 *Consider the following program* $\mathcal{R}$ *which defines some functions on lists of natural numbers:*

$$\text{dbl}(0) \rightarrow 0 \qquad\qquad \text{dbls}([]) \rightarrow []$$
$$\text{dbl}(s(x)) \rightarrow s(s(\text{dbl}(x))) \qquad \text{dbls}(x :: y) \rightarrow \text{dbl}(x) :: \text{dbls}(y)$$
$$\text{sel}(0, x :: y) \rightarrow x \qquad\qquad \text{indx}([], x) \rightarrow []$$
$$\text{sel}(s(x), y :: z) \rightarrow \text{sel}(x, z) \quad \text{indx}(x :: y, z) \rightarrow \text{sel}(x, z) :: \text{indx}(y, z)$$
$$\text{from}(x) \rightarrow x :: \text{from}(s(x))$$

The canonical replacement map for $\mathcal{R}$ *is:* $\mu_\mathcal{R}^{com}(f) = \emptyset$ *for all* $f \in \{0, s, [], ::, \text{from}\}$, $\mu_\mathcal{R}^{com}(\text{dbl}) = \mu_\mathcal{R}^{com}(\text{dbls}) = \mu_\mathcal{R}^{com}(\text{indx}) = \{1\}$ *and* $\mu_\mathcal{R}^{com}(\text{sel}) = \{1, 2\}$.

Theorem 3.3 ([5]) *Let* $\mathcal{R} = (\Sigma, R) = (\mathcal{C} \uplus \mathcal{F}, R)$ *be a left-linear TRS and* μ *be a* Σ-map such that $\mu_\mathcal{R}^{com} \sqsubseteq \mu$. *Let* t *be a term and* $s = c(\tilde{s})$ *for some* $c \in \mathcal{C}$. *If* $t \rightarrow^* s$, *there exists* $s' = c(\tilde{s'})$ *s.t.* $t \hookrightarrow^* s'$, *and* $s' \rightarrow^* s$.

Theorem 3.4 ([5]) *Let* $\mathcal{R} = (\Sigma, R)$ *be an orthogonal TRS and* μ *be a* Σ-map such that $\mu_\mathcal{R}^{com} \sqsubseteq \mu$. *Let* t *be a term and* $s = f(\tilde{s})$ *be a head-normal form. If* $t \rightarrow^* s$, *there exists a head-normal form* $s' = f(\tilde{s'})$ *s.t.* $t \hookrightarrow_{\mathcal{R}(\mu)}^* s'$, *and* $s' \rightarrow^* s$.

Hence, from Theorem 3.3, for left-linear TRSs, we have completeness in *head-evaluations* (i.e., reductions leading to a constructor head-normal form). For orthogonal TRSs, we have completeness in head-normalization (Theorem 3.4).

Example 3.5 *For* $\mathcal{R}$ *in Example 3.2, we get the following head-evaluation using* $\mu_\mathcal{R}^{com}$ *(redexes underlined; we mark some steps for further discussion):*

$$\text{sel}(s(0), \text{dbls}(\underline{\text{from}(0)}))$$
$$\hookrightarrow \text{sel}(s(0), \underline{\text{dbls}(0 :: \text{from}(s(0)))}) \qquad\qquad (*)$$
$$\hookrightarrow \text{sel}(s(0), \underline{\text{dbl}(0)} :: \text{dbls}(\text{from}(s(0)))) \qquad (**)$$
$$\hookrightarrow \underline{\text{sel}(0, \text{dbls}(\text{from}(s(0))))}$$
$$\hookrightarrow \text{sel}(0, \text{dbls}(\underline{s(0) :: \text{from}(s(s(0)))})) \qquad\qquad (*)$$
$$\hookrightarrow \underline{\text{sel}(0, \text{dbl}(s(0)) :: \text{dbls}(\text{from}(s(s(0)))))}$$
$$\hookrightarrow \underline{\text{dbl}(s(0))}$$
$$\hookrightarrow s(s(\text{dbl}(0)))$$

4 Strongly replacing-independent TRSs

In this section, we introduce the strongly replacing-independent TRSs, for which we have proven that any context-sensitive reduction is needed [7]. A term t is strongly μ-compatible ($\mathsf{scomp}_\mu(t)$) if $\widetilde{O^\mu}(t) = O_V(t)$. Alternatively $\mathsf{scomp}_\mu(t)$ holds if $O_\Sigma(t) = O^\mu(t)$. Clearly $\mathsf{scomp}_\mu(t) \Rightarrow \mathsf{comp}_\mu(t)$. A set of terms $T \subseteq \mathcal{T}(\Sigma, V)$ is said to be *weakly compatible* ($\mathsf{wcomp}(T)$), if, for all $t \in T$, $\mathsf{scomp}_{\mu_t}(t)$. T is strongly μ-compatible ($\mathsf{scomp}_\mu(T)$), if, for all $t \in T$, $\mathsf{scomp}_\mu(t)$.

Some terms have *no* replacement map μ which satisfies $\mathsf{scomp}_\mu(t)$. For instance, there is no replacement map which makes the term $\mathtt{f}(\mathtt{f}(\mathbf{x}, \mathbf{a}), \mathbf{y})$ strongly compatible. When such a $\Sigma(t)$-map exists, it only can be μ_t. The $\Sigma(T)$-map μ which makes a set T strongly μ-compatible must be $\mu = \mu_T$. However, the replacement restrictions for symbols in $\Sigma \backslash \Sigma(T)$ can be freely established without damaging the strong compatibility of T. We assume this fact in the remainder of our exposition with no explicit mention. A weakly compatible set of terms is not, in general, strongly compatible.

Example 4.1 *Both* $t = \mathtt{first}(0, \mathbf{x})$ *and* $t' = \mathtt{first}(\mathtt{s}(\mathbf{x}), \mathbf{y} :: \mathbf{z})$ *terms are strongly compatible w.r.t. μ_t and $\mu_{t'}$, respectively. Thus, the set $T = \{t, t'\}$ is weakly compatible. However, the set T is not strongly compatible w.r.t. $\mu_t \sqcup \mu_{t'}$.*

Weak compatibility is a modular property (i.e., given $T, S \subseteq \mathcal{T}(\Sigma, V)$, $\mathsf{wcomp}(T \cup S) \Leftrightarrow \mathsf{wcomp}(T) \wedge \mathsf{wcomp}(T)$), but scomp is not. We also have the following:

Proposition 4.2 *Let* $T \subseteq \mathcal{T}(\Sigma, V)$ *and* $\mu_T = \sqcup_{t \in T} \mu_t$. *Then* $\mathsf{scomp}_{\mu_T}(T)$ *iff* $\mathsf{wcomp}(T)$ *and for all* $t, t' \in T$ $\mu_t\!\downarrow_\Delta = \mu_{t'}\!\downarrow_\Delta$ *where* $\Delta = \Sigma(t) \cap \Sigma(t')$.

This proposition gives us a criterion to know whether a weakly compatible set of terms is strongly compatible. Note that, in Example 4.1, $\mu_t\!\downarrow_\Delta \neq \mu_{t'}\!\downarrow_\Delta$, where $\Delta = \Sigma(t) \cap \Sigma(t') = \{\mathtt{first}\}$, because $\mu_t(\mathtt{first}) = \{1\}$ and $\mu_{t'}(\mathtt{first}) = \{1, 2\}$.

Definition 4.3 (Weakly and strongly replacing-independent TRSs) *Let* $\mathcal{R} = (\Sigma, R)$ *be a TRS. $\mathcal{R}$ is weakly (strongly) replacing-independent if $L(\mathcal{R})$ is a weakly (strongly) compatible set of terms.*

If $\mathcal{R}$ is strongly replacing-independent, it is so w.r.t. $\mu_\mathcal{R}^{com}$. This is the *intended* replacement map when dealing with strongly replacing-independent TRSs. The TRS in Example 3.2 is strongly replacing-independent.

Theorem 4.4 ([7]) *Let $\mathcal{R}$ be an orthogonal, strongly replacing-independent TRS. Let t be a term. Then $O_\mathcal{R}^{\mu_\mathcal{R}^{com}}(t)$ is a set of needed redexes.*

This theorem motivates our interest in strongly replacing-independent TRSs: we can *only* perform needed $\mu_\mathcal{R}^{com}$-reductions when we work with this class of TRSs.

To transfom a TRS into a strongly replacing-independent TRS, first we obtain a weakly replacing-independent TRS (transformation W). From this one, we obtain a strongly replacing-independent TRS (transformation S).

132

4.1 From TRSs to weakly replacing-independent TRSs

If t is not strongly compatible, there is a μ_t-replacing variable occurrence $v.i \in O_V^{\mu_t}(t)$ which is the i-th argument of a function symbol $f \in \Sigma(t)$. By definition of μ_t, there exists a replacing argument of f which is *not* a variable at an occurrence $u.i \in O_\Sigma^{\mu_t}(t)$. We say that $u.i$ is a *disagreeing* occurrence in t. Denote as D_t the set of disagreeing occurrences of subterms in a term t: $D_t = \{u.i \in O_\Sigma^{\mu_t}(t) \mid t = C[f(\tilde{t})]_u \wedge (\exists v.i \in O_V^{\mu_t}(t). t = C'[f(\tilde{s})]_v)\}$. To eliminate i from $\mu_t(f)$, we need to *remove* such disagreeing occurrences. Let C_D^t be the occurrences of strongly compatible subterms in t: $C_D^t = \{u \in O(t) \mid t|_u \text{ is strongly compatible}\}$. We remove strongly compatible (proper) subterms containing disagreeing occurrences: U_D^t is the set of occurrences of maximal strongly compatible subterms in a term t which contain the disagreeing occurrences. $U_D^t = (maximal(D_t)\downarrow \cap minimal(C_D^t))\backslash\{\epsilon\}$. Note that, if t is strongly compatible, then $minimal(C_D^t) = \{\epsilon\}$ and therefore $U_D^t = \emptyset$.

If t is a *lhs* of a rule of a TRS, this elimination will change the matchings in the rewriting process. In order to keep the semantics of the TRS, new function symbols *match* gather the removed subterms to complete the delayed matching.

Definition 4.5 (Transformation W) *Let* $\mathcal{R} = (\Sigma, R)$ *be a TRS. The TRS* $W(\mathcal{R}) = (\Sigma \uplus M, R')$ *is:* $R' = \cup_{l \to r \in R} w(l \to r)$*, where*

```
w(l → r) =
    if U_D^l = Ø then {l → r} else
    let u_D ∈ U_D^l
        X ∉ Var(l) be a fresh variable
        {y_1, ..., y_p} = Var(l[ ]_{u_D}), and
        match ∈ M be a new p + 1-ary function symbol
    in {match(l|_{u_D}, y_1, ..., y_p) → r} ∪ w(l[X]_{u_D} → match(X, y_1, ..., y_p))
```

Example 4.6 *Let us consider the following TRS $\mathcal{R}$:*
$$f(c(d(x)), d(c(y))) \to x$$
$$f(c(x), f(y, c(b))) \to y$$
We apply w *to each rule. For* $l = f(c(d(x)), d(c(x)))$*, we have* $D_l = \{1.1, 2.1\}$*, $minimal(C_D^l) = \{1, 2\}$ and $U_D^l = \{1, 2\}$. We choose* $u_D = 1$ *and we get:*
$$f(X, d(c(y))) \to match(X, y) \qquad match(c(d(x)), y) \to x$$
Each lhs is strongly compatible now. For $l' = f(c(x), f(y, c(b)))$*, we have:* $D_{l'} = \{1, 2.2.1\}$*, $minimal(C_D^{l'}) = \{1, 2\}$ and $U_D^{l'} = \{1, 2\}$. Choosing* $u_D = 1$*, we get*
$$f(X, f(y, c(b))) \to match'(X, y) \qquad match'(c(x), y) \to y$$

Theorem 4.7 *Let $\mathcal{R}$ be a TRS. Then $W(\mathcal{R})$ is a weakly replacing-independent TRS. If $\mathcal{R}$ is weakly replacing-independent, then $W(\mathcal{R}) = \mathcal{R}$.*

Theorem 4.8 (Correctness and completeness) *Let $\mathcal{R} = (\Sigma, R)$ be a TRS, and $W(\mathcal{R}) = (\Sigma \uplus M, R')$. Let $t, s \in \mathcal{T}(\Sigma, V)$. Then, $t \to_\mathcal{R}^* s$ iff $t \to_{W(\mathcal{R})}^* s$.*

In general, W does *not* preserve orthogonality or confluence of the original TRS but only left-linearity. For instance, $W(\mathcal{R})$ in Example 4.6 is orthogonal. However, in the second step of Example 4.6, we could choose $u_D = 2$ instead of $u_D = 1$. Thus we obtain the following *non-orthogonal* weakly replacing-independent TRS:

$$f(X, d(c(y))) \rightarrow match(X, y) \qquad match(c(d(x)), y) \rightarrow x$$
$$f(c(x), X) \rightarrow match'(X, x) \qquad match'(f(y, c(b)), x) \rightarrow y$$

Therefore, we must check for confluence of $W(\mathcal{R})$ (by using the standard methods) in order to make a practic use of the transformation.

4.2 From weakly to strongly replacing independent TRSs

W solves disagreements *inside* each *lhs*. In order to make a TRS strongly replacing-independent, we need to eliminate disagreements among *lhs*'s of *different* rules.

Example 4.9 *Let us consider the weakly replacing-independent TRS $\mathcal{R}$:*

$$first(0, x) \rightarrow [\,]$$
$$first(s(x), y :: z) \rightarrow y :: first(x, z)$$

The lhs's $l = first(0, x)$ and $l' = first(s(x), y :: z)$ of $\mathcal{R}$ do not conform a strongly compatible set of terms (see Example 4.1). By Proposition 4.2, this is because of $\mu_l(first) = \{1\}$ and $\mu_{l'}(first) = \{1, 2\}$. In order to convert $\{l, l'\}$ into a strongly compatible set of terms, we must eliminate the subterm $y :: z$ from l' and to replace it by a fresh variable X. In this way, we obtain $\{first(0, x), first(s(x), X)\}$ which is a strongly compatible set.

We need to keep the semantics of the original TRS unchanged. We add a new symbol match *which is intended to perform the matching of the second argument with the pattern $x :: y$. We obtain the strongly replacing-independent TRS $\mathcal{R}'$:*

$$first(0, x) \rightarrow [\,] \qquad\qquad match(y :: z, x) \rightarrow y :: first(x, z)$$
$$first(s(x), X) \rightarrow match(X, x)$$

We generalize this procedure. Let us consider a TRS $\mathcal{R} = (\Sigma, R)$, and $l \in L(\mathcal{R})$ in the following definitions:

- $D_l = \{l' \in L(\mathcal{R}) \mid \mu_l \downarrow_\Delta \neq \mu_{l'} \downarrow_\Delta \text{ where } \Delta = \Sigma(l) \cap \Sigma(l')\}$
- $\Sigma_D(l) = \{f \in \Sigma(l) \mid \exists l' \in D_l . f \in \Sigma(l') \wedge \mu_l(f) \neq \mu_{l'}(f)\}$
- For all $f \in \Sigma(l)$, $D_l^f = \{l' \in D_l \mid f \in \Sigma(l')\}$
- For all $f \in \Sigma_D(l)$, $\mu_D^l(f) = \cup_{l' \in D_l^f} \mu_l(f) \backslash \mu_{l'}(f)$
- $U_D^l = \{u.i \in O_\Sigma^{\mu_l}(l) \mid l = C[f(\tilde{t})]_u \wedge f \in \Sigma_D(l) \wedge i \in \mu_D^l(f)\}$
- $U_D^R = \{U_D^l \mid l \rightarrow r \in R\}$

Roughly speaking, U_D^l is the set of occurrences of subterms in l which should be *removed* from l in order to eliminate all disagreements introduced by l in $L(\mathcal{R})$. They are said *positive* disagreements of l, because by removing subterms from l itself, we can eliminate them.

Definition 4.10 (Transformation S) *Let $\mathcal{R} = (\Sigma, R)$ be a weakly replacing-independent TRS. The TRS $S(\mathcal{R}) = (\Sigma \cup M, R')$ is: $R' = S_0(R, U_D^R)$ where $S_0(\emptyset, X) = \emptyset$, $S_0(\{l \rightarrow r\} \cup R, \{U_D^l\} \cup U_D^R) = s(l \rightarrow r, U_D^l) \cup S_0(R, U_D^R)$ and*

$s(l \to r, U_D^l) =$
    if $U_D^l = \emptyset$ then $\{l \to r\}$ else
    let $W = maximal(U_D^l) = \{v_1, \ldots, v_m\}$
        $X_1, \ldots, X_m$ be fresh, distinct variables
        $Y = \{y_1, \ldots, y_p\} = Var(l[\;]_{v_1} \cdots [\;]_{v_m})$, and
        $match \in M$ be a new $m + p$-ary function symbol
    in $\{match(l|_{v_1}, \ldots, l|_{v_m}, y_1, \ldots, y_p) \to r\} \cup$
        $s(l[X_1]_{v_1} \cdots [X_m]_{v_m} \to match(X_1, \ldots, X_m, y_1, \ldots, y_p), U_D^l \setminus W)$

Example 4.11 *Let us consider the following weakly replacing-independent TRS:*
    $g(a, x, f(a, b)) \to b$
    $f(x, g(x, c, d)) \to a$
*As we can see, $l = g(a, x, f(a, b))$ has a positive (g-)disagreement and (f-)disagreement
with $l' = f(x, g(x, c, d))$ and l' has a positive (g)-disagreement with l. We have:*
    $D_l = \{l'\}$, $\Sigma_D(l) = \{f, g\}$, $\mu_D^l = \mu_l \setminus \mu_{l'} = \langle\{1, 2\}, \{1, 3\}\rangle \setminus \langle\{2\}, \{2, 3\}\rangle =$
    $\langle\{1\}, \{1\}\rangle$, $U_D^l = \{1, 3.1\}$.
    *Also $D_{l'} = \{l\}$, $\Sigma_D^{l'} = \{f, g\}$, $\mu_D^{l'} = \mu_{l'} \setminus \mu_l = \langle\{2\}, \{2, 3\}\rangle \setminus \langle\{1, 2\}, \{1, 3\}\rangle =$
    $\langle\emptyset, \{2\}\rangle$, $U_D^{l'} = \{2.2\}$.*
Thus for l, we get $W = U_D^l$, $Y = \{x\}$, match is a 3-ary symbol, and
    $s(l, U_D^l) = \{g(X, x, f(Y, b)) \to match(X, Y, x), \ match(a, a, x) \to b\}$.
For l', $W = U_D^{l'}$, $Y = \{x\}$, match' is a 2-ary symbol, and
    $s(l', U_D^{l'}) = \{f(x, g(x, X, d)) \to match'(X, x), \ match'(c, x) \to a\}$.
Thus, $S(\mathcal{R})$ is:
    $g(X, x, f(Y, b)) \to match(X, Y, x)$ $match(a, a, x) \to b$
    $f(x, g(x, X, d)) \to match'(X, x)$ $match'(c, x) \to a$

Theorem 4.12 *If $\mathcal{R}$ is a weakly replacing-independent TRS, then $S(\mathcal{R})$ is strongly
replacing-independent. If $\mathcal{R}$ is strongly replacing-independent, then $S(\mathcal{R}) = \mathcal{R}$.*

S can fail if the input TRS is not weakly replacing-independent.

Example 4.13 *Let us consider $\mathcal{R}$ in Example 4.6. Note that $\Delta = \Sigma(l) \cap \Sigma(l') =
\{c, f\}$ and $\mu_l \downarrow_\Delta = \langle\{1\}, \{1, 2\}\rangle = \mu_{l'} \downarrow_\Delta$. Therefore, $D_l = D_{l'} = \emptyset$, hence $U_D^l =
U_D^{l'} = \emptyset$ and $S(\mathcal{R}) = \mathcal{R}$, but $\mathcal{R}$ is not strongly replacing-independent.*

Theorem 4.14 (Correctness and completeness) *Let $\mathcal{R} = (\Sigma, R)$ be a weakly
replacing-independent TRS, and $S(\mathcal{R}) = (\Sigma \uplus M, R')$. Let $t, s \in \mathcal{T}(\Sigma, V)$. Then,
$t \to_\mathcal{R}^* s$ iff $t \to_{S(\mathcal{R})}^* s$.*

S preserves left-linearity. S preserved non-overlaps in Examples 4.9 and 4.11.
Unfortunately, in general, S does *not* preserve either orthogonality or confluence.

Example 4.15 *The orthogonal, weakly replacing-independent TRS $\mathcal{R}$:*
    $h(x, b, c) \to x$
    $h(a, x, b) \to x$
    $h(b, c, x) \to x$
is transformed into $S(\mathcal{R})$:

$$h(x, X, Y) \to \text{match}(X, Y, x) \qquad \text{match}(b, c, x) \to x$$
$$h(X, x, Y) \to \text{match}'(X, Y, x) \qquad \text{match}'(a, b, x) \to x$$
$$h(X, Y, x) \to \text{match}''(X, Y, x) \qquad \text{match}''(b, c, x) \to x$$

which is not orthogonal. It is not confluent, since $h(a, b, c) \to_{S(\mathcal{R})}^* a$, but also $h(a, b, c) \to_{S(\mathcal{R})}^* \text{match}'(a, c, b)$ and $h(a, b, c) \to_{S(\mathcal{R})}^* \text{match}''(a, b, c)$.

Therefore, we should also test confluence of $S(\mathcal{R})$ (using any standard method) to safely use it. W and S could be combined: Let $\mathcal{R}$ be as in Example 4.6. $S(W(\mathcal{R}))$ is:

$$f(X, d(Y)) \to \text{match}''(Y, X) \qquad f(X, f(y, c(Y))) \to \text{match}'''(Y, X, y)$$
$$\text{match}(c(X), y) \to \text{match}^{iv}(X, y) \qquad \text{match}'(c(x), y) \to y$$
$$\text{match}''(c(y), X) \to \text{match}(X, y) \qquad \text{match}'''(b, X, y) \to \text{match}'(X, y)$$
$$\text{match}^{iv}(d(x), y) \to x$$

which is an orthogonal TRS. Therefore, the previous results ensure that $S(W(\mathcal{R}))$ is equivalent to $\mathcal{R}$, but we can perform optimal reductions by using the canonical replacement map because it is a strongly replacing-independent TRS.

5 Program transformation for complete evaluations

Regarding normalization of terms, if we restrict ourselves to values, csr is powerful enough to compute them. Given a set $B \subseteq C$, the replacement map $\mu_{\mathcal{R}}^B$ is $\mu_{\mathcal{R}}^B = \mu_{\mathcal{R}}^{com} \sqcup \mu_B$, where $\mu_B(c) = \mathbb{N}_{ar(c)}^+$ for all $c \in B$ and $\mu_B(f) = \emptyset$ if $f \notin B$.

Theorem 5.1 ([5]) Let $\mathcal{R} = (\Sigma, R) = (\mathcal{C} \uplus \mathcal{F}, R)$ be a left-linear TRS, $B \subseteq C$ and μ be a Σ-map such that $\mu_{\mathcal{R}}^B \sqsubseteq \mu$. Let $t \in \mathcal{T}(\Sigma, V)$, and $\delta \in \mathcal{T}(B, V)$. Then $t \to^* \delta$ iff $t \hookrightarrow^* \delta$.

By taking $\mu_{\mathcal{R}}^{com}$ as given in Example 3.2, and $B = \{0, s\}$, then $\mu_{\mathcal{R}}^B(s) = \{1\}$ (recall that $\mu_{\mathcal{R}}^{com}(s) = \emptyset$). We continue the head-evaluation of Example 3.5,

$$s(s(\underline{\text{dbl}(0)})) \hookrightarrow s(s(0))$$

to get the complete evaluation. The non-terminating or useless computations which could start in the steps $(*)$ and $(**)$ in Example 3.5 are still avoided, because $\mu_{\mathcal{R}}^B(::) = \emptyset$. Moreover, by using the results in [12] we can prove that $\mathcal{R}$ is $\mu_{\mathcal{R}}^B$-terminating. Unfortunately, we cannot ensure optimality of the $\mu_{\mathcal{R}}^B$-derivation, since $\mu_{\mathcal{R}}^{com} \sqsubseteq \mu_{\mathcal{R}}^B$ and Theorem 4.4 does not apply. More problematic situations arise.

Example 5.2 Let us consider $t = \text{indx}(s(0) :: [], \text{dbls}(\text{from}(0)))$. By using $\mathcal{R}$ in Example 3.2, we can head-evaluate t under $\mu_{\mathcal{R}}^{com}$:

$$\text{indx}(s(0) :: [], \text{dbls}(\text{from}(0)))$$
$$\hookrightarrow \text{sel}(s(0), \text{dbls}(\text{from}(0))) :: \text{indx}([], \text{dbls}(\text{from}(0)))$$

If we want to compute the value of t, we take $B = \{0, s, [], ::\}$. Hence, $\mu_{\mathcal{R}}^B(s) = \{1\}$ and $\mu_{\mathcal{R}}^B(::) = \{1, 2\}$. This allows us to continue until the end:

$$\texttt{sel}(\texttt{s}(0),\texttt{dbls}(\texttt{from}(0))) :: \texttt{indx}([],\texttt{dbls}(\texttt{from}(0)))$$
$$\hookrightarrow \texttt{sel}(\texttt{s}(0),\texttt{dbls}(\underline{\texttt{from}(0)})) :: []$$
$$\hookrightarrow \texttt{sel}(\texttt{s}(0),\texttt{dbls}(\underline{0 :: \texttt{from}(\texttt{s}(0))})) :: [] \qquad (*)$$
$$\hookrightarrow \texttt{sel}(\texttt{s}(0),\underline{\texttt{dbl}(0) :: \texttt{dbls}(\texttt{from}(\texttt{s}(0))))} :: [] \qquad (**)$$
$$\hookrightarrow \texttt{sel}(0,\texttt{dbls}(\underline{\texttt{from}(\texttt{s}(0)))}) :: []$$
$$\hookrightarrow \texttt{sel}(0,\texttt{dbls}(\underline{\texttt{s}(0) :: \texttt{from}(\texttt{s}(\texttt{s}(0)))})) :: [] \qquad (*)$$
$$\hookrightarrow \texttt{sel}(0,\underline{\texttt{dbl}(\texttt{s}(0)) :: \texttt{dbls}(\texttt{from}(\texttt{s}(\texttt{s}(0)))))} :: []$$
$$\hookrightarrow \underline{\texttt{dbl}(\texttt{s}(0))} :: []$$
$$\hookrightarrow \texttt{s}(\underline{\texttt{s}(\texttt{dbl}(0))}) :: []$$
$$\hookrightarrow \texttt{s}(\texttt{s}(0)) :: []$$

However, $\mathcal{R}$ is not $\mu_{\mathcal{R}}^{\mathcal{B}}$-terminating now: Since $\mu_{\mathcal{R}}^{\mathcal{B}}(::) = \{1,2\}$, the repeated application of a from-rule in the $(*)$ terms goes into a loop. Optimality of derivations is also compromised: we could perform an unbound number of (useless) reductions for the redex $\texttt{double}(0)$ *in* $(**)$ *which are not needed.*

The unpleasant situation sketched in Example 5.2 is solved by giving a new program transformation.

5.1 The transformation V

If we deal with typed TRSs, Theorem 5.1 is very easy to use, since, given a term $t = f(\tilde{t})$, we are able to establish the maximal set of constructors $\mathcal{B} \subseteq \mathcal{C}$ which should be considered. In this section we assume the existence of some valid type system [9]. Basic types are denoted as nat, bool, etc. Symbols $f \in \Sigma$ are typed by: $f : \tau_1 \times \ldots \times \tau_k \to \tau$. The *type* of f is $type(f) = \tau$. Types of arguments of f are gathered in $typearg(f) = \{\tau_1, \ldots, \tau_k\}$. Variables $x \in V$ also have a type, $type(x)$. We also assume that all terms are well typed everywhere. The type of a term t is the type of its outermost symbol.

We need to isolate the replacement restrictions which are needed to perform the head-evaluation of an operation rooted term $t = f(\tilde{t})$ for some $f \in \mathcal{F}$ from the restrictions which are needed to allow them within a constructor context $C[] \in \mathcal{T}(\mathcal{B}, V)$ for some $\mathcal{B} \subseteq \mathcal{C}$. *Below the outermost defined symbols, reductions should be performed only up to head-evaluation.* To deal with this task, we introduce the following notations:

- $outer_{\mathcal{F}}(t) = \{root(t|_u) \in \mathcal{F} \mid \forall v < u.\ root(t|_v) \notin \mathcal{F}\}$ is the set of outermost defined symbols in t.
- $Var_{\mathcal{B}}(t) = \{x \in Var(t) \mid \exists u \in O(t).\ t|_u = x \wedge \forall v < u.\ root(t|_v) \in \mathcal{B}\}$ is the set of $\mathcal{B}$-*variables*, i.e., variables of t having a maximal proper prefix which only points to symbols in $\mathcal{B}$. We also define $\mathcal{B}_\tau = \{c \in \mathcal{B} \mid type(c) = \tau\}$.
- The set of possible types for outermost defined functions arising by instantiation of a variable x is $Type_{\mathcal{B}}(type(x))$ where
$$Type_{\mathcal{B}}(\tau) = \{\tau\} \cup \bigcup_{c \in \mathcal{B}_\tau} Type_{\mathcal{B}}(\tau')$$
$$\tau' \in typearg(c)$$
- $Vouter_{\mathcal{B}}(t) = \bigcup_{x \in Var_{\mathcal{B}}(t)} \{f \in \mathcal{F} \mid type(f) \in Type_{\mathcal{B}}(type(x))\}$ are the defined symbols which can become outermost by instantiating $\mathcal{B}$-variables of t.

Example 5.3 *Let us consider the TRS in Example 3.2. We calculate $Vouter_\mathcal{B}(x)$.*
Let $type(x) = $ nat and $\mathcal{B} = \{0, \mathbf{s}\}$. Since $Type_\mathcal{B}(type(x)) = \{\text{nat}\} \cup Type_\mathcal{B}(\text{nat}) =$
$\{\text{nat}\}$, we have $Vouter_\mathcal{B}(x) = \{\text{dbl}, \text{sel}\}$.

Given a TRS $\mathcal{R} = (\Sigma, R) = (\mathcal{F} \uplus \mathcal{C}, R)$, $\mathcal{B} \subseteq \mathcal{C}$ and $f \in \mathcal{F}$, $outrhs_\mathcal{R}(f) \subseteq \mathcal{F}$
contains the outermost defined symbols in rhs's of the f-rules: $outrhs_\mathcal{R}(f) =$
$\cup_{f(\tilde{l}) \to r \in R} outer_\mathcal{F}(r)$. Now $Vrhs(f) \subseteq \mathcal{F}$ is the set of outermost defined symbols which can appear by instantiation of $\mathcal{B}$-variables in rhs's of the f-rules:
$Vrhs(f) = \cup_{f(\tilde{l}) \to r \in R} Vouter_\mathcal{B}(r)$. If $\mathcal{F}_\mathcal{R} : \mathcal{P}(\mathcal{F}) \to \mathcal{P}(\mathcal{F})$ is:

$$\mathcal{F}_\mathcal{R}(F) = F \cup \bigcup_{g \in F} \mathcal{F}_\mathcal{R}(outrhs_\mathcal{R}(g)) \cup \bigcup_{g \in F} \mathcal{F}_\mathcal{R}(Vrhs(g)).$$

the set $\mathcal{F}_\mathcal{R}^f = \mathcal{F}_\mathcal{R}(\{f\})$ contains the defined symbols which can turn outermost
when a f-rooted (well typed) term $f(\tilde{t})$ is rewritten.

Example 5.4 *Given $\mathcal{R}$ in Example 3.2, let us obtain $\mathcal{F}_\mathcal{R}^\text{sel}$ and $\mathcal{F}_\mathcal{R}^\text{indx}$.*

- *We have that $outrhs_\mathcal{R}(\text{sel}) = \{\text{sel}\}$ and $Vrhs(\text{sel}) = \{\text{sel}, \text{dbl}\}$. Thus,*
  $\mathcal{F}_\mathcal{R}^\text{sel} = \mathcal{F}_\mathcal{R}(\{\text{sel}\}) = \{\text{sel}\} \cup \mathcal{F}_\mathcal{R}(\{\text{sel}\}) \cup \mathcal{F}_\mathcal{R}(\{\text{dbl}\}) = \{\text{sel}, \text{dbl}\}$.
- *$outrhs_\mathcal{R}(\text{indx}) = \{\text{sel}, \text{indx}\}$ and $Vrhs(\text{indx}) = \emptyset$. Thus,*
  $\mathcal{F}_\mathcal{R}^\text{indx} = \mathcal{F}_\mathcal{R}(\{\text{indx}\}) = \{\text{indx}\} \cup \mathcal{F}_\mathcal{R}(\{\text{sel}\}) = \{\text{indx}, \text{sel}, \text{dbl}\}$.

The formal treatment of the transformation which we are going to introduce
becomes simpler, if we do not look for the least increment of the number of
rules of the TRS. For instance, by introducing new rules $f'(\tilde{l}) \to r'$ to deal
with *each* defined symbol f' which stands for the outermost version of a symbol
$f \in \mathcal{F}$, the definition of the transformation would be easier, but we also get
undesirable consequences. For example, in the evaluation of $t = \text{indx}(\mathbf{s}(0) ::$
$[], \text{dbls}(\text{from}(0)))$ as given in Example 5.2, the symbol **from** does *not* become
outermost. Thus, we do not need the rule:
   $\text{from}'(x) \to \bar{\mathbf{T}}(x) ::' \text{from}'(\mathbf{s}(x))$
(the meaning of $\bar{\mathbf{T}}$ is explained below) which introduces *non-termination*, because
we need that $::'$ (the 'outermost' version of $::$) be replacing in both its first and
second arguments in order to obtain completeness in evaluations. However, this
rule does *not* add computational power to the transformation, because **from**' will
never arise in the evaluation. For this reason, we perform a more accurated analysis of the required additional rules. We define now the program transformation.
First, we give the new signature.

Definition 5.5 *Given a TRS $\mathcal{R} = (\Sigma, R) = (\mathcal{C} \uplus \mathcal{F}, R)$, $f \in \mathcal{F}$ and $\mathcal{B} \subseteq \mathcal{C}$,*
$\Sigma_\mathcal{B}^f = \Sigma \uplus \mathcal{F}' \uplus \mathcal{B}'$, where: $c' \in \mathcal{B}' \Leftrightarrow c \in \mathcal{B} \wedge ar(c') = ar(c)$ and $g' \in \mathcal{F}' \Leftrightarrow$
$g \in \mathcal{F}_\mathcal{R}^f \wedge ar(g') = ar(g)$. c' represents the constructors above the outermost
applications of defined symbols. g' represents outermost applications of $g \in \mathcal{F}_\mathcal{R}^f$.

The (partial) function $\tau_\mathcal{B}^f$ transforms terms in $\mathcal{T}(\Sigma, V)$ into terms in $\mathcal{T}(\Sigma_\mathcal{B}^f, V)$:
$\tau_\mathcal{B}^f(x) = x$, $\tau_\mathcal{B}^f(g(\tilde{t})) = g'(\tilde{t})$ if $g \in \mathcal{F}_\mathcal{R}^f$. Finally, $\tau_\mathcal{B}^f(c(\tilde{t})) = c'(\tau_\mathcal{B}^f(\tilde{t}))$ if $c \in \mathcal{B}$.
$\tau_\mathcal{B}^f$ is only defined on a subset $ev_\mathcal{B}^f(\Sigma, V)$ of terms which is given as follows:

$V \subseteq ev_{\mathcal{B}}^f(\Sigma, V)$, $g(\tilde{t}) \in ev_{\mathcal{B}}^f(\Sigma, V)$ if $g \in \mathcal{F}_{\mathcal{R}}^f$ and $c(\tilde{t}) \in ev_{\mathcal{B}}^f(\Sigma, V)$ if $c \in \mathcal{B}$ and $t_1, \ldots, t_{ar(c)} \in ev_{\mathcal{B}}^f(\Sigma, V)$. If we do not require $V \subseteq ev_{\mathcal{B}}^f(\Sigma, V)$, then we are defining the set $gev_{\mathcal{B}}^f(\Sigma, V)$. Note that, if t can be evaluated to a value $\delta \in \mathcal{T}(\mathcal{B}, V)$ $(\delta \in \mathcal{T}(\mathcal{B}))$, then $t \in ev_{\mathcal{B}}^f(\Sigma, V)$ $(t \in gev_{\mathcal{B}}^f(\Sigma, V))$.

The transformation introduces rules to deal with our differentiation of symbols. Rules for outermost defined symbols $f' \in \mathcal{F}'$ introduce new outermost constructors $c' \in \mathcal{B}'$ and outermost defined symbols $f' \in \mathcal{F}'$. Rules for inner defined symbols $f \in \mathcal{F}$ are exactly the original ones of the TRS.

Definition 5.6 (Transformation V) *Let $\mathcal{R} = (\Sigma, R) = (\mathcal{C} \uplus \mathcal{F}, R)$ be a TRS, $f \in \mathcal{F}$ and $\mathcal{B} \subseteq \mathcal{C}$. Then $\mathsf{V}_{\mathcal{B}}^f(\mathcal{R}) = (\Sigma_{\mathcal{B}}^f \uplus \{\bar{\mathsf{T}}\}, R \cup S_{\mathcal{B}} \cup T_{\mathcal{B}})$, where:*

- *$\bar{\mathsf{T}}$ with $ar(\bar{\mathsf{T}}) = 1$ is a fresh, defined symbol whose rules perform the renaming of external constructors $c \in \mathcal{B}$ to constructors $c' \in \mathcal{B}'$ and outermost application of $g \in \mathcal{F}_{\mathcal{B}}^f$ to outermost applications of the corresponding $g' \in \mathcal{F}'$.*
- *$S_{\mathcal{B}} = \{g'(\tilde{l}) \to \kappa_{\mathcal{B}}^f(r) \mid g(\tilde{l}) \to r \in R \wedge g \in \mathcal{F}_{\mathcal{R}}^f \wedge r \in ev_{\mathcal{B}}^f(\Sigma, V)\}$, where $\kappa_{\mathcal{B}}^f(x) = \bar{\mathsf{T}}(x)$, $\kappa_{\mathcal{B}}^f(g(\tilde{t})) = g'(\tilde{t})$ if $g \in \mathcal{F}_{\mathcal{R}}^f$, and $\kappa_{\mathcal{B}}^f(c(\tilde{t})) = c'(\kappa_{\mathcal{B}}^f(\tilde{t}))$ if $c \in \mathcal{B}$.*
  $T_{\mathcal{B}} = \{\bar{\mathsf{T}}(c(x_1, \ldots, x_k)) \to c'(\bar{\mathsf{T}}(x_1), \ldots, \bar{\mathsf{T}}(x_k)) \mid c \in \mathcal{B}\} \cup \{\bar{\mathsf{T}}(g(x_1, \ldots, x_k)) \to g'(x_1, \ldots, x_k) \mid g \in \mathcal{F}_{\mathcal{R}}^f\}$

To simplify the notation, we usually write V instead of $\mathsf{V}_{\mathcal{B}}^f$, when f and $\mathcal{B}$ are clear from the context. The following examples illustrate our transformation.

Example 5.7 *If we take $f = \mathtt{sel}$ and $\mathcal{B} = \{0, \mathtt{s}\} \subseteq \{0, \mathtt{s}, [], ::\} = \mathcal{C}$, the additional rules for the evaluation of $t = \mathtt{sel}(Num, ListNum)$ are:*

$$\mathtt{dbl'(0)} \to \mathtt{0'} \qquad\qquad \mathtt{sel'(0, x :: y)} \to \mathtt{x}$$
$$\mathtt{dbl'(s(x))} \to \mathtt{s'(s'(dbl'(x)))} \quad \mathtt{sel'(s(x), y :: z)} \to \mathtt{sel'(x, z)}$$

$$\bar{\mathsf{T}}(0) \to \mathtt{0'} \qquad\qquad \bar{\mathsf{T}}(\mathtt{dbl(x)}) \to \mathtt{dbl'(x)}$$
$$\bar{\mathsf{T}}(\mathtt{s(x)}) \to \mathtt{s'}(\bar{\mathsf{T}}(x)) \qquad \bar{\mathsf{T}}(\mathtt{sel(x, y)}) \to \mathtt{sel'(x, y)}$$

Example 5.8 *If we take $f = \mathtt{indx}$ and $\mathcal{B} = \{0, \mathtt{s}, [], ::\} = \mathcal{C}$, the additional rules for the evaluation of $t = \mathtt{indx}(ListNum, ListNum)$ are:*

$$\mathtt{dbl'(0)} \to \mathtt{0'} \qquad\qquad \mathtt{indx'([], x)} \to \mathtt{[]'}$$
$$\mathtt{dbl'(s(x))} \to \mathtt{s'(s'(dbl'(x)))} \quad \mathtt{indx'(x :: y, z)} \to \mathtt{sel'(x, z)} ::' \mathtt{indx'(y, z)}$$
$$\mathtt{sel'(0, x :: y)} \to \mathtt{x}$$
$$\mathtt{sel'(s(x), y :: z)} \to \mathtt{sel'(x, z)}$$

$$\bar{\mathsf{T}}(0) \to \mathtt{0'} \qquad\qquad \bar{\mathsf{T}}(\mathtt{dbl(x)}) \to \mathtt{dbl'(x)}$$
$$\bar{\mathsf{T}}(\mathtt{s(x)}) \to \mathtt{s'}(\bar{\mathsf{T}}(x)) \qquad \bar{\mathsf{T}}(\mathtt{indx(x, y)}) \to \mathtt{indx'(x, y)}$$
$$\bar{\mathsf{T}}([]) \to \mathtt{[]'} \qquad\qquad \bar{\mathsf{T}}(\mathtt{sel(x, y)}) \to \mathtt{sel'(x, y)}$$
$$\bar{\mathsf{T}}(\mathtt{x :: y}) \to \bar{\mathsf{T}}(x) ::' \bar{\mathsf{T}}(y)$$

Given a Σ-map μ, we define the replacement map μ' which is used in the transformed TRS $\mathsf{V}(\mathcal{R})$ to obtain *complete* evaluations (leading to values) provided that μ is complete for head-evaluations. To obtain it we use a function.

Definition 5.9 *Let* $\mathcal{R} = (\Sigma, R) = (\mathcal{C} \uplus \mathcal{F}, R)$ *be a TRS,* $f \in \mathcal{F}$, *and* $\mathcal{B} \subseteq \mathcal{C}$. *Let* μ *be a* Σ-map. *The function* $rmap_{\mathcal{B}}^{f} : M_{\Sigma} \to M_{\Sigma_{\mathcal{B}}^{f} \uplus \{\bar{\mathsf{T}}\}}$ *is given by:* $rmap_{\mathcal{B}}^{f}(\mu) = \mu \sqcup \mu' \sqcup \mu_{\mathcal{B}'}$, *where* $\mu'(g') = \mu(g)$ *for all* $g \in \mathcal{F}_{\mathcal{R}}^{f}$ *and* $\mu'(g) = \emptyset$ *for any other symbol.* $\mu_{\mathcal{B}'}(c') = \mathbb{N}_{ar(c')}^{+}$ *for all* $c' \in \mathcal{B}'$, *and* $\mu_{\mathcal{B}'}(g) = \emptyset$ *for any other symbol.*

Note that, if $\mu' = rmap_{\mathcal{B}}^{f}(\mu)$, then $\mu'(\bar{\mathsf{T}}) = \emptyset$.

Example 5.10 *Let us consider the TRS* $\mathcal{R}$ *in Example 3.2. If* $f = \texttt{indx}$, $\mathcal{B} = \{0, \texttt{s}, [], ::\}$, *and* $\mu' = rmap_{\mathcal{B}}^{f}(\mu_{\mathcal{R}}^{com})$, *then* $\mu'(\texttt{s}) = \mu'(::) = \mu'(\texttt{from}) = \mu'(\bar{\mathsf{T}}) = \emptyset$, $\mu'(\texttt{s}') = \mu'(\texttt{dbl}) = \mu'(\texttt{dbl}') = \mu'(\texttt{dbls}) = \mu'(\texttt{indx}) = \mu'(\texttt{indx}') = \{1\}$, $\mu'(::') = \mu'(\texttt{sel}) = \mu'(\texttt{sel}') = \{1, 2\}$.

We have that μ-replacing redex occurrences of t are exactly the same than $rmap_{\mathcal{B}}^{f}(\mu)$-replacing redex occurrences (w.r.t. $V(\mathcal{R})$) of $\tau_{\mathcal{B}}^{f}(t)$. Thus, $rmap_{\mathcal{B}}^{f}(\mu)$ computes below an outermost defined symbol exactly in the same degree than μ does. Thus, we avoid useless computations.

Proposition 5.11 *Let* $\mathcal{R} = (\Sigma, R) = (\mathcal{F} \uplus \mathcal{C}, R)$ *be a TRS,* $f \in \mathcal{F}$ *and* $\mathcal{B} \subseteq \mathcal{C}$. *Let* $t = C[t_1, \dots, t_n] \in \mathcal{T}(\Sigma, V)$, $u_1, \dots, u_n \in O(t)$ *be such that* $C[x_1, \dots, x_n] \in \mathcal{T}(\mathcal{B}, V)$ *and* $root(t_i) \in \mathcal{F}_{\mathcal{R}}^{f}$, $t_i = t|_{u_i}$ *for* $1 \le i \le n$. *Let* μ *be a* Σ-map *and* $\mu' = rmap_{\mathcal{B}}^{f}(\mu)$. *Then,* $O_{V(\mathcal{R})}^{\mu'}(\tau_{\mathcal{B}}^{f}(t)) = \cup_{1 \le i \le n} u_i.O_{\mathcal{R}}^{\mu}(t_i)$.

If $\mathcal{R}$ is an orthogonal strongly replacing-independent TRS, computations in $V(\mathcal{R})$ using $rmap_{\mathcal{B}}^{f}(\mu_{\mathcal{R}}^{com})$ are needed as long as computations in $\mathcal{R}$ using $\mu_{\mathcal{R}}^{com}$ are.

To utilize $V(\mathcal{R})$ in evaluating a term $f(\tilde{t})$, we can directly evaluate $\bar{\mathsf{T}}(f(\tilde{t}))$. V preserves confluence of $\mathcal{R}$ (but not orthogonality) when evaluating a term $t = f(\tilde{t})$ for which V was defined. Thus, we can apply the rules careless: no undesired reduction sequence will arise.

Example 5.12 *Let us consider the TRS* $\mathcal{R}$ *in Example 3.2. Let* $f = \texttt{indx}$ *and* $\mathcal{B} = \{0, \texttt{s}, [], ::\}$. *Let* $\mu' = rmap_{\mathcal{B}}^{f}(\mu_{\mathcal{R}}^{com})$ *(see Example 5.10). By using* $V(\mathcal{R})$ *(see Example 5.8) and* μ', *we have:*

$$\bar{\mathsf{T}}(\texttt{indx}(\texttt{s}(0) :: [], \texttt{dbls}(\texttt{from}(0))))$$
$$\hookrightarrow \underline{\texttt{indx}'(\texttt{s}(0) :: [], \texttt{dbls}(\texttt{from}(0)))}$$
$$\hookrightarrow \texttt{sel}'(\texttt{s}(0), \texttt{dbls}(\texttt{from}(0))) ::' \underline{\texttt{indx}'([], \texttt{dbls}(\texttt{from}(0)))}$$
$$\hookrightarrow \underline{\texttt{sel}'(\texttt{s}(0), \texttt{dbls}(\texttt{from}(0)))} ::' []'$$
$$\hookrightarrow \texttt{sel}'(\texttt{s}(0), \texttt{dbls}(\underline{0 :: \texttt{from}(\texttt{s}(0)))})) ::' []' \qquad (*)$$
$$\hookrightarrow \texttt{sel}'(\texttt{s}(0), \underline{\texttt{dbl}(0) :: \texttt{dbls}(\texttt{from}(\texttt{s}(0)))})) ::' []' \qquad (**)$$
$$\hookrightarrow \underline{\texttt{sel}'(0, \texttt{dbls}(\texttt{from}(\texttt{s}(0))))} ::' []'$$
$$\hookrightarrow \texttt{sel}'(0, \texttt{dbls}(\underline{\texttt{s}(0) :: \texttt{from}(\texttt{s}(\texttt{s}(0))))})) ::' []' \qquad (*)$$
$$\hookrightarrow \texttt{sel}'(0, \underline{\texttt{dbl}(\texttt{s}(0)) :: \texttt{dbls}(\texttt{from}(\texttt{s}(\texttt{s}(0))))})) ::' []'$$
$$\hookrightarrow \underline{\bar{\mathsf{T}}(\texttt{dbl}(\texttt{s}(0)))} ::' []'$$
$$\hookrightarrow \underline{\texttt{dbl}'(\texttt{s}(0))} ::' []'$$
$$\hookrightarrow \texttt{s}'(\texttt{s}'(\underline{\texttt{dbl}'(0)})) ::' []'$$
$$\hookrightarrow \texttt{s}'(\texttt{s}'(\underline{0'})) ::' []'$$

Note that, from (∗) and (∗∗), no harmful or wasteful computations can be initiated. The cs-derivation does really behave as being essentially guided by $\mu_{\mathcal{R}}^{com}$ (Proposition 5.11). Thus, neededness of computations is preserved.

Theorem 5.13 (Correctness and completeness) *Let* $\mathcal{R} = (\Sigma, R) = (\mathcal{C} \uplus \mathcal{F}, R)$ *be a left-linear TRS. Let* $f \in \mathcal{F}, \mathcal{B} \subseteq \mathcal{C}, t = f(\tilde{t}) \in \mathcal{T}(\Sigma, V),$ *and* $\delta \in \mathcal{T}(\mathcal{B})$. *Let* $\mathcal{R}' = \mathsf{V}(\mathcal{R})$. *Let* μ *be a* Σ-*map such that* $\mu_{\mathcal{R}}^{com} \sqsubseteq \mu,$ *and* $\mu' = rmap_{\mathcal{B}}^f(\mu)$. *Then* $t \rightarrow_{\mathcal{R}}^* \delta$ *iff* $\tau_{\mathcal{B}}^f(t) \hookrightarrow_{\mathcal{R}'(\mu')}^* \tau_{\mathcal{B}}^f(\delta)$.

6 Conclusions and future work

We have introduced the class of *weakly replacing-independent* TRSs, a superclass of strongly replacing-independent TRSs which covers many usual functional programs. The transformation W yields a weakly replacing-independent TRS from an arbitrary TRS. S produces a strongly replacing-independent TRS from a weakly replacing-independent TRS. This allows us to eventually obtain benefit from the nice properties of strongly replacing-independent TRSs. In particular, neededness of computations when using orthogonal strongly replacing-independent TRSs. The transformations have been proven both correct and complete, but orthogonality is not preserved, in general.

We have also defined a program transformation V which allows us to raise the good properties of csr concerning head-evaluations to complete evaluations. In [3] we found a transformation to achieve lazy evaluations in a transformed TRS by using *eager* rewriting. This transformation is more complex than our V transformation. In the worst case for that transformation, it adds $3 + n \ r + n \ 2^l + 2 \ s$ rules to the original TRS $\mathcal{R} = (\Sigma, R)$ (see [3]), where n is the number of rules in R, s is the number of symbols in Σ, r is the maximal number of nonvariable nonreplacing occurrences in the rhs's of the TRS, and l is the maximal number of nonvariable nonreplacing occurrences[3] in the lhs's in R. The transformation V only introduces $n + s$ new rules in the worst case. This is because we obtain advantages in compiling to csr instead of rewriting as in [3]. However, a more detailed comparison of time complexity (to obtain the transformed TRS) would be required for a fair comparison.

Strongly replacing-independent TRSs have some links with the *path sequential* TRSs of Sekar et al. in [10]. The strict prefix $sprefix_t(u)$ of an occurrence u in a term t is the chain of symbols laying in occurrences $v < u$. Roughly speaking, a constructor-based TRS $\mathcal{R}$ is path sequential if, for all $l, l' \in L(\mathcal{R})$, and $u \in O(l) \cap O(l')$ such that $sprefix_l(u) = sprefix_{l'}(u)$, $u \in O_\Sigma(l)$ iff $u \in O_\Sigma(l')$. Path sequential TRSs are a particular class of strongly sequential TRSs [2, 10]. It is not difficult to see that constructor-based strongly replacing-independent TRSs are path sequential. However, computations with strongly replacing-independent TRSs are simpler. In [10], a method to transform a constructor-based strongly sequential TRS into a path sequential TRS is given. Our transformations W and

---

[3] There is an easy correspondence between the predicate Λ which is used in [3] to specify replacement restrictions and our replacement map μ. Nevertheless, *lazy rewriting* which is defined from Λ is quite different from csr.

S are simpler and they apply to any TRS. An interesting topic is using W and S to connect strongly sequential and strongly replacing-independent TRSs. Since our transformations do not preserve orthogonality, we are interested in giving conditions to ensure its preservation, or even to modify them to obtain this behavior. Nevertheless, after [11], orthogonality is not required to have strong sequentiality, hence normalizing strategies. Thus, the topic is also an interesting subject for further research, even for the current version of the transformations.

References

1. N. Dershowitz and J.P. Jouannaud. Rewrite Systems. In J. van Leeuwen, editor, *Handbook of Theoretical Computer Science*, volume B: Formal Models and Semantics, pages 243-320. Elsevier, Amsterdam and The MIT Press, Cambridge, MA, 1990.

2. G. Huet and J.J. Lévy. Computations in orthogonal term rewriting systems. In J.L. Lassez and G. Plotkin, editors, *Computational logic: essays in honour of J. Alan Robinson*, pages 395-414 and 415-443. The MIT Press, Cambridge, MA, 1991.

3. J.F.Th. Kamperman and H.R. Walters. Lazy Rewriting and Eager Machinery. In J. Hsiang, editor, *Proc. of 6th International Conference on Rewriting Techniques and Applications, RTA'95*, LNCS 914:147-162, Springer-Verlag, Berlin, 1995.

4. J.W. Klop. Term Rewriting Systems. In S. Abramsky, D.M. Gabbay and T.S.E. Maibaum. *Handbook of Logic in Computer Science*, volume 3, pages 1-116. Oxford University Press, 1992.

5. S. Lucas. Context-sensitive computations in functional and functional logic programs. *Journal of Functional and Logic Programming*, 1997, *to appear*.

6. S. Lucas. Fundamentals of context-sensitive rewriting. In M. Bartŏsek, J. Staudek and J. Wiedermann, editors, *Proc. of XXII Seminar on Current Trends in Theory and Practice of Informatics, SOFSEM'95*, LNCS 1012:405-412, Springer-Verlag, Berlin, 1995.

7. S. Lucas. Needed Reductions with Context-Sensitive Rewriting. In M. Hanus and K. Meinke, editors, *Proc. of 6th International Conference on Algebraic and Logic Programming, ALP'97*, LNCS to appear.

8. M.J. O'Donnell. Equational Logic as a Programming Language. The MIT Press, Cambridge, Massachusetts, 1985.

9. C. Reade. Elements of Functional Programming. Addison-Wesley Publishing Company, 1993.

10. R.C. Sekar, S. Pawagi and I.V. Ramakrishnan. Transforming Strongly Sequential Rewrite Systems with Constructors for Efficient Parallel Execution. In N. Dershowitz, editor, *Proc. of 3rd International Conference on Rewriting Techniques and Applications, RTA'89*, LNCS 355:404-418, Springer-Verlag, Berlin, 1989.

11. Y. Toyama. Strong Sequentiality of Left-Linear Overlapping Rewrite Systems. In *Proc. of 7th IEEE Symposium on Logic in Computer Science*, Santa Cruz, CA, pages 274-284, 1992.

12. H. Zantema. Termination of Context-Sensitive Rewriting. In H. Comon, editor, *Proc. of 8th International Conference on Rewriting Techniques and Applications, RTA'97*, LNCS 1232:172-186, Springer-Verlag, Berlin, 1997.

Inline expansion: *when* and *how*?

Manuel Serrano

Manuel.Serrano@cui.unige.ch
http://cuiwww.unige.ch/~serrano/

Centre Universitaire d'Informatique, University of Geneva
24, rue General-Dufour, CH-1211 Geneva 4, Switzerland

Abstract. Inline function expansion is an optimization that may improve program performance by removing calling sequences and enlarging the scope of other optimizations. Unfortunately it also has the drawback of enlarging programs. This might impair executable programs performance. In order to get rid of this annoying effect, we present, an easy to implement, inlining optimization that minimizes code size growth by combining a compile-time algorithm deciding *when* expansion should occur with different expansion frameworks describing *how* they should be performed. We present the experimental measures that have driven the design of inline function expansion. We conclude with measurements showing that our optimization succeeds in producing faster codes while avoiding code size increase.

Keywords: Compilation, Optimization, Inlining, Functional languages.

1 Introduction

Inline function expansion (henceforth "inlining") replaces a function invocation with a modified copy of the function body. Studies of compilation of functional or object-oriented languages show that inlining is one of the most valuable optimizations [1, 4]. Inlining can reduce execution time by removing calling sequences and by increasing the effectiveness of further optimizations:

- Function call sequences are expensive because they require many operations (context save/restore (i.e. memory fetches) and jumps). For small functions, the call sequence can be more expensive than the function body.
- Inlining can improve the effectiveness of the other compiler optimizations because inlined function bodies are modified copies. The formal function parameters are replaced with (or bound to) the actual parameters. Known properties of the actual parameters can then be used to optimize the duplicated function body. For instance, inlining helps the compilation of polymorphic functions because modified versions may become monomorphic. Finally, inlining helps the optimization of both the called and the calling function. Information about actual parameters can be used to improve the compilation of an inlined function body; information about the result of an inlined function can be used to improve the calling function.

As inlining duplicates function bodies, it has an obvious drawback: it increases the size of the program to be compiled and possibly the size of the produced object file. In this case, compilation becomes more time consuming (because after inlining the compiler must compile larger abstract syntax trees) and, in the worst case, execution can become slower. On modern architectures, best performance is obtained when a program fits into both the instruction and data caches. Clearly, smaller executables are more likely to fit into the instruction cache.

To prevent code explosion, inlining expansion cannot be applied to all function calls. The most difficult part of the inlining optimization is the design of a realistic inlining decision algorithm. This paper focuses on this issue. It presents a compile-time algorithm which allows fine control of code growth and does not require profiling information or user annotations.

Functional languages are characterized by extensive use of functions and particularly recursive functions. Both types of functions can be inlined within a unique framework but a refined expansion can be achieved for recursive functions. This paper presents an efficient framework for inlining recursive functions. Experimental measurements show this framework to be one of the keys to controlling code size growth. This is done by a combination of an inlining decision algorithm (deciding *when* to perform the expansions) and *ad-hoc* expansion frameworks (describing *how* to perform the expansions).

Inlining may impair code production because of los of high level informations. For instance, Cooper *et al.* report in [5] that inlining discards aliasing informations in Fortran programs, so that compilers are unable to avoid interlock during executions. Davison and Holler show in [6] that inlining for C may increase register save and restore operations because of C compilers artifacts. On our part, we have never noticed decreases of performance when activating inlining optimization.

This paper is organized as follows: section 2 presents a study of previous algorithms and schemes. Section 3 presents our new algorithm. Section 4 presents the different inlining frameworks. Section 5 reports on the impact of the inlining expansion optimization in Bigloo, our Scheme compiler.

2 Inline expansion: *when*

2.1 Previous approaches

This section contains a presentation of the main inlining decision rules and algorithms previously published. The remarks made in this section are the basis for the design of the algorithm presented in section 3.

User inlining indications Some systems (e.g. gcc) or language definitions (e.g. C++) allow programs to contain inlining annotations.

Rule 1 (inlining annotation) *Let d be the definition of a function f; a call to f is inlined if d has an "inline" annotation.*

Inlining annotations are useful to implement some parts of the source language (for instance, in Bigloo [12], our *Scheme & ML* compiler, inlining annotations are used intensively in the libraries for accessing and mutating primitives like `car`, `cdr`, `vector-ref` or `vector-set!`) but cannot replace automatic inlining decisions. By contrast an automatic inlining decision algorithm can choose to inline a function at a call site, but also not to do it at another call site. User inlining annotations are attached to function definitions and, as a consequence, are not call site dependent. As a result, misplaced inlining annotations can lead to code size explosion. Furthermore, inlining annotations require the programmer to have a fair understanding of the compiler strategy in order to be able to place annotations judiciously.

Size-based criteria Simpler inlining decision algorithms [14, 4] are based on the body size of called functions:

Rule 2 (body-size) *Let $\mathcal{K}$ be a constant threshold, f a function, s the body size of f; a call to f is inlined if s is less than $\mathcal{K}$.*

Rule 2 succeeds in limiting the code size growth without recursive function definitions because any function call of a program cannot be replaced by an expression bigger than $\mathcal{K}$. Hence, inlining expansion of a program containing c calls can increase the code size by at most $c \times \mathcal{K}$. In order to prevent infinite loops when inlining recursive functions, rule 2 has to be extended:

Rule 3 (body-size & nested-call) *Let f be a function, k a call to f; k is inlined if f satisfies rule 2 and if k is not included in the body of f.*

This rule helps preventing code explosion and is fairly easy to implement, but it is very restrictive. It may prevent inlining of functions which could have been inlined without code growth. For example, let's study the following Scheme definition:

```
(define (plus x₁ x₂ x₃ ... xₙ) (+ x₁ x₂ x₃ ... xₙ))
```

Let n be larger than the constant threshold $\mathcal{K}$. Therefore, this `plus` function cannot be inlined because it is said to be too large (its body size is greater than $\mathcal{K}$). However, inlining calls to `plus` does not increase the compiled code size because the body size of `plus` is not greater than any call to `plus`. From this remark, Appel presents in [1] an improvement of Rule 3:

Rule 4 (body-size vs call-size) *If the body of a function f is smaller than the overhead required for a function call, then f may be inlined without increasing the program size.*

Savings estimates The inlining of a call to a function f replaces the formal parameters by the actual parameters and some of them may have special properties (constants, for instance). Other optimizations such as *constant folding* may be able to shrink the modified version of the body of f. Since Rule 4 neglects this, we define:

Rule 5 (saving estimations) *If the body of f, after inlining, will shrink by further optimizations to become smaller than the overhead required for a function call, then the call to f may be inlined.*

Two implementations of this approach have been described. The first one, due to Appel [1], estimates the savings of the other optimizations without applying them. The second, due to Dean and Chambers [7], uses an *inline-trial* scheme: rather than just estimating the savings of other optimizations, these are applied and the savings are measured by inspecting the result of the compilation. To limit the number of required compilations, each inlining decision is stored in a persistent database. Before launching a full compilation of a call site function, the inlining decision algorithm scans its database to find a similar call (a call to the same function with the same kind of parameters). Rule 5 has, however, two important drawbacks:

- The two techniques estimate the impact of the other optimizations on the body of a called function f in the context of a specific call site included in a function g. Neither computes the savings of applying the other compiler optimizations on the body of g, due to the added expense. However, after inlining, additional information may be known about a function result. For instance, in the following Scheme program:

```
1: (define (inc i x)          6:    ...
2:     (if (fixnum? i)         7:        (let ((y (inc 1 x)))
3:         (fixnum+ i x)       8:            (if (fixnum? y)
4:         (flonum+ i x)))     9:                ...)))
5: (define (foo x)
```

  Inlining the call to inc in foo (line 7) allows better compilation of the body of inc because, since i is bound to the fixnum constant 1, the test (fixnum? i) (line 2) can be removed. After inlining and test reduction, it appears that y can only be bound to a fixnum. This information can be used to improve the compilation of foo (by removing, for instance, the line 8 test).
- The saving estimations can only be computed for local optimizations. Global optimizations (such as *inter-procedural register allocations* or *control flow analysis*) require compilation of the whole program and their results are mostly unpredictable. Because these optimizations are often slow, it is, in practice, impossible to apply them each time a function could be inlined.

Because saving estimations are computed on an overly restricted set of optimizations, we think rule 5 is not highly efficient. It fails to measure the real impact of inlining in further optimizations.

Profile-based decision Some inlining decision algorithms use profile information. Programs are run with various sets of input data and statistics are gathered. Inlining decisions are taken based on these statistics. Two papers present such works [11, 8]. They are based on the same rule that can be merged with rule 2 to prevent excessive code growth:

Rule 6 (profiling statistics) *When profiling statistics show that the execution time of an invocation of a function f is longer than the execution time of the evaluation of the body of f, f could be inlined.*

We do not think profile-based decision algorithms are practical because they require too much help from the programmer. A judicious set of executions must be designed and many compilations are needed.

3 The inlining decision algorithm

From the remarks of Section 2.1, we have designed our own inlining decision algorithm.

3.1 The input language

The input language of our algorithm is very simple. It can be seen as a small Scheme [9] language with no higher order functions. It is described in the grammar below:

Syntactic categories

v	$\in$ VarId	(Variables identifier)
f	$\in$ FunId	(Functions identifier)
Λ	$\in$ Exp	(Expressions)
k	$\in$ Cnst	(Constant values)
Π	$\in$ Prgm	(Program)
Γ	$\in$ Def	(Definition)

$$\Lambda ::= k$$
$$| \; v$$
$$| \; (\text{let } ((v \; \Lambda) \ldots) \; \Lambda)$$
$$| \; (\text{set! } v \; \Lambda)$$
$$| \; (\text{labels } ((f \; (v \ldots v) \; \Lambda) \ldots) \; \Lambda)$$
$$| \; (\text{if } \Lambda \; \Lambda \; \Lambda)$$
$$| \; (\text{begin } \Lambda \ldots \Lambda)$$
$$| \; (f \; \Lambda \ldots \Lambda)$$
$$| \; (+ \; \Lambda \; \Lambda)$$

Concrete syntax

$$\Pi ::= \quad \Gamma \ldots \Gamma \; \Lambda$$
$$\Gamma ::= \quad (\text{define } (f \; v \ldots v) \; \Lambda)$$

A program is composed of several global function definitions and of one expression used to initiate computations. Local recursive functions are introduced by the `labels` special form. Other constructions are regular Scheme constructions.

3.2 Principle of the algorithm

Our algorithm uses static information. The decision to expand a call site depends on the size of the called function, the size of the call (i.e. the number of actual parameters) and the place where the call is located. Our decision algorithm does not require user annotation or profiling statistics. Inspired by [1, page 92] the idea of the algorithm is to allow code growth by a certain factor for each call site of the program. When a call is inlined, the algorithm is recursively invoked on the body result of the substitution. The deeper the recursion becomes, the smaller the factor is.

We illustrate the algorithm's behavior on the following example:

```
1: (define (inc-fx x) (+ x 1))          6:        (inc-fx x)
2: (define (inc-fl x)                    7:        (inc-fl x)))
3:    (inc-fx (inexact->exact x)))       8: (define (foo x) (inc x))
4: (define (inc x)                       9: (foo 4)
5:    (if (fixnum? x)
```

Suppose that at recursion depth zero we permit call sites to become 4 times larger and we make each recursive call to the inlining algorithm divide this multiplicative factor by 2 (later on, we will study the impact of the choice of the regression function). The line 8 call to inc has a size of 2 (1 for the called function plus 1 for the formal argument). The body size of inc is 7 (1 for the conditional, 2 for the test and 2 for each branch of the conditional). Hence, the call is expanded. Before expanding the body of inc in line 8, the inlining process is launched on the body of the function with a new multiplicative factor of 2 (half the initial factor of 4). The inlining process reaches line 6, the call to inc-fx. The size of the body of this function is 3 (1 for the + operator call and 1 for each actual argument), the call size is 2 hence this call is expanded. No further inlining can be performed on the body of inc-fx because + is a primitive operator. The inlining process then reaches the call of line 7. The call to inc-fl is inlined, the multiplicative factor is set to 1 and the inner call to inc-fx (line 3) is reached. This call cannot be expanded because the amount of code growth is less than the body of inc-fx. After the inlining process completes, the resulting code is:

```
1: (define (inc-fx x) (+ x 1))          4:        (+ x 1)
2: (define (foo x)                       5:        (inc-fx (inexact->exact x))))
3:    (if (fixnum? x)                     6: (foo 4)
```

Dead functions have been removed (inc and inc-fl) and, as one can notice, the total size of the program is now smaller *after* inline expansion. Experimental results (see section 5) show that this phenomenon is frequent: in many situations, our inline expansion reduces the resulting code size.

3.3   The algorithm

The main part of the algorithm is a graph traversal of the abstract syntax tree. All function definitions are scanned in a random order (the scanning order has no impact on the result of the optimization). The inlining process, $\mathcal{I}_{ast}$ (algorithm 3.1), takes three arguments: a multiplicative factor (k), a set of functions ($\mathcal{S}$) and an abstract syntax tree (Λ). It returns new abstract syntax trees.

Function calls satisfying the $\mathcal{I}_{app?}$ predicate are inlined using the $\mathcal{I}_{app}$ function (algorithm 3.2). As one can notice, the inlining decision is context dependent. A given function can be inlined on one call site and left unexpanded on another site. A function call is inlined if its code size growth factor is strictly

```
K:   an external user parameter

I( Π )=
   ∀f∈Π↓definitions
      f↓body ← Iast( K, ∅, f↓body )

Iast( k, S, Λ )=
   case Λ
     [ k ]:
        Λ
     [ v ]:
        Λ
     [ (let ((v0 Λ0) ...) Λ) ]:
        let Λ'0=Iast( k, S, Λ0 ), ...
           [ (let ((v0 Λ'0) ...) Iast( k, S, Λ )) ]
     [ (set! v Λ) ]:
        [ (set! v Iast( k, S, Λ )) ]
        ⋮
     [ (f a0 ...) ]:
        let a'0=Iast( k, S, a0 ), ...
           Iapp( k, S, f, a'0, ... )
   end
```

Algorithm 3.1: The abstract syntax tree walk

smaller than the value of k. This criteria is strong enough to avoid infinite recursions. This current version of $I_{app?}$ does not make use of the S argument. Later versions (Section 4.2) will. The expansion of a call to a function f is computed by I_{let} (algorithm 3.2). It replaces the call by a new version of the body of f. This new version is a copy of the original body, α-converted and recursively inlined. To recursively enter the inlining process, a new factor is computed. Section 5.1 will study the impact of the Dec function on the inlining process.

```
Iapp( k, S, f, Λ0, ..., Λn )=
   if Iapp?( k, S, f, n + 1 )
      then Ilet( k, S, f, Λ0, ..., Λn )
      else [ (f Λ0 ... Λn) ]

Iapp?( k, S, f, csize )=
   function-size( f↓body ) < k * csize

Ilet( k, S, f, Λ0, ... )=
   let x0=f↓formals0, ...
      [ (let ((x0 Λ0) ...) Iast( Dec( k ), {f}∪S, f↓body )) ]
```

Algorithm 3.2: The let-inline expansion

3.4 Inlining in presence of higher-order functions

Inlining a function call requires knowing which function is called in order to access its body. In the presence of higher-order functions, the compiler sometimes does not know which function is invoked. The algorithm presented above can be extended to accept higher-order functions by adding the straightforward rule that calls to unknown functions are not candidates to expansion. In order to enlarge the set of the possibly inlined function calls of higher order languages, Jagannathan and Wright have proposed in [10] to apply a control flow analysis before computing the inline expansion. For each call site of a program, the control flow analysis is used to determine the set of possibly invoked functions. When this set is reduced to one element the called function can be inlined. This work is complementary to the work presented here. Jagannathan and Wright enlarge the set of inlining candidates, while we propose an algorithm to select which calls to inline from this set.

4 Inline expansion: *how*

Section 2 described the algorithm to decide *when* a function call should be inlined. In this section we show *how* a functional call should be inlined. Functions are divided into two classes: *non-recursive* and *recursive* ones.

4.1 Inlining of non-recursive functions (let-inlining)

The inlining of a call to a non-recursive function has been shown in algorithm 3.2. Non-recursive function inlining is a simple β-reduction: it binds formal parameters to actual parameters and copies the body of the called function.

4.2 Inlining of recursive functions (labels-inlining)

Self-recursive functions can be inlined using the transformation $\mathcal{I}_{let}$ but a more valuable transformation can be applied: rather than unfolding recursive calls to a certain depth, local recursive definitions are created for the inlined function (following the scheme presented in [13]). When inlining a recursive function f, $\mathcal{I}_{labels}$ (algorithm 4.1) creates a local definition and replaces the original target of the call with a call to the newly created one. It is more valuable to introduce local functions than unrolling some function calls because the constant propagation and other local optimizations are no longer limited to the depth of the unrolling; they are applied to the whole body of the inlined function. The previous definitions of functions $\mathcal{I}_{app}$ and $\mathcal{I}_{app?}$ have to be modified. Recursive calls should not be further unfolded. This is avoided by making use of the $\mathcal{S}$ argument in the $\mathcal{I}_{app?}$ function.

We show the benefit of the $\mathcal{I}_{labels}$ on the following Scheme example:

```
(define (map f 1) (if (null? 1) '() (cons (f (car 1)) (map f (cdr 1)))))
(define (succ x) (+ x 1))
(define (map-succ 1) (map succ 1))
```

```
I_app( k, S, f, Λ_0, ..., Λ_n )=
  if I_app?( k, S, f, n + 1 )
    then if f is a self recursive function ?
           then I_labels( k, S, f, Λ_0, ..., Λ_n )
           else I_let( k, S, f, Λ_0, ..., Λ_n )
    else [[ (f Λ_0 ... Λ_n) ]]

I_app?( k, S, f, csize )=
  if f∈S
    then false
    else function-size( f↓_body ) < k * csize

I_labels( k, S, f, Λ_0, ..., Λ_n )=
  let λ'=I_ast( Dec( k ), {f}∪S, f↓_body ),
  let x_0=f↓_formals_0, ...
    [[ (labels ((f (x_0 ...) λ')) (f Λ_0 ... Λ_n)) ]]
```

Algorithm 4.1: The labels-inline expansion

When inlining **map** into **map-succ**, the compiler detects that **map** is self-recursive, so it inlines it using a local definition:

```
(define (map-succ l)
  (labels ((map (f l)
    (if (null? l) '() (cons (f (car l)) (map f (cdr l)))))))
  (map succ l)))
```

A further pass of the compiler states that the formal parameter **f** is a loop invariant, so **f** is replaced with its actual value **succ**. Then, **succ** is open-coded and we finally get the equivalent definition:

```
(define (map-succ l)
  (labels ((map (l)
    (if (null? l) '() (cons (+ 1 (car l)) (map (cdr l)))))))
  (map l)))
```

Thanks to the labels-inline expansion and to constant propagation, closure allocations are avoided and computed calls are turned into direct calls. The whole transformation speeds up the resulting code and it may reduce the resulting code size because the code for allocating closures is no longer needed.

4.3 Inlining as loop unrolling (unroll-inlining)

We have experimented an *ad-hoc* inlining scheme for loops. Here we consider a loop to be any recursive function with one single inner recursive call. When a loop is to be inlined, a local recursive function is created (according to the I_{labels} transformation) followed by a traditional unrolling. This new expansion scheme requires the slight modifications to I_{app} and $I_{app?}$ given in algorithm 4.2. The unrolling is actually a simple mix between the previous inlining frameworks. The transformation I_{labels} is applied once, followed by as many I_{let} transformations as the multiplicative factor k allows. We illustrate the unroll-inline transformation on the preceding `map-succ` example:

```
 1: (define (map-succ 1)           6:         (if (null? l2) '()
 2:  (labels ((map (l1)            7:          (cons (+ 1 (car l2))
 3:    (if (null? l1) '()          8:           (map (cdr l2))
 4:     (cons (+ 1 (car l1))       9:           ))))))
 5:      (let ((l2 (cdr l1)))     10:    (map 1)))
```

$$\mathcal{I}_{app}(\ k,\ \mathcal{S},\ f,\ \Lambda_0,\ ...,\ \Lambda_n\ )=$$
$$\text{if } \mathcal{I}_{app?}(\ k,\ \mathcal{S},\ f,\ n+1\ )$$
$$\qquad \textbf{then if } f \text{ is a self recursive function ? and } f \notin \mathcal{S}$$
$$\qquad\qquad \textbf{then } \mathcal{I}_{labels}(\ k,\ \mathcal{S},\ f,\ \Lambda_0,\ ...,\ \Lambda_n\ )$$
$$\qquad\qquad \textbf{else } \mathcal{I}_{let}(\ k,\ \mathcal{S},\ f,\ \Lambda_0,\ ...,\ \Lambda_n\ )$$
$$\qquad \textbf{else } [\![\ (f\ \Lambda_0\ ...\ \Lambda_n)\ ]\!]$$

$$\mathcal{I}_{app?}(\ k,\ \mathcal{S},\ f,\ csize\ )=$$
$$\textit{function-size}(\ f{\downarrow}_{body}\ ) < k * csize$$

Algorithm 4.2: The unroll-inline expansion

4.4 Related work

Little attention has been formerly given to *how* the expansion should be performed. Previous works have considered it as a straightforward β-reduction. Inlining of recursive functions has been mainly addressed into three previous papers:

- In the paper [3] H. Baker focuses on giving a semantics to the inlining of recursive functions. Inlining of recursive functions is thought as a loop unrolling by unfolding calls until a user determined depth level. The paper neither studies the impact of this inlining framework on run time performance nor attempts to present optimized transformations. We even think that the proposed transformations would probably slow down executions (because they introduce higher order functions which are difficult to implement efficiently).

- We have made a previous presentation of the labels-inline transformation in [13]. It does not focus on the inlining optimization and it merely presents the transformation without studying its impact.

- The labels-inline transformation has been used by A. Appel in [2]. His approach differs a little bit from our because Appel introduces header around every loop independently of the inlining optimization. We think this has two drawbacks. First, un-inlined loops have to be cleaned up (that is, headers have to be removed) otherwise there is an extra call overhead. More importantly, introducing header make functions abstract syntax tree bigger. Since the inlining algorithm uses functions size to decide to inline a call, loops with header introduced are less likely to be inlined.

5 Experimental results

For experimental purposes, we used ten different Scheme programs, written by different authors, using various programming styles. Experiments have been conducted on a DEC ALPHA 3000/400, running DEC OSF/1 V4.0 with 64 Megabytes of memory.

programs	nb lines	author	description
Bague	104	P. Weis	Baguenodier game.
Queens	132	L. Augustsson	Queens resolution.
Confo	596	M. Feeley	Lattice management.
Boyer	640	R. Gabriel	Boyer completion.
Peval	643	M. Feeley	Partial evaluator.
Earley	672	M. Feeley	Earley parser.
Matrix	753	-	Matrix computation.
Pp	757	M. Serrano	Lisp pretty-printer.
Maze	879	O. Shivers	Maze game escape.
Nucleic	3547	M. Feeley	Molecular placement.

In order to be as architecture-independent as possible, we have measured duration in both user plus system cpu time and number of cpu cycles (using the **pixie** tool). For all our measures, even when the multiplicative factor is set to 0, primitive operators (such as + or `car`) are still inlined.

5.1 Selecting the $\mathcal{D}ec$ regression function

We have studied the impact of the $\mathcal{D}ec$ function, first used in algorithm 3.2. We have experimented with three kind of regression functions: decrementations: $\lambda_{-\mathcal{N}}=(\lambda\ (k)\ (-\ k\ \mathcal{N}))$, divisions: $\lambda_{/\mathcal{N}}=(\lambda\ (k)\ (/\ k\ \mathcal{N}))$ and two *step* functions: $\lambda_{=0}=(\lambda\ (k)\ 0)$ and $\lambda_{=k_{init}/\mathcal{N}}=(\lambda\ (k)\ (if\ (=\ k\ k_{init})\ (/\ k\ \mathcal{N})\ 0))$.

For each of these functions, we have measured the code size growth and the speed improvement. Since measurement showed that varying $\mathcal{N}$ has a small impact, we just present measurements where $\mathcal{N}$ has been set to two.

We present results for only three programs, **Queens**, **Peval** and **Conform** because they are representative of the whole 10 programs. The X axis represents the initial value of the k multiplicative factor. The Y axis of the upper graphics represents the normalized object file size. The Y axis of the lower graphics represents the normalized durations (cpu cycles).

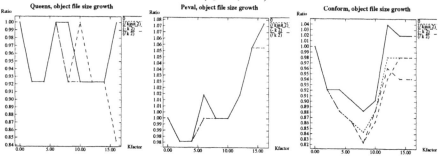

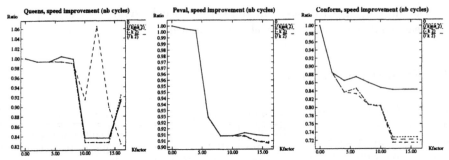

Two remarks can be made on these measurements:

- The regression function $\lambda_{=0}$ produces less efficient executables (see for instance **Conform**) than others regression functions. This proves that a recursive inlining algorithm (an algorithm trying to inline the result of an inlined call) gives better results that a non recursive one.
- $\lambda_{=k_{init}/\mathcal{N}}$, $\lambda_{-\mathcal{N}}$ and $\lambda_{/\mathcal{N}}$ lead to about the same results. This demonstrates that only the very first recursive steps of the inlining are important. Functions like $\lambda_{-\mathcal{N}}$ or $\lambda_{/\mathcal{N}}$ have the drawback to authorize large code size expansion (about $2^{\frac{1}{\mathcal{N}}*\log_2 k^2}$ in the worst case for $\lambda_{/\mathcal{N}}$). *Step* functions like $\lambda_{=k_{init}/\mathcal{N}}$ are much more restrictive ($k^2/\mathcal{N}$ in the worst case). Choosing *step* functions leads to small and efficient compiled programs.

5.2 The general measurements

The second step of our experiment has been to study the impact of the let-inline, labels-inline and unroll-inline expansions. The results summarized in Figure 1 show the speedups and the code size increases for the 10 programs in each of the 3 frameworks. For each of them we have computed a speedup, measured as the ratio of the speed of the inlined divided by the speed of the same program with inlining disabled, and a size, measured as the ratio of the size of the inlined program divided by the size of the original program. The experiment was performed for all values of $\mathcal{N}$ (see Section 5.1 for the definition of $\mathcal{N}$) between 1 and 15. The Figure shows the results of the best speedup for each program and framework. Furthermore, we computed speedups and size increases with respect to number of cycles and actual time elapsed. Thus, in Figure 1, *cycle*/speed refer to the ratio of cycles and *cycle*/size refers to the ratio of sizes, while *sys+cpu*/speed refers to the ratio of times and *sys+cpu*/size refers to the ratio of size. Note that for a given program and framework, the value of $\mathcal{N}$ giving the best speedup is sometimes different if we measure it in cycles or elapsed time, thus the size increases may also differ.

Labels-inlining Labels-inlining is an important issue in order to minimize object file size. In the worst case, labels-inlining behaves as let-inlining, enlarging object file size, but in general, it succeeds in limiting or even avoiding expansions. This good behavior does not impact on speedup ratios.

Programs	let				labels				unroll			
	cycle		sys+cpu		cycle		sys+cpu		cycle		sys+cpu	
	speed	size	speed	size	speed	size	speed	size	speed	size	speed	size
bague	0.67	1.18	0.66	1.18	0.69	1.18	0.66	1.18	0.69	1.18	0.66	1.18
queens	0.86	1.53	0.89	1.53	0.82	0.92	0.85	0.92	0.81	0.92	0.89	0.92
conform	0.72	1.21	0.83	1.17	0.72	0.96	0.76	0.96	0.72	0.98	0.76	0.98
boyer	0.89	1.00	1.00	1.00	0.89	0.90	0.89	0.90	0.89	0.90	0.89	0.90
peval	0.98	1.05	1.00	1.00	0.90	1.05	0.90	1.00	0.96	1.13	0.94	1.03
earley	0.95	1.00	0.97	1.00	0.95	1.00	0.97	1.00	0.95	1.00	0.97	1.00
matrix	0.93	1.11	0.88	1.11	0.94	0.88	0.92	0.91	0.94	0.94	0.90	0.94
pp	0.94	1.22	0.90	1.11	0.95	1.10	0.92	1.07	0.95	1.14	0.92	1.09
maze	0.71	0.84	0.73	0.84	0.70	0.80	0.73	0.84	0.71	0.80	0.73	0.80
nucleic	0.99	1.15	0.95	1.15	0.98	1.15	0.98	1.10	0.98	1.15	1.00	1.00
Average	0.86	1.13	0.88	1.11	0.85	0.99	0.86	0.99	0.86	1.01	0.87	0.98

Fig. 1. Best speedups

Except for a very few programs, let-inlining does not succeed in producing faster (less cpu cycle consuming) executables than labels-inlining but it enlarges too much the object file size. For instance, the let-inlining aborts on **Earley** and **Matrix** for very high initial values of the multiplicative factor k because the abstract syntax trees of these programs become excessively large.

Unroll-inlining Few improvements come from unroll-inlining. Only **Boyer** and **Maze** are improved when this framework is used. One explanation for this result is that unroll-inlining is barely applied because most loops have only one argument (after removal of invariant parameters) and thus they can then be inlined only if their body is very small.

This is a slightly disappointing result but even the benefits of classical loop unrolling optimizations are not well established. For instance, experience with gcc in [14] is that "[general loop unrolling] usually makes programs run more slowly". On modern architectures performing dynamic instruction scheduling, loop unrolling that increases the number of tests can severely slow down execution. This was partially shown by the measures of the labels-inlining impact that showed that it is more valuable to specialize a loop rather than to unfold outer loop calls.

5.3 Related work

The inlining impact depends on the cost of function calls and thus is highly architecture-dependent. Hence, comparison with previous measures reported on inlining speedup, made on different architectures, is difficult. Furthermore, we think that it does not make sense to compare the inlining impact for very different languages. For instance, since a typical C program does not make extensive use of small functions such as a Scheme and ML program, an inlining optimizer for C should probably not adopt a framework tuned for a functional language. We limit the present comparison to a few publications.

- C. Chambers shows that inlining reduces the object file size produced by the Self compiler [4] by a very large factor (in the best case, inlining reduces the object file size from a factor of 4) while making programs run much faster (between 4 to 55 times faster). The explanation is found in [4, section B.3.1]: "In SELF, the compiler uses inlining mostly for optimizing user-defined control structures and variable accesses, where the resulting inlined control flow graph is usually much smaller than the original un-inlined graph. These sorts of inlined constructs are already 'inlined' in the traditional language environment. Inlining of larger 'user-level' methods or procedures does usually increase compile time and compiled code space as has been observed in traditional environments...".
- We share with Jagannathan and Wright [10] three test programs: **Maze**, **Boyer** and **Matrix**. For all of them, we have measured the same speed improvement but our techniques do not increase the object file size while that of Jagannathan and Wright enlarges it by 20%.
- In [2] Appel reports on an average speedup of 5% for the labels-inlining. Our measures do not allow us to conclude in a same way. We have found that the main effect of the labels-inlining is to reduce the size of the inlined programs. As suggested by Appel his improvement may come from the reduction of the closure allocations. Less closures are allocated because in a CPS style, labels-inlining and its hoisting of loop invariant arguments may avoid the construction of some continuations.

Conclusion

We have shown in this paper that the combination of a decision algorithm with different expansion frameworks makes the inline expansion optimization more valuable. It improves run time performances (about 15% on average) while avoiding its traditional drawback, the object code size growth. The decision-making algorithm we have presented is based on static compile time informations and does not require user annotations or profiling data. The expansion framework allows inlining of recursive functions. Both are easy to implement. In Bigloo, our Scheme compiler, the decision-making algorithm and the different expansion strategies constitute less than 4% of the whole source code.

Acknowledgments

Many thanks to Christian Queinnec, Xavier Leroy, Jeremy Dion, Marc Feeley, Jan Vitek and Laurent Dami for their helpful feedbacks on this work.

References

1. A. Appel. **Compiling with continuations**. Cambridge University Press, 1992.
2. A. Appel. **Loop Headers in λ-calculus or CPS**. *Lisp and Symbolic Computation*, 7:337–343, December 1994.
3. H. Baker. **Inlining Semantics for Subroutines which are recursive**. *ACM Sigplan Notices*, 27(12):39–46, December 1992.
4. C. Chambers. **The Design and Implementation of the SELF Compiler, an Optimizing Compiler for Object-Oriented Programming Languages**. Technical report stan-cs-92-1240, Stanford University, Departement of Computer Science, March 1992.
5. K. Cooper, M. Hall, and L. Torczon. **Unexpected Side Effects of Inline Substitution: A Case Study**. *ACM Letters on Programming Languages and Systems*, 1(1):22–31, 1992.
6. J. Davidson and A. Holler. **Subprogram Inlining: A Study of its Effects on Program Execution Time**. *IEEE Transactions on Software Engineering*, 18(2):89–101, February 1992.
7. J. Dean and C. Chambers. **Towards Better Inlining Decisions Using Inlining Trials**. In *Conference on Lisp and Functional Programming*, pages 273–282, Orlando, Florida, USA, June 1994.
8. W. Hwu and P. Chang. **Inline Function Expansion for Compiling C Programs**. In *Conference on Programming Language Design and Implementation*, Portland, Oregon, USA, June 1989. ACM.
9. IEEE Std 1178-1990. **IEEE Standard for the Scheme Programming Language**. Institute of Electrical and Electronic Engineers, Inc., New York, NY, 1991.
10. S. Jagannathan and A. Wright. **Flow-directed Inlining**. In *Conference on Programming Language Design and Implementation*, Philadelphia, Penn, USA, May 1996.
11. R.W. Scheifler. **An Analysis of Inline Substitution for a Structured Programming Language**. *CACM*, 20(9):647–654, September 1977.
12. M. Serrano. **Bigloo user's manual**. RT 0169, INRIA-Rocquencourt, France, December 1994.
13. M. Serrano and P. Weis. **$1 + 1 = 1$: an optimizing Caml compiler**. In *ACM SIGPLAN Workshop on ML and its Applications*, pages 101–111, Orlando (Florida, USA), June 1994. ACM SIGPLAN, INRIA RR 2265.
14. R. Stallman. **Using and Porting GNU CC**. for version 2.7.2 ISBN 1-882114-66-3, Free Software Foundation, Inc., 59 Temple Place - Suite 330, Boston, MA 02111-1307, USA, November 1995.

Higher-Order Value Flow Graphs

Christian Mossin

DIKU, University of Copenhagen[**]

Abstract. The concepts of value- and control-flow graphs are important for program analysis of imperative programs. An imperative value flow graph can be constructed by a single pass over the program text. No similar concepts exist for higher-order languages: we propose a method for constructing value flow graphs for typed higher-order functional languages. A higher-order value flow graph is constructed by a single pass over an explicitly typed program. By using standard methods, single source and single use value flow problems can be answered in linear time and all sources-all uses can be answered in quadratic time (in the size of the flow graph, which is equivalent to the size of the explicitly typed program). On simply typed programs, the precision of the resulting analysis is equivalent to closure analysis [10,11,8]. In practice, it is a reasonable assumption that typed programs are only bigger than their untyped equivalent by a constant factor, hence this is an asymptotic improvement over previous algorithms.
We extend the analysis to handle polymorphism, sum types and recursive types. As a consequence, the analysis can handle (explicit) dynamically typed programs. The analysis is polyvariant for polymorphic definitions.

Keywords: program analysis, type system, efficiency, polymorphism, recursive types, polyvariance.

1 Introduction

Flow analysis of a program aims at approximating at compile-time the flow of values during execution of the program. This includes relating definitions and uses of first-order values (eg. which booleans can be consumed by a given conditional) but also flow of data-structures and higher-order values (eg. which function-closures can be applied at a given application). Values are abstracted by a label of the occurrence of the value — i.e. the label of first-order values uniquely identifies the occurrence of the value, while data-structures and closures are abstracted by the label of the constructor resp. lambda.

Flow information is directly useful for program transformations such as constant propagation or firstification, and, by interpreting the value flow in an appropriate domain, for many other program analyses. Furthermore, information about higher-order value flow can allow first-order program analysis techniques to be applicable to higher-order languages.

[**] Universitetsparken 1, DK-2100 Copenhagen Ø, Denmark, e-mail: mossin@diku.dk

We present a flow analysis for typed, higher-order functional languages. The analysis constructs a value flow graph which is linear in the size of the explicitly typed program. Single queries (single-source or single-sink data-flow) can be performed on this graph by standard reachability algorithms in linear time and, similarly, full flow information can be obtained in quadratic time.

On simply typed programs our analysis is equivalent in strength to closure analysis [10,11] and the constraint based analysis of Palsberg [8]. Since explicitly typed programs are typically only a constant bigger than the underlying untyped program, this gives (under the assumption that all types are bounded by a constant) an asymptotic improvement over previously published algorithms.

Independently of this work, Heintze and McAllester [4] developed a constraint based analysis with the same properties as our (i.e. linear time single query flow analysis of simply typed programs) — a careful examination reveals that the analyses are indeed similar. The presentations, however, are fundamentally different. In particular, Heintze and McAllester do not develop an explicit flow graph and the concept of types only occurs in the complexity argument. In our approach, types are a integral part of the analysed program. This makes our analysis easier to extend: in this paper we show how to deal with *polymorphism* (Heintze and McAllester give an ad hoc solution basically unfolding all polymorphic definitions), *recursive* types (Heintze and McAllester shows how lists can be handled, but it is not clear how to generalise to arbitrary recursive types) and *sum* types (not considered beyond lists by Heintze and McAllester).

We add polymorphism, sums and recursive types by considering these constructs as new value/consumer pairs: abstraction/instantiation, injection/projection and fold/unfold. Being able to handle languages with sums and recursive types allows us to specify the analysis for languages with an explicit *dynamic* type system — thus making the analysis applicable for untyped as well as typed languages.

The analysis is polyvariant for polymorphic definitions: monomorphic program analysis lose precision at function definitions by mixing information from different call-sites. Our analysis avoids this for arguments of polymorphic type.

2 Language

We will start with a simply typed lambda calculus extended with booleans, pairs and recursion. The types of the language are

$$t ::= \text{Bool} \mid t \to t' \mid t \times t'$$

We present the language using the type system of figure 1. In order to refer to subexpression *occurrences*, we assume that terms are *labelled*. We assume that labelling is preserved under reduction — hence, a label does not identify a single occurrence of a sub-expression, but a set of subexpressions (intuitively redexes of the same original subexpression).

The semantics of the language is given by the reduction rules in figure 2. As usual we write $\longrightarrow^*$ for the reflexive and transitive closure of $\longrightarrow$. We assume for

$$\text{Id} \;\; \overline{A, x : t \vdash x : t} \qquad \text{Bool-intro} \;\; \overline{A \vdash \text{True}^l : \text{Bool}} \qquad \overline{A \vdash \text{False}^l : \text{Bool}}$$

$$\text{Bool-elim} \;\; \frac{A \vdash e : \text{Bool} \quad A \vdash e' : t \quad A \vdash e'' : t}{A \vdash \text{if}^l \; e \; \text{then} \; e' \; \text{else} \; e'' : t} \qquad \text{fix} \;\; \frac{A, x : t \vdash e : t}{A \vdash \text{fix}^l x.e : t}$$

$$\rightarrow\text{-intro} \;\; \frac{A, x : t \vdash e : t'}{A \vdash \lambda^l x : t.e : t \rightarrow t'} \qquad \rightarrow\text{-elim} \;\; \frac{A \vdash e : t' \rightarrow t \quad A \vdash e' : t'}{A \vdash e @^l e' : t}$$

$$\times\text{-intro} \;\; \frac{A \vdash e : t \quad A \vdash e' : t'}{A \vdash (e, e')^l : t \times t'} \qquad \times\text{-elim} \;\; \frac{A \vdash e : t \times t' \quad A, x : t, y : t' \vdash e' : t''}{A \vdash \text{let}^l \; (x, y) \; \text{be} \; e \; \text{in} \; e' : t''}$$

Fig. 1. Type System

Contexts:

$$C ::= [\,] \mid \lambda^l x : t.C \mid C @^l e \mid e @^l C \mid \text{fix}^l x.C \mid$$
$$\quad \text{if}^l \; C \; \text{then} \; e' \; \text{else} \; e'' \mid \text{if}^l \; e \; \text{then} \; C \; \text{else} \; e'' \mid \text{if}^l \; e \; \text{then} \; e' \; \text{else} \; C \mid$$
$$\quad (C, e')^l \mid (e, C)^l \mid \text{let}^l \; (x, y) \; \text{be} \; C \; \text{in} \; e' \mid \text{let}^l \; (x, y) \; \text{be} \; e \; \text{in} \; C$$

Reduction Rules:

$$
\begin{array}{lll}
(\beta) & (\lambda^{l'} x.e) @^l e' \longrightarrow e[e'/x] \\
(\delta\text{-if}) & \text{if}^l \; \text{True}^{l'} \; \text{then} \; e \; \text{else} \; e' \longrightarrow e \\
& \text{if}^l \; \text{False}^{l'} \; \text{then} \; e \; \text{else} \; e' \longrightarrow e' \\
(\delta\text{-let-pair}) & \text{let}^l \; (x, y) \; \text{be} \; (e, e')^{l'} \; \text{in} \; e'' \longrightarrow e''[e/x][e'/y] \\
(\delta\text{-fix}) & \text{fix}^l x.e \longrightarrow e[\text{fix}^l x.e/x] \\
(\text{Context}) & C[e] \longrightarrow C[e'] & \text{if} \; e \longrightarrow e'
\end{array}
$$

Fig. 2. Semantics

all expressions that bound and free variables are distinct, and that this property is preserved (by α-conversion) during reduction.

We will refer to abstractions, booleans and pairs as data, and applications, conditionals and 'let (x, y) be (e, e') in e'''' as consumers — thus β, δ-if and δ-let-pair reductions are data-consumptions. Data flow analysis seeks a safe approximation to possible consumptions during *any* reduction of a term.

3 Flow Graphs

A *typed flow graph* for a type derivation $\mathcal{T}$ for an expression e is a graph (V, E) where V is a set of nodes and E is a set of edges.[1]. Each judgement $A \vdash e' : t$ in

---

[1] The reader might want to think of graphs as graphical representation of constraint sets: nodes n as variable and edges from n_1 to n_2 as constraints $n_1 \leq n_2$

$\mathcal{T}$ is represented by a set of nodes: one node for each constructor (Bool, $\times$, $\to$) in t. The node associated with the top type constructor of t is named according to e while the rest are anonymous (but still conceptually associated with this named node). Collections of nodes associated with different judgements are called *multinodes* (or just *m-nodes*) and are connected by collections of edges called *cables* which intuitively carry values of the appropriate type. It is convenient to think of such an *m-node* as a parallel "plug". We will use N for m-nodes and n for single nodes. Each variable (bound or free) in the analysed expression e will give rise to *one* variable m-node and each *occurrence* of a variable gives rise to a *box* m-node. Every other subexpression e' of e will give rise to a *syntax* m-node and a *box* m-node. The latter is referred to as the *root* of the graph associated with e' and represents the result of evaluating e'.

The set of edges between two m-nodes form a *cable*. To be precise, we define a t-cable as follows:

1. A Bool-cable is a single edge (wire): $\longrightarrow$

2. A $(t \to t')$-cable is $\overset{1}{\underset{2}{\rightleftarrows}}$ where $\overset{1}{\Longrightarrow}$ is a t-cable, $\overset{1}{\Longleftarrow}$ is its flipped

   version and $\overset{2}{\Longrightarrow}$ is a t'-cable.

3. A $(t \times t')$-cable is $\overset{1}{\underset{2}{\Longrightarrow}}$ where $\overset{1}{\Longrightarrow}$ is a t-cable and $\overset{2}{\Longrightarrow}$ is a t'-cable.

By "flipped" we mean inverting the direction of all wires in the cable, but not changing the top to bottom order of wires. We will use w for wires (edges) in E.

Edges are also considered paths (of length one). Composition of paths p_1 and p_2 is written $p_1 \cdot p_2$. If c is one of the following cables

$$\overset{w}{\longrightarrow} \qquad \overset{\overset{\overset{\longleftarrow}{w}}{\longrightarrow}}{\Longrightarrow} \qquad \overset{\overset{\overset{\longrightarrow}{w}}{\longrightarrow}}{\Longrightarrow}$$

the edge w is called the *carrier* of c. A path $w \cdot p \cdot w'$ is a *def-use* path if it starts from a data m-node, ends at a consumer m-node and w and w' are carriers. If w is an edge in a cable c, we say that it is a *forward* edge if it has the same orientation as the carrier of c, and a *backward* edge if it has the opposite orientation.

3.1 Simple Types

Figure 3 defines a function $\mathcal{G}$ from type derivations to typed flow graphs. Each right-hand side of the definition has a root m-node which is the m-node to be connected at recursive calls. Note that each data m-node generates a new carrier starting at the m-node and connects the sub-cables, while a consumer m-node terminates a carrier (and connects sub-cables). Furthermore, note that whenever two cables are connected, they have the same type.

- The variable case constructs a root m-node and connects the (unique) variable m-node to the root.

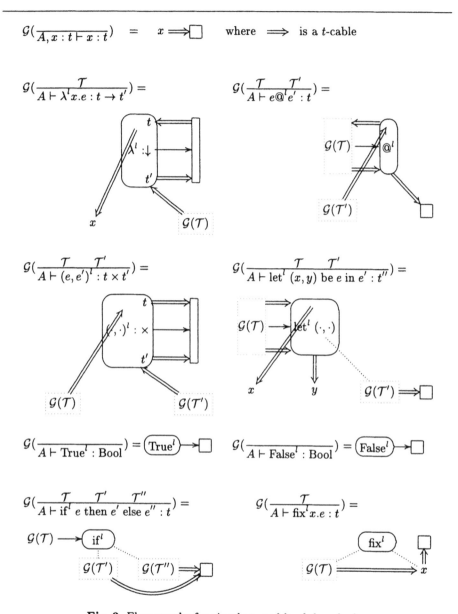

Fig. 3. Flow graphs for simply typed lambda calculus

- The case for $\mathcal{G}(\dfrac{\mathcal{T}}{A \vdash \lambda^l x.e : t \to t'})$ constructs a λ^l value m-node. A $t \to t'$ cable (call it c) leaves this m-node towards the root m-node of the graph indicating that the lambda itself is the result of the expression. A t cable connecting to the argument sub-cable of c goes towards the unique variable m-node for the bound variable. Similarly, a cable leaving the root of the graph for e connects to the result sub-cable of c.
  In the case for $e@^l e'$ a $t \to t'$ cable c enters a $@^l$ consumer m-node from the root of $\mathcal{G}(\mathcal{T})$ (where $\mathcal{T}$ is the derivation for e and $\mathcal{T}'$ is the derivation for e' — similar in the later cases). The root of $\mathcal{G}(\mathcal{T}')$ is connected at the $@^l$ m-node to the argument sub-cable of c and the result sub-cable of c is connected to the root of the graph.
- In the case for pairs, the cables from the roots of the components are combined at a $(\cdot, \cdot)^l$ value m-node. The cable leaving the $(\cdot, \cdot)^l$ has a pair type and goes to the root. The case for 'let^l (x, y) be e in e'' lets a pair cable from $\mathcal{G}(\mathcal{T})$ enter a 'let^l $(\cdot, \cdot)$' consumer m-node and sends the sub-cables on to the (unique) m-nodes for the bound variables. The graph $\mathcal{G}(\mathcal{T}')$ connects directly to the root (since e' will usually have occurrences of x or y, the graph will usually be connected). The dotted edge from the 'let^l $(\cdot, \cdot)$' m-node to $\mathcal{G}(\mathcal{T}')$ is only included to aid readability and is not part of the graph.
- The cases for booleans and 'if' should be straightforward — note that both branches of conditionals connect to the root, indicating that we do not know which branch will be taken.
- Applying $\mathcal{G}$ to $\dfrac{\mathcal{T}}{A \vdash \text{fix}^l x.e : t}$ connects $\mathcal{G}(\mathcal{T})$ to x indicating that the result of evaluating e is bound to x. We then connect x to the root. Note, that the 'fix' m-node is not connected to the graph — thus variable, data, consumer and box m-nodes suffice (the 'fix' m-node is only included for readability).

The *interface* of a graph $G = \mathcal{G}(\dfrac{\mathcal{T}}{A \vdash e : t})$ consists of the root m-node of G and the variable m-nodes x where x is free in e. Note that there is a one-to-one correspondence between type constructors in $A \vdash e : t$ and nodes in the interface of G. An occurrence of a type constructor in $x_1 : t_1, \cdots, x_n : t_n \vdash e : t$ is called positive (negative) if it occurs positively (negatively) in $t_1 \to \cdots \to t_n \to t$.[2] A node occurs positively (negatively) in the interface of $\mathcal{G}(\dfrac{\mathcal{T}}{A \vdash e : t})$ if the corresponding type constructor occurs positively (negatively) in $A \vdash e : t$.

Example 1. Applying $\mathcal{G}$ to the unique derivation of

$$\vdash \text{let}^{l_1} (f, x) \text{ be } (\lambda^{l_2} y.y, \text{True}^{l_3})^{l_4} \text{ in } f@^{l_5} x : \text{Bool}$$

results in the following typed flow graph:

---

[2] Assume the syntax tree for a type t. If the path from the root of the tree to a type constructor c (one of Bool, $\times$ or $\to$) follows the argument branch of $\to$ constructors an even (odd) number of times then c is said to occur positively (negatively) in t.

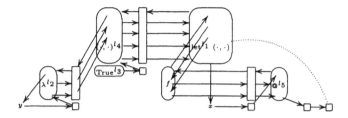

The reader is encouraged to follow the def-use path from λ^{l_2} to $@^{l_5}$ and the path from the True^{l_3} to the root of the graph.

3.2 Polymorphism

To add polymorphism, we extend the language of types as follows[3]:

$$t ::= \tau \mid \text{Bool} \mid t \to t' \mid t \times t' \mid \forall \tau.t$$

where we use τ for type variables. We add explicit syntax for generalisation and instantiation. The extension to the language is defined by the type rules

$$\forall\text{-I} \ \frac{A \vdash e : t}{A \vdash \Lambda^l \tau.e : \forall \tau.t} \ (\tau \text{ not free in } A) \qquad \forall\text{-E} \ \frac{A \vdash e : \forall \tau.t'}{A \vdash e\{t\}^l : t'[t/\tau]}$$

and the reduction rule:

$$(\beta) \ (\Lambda^l \tau.e)\{t\}^{l'} \longrightarrow e$$

where Λ is data and $\{\}$ is a consumer.

Intuitively, a type variable τ can carry any value since it might be instantiated to any type. For graphs, however, the opposite intuition is more fruitful: *no* value is carried along a τ-cable, since, as long as the value has type τ, it *cannot* be used. This approach relies on the same intuition as "Theorems for Free", that a function cannot touch arguments of polymorphic type [12]. Thus a τ-cable is no cable at all and the appropriate connections are made at the instantiation m-node. A $\forall \tau.t$ cable is a t-cable.

Since t-cables and $\forall \tau.t$-cables are the same, a quantification m-node just passes on its incoming cable:

$$\mathcal{G}\left(\frac{\tau}{A \vdash \Lambda^l \tau.e : \forall \tau.t}\right) \ = \ \mathcal{G}(\mathcal{T}) \Longrightarrow \boxed{\Lambda^l} \Longrightarrow \square$$

An instantiation m-node has an ingoing $\forall \tau.t'$ cable and an outgoing $t'[t/\tau]$ cable. All wires of the $\forall \tau.t'$ cable are connected to the similar wires in the $t'[t/\tau]$ cable. The remaining edges of the $t'[t/\tau]$ cable form t cables — these

---

[3] Since we are analysing programs that are already typed, System F gives a smoother presentation — the program might well be typed without using the full power (e.g. by allowing polymorphism only in let-bound expressions).

are connected such that negative occurrences of t are connected to all positive occurrences of t

To be precise, assume that t' has n occurrences of τ and write the occurrences as $\tau^{(1)}, \cdots \tau^{(n)}$ and the similar occurrences of t in $t'[t/\tau]$ as $t^{(1)}, \cdots t^{(n)}$. For any pair $\tau^{(i)}, \tau^{(j)}$ where $\tau^{(i)}$ occurs negatively and $\tau^{(j)}$ occurs positively in t', add a t-cable from $t^{(i)}$ to $t^{(j)}$.

Example 2. Consider

$$\lambda^{l_1} id.(id\{\text{Bool}\}^{l_2} @^{l_3} \text{True}^{l_4}, id\{\text{Bool} \times \text{Bool}\}^{l_5} @^{l_6} (\text{False}^{l_7}, \text{False}^{l_8})^{l_9})^{l_{10}}$$
$$@\Lambda^{l_{11}}\tau.\lambda^{l_{12}}x.x$$

where we assume that id is given type $\forall \tau.\tau \to \tau$. The graph fragment for the argument $\Lambda^{l_{11}}\tau.\lambda^{l_{12}}x.x$ looks as follows

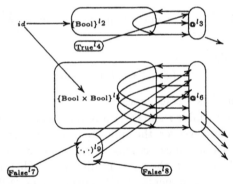

The dashed edges are not part of the graph and are only included to make the graph more readable since it would otherwise be completely unconnected[4].

The graph fragment for the applications of id looks as follows:

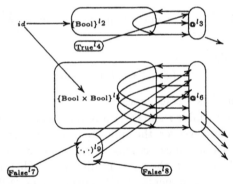

(we have left out superfluous box-nodes).

3.3 Sum Types

Sum types have the following syntax:

$$t ::= \text{Bool} \mid t \to t' \mid t \times t' \mid t + t' \mid 1$$

Again, we associate syntax with the type rules:

$$1 \frac{}{A \vdash u^l : 1} \qquad +\text{-I} \frac{A \vdash e : t}{A \vdash \text{inl}^l(e) : t + t'} \qquad \frac{A \vdash e : t'}{A \vdash \text{inr}^l(e) : t + t'}$$

$$+\text{-E} \frac{A \vdash e : t + t' \quad A, x : t \vdash e' : t'' \quad A, y : t' \vdash e'' : t''}{A \vdash \text{case}^l \, e \text{ of } \text{inl}(x) \mapsto e'; \text{ inr}(y) \mapsto e'' : t''}$$

---

[4] While the dashed edges are not necessary to find def-use paths, they can be included if we want information about which values a given variable can be bound to.

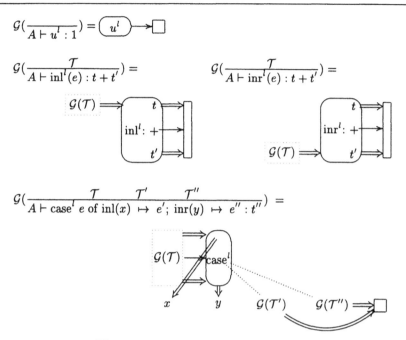

Fig. 4. Typed flow graphs for sum types

The reduction rules for the constructs are as follows:

$$(\delta\text{-case}) \quad \text{case}^{l'} \text{ inl}^l(e) \text{ of inl}(x) \mapsto e'; \text{ inr}(y) \mapsto e'' \longrightarrow e'[e/x]$$
$$\text{case}^{l'} \text{ inr}^l(e) \text{ of inl}(x) \mapsto e'; \text{ inr}(y) \mapsto e'' \longrightarrow e''[e/y]$$

where 'inl' and 'inr' construct data and 'case' is a consumer.

To extend typed graphs with sum types, we first have to define cables carrying values of sum type:

A $(t+t')$-cable is $\overset{1}{\underset{2}{\Rrightarrow}}$ where $\overset{1}{\Rightarrow}$ is a t-cable and $\overset{2}{\Rightarrow}$ is a t'-cable.

The carrier cable represents the flow of the 'inl'/'inr' data.

In figure 4 we extend the definition of $\mathcal{G}$ with the new syntactic constructs. The constructs should be straightforward: the unit u^l is treated like other constants, $\text{inl}^l(e)$ and $\text{inr}^l(e)$ connect the root of $\mathcal{G}(\mathcal{T})$ to the appropriate sub-cable of the sum-cable — nothing flows into the other sub-cable. Finally, the case-construct decomposes the sum (in a manner similar to 'let^l $(\cdot,\cdot)$') and connects the branches to the root (similarly to 'if').

3.4 Recursive Types

Recursive types add the ability to define integers, lists etc.:

$$t ::= \tau \mid \text{Bool} \mid t \to t' \mid t \times t' \mid t + t' \mid \mu\tau.t$$

where we have retained the sum types from above (since they are required to make practical use of recursive types).

Usually, recursive types are added to type systems by adding the equivalence $\mu\tau.t = t[\mu\tau.t/\tau]$ We make applications of this equivalence explicit in the language by adding syntax with the following type rules:

$$\text{fold } \frac{A \vdash e : t[\mu\tau.t/\tau]}{A \vdash \text{fold}^l(e) : \mu\tau.t} \qquad \text{unfold } \frac{A \vdash e : \mu\tau.t}{A \vdash \text{unfold}^l(e) : t[\mu\tau.t/\tau]}$$

We consider 'fold' as data and 'unfold' as a consumer and add the reduction rule:

$$(\delta\text{-rec}) \text{ unfold}^{l'}(\text{fold}^l(e)) \longrightarrow e$$

As with polymorphism, τ cables are empty — this makes even more sense with recursive types as no variable will ever have type τ and hence the values that a variable can evaluate to can be read from the graph even without τ-cables.

A $\mu\tau.t$ cable has to carry the information from all unfoldings of the type, hence we need a t cable to carry the information of t as well as instantiations with $\mu\tau.t$ of positive occurrences of τ, and a flipped t cable to carry the information of instantiations of negative occurrences of τ. Similarly, we need a wire in each direction carrying 'fold' values. Thus

A $\mu\tau.t$ cable is $\overset{2}{\underset{1}{\rightrightarrows}}\rightleftarrows$ where $\overset{1}{\Longrightarrow}$ is a t-cable, $\overset{1}{\Longleftarrow}$ is its flipped version and $\overset{2}{\Longrightarrow}$ is a t-cable.

The forward single edge is the carrier and carries the label of the applied fold operation; the backward single edge carries the labels of all fold operation that can occur in argument position.

Fold and unfold m-nodes are dual and parameterised by the recursive type involved. An unfold m-node has an incoming $\mu\tau.t$ cable and an outgoing $t[\mu\tau.t/\tau]$ cable. Let superscripts index the occurrences of τ in t as in the polymorphic case. We connect the edges of the positive sub cable of the incoming cable to the nodes of the outermost t on the outgoing side. Furthermore, the incoming $\mu\tau.t$ cable is connected to all $\mu\tau.t^{(i)}$ — directly if $\tau^{(i)}$ is a positive occurrence of τ in t and "switched" if $\tau^{(i)}$ is a negative occurrence. The fold m-node has an incoming $t[\mu\tau.t/\tau]$ cable and an outgoing $\mu\tau.t$ cable. Connections are made similarly.

Example 3. The 'fold' m-node for folding $(\mu\tau.\tau \to \tau) \to (\mu\tau.\tau \to \tau)$ to $\mu\tau.\tau \to \tau$ and the dual 'unfold' m-node for unfolding $\mu\tau.\tau \to \tau$ to $(\mu\tau.\tau \to \tau) \to (\mu\tau.\tau \to \tau)$ are given below. The type constructors are included to remind the reader of the kind of labels carried by the individual wires.

fold: unfold:

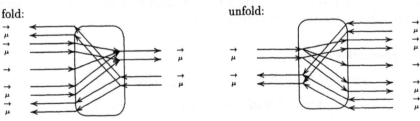

$$Bool! : \mathsf{Bool} \rightsquigarrow \mathsf{D} \qquad Fun! : \mathsf{D} \rightarrow \mathsf{D} \rightsquigarrow \mathsf{D} \qquad Pair! : \mathsf{D} \times \mathsf{D} \rightsquigarrow \mathsf{D}$$
$$Bool? : \mathsf{D} \rightsquigarrow \mathsf{Bool} \qquad Fun? : \mathsf{D} \rightsquigarrow \mathsf{D} \rightarrow \mathsf{D} \qquad Pair? : \mathsf{D} \rightsquigarrow \mathsf{D} \times \mathsf{D}$$

$$\frac{c_1 : t_1 \rightsquigarrow t_1' \quad c_2 : t_2 \rightsquigarrow t_2'}{c_1 \times c_2 : t_1 \times t_2 \rightsquigarrow t_1' \times t_2'} \qquad \frac{c_1 : t_1 \rightsquigarrow t_1' \quad c_2 : t_2 \rightsquigarrow t_2'}{c_1 \rightarrow c_2 : t_1' \rightarrow t_2 \rightsquigarrow t_1 \rightarrow t_2'} \qquad \text{Sub} \; \frac{A \vdash e : t \quad c : t \rightsquigarrow t'}{A \vdash [c]^l e : t'}$$

Fig. 5. Dynamic Typing

3.5 Dynamic Types

For dynamic typing we need simple types plus the special type D:

$$t ::= \mathsf{D} \mid \mathsf{Bool} \mid t \rightarrow t' \mid t \times t'$$

The necessary extensions to the type system of figure 1 are given in figure 5 (for more details see Henglein [5]).

The conversions $Bool!, Fun!, Pair!$ correspond to tagging operations: they take an untagged value which the type system guarantees has a given type (eg. Bool) and throws it into the common pool of values about which the type system knows nothing. In this pool values have tags that can be checked at run time. Conversions $Bool?, Fun?, Pair?$ check the tag of a value and provide the untagged value of which the type inference now knows the type.

Using recursive types and sum types, we already have sufficient power to specify dynamic types. Type D is equivalent to

$$\mu\tau.((\tau \rightarrow \tau) + ((\tau \times \tau) + \mathsf{Bool}))$$

The conversions are expressible in our language. E.g. $[Bool!]^l$ is $\text{fold}^l \circ \text{inr}^l \circ \text{inr}^l$ and $[Bool?]^l$ is $\text{outr}^l \circ \text{outr}^l \circ \text{unfold}^l$ where outr^l is a shorthand for

$$\lambda^l x.\text{case}^l \; x \; \text{of} \; \text{inl}(y) \; \mapsto \; error; \; \text{inr}(z) \; \mapsto \; z$$

(having different labels on the sum and recursive type operators would not give any additional information, so we just assume that they are the same).

By the coding of dynamic types using sums and recursive types, we find that a D-cable consists of 6 forward and 6 backward edges (the 6 are $\rightarrow$, $+$, $\times$, $+$, Bool, μ). Since the labels carried by the sum and μ edges are the same, we can replace them with one forward and one backward edge carrying tag-labels:

where the edges read from top to bottom carry labels of type: !, $\rightarrow$, $\times$, Bool, !, $\rightarrow$, $\times$ and Bool. Now the tagging and untagging m-nodes can be found by combining m-nodes for sum and recursive types.

Example 4. The $[Fun!]^l$ m-node (equivalent to $\text{fold}^l \circ \text{inl}^l$) is given in figure 6 (where the left-hand side is a $\mathsf{D} \rightarrow \mathsf{D}$ cable and the right-hand side is a D cable).

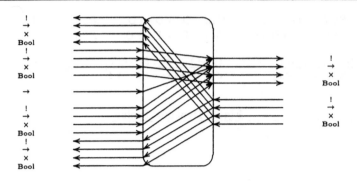

Fig. 6. The $[Fun!]^l$ m-node

3.6 Soundness

A flow graph is a sound abstraction of the definitions and uses of data during evaluation of an expression e, if (a) whenever there is a redex in e, there is a path starting from the data being consumed and ending at the consumer and (b) reduction does not add extra paths. We state soundness for the system with polymorphism, sums and recursive types. Soundness for the dynamic system follows by the construction. The proof of the following theorem can be found in [7].

Theorem 5. *Let C, e_1, e_2, T_1, A, t be given such that* $\dfrac{T_1}{A \vdash C[e_1] : t}$ *and e_1 reduces to e_2 by a β or δ redex. Then there exists T_2 such that*

1. $\dfrac{T_2}{A \vdash C[e_2] : t}$
2. *if the redex lets l consume l' then there is a def-use path from m-node l' to m-node l in $\mathcal{G}(\dfrac{T_1}{A \vdash C[e_1] : t})$ and*
3. $\{(l_1, l_2) \mid$ *there is a def-use path from l_1 to l_2 in $\mathcal{G}(\dfrac{T_1}{A \vdash C[e_1] : t})\}$*

   $\supseteq \{(l_1, l_2) \mid$ *there is a def-use path from l_1 to l_2 in $\mathcal{G}(\dfrac{T_2}{A \vdash C[e_2] : t})\}$*

4 Discussion

4.1 Algorithm

So far we have only discussed the construction of flow graphs. It should be clear, however, that the usual flow problems ("Where is a given occurrence of a value used?", "Which values are used by a given consumer?" and the full flow problem) can be solved by standard reachability algorithms. Single data or single consumer problems can be answered in linear time while the full flow problem can be answered in quadratic time. In the same way, we can answer questions such as "which values can a given expression evaluate to?", or "which values can a given variable be bound to?", though some care should be taken for the latter query in the polymorphic case (as mentioned in section 3.2).

We can leave out wires for polymorphism, sums, recursiveness etc. if tracing this is not necessary. Further, if only what is usually known as control flow information[5] is needed then more can be left out. A $\mu\tau.t$-cable does not need the backward t-cable and μ-edge if there are no negative occurrences of τ in t.

It is also possible to reduce the size of graphs by eliminating unnecessary nodes: most box-nodes and the quantification nodes can immediately be removed, but if we are only interested in part of the flow (e.g. only higher-order flow) more can be removed. By reachability (see Ayers [2]) we can remove cables in 'if' and 'case' provided the flow graph can prove that all values destructed will be True or all values will be False (resp. inl(·) or inr(·)). Furthermore, if we are only interested in the input/output behaviour, the graph can be reduced to depend only on the size of the interface (i.e. constant under assumption that types are bounded). This is useful if further polyvariance is desired as cloning the graphs for a definition will be cheap (this option is discussed by Heintze and McAllester [4]).

4.2 Precision

It was shown in [6] that the simply typed fragment of this analysis (that is the analysis presented in section 3.1) was equivalent to closure analysis of the same program. The equivalence extends in a straightforward manner to sum types.

Assume that e is polymorphically typed. Our analysis can yield better results than closure analysis when analysing e: using the polymorphic type information gives us a degree of polyvariance. Consider the identity function $id = \lambda^{l_1} x.x$ of type $\forall \tau.\tau \to \tau$ and assume two call sites $id@^{l_2}\mathrm{True}^{l_3}$ and $id@^{l_4}\mathrm{False}^{l_5}$. Closure analysis will find that the result of both applications can be l_3 or l_5. Our analysis will create two instantiation nodes and hence keep the applications separate: the result will be l_3 for the first application and l_5 for the second. If the identity function was given type Bool $\to$ Bool instead, we would get the same (sub-optimal) result as closure analysis. This loss of polyvariance would also arise if the identity was specified as $\lambda^{l_1} x.\mathrm{if}^{l_2} x$ then x else x since this can only be given a monomorphic type.

Consider recursive types. Our analysis is *potentially* as good as closure analysis. Heintze shows that flow analysis based on recursive types is equivalent to closure analysis [3]. It is not difficult to show that our analysis is equivalent to recursive type based analysis, *except* that the base types chosen in advance. This implies that for every untyped term e, there *exists* a type derivation for e such that the resulting graph contains information equivalent to closure analysis.

Example 6. Consider lists. The usual type for lists of element of type t is $\mu\tau.((t \times \tau) + 1)$. Using this type, $[\mathrm{True}^{l_1}, \mathrm{False}^{l_2}]$ is shorthand for

$$\mathrm{fold}(\mathrm{inl}((\mathrm{True}^{l_1}, \mathrm{fold}(\mathrm{inl}((\mathrm{False}^{l_2}, \mathrm{fold}(\mathrm{inr}(u^{l_0}))^{l_6})))^{l_7}))$$

---

[5] We prefer to think of this as value flow of control structures

(where we have left out some unnecessary labels). Using this type for lists, our analysis will find that fst([True^{l_1}, False^{l_2}]) (where fst is shorthand for λx.let (f, s) be (case unfold(x) of inl$(y) \mapsto y$; inr$(z) \mapsto error$) in f) can result in l_1 as well as l_2. Using a different type for lists (such as $(t \times \mu\tau.((t \times \tau)+1))+1$) will yield the precise result in this case.

4.3 Related Work

Independently of this work, Heintze and McAllester developed a flow analysis which has the same complexity as ours on simply typed programs [4] (on untyped programs it might not terminate). Their analysis is derived by transforming the constraint formulation of flow analysis [8] to avoid computation of dynamic transitive closure. For each node n there are potentially nodes $dom(n)$ and $ran(n)$. Due to the boundedness of standard types, the number of nodes is similarly bounded — this corresponds directly to our m-nodes.

Types, however, are treated fundamentally different in their presentation. While types is an integrated part of the generation of our flow graphs, it only appears in the proof of termination/complexity of their algorithm. We believe that this difference make it difficult to extend their system. In particular:

Polymorphism Since their algorithm does not need the types, it is directly applicable to polymorphically typed programs. Complexity results, however, are preserved only if the monotypes of the expanded program is bounded by a constant. While this is not unreasonable for let-polymorphic languages, our solution preserves the complexity results if the size of types of the *original* program is bounded by a constant. Furthermore, we get polyvariance for free.

Recursive types Heintze and McAllester shows how their analysis can be extended to handle lists. It is not clear, however, how to generalise to arbitrary recursive types — for types $\mu\tau.t$ where τ occurs negatively in t the backward cable is a necessary and non-obvious extension which does not fit easily into their framework. As a consequence their analysis is not applicable to dynamically typed programs (as mentioned above, termination is not guaranteed if the analysis is applied to untyped terms).

We find that our improvements rely heavily on our formalism and in particular on the availability of types at graph construction time.

The notion of *well-balanced path* by Asperti and Laneve [1] corresponds directly to the usual constraint formulation of flow analysis. Asperti and Laneve refine the concept of well-balanced path to *legal path* which captures exactly the set of virtual redexes in a term — a notion of *exact* flow analysis useful for optimal reduction. If we place a restriction similar to legality on the paths of our graphs, we will obtain an exact flow analysis — as a direct consequence of the precision, the analysis will be non-elementary recursive. We hope to find a formulation of the legality restriction, that is amenable to abstraction and hence develop analyses strictly more precise than closure analysis, but with a non-prohibitive complexity. In particular, we hope to find the first-order analysis of Horowitz, Reps and Sagiv [9] as a special case.

5 Conclusion

We have presented a notion of flow graph for higher-order programs. Under assumption that the size of all types is bounded by a constant, the resulting flow analysis presents an asymptotic improvement over earlier work. Heintze and McAllester have independently of this work reported similar results, but in contrast to their work, our approach handles recursive types and is hence applicable to untyped programs (if a dynamic type discipline is enforced). Furthermore, we handle polymorphism in a more general way which entails a desirable degree of polyvariance.

Acknowledgements This paper extends work presented in my Ph.D.-thesis [6]. I would like to thank my supervisor Fritz Henglein for many rewarding discussions and my official opponents, Alex Aiken, Nils Andersen and Peter Sestoft for their comments and suggestions.

References

1. A. Asperti and C. Laneve. Paths, computations and labels in the λ-calculus. In *RTA'93*, volume 690 of *LNCS*, pages 152–167. Springer-Verlag, 1993.
2. A. Ayers. Efficient closure analysis with reachability. In *Proc. Workshop on Static Analysis (WSA), Bordeaux, France*, pages 126–134, Sept. 1992.
3. N. Heintze. Control-flow analysis and type systems. In A. Mycroft, editor, *Symposium on Static Analysis (SAS)*, volume 983 of *LNCS*, pages 189–206, Glasgow, 1995.
4. N. Heintze and D. McAllester. Control-flow analysis for ML in linear time. In *International Conference on Functional Programming (ICFP)*, 1997. To appear.
5. F. Henglein. Dynamic typing: Syntax and proof theory. *Science of Computer Programming (SCP)*, 22(3):197–230, 1994.
6. C. Mossin. *Flow Analysis of Typed Higher-Order Programs*. PhD thesis, DIKU, University of Copenhagen, January 1997.
7. C. Mossin. Higher-order value flow graphs. Technical report, DIKU, 1997.
8. J. Palsberg. Global program analysis in constraint form. In S. Tison, editor, *19th International Colloquium on Trees in Algebra and Programming (CAAP)*, volume 787 of *LNCS*, pages 276–290. Springer-Verlag, 1994.
9. T. Reps, S. Horwitz, and M. Sagiv. Precise interprocedural dataflow analysis via graph reachability. In *Conference Record of the 22nd ACM Symposium on Principles of Programming Languages*, pages 49–61, San Francisco, CA, Jan. 1995.
10. P. Sestoft. Replacing function parameters by global variables. Master's thesis, DIKU, University of Copenhagen, Denmark, October 1988.
11. P. Sestoft. *Analysis and Efficient Implementation of Functional Languages*. PhD thesis, DIKU, University of Copenhagen, Oct. 1991.
12. P. Wadler. Theorems for free! In *Proc. Functional Programming Languages and Computer Architecture (FPCA), London, England*, pages 347–359. ACM Press, Sept. 1989.

Intuitionistic Implication in Abstract Interpretation

Roberto Giacobazzi   Francesca Scozzari

Dipartimento di Informatica, Università di Pisa
Corso Italia 40, 56125 Pisa, Italy
E-mail: {giaco, scozzari}@di.unipi.it
Ph.: +39-50-887283   Fax: +39-50-887226

Abstract. In this paper we introduce the notion of Heyting completion in abstract interpretation, and we prove that it supplies a logical basis to specify relational program analyses by means of intuitionistic implication. This provides a uniform algebraic setting where abstract domains can be specified by simple logic formulas, or as solutions of recursive abstract domain equations, involving few basic operations for domain construction. We apply our framework to study directionality in type inference and groundness analysis in logic programming.

Keywords: *Abstract interpretation, directional types, domains, intuitionistic logic, logic programming, static analysis.*

1   Introduction

One of the most attractive features of abstract interpretation is the ability to systematically derive program analyses from formal semantics specifications. Analyses can be composed, refined and decomposed according to the need. A key role in this construction is played by abstract domains: *Modifying domains corresponds to modify analyses*. A number of operations were designed to systematically construct new abstract domains, by refinement ([12,14,15,17,18,21,26]), decomposition ([10]) and compression ([19]), and some of them are included as tools for design aid in modern systems for program analysis, like in GAIA ([12]), PLAI ([9]), and System Z ([27]), providing high-level facilities to tune the analysis in accuracy and costs. Most of these operations arise from the common logical operations on program properties. For instance, the well known *reduced product* ([14]) of two domains is the most abstract domain which is approximated by both the given domains. From the analysis point of view, it corresponds to the simplest analysis which is more precise than the two given analyses, i.e. which derives at least the same properties. The *disjunctive completion* ([14,15]) of a domain is the most abstract domain able to deal with disjunctions of properties in the given domain.

The possibility to tune the analysis in independent attribute and relational mode is probably one of the most attractive feature of this technology. The efficient but less precise *independent attribute* analysis method assigns properties to program objects, independently from the properties of other objects. This method is generalized by the more precise but costly *relational* one, which exploits at each program point the relations between the properties of program objects ([23]). This can be achieved by including relations or functions as domain objects. The very first example of domain constructor for relational analysis by abstract interpretation is Cousot's *reduced (cardinal) power* [14], where monotone functions are used to represent dependency information between properties of program objects. Although the notion of dependency is fundamental in analysis, e.g. for the efficient execution of programs on parallel computers, this construction is rarely applied in the literature, even if, as we prove in this paper, surprisingly, most well known domains for relational program analysis can be specified in this way. This is probably due to the lack of a clean logical interpretation for reduced power. While reduced product and disjunctive completion have both a clean and immediate logical interpretation as conjunction and disjunction of program properties, there is no known logical interpretation for most of the relational combinators, in particular for reduced power.

In this paper we fill this gap by introducing a new operation for abstract domain refinement, which is *Heyting completion*. The idea is to consider the space of all intuitionistic implications built from every pair of elements of the given domain. This domain has an immediate logical interpretation as the collection of intuitionistic formulas built, without nested implication, in the fragment $\wedge, \rightarrow$. We prove that this operation provides a logical foundation for Cousot's reduced power of abstract domains. Moreover, this has the advantage of making applicable relevant results in intuitionistic logic to abstract domain manipulation. We study the algebraic properties of Heyting completion in relation with reduced product and disjunctive completion. The result is an advanced algebra of domain operations, where abstract domains can be specified by simple logic formulas, using few basic operations for domain construction, all characterized by a clean logical interpretation. In this algebraic setting, we study the solutions of implicational domain equations, i.e. equations between abstract domains involving Heyting completion as basic domain constructor. A new family of abstract domains for analysis is introduced as solutions of these equations. These domains are closed under dependency construction, and somehow represent an upper bound on how much this information can be derived systematically from a given domain. This provides also a first account on the possibility to study domains for analysis as solutions of recursive domain equations, as traditionally done for domains in denotational semantics.

We apply Heyting completion as domain refinement to directional type inference in logic programming. Type inference is general enough to include relevant examples of analyses in logic programs. We prove that the same construction by Heyting completion surfaces most of the well known applications of type inference, from groundness ([3]) to more structured directional types ([6,1]). This approach to directionality by systematic domain refinement has the advantage of being independent from specific applications. This supplies a better comprehension on the nature of directionality in these analyses, and suggest how to construct new domains for program analysis.

2 Related works

In the very last section of [14], Cousot and Cousot introduced the notion of reduced power, as a domain of monotone functions between two given abstract domains. This construction was reconsidered in [18], where some properties on the lattice structure of reduced power are studied. The main result in [18] is a necessary and sufficient condition on the abstract domain A, such that its reduced power with A itself is isomorphic to a space of closure operators on A. None of these papers however gave a logical interpretation for the operation of reduced power, in particular in relation with other known operations for domain manipulation. In addition, none of them characterize the notion of domains closed under dependency construction. Nielson's *tensor product* [26] is also known as a basic operator for relational analyses construction. However this operation is not directly comparable, in the sense of abstract interpretation (i.e. it provides neither more abstract nor more concrete domains) with reduced power, as proved in [18]. On the side of program analysis, Codish and Demoen [8] firstly used the directional information obtainable for groundness analysis in *Pos* (also called *Prop*) ([3]), to implement efficient type inference algorithms by abstract interpretation. Their results however are not immediately applicable to other program properties, due to the lack of a suitable domain completion, generalizing their construction.

3 Preliminaries

3.1 Notation and basic notions

Let A, B and C be sets. The powerset of A is denoted by $\wp(A)$. If $X \subseteq A$, $\overline{X}$ is the set-theoretic complement of X. If A is a poset or a pre-ordered set, we usually denote $\leq_A$ the corresponding partial order. If A is pre-ordered and $I \subseteq A$ then $\downarrow I = \{x \in A \mid \exists y \in I.\ x \leq_A y\}$. For $x \in A$, $\downarrow x$ is a shorthand for $\downarrow \{x\}$. $\wp^{\downarrow}(A)$ denotes the set of *order-ideals* of A, where $I \subseteq A$ is an order-ideal if $I = \downarrow I$. $\wp^{\downarrow}(A)$ is a complete lattice with respect to set-theoretic inclusion, where the join is set union and the meet is set intersection. We write $f : A \longmapsto B$ to mean that f is a total function from A to B. If $C \subseteq A$ then $f(C) = \{f(x) \mid x \in C\}$. By $g \circ f$ we denote the composition $\lambda x.g(f(x))$. Let $\langle A, \leq_A, \vee_A, \wedge_A, \top_A, \bot_A \rangle$ and $\langle B, \leq_B, \vee_B, \wedge_B, \top_B, \bot_B \rangle$ be complete lattices. A function $f : A \longmapsto B$ is *(co-)additive* if for any $C \subseteq A$, $f(\vee_A C) = \vee_B f(C)$ $(f(\wedge_A C) = \wedge_B f(C))$. f is *(co-)continuous* when the above statement on (co-)additivity holds for chains C only. If A is a complete lattice, the *pseudo-complement* of a *relatively to* b, if it exists, is the unique element $a \to b \in A$ such that for any $x \in A$: $a \wedge_A x \leq_A b$

iff $x \leq_A a \to b$. A is *relatively pseudo-complemented* if $a \to b$ exists for every $a, b \in A$. The *pseudo-complement* of a, if it exists, is $a \to \perp_A$ (see [5]).

3.2 Abstract interpretation, Galois connections and closure operators

The standard Cousot and Cousot theory of abstract interpretation is based on the notion of Galois connection ([13]). If C and A are posets and $\alpha : C \longmapsto A$, $\gamma : A \longmapsto C$ are monotone, such that $\forall c \in C. \ c \leq_C \gamma(\alpha(c))$ and $\forall a \in A. \ \alpha(\gamma(a)) \leq_A a$, then we call the quadruple $\langle C, \gamma, A, \alpha \rangle$ a *Galois connection* (G.c.) between C and A. If in addition $\forall a \in A. \ \alpha(\gamma(a)) = a$, then $\langle C, \gamma, A, \alpha \rangle$ is a *Galois insertion* (G.i.) of A in C. In the setting of abstract interpretation, C and A are called, respectively, *concrete* and *abstract domain*, and they are assumed to be complete lattices. Any G.c. $\langle C, \gamma, A, \alpha \rangle$ can be lifted to a G.i. identifying in an equivalence class those objects in A having the same image (meaning) in C. This process is known as *reduction* of the abstract domain. In the rest of the paper, L is a complete lattice $\langle L, \leq_L, \vee_L, \wedge_L, \top_L, \perp_L \rangle$ playing the role of the concrete domain.

An (*upper*) *closure operator* on L is an operator $\rho : L \longmapsto L$ monotonic, idempotent and extensive (viz. $\forall x \in L. \ x \leq_L \rho(x)$) [24]. Each closure operator ρ is uniquely determined by the set of its fixpoints, which is its image $\rho(L)$. Hence, in the following, when closures are used to denote abstract domains, they will be denoted as sets, with Roman capital letters. $X \subseteq L$ is the set of fixpoints of a closure operator on L iff X is a *Moore-family* of L, i.e. $\top_L \in X$ and X is completely meet-closed (viz. for any non-empty $Y \subseteq X$, $\wedge_L Y \in X$). For any $X \subseteq L$, we denote by $\lambda(X)$ the *Moore-closure* of X, i.e. the least subset of L containing X, which is a Moore-family of L. $\rho(L)$ is a complete lattice with respect to $\leq_L$, but, in general, it is not a complete sublattice of L, since the join in $\rho(L)$ might be different from $\vee_L$. $\rho(L)$ is a complete sublattice of L iff ρ is additive. We denote by $\langle uco(L), \sqsubseteq, \sqcap, \sqcup, \lambda x. \top, \lambda x. x \rangle$ the complete lattice of all upper closure operators on L, where the ordering is pointwise i.e., $\rho \sqsubseteq \eta$ iff $\forall x \in L. \ \rho(x) \leq_L \eta(x)$, or equivalently $\eta(L) \subseteq \rho(L)$.

The equivalence between G.i. and closure operators is well known [5]. However, closure operators are often more practical and concise than G.i.'s to reason about abstract domains, being independent from representation choices for domain objects ([14]). Any G.i. $\langle L, \gamma, A, \alpha \rangle$ is uniquely determined (up to isomorphism) by the closure operator $\gamma \circ \alpha$, and, conversely, any closure operator uniquely determines a G.i. (up to isomorphism). The complete lattice of all abstract domains (identified up to isomorphism) on L is therefore isomorphic to $uco(L)$. Thus, in the rest of the paper, we often abuse notation and consider an abstract domain and the corresponding closure as the same object, so whenever we will say that D is an abstraction of C, we will mean that D is isomorphic to $\rho(C)$, for some closure $\rho \in uco(C)$. The order relation on $uco(L)$ corresponds precisely to the order used to compare abstract domains with regard to their precision: If A and B are abstractions of L, then A is *more precise* than B iff $A \sqsubseteq B$ as closures.

4 Refinement by pseudo-complements

An abstract domain for analysis is usually a set of objects, equipped with a partial order. In this structure the information is associated with both the domain objects and the way they are ordered—the top-element representing no information. An *abstract domain refinement* is intended to discover the information apparently hidden in a domain, by exploiting both the domain objects and their relation. Filé et al. studied this notion in [16], as a generalization for most of the well known operations for domain refinement, like *reduced product*, and *disjunctive completion*. A domain refinement is a mapping $\Re : uco(L) \longmapsto uco(L)$, such that for any abstract domain $A \in uco(L)$: $\Re(A)$ contains more information than A (i.e., $\Re$ is *reductive* $\Re(A) \sqsubseteq A$), and $\Re$ is monotonic. Idempotent domain refinements play an important role in this theory, as they upgrade domains all at once. This last condition clearly defines *idempotent refinements as lower closure operators* on $uco(L)$, i.e. monotonic, idempotent and reductive operators. In the following the set of lower closure operations on L is denoted $lco(L)$. Their properties follow by duality from those above for upper closure operators.

In this section we are interested in determining complementary information in abstract interpretation by domain refinement. This information may be useful to enhance domains, e.g. to represent negative information. Given two domain objects a and b, we are interested in characterizing, by a simple domain transformation, an object c such that, when combined with a, the result is approximated by b.

Example 1. Consider the following lattice L for *sign analysis*, which is an abstract interpretation of $\wp(\mathbb{Z})$, and one of its strict abstractions A, both depicted below. The objects in L and A have the obvious meaning as fixpoints of closures on $\wp(\mathbb{Z})$. $- \in L$ represents the necessary information which, when combined with $+ \in A$, gives $\emptyset$ as result.

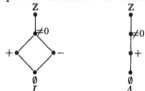

The refinement by complements was introduced in [16]. This refinement is based on the notion of complement, viz. a^* is a complement for a in L if $a \wedge_L a^* = \bot_L$ and $a \vee_L a^* = \top_L$. When the complement exists unique for an element a, it summarizes the common information shared by all the elements c such that $c \wedge_L a = \bot_L$. The previous example shows that the requirement of complementation that $a \vee_L a^* = \top_L$ is too strong to enhance the simple domain of signs A (note that, in Example 1, $-$ is not the complement for $+$ in L). We weaken the definition of complementation in two ways. First, by relaxing that $a \vee_L a^* = \top_L$, the above observation boils down to the well known notion of pseudo-complement, which, when it exists, is unique, indeed $a \rightarrow \bot_L = \vee_L\{c \mid a \wedge_L c = \bot_L\}$. Second, we relativize this notion by considering relative pseudo-complements, which, when they exist, are uniquely given by $a \rightarrow b = \vee_L\{c \mid a \wedge_L c \leq_L b\}$.

Definition 2. Let $A, B \subseteq L$. We define $A \longrightarrow B = \{a \rightarrow b \in L \mid a \in A, b \in B\}$.

It is worth noting that in the above definition we do not require any further hypothesis on the structure of L, apart being a complete lattice. Hence, although $a \to b = \vee_L\{c \mid a \wedge_L c \leq_L b\}$ always exists unique in complete lattices, it may in general fail to be the pseudo-complement of a relative to b. The following example shows this phenomenon.

Example 3. Consider the following simple lattice L for *overflow analysis* of integer variables, which is an abstract interpretation of the standard lattice for *interval analysis* in [13]. In this example, $m \in \mathbb{N}$ is a constant, playing the role of *maxint*.

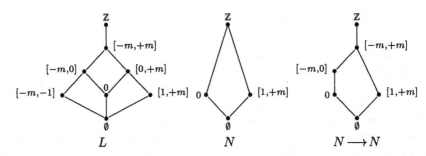

Note that L is neither distributive, nor pseudo-complemented. If N is the domain depicted above, which is a strict abstraction of L, although being defined, $0 \to \emptyset = 0 \to [1, +m] = [-m, +m]$ is neither the pseudo-complement of 0, nor the pseudo-complement of 0 relative to $[1, +m]$. In the case of $[1, +m] \to 0 = [1, +m] \to \emptyset$ instead, we obtain precisely the relative pseudo-complement which is indeed $[-m, 0]$. Note that when an object $a \to b$ is not the relative pseudo-complement, it still provides an approximation for the information which is complementary to a. In this case, the complementary information for 0, which should be given by the union of the intervals $[-m, -1] \cup [1, +m]$, is approximated by their convex hull $0 \to \emptyset = [-m, +m]$.

We extend the domain transformation $\longrightarrow$ to a binary abstract domain refinement. Given two abstract domains X and Y, this is precisely captured by the least Moore family (viz. abstract domain) containing $X \longrightarrow Y$.

Definition 4. Let $A, B \in uco(L)$. The *Heyting completion of A wrt B*, denoted by $A \xrightarrow{\wedge} B$, is $\curlywedge(A \longrightarrow B)$.

Theorem 5. Let $A \in uco(L)$. $\lambda X, Y.\ X \xrightarrow{\wedge} Y$ is argumentwise monotonic on $uco(L)$, and $\lambda X.\ A \xrightarrow{\wedge} X$ is reductive on $uco(L)$.

In the following, the Heyting completion of a domain X is $X \xrightarrow{\wedge} X$. Note that, while the Heyting completion operator $\lambda X.\ X \xrightarrow{\wedge} X : uco(L) \longmapsto uco(L)$ is monotonic, it is not an idempotent refinement. For instance, in Example 3, we have that $[0, +m] \notin N \xrightarrow{\wedge} N$, but $[0, +m] \in (N \xrightarrow{\wedge} N) \xrightarrow{\wedge} (N \xrightarrow{\wedge} N)$.

5 Algebraic properties

In this section we show some basic algebraic properties of Heyting completion with respect to other domain operations. To this aim, we embed the lattice of abstract domains into an algebra of primitive operators for domain refinement. In particular, we consider the meet operation ($\sqcap$) of closure operators, which is (isomorphic to) the well known *reduced product* ([14]) of abstract domains, together with the above Heyting completion, and the operation for *disjunctive completion* ($\curlyvee$) ([14,15,19]).

In the rest of the paper, $A, B, C \in uco(L)$, and denote generic abstract domains.

Proposition 6.

1. $A \xrightarrow{\wedge} \{\top_L\} = \{\top_L\}$
2. $\{\top_L\} \xrightarrow{\wedge} A = A$
3. $(A \xrightarrow{\wedge} C) \sqcap (B \xrightarrow{\wedge} C) = \curlywedge((A \cup B) \longrightarrow C)^1$

Complete Heyting algebras play a central role in our construction, as they correspond precisely to the models of propositional intuitionistic logic. L is a *complete Heyting algebra* (cHa), if for each $X \subseteq L$ and $y \in L$, $y \wedge_L (\vee_L X) = \vee_L \{ y \wedge_L x \mid x \in X \}$. If L is cHa, then it is relatively pseudo-complemented, and $\rightarrow$ models intuitionistic implication. Hence, $A \xrightarrow{\wedge} A$ is the most abstract domain containing the implications $a \rightarrow b$ for $a, b \in A$.

Proposition 7. *Let L be a cHa.*

1. $A \xrightarrow{\wedge} (C \sqcap B) = (A \xrightarrow{\wedge} C) \sqcap (A \xrightarrow{\wedge} B)$
2. $(A \sqcap B) \xrightarrow{\wedge} C = A \xrightarrow{\wedge} (B \xrightarrow{\wedge} C)$
3. $A \xrightarrow{\wedge} \curlywedge(X) = \underset{x \in X}{\sqcap} A \xrightarrow{\wedge} \{\top_L, x\}$ *if $X \subseteq L$.*

Note that by (3) in Proposition 7, Heyting completion can be constructed from *atomic domains*, i.e., closures of the form $\{\top_L, x\}$, by considering only the elements x in a generating[2] set X. In this case, if $x \in L$, then $A \xrightarrow{\wedge} \{\top_L, x\}$ is the most abstract domain which contains the pseudo-complements of the elements in A in the interval lattice $[x, \top_L] \subseteq L^3$.

The disjunctive completion was introduced in [14] to express *merge over all paths* data-flow analysis in fixpoint form. The idea is to lift a given abstract domain A, to the least (most abstract) domain which includes A and which is a complete (join-) sublattice of L, viz. no approximation is induced by considering the join of abstract objects. The disjunctive completion of A is defined as the most abstract domain which is an additive closure and includes A (cf. [14,19]):

---

[1] Note that $A \cup B$ may not be, in general, a Moore-family.
[2] $A \subseteq L$ is generated by $X \subseteq A$ if $A = \curlywedge(X)$.
[3] if $a, b \in L$, the *interval lattice* $[a, b]$ is the complete sub-lattice of L: $\{x \in L \mid a \leq_L x \leq_L b\}$.

$\Upsilon(A) = \sqcup\{ X \in uco(L) \mid X \sqsubseteq A \text{ and } X \text{ is additive} \}$. The following result specifies the disjunctive completion of an abstract domain A when the concrete domain L is either collecting or a cHa with A finite. Note that *collecting domains*, i.e., domains of the form $\wp(S)$ for some set S, are typical concrete domains in collecting semantics for program analysis (e.g. [15,22,25]).

Proposition 8. *If L is collecting or L is a cHa and A is finite, then $\Upsilon(A) = \{\vee_L X \mid X \subseteq A\}$.*

Next result follows immediately from the logical properties of intuitionistic implication, and it specifies the relation between disjunctive and Heyting completions.

Proposition 9. *If L is collecting or L is a cHa and A is finite, $\Upsilon(A) \xrightarrow{\Lambda} B = A \xrightarrow{\Lambda} B$.*

The inverse operation to disjunctive completion, which is called *disjunctive optimal basis*, was introduced in [19]. Given an abstract domain A, the idea is to find the most abstract domain X (when it exists) such that $\Upsilon(A) = \Upsilon(X)$. This domain, denoted $\Omega(A)$, is such that $A \sqsubseteq \Omega(A)$. Giacobazzi and Ranzato proved in [19] that $\Omega(A)$ exists under some hypotheses, e.g. when L or A are finite, or when L is collecting, and $\Omega(A) = \lambda(\{ x \in A \mid \forall Y \subseteq A.\ x = \vee_L Y \Rightarrow x \in Y \})$.

Corollary 10. *If L is collecting or L is a cHa and A is finite, then $A \xrightarrow{\Lambda} B = \Omega(A) \xrightarrow{\Lambda} B$.*

This result specifies that $A \xrightarrow{\Lambda} B$ can always be obtained by considering the more abstract, and hence less expensive, domain $\Omega(A)$. This because, the implicational information generated by the disjunctive information in A, i.e. those objects $x \to b$ where $x \in A$ is such that there exists $C \subseteq A$ and $x = \vee_L C$, can be reconstructed by conjunction of relative pseudo-complements of the form $c \to b$, with $c \in C$. Here, the disjunctive optimal basis plays the role of the least domain generating A by disjunctive completion. By combining the above result with (3) in Proposition 7, we obtain the following result, with $X \subseteq L$ playing the role of generating set. This result may be useful to implement Heyting completion of abstract domains, from the most abstract arguments.

$$A \xrightarrow{\Lambda} \lambda(X) = \underset{x \in X}{\sqcap}\ \Omega(A) \xrightarrow{\Lambda} \{\top_L, x\}.$$

Note that, the implementation of the Heyting completion $A \xrightarrow{\Lambda} B$ involving the disjunctive optimal basis of A and an atomic decomposition of B, requires a lower number of reductions to identify pairs $a \to b$ having the same meaning. In particular, whenever $A = \wp(S)$ for some set S and A is a disjunctive domain, then an upper bound to the number of elements in $A \xrightarrow{\Lambda} A$ is not $|A|^2$, but $2|A|$. This because $|\Omega(A)| = log(|A|)$, $A = \lambda(\{ S \setminus \{ x \} \mid x \in S \})$ and $|\{ S \setminus \{ x \} \mid x \in S \}| = log(|A|)$. In this case $|A \xrightarrow{\Lambda} A| \leq 2|A|$.

6 Reduced power and Heyting completion

Reduced power was introduced by Cousot and Cousot in [14], under the hypothesis that the concrete domain is some Boolean lattice of assertions. This construction was generalized in [18], where weaker hypotheses (e.g. cHa's) are considered for the existence of reduced power of domains. We follow this presentation, and we call *dependencies* the objects in the reduced power of domains.

We are interested in the case of *autodependencies*, which are monotone functions from an abstract domain A into itself. Monotone functions are considered equivalent, and therefore reduced, if they represent the same dependency between the objects of A. If $A = \rho_A(L)$ for $\rho_A \in uco(L)$, an autodependency is specified by the function $\lambda x. \, \rho_A(d \wedge_L x) : A \longmapsto A$, with $d \in L$. The set of all such dependencies is the reduced power $A^A = \{\, \lambda x \in A. \, \rho_A(d \wedge_L x) \mid d \in L \,\}$. Note that considering autodependencies in A^A is not a serious restriction, because $A^B \subseteq (A \sqcap B)^{(A \sqcap B)}$ ([18]). Next result extends Theorem [14, 10.2.0.1] to cHa's and proves that A^A refines A.

Theorem 11 ([18]). *Let L be a cHa and $A = \rho_A(L)$ for $\rho_A \in uco(L)$. Then $\langle L, \alpha, A^A, \gamma \rangle$ is a G.i. where $\alpha = \lambda d \in L. \, (\lambda x \in A. \, \rho_A(d \wedge_L x))$. Moreover $A^A \sqsubseteq A$.*

The following technical lemma is essential to give a representation result for dependencies in A^A, in terms of relative pseudo-complements.

Lemma 12. *Let L be a cHa and $\rho \in uco(L)$. Then, for any $d \in L$: $\gamma(\lambda x \in \rho(L). \, \rho(d \wedge_L x)) = \bigwedge_{a \in \rho(L)} (a \to \rho(d \wedge_L a))$.*

The following representation result for autodependencies is the main result of this section, and it specifies that, for autodependencies, reduced power is equivalent to Heyting completion.

Theorem 13. *If L is a cHa and $A = \rho_A(L)$ for $\rho_A \in uco(L)$, then $A^A = A \xrightarrow{\wedge} A$.*

This result proves a strong link between two apparently unrelated domain refinements, namely between domain refinement by reduced power, and domain completion by relative pseudo-complements.

7 Examples

7.1 Implicational groundness analysis

Pos is the domain most widely used for groundness analysis of logic programs ([3]). *Pos* is able to characterize both pure groundness, i.e. whether a variable is instantiated to ground terms during program execution, and the relations between the groundness of different program variables, providing in this sense a clear example of relational analysis. In this section we show that the domain *Pos* of positive Boolean functions can be interpreted as an implicational domain. *Pos* is the result of Heyting completion of a simpler domain for pure groundness. This domain is obtained by lifting Jones and Søndergaard's domain for pure groundness analysis $\mathcal{G}$ ([22]) by disjunctive completion. The disjunctive completion gives here the least amount of disjunctive information which is typical of *Pos*.

We fix a first-order language $\mathcal{L}$, with variables ranging in $\mathcal{V}$. The set of terms and idempotent substitutions, viz. mappings from $\mathcal{V}$ to terms in $\mathcal{L}$, are denoted respectively $T_\mathcal{L}$ and *Sub*. Objects in $T_\mathcal{L}$ and *Sub* are partially ordered by instantiation: $a \leq b$ iff $\exists \theta \in Sub. \ a = b\theta$. For any syntactic object s, $var(s)$ denotes the set of its variables.

Let $Var \subseteq \mathcal{V}$ be a finite set, representing the set of interesting variables. *Pos* is the set of (classic) propositional formulas built on Var and the constant *true*, by using the connectives $\wedge, \vee, \rightarrow$. The interpretation of the connectives is the classical one: $\phi \leq \psi$ if and only if ψ is a logical consequence of ϕ. We say that $I \subseteq Var$ is a model for ϕ, denoted $I \models \phi$, if ϕ is true in the interpretation which assigns *true* to all the variables in I and *false* to the other ones [3]. For the sake of simplicity we write θ **grounds** ϕ to denote $\{\, x \in Var \mid var(\theta(x)) = \emptyset \,\} \models \phi$, for $\theta \in Sub$.

Because logic programs compute substitutions, the concrete domain we consider is $\wp^\downarrow(Sub)$, which is a cHa. *Pos* is an abstraction of $\wp^\downarrow(Sub)$, and the concretization function is $\gamma_{Sub}(\phi) = \{\, \theta \in Sub \mid \forall \sigma \leq \theta. \ \sigma \text{ grounds } \phi \,\}$ ([11]). $\mathcal{G} \subset Pos$ is the standard domain for pure groundness analysis defined in [22], which is a strict abstraction of *Pos*, including formulas on Var with the only connective $\wedge$. As usual, we identify *Pos* and $\mathcal{G}$ with the corresponding closures on $\wp^\downarrow(Sub)$: $\gamma_{Sub}(Pos)$ and $\gamma_{Sub}(\mathcal{G})$.

Theorem 14. $Pos = \Upsilon(\mathcal{G}) \xrightarrow{\wedge} \Upsilon(\mathcal{G})$.

Note that, by Proposition 9, $Pos = \mathcal{G} \xrightarrow{\wedge} \Upsilon(\mathcal{G})$. For $Var = \{x, y\}$, the domains $\mathcal{G}$, $\Upsilon(\mathcal{G})$ and *Pos* are depicted below.

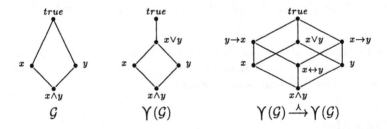

7.2 Directionality in type inference

In this section we consider the problem of inferring types in logic programs by abstract interpretation. Given a domain for (basic) type analysis, we show how the Heyting completion of such a domain captures the notion of directionality among types and, more in general, how this construction surfaces directionality in any property closed under instantiation. In this case, Heyting completion supplies a domain for type inference, including the same dependency information between types as traditionally obtained in standard results on directional type checking by verification methods [1].

The operational semantics of a logic program P, viz. a finite set of Horn clauses in $\mathcal{L}$, is defined by SLD-resolution. If G is a goal, viz. a conjunction of atoms in $\mathcal{L}$, then we write $G \xrightarrow{\vartheta}^*_P \square$ iff $\vartheta \in Sub$ is a computed answer substitution for G in P ([2]). A type is a set of terms closed under substitution [1]. Hence, the concrete domain in which we interpret types is $\wp^{\downarrow}(T_{\mathcal{L}})$. An (abstract) domain of types $\mathcal{T}$ is therefore any abstraction of $\wp^{\downarrow}(T_{\mathcal{L}})$.

A type for a predicate p of arity n is an n-tuple of types. In the following, for the sake of simplicity, we assume that all predicates in the program have the same arity n, and abuse $T_{\mathcal{L}}$ to denote n-tuples of terms. A *directional type* for a predicate p has the form $\langle I, O \rangle$ where I and O are types for p. The type I is the "input" type and type O is the "output" type of p. A predicate p has type $\langle I, O \rangle$ in a program P (denoted $p \in \langle I, O \rangle$) if for any goal $p(t)$, $t \in I \Rightarrow \theta(t) \in O$ for any answer substitution θ (cf. [1]). Next result relates the Heyting completion refinement to the notion of directional type. The idea is to prove that an implicational type $\tau_1 \to \tau_2$ models exactly the above notion of directional type.

Theorem 15. *Let P be a program, $\mathcal{T}$ be a domain of types, $\tau_1, \tau_2 \in \mathcal{T}$ and p be a predicate. Then $(\forall \theta.\ p(\bar{X}) \xrightarrow{\theta}^*_P \square \Rightarrow \bar{X}\theta \in \tau_1 \to \tau_2) \Leftrightarrow (\forall \bar{t} \in \tau_1.\forall \sigma.\ p(\bar{t}) \xrightarrow{\sigma}^*_P \square \Rightarrow \bar{t}\sigma \in \tau_2)$.*

Corollary 16. *In the hypothesis of Theorem 15, p has type $\tau_1 \to \tau_2$ in $\mathcal{T} \xrightarrow{\wedge} \mathcal{T}$ iff $p \in \langle \tau_1, \tau_2 \rangle$.*

Clearly, the domain $\mathcal{T} \xrightarrow{\wedge} \mathcal{T}$ is still closed under instantiation. Directional types in $\mathcal{T} \xrightarrow{\wedge} \mathcal{T}$, that satisfy the theorem above, can be obtained by abstract interpretation, with abstract domain $\mathcal{T} \xrightarrow{\wedge} \mathcal{T}$, by means of any bottom-up/top-down analyzer which is able to approximate correct or even computed answer substitutions (e.g. [4,7]).

Example 17. Let us consider the program $P = \{p(X, X)., r(2, Y) : -p(2, Y).\}$ and the following simple domain of basic types $\mathcal{T}$, where symbols I (integer) and B (Boolean) have the obvious meaning as fixpoints of a closure operator on $\wp^{\downarrow}(T_{\mathcal{L}})$. A standard type inference which can be obtained from the above domain

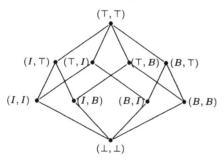

of types $\mathcal{T}$, returns the following type patterns: $\{p(\top, \top), r(I, \top)\}$. Although correct, this result is not very precise. By abstract interpretation in the refined domain $\mathcal{T} \xrightarrow{\wedge} \mathcal{T}$, we obtain the more precise type patterns: $\{p(X, X)., r(I, I)\}$, where $p(X, X)$ is a shorthand for $\bigwedge_{(\tau_1, \tau_2) \in \mathcal{T}} p(\tau_1, \tau_2) \to p(\tau_1 \cap \tau_2, \tau_1 \cap \tau_2)$, i.e. $p(I, \top) \to p(I, I) \wedge p(\top, I) \to p(I, I) \wedge p(B, \top) \to p(B, B) \wedge p(\top, B) \to p(B, B)$.

7.3 From types back to groundness

A similar result of the above one was proved in [18] in the particular case of ground dependency analysis, with no disjunctive information. The authors proved that the abstract domain $Def \subset Pos$ ([3]), which contains formulas whose models are closed under intersection, is, in view of Theorem 13, precisely $\mathcal{G} \xrightarrow{\wedge} \mathcal{G}$. Hence in this case, pure groundness $\mathcal{G}$ or disjunctive groundness $\curlyvee(\mathcal{G})$ can be both viewed as some basic type definition, and ground dependency, both in Def and Pos, can be interpreted as directional type inference. The key point here is that the concrete domain is some lattice of order-ideals, i.e. sets of objects closed under instantiation, which are non-Boolean cHa. A different concrete domain would change completely the interpretation of directionality. Consider the Boolean concrete domain $\wp(Sub)$. If $Var = \{x, y\}$ we have the following domain $\mathcal{G} \xrightarrow{\wedge} \mathcal{G}$, which differs from the analogous completion Def on the non-Boolean lattice $\wp^{\downarrow}(Sub)$.

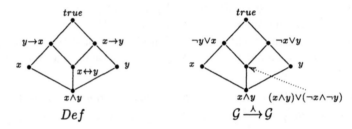

While $\mathcal{G} \xrightarrow{\wedge} \mathcal{G}$ is no longer able to express ground dependencies, it is now able to express negative groundness information. This because intuitionistic implication is replaced by classical one. This is a consequence of the peculiar nature of the concrete (collecting) domain, which is a Boolean lattice. In this case, the relative pseudo-complements introduced by the Heyting completion provide negation of properties. This because, in Boolean lattices, $a \to b = \neg a \vee b$, for instance $\neg x \vee y = x \to x \wedge y = \overline{\gamma_{Sub}(x)} \cup \gamma_{Sub}(x \wedge y)$, while this is not the case in complete Heyting algebras. For instance, the empty substitution belongs to $\neg x \vee y$, but it provides no groundness information. Clearly, because the set-theoretic complement of a set closed under instantiation is not, in general, closed under instantiation, then $\mathcal{G} \xrightarrow{\wedge} \mathcal{G}$ is not here an abstraction of $\wp^{\downarrow}(Sub)$. In this sense, the analysis obtained from $\mathcal{G} \xrightarrow{\wedge} \mathcal{G}$ cannot be regarded as type inference.

8 Implicational domain equations

In this section we consider the idempotent extension of Heyting completion. Given an abstract domain A, we are interested in the least abstract domain X which is more concrete than A and it is closed under $\xrightarrow{\wedge}$, i.e. the least (most abstract) solution (if any) of the implicational domain equation

$$X = A \sqcap (X \xrightarrow{\wedge} X) \tag{1}$$

We consider the algebra $\langle uco(L), \sqcap, \Upsilon, \xrightarrow{\curlywedge}\rangle$, involving conjunction of domains by reduced product, disjunctive completion and Heyting completion, which are all monotonic operators on domains. Note that the least fixpoint of $\lambda X.\ A \sqcap (X \xrightarrow{\curlywedge} X)$ is L, which is the identical closure $\lambda x.x$. We are interested in the greatest fixpoint of $\lambda X.\ A \sqcap (X \xrightarrow{\curlywedge} X)$ in $uco(L)$, which exists and it is the domain corresponding to the least closure ordinal of the above operator, in the following family of domains: $B_1 = A$, $B_{\alpha+1} = A \sqcap (B_\alpha \xrightarrow{\curlywedge} B_\alpha) = B_\alpha \xrightarrow{\curlywedge} B_\alpha$ and $B_\alpha = \sqcap_{\gamma<\alpha} B_\gamma$ if α is a limit ordinal.

Theorem 18. *Let L be a cHa and $X \sqsubseteq A$.*

1. *X is a solution of (1) iff it is a subalgebra of L with respect to the relative pseudo-complement.*
2. *X is a complete Heyting subalgebra of L iff it is a solution of (1) and it is disjunctive.*

It is worth noting that the operator associated with the equation (1), $\lambda X.\ A \sqcap (X \xrightarrow{\curlywedge} X)$ is not, in general, co-continuous in $uco(L)$, as shown by the following example. Hence ω may not in general be its least closure ordinal.

Example 19. Consider the following complete lattice $L = \mathbb{N} \cup \{\omega, \top, c\}$ depicted below, and the family of its abstractions $A_i \in uco(L)$, such that for any $i \in \mathbb{N}$, $A_i = \{n \in \mathbb{N} \mid n \leq i\} \cup \{\top\}$.

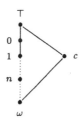

$\{A_i\}_{i\in\mathbb{N}}$ is a chain, and for any $i \in \mathbb{N}$, $A_i = A_i \xrightarrow{\curlywedge} A_i$, but $\sqcap_{i\in\mathbb{N}} A_i = \mathbb{N}\cup\{\omega\}$ is not dependency closed, since $c = 0 \to \omega \in (\sqcap_{i\in\mathbb{N}} A_i) \xrightarrow{\curlywedge} (\sqcap_{i\in\mathbb{N}} A_i)$. Note that L above is not a cHa. However, unfortunately, it is not co-continuous even if the concrete domain is a Boolean algebra. It is sufficient to consider $L = \langle \wp(\omega), \omega, \emptyset, \cap, \cup, \subseteq\rangle$, and the chain of domains $A_i = \curlywedge(\cup_{1\leq j\leq i}\{\emptyset, \omega, \omega\setminus\{i\}, \{i\}\}) \in uco(\wp(\omega))$, for $i \geq 1$. Note that $\sqcap_{i\geq 1} A_i = \curlywedge(\cup_{i\geq 1} A_i)$ and $\{0\}, \emptyset \in \sqcap_{i\geq 1} A_i$ but, being $\cap$-irreducible, $\{0\} \to \emptyset = \omega\setminus\{0\} \notin \sqcap_{i\geq 1}(A_i \xrightarrow{\curlywedge} A_i)$.

Clearly, co-continuity is ensured when L is a finite domain, because $uco(L)$ is finite too, or when $uco(L)$ satisfies the descending chain condition, i.e. it does not contains infinite descending chains. Because $uco(L)$ is a domain of functions, both of these conditions are far too restrictive for a concrete domain for semantics and analysis. However, co-continuity is maintained when the descending chain condition holds on the concrete domain L, as proved by the next result. Note that the operator we want to prove co-continuous is defined on $uco(L)$ and our condition, in general, does not imply that $uco(L)$ enjoys the descending chain property.

Theorem 20. *If L enjoys the descending chain property, the operator $\lambda X. A \sqcap (X \xrightarrow{\Lambda} X)$ is co-continuous in $uco(L)$.*

Next result characterizes a generic solution, and the most abstract solution to the equation (1), under the hypothesis that L is a collecting domain.

Theorem 21. *Let $L = \wp(S)$ for some set S. $A = A \xrightarrow{\Lambda} A$ iff A is disjunctive and complemented, viz. $A = \curlyvee(A)$ and $A = A \sqcap (A \xrightarrow{\Lambda} \{\top_L, \bot_A\})$. Moreover $\curlyvee(A \sqcap (A \xrightarrow{\Lambda} \{\top_L, \bot_A\}))$ is the most abstract solution domain for (1).*

9 Conclusions and future work

A logical interpretation for the basic operations for domain refinement gives rise to an algebra, where domains, and therefore analyses, can be manipulated in a logical framework. Hence, analyses can be specified in equational form, as domains in denotational semantics. Domains are no longer specified in terms of their elements, but in terms of the property they have to meet. Heyting completion is, in this construction, the basic step to build relational analyses. The logic interpretation of domain refinements has another interesting application. Hankin and Le Metayer ([20]) proved that some properties of data-structures during program execution can be inferred by a simple type system, in a kind of *proof theoretic* approach to program analysis. We believe that there is a link between systematic refinements of domains and corresponding refinements of proof systems for data-flow analysis, i.e., there is a proof-theoretic counterpart of our Heyting completion.

References

1. A. Aiken and T.K. Lakshman. Directional type checking of logic programs. In *Proc. 1ˢᵗ Static Analysis Symp. SAS'94*, LNCS 864, pp. 43–60. Springer, 1994.
2. K. R. Apt. Introduction to logic programming. In *Handbook of Theoretical Computer Science*, Vol. B, pp. 495–574. Elsevier, 1990.
3. T. Armstrong, K. Marriott, P. Schachte, and H. Søndergaard. Boolean functions for dependency analysis: algebraic properties and efficient representation. In *Proc. 1ˢᵗ Static Analysis Symp. SAS'94*, LNCS 864, pp. 266–280. Springer, 1994.
4. R. Barbuti, R. Giacobazzi, and G. Levi. A general framework for semantics-based bottom-up abstract interpretation of logic programs. *ACM TOPLAS*, 15(1):133–181, 1993.
5. G. Birkhoff. Lattice theory. In *AMS Colloquium Publication, third ed.* AMS Press, 1967.
6. F. Bronsard, T.K. Lakshman, and U.S. Reddy. A framework of directionality for proving termination of logic programs. In *Proc. 1992 Joint Int'l Conf. and Symp. Logic Prog.*, pp. 321–335. MIT Press, 1992.
7. M. Bruynooghe. A practical framework for the abstract interpretation of logic programs. *J. of Logic Programm.* 10:91–124, 1991.
8. M. Codish and B. Demoen. Deriving type dependencies for logic programs using multiple incarnations of *Prop*. In *Proc. 1ˢᵗ Static Analysis Symp. SAS'94*, LNCS 864. Springer, 1994.

9. M. Codish, A. Mulkers, M. Bruynooghe, M. García de la Banda, and M.Hermenegildo. Improving abstract interpretations by combining domains. *ACM TOPLAS*, 17(1):28–44, 1995.

10. A. Cortesi, G. Filé, R. Giacobazzi, C. Palamidessi, and F. Ranzato. Complementation in abstract interpretation. *ACM TOPLAS* 19(1):7–47, 1997.

11. A. Cortesi, G. Filè, and W. Winsborough. *Prop* revisited: Propositional formulas as abstract domain for groundness analysis. In *Proc. 6th IEEE LICS*, pp. 322–327. IEEE Comp. Soc. Press, 1991.

12. A. Cortesi, B. Le Charlier, and P. Van Hentenryck. Combinations of abstract domains for logic programming. In 21st *ACM POPL*, pp. 227–239. ACM Press, 1994.

13. P. Cousot and R. Cousot. Abstract interpretation: a unified lattice model for static analysis of programs by construction or approximation of fixpoints. In 4th *ACM POPL*, pp. 238–252. ACM Press, 1977.

14. P. Cousot and R. Cousot. Systematic design of program analysis frameworks. In 6th *ACM POPL*, pp. 269–282. ACM Press, 1979.

15. P. Cousot and R. Cousot. Higher-order abstract interpretation (and application to comportment analysis generalizing strictness, termination, projection and per analysis of functional languages). In *Proc. 1994 Int'l Conf. on Comp. Lang. IC-CL'94*, pp. 95–112. IEEE Comp. Soc. Press, 1994.

16. G. Filé, R. Giacobazzi, and F. Ranzato. A unifying view on abstract domain design. *ACM Comp. Surveys*, 28(2):333–336, 1996.

17. G. Filé and F. Ranzato. Improving abstract interpretations by systematic lifting to the powerset. In *Proc. 1994 Int'l Logic Prog. Symp.*, pp. 655–669. MIT Press, 1994.

18. R. Giacobazzi and F. Ranzato. Functional dependencies and Moore-set completions of abstract interpretations and semantics. In *Proc. 1995 Int'l Logic Prog. Symp.*, pp. 321–335. MIT Press, 1995.

19. R. Giacobazzi and F. Ranzato. Compositional optimization of disjunctive abstract interpretations. In *Proc. ESOP'96*, LNCS 1058, pp. 141–155. Springer, 1996.

20. C. Hankin and D. Le Metayer. Deriving algorithms from type inference systems: Applications to strictness analysis. In 21st *ACM POPL*, pp. 202–212. ACM Press, 1994.

21. T.P. Jensen. Disjunctive strictness analysis. In 7th *IEEE LICS*, pp. 174–185. IEEE Comp. Soc. Press, 1992.

22. N. D. Jones and H. Søndergaard. A Semantics-based Framework for the Abstract Interpretation of Prolog. In S. Abramsky and C. Hankin, eds., *Abstract Interpretation of Declarative Languages*, pp. 123–142. Ellis Horwood Ltd, 1987.

23. N.D. Jones and S.S. Muchnick. Complexity of flow analysis, inductive assertion synthesis and a language due to Dijkstra. In S. Muchnick and N.D. Jones, eds., *Program Flow analysis: Theory and Applications*, pp. 380–393. Prentice-Hall, 1981.

24. J. Morgado. Some results on the closure operators of partially ordered sets. *Port. Math.*, 19(2):101–139, 1960.

25. A. Mycroft and F. Nielson. Strong abstract interpretation using power domains. In *Proc. 10th ICALP*, LNCS 154, pp. 536–547. Springer, 1983.

26. F. Nielson. Tensor products generalize the relational data flow analysis method. In *Proc. 4th Hung. Comp. Science Conf.*, pp. 211–225, 1985.

27. K. Yi and W.L. Harrison. Automatic generation and management of interprocedural program analyses. In 20th *ACM POPL*, pp. 246–259. ACM Press, 1993.

An Open-Ended Finite Domain Constraint Solver

Mats Carlsson[1], Greger Ottosson[2], and Björn Carlson[3]

[1] SICS, PO Box 1263, S-164 29 KISTA, Sweden
[2] Computing Science Dept., Uppsala University
PO Box 311, S-751 05 UPPSALA, Sweden
[3] Xerox PARC, 3333 Coyote Hill Road, Palo Alto, CA 94304, USA

Abstract. We describe the design and implementation of a finite domain constraint solver embedded in a Prolog system using an extended unification mechanism via attributed variables as a generic constraint interface. The solver is essentially a scheduler for *indexicals*, i.e. reactive functional rules encoding local consistency methods performing incremental constraint solving or entailment checking, and *global constraints*, i.e. general propagators which may use specialized algorithms to achieve a higher degree of consistency or better time and space complexity.

The solver has an open-ended design: the user can introduce new constraints, either in terms of indexicals by writing rules in a functional notation, or as global constraints via a Prolog programming interface. Constraints defined in terms of indexicals can be linked to 0/1-variables modeling entailment; thus indexicals are used for constraint solving as well as for entailment testing. Constraints can be arbitrarily combined using the propositional connectives by automatic expansion to systems of reified constraints.

Keywords: Implementation of Constraint Systems, Constraint Programming, Finite Domains, Indexicals, Global Constraints.

1 Introduction

We describe the design and implementation of the SICStus Prolog [11] finite domain constraint solver. The solver is essentially a scheduler for two entities: *indexicals* [24], i.e. reactive functional rules performing incremental constraint solving or entailment checking within the framework of the Waltz filtering algorithm [26], and *global constraints*, i.e. general propagators which may use specialized constraint solving algorithms.

An indexical for solving a constraint $C(X_1, \ldots, X_n)$ has the form X_i in r, where the expression r, called *range*, specifies the feasible values for X_i in terms of the feasible values for $X_1, \ldots, X_{i-1}, X_{i+1}, \ldots, X_n$. The basic idea is to express C as n indexicals, one for each X_i, encoding a local consistency method for solving C. Each indexical is a *projection* of C onto X_i; hence, indexicals are also known as *projection constraints* [21], and have been used in several implementations [9,21,6]. Ranges are defined using a "constraint programming assembly language", which gives the programmer precise control over the level of consistency, and can yield more efficient solutions than relying on the solver's built-in constraints.

An important feature of any constraint solver is *reification*, i.e. the ability to link a constraint to a 0/1-variable reflecting the truth value of the constraint. Thus constraints can be combined using propositional connectives to model cardinality and disjunction simply by flattening to systems of reified constraints and arithmetic constraints over their 0/1-variables. Reification subsumes several frequently used operations such as blocking implication [20] and the cardinality operator [23]. These 0/1-variables may be used in other constraints, thus complex constraints can often be decomposed into a system of many reified, simple constraints.

A crucial operation in reification is entailment detection. It has been shown that indexicals can be used not only for solving constraints, but also for incremental entailment detection [24,5]. The solver handles both kinds of indexicals, ensuring that certain preconditions are satisfied before admitting them for execution. We have built a general reification mechanism for constraints defined by indexicals on top of this idea.

A problem with local propagation methods is the small grain size: each invocation of an indexical does relatively little work (at most *one* domain is pruned), and the overhead of scheduling indexicals for execution becomes noticeable. Furthermore, consider a constraint C expressing some complex relation. Expressing this in terms of primitive constraints, usually through library constraints defined with indexicals, perhaps combined with reification, means spawning many small constraints each maintaining local consistency. However, the consistency for C as a whole can be poor and the large amount of suspensions incurs a scheduling overhead. The alternative is to treat C as a single *global* constraint, using a specialized algorithm that exploits the structure of the problem and retains a high degree of consistency. Also, specialized algorithms that outperform local propagation are available for important classes of constraints. We have addressed these problems by defining a clean interface by which global constraints can be defined in Prolog.

The solver has an open-ended design: the user can introduce new constraints, either in terms of indexicals by writing rules in a functional notation, or as global constraints via a Prolog programming interface.

Constraints defined in terms of indexicals can be linked to 0/1-variables modeling entailment; thus indexicals are used for constraint solving as well as for entailment testing. Constraints can be arbitrarily combined using the propositional connectives by automatic expansion to systems of reified constraints.

Our work has the following contributions.

- It is the first full implementation of an idea [24] to use indexicals to specify the four aspects of a reified constraint, viz. solving the constraint or its negation, and detecting entailment or disentailment of the constraint.
- It is a loosely coupled integration of indexicals into the Prolog abstract machine, with truly minimal extensions on the Prolog side.

- It provides an API for defining global constraints in Prolog.
- It provides mixed execution strategies with indexicals encoding local consistency methods within a Waltz-like algorithm combined with global constraints encoding specialized consistency algorithms. We maintain separate scheduling queues for the two; a global constraint is only resumed when no indexicals are scheduled for execution.
- It extends the indexical language with constructs that e.g. admit arbitrary binary relations to be encoded.
- It shows that a fully-fledged open-ended finite domain system with negative integers, non-linear arithmetic, reification, mixed execution strategies, loosely coupled to a Prolog abstract machine, is possible with competitive performance.

These contributions will be described in detail later. The rest of the paper is structured as follows. Section 2 defines the constraint system and our extended indexical language. Section 3 describes the architecture of the constraint solver, how the Prolog engine had to be extended to provide services specific for FD constraints, and briefly how constraints are compiled to calls to library constraints and/or to indexicals. Section 4 describes the global constraint API. In Sec. 5, we evaluate the basic performance of our reification mechanism, and compare the performance of our solver with four similar systems. Section 6 compares our results with other work. We end with some conclusions about our work.

2 The Constraint System

2.1 Domain Constraints, Indexicals, Entailment and Disentailment

The constraint system is based on domain constraints and indexicals. A *domain constraint* is an expression $X \in I$, where I is a nonempty set of integers. A set S of domain constraints is called a *store*. $[X]_S$, the *domain of X in S*, is defined as the intersection of all I such that $X \in I$ belongs to S (if no such $X \in I$ belongs to S, $[X]_S = \mathcal{Z}$). A store S' is an *extension* of a store S iff $\forall X : [X]_{S'} \subseteq [X]_S$.

The following definitions, adapted from [25], define important notions of consistency and entailment of constraints wrt. stores. Let $[[X]]_S$ denote the interval $\min([X]_S) .. \max([X]_S)$:

A constraint C is *domain-consistent wrt. S* iff, for each variable X_i and value V_i in $[X_i]_S$, there exist values V_j in $[X_j]_S$, $1 \le j \le n, i \ne j$, such that $C(V_1, \ldots, V_n)$ is true. A constraint C is *domain-entailed by S* iff, for all values V_j in $[X_j]_S$, $1 \le j \le n$, $C(V_1, \ldots, V_n)$ is true. A constraint C is *interval-consistent wrt. S* iff, for each variable X_i there exist values V_j in $[[X_j]]_S$, $1 \le j \le n, i \ne j$, such that $C(V_1, \ldots, \min([X_i]_S), \ldots, V_n)$ and $C(V_1, \ldots, \max([X_i]_S), \ldots, V_n)$ are both true. A constraint C is *interval-entailed by S* iff, for all values V_j in $[[X_j]]_S$, $1 \le j \le n$, $C(V_1, \ldots, V_n)$ is true. Finally, a constraint is *domain-disentailed (interval-disentailed) by S* iff its negation is domain-entailed (interval-entailed) by S.

$$N ::= x \mid i, \text{ where } i \in \mathcal{Z} \mid \infty \mid -\infty$$

$$T ::= N \mid T + T \mid T - T \mid T * T \mid \lceil T/T \rceil \mid \lfloor T/T \rfloor \mid T \bmod T$$
$$\mid \ \min(x) \mid \max(x) \mid \text{card}(x)$$

$$R ::= T..T \mid R \cap R \mid R \cup R \mid R \ ? \ R \mid \backslash R$$
$$\mid \ R + T \mid R - T \mid R \bmod T$$
$$\mid \ \text{unionof}(x, R, R) \mid \text{switch}(T, F) \mid \text{dom}(x)$$
$$\mid \ \text{a finite subset of } \mathcal{Z}$$

$$F ::= \text{a finite mapping from } \mathcal{Z} \text{ to } R$$

Fig. 1. Syntax of range expressions

An indexical has the form x in r, where r is a *range* (generated by R in Fig. 1). When applied to a store S, x in r evaluates to a domain constraint $x \in r_S$, where r_S is the value of r in S (see below).

The value of a term t in S, t_S, is an integer computed by the scalar functions defined by T in Fig. 1. The expressions $\min(y), \max(y)$, and $\text{card}(y)$ evaluate to the minimum, maximum, and size of $[y]_S$, respectively.

The value of a range r in S, r_S, is a set of integers computed by the functions defined by R in the figure. The expression $\text{dom}(y)$ evaluates to $[y]_S$. The expression $t..t'$ denotes the interval between t_S and t'_S, and the operators $\cup, \cap$ and $\backslash$ denote union, intersection and complement respectively. The conditional range $r \ ? \ r'$ [21,4] evaluates to r'_S if $r_S \neq \emptyset$ and $\emptyset$ otherwise. The expressions $r + t$, $r - t$, and $r \bmod t$ denote the integer operators applied point-wise.

We have introduced two new range expressions that make it possible to encode arbitrary binary relations as indexicals:

- The value of the expression $\text{switch}(t, f)$ in S is the set $f(t_S)_S$, if t_S is in the domain of f, or $\emptyset$ otherwise. This is implemented as a simple hash table.
- The value of the expression $\text{unionof}(x, d, e)$ is $\bigcup_{x \in d_S} e_S$ i.e. x is quantified by the expression and is assumed to occur in e only. The implementation resembles a "for" loop over the elements of d_S.

For example, let $p(X, Y)$ denote the binary relation

$$\{(1, 1), (2, 1), (2, 2), (3, 1), (3, 2), (3, 3)\}$$

Using the new range expressions, $p(X, Y)$ can be encoded by the two indexicals

```
X in unionof(B,dom(Y),switch(B,[1-{1,2,3},2-{2,3},3-{3}])),
Y in unionof(B,dom(X),switch(B,[1-{1},2-{1,2},3-{1,2,3}])).
```

$[x]_S$ related to r_S	r monotone in S	r anti-monotone in S
$[x]_S \cap r_S = \emptyset$	inconsistent	may become entailed
$[x]_S \subseteq r_S$	may become inconsistent	entailed
$[x]_S \neq ([x]_S \cap r_S) \neq \emptyset$	may become inconsistent	may become entailed

Table 1. Entailment/Inconsistency of x in r in a store S

2.2 Monotonicity of Indexicals

A range r is *monotone in S* iff for every extension S' of S, $r_{S'} \subseteq r_S$. A range r is *anti-monotone in S* iff for every extension S' of S, $r_S \subseteq r_{S'}$. By abuse of notation, we will say that x in r is (anti-)monotone iff r is (anti-)monotone.

The consistency and entailment of x in r in a store S is checked by considering the relationship between $[x]_S$ and r_S, together with the monotonicity of r in S (see Tab. 1). Suppose an indexical x in r is executed in store S where r is monotone in S. If $[x]_S \cap r_S = \emptyset$, an inconsistency is detected. Otherwise, if $[x]_S \subseteq r_S$, $[x]_S$ is already contained in the set of values that are compatible with r_S. Otherwise, $[x]_S$ contains some values that are incompatible with r_S. Hence, $x \in r_S$ is added to S, and we say that x is *pruned*.

3 The Constraint Solver

3.1 Design

The solver is essentially a scheduler for two entities: indexicals performing constraint solving within the framework of the Waltz filtering algorithm [26], and global constraints, i.e. general propagators which may use specialized consistency algorithms. At the heart of the solver is an evaluator for indexicals, i.e. an efficient implementation of the decision table shown in Tab. 1.

Indexicals and global constraints can be added by the programmer, giving precise control over aspects of the operational semantics of constraints. Trade-offs can be made between the computational cost of the constraints and their pruning power. They can yield more efficient solutions than relying on the solver's built-in constraints.

The indexical language provides many degrees of freedom for the user to select the level of consistency to be maintained depending on application-specific needs. For example, the constraint $X = Y + C$ may be defined as indexicals maintaining domain-consistency or interval-consistency as eqcd/3 or eqci/3 respectively of Fig. 2. The notation is explained in Sec. 3.2.

It is of course possible to write indexicals which don't make sense. Basically, an indexical only has declarative meaning if the set denoted by the range is monotonically decreasing. Consider the definition of a constraint C containing an indexical X in r. Let $\mathcal{T}(X, C, S)$ denote the set of values for X that can make C true in some ground extension of the store S. Then the indexical should obey the following coding rules:

```
eqcd(X,Y,C) +:
    X in dom(Y)+C,
    Y in dom(X)-C.

eqci(X,Y,C) +:
    X in min(Y)+C..max(Y)+C,
    Y in min(X)-C..max(X)-C.
```

Fig. 2. Indexicals expressing $X = Y + C$

1. if r is ground, $r_S = \mathcal{T}(X, C, S)$
2. if r is monotone, $r_S \supseteq \mathcal{T}(X, C, S)$
3. all arguments of C except X should occur in r

Fig. 3. Coding rules for a propagating indexicals X in r

Rule 1 says that it is safe to consider C entailed after pruning X if r is ground. This is a significant optimization [5], and is exploited as follows: Indexicals that are projections of the same constraint, as e.g. in eqcd/3 in Fig. 2, are connected by references to a common flag. Whenever one of the indexicals is decided entailed, the flag is set. Before any indexical is executed, its associated entailment flag is checked and if set the indexical is ignored. The same optimization is used elsewhere [9,6].

Rule 2 is implied by rule 1 as follows: For all extensions S' of S that make r ground, if r is monotone, $r_{S'} \subseteq r_S$ and hence $\mathcal{T}(X, C, S') \subseteq r_S$. Rule 2 follows from this since, by definition, $\mathcal{T}(X, C, S)$ is the union of all $\mathcal{T}(X, C, S')$. The solver relies on this rule by requiring that X in r be monotone before admitting it for execution.

Finally, rule 3 is a natural consequence of rule 1 for any reasonable constraint.

It has been shown that anti-monotone indexicals can be used for expressing logical conditions for entailment detection [5]. As we will show in the following section, a reification mechanism can be built on top of indexicals. Coding rules analogous to those in Fig. 3 apply for indexicals detecting entailment.

The solver has been extended to handle both kinds of indexicals, and ensures that the (anti-)monotonicity precondition is satisfied before admitting any indexical for execution. This is achieved by suspending the indexicals until certain variables are ground. The set of variables to suspend on is easily computed at compile time [5]. For example, in eqcd/3 in Fig. 2, the first indexical is not admitted for execution until C is known.

We maintain separate separate scheduling queues for indexicals and global constraints; a global constraint is only resumed when no indexicals are scheduled for execution. Thus, global constraints can be seen as having lesser priority than indexicals. This is reasonable, since indexicals are cheap to invoke (but may perform little useful work), while specialized algorithms for global constraints can be expensive (but yield many conclusions when invoked). Some other systems can assign different priorities to individual constraints [12,22].

The solver also provides the usual predefined search strategies (fixed order, fail-first principle, branch and bound for minimization or maximization) and utility predicates for accessing domains, execution statistics, controlling aspects of the answer constraint, etc.

3.2 FD Predicates and Reification

We have minimally extended the Prolog system by admitting the definition of constraints as the one shown in Fig. 2. The constraints become known to the Prolog system as *FD predicates*, and when called, the Prolog engine simply escapes to the constraint solver. In our design, contrary to e.g. clp($\mathcal{FD}$), indexicals can only appear in the context of FD predicate definitions; they are not constraints but projections of constraints.

The definitions in Fig. 2 provide methods for solving $X = Y + C$ constraints. If we want to reify such constraints, however, we need methods for detecting entailment and disentailment, and for solving the negated constraint. Thus, FD predicates may contain up to four "clauses" (for solving the constraint or its negation, and for checking entailment or disentailment). The role of each clause is reflected in the "neck" operator. Indexicals used for constraint solving are called *propagating*. Those used for entailment checking are called *checking*. Table 2 summarizes the different cases. Figure 4 shows the full definition of our example constraint with all four clauses for domain-consistency and -entailment. The reified constraint may be used as follows, expressing the constraint $U + V = 5 \Leftrightarrow B$:

```
?- eqcd(U,V,5) iff B.
```

The implementation spawns two coroutines corresponding to the clauses for detecting entailment and disentailment. Eventually, one of them will bind B to 0 or 1. A third coroutine is spawned, waiting for B to become bound, at which time the clause for posting the constraint (or its negation) is activated. In the mean time, the constraint may have been detected as (dis)entailed, in which case the third coroutine is dismissed.

role	neck symbol	indexical type	precondition
solve C	+:	propagating	monotone
solve $\neg C$	-:	propagating	monotone
check C	+?	checking	anti-monotone
check $\neg C$	-?	checking	anti-monotone

Table 2. Roles of FD predicate clauses

Alternative encodings of reification are described in Sec. 5.1.

```
eqcd(X,Y,C) +: % positive constraint solving
    X in dom(Y)+C,
    Y in dom(X)-C.
eqcd(X,Y,C) -: % negative constraint solving
    X in \{Y+C},
    Y in \{X-C}.
eqcd(X,Y,C) +? % entailment detection
    X in {Y+C}.
eqcd(X,Y,C) -? % disentailment detection
    X in \dom(Y)+C.
```

Fig. 4. Indexicals for reifying $X = Y + C$

3.3 Prolog Engine Extensions

The Prolog engine had to be extended to be able to cope with calls to FD predicates. This was done by introducing the FD predicate as a new predicate type known to the Prolog emulator. The emulator's call instruction dispatches on the type of the predicate being called, and if FD predicates are called as Prolog goals, the emulator will escape to the solver. No new abstract machine instructions were introduced.

FD predicate definitions are compiled by a source-to-source translation mechanism into directives that will store the object code and insert the new predicate into the Prolog symbol table. The Prolog compiler proper was not extended at all. Indexical ranges are compiled into postfix notation, which is then translated by the loader into byte code for a threaded-code stack machine. A small set of solver primitives provides the necessary back-end, managing memory, storing byte code in-core, etc.

The interface between the Prolog engine and the solver is provided in part by the attributed variables mechanism [13], which has been used previously to interface several constraint solvers into CLP systems [10,12,25,9,6,22]. This mechanism associates solver-specific information with variables, and provides hooks for extended unification and projection of answer constraints.

Thus, the only extension to the Prolog kernel was the introduction of a new predicate type, a truly minimal and modular extension.

3.4 Macro-expansion of Goals

The indexical language can be regarded as a low-level language for programming constraints. It is usually not necessary to resort to this level of programming—most commonly used constraints are available via library calls and/or via macro-expansion.

A very common class of constraints are equations, disequations and inequations, and propositional combinations of these. These are translated by a built-in macro-expansion mechanism into sequences of library constraint goals. The expanded code is linear in the size of the source code. Similar expansions are used in most other systems. Again, the Prolog compiler proper is not aware of this macro-expansion. For example, the Prolog clause:

```
p(X, Y, Z) :-
        X+2*Y+3*Z#>=4 #\/ 4*X+3*Y+2*Z #=< 1.
```

is expanded to:

```
p(X, Y, Z) :-
        scalar_product([-1,1,2,3], [D,X,Y,Z], #=, 0),
        4 #=< D iff E,
        scalar_product([-1,4,3,2], [F,X,Y,Z], #=, 0),
        F #=< 1 iff G,
        clpfd:'p\\/q'(E, G, 1).
```

4 The Global Constraint Interface

We have developed a programming interface by means of which new global constraints can be defined in Prolog. Constraints defined in this way can take arbitrary arguments and may use any constraint solving algorithm, provided it makes sense.

The interface maintains a private state for each invocation of a global constraint. The state may e.g. contain the domains of the most recent invocation, admitting consistency methods such as AC-4 [15]. The interface also provides means to access the domains of variables and operations on the internal domain representation.

To make the solver aware of a new global constraint, the user must assert a Prolog clause

```
dispatch_global(Constraint,
                State0,
                State, Actions) :- Body.
```

which the solver will call whenever a constraint of the new type is posted or resumed. A dispatch_global goal is true if *Constraint* is the constraint term itself, *State0* is the current state of the invocation, the conjunction *Body* succeeds, unifying *State* with the updated state and *Actions* with a list of requests to the solver. Such requests include notifications that the constraint has been detected entailed or disentailed, requests to prune variables, and requests to rewrite the constraint into some simpler constraints. *Body* is not allowed to change the state of the solver e.g. by doing recursive constraint propagation, as the scheduling queues are under the control of the solver and not globally accessible.

A global constraint invocation is posted to the solver by calling fd_global(*Constraint, State, Susp*) where *Constraint* is the constraint, *State* the initial state of the invocation, and *Susp* encodes how the constraints should be suspended on the variables occurring in it. A full example is shown in Fig. 5.

```
le_iff(X,Y,B) :-
    B in 0..1,          % suspend on bounds of X,Y and on value of B
    fd_global(le(X,Y,B), [], [minmax(X),minmax(Y),val(B)]).

:- multifile dispatch_global/4.
dispatch_global(le(X,Y,B), [], [], Actions) :-
    le_solver(B, X, Y, Actions).

le_solver(B, X, Y, Actions) :- var(B), !,
    (   fd_max(X, Xmax), fd_min(Y, Ymin), Xmax=<Ymin
    ->  Actions = [exit,B=1]          % entailed, B=1
    ;   fd_min(X, Xmin), fd_max(Y, Ymax), Xmin >Ymax
    ->  Actions = [exit,B=0]          % entailed, B=0
    ;   Actions = []                  % not entailed, no pruning
    ).
le_solver(0, X, Y, [exit,call('x>y'(X,Y))]).  % rewrite to X#>Y
le_solver(1, X, Y, [exit,call('x=<y'(X,Y))]). % rewrite to X#=<Y
```

Fig. 5. $x \leq y \Leftrightarrow b$ as a global constraint

Reification cannot be expressed in this interface; instead, reification of a global constraint may be achieved by explicitly passing it a 0/1-variable. Figure 5 illustrates this technique too.

Many of the solver's built-in constraints are implemented via this programming interface, for example:

- non-linear arithmetic constraints,
- constraints expressing sums and scalar products of a list of domain variables,
- all_different(L), constraining the elements of the list L to take distinct values. We have implemented a weak version simulating pairwise inequalities as well as a strong version based on Régin's algorithm [19].
- element(I, L, Y), constraining the I:th element of L to be equal to Y, uses a consistency algorithm based on AC-4.
- cumulative(S, D, R, L), modelling a set of tasks with start times S, durations D, and resource need R, sharing a resource with capacity L [1]. The implementation is based on several OR methods [7,2].

5 Performance Evaluation

The performance evaluation of our solver is structured as follows. First, we compare our low-level implementation of reification with alternative schemes. Then, we measure the general performance of our solver on a set of benchmark programs, and compare it with four similar CLP systems.

5.1 The Reification Mechanism

The mechanism as described in Sec. 3.2 is but one of several possible implementation options. There are well-known techniques in OR for reifying linear arithmetic constraints [27]. Sidebottom showed how reification can be encoded into indexicals using the conditional range operator [21]. Finally, reification can be expressed by a global constraint.

We measured the performance of these four schemes on the simple example $x, y \in 1..10$, $x \le y \Leftrightarrow b$. Having posted this constraint, a failure driven loop was executed 10000 times, executing each of the relevant cases ($b = 1$, $b = 0$, entailment, disentailment). The four constraint formulations are listed in Figs. 5 and 6. The constant 10000 that occurs in the version using the OR method is an arbitrarily chosen sufficiently large constant. Our low-level reification mechanism was the fastest, with conditional ranges being some 17% slower, The OR method method some 76% slower, and the global constraint formulation some 82% slower.

```
le1(X,Y,B) :-              % low-level method
    X #=< Y iff B.

le2(X,Y,B) :-              % OR method
    B in 0..1,
    Xmax #=  X + 10000*B,
    Xmax #=< Y + 10000,
    Y    #<  Xmax.

le3(X,Y,B) +:              % conditional range method
    X in ((1..B) ? (inf..max(Y))) \/ ((B..0) ? (min(Y)+1..sup)),
    Y in ((1..B) ? (min(X)..sup)) \/ ((B..0) ? (inf..max(X)-1)),
    B in ((min(X)..max(Y)) ? (1..1)) \/ ((min(Y)+1..max(X)) ? (0..0)).
```

Fig. 6. Three encodings of $x \le y \Leftrightarrow b$

5.2 Benchmark Results

The first part of Tab. 3 shows execution times for a set of small, well-known benchmark programs, with numbers in parentheses indicating relative times wrt. SICStus. The programs have been chosen to be clean and fairly representative of real-world problems, and coded straight-forwardly in a way a programmer without deep system specific knowledge would. Naive variable ordering has been used for all problems, as different first-fail implementations tend to break ties in slightly different ways. Where applicable, built-in constraints such as all_different/1, element/3 and atmost/3 have been used, whereas more complex global constraints are not used in these programs. For example, in the Squares 21 (packing 21 squares into a large square) benchmark, the constraint that no square can overlap with any other square is expressed with cardinality over four inequations and not with CHIP's diffn/1 constraint. Thus, the collected figures represent a notion of the basic performance of a system.

The systems tested besides SICStus are CHIP version 5.0.0, ECL^{i}PS^e version 3.5.2, B-Prolog version 2.1 [29] and clp($\mathcal{FD}$) version 2.21. All benchmarks have been run on (or normalized to) a SUN SPARCstation 4 with a 85MHz microSPARC CPU and the times shown are in milliseconds. The performance comparison has been limited to the above systems since these are the Prolog based systems that were available to us, but could easily be extended. Furthermore, SICStus and Oz [22] have almost identical performance on the alpha, eq10 and eq20 benchmarks [28].

Of the eight programs, the last two, Magic 20 (magic series of length 20) and Squares 21 (packing 21 squares into a large square) need reification, which is not supported in clp($\mathcal{FD}$), B-Prolog and only partly supported in CHIP. The figure for Magic 20 with clp($\mathcal{FD}$) is with reification implemented using the OR method, in CHIP using conditional clauses and in B-Prolog reification has been done using delay-clauses. Squares 21 could not be run on B-Prolog due to lack of support for non-linear arithmetic, and on clp($\mathcal{FD}$) due to memory allocation problems that we were unable to debug.

Benchmarks

Problem	clp($\mathcal{FD}$)	B-Prolog	CHIP	ECL^{i}PS^e	SICStus
Alpha	3900 (0.23)	14800 (0.89)	42600 (2.55)	100000 (5.99)	16700
Cars$^{50\ times}$	970 (0.20)	2400 (0.50)	3700 (0.77)	4400 (0.92)	4800
Eq10$^{50\ times}$	2000 (0.35)	3900 (0.70)	6100 (1.09)	9100 (1.63)	5600
Eq20$^{50\ times}$	3400 (0.40)	11000 (1.29)	11500 (1.35)	18000 (2.12)	8500
Queens-8 all$^{10\ times}$	850 (0.20)	1000 (0.23)	1800 (0.42)	7500 (1.74)	4300
Queens-16 one$^{10\ times}$	5500 (0.21)	10000 (0.38)	12500 (0.48)	60000 (2.31)	26000
Magic 20	630 (1.05)	3800 (6.33)	6800 (11.3)	3300 (5.50)	600
Squares 21	n/a	n/a	59000 (1.98)	171000 (5.74)	29800
Arithmetic Mean	(0.38)	(1.5)	(3.2)	(3.2)	(1.0)
Harmonic Mean	(0.28)	(0.56)	(1.0)	(2.16)	(1.0)

Constraint Executions

1M prunings	806 (0.08)	5400 (0.55)	957 (0.09)	42710 (4.38)	9760

Table 3. Performance results for selected problems

The second part of Tab. 3 shows the performance on the unsatisfiable constraints $x, y \in 1..500000$, $x < y$, $y < x$. Posting these constraints will make the last two constraints trigger each other iteratively until failure, i.e. one million invocations and prunings. This gives an idea of the raw speed of the solvers on *intervals*.

Although the results show some peaks, e.g. for Alpha, Magic 20 and 1M, we conclude that SICStus shows performance comparable with that of all systems tested. SICStus performs significantly better than ECL^{i}PS^e, while it is lagging behind clp($\mathcal{FD}$). It is worth noting that SICStus performs quite well on the benchmarks that use reification, which shows that low-level support for reification is valuable.

6 Comparison with Other Work

A full comparison with all existing finite domain constraint solvers is clearly outside the scope of this paper. In this section, we will focus on particular features of our solver and how they relate to some other known systems.

Indexicals Indexicals were first conceived in the context of cc($\mathcal{FD}$) [24,25]. The vision was to provide a rational, *glass box* reconstruction of the FD part of CHIP[10], replacing a host of ad-hoc concepts by a small set of powerful concepts and combinators such as blocking implication and the cardinality operator. Indexicals were a key component of the design, but seem to have been abandoned later. Unfortunately, no implementation of cc($\mathcal{FD}$) is available for comparison. Other systems [9,21,6] have been solely based on indexicals. Notably, clp($\mathcal{FD}$) [9] demonstrated the feasibility of the indexical approach, achieving excellent performance by compiling to C. Our design is the first to be based on a mixture of indexicals and global constraints, compiling indexicals to byte code for a threaded-code stack machine. The comparison with clp($\mathcal{FD}$) indicates that indexicals require a tight integration, compiled to C or native code, to achieve truly competitive performance.

The indexical scheme can be readily extended, with for example conditional ranges [21,6], with "foreach" constructs as in our design, or with arbitrary functions written in C [9]. A generalization of indexicals to *m-constraints* encoding path-consistency methods was proposed in [8].

Reification CLP(BNR) [16] was the first system to allow propositional combinations of arithmetic constraints by means of reification. This is now allowed by many systems including ours [21,12,22,17]. Other systems provide blocking implication [10,25] or cardinality [25]. Only research prototypes have no reification support.

We have provided a full implementation of an idea [24] to use indexicals to specify the four aspects of a reified constraint, viz. solving the constraint or its negation, and detecting entailment or disentailment of the constraint.

Global constraints It is well known that local constraint propagation, even with reification, can be too weak. A constraint involving many variables, e.g. the constraint that the elements of a list all be distinct, may be modeled by $O(N^2)$ disequations. If the same constraint is expressed as a single, global constraint, we get much better ($O(N)$) space complexity, much smaller scheduler overhead, and the opportunity to employ a specialized, complete filtering algorithm [19] instead of merely mimicking the pairwise disequations. The need for specialized algorithms is most obvious on hard combinatorial problems [1,3,18], while the space complexity aspects can dominate on large instances of otherwise easy problems.

Consequently, solvers based solely on indexicals can hardly be competitive on these classes of problems. On the other hand, indexicals admit rapid prototyping of user-defined constraints: defining a global constraint usually requires much more programming effort. Also, in our implementation, an indexical formulation often outperforms a global one if the constraint involves few variables. The break-even point has not been determined.

Most solvers are based solely on what we have called global constraints, as e.g. [12,22,17,10,14]. Ours is based on a mixed approach, combining the best of both worlds.

Programming interfaces Any system that is not completely closed needs a programming interface for defining new constraints. In indexical-based systems, the indexical language provides such an interface. clp($\mathcal{FD}$) [9] allows the use of arbitrary C functions in indexicals. ECL^{i}PS^e [12] uses attributed variables as a generic constraint interface. By accessing these attributed variables and calling internal coroutining primitives, user-defined constraints can be programmed. Oz [22], Ilog Solver [14] and CHIP [10] provide programming interfaces in terms of C++ classes. CHIP also provides declarations that allow the user to use arbitrary Prolog code as constraints; we provide the same ability via a simple API.

Negative numbers In many finite domain constraint solvers, the constraints are over natural numbers [22,9,25,6,10]. The extension to the full integer domain strictly extends the expressive power of the language so that it can reason e.g. about differences, but complicates the non-linear arithmetic constraints somewhat. We share this extensions with some other systems [12,16,21,17].

Host language integration The design of clp($\mathcal{FD}$) [9] extends the underlying Prolog engine with several new abstract machine instructions supporting constraints, and compiles all source code to C.

AKL($\mathcal{FD}$) [6] integrated the indexical approach into a concurrent constraint language with deep guards and a generic constraint interface on the level of C. Constraint system specific methods for e.g. garbage collection must be provided in this interface.

As in ECL^{i}PS^e, we used attributed variables as a generic constraint interface, and minimally extended the Prolog engine by the FD predicate mechanism, handling all compilation issues by source-to-source translation.

7 Conclusions

We describe the design and implementation of the SICStus Prolog finite domain constraint solver. The solver has an open design, supports reification, and allows constraints to be added by the user by two complementary mechanism: (a) as indexicals that perform incremental constraint solving and entailment checking within a Waltz-like algorithm, and (b) as global constraints via a Prolog programming interface, admitting specialized consistency methods. We describe a loosely coupled integration of finite domain constraints into the Prolog abstract machine; thus the techniques can be generalized to other constraint systems. We extend the indexical language, thus enabling the encoding of arbitrary binary relations as indexicals. We compare the performance and functionality of the design with other work.

We have shown that a fully-fledged open-ended finite domain system with negative integers, non-linear arithmetic, reification, mixed execution strategies, loosely coupled to a Prolog abstract machine, is possible with competitive performance.

Acknowledgements

The research reported herein was supported in part by the Advanced Software Technology Center of Competence at Uppsala University (ASTEC), and in part by the Swedish Institute of Computer Science (SICS).

References

1. A. Aggoun and N. Beldiceanu. Extending CHIP in order to solve complex scheduling and placement problems. *Mathl. Comput. Modelling*, 17(7):57–73, 1993.
2. P. Baptiste and C. Le Pape. A theoretical and experimental comparison of constraint propagation techniques for disjunctive scheduling. In *Proceedings of the Seventeenth International Joint Conference on Artificial Intelligence (IJCAI-95)*, Montreal, Canada, August 1995.
3. N. Beldiceanu and E. Contejean. Introducing global constraints in CHIP. *Mathl. Comput. Modelling*, 20(12):97–123, 1994.
4. B. Carlson and M. Carlsson. Compiling and Executing Disjunctions of Finite Domain Constraints. In *Proceedings of the Twelfth International Conference on Logic Programming*. MIT Press, 1995.
5. B. Carlson, M. Carlsson, and D. Diaz. Entailment of finite domain constraints. In *Proceedings of the Eleventh International Conference on Logic Programming*. MIT Press, 1994.
6. B. Carlson, M. Carlsson, and S. Janson. The implementation of AKL(FD). In *Logic Programming: Proceedings of the 1995 International Symposium*. MIT Press, 1995.
7. Y. Caseau and F. Laburthe. Improved clp scheduling with task intervals. In P. Van Hentenryck, editor, *Logic Programming, Proceedings of the Eleventh International Conference on Logic Programming*, pages 369–383, Santa Margherita Ligure, Italy, 1994. MIT Press.
8. Philippe Codognet and Giuseppe Nardiello. Enhancing the constraint-solving power of clp(FD) by means of path-consistency methods. In A. Podelski, editor, *Constraints: Basics and Trends*, volume 910 of *Lecture Notes in Computer Science*, pages 37–61. Springer-Verlag, 1995.
9. D. Diaz and P. Codognet. A Minimal Extension of the WAM for CLP(FD). In *Proceedings of the International Conference on Logic Programming*, pages 774–790, Budapest, Hungary, 1993. MIT Press.

10. M. Dincbas, P. van Hentenryck, H. Simonis, A. Aggoun, T. Graf, and F. Berthier. The Constraint Logic Programming Language CHIP. In *Proceedings of the International Conference on Fifth Generation Computer Systems*, 1988.

11. Mats Carlsson et al. SICStus Prolog User's Manual. SICS Research Report, Swedish Institute of Computer Science, 1995.
    URL: http://www.sics.se/isl/sicstus.html.

12. Micha Meier et al. ECLiPSe user manual. ECRC Research Report ECRC-93-6, European Computer Research Consortium, 1993.

13. C. Holzbaur. *Specification of Constraint Based Inference Mechanism through Extended Unification*. PhD thesis, Dept. of Medical Cybernetics and AI, University of Vienna, 1990.

14. ILOG. ILOG Solver C++. Reference manual, ILOG S.A., 1993.

15. R. Mohr and T.C. Henderson. Arc and path consistency revisited. *Artificial Intelligence*, 28:225–233, 1986.

16. W. Older and A. Vellino. Constraint arithmetic on real intervals. In *Constraint Logic Programming: Selected Research (eds. Benhamou and Colmerauer)*. MIT Press, 1993.

17. PrologIA. Le manuel de Prolog IV. Reference manual, PrologIA S.A., 1997.

18. J.-F. Puget and M. Leconte. Beyond the glass box: Constraints as objects. In J. Lloyd, editor, *Proceedings of the International Logic Programming Symposium (ILPS-95)*, pages 513–527, Portland, 1995.

19. J.-C. Régin. A filtering algorithm for constraints of difference in CSPs. In *Proc. of the Twelfth National Conference on Artificial Intelligence (AAAI-94)*, pages 362–367, 1994.

20. Vijay A. Saraswat. *Concurrent Constraint Programming Languages*. PhD thesis, Carnegie-Mellon University, January 1990.

21. Gregory Sidebottom. *A Language for Optimizing Constraint Propagation*. PhD thesis, Simon Fraser University, November 1993.

22. Gert Smolka. The Oz programming model. In J. van Leeuwen, editor, *Computer Science Today*, volume 1000 of *Lecture Notes in Computer Science*, pages 324–343. Springer-Verlag, 1995.

23. Pascal Van Hentenryck and Yves Deville. The cardinality operator: a new logical connective in constraint logic programming. In *International Conference on Logic Programming*. MIT Press, 1991.

24. Pascal Van Hentenryck, Vijay Saraswat, and Yves Deville. Constraint processing in cc(FD). Draft, Computer Science Department, Brown University, 1991.

25. Pascal Van Hentenryck, Vijay Saraswat, and Yves Deville. Design, implementation and evaluation of the constraint language cc(FD). In A. Podelski, editor, *Constraints: Basics and Trends*, volume 910 of *Lecture Notes in Computer Science*. Springer-Verlag, 1995.

26. D. Waltz. *The Psychology of Computer Vision (Ed. P. Winston)*, chapter Understanding line drawings of scenes with shadows. McGraw-Hill, New York, 1975.

27. H.P. Williams. *Model Building in Mathematical Programming*. J. Wiley and sons, New York, 1978.

28. Jörg Würtz, 1997. Personal Communication.

29. Neng-Fa Zhou. B-Prolog User's Manual Version 2.1. Technical report, Kyushu Institute of Technology, 1997.
    URL: http://www.cad.mse.kyutech.ac.jp/people/zhou/bprolog.html.

Semantics and Compilation of Recursive Sequential Streams in $8_{1/2}$

Jean-Louis Giavitto, Dominique De Vito, Olivier Michel

LRI u.r.a. 410 du CNRS,
Bâtiment 490, Université Paris-Sud, 91405 Orsay Cedex, France
Tel: +33 1 69 15 64 07   *e-mail:* giavitto@lri.fr

Abstract. Recursive definition of streams (infinite lists of values) have been proposed as a fundamental programming structure in various fields. A problem is to turn such expressive recursive definitions into an efficient imperative code for their evaluation. One of the main approach is to restrict the stream expressions to interpret them as a temporal sequence of values. Such *sequential* stream rely on a *clock analysis* to decide at what time a new stream value must be produced. In this paper we present a denotational semantics of recursively defined sequential streams. We show how an efficient implementation can be derived as guarded statements wrapped into a single imperative loop.
Keywords: stream, clock, compilation of dataflow graphs.

1   Introduction

To simplify the formal treatment of a program, Tesler and Enea [1] have considered single assignment languages. To accommodate loop constructs, they extend the concept of variable to an infinite sequence of values rather than a single value. This approach takes advantage of representing iterations in a "mathematically respectable way" [2] and to quote [3]: "series expressions are to loops as structured control constructs are to gotos". Such infinite sequences are called *streams* and are manipulated as a whole, using filters, transductors, etc.

This approach has led to the development of the stream data structure and the dataflow paradigm, according to a large variety of circumstances and needs. Since the declarative programming language Lucid [4], more and more declarative stream languages have been proposed: Lustre [5] and Signal [6] in the field of real-time programming, Crystal [7] for systolic algorithms, Palasm [8] for the programming of PLD, Daisy [9] for VLSI design, $8_{1/2}$ [10] for parallel simulation, Unity [11] for the design of parallel programs, etc. Moreover, declarative definitions of streams can be a by-product of the data-dependence analysis of more conventional languages like Fortran. In this case, a stream corresponds to the successive values taken by a variable, e.g. in a loop.

1.1   Synchronous Streams

Synchronous streams in Lustre or Signal have been proposed as a tool for programming reactive systems. In these two languages, the succession of elements in a stream is tightly coupled with the concept of time: the evaluation order of the elements in a stream is the same as the order of occurrence of the elements in the stream [12]. This is not true in Lucid, where the computation of element i in a stream A may require the computation of an element $j > i$ in A. In addition, synchronization between occurrences of events in different streams is a main concern in Lustre and Signal. Lustre and Signal rely on a *clock analysis* to ensure that synchronous expressions receive their arguments at the same time (see [13] and [14] for a general introduction to synchronous programming). For example, the expression $A + B$ where A and B are streams, is allowed in Lustre or Signal only if the production of the elements in A and B takes place at the same instants (and so does the computation of the elements of $A + B$). This requires that the streams A, B and $A + B$ share a common reference in time: a *clock*. Timed flow, synchrony, together with a restriction on stream expressions to ensure bounded memory evaluation [15], make Lustre and Signal especially suitable tools to face real-time applications.

1.2 Sequential Streams

Sequential streams in $8_{1/2}$ share with the previous approach the idea of comparing the order of occurrence of events in different streams. But, in contrast with the previous approach, the expression $A + B$ is always allowed in $8_{1/2}$ emphasizing on a single common global time. The instants of this time are called *ticks*. The $8_{1/2}$ clock of the stream is specified by the sequence of ticks where a computation must occurs to ensure that, at each instant of the global clock, the relationship between the instantaneous values of the streams A, B, and $A + B$ is satisfied. Given streams A and B, it suffices to recompute the value of $A + B$ whenever a change happen to A or to B. The value of a stream can be observed at any time and this value is the value computed at the last change.

The idea of a clock in $8_{1/2}$ corresponds more closely to the time where values are computed rather than to the time when they must be consumed. In addition, a stream value can be accessed at any time. This makes $8_{1/2}$ unable to express real-time synchronization constraints (for example, asserting that two streams must have the same clock, like the *synchro* primitive in Signal), but makes more easy arbitrary combinations of *trajectories* in the simulation of dynamical systems [16]. We call $8_{1/2}$ streams *sequential streams* to stress that they have a strict temporal interpretation of the succession of the elements in the stream (like Lustre and Signal and unlike Lucid) without constraining to synchronous expressions.

1.3 Compiling Recursive Stream Equations into a Loop

The clock of a synchronous stream is a temporal predicate which asserts that the current value of the stream is changing. The inference, at compile time, of the clock of a stream makes the compiler able to check for consistencies (for example no temporal shortcuts between stream definitions) and to generate straight code for the computation of the stream values instead of using a more expensive demand-driven evaluation strategy.

Compiling a set of recursive stream equations consists in generating the code that enumerates the stream values in a strict ascending order. The idea is just to wrap a loop, that enumerates the ticks, around the guarded expression that computes the stream values at a given tick. This is possible because we only admit operators on streams satisfying a preorder restriction. The problem is to derive a static scheduling of the computations and to generate an efficient code for the guards corresponding to the clocks of the stream expressions.

Structure of the paper. In the following section, we sketch $\mathcal{L}$ a declarative language on sequential streams. In section 3 we give a denotational semantics of $\mathcal{L}$ based on an extension of Kahn's original semantics for dataflow networks [17]. The main difference between our semantics and that of Plaice [18] or Jensen [19] relies in a simpler presentation of clocks. Moreover, our proposition satisfies a property of consistency between clock and stream values: if the clock ticks, the corresponding stream value is defined. Section 4 presents the translation of the clock definitions from the denotational semantics to a boolean expression using C as the target language. The process involves the resolution of a system of boolean expressions. Section 5 presents a benchmarks corresponding to the performances of a $8_{1/2}$ program compiled using the previous tools compared to an equivalent hand-coded C program: it compares quite well. Finally, section 6 examines related works.

2 Recursively Defined Sequential Streams

Conventions. We adopt the following notations. The value of a stream is a function from a set of instants called *ticks*, to values called *scalar values*. We restrict ourself in this paper to totally ordered unbounded countable set of ticks and therefore we use $\mathbb{N}$ to represent this set ([20] and [21] show possible uses of a partially ordered set of instants). The *current value* of a stream A refers to the scalar value at some tick t and is denoted by $A(t)$. The current value of a stream may be undefined, which is denoted by *nil*. A sequential stream is more than a function from ticks to scalar values: we have to represent the instants where a computation takes place to maintain the relationship asserted by the definition of the stream. The set of ticks characterizing the activity of the stream A is called its *clock* and written $cl(A)$. For $t \neq 0$, if $t \notin cl(A)$, then $A(t) = A(t-1)$ because no change of value occurs and therefore the current value is equal to the previous value. If $0 \notin cl(A)$, then $A(0) = nil$. So, a stream A described by $>$; ; 1; ; 2; ; 3; ... $>$ means that $A(0) = nil$, $A(1) = nil$, $A(2) = 1$, $A(3) = 1$, $A(4) = 2$, $A(5) = 2$, $A(6) = 3$, *etc.* The clock of A is the set $cl(A) = \{2, 4, 6 \ldots\}$. With this notation, ticks are separated by ";" and a value is given only if the corresponding tick is in the clock of the stream.

2.1 A Sequential Stream Algebra

The language $\mathcal{L}$ represents the core of $8_{1/2}$ w.r.t the definition of streams. The set of expressions in $\mathcal{L}$ is given by the grammar:

$$e ::= c \mid \texttt{Clock}\, n \mid x \mid e_1 \, op \, e_2 \mid \$e \mid e_1 \, \textbf{when} \, e_2$$

where c ranges over integer and boolean constants (interpreted as constant streams), n ranges over $\mathbb{N}$, x over the set of variables ID and op over integer and boolean operations such as $+, \wedge, ==, <$ etc.

Constant streams. Scalar constants, like 0 or *true*, are overloaded to denote also a constant stream with clock reduced to the singleton $\{0\}$ and current value always equal to the scalar c: $c(t) = c$. A construct like $\texttt{Clock}\, n$ represents a predefined boolean stream with current value always equal to *true* and with an unbounded clock (the precise clock is left unspecified).

Arithmetic expressions. An expression like $e_1 \, bop \, e_2$ extends the scalar operator *bop* to act in a point-wise fashion on the elements of the stream: $\forall t, (A \, bop \, B)(t) = A(t) \, bop \, B(t)$. The clock of $A \, bop \, B$ is the set of ticks t necessary to maintain this assertion (in a first approximation, it is the union of the clocks of A and B, Cf. section 3).

Delay. The delay operator $, is used to shift "in time" the values of an entire stream. It gives access to the previous stream value. This operator is the only one that does not act in a point-wise fashion. Consequently, only past values can be used to compute a current stream value, and references to past values are relative to the current one. So, only the last p values of a stream have to be recorded where p is a constant computable at compile time. This restriction enables a finite memory assumption and enforces a temporal interpretation of the sequence of elements in a stream.

Sampling. The **when** operator is a trigger, corresponding to the temporal version of the **if then else** construct. It appears also in Lustre and Signal. The values of the stream A **when** B are those of A sampled at the ticks where B takes the value *true* (Cf. Tab. 1).

Table 1. Some examples of streams expression.

1 : >	1;	;	;	;	; ··· >
true : >	true;	;	;	;	; ··· >
Clock 2 : >	true;	; true;	; true;	··· >	
1 when Clock 2 : >	1;	; 1;	; 1;	··· >	
$1 : >	;	;	;	;	; ··· >
$(1 when Clock 2) : >	;	; 1;	; 1;	··· >	

2.2 Recursively Defined Sequential Streams

A stream definition in $\mathcal{L}$ is given through an equation $x = e$ where x is a variable and e a stream expression. This definition can be read as an equation being satisfied between x and the stream arguments of e.

A definition can be guarded to indicate that it is valid only for some ticks:

$$A@0 = 33, \quad A = (\$A + 1) \text{ when Clock } 0 \ .$$

The first equation is guarded by @0 which indicates that this equation is only valid for the first tick in the clock of A (that is, the first tick of A is also the first tick of the constant stream 33, which is the tick $t = 0$). The second equation is "universally" quantified and defines the stream when no guarded equation applies. In this paper, the only language we consider for temporal guards is @n where n is an integer which denotes the nth tick in a clock. A $\mathcal{L}$ program is a set of such definitions (i.e. guarded or non-guarded equations). For a given identifier x, there can only be a single universally quantified equation and at most one equation quantified by n.

An example of a reactive system using sequential streams. A "wlumf" is a "creature" whose behavior (mainly eating) is triggered by the level of some internal state (see [22] for such model in ethological simulation) More precisely, a wlumf is *hungry* when its *glycaemia* subsides under the level value 3. It can *eat* when there is some *food* in its environment. Its metabolism is such that when it eats, the glycaemia goes up to the level 10 and then decreases to zero at a rate of one unit per time step. Essentially, a wlumf is made of counters and flip-flop triggered and reset at different rates. The operator {...} is used to group sets of logically related stream definitions but we shall not be concerned with this aspect of the language for the rest of the paper .

System $wlumf = \{$

   $hungry@0 = false$

   $hungry = glycemia < 3$

   $glycemia@0 = 6$

   $glycemia = $ if eat then 10

     else $\max(0, \$glycemia-1)$ when $(\text{Clock}\,0)$ fi

   $eat@0 = false$

   $eat = \$hungry \;\&\&\; environment.food$

$\}$

System $environment = \{$

   $t@0 = 0$

   $t = \$t + 1$ when $\text{Clock} - 4$

   $food = (0 == (t\%2))$

$\}$

Fig. 1. The dynamical behaviour of an artificial creature, the "wlumf". The operator % is for modulo and $==$ for testing equality. So *food* is *true* or *false* depending on the parity of the counter t which progresses randomly at an average rate of $1/4$. The operator && is the logical and.

3 A Denotational Semantics for $\mathcal{L}$

For the sake of simplicity, we assume that guarded equations are only of the form $x@0 = e$. Therefore, we replace a definition $x@0 = e_1$, $x = e_2$ by a single equation $x = e_1$ fby e_2 where fby is a new operator waiting for the first tick in the clock of e_1 and then switching to the stream e_2. The denotational semantics of $\mathcal{L}$ is based on an extension of Kahn's original semantics for dataflow networks [17]. The notations are slightly adapted from [23].

3.1 Stream Values and Clocks

The basic domain consists of finite and infinite sequences over the sets of integer and boolean values extended with the value *nil* to represent the absence of a value: SCVALUE $= Bool \cup Int \cup \{nil\}$ and VALUE $=$ SCVALUE* $\cup$ SCVALUE$^\infty$. The operation "." denotes the concatenation of finite or infinite sequences. In VALUE, u approximates v, written $u \preceq v$ if $v = u.w$. This order is chosen against the more general Scott order (e.g. used for defining domains of functions [23]) in accordance with our interpretation of the succession of elements in the stream as the progression in time of the evaluation process.

A first idea to describe timed stream is to associate to the sequence of values, a sequence of boolean flags telling if an element is in the clock of the stream (flag true: $\top$) or not (flag false: $\bot$). In other words, a sequence of booleans $\{\bot, \top\}$ is used to represent $cl()$. For example, the sequence representing the clock of Clock 2 is: $\top \bot \top \bot \top \ldots$ Thus: $\text{ScClock} = \{\bot, \top\}$ and $\text{Clock} = \text{ScClock}^* \cup \text{ScClock}^\infty$. We choose to completely order ScClock by $\bot < \top$. The motivation to completely order the domain ScClock is the following: there is no particular reason for a stream definition evaluating into a sequence of undefined values, not to have a defined clock (with no true values). Moreover, if we cannot evaluate the current value of a clock, we obviously cannot evaluate the current value of the corresponding stream and this is observationally equivalent to the value $\bot$ in the clock sequence.

By convention, if s is a Clock, then $t \in s$ means $s(t) = \top$ and $t \notin s$ means $s(t) = \bot$. We extend the logical or $\vee$ by $\underline{\vee}$ and the logical and $\wedge$ by $\underline{\wedge}$ to operate point-wise on Clock: that is, $(s \underline{\wedge} s')(t) = s(t) \wedge s'(t)$ and $(s \underline{\vee} s')(t) = s(t) \vee s'(t)$. The ordering of clocks is also the prefix ordering.

In the work of Plaice [18] or Jensen [19], the definition of the clock of a stream is loosely coupled with the value of the stream, in the following sense: a tick can be in the clock of a stream while the current value of the stream is undefined. The simplest example is the expression $\$e$ which has the same clock of e but with an undefined value for the first tick in $cl(e)$. On the contrary, we ask for a denotational semantics that ensures that:

$$t \in cl(e) \Rightarrow e(t) \neq nil \qquad (1)$$

A property like (1) is natural and certainly desirable but cannot be directly achieved. This is best shown on the following example. Consider the stream defined by:

$$A = 1 \text{ fby } ((\$A + 1) \text{ when } (\text{Clock } 0)) \qquad (2)$$

which is supposed to define a counter increasing every ticks. But, if we assume property (1), then $cl(A)$ can be proved to be $\{0\}$. As a matter of fact, $0 \in cl(A)$ because $0 \in cl(1)$ and obviously the first tick in $cl(e)$ is also in $cl(e \text{ fby } e')$. Furthermore, a delayed stream $\$e$ cannot have a defined value the first time e has a defined value. So, using property (1), it comes that $0 \notin cl(\$A)$. Furthermore, the value of e when $clock 0$ is defined only when e has a defined value. So, again using property (1), we infer that

$$cl(A) = \top.Ok(cl(\$A + 1)) = \top.Ok(cl(\$A)) \qquad (3)$$

where the predicate Ok tells if the clock has already ticked: $Ok(\bot.s) = \bot.Ok(s)$ and $Ok(\top.s) = True$ (the sequence $True$ is the solution of the equation $True = \top.True$). The clock of $\$A$ depends of the clock of A and more precisely, except for the first tick in $cl(A)$, we have $cl(\$A) = cl(A)$. So, for $t \neq 0$, equation (3) rewrites in:

$$t \neq 0, \quad cl(A)(t) = Ok(cl(A))(t) \qquad (4)$$

Equation (4) is a recursive equation with solutions in Clock. This equation admits several solutions but the least solution, with respect to the structure of Clock, is $cl(A) = \top.False$ (where $False = \bot.False$). This is a problem because we expect the solution $True$.

The collapse of the clock is due to the confusion of two predicates : "having a definite value at tick t" and "changing possibly of value at tick t". Then, to develop a denotational semantics exhibiting a property similar to (1), our idea is to split the clock of a stream A in two sequences $\mathcal{D}(A)$ and $\mathcal{C}(A)$ with the following intuitive interpretation: $\mathcal{D}(A)$ indicates when the first non nil value of A becomes available for further computations and $\mathcal{C}(A)$ indicates that some computations are necessary to maintain the relationship asserted by the stream definition.

3.2 Semantics of Expressions

We call environment a mapping from variables to CLOCK or VALUE. An element ρ of ENV is a mapping ID $\rightarrow$ CLOCK $\times$ CLOCK $\times$ VALUE. Such an element really represents three environments linking a variable to the two sequences representing its clock and the sequence representing its value.

The semantics of $\mathcal{L}$ expressions is defined by the three functions:

$$\mathcal{D}[\,], \mathcal{C}[\,], \mathcal{V}[\,] : \text{EXP} \rightarrow \text{ENV} \rightarrow \text{VALUE} .$$

The reason of using an element of ENV instead of an environment, is the value of an expression involving variable may depend of the clocks $\mathcal{D}[\,]$ and $\mathcal{C}[\,]$ of this variable. By convention, if $\rho \in$ ENV, then ρ_d, ρ_c and ρ_v represents the components of ρ, that is: $\rho(x) = (\rho_d(x), \rho_c(x), \rho_v(x))$. In addition, we omit the necessary injections between the basic syntactic and semantic domains when they can be recovered from the context.

A constant c denotes the following three sequences:

$$\mathcal{D}[c]\rho = True, \quad \mathcal{C}[c]\rho = \top.False, \quad \mathcal{V}[c]\rho = c^\infty,$$

where c^∞ denotes an infinite sequence of c's, i.e. $c^\infty = c.c^\infty$. The intuitive meaning is that the current values of a constant stream are available from the beginning of time, a computation being needed only at the first instant to build the initial value of the constant stream and the current values being all the same. Some other constants are needed if we want to have streams with more than singleton clocks. This is the purpose of the constant stream Clock n which has an unbounded clock:

$$\mathcal{D}[\text{Clock } n]\rho = True, \quad \mathcal{C}[\text{Clock } n]\rho = dev(n), \quad \mathcal{V}[\text{Clock } n]\rho = True,$$

where $dev(n)$ is some device computing a boolean sequence depending on n, beginning by $\top$ and with an unbounded number of $\top$ values. Variables are looked up in the corresponding environment:

$$\mathcal{D}[x]\rho = \rho_d(x), \quad \mathcal{C}[x]\rho = \rho_c(x), \quad \mathcal{V}[x]\rho = \rho_v(x) .$$

The predefined arithmetic and logical operators are all strict:

$$\mathcal{D}[e_1 \, bop \, e_2]\rho = \mathcal{D}[e_1]\rho \wedge \mathcal{D}[e_2]\rho$$
$$\mathcal{C}[e_1 \, bop \, e_2]\rho = \mathcal{D}[e_1 \, bop \, e_2]\rho \wedge (\mathcal{C}[e_1]\rho \vee \mathcal{C}[e_2]\rho)$$
$$\mathcal{V}[e_1 \, bop \, e_2]\rho = \mathcal{V}[e_1]\rho \, bop \, \mathcal{V}[e_2]\rho$$

that is, the value of $e_1 \, bop \, e_2$ can be computed only when both e_1 and e_2 have a value. This value changes as soon as e_1 or e_2 changes its value, when both are defined. Notice that the definition of $\mathcal{C}[e]\rho$ takes the form $\mathcal{D}[e]\rho\wedge(\ldots)$ in order to ensure the property:

$$\forall t, \mathcal{C}[e]\rho(t) \Rightarrow \mathcal{D}[e]\rho(t) \tag{5}$$

(Cf. section 3.3). For a delayed stream, the equations are:

$$\mathcal{D}[\$e]\rho = delD(\mathcal{D}[e]\rho), \quad \mathcal{C}[\$e]\rho = \mathcal{D}[\$e]\rho \wedge \mathcal{C}[e]\rho$$
$$\mathcal{V}[\$e]\rho = delV(nil, nil; \mathcal{V}[e]\rho, \mathcal{C}[e]\rho)$$

where *delD* and *delV* are auxiliary functions defined by (s, s'' are sequences and p, p' are scalar values $\neq nil$):

$$delD(\bot.s) = \bot.delD(s)$$
$$delD(\top.s) = \bot.s$$
$$delV(nil, nil; v.s, \bot.s') = nil.delV(nil, nil; s, s')$$
$$delV(nil, nil; v.s, \top.s') = nil.delV(v, v; s, s')$$
$$delV(p, p'; v.s, \bot.s') = p.delV(p, p'; s, s')$$
$$delV(p, p'; v.s, \top.s') = p'.delV(p', v; s, s')$$

In other words, if t is the first tick for which A has a defined value, then the value of $\$A$ becomes available at $t + 1$. The computation needed for $\$A$ takes place at the same instants, as for A, except the first instant, and the values are shifted in time accordingly.

The sampling operator is specified by:

$$\mathcal{D}[e_1 \text{ when } e_2]\rho = \mathcal{D}[e_1]\rho \wedge \mathcal{D}[e_2]\rho$$
$$\mathcal{C}[e_1 \text{ when } e_2]\rho = \mathcal{D}[e_1 \text{ when } e_2]\rho \wedge (\mathcal{C}[e_2]\rho \wedge \mathcal{V}[e_2]\rho)$$
$$\mathcal{V}[e_1 \text{ when } e_2]\rho = trigger(nil; \mathcal{V}[e_1]\rho, \mathcal{C}[e_1 \text{ when } e_2]\rho)$$

where *trigger* is defined as:

$$trigger(p; v.s, \bot.s') = p.trigger(p; s, s')$$
$$trigger(p; v.s, \top.s') = v.trigger(v; s, s')$$

The value of the sampling operator can be defined only when both operands are defined. The clock is defined by the (sub)clock of e_2 when e_2 takes the value $\top$.

Finally, the `fby` construct takes the first defined element in its first argument and then "switches" to its second argument:

$$\mathcal{D}[e_1 \text{ fby } e_2]\rho = \mathcal{D}[e_1]\rho$$
$$\mathcal{C}[e_1 \text{ fby } e_2]\rho = \mathcal{D}[e_1]\rho \wedge fbyC(\mathcal{C}[e_1]\rho, \mathcal{C}[e_2]\rho)$$
$$\mathcal{V}[e_1 \text{ fby } e_2]\rho = fbyV(\mathcal{C}[e_1]\rho, \mathcal{V}[e_1]\rho, \mathcal{V}[e_2]\rho)$$

where:

$$fbyC(\bot.s, b.s') = \bot.fbyC(s, s')$$
$$fbyC(\top.s, b.s') = \top.s'$$
$$fbyV(\bot.w, v.s, v'.s') = v.fbyV(w, s, s')$$
$$fbyV(\top.w, v.s, v'.s') = v.s'$$

3.3 Semantics of Programs

The semantics of a set of recursive equations $\{\ldots, x_i = e_i, \ldots\}$ is composed of an element $\rho \in \text{ENV}$ assigning domain, clock and values to each stream variables x_i in the program. It can be computed as the least fixed point of the function

$$F(\rho) = [\ldots, x_i \mapsto (\mathcal{D}[e_i]\rho, \mathcal{C}[e_i]\rho, \mathcal{V}[e_i]\rho), \ldots]$$

where $[\dots, x \mapsto v, \dots]$ stands for an environment which maps x to v. All auxiliary functions involved are monotone and continuous. Then, the fixed point can be calculated in the standard way as the least upper bound of a sequence of iterations F^n starting from the empty environments. We write $(\mathbf{D}(x), \mathbf{C}(x), \mathbf{V}(x))$ for the value associated to x in the meaning of a program.

The simple form of the semantics may accommodate several variations to specify other stream algebra. The affirmation (5) holds for any environment ρ, and then it holds also for the fixpoint:

$$\forall t,\ \mathbf{C}(e)(t) \Rightarrow \mathbf{D}(e)(t) \tag{6}$$

A proof by induction on the structure of an expression shows that a property similar to (1) holds between $\mathcal{C}[\![e]\!]$ and $\mathcal{V}[\![e]\!]$ for any expression e in a program: $\forall t,\ \mathbf{C}(e)(t) \Rightarrow \mathbf{V}(e)(t) \neq nil$. Another result will be extremely useful for the implementation. Once defined, the current value of a stream may change on tick t only if the clock of the stream takes the value $\top$ at t:

$$\forall t,\ \mathbf{D}(e)(t-1) \wedge \mathbf{V}(e)(t-1) \neq \mathbf{V}(e)(t) \Rightarrow \mathbf{C}(e)(t) \tag{7}$$

the proof is by induction on terms in $\mathcal{L}$.

Example of a counter. As an example, we consider the semantics of the clock of the program (2). We assume that $dev(0) = True$. The semantics of the counter A is defined by the following equations:

$$\mathbf{D}(A) = \mathbf{D}(1 \texttt{ fby } ((\$A+1)\texttt{ when Clock }0)) = \mathbf{D}(1) = True$$
$$\mathbf{C}(A) = \mathbf{C}(1 \texttt{ fby } ((\$A+1)\texttt{ when Clock }0))$$
$$= fbyC(\mathbf{C}(1), \mathbf{C}((\$A+1)\texttt{ when Clock }0))$$
$$= fbyC(\top.False, \mathbf{D}((\$A+1\texttt{ when Clock }0) \wedge (\mathbf{C}(\texttt{Clock }0) \wedge True))\ .$$

We have $\mathbf{D}((\$A+1)\texttt{ when Clock }0) = \mathbf{D}(\$A+1) \wedge \mathbf{D}(\texttt{Clock }0) = \mathbf{D}(\$A+1) = \mathbf{D}(\$A) \wedge True = \mathbf{D}(\$A) = \bot.True$ because $\mathbf{D}(A) = True$. So, as expected:

$$\mathbf{C}(A) = True \wedge fbyC(\top.False, \bot.True \wedge (\mathbf{C}(\texttt{Clock }0) \wedge True))$$
$$= fbyC(\top.False, \bot.True) = True\ .$$

4 Compiling Recursive Streams into a Loop

We implement a sequence s as *the successive values of one memory location* associated with (the current value of) s. We emphasize that successive means here successive *in time*. The idea is to translate a set of equations $\{\dots, x = e, \dots\}$ into the imperative program (in a C like syntax):

```
for(;;)  { ...; xd = ed; xc = ec; xv = ev;  ...; }
```

where x_d is associated to the current value of $\mathbf{D}(x)$, etc. This implementation is far from the representation needed for Lucid (or for the lazy lists of Haskell) where several elements of a sequence can be present at the same time in the memory so that a garbage collector is involved to remove useless elements from the memory.

With the denotational semantics defined above, this representation implies the update of the three memory locations at each tick (i.e. for each element in the sequence). However, property (6) implies that it is sufficient to update the memory location representing $\mathbf{C}(e)$ only when $\mathbf{D}(e)(t)$ evaluates to true. And property (7) implies that is is sufficient to evaluate $\mathbf{V}(e)(t)$ when $\mathbf{C}(e)(t)$ evaluates to true. These two conditions are sufficient but not necessary (e.g. Clock 0 has an unbounded clock but its current value is always $\top$). So, a $\mathcal{L}$ program can be translated into the following C skeleton:

```
for(;;)  { ...; if(x_d = e_d) { if(x_c = e_c) { x_v = e_v; }} ...; }
```

However, translating a set of definitions into imperative assignments is not straightforward because of the recursive definitions: how to evaluate fixed points of sequences expressions without 1) handling explicitly infinite sequences and 2) iterations. In the rest of the section, we will build the tools that are necessary for this translation.

4.1 LR(1) Functions

We say that a function $f : \text{SCVALUE} \times \text{VALUE}^n \to \text{VALUE}$ is LR(1) if:

$$f(m; v_1.s_1, \ldots, v_n.s_n) = f'(m, v_1, \ldots, v_n) . f(f''(m, v_1, \ldots, v_n); s_1, \ldots, s_n)$$

where f' and f'' are functions from scalar values to scalar values: $f', f'' : \text{SCVALUE}^{n+1} \to \text{SCVALUE}$. Being LR(1) means that computing f on sequences can be a left to right process involving only computation on scalars, with only one memory location, assuming that the arguments are also provided from left to right.

Suppose F is LR(1); to solve the equation $v.s = F(m; v.s)$ on sequences (v and s are unknown, m is a parameter) it is then sufficient to solve the equation

$$v = F'(m; v) \tag{8}$$

on scalars and then to proceed with the resolution of $s = F(F''(m, v); s)$. Thus we have to consider the two sequences:

$$v_i = F'(m_i; v_i), \qquad m_i = F''(m_{i-1}, v_{i-1}), \quad i \geq 1$$

obtained by enumerating the successive solutions of (8) starting from an initial value m_0. The sequence of v_i's is obviously a solution of $s = F(s)$ and moreover, it is the least solution for $\preceq$. The equation (8) is called the I-equation associated with the equation $s = F(s)$ (I stands for "instantaneous"). It is easy to show that all the functions involved in the semantics of an expression given in section 3 are LR(1). This provides the basis for the implementation of declarative sequential streams into an imperative code.

4.2 Guarded LR(1) Semantic Equations

It is easy to rephrase the semantic definition of each $\mathcal{L}$ construct given in section 3 to make explicit properties (6), (7) and LR(1). The semantic equations are rephrased in Fig. 2 but due to the lack of place, we omit to rephrase some auxilliary functions. We have explicitly stated the values for a tick t in order to give directly the expressions e_d, e_c and e_v corresponding to C skeleton. The notation $s(t)$ refers to the tth element in sequence s, where element numbering starts 0. Semantics of systems remains the same. We will omit the tedious but straightforward proof by induction on terms to check that the two semantic definitions compute the same thing.

for commodity, let $\quad \mathcal{D}[\![e]\!]\rho(-1) = \bot, \quad \mathcal{C}[\![e]\!]\rho(-1) = \bot, \quad \mathcal{V}[\![e]\!]\rho(-1) = nil$
for any expression e and environment ρ, and assume $t > -1$ below:

$\mathcal{D}[\![c]\!]\rho(t) = \top \qquad \mathcal{C}[\![c]\!]\rho(t) = (t == 0) \qquad \mathcal{V}[\![c]\!]\rho(t) = c$

$\mathcal{D}[\![\texttt{Clock } n]\!]\rho(t) = \top \qquad \mathcal{C}[\![\texttt{Clock } n]\!]\rho(t) = dev(n, t) \qquad \mathcal{V}[\![\texttt{Clock } n]\!]\rho(t) = \top$

$\mathcal{D}[\![x]\!]\rho(t) = \rho(x)(t) \qquad \mathcal{C}[\![x]\!]\rho(t) = \rho(x)(t) \qquad \mathcal{V}[\![x]\!]\rho(t) = \rho(x)(t)$

$\mathcal{D}[\![e_1 \text{ bop } e_2]\!]\rho(t) = \mathcal{D}[\![e_1]\!]\rho(t) \wedge \mathcal{D}[\![e_2]\!]\rho(t)$
$\mathcal{C}[\![e_1 \text{ bop } e_2]\!]\rho(t) = if \ \ \mathcal{D}[\![e_1 \text{ bop } e_2]\!]\rho(t) \ \ then \ \ \mathcal{C}[\![e_1]\!]\rho(t) \vee \mathcal{C}[\![e_2]\!]\rho(t) \ \ else \ \ \bot$
$\mathcal{V}[\![e_1 \text{ bop } e_2]\!]\rho(t) = if \ \ \mathcal{C}[\![e_1 \text{ bop } e_2]\!]\rho(t) \ \ then \ \ \mathcal{V}[\![e_1]\!]\rho(t) \text{ bop } \mathcal{V}[\![e_2]\!]\rho(t)$
$\qquad\qquad\qquad\qquad else \ \ \mathcal{V}[\![e_1 \text{ bop } e_2]\!]\rho(t-1)$

$\mathcal{D}[\![\$e]\!]\rho(t) = \mathcal{D}[\![e]\!]\rho(t-1)$
$\mathcal{C}[\![\$e]\!]\rho(t) = if \ \ \mathcal{D}[\![\$e]\!]\rho(t) \ \ then \ \ \mathcal{C}[\![e]\!]\rho \ \ else \ \ \mathcal{C}[\![\$e]\!]\rho(t-1)$
$\mathcal{V}[\![\$e]\!]\rho(t) = if \ \ \mathcal{C}[\![\$e]\!]\rho(t) \ \ then \ \ delV(nil, nil; \mathcal{V}[\![e]\!]\rho, \mathcal{C}[\![e]\!]\rho)(t) \ \ else \ \ \mathcal{V}[\![\$e]\!]\rho(t-1)$

$\mathcal{D}[\![e_1 \text{ when } e_2]\!]\rho(t) = \mathcal{D}[\![e_1]\!]\rho(t) \wedge \mathcal{D}[\![e_2]\!]\rho(t)$
$\mathcal{C}[\![e_1 \text{ when } e_2]\!]\rho(t) = if \ \ \mathcal{D}[\![e_1 \text{ when } e_2]\!]\rho(t) \ \ then \ \ \mathcal{C}[\![e_2]\!]\rho(t) \wedge \mathcal{V}[\![e_2]\!]\rho(t) \ \ else \ \ \bot$
$\mathcal{V}[\![e_1 \text{ when } e_2]\!]\rho(t) = if \ \ \mathcal{C}[\![e_1 \text{ when } e_2]\!]\rho(t) \ \ then \ \ \mathcal{V}[\![e_1]\!]\rho(t) \ \ else \ \ \mathcal{V}[\![e_1 \text{ when } e_2]\!]\rho(t-1)$

$\mathcal{D}[\![e_1 \text{ fby } e_2]\!]\rho(t) = \mathcal{D}[\![e_1]\!]\rho(t)$
$\mathcal{C}[\![e_1 \text{ fby } e_2]\!]\rho(t) = if \ \ \mathcal{D}[\![e_1 \text{ fby } e_2]\!]\rho(t) \ \ then \ \ fbyC(\mathcal{C}[\![e_1]\!]\rho, \mathcal{C}[\![e_2]\!]\rho)(t) \ \ else \ \ \bot$
$\mathcal{V}[\![e_1 \text{ fby } e_2]\!]\rho(t) = if \ \ \mathcal{C}[\![e_1 \text{ fby } e_2]\!]\rho(t) \ \ then \ \ fbyV(\mathcal{C}[\![e_1]\!]\rho, \mathcal{V}[\![e_1]\!]\rho, \mathcal{V}[\![e_2]\!]\rho)(t)$
$\qquad\qquad\qquad\qquad else \ \ \mathcal{V}[\![e_1 \text{ fby } e_2]\!]\rho(t-1)$

Fig. 2. Semantics of $\mathcal{L}$ in an explicit LR(1) form.

4.3 I-system Associated with a Program

Each equation $x = F(x)$ in a $\mathcal{L}$ program is directly interpreted through the semantics of an expression, as three equations defining $\mathcal{D}[\![x]\!]$, $\mathcal{C}[\![x]\!]$ and $\mathcal{V}[\![x]\!]$, the images of x by the program meaning. Each right hand-side, written respectively $F_d[x]$, $F_c[x]$ and $F_v[x]$, corresponds to a LR(1) function and therefore can be decomposed into the F' and F'' forms. In order to implement the various environments simply as a set of memory locations, we write x_d, x_c and x_v for the current value of $\mathcal{D}[\![x]\!]$, $\mathcal{C}[\![x]\!]$ and $\mathcal{V}[\![x]\!]$ and x_{md}, x_{mc} and x_{mv} for the first argument in F'. The three I-equations associated with $x = F(\dots)$ can then be rephrased as:

$$x_d = F'_d[x](x_{md}; \dots), \quad x_c = F'_c[x](x_{mc}; \dots), \quad x_v = F'_v[x](x_{mv}; \dots) \ .$$

For each variable in the program there is one equation defining x_d, one for x_c and one for x_v. The expression defining x_c has the form: *if* x_d *then* $\dots$ *else* x_{mc} and the expression defining x_v follow the pattern *if* x_c *then* $\dots$ *else* x_{mv}, except for the constants. The variables x_{mc} and x_{mv} are in charge to record the value x_c or x_v at the previous tick (or equivalently, they denote the one-tick shifted sequence that appears in the right hand side of the semantic equations). The expressions "$\dots$" that appear in the *if* *then* *else* expression are also LR(1) functions of the sequences x_{md}, x_{mc}, x_{mv}, x_d, x_c and x_v. Thus they may require some additional scalar variables x'_m.

The set of I-equations associated with a program is called the I-system associated with the program. Suppose we can solve an I-system, then a sketch of the code implementing the computation of a $\mathcal{L}$ program is given in Fig. 3.

```
    data declarations corresponding to the  x_d, x_c, x_v's
    data declarations corresponding to the  x_mc, x_mv's
    for(;;) {
        solve the I-system and update the  x_d, x_c, x_v's
        update the x_md, x_mc, x_mv's according to the function  F'''_...[x]
    }
```

Fig. 3. Sketch of the code implementing the computation of a $\mathcal{L}$ program.

4.4 Solving Efficiently an I-system

The problem of computing the least fixed point of a set of equations on sequences has now be turned into the simpler problem of computing the least solution of the I-system, a set of equations between scalar values. A straightforward solution is to compute it by fixed point iterations. If l is the number of expressions in the program, the iterations must become stationary after at most l steps, because the scalar domains are all flat. The problem is that this method may require l steps (l can be large) and that each step may require the computation of all the l expressions in the program.

Consider the dependence graph of an I-system: vertices correspond to variables and an edge from x to y corresponds to the use of x in the definition of y. This graph may be cyclic if the given definitions are recursive. For instance in $a@0 = b, a = \$a$ or b which defines a signal a always $true$ after the first true value in b, $C[a]$ depends of $C[a]$ (and also of $C[b]$ which imposes its clock).

Without recursive equations, solving the I-system is easily done by simple substitutions: a topological sort can be used to order the equations at compile time. Non strict operators, like the conditional expression if...then...else..., can rise a problem because they induce a dependence graph depending on the value of the argument, value which is known only at evaluation time. Most of the time, it is possible to consider the union of the dependence graphs without introducing a cycle (which enables a static ordering of the equations). For the remaining rare cases, more sophisticated techniques, like conditional dependence graphs [24], can be used to infer a static scheduling. Solving the sorted system reduces to compute, in the order given by the topological sort, each right hand side and update the variables in the left hand side. In addition, the environment is implicitly implemented in the $x_d, x_c, x_v, \ldots$ variables.

For cyclic dependence graphs, the vertices can be grouped by *maximal strongly connected components*. The maximal strongly components form an acyclic graph corresponding to a partition of the initial I-system into several sub-systems. We call this graph the c-graph of the system (c stands for "component"). A *root* in the c-graph is a minimal element, that is, a node without predecessor (because c-graphs are acyclic, at least a root must exist). Each root of the c-graph represents a valid sub-system of the I-system, that is, a system where all variables present are defined (this is because roots are minimal elements). The solution of the entire I-system can be obtained by solving the sub-systems corresponding to the roots, propagating the results and then iterating the process. The processing order of the components can be determined by a topological sort on the c-graph.

So, we have turned the problem of solving an I-system into the problem of solving a root, that is: solving a subsystem of the initial system that corresponds to a maximal strongly connected component without a predecessor. In a root, we make a distinction between two kinds of nodes: the V-nodes corresponding to expressions computing the current value of some stream and the B-nodes generated by the computation of the current boolean value for the clock of some stream. It can be seen that if there is a cycle between V-nodes, there is also a corresponding cycle involving only B-nodes (because the computation of $\mathcal{D}[e]$ and $\mathcal{C}[e]$ involves the same arguments as the computation of $\mathcal{V}[e]$ for any expression e).

First, we turn our attention on cycles involving only B-nodes: they correspond to $\lambda x.x$, $\wedge$, $\vee$ and $if \quad then \quad else$ operations between SCCLOCK. We assume that the root is reduced, that is, each argument of a B-node is an output of another B-node in the root (e.g., expressions like $\top \wedge x$ are reduced to x before consideration). Then, the output of any node in the root reduces to $\bot$. This is because a B-node op is strict (i.e. $op(\ldots, \bot, \ldots) = \bot$). Consequently, the fixed point is reached after one iteration.

Now, we turn our attention on cycles involving only V-nodes. Circular equations between values result also in circular equations between domains and clocks. The associated clock then evaluates to *false* so there is no need to compute the associated value (which therefore remains *nil*).

A cycle involving both V-nodes and B-nodes is not possible inside a reduced root because there is no operator that promotes a clock into a value (clocks are hidden objects to the programmer, appearing at the semantical and implementation levels only).

5 Evaluation

The approach described in this paper has been fully implemented in the experimental environment of the $8_{1/2}$ language [25–27] (available at ftp://ftp.lri.fr/LRI/soft/archi/Softwares/8,5). The current compiler is written in C and in CAML. It generates either a target code for a virtual machine implemented on a UNIX workstation or directly a straight C code (no run-time memory management is necessary).

To evaluate the efficiency of our compilation scheme, we have performed some tests. We have chosen to compare the sequential generated C code from the $8_{1/2}$ equations with the hand-coded corresponding C implementation (because the application domain of $8_{1/2}$ is the simulation of dynamical systems, tests include a standard example of the numerical resolution of a partial differential equation through an explicit scheme and an implementation of the Turing's equations of diffusion-reaction). We details the results of the benchmark for the numerical resolution of a parabolic partial differential equation governing the heat diffusion in a thin uniform rod (Cf. Tab. 2).

The mean execution time corresponding to the compiler generated code without optimization is about 2.9 times slower than the hand-written one. The slight variation of the ratio with the number of iterations (which is the tick at which the program stops) are explained by a cache effect [28].

Four optimizations can be made on the generated C code to improve the performances. The first two concern the management of arrays (array shifting instead of gather/scatter and array sharing instead of copying for the concatenation) and does not interfere with the stream compilation scheme.

The last two optimizations have to do with the management of streams. For each delay $\$F$ appearing in the $8_{1/2}$ code, a copy has to be performed. The current value of a stream F is copied as many times as F is referenced by the delay operator. So, the sharing of delay expressions removes the useless copies. Moreover, the copy of expressions referenced by a delay operator (x_d into x_{md}, etc.) can be time-consuming,

Table 2. The heat diffusion resolution. Each element represents the ratio of the generated code execution time by the hand-written one. They both have been compiled using the GNU C compiler with the optimization option set -O. The evaluation has been performed on a *HP-UX 9000/705 Series* under the *HP-UX 9.01* operating system. The first number represents the ratio without high-level optimizations, the second with the four optimizations sketched. The ratio does not depend of the number of iterations, i.e. the number of stream elements that are computed, which shows the strict temporal nature of the stream evaluation scheme.

Number of iterations → Size of the rod ↓	100	500	1000	5000	10000
10	5.66	5.13	4.87	4.96	4.93
	3.89	3.59	3.65	3.70	3.66
100	2.27	2.17	2.17	2.15	2.15
	1.34	1.26	1.26	1.25	1.25
1000	2.80	2.76	2.76	2.76	2.76
	1.10	1.09	1.08	1.08	1.08
10000	2.62	2.60	2.61	2.60	2.61
	1.01	1.01	1.01	1.00	1.01

especially when large arrays are manipulated. However, the copy of the value of a stream F is not required, under some conditions (a similar optimization is described in Lustre [29]). If these conditions are not met, it is however possible to discard the delay copy. But it is necessary to have a temporary variable associated with the stream $\$F$. This kind of delay optimization consists in the definition of a single variable for each of the streams F and $\$F$ and to alternatively let it play the role of F or $\$F$ (a similar optimization is proposed in Sisal [30]).

The second number in Tab. 2 underlines the impact of these improvements: the mean ratio decreases to 1.5. Actually, it goes as far as 1.1 if we do not take into account the tests for which the rod has less than 100 elements, that is a size such that control structures are not negligible. However, it must be noted that there is a large room for further optimizations. More benchmarks can be found in [28].

6 Conclusion

Denotational semantics of recursive streams goes back to [17]. Equivalence between the denotational semantics and the operational behavior of a dataflow networks is studied in the work of [31]. Denotational semantics of timed flow begins in the framework of Lustre with [32,18]. A very general framework has been formulated in [33] but its sophistication makes its use uneasy. The work of Jensen [19] formalizes clock analysis in terms of abstract interpretation and extends the works of Plaice and Bergerand. We should mention the work of Caspi and Pouzet [34]: the clock calculus there is different than most other in not using fixpoints. Our proposal fills a gap left open in these approaches by providing a denotational semantics of clock tightly coupled with the denotational semantics of values. Notice that there is a great difference between our handling of time and the synchronous concept of time in reactive systems: our clocks indicates when the value of a stream has to be recalculated as a result of other changes in the system, while clocks in reactive systems tells when the value of a signal is present.

If $\mathbf{D}(x)$ or $\mathbf{C}(x)$ reduces to *False*, there is no value produced in the sequence $\mathbf{V}(x)$. This situation is a kind of deadlock. Deadlocks detection in declarative stream definitions are studied in [35,36] and for lazy lists in [37]. Thanks to the ROBDD [38] representation of clocks, it is possible to detect at compile-time some cases of such definitions. Clock reducing to *True* can also be detected and their implementation optimized. Signal has developed a sophisticated clock calculus to solve clock equations (dynamical system over $Z/3Z$ and Grobner bases). This approach is powerful but computation consuming. Its extension to our own stream algebra is not obvious and must be carefully studied.

The transformation of stream expressions into loops is extensively studied in [3]. The expressions considered do not allow recursive definitions of streams. Our proposition handles this important extension as well as "off-line cycle" expressions and is based upon the formal semantics of the expressions. We share the preorder restriction, i.e.: the succession of stream elements must be processed in time ascending order (this is not the case in Lucid). We focus also on unbounded streams and therefore we do not consider operations like concatenation of bounded streams. The work in [39] considers the static scheduling of a class of dataflow graphs used in digital signal processing. The translation of a (recursive) stream definition into a (cyclic) dataflow graph is straight-forward. Their propositions apply but are limited to the subset of "on-line" programs [40]. This restriction excludes the sampling operator and requires the presence of, at least, one delay on each cycle of the dataflow graph.

The benchmarks performed validate the approach used in the compilation of the clock expressions although all the needed optimizations are not currently implemented. When made by hand, the ratio between the C version and the $8_{1/2}$ version lies between 1.1 and 2.3 (in favor of C) for the benchmark programs. As an indication, the hand-written C program for the Turing example of diffusion-reaction has 60 lines of code whereas the $8_{1/2}$ program is only 15 lines long (which are the straight transcription of the mathematical equations governing the process). Thus the price to pay for high expressivity (declarative definition of high-level objects) is not always synonym of low efficiency provided that some carefully tuned optimization techniques are used. Nevertheless, the cost of the control structures cannot be neglected and several optimizations must be performed [27].

Acknowledgments. The authors wish to thank Jean-Paul Sansonnet, the members of the *Parallel Architectures* team in LRI and the anonymous reviewers for their constructive comments.

References

1. G. L. Tesler and H. J. Enea. A language design for concurrent processes. In *AFIPS Conference Proceedings*, volume 32, pages 403–408, 1968.
2. W. W. Wadge and E. A. Ashcroft. *Lucid, the Data flow programming language.* Academic Press U. K., 1985.
3. R. C. Waters. Automatic transformation of series expressions into loops. *ACM Trans. on Prog. Languages and Systems*, 13(1):52–98, January 1991.
4. W. W. Wadge and E. A. Ashcroft. Lucid - A formal system for writing and proving programs. *SIAM Journal on Computing*, 3:336–354, September 1976.

5. P. Caspi, D. Pilaud, N. Halbwachs, and J. A. Plaice. LUSTRE: A declarative language for programming synchronous systems. In *Conference Record of the Fourteenth Annual ACM Symposium on Principles of Programming Languages*, pages 178–188, Munich, West Germany, January 21–23, 1987. ACM SIGACT-SIGPLAN, ACM Press.

6. P. Le Guernic, A. Benveniste, P. Bournai, and T. Gautier. Signal, a dataflow oriented language for signal processing. *IEEE-ASSSP*, 34(2):362–374, 1986.

7. M. C. Chen. A parallel language and its compilation to multiprocessor machines or VLSI. In *Principles of Programming Languages*, pages 131–139, Florida, 1986.

8. N. Schmitz and J. Greiner. Software aids in PAL circuit design, simulation and verification. *Electronic Design*, 32(11), May 1984.

9. S. D. Johnson. *Synthesis of Digital Designs from Recursion Equations*. ACM Distinguished Dissertations. ACM Press, 1983.

10. J.-L. Giavitto. A synchronous data-flow language for massively parallel computer. In D. J. Evans, G. R. Joubert, and H. Liddell, editors, *Proc. of Int. Conf. on Parallel Computing (ParCo'91)*, pages 391–397, London, 3-6 September 1991. North-Holland.

11. K. Chandy and J. Misra. *Parallel Program Design - a Foundation*. Addison Wesley, 1989.

12. J. A. Plaice, R. Khédri, and R. Lalement. From abstract time to real time. In *ISLIP'93: Proc. of the 6th Int. Symp. on Lucid and Intensional programming*, 1993.

13. A. Benveniste and G. Berry. Special section: Another look at real-time programming. *Proc. of the IEEE*, 79(9):1268–1336, September 1991.

14. N. Halbwachs. *Synchronous programming of reactive systems*. Kluwer Academic publishers, 1993.

15. Paul Caspi. Clocks in dataflow languages. *Theoretical Computer Science*, 94:125–140, 1992.

16. O. Michel, J.-L. Giavitto, and J.-P. Sansonnet. A data-parallel declarative language for the simulation of large dynamical systems and its compilation. In *SMS-TPE'94: Software for Multiprocessors and Supercomputers*, Moscow, 21-23 September, 1994. Office of Naval Research USA & Russian Basic Research Foundation.

17. Gilles Kahn. The semantics of a simple language for parallel programming. In *proceedings of IFIP Congress'74*, pages 471–475. North-Holland, 1974.

18. J. A. Plaice. *Sémantique et compilation de LUSTRE un langage déclaratif synchrone*. PhD thesis, Institut national polytechnique de Grenoble, 1988.

19. T. P. Jensen. Clock analysis of synchronous dataflow programs. In *Proc. of ACM Symposium on Partial Evaluation and Semantics-Based Program Evaluation*, San Diego CA, June 1995.

20. H. R. Andersen and M. Mendler. An asynchronous process algebra with multiple clocks. In D. Sannella, editor, *Programming languages and systems - ESOP'94*, volume 788 of *Lecture Notes in Computer Sciences*, pages 58–73, Edinburgh, U.K., April 1994. Springer-Verlag.

21. P.-A. Nguyen. Représentation et construction d'un temps asynchrone pour le langage 81/2, Avril-Juin 1994. Rapport d'option de l'Ecole Polytechnique.

22. Patti Maes. A bottom-up mechanism for behavior selection in an artificial creature. In Bradford Book, editor, *proceedings of the first international conference on simulation of adaptative behavior*. MIT Press, 1991.

23. P. D. Mosses. *Handbook of Theoretical Computer Science*, volume 2, chapter Denotational Semantics, pages 575–631. Elsevier Science, 1990.

24. A. Benveniste, P. Le Guernic, and C. Jacquemot. Synchronous programming with events and relations: the SIGNAL language and its semantics. *Science of Computer Programming*, 16:103–149, 1991.

25. O. Michel. Design and implementation of $81/2$, a declarative data-parallel language. *Computer Languages*, 22(2/3):165–179, 1996. special issue on Parallel Logic Programming.

26. O. Michel, D. De Vito, and J.-P. Sansonnet. $81/2$: data-parallelism and data-flow. In E. Ashcroft, editor, *Intensional Programming II:Proc. of the 9th Int. Symp. on Lucid and Intensional Programming*. World Scientific, May 1996.

27. D. De Vito and O. Michel. Effective SIMD code generation for the high-level declarative data-parallel language $81/2$. In *EuroMicro'96*, pages 114–119. IEEE Computer Society, 2-5September 1996.

28. D. De Vito. Semantics and compilation of sequential streams into a static SIMD code for the declarative data-parallel language $81/2$. Technical Report 1044, Laboratoire de Recherche en Informatique, May 1996. 34 pages.

29. N. Halbwachs, P. Raymond, and C. Ratel. Generating efficient code from dataflow programs. In Springer Verlag, editor, *3rd international symposium, PLILP'91, Passau, Germany*, volume 528 of *Lecture Notes in Computer Sciences*, pages 207–218, August 1991.

30. D. C. Cann and P. Evripidou. Advanced array optimizations for high performance functional languages. *IEEE Trans. on Parallel and Distributed Systems*, 6(3):229–239, March 1995.

31. A. A. Faustini. An operational semantics of pure dataflow. In M. Nielsen and E. M. Schmidt, editors, *Automata, languages and programing: ninth colloquium*, volume 120 of *Lecture Notes in Computer Sciences*, pages 212–224. Springer-Verlag, 1982. equivalence sem. op et denotationelle.

32. J.-L. Bergerand. *LUSTRE: un langage déclaratif pour le temps réel*. PhD thesis, Institut national polytechnique de Grenoble, 1986.

33. A. Benveniste, P. Le Guernic, Y. Sorel, and M. Sorine. A denotational theory of synchronous reactive systems. *Information and Computation*, 99(2):1992–230, 1992.

34. Paul Caspi and Marc Pouzet. Synchronous Kahn networks. In *Proceedings of the 1996 ACM SIGPLAN International Conference on Functional Programming*, pages 226–238, Philadelphia, Pennsylvania, 24–26 May 1996.

35. W. W. Wadge. An extensional treatment of dataflow deadlock. *Theoretical Computer Science*, 13(1):3–15, 1981.

36. E. A. Lee and D. G. Messerschmitt. Synchronous dataflow. *Proc. of the IEEE*, 75(9), September 1987.

37. B. A. Sijtsma. On the productivity of recursive list definitions. *ACM Transactions on Programming Languages and Systems*, 11(4):633–649, October 1989.

38. R. E. Bryant. Graph based algorithms for boolean function manipulation. *IEEE Trans. on Computers*, C-35(8):677–691, August 1986.

39. K. K. Parhi and D. G. Messerschmitt. Static rate-optimal scheduling of iterative data-flow programs via optimum unfolding,. *IEEE Trans. on Computers*, 40(2), February 1991.

40. A. Aho, J. Hopcroft, and J. Ullman. *The design and analysis of computer algorithms*. Addison-Wesley, 1974.

—oOo—

Implementation of Term Rewritings with the Evaluation Strategy

Kazuhiro Ogata and Kokichi Futatsugi

JAIST ({ogata, kokichi}@jaist.ac.jp)
Tatsunokuchi, Ishikawa 923-12, JAPAN

Abstract. The evaluation strategy (the E-strategy) is more flexible than lazy, eager or any other fixed order of evaluation because each operation can have its own local strategy. An efficient implementation of the E-strategy based on strategy lists is proposed. A strategy list for a term t is basically a sequence of all eager positions (reachable nodes) in t. The order of the strategy list corresponds to the order of the evaluation of t. The E-strategy can control parallel rewritings as well as sequential ones. The parallel extension of the E-strategy is also described.

Keywords: term rewriting systems, reduction strategies, the E-strategy.

1 Introduction

A *reduction strategy* is a function that takes a set of rewrite rules (a term rewriting system; TRS) and a ground term as arguments, and prescribes which redices in the term have to be rewritten next. It also prescribes which one of these rules has to be applied if there are more than one applicable rules for the redex. It affects termination, space efficiency and rewriting speed in no small way. Outermost reduction strategies [10] (also called lazy evaluation) often have a better termination behavior than innermost reduction strategies (also called eager evaluation), while innermost reduction strategies [11, 13] can be implemented much more efficiently than outermost reduction strategies. A decision what kind of reduction strategies to adopt is a significant issue in implementing reducers or rewrite engines, which is one of primary factors that decides a character of the rewrite engines.

The functional strategy [16, 20], which is a variant of lazy evaluation, is used to implement lazy functional programming languages such as Miranda and Haskell. Though it is more efficiently implementable than pure lazy evaluation, the straightforward implementation of the functional strategy is not so even efficient both in space and time. So, eager evaluation is used to evaluate some points in the program instead of the functional strategy. The points in the program, where evaluation orders do not change the termination behavior of the program, are gained according to the strictness information provided by a strictness analyzer or by the programmer [20]. The superfluous costs related to lazy evaluation also remain even if the whole points in the program can be evaluated eagerly.

OBJ [7, 9] is an algebraic specification language including an executable functional programming language as its sublanguage. The reduction strategy used in OBJ is the *evaluation strategy* (the *E-strategy*) that is more flexible than lazy, eager or any other fixed order of evaluation because each operation can have its own *local strategy*. The E-strategy can control parallel rewritings as well as sequential ones [8].

TRAM (Term Rewriting Abstract Machine) [17] is an abstract machine for order-sorted conditional TRSs (OSCTRSs). The OSCTRSs [14] can serve as a general computation model for advanced algebraic specification languages such as OBJ or *CafeOBJ* [2]. TRAM adopts the E-strategy as its reduction strategy. In TRAM, left-hand sides (LHSs) of rewrite programs (i.e. TRSs) are encoded into *discrimination nets* [4]. Terms to be rewritten using the rules are compiled into pairs of self modifying programs (*matching programs*) and *strategy lists*. The matching program matchs the original term with the discrimination net (i.e. LHSs). A strategy list for a term t is basically a sequence of eager positions in t. The eager positions in t are the reachable nodes in t by traversing t according to given local strategies of the operations. The order of the sequence corresponds to one of the traverse of t for finding redices according to the local strategies. In this paper, we give the definition of strategy lists and define the reduction machinery with the E-strategy based on the strategy lists. In the implementation of TRAM, the strategy list for a term is a sequence of labels (addresses) of the matching program. Right-hand sides (RHSs) of rewrite programs are compiled into pairs of matching program templates and strategy list templates. In this paper, we also describe the implementation of the E-strategy used in TRAM. The implementation can remove completely the superfluous costs related to lazy evaluation if all operations have eager local strategies. TRAM also supports parallel rewritings by extending the E-strategy for specifying parallel rewritings [18]. The parallel extension of the E-strategy is also described.

We suppose the reader familiar with the basic concepts of TRSs and refer to [5, 15].

2　The E-strategy

The *E-strategy* [7, 9] lets each operation have its own *local strategy*. The local strategies indicate the order of rewritings of terms whose top operations have the strategies. The order is specified by using lists of numbers ranging from zero through the number of the arguments of the operations. Non-zero number n and zero in the lists mean that nth arguments of the terms and the terms themselves are reduced (evaluated) to a variant of normal forms respectively. We call the variant of normal forms *E-normal forms* (*ENFs*). Arguments of the terms whose corresponding numbers do not appear in the lists might or might not be evaluated on demand or lazily.

The following TRAM program, which is similar to a OBJ's module, defines a function that returns the nth element of an infinite natural number's list:

Example 1.

    sorts: *Zero NzNat Nat List* .

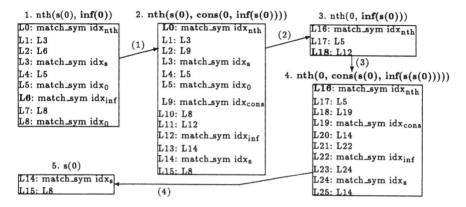

Fig. 1. Reduction sequence for the term $nth(s(0), inf(0))$

order: $Zero < Nat \ \ NzNat < Nat$.
ops: $0 : -> Zero \ \ s : Nat -> NzNat$
    $cons : Nat \ List -> List \ \{ \textbf{strat:} \ (1 \ 0) \ \}$
    $inf : Nat -> List$
    $nth : Nat \ List -> Nat$.
vars: $X \ Y : Nat \ \ L : List$.
rules: $inf(X) -> cons(X, inf(s(X)))$
    $nth(0, cons(X, L)) -> X$
    $nth(s(X), cons(Y, L)) -> nth(X, L)$.

The operation *cons* has the local strategy $(1 \ 0)$ that indicates a term whose top operation is *cons* is tried to be rewritten to another after evaluating the first argument of the term to ENF when the term is evaluated. If the term is rewritten to another, the new one will be evaluated according to the local strategy of its top operation. The second argument might or might not be evaluated lazily. The eager local strategy $(1 \ 2 \ldots 0)$ is attached to each of operations to which explicit local strategies are not specified. Figure 1 shows the reduction sequence for the term $nth(s(0), inf(0))$ using the above program. The ENF of the term $inf(0)$ is $cons(0, inf(s(0)))$ in the reduction step (1) in Fig. 1.

3 Reduction by the E-strategy

We first define *lazy, proper eager* and *pseudo-eager paths*, and *lazy, proper eager* and *pseudo-eager positions* in terms [12]. A path in a term is represented as a sequence of positive integers. Let p be a path in a term t, $p.0$ is a position in t and $t|_p = t|_{p.0}$.

Definition 1.

- For any term t, ϵ (the empty sequence) is a proper eager path in t.

- If p is a proper eager path in t, $t|_p = f(t_1, \ldots, t_n)$, f's local strategy is $(a_1 \ldots a_l)$, and m $(1 \leq m \leq l+1)$ is the minimum index such that $a_m = 0$ (suppose that $a_{l+1} = 0$), then $p.a$ is a proper eager or a pseudo-eager path in t if $a \in (a_1 \ldots a_{m-1})$ or $a \in (a_{m+1} \ldots a_l)$ and $a \neq 0$, respectively. If $0 \in (a_1 \ldots a_l)$, $p.0$ is a proper eager position in t and is also a pseudo-eager position in t if there are multiple occurrences of zeros in $(a_1 \ldots a_l)$.
- If p is a pseudo-eager path in t, $t|_p = f(t_1, \ldots, t_n)$ and f's local strategy is $(a_1 \ldots a_l)$, then $p.a$ is an pseudo-eager path in t if $a \in (a_1 \ldots a_l)$ and $a \neq 0$. If $0 \in (a_1 \ldots a_l)$, $p.0$ is an pseudo-eager position in t.
- All other paths and positions are lazy.

Note that $p.0$ is not necessarily a proper eager or a pseudo-eager position in t even if p is a proper eager or a pseudo-eager path in a term t. We say that subterms at proper eager or pseudo-eager positions in a term t are proper eager or pseudo-eager in t, and the others are lazy in t. When reducing a term with the E-strategy, proper eager subterms are evaluated eagerly, and pseudo-eager and lazy ones might or might not be evaluated lazily. For example, given the program in Ex. 1 and the term $t = nth(s(0), cons(0, inf(s(0))))$, the paths ϵ, 1, 1.1, 2, 2.1 in t and the positions 0, 1.0, 1.1.0, 2.0, 2.1.0 in t are proper eager; the paths 2.2, 2.2.1, 2.2.1.1 in t and the positions 2.2.0, 2.2.1.0, 2.2.1.1.0 in t are lazy. There are no pseudo-eager paths and positions in t.

We refer to proper eager or pseudo-eager positions as eager positions. We define order between two eager positions in a term.

Definition 2. Given two eager positions $p = a.p'$ and $q = b.q'$ in a term $t = f(t_1, \ldots, t_n)$, p is *earlier* than q in t if a appears before b in f's local strategy or p' is earlier than q' in t_a if $a = b$.

If p is earlier than q in a term t, basically $t|_p$ is evaluated earlier than $t|_q$ when evaluating t with the E-strategy. For example, given the term $t = nth(s(0), cons(0, inf(s(0))))$ under the program in Ex. 1, 1.1.0 is earlier than 2.1.0 in t.

The *strategy list* for a term t, written $slst(t)$, is a sequence of eager positions in t. It is defined as follows:

Definition 3. Given a term $t = f(t_1, \ldots, t_n)$, if f's local strategy is $(a_1 \ldots a_l)$, then $slst(t)$ is $seq_{a_1} ++ \ldots ++ seq_{a_l}$ such that

$$seq_{a_i} = \begin{cases} [0] & \text{if } a_i = 0 \\ a_i.slst(t_{a_i}) & \text{otherwise} \end{cases}$$

where $i = 1, \ldots, l$, $++$ concatenates two sequences, $p.[q_1, \ldots, q_n] = [p.q_1, \ldots, p.q_n]$, and $p.[\,] = [\,]$. If f's local strategy is empty, then $slst(t)$ is empty. The strategy list for a context $t[\,]_p$, written $slst(t[\,]_p)$, is gained by excluding all eager positions in $t|_p$ from $slst(t)$.

The strategy list for a term t contains all eager positions in t, or the basically equivalence to all subterms evaluated eagerly when evaluating t with the E-strategy. The order of $slst(t)$ corresponds to the order of the evaluation of t.

If p appears before q in $slst(t)$, p is earlier than q in t. For example, given the term $t = nth(s(0), cons(0, inf(s(0))))$ under the program in Ex. 1, $slst(t) = [1.1.0, 1.0, 2.1.0, 2.0, 0]$ and $slst(t[\ ]_{2.1.0}) = [1.1.0, 1.0, 2.0, 0]$.

Operationally, the reduction of a term with the E-strategy can be described in rewrite rules (a TRAM Program) as follows:

Definition 4.

> **sorts:** *Zero NzNat Nat Bool Term Lstrat* $\cdots$.
> **order:** *Zero* < *Nat NzNat* < *Nat* $\cdots$.
> **ops:** *eval* : *Term* $->$ *Term* // evaluates a term t
>   *reduce* : *Term Lstrat* $->$ *Term* // reduces t by t's top op's strategy
>   *strategy* : *Term* $->$ *Lstrat* // returns t's top op's strategy
>   *isRedex* : *Term* $->$ *Bool* // returns true if t is a redex
>   *rhs* : *Term* $->$ *Term* // returns the corresponding contractum
>   *arg* : *Term NzNat* $->$ *Term* // returns the ith arg
>   *replace* : *Term NzNat Term* $->$ *Term* // replaces ith arg with another
>   *nil* : $->$ *Lstrat*   *c* : *Nat Lstrat* $->$ *Lstrat*
> $\cdots$.
> **vars:** T : *Term* L : *Lstrat* X : *NzNat* $\cdots$.
> **rules:** *eval*(T) $->$ *reduce*(T, *strategy*(T))
>   *reduce*(T, *nil*) $->$ T
>   *reduce*(T, *c*(0, L)) $->$ if(*isRedex*(T), *eval*(*rhs*(T)), *reduce*(T, L))
>   *reduce*(T, *c*(X, L)) $->$ *reduce*(*replace*(T, X, *eval*(*arg*(T, X))), L)
> $\cdots$.

The straightforward implementation of the above reduction machinery is extremely inefficient because the search space for finding redices is huge. The implementations used in OBJ3 [9] and CafeOBJ [2] make use of *evaluated flags*, which are attached to once evaluated terms, so as to prune the greater part of the huge space. The reduction of a term with the E-strategy and the evaluated flags is defined as follows:

Definition 5.

> **sorts:** $\cdots$.
> **order:** $\cdots$.
> **ops:** $\cdots$
>   *setFlag* : *Term* $->$ *Term* // marks an evaluated flag on t's top op
>   *evaluated* : *Term* $->$ *Bool* // returns true if t has been evaluated
> $\cdots$.
> **vars:** $\cdots$.
> **rules:** *eval*(T) $->$ if(*evaluated*(T), T, *reduce*(T, *strategy*(T)))
>   *reduce*(T, *nil*) $->$ *setFlag*(T)
>   *reduce*(T, *c*(0, L)) $->$ if(*isRedex*(T), *eval*(*rhs*(T)), *reduce*(T, L))
>   *reduce*(T, *c*(X, L)) $->$ *reduce*(*replace*(T, X, *eval*(*arg*(T, X))), L)
> $\cdots$

The following relation between the two reducers $eval_4$ and $eval_5$ (where $eval_N$ stands for $eval$ defined in Def. N) holds under the restricted E-strategy:

Theorem 6. *If all local strategies in a rewrite program R end with zero or are empty, the reduction of a term with respect to (w.r.t.) R with $eval_5$ is operationally equal to one of the term w.r.t. R with $eval_4$. In other words, for any term t, $eval_5(t) = eval_4(t)$.*

Proof. We will give the proof on another paper.

On the reduction of terms with $eval_5$, the following holds:

Theorem 7. *For any rewrite program R with a collection of local strategies $S = \{es_1, \ldots, es_n\}$, $eval_5(t)$ w.r.t. R with $S' = \{es'_1, \ldots, es'_n\}$ is equal to $eval_5(t)$ w.r.t. R with S for any term t, such that each es'_i is gained by folding multiple successive occurrences of zeros to one occurrence after excluding second and later occurrences of any positive integer from es_i.*

Proof. Suppose that f's local strategy is $es = (\ldots a \ldots a \ldots)$ (a is a positive integer and the former is the first occurrence of a in es) and consider the reduction of a term $t = f(t_1, \ldots, t_n)$. Since the evaluated flag is marked on the result t'_a of $eval_5(t_a)$ for the first occurrence of a, $eval_5(t'_a)$ for the second or later occurrence of a just returns its argument t'_a and the second or later occurrence of a does not affect the reduction of t. The second or later in the multiple successive occurrences of zeros in es does not affect the reduction of t because any subterms in t does not change if t is not a redex at the first occurrence of zero and the suffix after the first occurrence of zero does not need if t is a redex. $\square$

Under the reduction of terms with the restricted E-strategy such that all local strategies end with zero or are empty, we can say that second and later occurrences of any positive integer, and second and later in multiple successive occurrences of zeros in each local strategy do not affect the reduction from theorem 7 and 6. Then, the *regular E-strategy* is defined as follows:

Definition 8. The *regular E-strategy* is the E-strategy such that each local strategy is empty or it ends with zero and there is at most one occurrence of each positive integer and no multiple successive occurrences of zeros in it.

Under the regular E-strategy, the strategy list for a term $t[s]_p$ can be seq_1 ++ $p.slst(s)$ ++ seq_2 from Def. 3, and then, $slst(t[\ ]_p) = seq_1$ ++ seq_2 because there is at most one occurrence of each positive integer in each local strategy in the regular E-strategy. The implementation of (Parallel) TRAM supports the regular E-strategy.

We define the one-step rewrite relation $\xrightarrow{ER'}$ before we give the definition of the one-step rewrite relation $\xrightarrow{ER}$ that is useful for implementing efficiently the regular E-strategy.

Definition 9. t rewrites to t' w.r.t. a rewrite program R with the regular E-strategy, written $t \xrightarrow{ER'} t'$, if $\exists u \to v \in R$, a substitution σ, an eager position p_i such that

- $t|_{p_i} = u^\sigma$
- $t' = t[v^\sigma]_{p_i}$
- there are no redices at any eager position in the prefix $[p_1, \ldots, p_{i-1}]$ just before p_i of $slst(t)$.

If a term s is gained such that $t \xrightarrow{ER'*} s$ and there are no redices at any eager position in $slst(s)$, starting from a term t, then s may be not equal to $eval_5(t)$. In other words, the reduction based on $\xrightarrow{ER'}$ is different from one with $eval_5$. Suppose that t is an input term and $t \xrightarrow{ER'} t'$ at an eager position p by using a rewrite rule $u \to v$ and a substitution σ. As described above, $slst(t)$ $(= slst(t[u^\sigma]_p))$ is seq_1 $++$ $p.slst(u^\sigma)$ $++$ seq_2 and $slst(t')$ $(= slst(t[v^\sigma]_p))$ is seq_1 $++$ $p.slst(v^\sigma)$ $++$ seq_2. After the rewriting, the redex at the leftmost one of the eager positions in seq_1 will be rewritten first if there are redices at some eager positions in seq_1 in the reduction based on $\xrightarrow{ER'}$, while the redex will not be rewritten first even if there are redices at some eager positions in seq_1 in the reduction based on $eval_5$. In the reduction based on $eval_5$, the redex at the leftmost one of the eager positions in $p.slst(v^\sigma)$ $++$ seq_2 will be rewritten first. We call $p.slst(v^\sigma)$ $++$ seq_2 the *unevaluated strategy list* for t', written $ueslst(t')$, after the rewriting $t \xrightarrow{ER'} t'$.

Here, we give the definition of the one-step rewrite relation $\xrightarrow{ER}$ based on unevaluated strategy lists.

Definition 10. t rewrites to t' w.r.t. a rewrite program R with the regular E-strategy, written $t \xrightarrow{ER} t'$, if $\exists u \to v \in R$, a substitution σ, an eager position p_i such that

- $t|_{p_i} = u^\sigma$
- $t' = t[v^\sigma]_{p_i}$
- there are no redices at any eager position in the prefix $[p_1, \ldots, p_{i-1}]$ just before p_i of $ueslst(t)$.

Since $ueslst(t)$ can be seq_1 $++$ $p.slst(u^\sigma)$ $++$ seq_2 because $ueslst(t)$ is a suffix of $slst(t)$, $p.slst(v^\sigma)$ $++$ seq_2 is the $ueslst(t')$ after the rewriting. After the rewriting, $p.slst(v^\sigma)$ $++$ seq_2 is given to t' as its unevaluated strategy list.

The unevaluated strategy list for an input term is the same as the strategy list for the term. Given a term t and a rewrite program R with the regular E-strategy, if there are no redices in $ueslst(t)$, then t is in ENF w.r.t. R. For example, the term $cons(0, inf(s(0)))$ is in ENF w.r.t. the program in Ex. 1.

4 Implementing the E-strategy Based on Strategy Lists

On many conventional architectures, the recursive implementation of the reduction machinery according to Def. 5 is inefficient even if the greater part of the search space for finding redices is pruned by using evaluated flags. In this section, we propose more efficient implementation of the (regular) E-strategy based on (unevaluated) strategy list defined in the previous section. The implementation of the E-strategy is used in TRAM.

When the unevaluated strategy list for t' $(= t[v^\sigma]_{p_i})$ is gained after $t \xrightarrow{ER} t'$ at p_i, some eager positions (some pseudo-eager positions in $t|_{p_i}$) at the head in $[p_{i+1}, \ldots, p_k]$ (suppose that $ueslst(t) = [p_1, \ldots, p_i, \ldots, p_k]$) have to be removed if they are in $t|_{p_i}$. So, the number of elements that have to be removed from $[p_{i+1}, \ldots, p_k]$ in order to gain the unevaluated strategy list for t' $(= t[v^\sigma]_{p_i})$ is added to each element of the (unevaluated) strategy list. The (unevaluated) strategy list $[p_1, \ldots, p_i, \ldots, p_k]$ for t is turned into $[\langle p_1, x_1 \rangle, \ldots, \langle p_i, x_i \rangle, \ldots, \langle p_k, x_k \rangle]$. Then, after the rewriting, the unevaluated strategy list for t' $(= t[v^\sigma]_{p_i})$ is $slst(v^\sigma)$ ++ $[\langle p_{i+x_i+1}, x_{i+x_i+1} \rangle, \ldots, \langle p_k, x_k \rangle]$.

The reduction of a term with the regular E-strategy based on Def. 10 is defined as follows:

Definition 11.

> **sorts:** *Zero NzNat Nat Bool Term Pos SList Pair* $\cdots$.
> **order:** *Zero* < *Nat NzNat* < *Nat* $\cdots$.
> **ops:** *eval* : *Term* $\to$ *Term* // evaluates a term t
>   *reduce* : *Term EList* $\to$ *Term* // reduces t based on the strategy list
>   *getSList* : *Term* $\to$ *SList* // gains the strategy list for t
>   *sub* : *Term Pos* $\to$ *Term* // returns the subterm at the position
>   *replace* : *Term Pos Term* $\to$ *Term*
>   // replaces the subterm at the position with another term
>   *cat* : *SList SList* $\to$ *SList* // concatenate two sequences
>   *p* : *Pos Nat* $\to$ *Pair* // elements of SList
>   *nil* : $\to$ *SList* *c* : *Pair SList* $\to$ *SList*
>   *glue* : *Nat Term Pos SList* $\to$ *Term* // an auxiliary function
> $\cdots$.
> **vars:** T : *Term* L : *EList* P : *Pos* X : *Nat* U : *Pair cdots* .
> **rules:** $eval(T) \to reduce(T, getSList(T))$
> $reduce(T, nil) \to T$
> $reduce(T, c(p(P, X), L)) \to$
> $if(isRedex(sub(T, P)), glue(X, T, P, L), reduce(T, L))$
> $glue(0, T, P, L) \to$
> $reduce(replace(T, P, rhs(sub(T,P))), cat(getSList(rhs(sub(T,P))), L))$
> $glue(s(X), T, P, c(U, L)) \to glue(X, T, P, L)$
> $\cdots$.

Since the function *reduce* calls itself at the two tail positions, it can be implemented by using a loop that is more efficient than the recursive call.

Since we can precompute the template of the strategy list for each RHS (i.e. v of rewrite rules $u \to v$), the strategy list for an instance v^σ can be gained by instantiating the strategy list template for v. So, it is not necessary to construct the strategy list for the instance v^σ from scratch after each rewriting.

The subterm at p_i is added to each element in a strategy list for a term t so that the subterm $t|_{p_i}$ can be accessed efficiently. So, the strategy list $[\langle p_1, x_1 \rangle, \ldots, \langle p_i, x_i \rangle, \ldots, \langle p_k, x_k \rangle]$ for t is turned into $[\langle t|_{p_1}, p_1, x_1 \rangle, \ldots, \langle t|_{p_i}, p_i, x_i \rangle, \ldots, \langle t|_{p_k}, p_k, x_k \rangle]$. Therefore, the reduction machinery described in Def. 11 is modified as follows:

Definition 12.

> **sorts:** $\cdots$ *Triple* $\cdots$.
> **order:** $\cdots$.
> **ops:** $\cdots$
>> *inst : Term* $->$ *SList* // instantiates a strategy list template
>> *t : Term Pos Nat* $->$ *Triple* // elements of SList
>> *c : Triple SList* $->$ *SList*
>> *glue : Nat Term Term Pos SList* $->$ *Term* // an auxiliary function
>> $\cdots$.
> **vars:** $\cdots$ U : *Triple* S : *Term* $\cdots$.
> **rules:** *eval*(T) $->$ *reduce*$(T, getSList(T))$
>> *reduce*(T, nil) $->$ T
>> *reduce*$(T, c(t(S, P, X), L))$ $->$
>>> *if*$(isRedex(S), glue(X, T, S, P, L), reduce(T, L))$
>> *glue*$(0, T, S, P, L)$ $->$
>>> *reduce*$(replace(T, P, rhs(S))), cat(inst(rhs(S))), L))$
>> *glue*$(s(X), T, S, P, c(U, L))$ $->$ *glue*(X, T, S, P, L)
>> $\cdots$.

In TRAM, the reduction machinery with the regular E-strategy is implemented based on the reducer defined in Def. 12. In the next section, we describe the implementation of the E-strategy in TRAM as well as the outline of the TRAM architecture.

5 TRAM: Term Rewriting Abstract Machine

In this section, we present the implementation of the E-strategy used in TRAM after introducing the outline of TRAM [17].

5.1 Outline of the TRAM Architecture

TRAM consists of six regions (DNET, CR, CODE, SL, STACK and VAR) and three processing units (the rule compiler, the term compiler and the TRAM interpreter). DNET is the region for discrimination nets [4] encoded from the LHSs of rewrite programs. The RHSs of rewrite programs are compiled and allocated on CR. Matching programs compiled from subject terms are allocated on CODE. SL contains strategy lists for subject terms. STACK is the working place for pattern matching. VAR contains substitutions.

In TRAM, subject terms are compiled into sequences of abstract instructions (*matching programs*) that are self modifying programs.

Definition 13. The matching program L_T for a term T whose top operation is f of arity n is as follows:

L_T: match_sym idx_f
    L_1 // idx_f is the index for f.
    $\vdots$ // $L_i(i = 1, \ldots, n)$ is the label of
    L_n // the ith argument's matching program.

Figure 1 shows some terms and the corresponding matching programs. All applicable rewrite rules for T are gained by executing the program. The program is called by jumping the label L_T after pushing a continuation (a return address) onto STACK. match_sym tests whether f is in the root node of (a sub-tree of) DNET. If f is in the root, the continuations (the arguments) $L_n, \ldots, L_2$ are pushed onto STACK and the control is transferred to L_1. Backtracking is used so as to find all applicable rewrite rules for the term. The method for backtracking used in WAM [1] for Prolog is adopted.

Matching program templates are compiled from RHSs and are instantiated when the corresponding rules are used. The matching program at L9 through L15 in Fig. 1 is the instantiated one of the matching program template of $inf(X)$ $-> cons(X, inf(X))$ that is used in the rewriting (1) in Fig. 1.

Since TRAM supports order-sorted rewritings, the sort of the top operation of a term may have to be recalculated if some subterms in the term are rewritten by using rewrite rules whose both sides have different sorts, or some redices in the term are replaced with the corresponding contractums whose sorts are different from the redices'. In TRAM, when a redex is replaced with the corresponding contractum whose sort is different from the sort of the redex, the instruction match_sym in the matching program corresponding to the term that contains the redex as its argument is replaced with another instruction calc_sort. calc_sort recalculates the sort of the term according to the sorts of its arguments and replaces itself with match_sym. If the recalculated sort is different from the previous one, match_sym in the matching program that contains the term as its argument is replaced with calc_sort.

5.2 Implementing the E-strategy in TRAM

The implementation of the E-strategy in TRAM is based on the reduction machinery described in Def. 12. Elements of (unevaluated) strategy lists in TRAM are triples $\langle label, pslot, skip \rangle$ of matching programs' labels, parent slots holding the labels, and the number of elements to be skipped. The triples correspond to ones used in Def. 12. The last element of the strategy lists is the BINGO triple $\langle BINGO, result, \_ \rangle$. BINGO is the label of the instruction bingo that is executed when an ENF is got. The second of the BINGO triple is the parent slot of subject terms. The TRAM interpreter executes the matching program to reduce a subject term according to the strategy list until the BINGO triple. The strategy list for the term $nth(s(0), inf(0))$ in Fig. 1 is $[\langle L5, L4, 0 \rangle, \langle L3, L1, 0 \rangle, \langle L8, L7, 0 \rangle, \langle L6, L2, 0 \rangle, \langle L0, RESULT, 0 \rangle, \langle BINGO, L0, \_ \rangle]$.

When an applicable rewrite rule is got by executing the matching program for a subterm of a subject term, the strategy list template of the RHS of the rule is instantiated and the instantiated list is appended to the remaining strategy list of the subject term so that the unevaluated strategy list for the new term is gained after replacing the subterm (redex) with the corresponding contractum. [⟨L9, L2, 0⟩] is the instantiated one for the strategy list template of the rule $inf(X) \rightarrow cons(X, inf(s(X)))$ that is used in the rewriting (1) in Fig. 1. The unevaluated strategy list for the subject term $nth(s(0), cons(0, inf(s(0))))$ is [⟨L9, L2, 0⟩, ⟨L0, RESULT, 0⟩, ⟨BINGO, L0, _⟩] after the rewriting (1) is done.

Since any subterm bound to variables at proper eager positions in the LHS of a rewrite rule has been evaluated when the rule is used, it is not necessary to include any eager position in the subterm in the strategy list for an instance of the RHS. So, no information on such variables is included in strategy list templates for RHSs of rewrite rules. Variables at pseudo-eager or lazy positions in the LHS of a rewrite rule might be bound to as-yet nonevaluated subterms (or *thunks*). If such variables also occur at eager positions in the RHS, some eager positions in the thunks have to be included in the strategy list for an instance of the RHS. So, information on such variables is included in strategy list templates for RHSs of rewrite rules. In the current implementation of TRAM, thunks are represented as complete matching programs (complete DAGs). For example, the strategy list template for the rule $nth(s(X), cons(Y, L)) \rightarrow nth(X, L)$ includes information on L, but no information on X. If a rewrite rule has no variables that occur both at pseudo-eager or lazy positions in the LHS and at eager positions in the RHS, the strategy list template for the RHS can be constructed almost completely at the compile time since no information on variables is needed and the instantiation of the template is very easy. It leads to the efficient implementation that can remove completely the superfluous costs related to lazy evaluation if all operations have eager local strategies.

The TRAM interpreter executes the following instruction sequence when it begins to interpret the matching programs to reduce subject terms:

```
           init          // initializes TRAM's registers
    LOOP:  next          // pops a label from SL and puts it at L_Dummy
           jump L_Dummy
           go_ahead
           select        // selects one among the applicable rules
           rewrite       // replaces the redex with its contractum
           jump LOOP
```

next also pushes the go_ahead's label onto STACK. go_ahead is executed when an applicable rewrite rule is found. If there is no applicable rewrite rule, the control is transferred to LOOP. go_ahead triggers off backtracking if there is a choice point frame [1]. Otherwise it transfers the control to select. rewrite also appends the instantiated strategy list of the used rule to one for the subject term.

TRAM has been implemented on a workstation that carries 70MHz micro SPARC II. Several benchmark programs are examined on the workstation, which exhibit 50,000 to 100,000 rewrites per second. The current implementation of TRAM is about an order of magnitude faster than OBJ3 and CafeOBJ.

6 Parallel Extension of the E-strategy

The E-strategy can be extended so as to control parallel rewritings. The parallel extension of the E-strategy is called the *Parallel E-strategy*[18] that is a subset of the *Concurrent E-strategy*[8]. The local strategy of the Parallel E-strategy for an operation f of arity n is declared by using a list defined by the following extended BNF notation:

Definition 14.

$\langle$ParallelLocalStrategy$\rangle$ ::= ( ) | ($\langle$SerialElem$\rangle$* 0)
$\langle$SerialElem$\rangle$ ::= 0 | $\langle$ArgNum$\rangle$ | $\langle$ParallelElem$\rangle$
$\langle$ArgNum$\rangle$ ::= 1 | 2 | ... | n
$\langle$ParallelElem$\rangle$ ::= { $\langle$ArgNum$\rangle^+$ }

$\langle$ParallelElem$\rangle$ specifies some arguments of a term whose top operation is f that are reduced in parallel. Each element of $\langle$ParallelLocalStrategy$\rangle$ are evaluated in sequence from left. For example, a TRAM program computing Fibonacci numbers in parallel can be defined as follows:

Example 2.

sorts: *Zero NzNat Nat* .
order: *Zero* < *Nat NzNat* < *Nat* .
ops: *0* : $->$ *Zero s* : *Nat* $->$ *NzNat*
    padd : *Nat Nat* $->$ *Nat* { **strat:** ({1 2} 0) }
    fib : *Nat* $->$ *NzNat* .
vars: X Y : *Nat* .
rules: *padd*$(X, 0)$ $->$ X
    padd$(X, s(Y))$ $->$ $s(padd(X, Y))$
    fib(0) $->$ $s(0)$ *fib*$(s(0))$ $->$ $s(s(0))$
    fib$(s(s(X)))$ $->$ *padd*$(fib(X), fib(s(X)))$.

When the term *fib*$(s(s(0)))$ is reduced, first it is written to *padd*$(fib(0), fib(s(0)))$, and then two numbers are added after reducing *fib*(0) and *fib*$(s(0))$ in parallel.

In Parallel TRAM, each processor has its own TRAM interpreter and four mutable regions (CODE, SL, STACK and VAR). Two stable regions DNET and CR are shared with all processors. One of the processors is also an interface processor that also plays a role of the user interface by using the rule compiler and the term compiler.

A strategy list represents a process queue. A chunk of consecutive elements of the strategy list represents a process. Each process has two possible states: *active* and *pending*. Each process queue contains zero or more pending processes and zero or one active process. If there is an active process in a process queue, it is at the top of the queue. A processor whose process queue contains an active process is in *busy*. Otherwise it is in *idle*.

It is not necessary to change matching programs even though terms are reduced in parallel. Strategy lists control parallel rewritings by holding labels at which new parallel instructions are stored. The new parallel instructions are fork, join, exit, sleep and nop. fork creates a new process reducing a subterm in parallel and allocates the processor to it if there is an idle processor. Otherwise the caller processor reduces the new process, or the new process is *inlined*. join delays its caller process until all of its child processes terminate and makes the caller processor idle. exit terminates its caller process and reports the termination to its parent process. After executing exit, the caller processor resumes the pending process at the top of its process queue if there are pending ones in the queue. Otherwise the processor becomes idle by executing sleep. sleep makes its caller processor idle. nop does nothing. fork creating an empty process may appear in a strategy list by instantiating a strategy list template. nop is replaced with such a wasteful fork.

There are two kinds of triples that are elements of strategy lists in TRAM. One is for matching programs, the other for bingo. In addition to these ones, Parallel TRAM has five kinds of triples as elements of strategy lists. These new ones correspond to the new five parallel instructions: $\langle FORK, SIZE, A_J \rangle$, $\langle JOIN, PNUM, \_ \rangle$, $\langle EXIT, A_{PJ}, PID \rangle$, $\langle SLEEP, \_, \_ \rangle$ and $\langle NOP, \_, \_ \rangle$. FORK is the label of fork. $SIZE$ is the size of the forked process. A_J points to the JOIN triple corresponding to the FORK triple. JOIN is the label of join. $PNUM$ is a number of the caller's child processes that do not finish their work. EXIT is the label of exit. A_{PJ} points to the JOIN triple of the caller's parent process. PID is the processor ID of the caller's parent process. SLEEP is the label of sleep. NOP is the label of nop.

Parallel TRAM has been implemented on a multiprocessor workstation OMRON LUNA-88K[2] that carries four MC88100 RISC microprocessors. It was found to be about twice times faster than TRAM after executing some benchmark program on the two (sequential and parallel) versions of TRAM[18].

7   Related Work

Though lazy evaluation is fascinating because it has a good termination behavior, pure lazy evaluation is not efficiently implementable. So, efficiently implementable variants of lazy evaluation or methods for simulating lazy evaluation are proposed. One of the variants is the functional strategy [16, 20] that is used to implement lazy functional programming languages such as Miranda and Haskell. Kamperman and Walters provide a transformation technique for TRSs and input terms so that lazy evaluation can be simulated on the implementation of eager evaluation: *lazy rewriting on eager machinery*[12].

The E-strategy [7, 9] cannot only simulate lazy evaluation, but also is flexible such that it lets each operation have its own local strategy indicating the order of the evaluation of terms whose top operation have the strategy. The Clean [3, 20] system provides *strict annotations* so as to change locally the default functional strategy into eager evaluation. The main purpose of the strict annotations is to help a strictness analyzer to detect a lot of points in the program that can be evaluated eagerly for the gain in efficiency, but not to control the order of the evaluation for the gain in flexibility. The *laziness annotations* of lazy rewriting on eager machinery is similar to the strict annotations of the Clean system.

The implementations[6, 19, 20] of modern functional languages are completely lazy by nature, the superfluous costs related to lazy evaluation are remain even if the whole points in the program can be evaluated eagerly. In the implementation of lazy rewriting on eager machinery, there are no superfluous costs related to lazy evaluation if all arguments in the original TRS are annotated eager. However, the transformation adds a lot of extra rewrite rules to the original TRS. Since the implementation of the E-strategy is eager by nature, it can remove completely the superfluous costs related to lazy evaluation if all operations have eager local strategies. In addition, it is not necessary to add extra rewrite rules to the original TRS for lazy evaluation.

Since the current implementation of (Parallel) TRAM is extremely straightforward, it is inferior to modern rewrite engines such as ARM[11] in speed. The implementation has a couple of bottlenecks: one is the naive replacement of redices with the contractum and the other the naive representation of thunks. The (Parallel) TRAM system will be on a level or superior to the modern rewrite engines in speed by adopting the implementation techniques for the efficient replacement of redices with the contractum and the compact representation of thunks used in the modern rewrite engines[11, 19, 20] and removing these two bottlenecks.

8 Conclusions

We have defined the (unevaluated) strategy lists and have given the implementation of term rewritings with the (regular) E-strategy based on the strategy lists. The implementation can be realized by using a loop that is much more efficient than a recursive call on conventional architectures. The parallel extension of the E-strategy has been described.

References

1. Aït-Kaci, H.: Warren's Abstract Machine. A Tutorial Reconstruction. The MIT Press. 1991
2. CafeOBJ home page: http://ldl-www.jaist.ac.jp:8080/cafeobj
3. Brus, T. H., van Eekelen, M. C. J. D., van Leer, M. O. and Plasmeijer, M. J.: Clean - A Language for Functional Graph Rewriting. Proc. of the Conference on Functional Programming Langugaes and Computer Architecture. LNCS **274** Springer-Verlag. (1987) 364–384
4. Christian, J.: Flatterms, Discrimination Nets, and Fast Term Rewriting. *J. Automated Reasoning.* **10** (1993) 95–113

5. Dershowitz, N. and Jouannaud, J. P.: Rewrite Systems. In *Handbook of Theoretical Computer Science*. **B** (Ed. J. van Leeuwen). Elsevier Science Publishers. (1990) 243–320

6. Fairbairn, J. and Wray, S.: Tim: A Simple, Lazy Abstract Machine to Execute Supercombinators. Proc. of the Conference on Functional Programming Langugaes and Computer Architecture. LNCS **274** Springer-Verlag. (1987) 34–45

7. Futatsugi, K., Goguen, J. A., Jouannaud, J. P. and Meseguer, J.: Principles of OBJ2. Conference Record of the Twelfth Annual ACM Symposium on Principles of Programming Languages. (1984) 52–66

8. Goguen, J., Kirchner, C. and Meseguer, J.: Concurrent Term Rewriting as a Model of Computation. Proc. of the Workshop on Graph Reduction. LNCS **279** Springer-Verlag. (1986) 53–93

9. Goguen, J. A., Winkler, T., Meseguer, J., Futatsugi, K. and Jouannaud, J. P. : Introducing OBJ. Technical Report SRI-CSL-92-03. SRI International. 1992

10. Hoffmann, C. M. and O'Donnell M. J. : Programming with Equations. *ACM Trans. Prog. Lang. Syst.* **4** 1 (1982) 83–112

11. Kamperman, J. F. Th. and Walters, H. R.: ARM Abstract Rewriting Machine. Tech. Rep. CS-9330. CWI. Amsterdam. Netherlands. 1993. Available as ftp://ftp.cwi.nl/pub/gipe/reports/KW93.ps.Z

12. Kamperman, J. F. Th. and Walters, H. R.: Lazy Rewriting and Eager Machinery. Proc. of the International Conference on Rewriting Techniques and Applications. LNCS **914** Springer-Verlag. (1995) 147–162

13. Kaplan, S.: A Compiler for Conditional Term Rewriting Systems. Proc. of the International Conference on Rewriting Techniques and Applications. LNCS **256** Springer-Verlag. (1987) 25–41

14. Kirchner, C., Kirchner, H. and Meseguer, J.: Operational Semantics of OBJ-3. Proc. of the 15th International Colloquium on Automata, Languages and Programming. LNCS **317** Springer-Verlag. (1988) 287–301

15. Klop, J. W.: Term Rewriting Systems. In *Handbook of Logic in Computer Science*. **2** (Eds. S. Abramsky, Dov M. Gabbay and T. S. E. Maibaum). Oxford University Press. (1992) 1–116

16. Koopman, P. W. M., Smetsers, J. E. W., van Eekelen, M. C. J. D. and Plasmeijer, M. J.: Graph Rewriting Using the Annotated Functional Strategy. In *Term Graph Rewriting: Theory and Practice* (Eds. R. Sleep, R. Plasmeijer and M. van Eekelen). John Wiley & Sons Lts. 1993

17. Ogata, K., Ohhara, K. and Futatsugi, K.: TRAM: An Abstract Machine for Order-Sorted Conditional Term Rewriting Systems. Proc. of the 8th International Conference on Rewriting Techniques and Applications. (1997) (to appear)

18. Ogata, K., Kondo, M., Ioroi, S. and Futatsugi, K.: Design and Implementation of Parallel TRAM. Proc. of the Euro-Par'97. (1997) (to appear)

19. Peyton Jones, S. L.: Implementing Lazy Functional Languages on Stock Hardware: The Spinless Tagless G-machine. *J. Functional Programming.* **2** (2) (1992) 127–202

20. Plasmeijer, R. and van Eekelen, M.: *Functional Programming and Parallel Graph Rewriting.* Addison-Wesley. 1993

Reflections on Reflections

Gilles Barthe[1], John Hatcliff[2], and Morten Heine Sørensen[3]

[1] Centrum voor Wiskunde en Informatica (CWI)[†]
[2] Computer Science Department, Oklahoma State University[‡]
[3] Department of Computer Science, University of Copenhagen (DIKU)[§]

Abstract. In the functional programming literature, compiling is often expressed as a translation between source and target program calculi. In recent work, Sabry and Wadler proposed the notion of a *reflection* as a basis for relating the source and target calculi. A reflection elegantly describes the situation where there is a kernel of the source language that is isomorphic to the target language. However, we believe that the reflection criteria is so strong that it often excludes the usual situation in compiling where one is compiling from a higher-level to a lower-level language.

We give a detailed analysis of several translations commonly used in compiling that fail to be reflections. We conclude that, in addition to the notion of reflection, there are several relations weaker a reflection that are useful for characterizing translations. We show that several familiar translations (that are not naturally reflections) form what we call a *reduction correspondence*. We introduce the more general notion of a $(\mathcal{R}_1, \mathcal{R}_2, \mathcal{R}_3, \mathcal{R}_4)$-correspondence as a framework for describing relations between source and target calculi.

1 Introduction

In the functional programming literature, compiling is often expressed as a translation between source and target program calculi. The target calculus is typically based on continuation-passing style (CPS) terms [1,27], monadic-style terms [3,12], A-normal forms [10], or some other sort of intermediate language that makes explicit things such as intermediate values and closure operations. In recent work [23,24], Sabry and Wadler question: what is the appropriate relationship between source and target calculi?

Program calculi are often presented as equational theories. So one might answer the above question by stating that compiling should preserve the equality relation of the source calculi. That is,

$$M =_S N \text{ implies } M^* =_T N^* \tag{1}$$

where $=_S$ and $=_T$ denote the convertibility relation in the source and target calculi (respectively), and where M^* denotes the compilation of M. One might

---

[†] PO Box 94079, 1090 GB Amsterdam, The Netherlands, `gilles@cwi.nl`
[‡] 219 Math Sciences, Stillwater, OK, USA, 74078, `hatcliff@a.cs.okstate.edu`
[§] Universitetsparken 1, DK-2100 Copenhagen, Denmark, `rambo@diku.dk`

even require that the converse of the above implication holds (*i.e.*, that compiling preserves *and reflects* $=_S$).

However, it is usually more fruitful to focus on the reduction theories which typically underlie the equational theories. For example, one might require that

$$M \longrightarrow_S N \text{ implies } M^* \longrightarrow_T N^*. \tag{2}$$

If reductions are taken to represent computational steps or optimizations, this states that a series of computational steps in the source language can be expressed in the target language. Again, the converse may also be of interest: one would like that every optimization expressible in the target calculus be reflected in the source calculus as well. This is especially advantageous if the conceptual complexity of the target language (*e.g.*, CPS) is significantly greater than that of the source language. Such a result would allow one to reason about the optimizations in the target language while working only with the source language.

Sabry and Felleisen [22] popularized the use of a *decompiling* translation for establishing the converse of the implications. For example, for the latter implication at line (2), one might define a decompiling translation ♯ which maps target language terms back to source terms and require that

$$P \longrightarrow_T Q \text{ implies } P^\sharp \longrightarrow_S Q^\sharp.$$

This, along with some other simple properties describing the interaction between ∗ and ♯ is sufficient to establish the converse of line (2).

Now that there are two calculi (source and target) and two translations (compiling and decompiling) under consideration, there are are variety of ways in which these four components can be related. Sabry and Wadler sought to emphasize reduction properties over equational properties, and they adopted the topological notion of *Galois connection* as their foundation for judging the possible relationships. After noting that some Galois connections describe undesirable computational relationships, they proposed a special case of a Galois connection called a *reflection* as a basis for relating source and target calculi. They then showed that several compiling-related translations could be viewed as reflections between various source and target calculi.

However, a close examination of the definitions of Galois connection and reflection reveals what we feel are some overly strong computational properties. A reflection elegantly describes the situation where there is a kernel of the source language that is isomorphic to the target language. Yet we believe that the reflection criteria is so strong that it often excludes the usual situation in compiling where one is compiling from a higher-level to a lower-level language. In many such cases, it is simply impossible to obtain a reflection naturally.

The present work has two goals.

1. We reflect upon Sabry and Wadler's proposal of Galois connection and reflection, and give what we feel are the strengths and weaknesses of these properties as criteria for translations used in compiling. We conclude that, in addition to the notion of reflection, there are several relations weaker than

reflections that are useful for characterizing translations. We introduce the more general notion of a $(\mathcal{R}_1, \mathcal{R}_2, \mathcal{R}_3, \mathcal{R}_4)$-correspondence as a framework for describing these relations.

2. To support the assessment of relations between calculi, we study several well-known translations used in compiling that fail to be reflections.

   - *Simulating call-by-name under call-by-value using thunks:* Even though this familiar compiling technique is not a reflection, we show that it does establish a very tight relationship (which we call a *reduction correspondence*) between the reduction theories of the source and target calculi. This strengthens previous results reported by Hatcliff and Danvy [13].

   - *Simulating call-by-name under call-by-value using Plotkin's CPS translation:* We note that Plotkin's well-known call-by-name (CBN) CPS translation cannot form a reflection. We give an optimizing version of the CPS translation such as one would normally use in compiling, and show that it forms a reduction correspondence. This strengthens the results given by Plotkin to include a notion of decompiling (*i.e.*, a *direct-style* translation [5]), and a description of the relationship between source and target reduction theories.

   - *Simulating call-by-name under call-by-value using a Fischer-style CPS translation:* We present a Fischer-style CBN CPS translation where, in contrast to Plotkin's translation, a continuation is passed as the first argument to a function. We show that this translation produces terms with slightly different reductions properties than those produced by Plotkin's translation. Specifically, neither a reflection, nor a reduction correspondence holds. However, there is still a strong relationship between the source and target reduction theories, and one can show that the translation forms an *equational correspondence*. We also study the reduction properties of an optimizing Fischer-style CBN CPS translation. This appears to be the first in-depth study of Fischer-style call-by-name translations.

   - *Compiling call-by-value using CPS:* We return to Sabry and Wadler's result of a reflection between the call-by-value (CBV) sublanguage of Moggi's computational meta-language and CPS terms. We note that the reflection result is obtained using a non-standard target reduction theory instead of the conventional call-by-value theory. However, we show that one can obtain naturally a reduction correspondence using the conventional theory and an optimizing translation.

Based on this study and Sabry and Wadler's own observation that Sabry and Felleisen's rigorously justified Fischer-style CBV CPS transformation cannot give rise to a reflection, we question if *any* optimizing CPS translation appearing in the literature can be a reflection using conventional reduction theories.

The rest of the paper is organized as follows. Section 2 reviews and assesses Sabry and Wadler's definitions of Galois connection and reflection. Section 3 studies the thunk-based simulation of call-by-name under call-by-value. Section 4 studies the Plotkin and Fischer-style call-by-name CPS translation. Section 5 assesses results concerning the call-by-value CPS translations studied by Sabry and Wadler. Section 6 presents related work. Section 7 concludes.

2 Relationships Between Calculi

In this section, we review the definitions of Galois connection and reflection given by Sabry and Wadler [23]. We also adopt their introductory definitions and notation.

We write $\longrightarrow$ for compatible single-step reduction; $\longrightarrow\!\!\!\!\rightarrow$ for the reflexive and transitive closure of reduction; $=$ for the reflexive, transitive, and symmetric closure of reduction; and $\equiv$ for syntactic identity up to renaming of bound variables.

Assume a source calculus S with a reduction relation $\longrightarrow_S$, and a target calculus T with reduction relation $\longrightarrow_T$. Reductions are directed in such a way that they naturally correspond to evaluation steps or optimizations. Let the maps $* : S \to T$ and $\sharp : T \to S$ correspond to compiling and decompiling, respectively. Finally, let M, N range over terms of S, and P, Q range over terms of T.

2.1 Galois connection

Sabry and Wadler introduce the notion of Galois connection as the foundation for relating source and target calculi (via compiling and decompiling). The original topological notion of Galois connection [8] must be adapted slightly since reduction is not a partial-order but a pre-order [23].

Definition 1 (Galois connection [Sabry and Wadler]**).** Maps $*$ and $\sharp$ form a *Galois connection* from S to T whenever

$$M \longrightarrow\!\!\!\!\rightarrow_S P^\sharp \text{ if and only if } M^* \longrightarrow\!\!\!\!\rightarrow_T P.$$

There is an alternative characterization of a Galois connection.

Proposition 2 (Sabry and Wadler). *Maps $*$ and $\sharp$ form a Galois connection from S to T if and only if the following four conditions hold.*

$$
\begin{aligned}
&(1)\ M \longrightarrow\!\!\!\!\rightarrow_S M^{*\sharp}, \\
&(2)\ P \longleftarrow\!\!\!\!\!-_T P^{\sharp *}, \\
&(3)\ M \longrightarrow\!\!\!\!\rightarrow_S N \text{ implies } M^* \longrightarrow\!\!\!\!\rightarrow_T N^*, \\
&(4)\ P \longrightarrow\!\!\!\!\rightarrow_T Q \text{ implies } P^\sharp \longrightarrow\!\!\!\!\rightarrow_S Q^\sharp.
\end{aligned}
$$

What are the implications of using a Galois connection as a criteria for judging compiling translations? Consider the following discussion [24, p. 5].

Consider a source term M compiling to a target term M^*, and consider an optimization $M^* \longrightarrow\!\!\!\!\rightarrow_T P$ in the target.
1. A Galois connection guarantees the existence of a corresponding optimization $M \longrightarrow\!\!\!\!\rightarrow_S P^\sharp$ in the source.

2. Recompiling this yields a reduction $M^* \longrightarrow_T P^{\sharp^*}$ in the target.

Now consider the requirement of a Galois connection given in component (2) of Proposition 2.

Observation 3. *A Galois connection requires that decompiling ($\sharp$) followed by compiling ($*$) yields a term $P^{\sharp^*}$ that can be reduced to P.*

Thinking of reductions as optimizations, this means that $P^{\sharp*}$ must be *equally or less optimized* than P. That is, a Galois connection demands that decompiling followed by compiling puts you in a position that is the same or *poorer* (less optimized) than where you started.

2.2 Reflection

Sabry and Wadler recognize that component (2) of Proposition 2 represents an undesirable quality and they make the following observation [24, p. 5].

Observation 4 (Sabry and Wadler). *If this optimization (i.e., $P^{\sharp*}$) is to be at least as good as the original [term] P, we require that $P \longrightarrow_T P^{\sharp*}$.*

At this point there is a choice to be made regarding correcting the undesirable component (2) of Proposition 2.

1. One can simply drop the insistence that compiling and decompiling form a Galois connection, and instead require these translations to satisfy the properties of Proposition 2 *with direction of reductions in component (2) reversed*, i.e., require $P \longrightarrow_T P^{\sharp*}$.
2. One can keep the requirement of Galois connection, and also require that $P \equiv P^{\sharp*}$.

Sabry and Wadler take the latter option and refine the notion of Galois connection into a *reflection*.

Definition 5 (Reflection [Sabry and Wadler]). Maps $*$ and $\sharp$ form a *reflection* in S of T if they form a Galois connection and $P \equiv P^{\sharp*}$.

However, we believe that the first option is equally valid. Why should a situation where $P^{\sharp*}$ is more optimized than P be considered inappropriate for compiling? We return to this point after a more detailed assessment of reflections.

What are the implications of taking *reflection* as the criteria for judging compiling translations? The requirement that $P \equiv P^{\sharp*}$ has the following implications.

Observation 6 (Sabry and Wadler). *For a reflection, $\sharp$ is necessarily injective.*

Observation 7. *For a reflection, compiling must be surjective on the target language.*

More generally, a reflection guarantees that there is a kernel of the source language which is isomorphic to the target language. If S is the set of source terms, then $S^{*\sharp}$ is the relevant kernel. Sabry and Wadler show that Moggi's call-by-value monad translation, Plotkin's call-by-value CPS translation, and Girard's call-by-value translation to linear logic can be made into reflections. The framework of reflections gives an elegant description of the relationship between reduction theories in these cases.

However, if the target language is *isomorphic* to a kernel of the source language, one may question if the described compilation is truly interesting. The desire for an isomorphism seems to conflict with the typical situation in compiling where one is translating from a higher-level language to a lower-level language (with more implementation details and computational steps exposed). This is the case even when compiling to a relatively high-level intermediate language such as CPS or monadic-style terms (which we will later demonstrate).

The injectivity of decompiling requires that there exists a unique expressible computational state in the high-level language for each computational state in the target language. Many rigorously justified compiling translations appearing in the literature fail to have this property. For example, in each of the translations considered later in the paper, a single computational state in the source language may be realized by several intermediate computational states in the target language (involving instantiating continuations, opening thunks or closures, *etc.*). This type of relationship (which seems the norm for compiling) is ruled out in a reflection.

Sabry and Wadler note that in this type of situation, transformations that are not naturally reflections can be *made* into reflections by changing the source and target calculi. For example, when there are several intermediate states in the target language for each state in the source language, one may be able to obtain a reflection by changing the target calculus to include multiple-step reductions that skip over intermediate states and move directly between states isomorphic to source language states (this is the case with the Plotkin CBV CPS translation discussed in Section 5). This has the advantage of yielding a tighter relationship between (modified) source and target calculi. However, if either the source or target calculi has been modified, one must still relate the modified calculus to the original calculus, and one must reprove properties such as confluence, compatibility, *etc.* The multiple-step reductions required for establishing a reflection sometimes make these properties technically more complicated than in the conventional calculi (see Sabry and Wadler's treatment of Plotkin's CBV CPS translations [24]).

2.3 Characterizing the relation between source and target calculi

When characterizing the relation between source and target reduction theories, the four-component structure of Proposition 2 is quite useful. In describing the translations appearing in the remainder of the paper, it is convenient to use the following parameterized definition.

Definition 8. Maps $*$ and $\sharp$ form a $(\mathcal{R}_1, \mathcal{R}_2, \mathcal{R}_3, \mathcal{R}_4)$-correspondence between S and T if and only if the following four conditions hold.

(1) $M \; \mathcal{R}_1 \; M^{*\sharp}$
(2) $P \; \mathcal{R}_2 \; P^{\sharp *}$,
(3) $M \longrightarrow_S N$ implies $M^* \; \mathcal{R}_3 \; N^*$,
(4) $P \longrightarrow_T Q$ implies $P^\sharp \; \mathcal{R}_4 \; Q^\sharp$.

For example, a $(=_S, =_T, =_T, =_S)$-correspondence is equivalent to the notion of equational correspondence defined by Sabry and Felleisen [22], a $(\twoheadrightarrow_S, \twoheadleftarrow_T, \twoheadrightarrow_T, \twoheadrightarrow_S)$-correspondence is a Galois connection, and a $(\twoheadrightarrow_S, \equiv, \twoheadrightarrow_T, \twoheadrightarrow_S)$-correspondence is a reflection. The appropriate subscript (*i.e.*, S or T) is determined by the particular component of the correspondence, and we will often drop the subscripts on relations when no ambiguity results.

We noted earlier that the refining of Galois connection to reflection is one solution to the problematic component (2) of Proposition 2. We believe that reversing the direction of reductions in component (2) is equally justifiable and perhaps even more natural. Following this latter path leads to what we call a *reduction correspondence*.

Definition 9. A reduction correspondence is a $(\twoheadrightarrow, \twoheadrightarrow, \twoheadrightarrow, \twoheadrightarrow)$-correspondence.

Note that a reflection is intuitively the *intersection* of a Galois connection and a reduction correspondence.

Proposition 10. *If maps $* : S \rightarrow T$ and $\sharp : T \rightarrow S$ form a reflection, then they form a Galois connection and a reduction correspondence.*

3 Compiling CBN to CBV Using Thunks

To give a more concrete assessment of the relations of the previous section, we consider one of the oldest techniques in compiling: the implementation of call-by-name under call-by-value using thunks [15]. Here, we follow the presentation given in [13].

Figure 1 presents the source language Λ — the untyped λ-calculus under the theory of β-reduction. Figure 2 presents the target language Λ_τ — the untyped λ-calculus plus the suspension operators delay and force under the theory of β_v-reduction and thunk evaluation (τ-reduction). Intuitively, delay M suspends the computation of an expression M, and force M forces the evaluation of the suspension yielded by the evaluation of M. The notion of reduction $\beta_v\tau$ is Church-Rosser [13].

Figure 3 presents the compiling translation from Λ to Λ_τ.

Observation 11. *Terms in the image of the compiling translation $* : \Lambda \rightarrow \Lambda_\tau$ are in τ-normal form.*

248

$$\text{terms} \quad M, N ::= V \mid x \mid M\,N$$
$$\text{values} \quad V ::= \lambda x\,.\,M$$

$$(\beta) \qquad (\lambda x\,.\,M)\,N \longrightarrow M[x := N]$$

Fig. 1. The call-by-name language Λ

$$\text{terms} \quad M, N ::= V \mid M\,N \mid \textbf{force}\,M$$
$$\text{values} \quad V ::= x \mid \lambda x\,.\,M \mid \textbf{delay}\,M$$

$$(\beta_v) \qquad (\lambda x\,.\,M)\,V \longrightarrow M[x := V]$$
$$(\tau) \qquad \textbf{force}\,(\textbf{delay}\,M) \longrightarrow M$$

Fig. 2. The call-by-value language with thunks Λ_τ

$$* : \Lambda \to \Lambda_\tau$$
$$x^* = \textbf{force}\,x$$
$$(\lambda x\,.\,M)^* = \lambda x\,.\,M^*$$
$$(M\,N)^* = M^*\,(\textbf{delay}\,N^*)$$

Fig. 3. Compiling CBN to CBV using thunks

$$\text{terms} \quad P, Q ::= \textbf{force}\,x \mid \textbf{force}\,(\textbf{delay}\,P) \mid \lambda x\,.\,P \mid P\,(\textbf{delay}\,Q)$$

$$(\beta_v) \qquad (\lambda x\,.\,P)\,(\textbf{delay}\,Q) \longrightarrow P[x := \textbf{delay}\,Q]$$
$$(\tau) \qquad \textbf{force}\,(\textbf{delay}\,P) \longrightarrow P$$

Fig. 4. The compiled language of thunks Λ_{thunks}

$$\natural : \Lambda_{\text{thunks}} \to \Lambda$$
$$(\textbf{force}\,x)^\natural = x$$
$$(\textbf{force}\,(\textbf{delay}\,P))^\natural = P^\natural$$
$$(\lambda x\,.\,P)^\natural = \lambda x\,.\,P^\natural$$
$$(P\,(\textbf{delay}\,Q))^\natural = P^\natural\,Q^\natural$$

Fig. 5. Decompiling from the thunk language

This follows from the fact that in the translation, force is only applied to identifiers.

Since the notion of reduction $\beta_v\tau$ is Church-Rosser, it is sufficient to define the decompiling translation from Λ to Λ_τ on the set of terms in the image of the compiling translation closed under $\beta_v\tau$ reduction. These terms can be described by the grammar in Figure 4. Figure 4 also presents the reductions of the call-by-value language Λ_τ specialized to Λ_{thunks}. In analogy with the "administrative reductions" of CPS terms [21], one can view the τ-reduction of Figure 4 as an administrative reduction that manipulates suspensions (as opposed to the *source* reduction β_v of Figure 4 which corresponds to a reduction in the source language). Given this view, Observation 11 above implies that compiling generates terms that are in *administrative normal form*.

Figure 5 presents the decompiling translation. Decompiling simply removes the delay and force constructs.

Assessment: Is the translation a reflection? No. Having a reflection requires decompiling to be injective (Observation 6), and thunk decompiling is not injective. As in most cases in compiling, there are intermediate computational stages in the target language that are not uniquely expressible in the source language. For example, here are two target terms that decompile to the same source term:

$$(\texttt{force}\,(\texttt{delay}\,P))^\sharp \equiv P^\sharp.$$

This is to be expected since the source language does not make explicit the computation step where a suspension (*e.g.*, implemented as a closure) is forced (*e.g.*, by opening up the closure, restoring the saved environment, and evaluating).

From another point of view, having a reflection requires that compiling be surjective (Observation 7) on the language Λ_{thunks}. Surjectivity fails since Λ_{thunks} terms with τ-redexes such as $\texttt{force}\,(\texttt{delay}\,P)$ are not in the image of the compiling translation (Observation 11 states that terms in the image of compiling are τ-normal).[1]

The reflection criteria is often violated when compiling fails to commute with substitution up to identity. In the thunk setting, commuting up to identity would mean that

$$M^*[x := \texttt{delay}\,N^*] \equiv M[x := N]^*.[2]$$

However, only the weaker property

$$M^*[x := \texttt{delay}\,N^*] \longrightarrow_\tau M[x := N]^*$$

holds, *i.e.*, $M^*[x := \texttt{delay}\,N^*]$ yields a term that lies outside the image of the compiling translation (which breaks the surjectivity requirement). Here is an example.

$$((\lambda x\,.\,x)\,N)^* \quad = \quad (\lambda x\,.\,\texttt{force}\,x)\,(\texttt{delay}\,N^*) \tag{3}$$

---

[1] However, such terms are reachable via $\beta_v\tau$ from terms in the image of the translation.

[2] Note that the left-hand side above has the form of substitutions generated by β_v-reduction in the target language (see the β_v-reduction in Figure 4).

$$\longrightarrow_{\beta_v} (\texttt{force } x)[x := \texttt{delay } N^*] \qquad (4)$$

$$= \texttt{force}\,(\texttt{delay } N^*) \qquad (5)$$

$$\longrightarrow_{\tau} N^* \qquad (6)$$

Line (5) shows that substitution produces a term $\texttt{force}\,(\texttt{delay } N^*)$ that is not in τ-normal form. Thus, (following Observation 11) this term is not in the image of the compiling translation. Therefore, compiling is not surjective, and thus the thunk translation cannot give rise to a reflection.

However, there is a tight relationship between the reduction theories of the source and target language — there is a reduction correspondence.

Theorem 12 (Thunking).
The translations $* : \Lambda \rightarrow \Lambda_{thunks}$ *and* $\sharp : \Lambda_{thunks} \rightarrow \Lambda$ *form a*

$$(\equiv, \twoheadrightarrow, \twoheadrightarrow, \twoheadrightarrow)\text{-}correspondence.$$

This strengthens the result reported in [13] (an *equational correspondence*) to consider properties of reductions.

In summary, compiling with thunks is a very simple example where one cannot have a reflection because there is no source language kernel which is isomorphic to the target language (*e.g.*, Λ_{thunks}). However, the reduction correspondence is a quite strong relationship: *(i)* components (3) and (4) guarantee that each reduction sequence in the source language is mirrored in the target language (and vice versa), *(ii)* components (1) and (2) state that compiling and decompiling act in a complementary manner: whether starting in the source language or target language, the translations never return a term that is poorer than the original. And in contrast to a reflection, the term may even be better.

4 Compiling CBN to CBV Using CPS

In this section, we consider compiling CBN to CBV using CBN CPS translations. Such translations have been used as the foundation for compiling CBN and lazy languages in several different settings [3,4,7,11,20].

4.1 Plotkin's CBN CPS Translation

We first consider Plotkin's CBN CPS translation [21] based on the presentation given in [13].

The source language is the call-by-name language of Figure 1. The target language is the call-by-value language of Figure 2, omitting the suspension constructs $\texttt{delay}$ and $\texttt{force}$ from the syntax, and τ-reduction from the calculus. We will refer to the modified calculus as Λ_v.

Figure 6 presents the compiling translation: Plotkin's call-by-name CPS transformation (where y and k are fresh variables). As with thunks, decompiling is defined on the language of terms in the image of the compiling translation closed under the reduction theory of the target language Λ_v (*i.e.*, β_v-reduction).

$$V^* = \lambda k . k V^\dagger \qquad\qquad (\lambda x . M)^\dagger = \lambda x . M^*$$
$$x^* = \lambda k . x k$$
$$(M N)^* = \lambda k . M^* (\lambda y . y N^* k)$$

Fig. 6. Compiling CBN to CBV using Plotkin's CPS translation

$$
\begin{array}{rl}
\text{root terms} & R, S ::= \lambda k . A \\
\text{computations} & C ::= x \mid R \mid (\lambda x . R) S \\
\text{answers} & A ::= K (\lambda x . R) \mid C K \\
\text{continuations} & K ::= k \mid \lambda y . y R K
\end{array}
$$

$$
\begin{array}{rl}
(\beta_{src}) & (\lambda x . R) S \longrightarrow R[x := S] \\
(\beta_{ans.1}) & (\lambda y . y R K)(\lambda x . S) \longrightarrow (\lambda x . S) R K \\
(\beta_{ans.2}) & (\lambda k . A) K \longrightarrow A[k := K]
\end{array}
$$

Fig. 7. The compiled language of Plotkin CBN CPS terms $\Lambda^P_{\text{cbn-cps}}$

$$(\lambda k . A)^\natural = A^\natural \qquad\qquad (K (\lambda x . R))^\natural = K^\diamond[(\lambda x . R^\natural)]$$
$$(C K)^\natural = K^\diamond[C^\flat]$$
$$x^\flat = x$$
$$R^\flat = R^\natural$$
$$k^\diamond = [\cdot]$$
$$((\lambda x . R) S)^\flat = (\lambda x . R^\natural) S^\natural \qquad (\lambda y . y R K)^\diamond = K^\diamond[[\cdot] R^\natural]$$

Fig. 8. Decompiling from the Plotkin CBN CPS language

Figure 7 presents this language $\Lambda^P_{\text{cbn-cps}}$ and the reductions of Λ_v specialized to $\Lambda^P_{\text{cbn-cps}}$. For this language, we will assume three disjoint sets of identifiers.

$$x \in \text{Computation-Identifiers}$$
$$y \in \text{Value-Identifiers}$$
$$k \in \text{Continuation-Identifiers} = \{k\}$$

The first two are denumerably infinite, while the third need only contain exactly one identifier (a well-known property of CPS terms [5,6,22]).

Root terms expect a continuation and yield an answer. For every $M \in \Lambda$, $M^* = \lambda k . A$ for some answer A. *Answers* either throw a value to a continuation, or pass a continuation to a computation.

In the $\Lambda^P_{\text{cbn-cps}}$ reductions, β_{src}-reduction corresponds to β-reduction in the source calculus. The reductions $\beta_{ans.1}$ and $\beta_{ans.2}$ are administrative reductions — they simply manipulate continuations. Note that the syntactic categories of the language are closed under reduction.

Figure 8 presents the decompiling translation for $\Lambda^P_{\text{cbn-cps}}$. A key feature of this translation is that the translation of continuations $(\cdot)^\diamond$ yields call-by-name evaluation contexts E_n which can be described by the following grammar.

$$E_n ::= [\cdot] \mid E_n N$$

Assessment: Hatcliff and Danvy's factoring of Plotkin's CBN CPS translation into the thunk translation and Plotkin's CBV CPS translation illustrates that the thunk translation and the CBN CPS translation are structurally similar [13]. This is further evidenced in the discussion below.

The Plotkin CBN CPS translation fails to yield a reflection for essentially the same reason as the thunking translation. To make the connection more apparent, note that a term of the form $\lambda k . A$ can be viewed as a "CPS-thunk" since it is a computation waiting for a continuation before evaluation can proceed. The reduction $\beta_{ans.2}$ of Figure 7 is analogous to τ-reduction; it can be viewed as forcing a CPS-thunk by supplying a continuation.

As with thunks, decompiling fails to be injective because the reduction of CPS-thunks is not directly expressible in the source language. The following example shows two terms that decompile to the same source term.

$$((\lambda k . k\,(\lambda x . R))\,K)^{\natural} \equiv (K\,(\lambda x . R))^{\natural}$$

In contrast to the thunks case, the CPS language $\Lambda^{P}_{cbn\text{-}cps}$ has the additional administrative reduction $\beta_{ans.1}$ which describes the naming of intermediate values. This reduction is also not reflected explicitly in the source language Λ.

As with thunks, the CBN CPS compiling translation also fails to be surjective because it does not commute with substitution up to identity. Instead, one has

$$M^*[x := N^*] \longrightarrow_{\beta_{ans.2}} (M[x := N])^*$$

as the following sequence illustrates:

$$x^*[x := N^*] = (\lambda k . x\,k)[x := N^*] = \lambda k . N^*\,k \longrightarrow_{\beta_{ans.2}} N^*$$

where the last step follows by a simple case analysis of N.

So what is exactly is the correspondence between Λ and $\Lambda^{P}_{cbn\text{-}cps}$? Following the thunk analogy, one might expect a $(\equiv, \twoheadrightarrow, \twoheadrightarrow, \twoheadrightarrow)$-correspondence (*i.e.*, a reduction correspondence). However, one has the slightly weaker property.

Theorem 13 (Plotkin CBN CPS). *The translations* $* : \Lambda \to \Lambda^{P}_{cbn\text{-}cps}$ *and* $\natural :$ $\Lambda^{P}_{cbn\text{-}cps} \to \Lambda$ *form a*

$$(\equiv, =, \twoheadrightarrow, \twoheadrightarrow)\text{-}correspondence.$$

This strengthens the results of Plotkin [21] to include a notion of decompiling and an analysis of reduction properties (instead of only equational properties).

The following example illustrates why one has $=$ instead of $\twoheadrightarrow$ as the second component of the correspondence. Given the terms below which all correspond to the source term $x_1\,x_2$ (*i.e.*, $R_i^{\natural} = x_1\,x_2$ for $i = 1, 2, 3$)

$$R_1 = \lambda k . (\lambda k . (\lambda k . x_1\,k)\,k)\,(\lambda y . y\,(\lambda k . x_2\,k)\,k)$$
$$R_2 = \lambda k . (\lambda k . x_1\,k)\,(\lambda y . y\,(\lambda k . x_2\,k)\,k)$$
$$R_3 = \lambda k . x_1\,(\lambda y . y\,(\lambda k . x_2\,k)\,k)$$

$$M^* = \lambda k \,.\, (M \,:\, k)$$

$$x \,:\, K = x\,K$$
$$(\lambda x \,.\, M) \,:\, k = k\,(\lambda x \,.\, M^*)$$

$$(\lambda x \,.\, M)^\dagger = \lambda x \,.\, M^*$$

$$(\lambda x \,.\, M) \,:\, (\lambda y \,.\, y\,P\,K) = (\lambda x \,.\, M^*)\,P\,K$$
$$V\,N \,:\, K = V^\dagger\,N^*\,K$$
$$M\,N \,:\, K = M \,:\, (\lambda y \,.\, y\,N^*\,K)$$

Fig. 9. Compiling CBN to CBV using an optimizing Plotkin-style CPS translation

one has $R_2 \equiv R_1^{\sharp *} \equiv R_2^{\sharp *} \equiv R_3^{\sharp *}$. Thus,

$$R_1 \longrightarrow_{\beta_{ans.2}} R_1^{\sharp *} \quad \text{and} \quad R_3 \longleftarrow_{\beta_{ans.2}} R_3^{\sharp *}.$$

Conceptually, the mismatch between Theorem 12 and Theorem 13 follows from the fact that thunk compiling produces terms in administrative normal form (see Observation 11), where as the Plotkin CBN CPS transformation does not. Specifically, $\beta_{ans.2}$ redexes exist in terms in the image of the translation.

Figure 9 presents an optimizing version of the translation in Figure 6. The translation uses a two argument function $(\cdot \,:\, \cdot)$ (inspired by Plotkin's colon translation [21]) that accumulates a continuation term in the second argument, and in essence performs adminstrative reductions "on the fly". A simple induction shows that terms in the image of the translation are in administrative normal form (*i.e.*, they do not contain $\beta_{ans.1}$ or $\beta_{ans.2}$ redexes).

Taking the optimizing translation as the definition of compiling and referring to the example above, we now have $R_3 \equiv R_1^{\sharp *} \equiv R_2^{\sharp *} \equiv R_3^{\sharp *}$. Thus,

$$R_1 \longrightarrow_{\beta_{ans.2}} R_1^{\sharp *} \quad \text{and} \quad R_2 \longrightarrow_{\beta_{ans.2}} R_2^{\sharp *} \quad \text{and} \quad R_3 \longrightarrow_{\beta_{ans.2}} R_3^{\sharp *}.$$

Even with the optimizing translation, one still does not have a reflection. Decompiling is still not injective (the definition of decompiling has not changed), and compiling is not surjective on $\Lambda^P_{cbn\text{-}cps}$ (it does not commute with substitution up to identity). However, we now have a reduction correspondence which matches the previous result for thunks.

Theorem 14 (Optimizing Plotkin CBN CPS).
The translations $* : \Lambda \to \Lambda^P_{cbn\text{-}cps}$ *of Figure 9 and* $\sharp : \Lambda^P_{cbn\text{-}cps} \to \Lambda$ *form a*

$$(\equiv, \twoheadrightarrow, \twoheadrightarrow, \twoheadrightarrow)\text{-}correspondence.$$

4.2 Fischer-style CBN CPS Translation

In Plotkin's CBN CPS translation, continuations are passed as the second argument to functions. This can been seen by the form of the continuation $(\lambda y \,.\, y\,R\,K)$ where R and K are the first and second arguments to a function that will bind to y. In the full version of this paper [2], we give an alternative to the Plotkin CBN CPS translation where continuations are passed as the first argument to function. We call this alternative a "Fischer-style" translation because the idea of passing continuations as the first argument to functions originates with a CBV CPS translation given by Fischer [9]. Although one might imagine such a simple variation to be of no consequence, Sabry and Felleisen [22] have shown (in a call-by-value setting) that the Fischer-style allows more administrative reductions to be carried out at translation time by an optimizing translation. We carry this idea over to the call-by-name setting.

The Fischer-style CBN CPS translation fails to be a reflection for essentially the same reasons as the Plotkin CBN CPS translation: decompiling is not injective, and the translation does not commute with substitution up to identity. It gives rise to a $(\equiv, =, \twoheadrightarrow, =)$-correspondence.

Taking an optimizing translation to be the definition of compiling, one has a $(=, \twoheadrightarrow, \twoheadrightarrow, =)$-correspondence. We further show that that if one adds a single reduction to the source calculus, one actually has a $(\twoheadrightarrow, \twoheadrightarrow, \twoheadrightarrow, \twoheadrightarrow)$-correspondence using the optimizing translation.

5 CBV CPS Translations

Fischer CBV CPS translation: Sabry and Felleisen gave an in-depth analysis of an optimizing Fischer CBV CPS transformation [22]. As noted earlier, they made the insightful observation that the Fischer-style translation allows more administrative reductions to be performed than the Plotkin CBV CPS transformation. A modified version of this transformation was subsequently used by Flanagan et al.[10] to show how the essence of compiling with continuations could be captured using an extended source calculus instead of actually introducing continuations.

Sabry and Wadler note that this translation cannot form a reflection (see [24] for a nice discussion). In terms of our previous discussions, it fails to be a reflection because it does not commute with substitution up to identity. Some reductions (and associated substitutions) produce terms (representing intermediate computational steps dealing with passing continuations) that lie outside the image of the translation (i.e., surjectivity fails). Sabry and Wadler note that the proofs in the original presentation by Sabry and Felleisen [22] demontrate that the translation forms a $(\twoheadrightarrow, =, \twoheadrightarrow, \twoheadrightarrow)$ correspondence. They conclude their analysis of the translation by noting that "the Fischer translation [performs] too many administrative reductions to be a reflection" [24, p. 20]. They have recently shown that the translation gives rise to a Galois connection [25].

Plotkin CBV CPS translation: Sabry and Wadler show that an optimizing version of Plotkin's CBV CPS translation [21] forms a reflection if one takes Moggi's computational λ-calculus [19] as the source language. One may wonder how this CPS translation can form a reflection since all others that we have discussed cannot. The translation commutes with substitution up to identity, so this removes one obstacle. However β/β_v reduction still leads to terms which are not in the image of the translation. For example, consider the following compilation of a β_v-redex using Sabry and Wadler's optimizing translation.

$$((\lambda x \,.\, x)\, V)^* \quad = \quad \lambda k \,.\, (\lambda x \,.\, \lambda k \,.\, k\, x)\, V^\dagger\, k \tag{7}$$

$$\longrightarrow_{\beta_v} \lambda k . (\lambda k . k V^\dagger) k \tag{8}$$

$$\longrightarrow_{\beta_v} \lambda k . k V^\dagger \tag{9}$$

The term at line (8) necessarily lies outside the image of the optimizing translation because it contains an administrative redex. Therefore, one cannot have a reflection using the conventional β_v or β as the target calculi. Sabry and Wadler address this problem by using a non-standard calculus that glues together several β_v / β reductions. This follows their overall approach of modifying the associated calculi to obtain a reflection. Using this modified calculus one has the following reduction sequence.

$$((\lambda x . x) V)^* = \lambda k . (\lambda x . \lambda k . k x) V^\dagger k \tag{10}$$

$$\longrightarrow \lambda k . k V^\dagger \tag{11}$$

By combining the reductions into a single reduction, one moves past the offending term that lies outside the image of the translation. This fix cannot work with the other CPS translations because offending terms are created not only as the result of reduction, but as the result of *substitution* of terms which have leading λk's.

Even though one cannot have a reflection using the conventional β_v / β theory as the target calculus, in the full version of this paper we show that a reduction correspondence holds [2].

Based on the analysis of CPS translation throughout the paper, we question if *any* optimizing CPS translation can be a reflection with the conventional β_v / β calculus as the target calculus. Optimizing translations produce terms with no administrative redexes. When reducing CPS terms using β_v / β one must perform administrative reductions, that is, one cannot help but reach terms that lie outside the image of the translation. Since it seems that one must always create non-standard reduction theories to obtain reflections for CPS translations, the effectiveness of using reflection as a criteria for judging relationships between *existing standand calculi* when CPSing is not altogether clear.

6 Related Work

The most closely related results are those which use a compiling and decompiling translations to relate reduction or equational theories in source and target calculi. Of course, this includes the work of Sabry and Wadler which we have analyzed in detail [23,24]. This line of work can be traced back to Sabry and Felleisen's fundamental analysis of Fischer-style CBV CPS transformations, where they derive a equational theory that forms an equational correspondence with respect to Fischer-style CBV CPS terms under $\beta\eta$-equality. They showed that the derived theory forms an equational correspondence with Moggi's computational λ-calculus Λ_c.

Flanagan, Sabry, Duba, and Felleisen [10] showed that the properties of CPS terms that make them desirable for compiling could be captured using the equational theory derived by Sabry and Felleisen. That is, one could have the benefits of CPS with out resorting to the more complicated structure of CPS terms.

Hatcliff and Danvy incorporated many of these ideas in a general framework for reasoning about Plotkin-style CPS translations based on Moggi's computational meta-language [19]. They illustrated how CPS translations and associated meta-theory for various evaluation strategies such as call-by-name, call-by-value, and other mixed strategies (e.g., as might be applied to call-by-name strictness analyzed terms) could be derived using this framework. An equational correspondence between Moggi's meta-language and CPS terms plays a prominent rôle in establishing the general theory. In a work similar in spirit to Flanagan *et al.*, they demonstrated how Moggi's meta-language provides a foundation for partial evaluation of functional programs with computational effects [14]. Lawall and Thiemann have recently presented an alternate approach to the same goal by using the notion of reflection to justify the correctness of a partial evaluation for Moggi's computational λ-calculus Λ_c [18]. In an earlier work, Hatcliff and Danvy gave a detailed analysis of the relationship between thunks and Plotkin's CBN and CBV CPS translations [13]. In essence, they showed an equational correspondence between Λ and Λ_{thunks}, and demonstrated that Plotkin's CBN CPS translation could be factored through the thunk translation of Figure 3 and Plotkin's CBV CPS translation.

It was Danvy who first emphasized the importance of a *direct-style* (DS) or decompiling translation for CBV CPS terms [5]. Although he did not consider equational or reduction theories, he showed how CPS terms in a Scheme-like language could be mapped back to direct-style. Lawall and Danvy [17] later showed how the CPS and DS translations could be staged using an intermediate language similar to Moggi's computational λ-calculus. Although they did not consider equational or reduction theories, they paid special attention to the problem of preserving evaluation sequencing order in realistic languages like Scheme. It was this work that first introduced the notion of Galois connection to relate the compiling and decompiling CPS translations. Their notion of Galois connection is quite a bit different from Sabry and Wadler. The ordering used is not based on reduction (as is Sabry and Wadler's), but is induced directly from the translations and captures structural similarities between terms. The use of such intensional properties as the basis of the order seems to have some weaknesses. For example, Lawall and Danvy note that the order is not preserved by their translations that introduce and eliminate continuations.

7 Conclusion

The table below summarizes the relationships between the conventional source and target calculi induced by the translations we have discussed.

	conventional	optimizing
Thunks	$(\equiv, \twoheadrightarrow, \twoheadrightarrow, \twoheadrightarrow)$	
Plotkin CBN CPS	$(\equiv, =, \twoheadrightarrow, \twoheadrightarrow)$	$(\equiv, \twoheadrightarrow, \twoheadrightarrow, \twoheadrightarrow)$
Fischer CBN CPS	$(\equiv, =, \twoheadrightarrow, =)$	$(=, \twoheadrightarrow, \twoheadrightarrow, =)$
Plotkin CBV CPS	$(=, =, =, \twoheadrightarrow)$	$(\twoheadrightarrow, \twoheadrightarrow, \twoheadrightarrow, \twoheadrightarrow)$
Fischer CBV CPS	$(=, =, =, =)$	$(=, \twoheadrightarrow, \twoheadrightarrow, =)$

This work should be viewed as complementary to Sabry and Wadler's. The goal of both works is to establish technical tools and criteria for reasoning about and assessing how various compiling-oriented translations interact with reduction properties of program calculi. A difference is that Sabry and Wadler strive for a very tight relationship between source and target calculi reductions even if it means substantially modifying the source and target calculi. Our approach is to give a framework for describing the relationships that arise naturally between conventional calculi.

A benefit of Sabry and Wadler's approach is that the notions of Galois connection and reflection naturally lead to notions such as core source and target calculi that are isomorphic. Besides giving details of the properties of the translations from the table above, the full version of this paper illustrates how a similar notion of isomorphism can be captured in our framework by quotienting the conventional calculi [2].

A study of reduction theories such as ours and Sabry and Wadler's is not only of interest in compiling functional programs. For example, preserving reductions under CPS translation is important in techniques for inferring strong normalization from weak normalization [26]. There also appears to be strong connections to work on compilation of term-rewriting systems [16]. Both of these applications seem to involve translations that cannot form reflections.

Acknowledgements Thanks to Olivier Danvy, Sergey Kotov, Julia Lawall, Amr Sabry, Peter Thiemann, and Phil Wadler for helpful discussions.

References

1. Andrew W. Appel. *Compiling with Continuations*. Cambridge University Press, 1992.
2. Gilles Barthe, John Hatcliff, and Morten Heine Sørensen. Reflections on Reflections (full version). Forthcoming DIKU Technical Report. Available at http://www.cs.okstate.edu/~hatclif.
3. P. N. Benton. *Strictness Analysis of Lazy Functional Programs*. PhD thesis, Computer Laboratory, University of Cambridge, Cambridge, England, 1995.
4. Geoffrey Burn and Daniel Le Métayer. Proving the correctness of compiler optimisations based on a global program analysis. Technical report Doc 92/20, Department of Computing, Imperial College of Science, Technology and Medicine, London, England, 1992.
5. Olivier Danvy. Back to direct style. *Science of Computer Programming*, 22(3):183–195, 1994. Special Issue on ESOP'92, the Fourth European Symposium on Programming, Rennes, February 1992.
6. Olivier Danvy and Andrzej Filinski. Representing control, a study of the CPS transformation. Mathematical Structures in Computer Science, Vol. 2, No. 4, pages 361–391. Cambridge University Press, December 1992.
7. Olivier Danvy and John Hatcliff. CPS transformation after strictness analysis. *ACM Letters on Programming Languages and Systems*, 1(3):195–212, 1993.
8. B. A. Davey and H. A. Priestley. *Introduction to Lattices and Order*. Cambridge University Press, 1990.
9. Michael J. Fischer. Lambda-calculus schemata. In Talcott [28]. An earlier version appeared in the *Proceedings of the ACM Conference on Proving Assertions about Programs*, SIGPLAN Notices, Vol. 7, No. 1, January 1972.

10. Cormac Flanagan, Amr Sabry, Bruce F. Duba, and Matthias Felleisen. The essence of compiling with continuations. In David W. Wall, editor, *Proceedings of the ACM SIGPLAN'93 Conference on Programming Languages Design and Implementation*, SIGPLAN Notices, Vol. 28, No 6, pages 237–247, Albuquerque, New Mexico, June 1993. ACM Press.

11. Pascal Fradet and Daniel Le Métayer. Compilation of functional languages by program transformation. *ACM Transactions on Programming Languages and Systems*, 13:21–51, 1991.

12. John Hatcliff and Olivier Danvy. A generic account of continuation-passing styles. In Hans Boehm, editor, *Proceedings of the Twenty-first Annual ACM Symposium on Principles of Programming Languages*, Portland, Oregon, January 1994. ACM Press.

13. John Hatcliff and Olivier Danvy. Thunks and the λ-calculus. *Journal of Functional Programming*, 1995. (in press). The extended version of this paper appears as DIKU-Report 95/3.

14. John Hatcliff and Olivier Danvy. A computational formalization for partial evaluation. *Mathematical Structures in Computer Science*, 1996. (in press). To appear in a special issue devoted to selected papers from the *Workshop on Logic, Domains, and Programming Languages*. Darmstadt, Germany. May, 1995.

15. P. Z. Ingerman. Thunks, a way of compiling procedure statements with some comments on procedure declarations. *Communications of the ACM*, 4(1):55–58, 1961.

16. J. Kamperman and H. Walters. Minimal term rewriting systems. In M. Haveraaen, O. Owe, and O.-J. Dahl, editors, *Recent Trends in Data Type Specification*, volume 1130 of *Lecture Notes in Computer Science*, pages 274–290, 1996.

17. Julia L. Lawall and Olivier Danvy. Separating stages in the continuation-passing style transformation. In Susan L. Graham, editor, *Proceedings of the Twentieth Annual ACM Symposium on Principles of Programming Languages*, pages 124–136, Charleston, South Carolina, January 1993. ACM Press.

18. Julia L. Lawall and Peter Thiemann. Sound specialization in the presence of computational effects. To appear in the *Proceedings of TACS'97*.

19. Eugenio Moggi. Notions of computation and monads. *Information and Computation*, 93:55–92, 1991.

20. Chris Okasaki, Peter Lee, and David Tarditi. Call-by-need and continuation-passing style. In Talcott [28].

21. Gordon D. Plotkin. Call-by-name, call-by-value and the λ-calculus. *Theoretical Computer Science*, 1:125–159, 1975.

22. Amr Sabry and Matthias Felleisen. Reasoning about programs in continuation-passing style. In Talcott [28], pages 289–360.

23. Amr Sabry and Philip Wadler. A reflection on call-by-value. In *Proceedings of the 1996 ACM SIGPLAN International Conference on Functional Programming*, April 1996.

24. Amr Sabry and Philip Wadler. A reflection on call-by-value. Technical Report CIS-TR-96-08, Department of Computing and Information Sciences, University of Oregon, Eugene, Oregon, April 1996.

25. Amr Sabry and Philip Wadler. Personal communication. June 4, 1997.

26. Morten Heine Sørensen. Strong normalization from weak normalization in typed λ-calculi. *Information and Computation*, 133(1):35–71, 1997.

27. Guy L. Steele Jr. Rabbit: A compiler for Scheme. Technical Report AI-TR-474, Artificial Intelligence Laboratory, Massachusetts Institute of Technology, Cambridge, Massachusetts, May 1978.

28. Carolyn L. Talcott, editor. *Special issue on continuations*, LISP and Symbolic Computation, Vol. 6, Nos. 3/4. Kluwer Academic Publishers, 1993.

Evaluation Under Lambda Abstraction

Hongwei Xi

Department of Mathematical Sciences
Carnegie Mellon University
Pittsburgh, PA 15213, USA

email: hwxi+@cs.cmu.edu

Abstract. In light of the usual definition of values [18] as terms in weak head normal form (WHNF), a λ-abstraction is regarded as a value, and therefore no expressions under λ-abstraction can get evaluated and the sharing of computation under λ has to be achieved through program transformations such as λ-lifting and supercombinators. In this paper we generalise the notion of head normal form (HNF) and introduce the definition of *generalised head normal form* (GHNF). We then define values as terms in GHNF with flexible heads, and study a call-by-value λ-calculus λ_{hd}^v corresponding to this new notion of values. After establishing a version of the normalisation theorem in λ_{hd}^v, we construct an evaluation function $\mathbf{eval}_{hd}^v$ for λ_{hd}^v which evaluates under λ-abstraction. We prove that a program can be evaluated in λ_{hd}^v to a term in GHNF if and only if it can be evaluated in the usual λ-calculus to a term in HNF. We also present an operational semantics for λ_{hd}^v via a SECD machine. We argue that lazy functional programming languages can be implemented through λ_{hd}^v and an implementation of λ_{hd}^v can significantly enhance the degree of sharing in evaluation. This establishes a solid foundation for implementing run-time code generation through λ_{hd}^v.

Keywords: lambda-calculus, partial evaluation, run-time code generation

1 Introduction

SECD machines never evaluate expressions under a λ-abstraction, and this has some serious potential disadvantages. For instance, given a program

$$(\lambda x. + (x(0), x(1)))(\lambda y. I(I)(y)),$$

where $I = (\lambda z.z)$, the β-redex $I(I)$ gets reduced twice by either a call-by-value or a call-by-need SECD machine. This kind of duplication of evaluations can be avoided by extracting the maximal-free terms in a function at compile-time [17]. However, since evaluation can change the set of free variables in a term, the situation becomes complicated if such an expression is generated at run-time. This makes direct evaluation under λ-abstraction desirable.

Why is a value defined as a λ-abstraction or a variable in the usual call-by-value λ-calculus λ_v [18]?. Following [18], one crucial observation is that this form of values is closed under *value* substitutions in which values are substituted for free variables. This directly leads to the notion of residuals of β_v-redexes under β_v-reduction and the notion of parallel β_v-reduction, from which the Church-Rosser theorem for λ_v and the standardisation theorem for λ_v follow. An evaluation function for λ_v can then be defined and justified by the standardisation theorem for λ_v.

There exists another form of terms which is closed under substitutions. A term in head normal form (HNF) is of form $\lambda x_1...\lambda x_m.x(M_1)...(M_n)$; if x is x_i for some $1 \leq i \leq n$ then the term is in flexible HNF; flexible HNF is clearly closed under substitution.

If we define values as terms in flexible HNF, then we have to perform evaluation under λ-abstraction in order to reduce $(\lambda y.I(I)(y))$ to a value, which is $(\lambda y.y)$ in this case. Hence, call-by-value in this setting can avoid duplicating evaluations. Unfortunately, the new definition of values has some serious drawbacks as illustrated in Section 3. Modifying the notion of head normal form (HNF), we present the definition of generalised head normal form (GHNF). We then define values as terms in flexible GHNF and study a call-by-value λ-calculus λ_{hd}^v based on this definition. After proving a version of the normalisation theorem in λ_{hd}^v, we define an evaluation function which always evaluates a program to a term in GHNF if there exists one. Our main contribution is showing that a term can be reduced to a term in GHNF in the λ-calculus λ_{hd}^v if and only if it can be reduced to a term in HNF in the usual λ-calculus λ. We also present an operational semantics for λ_{hd}^v via a SECD machine, which can easily lead to a mechanical implementation (we have coded a prototype implementation).

Lazy functional programming languages can be implemented through the (call-by-name) λ-calculus. Executions of programs in realistic programming languages aim at returning observable values such as integers, booleans, (finite and infinite) lists, etc. Observable values are in HNF, and therefore, lazy functional programming languages can be implemented through the λ-calculus λ_{hd}^v since programs which output observable values can always be evaluated to terms in GHNF in λ_{hd}^v according to our main result. Other potential applications of λ_{hd}^v include partial evaluation and run-time code generation, which are discussed in the seventh section.

The next section presents some preliminaries. The third section presents the definitions of generalised head normal form and β_{hd}^v-redexes. The fourth section studies λ_{hd}^v, and its relations to λ. The fifth section presents an operational semantics of λ_{hd}^v via a SECD machine. The sixth section deals with extensions of λ_{hd}^v with recursion combinators, constructors and primitive operators. The rest of the paper discusses some related work and future directions.

We make the full version of our paper available through a pointer [21] so that the interested reader may verify proof details.

2 Preliminaries

In this section we briefly review the usual λ-calculus λ; we assume a basic familiarity of the reader with this material [4].

$$
\begin{array}{llll}
\text{variables} & x, y, z & & \\
\text{terms} & M, N & ::= & x \mid (\lambda x.M) \mid M(N) \\
\beta\text{-redexes} & R & ::= & (\lambda x.M)(N) \\
\text{contexts} & C & ::= & [] \mid (\lambda x.C) \mid M(C) \mid C(M) \\
\beta\text{-reduction} & C[(\lambda x.M)(N)] & \to_\beta & C[M\{x := N\}]
\end{array}
$$

The expression $C[M]$ stands for the term obtained by replacing $[]$ in C with M. The expression $M\{x := N\}$ denotes the result of substituting N for all free occurrences of x in M. We assume Barendregt's variable convention to avoid name collisions and treat α-conversions implicitly. We also introduce a new symbol $\bullet$ as a place holder and treat it as a variable. The body of a λ-abstraction $M = (\lambda x.M_1)$ is defined as $\mathrm{bd}(M) = M_1\{x := \bullet\}$; we write $\beta(M, N) = \mathrm{bd}(M)\{\bullet := N\}$ for the contractum of β-redex $R = M(N)$. We may use integers in our examples, but we only study pure λ-terms until Section 6. We shall use P for programs, i.e., closed *lambda*-terms.

For any decorated reduction notation of $\to$ in this paper, the corresponding decorated reduction notations of $\to^n$ and $\twoheadrightarrow$ stand for n steps and some (possibly zero) steps of such a reduction, respectively.

The following explicit notation of β-reduction enables us to write out the contracted β-redexes.

Definition 1. Given a β-redex R in M; $M \overset{R}{\to}_\beta N$ stands for the β-reduction step in which R gets contracted.

This notation generalises to other reductions.

Definition 2. *(HNF)* Given a term M; M has a head β-redex $(\lambda x.N_1)(N_2)$ if M is of form $\lambda x_1 \ldots \lambda x_m.(\lambda x.N_1)(N_2)(M_1) \ldots (M_n)$, where $m, n \geq 0$. We write $M \overset{h}{\to}_\beta N$ if $M \overset{R}{\to}_\beta N$ where R is the head β-redex in M. M is in HNF if M has no head β-redex, i.e., M is of form $\lambda x_1 \ldots \lambda x_m.x(M_1) \ldots (M_n)$, where $m, n \geq 0$; the HNF is flexible if x occurs in $x_1, \ldots, x_m$, and it is rigid otherwise.

Note that flexible HNF is closed under substitutions; if we define values as terms in flexible HNF, then a redex in the corresponding call-by-value calculus is of form $M(N)$, where M, N are in flexible HNF; we can prove that this λ-calculus is Church-Rosser and enjoys a version of standardisation theorem; unfortunately, normal forms in this λ-calculus may seem inappropriate to be regarded as outputs of programs; for instance, $(\lambda x.I(x(I)))(I)(0)$, is in normal form in this λ-calculus but we really wish to reduce it to 0; the reason is that $x(I)$ is not a value since it is not in *flexible* HNF. This obstacle will be overcome in the next section.

$$
\begin{aligned}
\mathrm{ghd}(M) &= M & \text{if } M \in \mathbf{Var}; \\
\mathrm{ghd}(\lambda x.M) &= \mathrm{ghd}(M) & \text{if } \mathrm{ghd}(M) \neq x \in \mathbf{Var}; \\
\mathrm{ghd}(\lambda x.M) &= 0 & \text{if } \mathrm{ghd}(M) = x \\
\mathrm{ghd}(\lambda x.M) &= n+1 & \text{if } \mathrm{ghd}(M) = n; \\
\mathrm{ghd}(\lambda x.M) &= \emptyset & \text{if } \mathrm{ghd}(M) = \emptyset; \\
\mathrm{ghd}(M(N)) &= \mathrm{ghd}(M) & \text{if } \mathrm{ghd}(M) \in \mathbf{Var}; \\
\mathrm{ghd}(M(N)) &= \mathrm{ghd}(N) & \text{if } \mathrm{ghd}(M) = 0 \text{ and } \mathrm{ghd}(N) \in \mathbf{Var}; \\
\mathrm{ghd}(M(N)) &= \emptyset & \text{if } \mathrm{ghd}(M) = 0 \text{ and } \mathrm{ghd}(N) \in \mathbf{Num}; \\
\mathrm{ghd}(M(N)) &= \emptyset & \text{if } \mathrm{ghd}(M) = 0 \text{ and } \mathrm{ghd}(N) = \emptyset; \\
\mathrm{ghd}(M(N)) &= n-1 & \text{if } \mathrm{ghd}(M) = n > 0; \\
\mathrm{ghd}(M(N)) &= \emptyset & \text{if } \mathrm{ghd}(M) = \emptyset.
\end{aligned}
$$

Table 1. The definition of general heads

Notations $\mathbf{x}$ denotes a sequence (possibly empty) of variables $x_1, \ldots, x_n$; $|\mathbf{x}| = n$ is the length of the sequence; $(\lambda \mathbf{x}.M)$ is $(\lambda x_1 \ldots \lambda x_n.M)$; $\mathbf{M}$ denotes a sequence (possibly empty) of terms $M_1, \ldots, M_n$; $|\mathbf{M}| = n$ is the length of M; $x(\mathbf{M})$ is $x(M_1) \ldots (M_n)$.

3 The generalised HNF

In this section we first present the definition of generalised HNF (GHNF); We then prove a few important properties on GHNF and introduce β_{hd}^v-redexes and their residuals under β_{hd}^v-reduction.

In the previous example, we cannot reduce the term $(\lambda x.I(x(I)))(I)(0)$ in the call-by-value λ-calculus where values are defined as terms in flexible HNF. The problem is that $I(x(I))$ is not a redex in such a λ-calculus since $x(I)$ is not in flexible HNF. This problem can be resolved if we treat $I(x(I))$ as a term with head x. Then $(\lambda x.I(x(I)))$ has a flexible head, and $(\lambda x.I(x)(I))(I)(0)$ can be reduced to 0, which is of the form we expect.

Definition 3. *(General Head and GHNF)* Let $\mathbf{Num} = \{0, 1, 2, \ldots\}$. The general heads of terms are defined in Table 1. Given a term M; M is in GHNF if $\mathrm{ghd}(M) \neq \emptyset$; M is rigid if $\mathrm{ghd}(M)$ is a variable; M is flexible if $\mathrm{ghd}(M)$ is a number; M is indeterminate if $\mathrm{ghd}(M) = \emptyset$.

It can be readily verified that $\mathrm{ghd}(M)$ is well-defined on every term $M \in \Lambda$. Therefore, GHNF is well-defined. If M is in HNF then M is in GHNF. The term $M = \lambda x.I(x(I))$ is in GHNF since $\mathrm{ghd}(M) = 0$, but M is not in HNF. The intuition behind this definition will be unfolded in Proposition 6.

Proposition 4. *Given M with $\mathrm{ghd}(M) \geq 0$ and N; then $\mathrm{ghd}(M\{x := N\}) = \mathrm{ghd}(M)$.*

Proposition 5. *Given a term M in GHNF and $M \twoheadrightarrow_\beta N$; then N is in GHNF and $\mathrm{ghd}(M) = \mathrm{ghd}(N)$.*

Both Proposition 4 and Proposition 5 follow from a structural induction on M. Since the general head of a term in flexible GHNF stays unchanged under both substitution and β-reduction, this yields some justification on taking flexible GHNF as the form of values in call-by-value λ-calculus λ^v_{hd} presented in the next section. The next proposition exhibits the intuition behind the definition of general head.

Proposition 6. *Given a term M in GHNF; then $M \overset{h}{\twoheadrightarrow}_\beta \mathrm{hnf}(M)$ for some term $\mathrm{hnf}(M)$; if $\mathrm{ghd}(M) = x$ then $\mathrm{hnf}(M)$ is of form $\lambda\mathbf{x}.x(\mathbf{N})$, where x does not occur in $\mathbf{x}$; if $\mathrm{ghd}(M) = n$ then $\mathrm{hnf}(M)$ is of form $\lambda\mathbf{x}\lambda x\lambda\mathbf{y}.x(\mathbf{N})$, where $|\mathbf{x}| = n$.*

Proof. Please see [4] for properties on head β-reduction. $\mathrm{hnf}(M)$ can be given by a structural induction on M.

Let values be defined as terms in flexible GHNF; given

$$M = (\lambda x.\lambda y.I(y)(x))(N),$$

where N is *not* a value; $\mathrm{ghd}(M) = 0$ and $\mathrm{ghd}(M(I)) = \emptyset$; since $M(I)$ is indeterminate, we need to be able to reduce it; M should not be reduced since it is a value; hence, we directly reduce $M(I)$ to $(\lambda x.I(I)(x))(N)$; this leads to the following definition of general body.

Definition 7. *(General Body)* For terms M with $\mathrm{ghd}(M) \geq 0$, its general body $\mathrm{gbd}(M)$ is defined as follows.

$$\begin{aligned}
\mathrm{gbd}(M_1(M_2)) &= \mathrm{gbd}(M_1)(M_2) \\
\mathrm{gbd}(\lambda x.M) &= M\{x := \bullet\} \quad \text{if } \mathrm{ghd}(M) = x; \\
\mathrm{gbd}(\lambda x.M) &= \lambda x.\mathrm{gbd}(M) \quad \text{if } \mathrm{ghd}(M) \in \mathbf{Num};
\end{aligned}$$

For example, $\mathrm{gbd}(\lambda x.\lambda y.I(y)(x)) = \lambda x.I(\bullet)(x)$. It is a routine verification that $\mathrm{gbd}(M)$ is well-defined for all M in flexible GHNF.

Definition 8. *(β^v_{hd}-redex)* A β^v_{hd}-redex is a term of form $M(N)$ where $\mathrm{ghd}(M) = 0$ and $\mathrm{ghd}(N) \in \mathbf{Num}$; $\beta^v_{hd}(M, N) = \mathrm{gbd}(M)\{\bullet := N\}$ is the contractum of the β^v_{hd}-redex; we write $M_1 \rightarrow_{\beta^v_{hd}} M_2$ if M_2 is obtained by replacing a β^v_{hd}-redex in M_1 with its contractum; a β^v_{hd}-reduction sequence is a possibly infinite sequence of form:

$$M_1 \rightarrow_{\beta^v_{hd}} M_2 \rightarrow_{\beta^v_{hd}} \cdots$$

The explicit notation of β^v_{hd}-reduction can be defined accordingly.

Proposition 9. *Given a term M in GHNF and $M \twoheadrightarrow_{\beta^v_{hd}} N$; then N in GHNF and $\mathrm{ghd}(M) = \mathrm{ghd}(N)$.*

Proof. This follows from a structural induction on M.

Hence, this partially justifies why a term M in GHNF can be regarded as a kind of head normal form under β_{hd}^v-reduction: $\mathrm{ghd}(M)$ is unchanged under β_{hd}^v-reduction.

Following the definition of residuals of β-redexes under β-reduction [4], we can then present the definition of residuals of β_{hd}^v-redexes under β-reduction and β_{hd}^v-reduction. Proposition 4 and Proposition 5 and Proposition 9 are needed to verify the correctness of such a definition. See [21] for details.

Note that we can also define β_{hd}^v-redexes as terms of form $M(N)$, where $\mathrm{ghd}(M) = 0$ and $\mathrm{ghd}(N) \in \mathbf{Num}$, or $\mathrm{ghd}(M) = 0$ and N is a variable. The obvious reason is that such a form is closed under $value$ substitution if a value is defined as a term in flexible GHNF or a variable. One disadvantage of adopting this definition is that the notion of residuals of β_{hd}^v-redexes under β-reduction is difficult to define. Besides, we will clearly see that if we can reduce a program to a GHNF via such an extended notion of β_{hd}^v-reduction then we can always do so without reducing any redex of form $M(N)$, where $\mathrm{ghd}(M) = 0$ and N is a variable.

4 The λ-calculus λ_{hd}^v and its relations to λ

In this section we present a call-by-value λ-calculus λ_{hd}^v in which values are defined as terms in flexible GHNF. We then mention that λ_{hd}^v is Church-Rosser and enjoys a version of normalisation theorem. Our main proof strategy is based on residual theory, which is quite different from the proof strategy in [18]. The reader who is interested in this subject can find further details in [20, 21].

λ_{hd}^v studies β_{hd}^v-reduction. $\lambda_{hd}^v \vdash M =_{\beta_{hd}^v} N$ if there exist

$$M = M_0, M_1, \ldots, M_{2n-1}, M_{2n} = N$$

such that $M_{2i-1} \twoheadrightarrow_{\beta_{hd}^v} M_{2i-2}$ and $M_{2i-1} \twoheadrightarrow_{\beta_{hd}^v} M_{2i}$ for $1 \le i \le n$.

Theorem 10. *(Church-Rosser) Given*

$$M \twoheadrightarrow_{\beta_{hd}^v} M_1 \quad and \quad M \twoheadrightarrow_{\beta_{hd}^v} M_2;$$

then $M_1 \twoheadrightarrow_{\beta_{hd}^v} N$ and $M_2 \twoheadrightarrow_{\beta_{hd}^v} N$ for some N.

Proof. A proof in the style of Tait/Martin-Löf can be given through parallel β_{hd}^v-reduction. We present a proof in [21] which uses the development separation technique studied in [20]. $\square$

Corollary 11. *Given $M \twoheadrightarrow_{\beta_{hd}^v} M_i$ for $i = 1, 2$; if M_1 and M_2 are in GHNF then $\mathrm{ghd}(M_1) = \mathrm{ghd}(M_2)$.*

Proof. By Theorem 10, there exists N such that $M_1 \twoheadrightarrow_{\beta_{hd}^v} N$ and $M_2 \twoheadrightarrow_{\beta_{hd}^v} N$. Hence, for $i = 1, 2$, $\mathrm{ghd}(M_i) = \mathrm{ghd}(N)$ by Proposition 9 since $\mathrm{ghd}(M_i) \ne \emptyset$. Therefore, $\mathrm{ghd}(M_1) = \mathrm{ghd}(M_2)$. $\square$

$$\lhd^v_{hd}(M) = \emptyset \text{ if } M \text{ is a variable};$$
$$\lhd^v_{hd}(\lambda x.M) = \lhd^v_{hd}(M);$$
$$\lhd^v_{hd}(M(N)) = \lhd^v_{hd}(M) \cup \lhd^v_{hd}(N) \cup (\mathcal{R}^v_{hd}(N) \times \mathcal{R}^v_{hd}(M))$$
$$\cup \{\langle M(N), L \rangle : L \in \mathcal{R}^v_{hd}(M) \cup \mathcal{R}^v_{hd}(N)\}$$
$$\text{if } M(N) \text{ is a } \beta^v_{hd}\text{-redex};$$
$$\lhd^v_{hd}(M(N)) = \lhd^v_{hd}(M) \cup \lhd^v_{hd}(N) \cup (\mathcal{R}^v_{hd}(N) \times \mathcal{R}^v_{hd}(M))$$
$$\text{if } \mathrm{ghd}(M) = 0 \text{ and } \mathrm{ghd}(N) \notin \mathbf{Num};$$
$$\lhd^v_{hd}(M(N)) = \lhd^v_{hd}(M) \cup \lhd^v_{hd}(N) \cup (\mathcal{R}^v_{hd}(M) \times \mathcal{R}^v_{hd}(N))$$
$$\text{if } \mathrm{ghd}(M) \neq 0.$$

Table 2. The definition of $\lhd^v_{hd}$

We say M has a general head $\mathrm{ghd}(N)$ if $M \twoheadrightarrow_{\beta^v_{hd}} N$ for some N in GHNF. By Corollary 11, a term has at most one general head. Clearly, $(\lambda x.x(x))(\lambda x.x(x))$ has no general head.

Definition 12. For every term M let $\mathcal{R}^v_{hd}(M)$ be the set of all β^v_{hd}-redexes in M; a relation $\lhd^v_{hd}(M)$ on $\mathcal{R}^v_{hd}(M)$ is defined in Table 2.

$\lhd^v_{hd}(M)$ is linear for every term M. We write $M \lhd^v_{hd} N$ in L if $\langle M, N \rangle \in \lhd^v_{hd}(L)$; we often leave L out if this causes no confusion; we say $R \in \mathcal{R}^v_{hd}(M)$ is the $\lhd^v_{hd}$-first β^v_{hd}-redex in M satisfying some property if R in M satisfies the property and there exists no $R' \lhd^v_{hd} R$ in M satisfying the same property.

Now we are ready to establish a version of normalisation theorem in λ^v_{hd}; we prove that the strategy is normalising which always contracts the $\lhd^v_{hd}$-first β^v_{hd}-redexes in terms; we then define an evaluation function which always evaluates a term M to a term in GHNF if $\lambda^v_{hd} \vdash M =_{\beta^v_{hd}} N$ for some N in GHNF.

If M is indeterminate then we call its $\lhd^v_{hd}$-first β^v_{hd}-redexes the *main* β^v_{hd}-redex in M. We present an equivalent definition of main β^v_{hd}-redexes below.

Definition 13. Given M with $\mathrm{ghd}(M) = \emptyset$; the main β^v_{hd}-redex $R^v_{hd}(M)$ in M is defined as follows.

$$R^v_{hd}(M) = \begin{cases} M & \text{if } M \text{ is a } \beta^v_{hd}\text{-redex}; \\ R^v_{hd}(M_1) & \text{if } M = \lambda x.M_1 \text{ and } \mathrm{ghd}(M_1) = \emptyset; \\ R^v_{hd}(M_1) & \text{if } M = M_1(M_2) \text{ and } \mathrm{ghd}(M_1) = \emptyset; \\ R^v_{hd}(M_2) & \text{if } M = M_1(M_2) \text{ and } \mathrm{ghd}(M_1) = 0 \\ & \text{and } \mathrm{ghd}(M_2) = \emptyset; \end{cases}$$

Clearly, $R^v_{hd}(M)$ is well-defined on every indeterminate term M. It is a routine verification that $R^v_{hd}(M)$ is the $\lhd^v_{hd}$-first in M.

Definition 14. If $M \xrightarrow{R}_{\beta^v_{hd}} N$ and $R = R^v_{hd}(M)$, then we write $M \xrightarrow{m}_{\beta^v_{hd}} N$. A β^v_{hd}-normalising sequence is a possibly infinite sequence of the following form.

$$M = M_0 \xrightarrow{m}_{\beta^v_{hd}} M_1 \xrightarrow{m}_{\beta^v_{hd}} \cdots$$

$$\begin{aligned}
\mathbf{eval}_{hd}^{v}(M) &= M && \text{if } ghd(M) \neq \emptyset; \\
\mathbf{eval}_{hd}^{v}(\lambda x.M) &= \lambda x.\mathbf{eval}_{hd}^{v}(M) && \text{if } ghd(M) = \emptyset; \\
\mathbf{eval}_{hd}^{v}(M(N)) &= \mathbf{eval}_{hd}^{v}(\beta_{hd}^{v}(M,N)) && \text{if } ghd(M) = 0 \text{ and } ghd(N) \geq 0; \\
\mathbf{eval}_{hd}^{v}(M(N)) &= \mathbf{eval}_{hd}^{v}(M(\mathbf{eval}_{hd}^{v}(N))) && \text{if } ghd(M) = 0 \text{ and } ghd(N) = \emptyset; \\
\mathbf{eval}_{hd}^{v}(M(N)) &= \mathbf{eval}_{hd}^{v}(\mathbf{eval}_{hd}^{v}(M)(N)) && \text{if } ghd(M) = \emptyset;
\end{aligned}$$

Table 3. The definition of $\mathbf{eval}_{hd}^{v}$

$$\begin{aligned}
\mathbf{eval}(M) &= M && \text{if } M \text{ in HNF}; \\
\mathbf{eval}(\lambda x.M) &= \lambda x.\mathbf{eval}(M) && \text{if } M \text{ is not in HNF}; \\
\mathbf{eval}(M(N)) &= \mathbf{eval}(\mathbf{eval}(M)N) && \text{if } M \text{ is not in HNF}. \\
\mathbf{eval}(M(N)) &= \mathbf{eval}(\beta(M,N)) && \text{if } M \text{ is a } \lambda\text{-abstraction in HNF};
\end{aligned}$$

Table 4. The definition of $\mathbf{eval}$

Let $\nu(M)$ denote the longest β_{hd}^{v}-normalising sequence from M, which can be of infinite length.

Theorem 15. (β_{hd}^{v}-normalisation) Given any $M \xrightarrow{\alpha}_{\beta_{hd}^{v}} N$, where N is in GHNF; then $\nu(M)$ is finite.

Proof. See [21] for details. □

For the sake of completeness, a version of standardisation theorem for λ_{hd}^{v} is also presented in [21]. Although normalisation theorem follows directly from standardisation theorem, the latter is far more complicated to prove than the former. This makes our proof of Theorem 15 in [21] quite attractive.

Corollary 16. Given $\lambda_{hd}^{v} \vdash M =_{\beta_{hd}^{v}} N$, where N is in GHNF; then $M \xrightarrow{m}_{\beta_{hd}^{v}} N_1$ for some N_1 and $ghd(N) = ghd(N_1)$.

Proof. Since $\lambda_{hd}^{v} \vdash M =_{\beta_{hd}^{v}} N$, $M \twoheadrightarrow_{\beta_{hd}^{v}} N_2$ and $N \rightarrow_{\beta_{hd}^{v}} N_2$ for some N_2 by Theorem 10. Since N is in GHNF, N_2 is also in GHNF by Proposition 9. Hence, Theorem 15 implies $\nu(M)$ is finite, i.e., $M \xrightarrow{m}_{\beta_{hd}^{v}} N_1$ for some N_1 in GHNF. By Corollary 11, $ghd(N) = ghd(N_1)$. □

We now define a β_{hd}^{v}-evaluation function $\mathbf{eval}_{hd}^{v}$ in Table 3, and then define the predicate M β_{hd}^{v}-*evaluates to* N *at time* t as follows.

1. M β_{hd}^{v}-evaluates to M at time 0 if $hd(M) \neq \emptyset$.
2. $\lambda x.M$ β_{hd}^{v}-evaluates to $\lambda x.N$ at time t if M β_{hd}^{v}-evaluates to N at time t.
3. If M β_{hd}^{v}-evaluates to M' at time t where $ghd(M') \neq 0$, then $M(N)$ β_{hd}^{v}-evaluates to $M'(N)$ at time t.

4. If M β^v_{hd}-evaluates to M' at time t where $\mathrm{ghd}(M') = 0$ and N β^v_{hd}-evaluates to N' at time t' where $\mathrm{ghd}(N') \in \mathbf{Var}$, then $M(N)$ β^v_{hd}-evaluates to $M'(N')$ at time $t + t'$;

5. If M β^v_{hd}-evaluates to M' at time t where $\mathrm{ghd}(M') = 0$, N β^v_{hd}-evaluates to N' at time t' where $\mathrm{ghd}(N') \geq 0$, and $\beta^v_{hd}(M', N')$ β^v_{hd}-evaluates to L are time t'', then $M(N)$ β^v_{hd}-evaluates to L are time $t + t' + t'' + 1$.

Theorem 17. *Given M which β-evaluates to a term at time t; then M β^v_{hd}-evaluates to N for some N in GHNF at some time $t' \leq t$.*

Proof. Please see [21]. □

Hence, $\mathbf{eval}^v_{hd}$ never takes more time to terminate than $\mathbf{eval}$ does. We expect that this is also the case if we study a call-by-need evaluation strategy for λ^v_{hd} and compare it with the call-by-need evaluation strategy in [3].

Theorem 18. *Given a term M; $\mathbf{eval}(M)$ is defined if and only if $\mathbf{eval}^v_{hd}(M)$ is defined.*

Proof. Please see [21]. □

We have shown that a program P β^v_{hd}-evaluates to a term in GHNF if and only if P β-evaluates to a term in HNF. If we extend λ^v_{hd} and λ with some base values such as integers and treat them as terms in HNF, then $\mathbf{eval}^v_{hd}(P)$ and $\mathbf{eval}(P)$ are both defined for every program P which outputs a base value b, and $\mathrm{ghd}(\mathbf{eval}^v_{hd}(P)) = \mathbf{eval}(P) = b$. After introducing constructors in Section 6, we shall see that (ω, ω) is also in GHNF with $\mathrm{ghd}((\omega, \omega)) = (\cdot, \cdot)$, where ω stands for some diverging computation; also $S = \mathbf{fix}(\lambda x.\mathbf{cons}(0, x))$, a stream with infinitely many 0's, is in GHNF with $\mathrm{ghd}(S) = \mathbf{cons}$; if a program P can be β-evaluated to such values, then $\mathbf{eval}^v_{hd}(P)$ allows us to observe the general head of such values. This suggests a new approach to implementing functional programming languages with call-by-name semantics, namely implementing λ^v_{hd}.

5 Operational Semantics

An operational semantics for λ^v_{hd} in the style of [18] is given in [21]. We have coded a primitive implementation of our SECD machine. We are planning to design a call-by-need λ-calculus corresponding to λ^v_{hd} and implement it. This is a subject of future work.

6 Extensions

We first add a recursion combinator to β^v_{hd}-calculus eliminating some syntactic overhead. Then we extend β^v_{hd}-calculus with constructors and primitive functions. All these extensions are compatible with our previous development of λ^v_{hd}, namely, we shall still have the Church-Rosser theorem, the normalisation theorem, and the relation between λ and λ^v_{hd}.

6.1 Recursion

We can use fixed point operator $Y = \lambda f.(\lambda x.f(x(x)))(\lambda x.f(x(x)))$ handling recursion; there is a prohibitively great deal of syntactic overhead involved if we use fixed point operators to do recursion directly; this suggests that we introduce **fix** as a recursion combinator with a δ-reduction: $\mathbf{fix}(f) \rightarrow f(\mathbf{fix}(f))$. Let $\mathrm{ghd}(\mathbf{fix}) = 0$; if $\mathrm{ghd}(f) \geq 0$ then $\mathbf{fix}(f)$ is a β^v_{hd}-redex and $\beta^v_{hd}(\mathbf{fix}, f) = f(\mathbf{fix}(f))$. A more practical approach is introducing *letrec*, which will be explored when we study implementations of λ^v_{hd} in the future.

6.2 Constructors

We treat base values such as integers and boolean values as constructors with 0 arity. We need to extend the definition of terms and the definition of ghd.

Definition 19. $c^n(M_1, \ldots, M_n)$ is a term if $M_1, \ldots, M_n$ are terms and c^n is constructor with arity n. Let **Const** be the set of all constructors.

$$\begin{aligned}
\mathrm{ghd}(M) &= c^n && \text{if } M = c^n(M_1, \ldots, M_n); \\
\mathrm{ghd}(M(N)) &= c^n && \text{if } \mathrm{ghd}(M) \in \mathbf{Const}; \\
\mathrm{ghd}(M(N)) &= \mathrm{ghd}(N) && \text{if } \mathrm{ghd}(M) = 0 \text{ and } \mathrm{ghd}(N) \in \mathbf{Const}.
\end{aligned}$$

This is a compatible extension of ghd. Let $S = \mathbf{fix}(\lambda x.\mathbf{cons}(0, x))$, then $\mathrm{ghd}(S) = \mathbf{cons}$; so S is in GHNF. This is justified in most actual implementations which allocate only one cell for **cons**, representing S as a cyclic data structure. Therefore, the λ^v_{hd}-calculus does not have the deficiency of the call-by-need λ-calculus [3], where S evaluates to $\mathbf{cons}(0, S)$ containing two distinct **cons** cells.

6.3 Primitive Functions

Primitive functions have to be handled individually according to their semantics. We use a few examples illustrating our points. Let Δ_n represent integer n for $n = 0, 1, \ldots$ and $\mathbf{t}, \mathbf{f}$ stand for truth values. Let $\mathbf{Int} = \{\Delta_0, \Delta_1, \ldots\}$ and $\mathbf{Bool} = \{\mathbf{t}, \mathbf{f}\}$.

Let *fun* be a primitive function on integers with arity 1. We intend to define $\mathrm{ghd}(\mathit{fun}) = \mathit{fun}$ and $\mathrm{ghd}(\mathit{fun}(M)) = M$ if M is a variable, but this definition has a serious flaw; assume that $\mathit{fun}(M)$ is a δ-redex if $\mathrm{ghd}(M)$ is some integer; then

$$\mathrm{ghd}((\lambda x.\mathit{fun}(x))(M)) = \mathrm{ghd}(M)$$

implies that $(\lambda x.\mathit{fun}(x))(M)$ is in GHNF; this prevents $\mathbf{eval}^v_{hd}$ from evaluating

$$(\lambda x.\mathit{fun}(x))(M)$$

to the value of $\mathit{fun}(M)$. Our solution to this dilemma is to modify the definition of general head; let $\mathrm{ghd}(\mathit{fun}(x)) = \langle x, \mathbf{Int}\rangle$ and $\lambda x.\mathit{fun}(x)$ have head $\langle 0, \mathbf{Int}\rangle$; $M(N)$ is regarded as a β^v_{hd}-redex if $M = \langle 0, \mathbf{Int}\rangle$ and $\mathrm{ghd}(N) \in \mathbf{Int}$. Clearly, **Int** can be replaced with other sets of constants. Also it is easy to see how to adjust the definition of ghd to handle such pairs. We write $\mathrm{ghd}(M) \in \mathbf{Pair}$ if M has a head which is a pair.

Basic Operators on Integers We show how addition (+) can be handled.

$$\text{ghd}(+(M, N)) = \begin{cases} \emptyset & \text{if ghd}(M) = \emptyset; \\ \langle\text{ghd}(M), \textbf{Int}\rangle & \text{if ghd}(M) \in \textbf{Var}; \\ \text{ghd}(M) & \text{if ghd}(M) \in \textbf{Pair}; \\ \emptyset & \text{if ghd}(M) = \textbf{Int and ghd}(N) = \emptyset; \\ \langle\text{ghd}(N), \textbf{Int}\rangle & \text{if ghd}(M) \in \textbf{Int and ghd}(N) \in \textbf{Var}; \\ \text{ghd}(N) & \text{if ghd}(M) = \textbf{Int and ghd}(N) \in \textbf{Pair}; \\ \emptyset & \text{if ghd}(M) \in \textbf{Int and ghd}(N) \in \textbf{Int}. \end{cases}$$

$+(M, N)$ is a δ-redex if $\text{ghd}(M), \text{ghd}(N) \in \textbf{Int}$. We also extend the definition of $\textbf{eval}^v_{hd}$, defining $\textbf{eval}^v_{hd}(+(M, N))$ as

$$\begin{cases} \Delta_{m+n} & \text{if ghd}(M) = \Delta_m \text{ and ghd}(N) = \Delta_n; \\ \textbf{eval}^v_{hd}(+(\textbf{eval}^v_{hd}(M), N)) & \text{if ghd}(M) = \emptyset; \\ \textbf{eval}^v_{hd}(+(M, \textbf{eval}^v_{hd}(N))) & \text{if ghd}(M) \neq \emptyset \text{ and ghd}(N) = \emptyset; \end{cases}$$

Other operations, such as subtraction $(-)$, multiplication $(\times)$ and equality $(=)$, can be handled in a similar fashion.

Conditional We introduce a conditional IF; $\text{IF}(M, N_1, N_2)$ is a term if M, N_1, N_2 are terms; then

$$\text{ghd}(\text{IF}(M, N_1, N_2)) = \begin{cases} \emptyset & \text{if ghd}(M) \in \textbf{Bool}; \\ \langle\text{ghd}(M), \textbf{Bool}\rangle & \text{if ghd}(M) \in \textbf{Var}; \\ \text{ghd}(M) & \text{if ghd}(M) \notin \textbf{Var} \cup \textbf{Bool}; \end{cases}$$

$\text{IF}(M, N_1, N_2)$ is a δ-redex if $\text{ghd}(M) \in \textbf{Bool}$. We extend the definition of $\textbf{eval}^v_{hd}$, defining

$$\textbf{eval}^v_{hd}(\text{IF}(M, N_1, N_2)) = \begin{cases} \textbf{eval}^v_{hd}(N_1) & \text{if ghd}(M) = \textbf{t}; \\ \textbf{eval}^v_{hd}(N_2) & \text{if ghd}(M) = \textbf{f}; \\ \textbf{eval}^v_{hd}(\text{IF}(\textbf{eval}^v_{hd}(M), N_1, N_2)) & \text{if ghd}(M) = \emptyset. \end{cases}$$

7 Related Work

λ^v_{hd} is closely related to the weak λ-calculus in [23] and the call-by-need λ-calculus in [3] in the following sense; we can define a kind of redex as a term of form $M(N)$ and its contractum as $[N/\bullet]\text{gbd}(M)$, where M is a term with $\text{ghd}(M) = 0$ and N is a variable or a *general* λ-abstraction(which is called *answer* in [3]); it can be readily verified that such a form is closed under value substitution if values are defined as variables or λ-abstractions; we can then define a kind of λ-calculus corresponding to such redexes; a close correspondence between this λ-calculus and the λ-calculi in [23] and [3] can be established accordingly; this provides a different approach to justifying the call-by-need λ-calculus presented in [3]; this observation partially motivated the paper. However, none of these previous λ-calculi allow direct evaluation of redexes under λ-abstractions; this may lead to a great deal of propagation of such redexes during evaluation.

The idea of "skipping over" arguments to formulate new redexes has already been presented in [14, 5], where an *item notation* is introduced to facilitate writing and reading. However, λ_{hd}^v is distinct from the λ-calculus λ_g[14] in a similar way that λ_v is distinct from λ. We did not adopt the item notation since we feel that the notion of residuals of β_{hd}^v-redexes under β_{hd}^v-reduction can be well expressed in our setting, which underpins our main proof strategy. This point can be appreciated if the reader studies [21] carefully.

The problem of sharing evaluation under λ-abstraction has lead to a great deal of study on λ-*lifting* [13] and *supercombinators* [10] under the title *full laziness* or *maximal laziness*. Because of the ability of evaluating under λ directly, $\mathbf{eval}_{hd}^v$ can achieve what is beyond the scope of either λ-lifting or supercombinators. Given a term

$$M = \lambda z.\lambda x.\lambda y. + (BIG(\mathrm{IF}(z, x, y)), \times(x, y))$$

and a program $P = (\lambda u. \ldots)(M(\mathbf{t})(\Delta_n))$, where BIG stands for some computationally complex strict function, and $(\lambda u. \ldots)$ is a term with general head 0. Note

$$\mathbf{eval}_{hd}^v(M(\mathbf{t})(\Delta_n)) = \lambda y. + (BIG_n, \times(x, y)),$$

where BIG_n is the value of $BIG(\Delta_n)$. Hence, $\mathbf{eval}_{hd}^v$ evaluates $BIG(\Delta_n)$ only once when evaluating P. Such a sharing of evaluation cannot be done using λ-lifting or supercombinators since term $\mathrm{IF}(z, x, y)$ contains variable y at compile time. In some sense, full laziness is really not full when evaluation under λ is allowed.

Another related subject is partial evaluation. We show that $\mathbf{eval}_{hd}^v$ works well with staged computation [6]. Let us define the power function $\mathbf{pow}$ as

$$\mathbf{fix}(\lambda f \lambda p \lambda n.\mathrm{IF}(= (p, \Delta_0), \Delta_1, \times(f\ n\ (-(p, 1)), n))).$$

Note $\mathbf{ghd}(\mathbf{pow}) = \langle \emptyset, \mathbf{Int} \rangle$. The followings can be readily verified.

$$\mathbf{eval}_{hd}^v(\mathbf{pow}(\Delta_0)) = \lambda n.(\lambda f.\lambda n.\Delta_1)(\mathbf{pow})(n)$$
$$\mathbf{eval}_{hd}^v(\mathbf{pow}(\Delta_1)) = \lambda n.(\lambda n. \times ((\lambda f.\lambda n.\Delta_1)(\mathbf{pow})(n), n))(n)$$
$$\mathbf{eval}_{hd}^v(\mathbf{pow}(\Delta_2)) = \lambda n.(\lambda n. \times ((\lambda n. \times ((\lambda f.\lambda n.\Delta_1)(\mathbf{pow})(n), n))(n), n))(n)$$

Note that $(\lambda f.\lambda n.\Delta_1)(\mathbf{pow})(n)$ is a term with general head Δ_1. This term can be replaced with Δ_1 through garbage collection in a real implementation. This example is very close to Example 2.4 in [6]. Suppose that we implement $\mathbf{eval}_{hd}^v$ using the above presented SECD machine; if a term $(\mathbf{pow}\ \Delta_n)$ is generated at *run-time* and needs to be evaluated, the machine always evaluates it to a GHNF before forming a closure; this is quite desirable since this amounts to some sort of partial evaluation at run-time. For the following function $\mathbf{dotprod}$ which computes the inner product of two vectors of some given length [12], the reader can also verify that $\mathbf{eval}_{hd}^v(\mathbf{dotprod}\ \Delta_n)$ is adequately expanded for every $\Delta_n \in \mathbf{Int}$. Note that $vec[n]$ yields the nth element in vector vec.

$$\mathbf{fix}(\lambda f \lambda n \lambda u \lambda v = \mathrm{IF}(= (n, 0), 0, +(f(-(n, 1))(u)(v), \times(u[n], v[n]))))$$

Also $\mathbf{eval}_{hd}^v$ does not suffer from any termination problems, which on the other hand, significantly limit the use of partial evaluators. Let us define Ackermann's function $\mathbf{acker}$ as

$$\mathbf{fix}(\lambda f \lambda m \lambda n.$$
$$\mathrm{IF}(=(m,0),+(n,1),f(-(m,1))(\mathrm{IF}(=(n,0),+(n,1),f(m)(-(n,1)))))$$

Given any $\Delta_m \in \mathbf{Int}$, $\mathbf{eval}_{hd}^v(\mathbf{acker}(\Delta_m))$ always terminates since no terms under the second IF can be evaluated when n is unknown. Thus, $\mathbf{eval}_{hd}^v$ is also promising to be used for run-time code generation purposes.

Our work also relates to [11]. We show that $\mathbf{eval}_{hd}^v$ can achieve *complete laziness* for the following example taken from [11] if we form closures instead of performing substitutions. This cannot be done by an evaluation strategy corresponding to full laziness as mentioned in [11]. Here lower case letters are variables and uppercase letters are closed expressions.

$$(\lambda f.f(B)(f(C)))((\lambda a.\lambda z.(\lambda g.g(a))(\lambda x.x(x)(z)))(A))$$

We assume that A is already in GHNF. Note that

$$(\lambda a.\lambda z.(\lambda g.g(a))(\lambda x.x(x)(z)))(A)$$

reduces to $(\lambda z.x(x)(z))$ with x bound to A; this term is not in flexible GHNF; therefore, the β-redex $x(x)$ with x bound to A needs to be reduced before we can bind z to B and C, avoiding evaluating it twice.

These examples suggest that $\mathbf{eval}_{hd}^v$ be a evaluation function which is able to perform some degree of *on-line* partial evaluation. This favors that a polished implementation of $\mathbf{eval}_{hd}^v$ is promising to enhance the performance of lazy functional programming languages in many cases.

8 Conclusions and Directions

We have presented a call-by-value λ-calculus λ_{hd}^v in which values are defined as terms in flexible generalised head normal form. λ_{hd}^v enjoys many similar properties as the λ-calculus λ does. Given a program P which outputs base values such as integers, $\lambda \vdash P =_\beta b$ for some base value b if and only if $\lambda_{hd}^v \vdash P =_{\beta_{hd}^v} M$ for some M in GHNF with b as its general head. Therefore, lazy functional programming languages can implement λ_{hd}^v, which suggests a significantly higher degree of sharing since evaluation can take place under λ-abstraction, viz. in the bodies of functions. We have also designed a SECD machine which can easily lead to an implementation of the evaluation function $\mathbf{eval}_{hd}^v$ for λ_{hd}^v.

A naïve implementation of $\mathbf{eval}_{hd}^v$ suffers a great deal from duplication of computation For instance, $(\lambda x \lambda y.y(x))(C)$ is a value in λ_{hd}^v; the computation in C will be duplicated if we propagate this value; this suggests that we investigate a call-by-need implementation of λ_{hd}^v, namely, using *let-binding* to handle such cases. We intend to extend λ_{hd}^v with explicit substitutions and study approaches to implementing λ_{hd}^v efficiently. Also we shall study relations between λ_{hd}^v and the *usual* call-by-value λ-calculus λ_v for it can be readily proven that β_{hd}^v-reduction preserves the β_v-equivalence in λ_v.

Clearly we shall lose the ability to compile abstractions to *fixed* native code sequence if we simply implement $\mathbf{eval}_{hd}^v$, which is very costly. Also we point out that $\mathbf{eval}_{hd}^v$ cannot yield full-laziness. For instance, the β_{hd}^v redex $I(I)$ in $(\lambda z.z(z))(\lambda y.y(I(I)))$ needs be evaluated twice by $\mathbf{eval}_{hd}^v$ while this can be simply avoided with the help of λ-lifting. This suggest that we combine $\mathbf{eval}_{hd}^v$ with the usual evaluation strategy for lazy functional programming. Through annotations in code [6], one may decide if $\mathbf{eval}_{hd}^v$ should be called before forming a closure. For instance, one may indicate that **pow** is a function which always β_{hd}^v-evaluates its first argument when it is available. In this line, we point out a more realistic example **sendto**, which sends a message to some address; one may wish not to form a closure when the address argument of **sendto** is known since **sendto** can then be significantly optimised; this amounts to some evaluation under λ. Such examples are abundant in programming languages, providing a rich area for further testing our idea.

Also it is suggested by the referees that a comparison of this work with Lamping's optimal reduction[15] is of certain interest.

We believe that studies on λ_{hd}^v can help enhance the performance of functional programming languages.

9 Acknowledgements

I gratefully acknowledge my discussion with Frank Pfenning regarding the subject of the paper, and thank him for his constructive comments on this work. I also thank Peter Andrews and Richard Statman for providing me with such a nice work environment. I also sincerely thank the referees for their constructive comments, which are given in unusual details.

References

1. M. Abadi, L. Cardelli, P.-L. Curien, and I.-I. Lévy (1991), Explicit substitutions, *Journal of Functional Programming*, 4(1), pp. 375-416.

2. S. Abramsky (1990), The lazy lambda calculus. In D. Turner, editor, *Declarative Programming*, Addison-Wesley Publishing Company.

3. Z.M. Ariola, M. Felleisen, J. Maraist, M. Odersky and P. Wadler (1996), A Call-by-Need Lambda Calculus, *Proceedings of the 22nd ACM Symposium on Principles of Programming Languages*, San Francisco, pp. 233-246

4. H.P. Barendregt, *The Lambda Calculus: Its Syntax and Semantics*, North-Holland, Amsterdam, 1984.

5. R. Bloo, F. Kamareddine and R. Nederpelt (1996), The Barendregt cube with definitions and generalised reduction, *Information and Computation*, vol 126(2), pp. 123-143. A useful lambda-notation, *Theoretical Computer Science*, vol. 155(1), pp 85-109.

6. R. Davies and F. Pfenning (1996), A Modal Analysis of Staged Computation, In Proceedings of the 23rd ACM Symposium on Principles of Programming Languages, pp. 206-209

7. A.J. Field and P.G. Harrison (1988), *Functional Programming*, Addison-Wesley Publishing Company.

8. J.R. Hindley (1978), Reductions of residuals are finite, *Trans. Amer. Math. Soc. 240*, pp. 345-361.

9. G. Huét (1994), Residual Theory in λ-Calculus: A Formal Development, *Journal of Functional Programming Vol. 4*, pp. 371–394.

10. R.J.M. Hughes (1984), The design and implementation of programming languages, *Ph.D. thesis, University of Oxford*.

11. C.K. Holst and C.K. Gomard (1991), Partial Evaluation is Fuller Laziness, in *Proceedings of the Symposium on Partial Evaluation and Semantics-Based Program Manipulation*, pp. 223-233.

12. R. Glück and J. Jørgensen (1995), Efficient multi-level generating extensions for program specialisation. In S.D. Swierstra and M. Hermenegildo, editors, *Programming Languages, Implementations Logics and Programs, Springer-Verlag LNCS 982*, pp. 259-278.

13. T. Johnsson (1985), Lambda lifting: transforming programs to recursive equations, In *Proceedings of the Conference on Functional programming Languages and Computer Architecture*, Nancy, pp. 190-203.

14. F. Kamareddine and R. Nederpelt (1996), A useful lambda-notation, *Theoretical Computer Science*, vol. 155(1), pp 85-109.

15. J. Lamping (1990), An Algorithm for Optimal Lambda Calculus Reduction, In *Seventeenth ACM Symposium on Principles of Programming Languages*, pp 16-30.

16. P.J. Landin (1964), The mechanical evaluation of expressions, *BCS Computing Journal 6(4)*, pp. 308-320.

17. S.L. Peyton Jones (1991), A fully-lazy λ-lifter in Haskell, *Software practice and experience 21*.

18. G.D. Plotkin (1975), Call-by-name, call-by-value and the lambda-calculus, *Theoretical Computer Science 1*, pp. 125-159.

19. C. Reade (1989), *Elements of Functional Programming*, Addison-Wesley Publishing Company.

20. H. Xi (1996), Separating developments in λ-calculus:
    http://www.cs.cmu.edu/~hwxi/papers/SepDev.ps

21. H. Xi (1996), Evaluation under lambda abstraction:
    http://www.cs.cmu.edu/~hwxi/papers/EvUdLam.ps

22. H. Xi (1997), Generalized Lambda-Calculi:
    http://www.cs.cmu.edu/~hwxi/papers/GLam.ps

23. N. Yoshida (1993), Optimal reduction in weak λ-calculus with shared environments. In *Proc. ACM conference on Functional Programming Languages and Computer Architecture*, Copenhagen.

Selective Recomputation for Handling Side-Effects in Parallel Logic Programs

Zhiyi Huang, Chengzheng Sun and Abdul Sattar

Knowledge Representation and Reasoning Unit
School of Computing & Information Technology
Griffith University, Nathan, Qld 4111, Australia

Abstract. *In contrast to merely AND- and merely OR- parallel execution models/systems, the side-effect problem in AND/OR parallel execution of Prolog programs is intricate and need to be carefully investigated. To decrease the non-trivial recomputation occurred in previous approach, this paper presents a Selective Recomputation(SR) approach for handling side-effects in the OR-forest model which can exploit both AND- and OR-parallelism. Firstly, the background and motivation is introduced. Secondly, the complex side-effects orderings in AND/OR parallel execution models/systems are clearly described using an innovative concept – side-effect execution permit token. Thirdly, recomputation line is proposed to divide an AND-parallel child tree into non-recomputation part and recomputation part. Therefore, the recomputation is only confined to the recomputation part of an AND-parallel child tree, instead of the entire tree. And the non-recomputation part can be explored in parallel as pure child tree. Finally, by adopting the delayed execution of soft side-effect built-ins, the non-recomputation part is enlarged and thus the recomputation is minimized and parallelism is maximized. Through comparison and analysis, we conclude the SR approach can solve the side-effect problem with minimum recomputation and maximum parallelism. The idea of SR is applicable to other AND/OR parallel execution models/systems as well.*

Keywords: Logic Programming, Parallel Processing, AND-parallelism, OR-parallelism, OR-forest, Side-effect

1 Introduction

Since the first effort in 1981 [15], a lot of works have been done [13, 1, 17, 10, 18, 6, 16, 3, 19] in the area of parallel execution of logic programs. The major difference among the parallel execution models/systems is that they exploit different forms of parallelism in different ways. In logic programs there are three major forms of parallelism: OR-parallelism (ORP), AND-parallelism which is classified into Independent AND-parallelism (IAP) and Dependent AND-parallelism (DAP), and unification parallelism which is a fine grain parallelism and seldom exploited. By the forms of parallelism exploited, parallel execution models/systems can be divided into: OR-parallel execution models/systems which merely exploit ORP, e.g., Aurora [13] and Muse [1]; AND-parallel execution models/systems which merely exploit AND-parallelism, e.g., &-Prolog [10], and DASWAM [18]; AND/OR parallel execution models/systems which exploit both AND- and OR- parallelism, e.g., Andorra-I [17], ACE [16], IDIOM [6], and OR-forest [19, 21]. Efficiently exploiting all the major forms of parallelism is one of the goals the researchers in this area are pursuing. This is an arduous task which needs concerted efforts. There were some successful attempts to exploit both OR-parallelism and Dependent AND-parallelism (especially the determinate DAP), e.g., Andorra-I, IDIOM and EAM. Since the communication cost rapidly increases with extensive use of DAP (especially non-determinate DAP), we focus on the exploitation of IAP and ORP in OR-forest model [19, 21].

The goal of our research is to design and implement a parallel logic programming system supporting both AND- and OR- parallel execution of logic programs. Based on the OR-forest model, a number of subjects have been studied [5, 20, 21, 11, 12]. In addition to above research work, we think it is very important to support parallel execution of Prolog without any restriction/presumption. Prolog is chosen as one of the languages to be implemented in our system due to its established leading position in supporting a wide range of practical applications. Not only does this choice save us a significant burden of designing a new language, but also ensures the practical usefulness and wide acceptance of the resulting system.

However, Prolog is a declarative programming language with a particular sequential operational semantics. They involve a simple, sequential execution model in which atomic goals within a clause body are executed in order, from left to right, and multiple clauses within a single procedure are tried one at a time, from top to bottom. In addition, Prolog has some extra-logical features which bring side-effects as part of execution result of a logic program. The extra-logical built-ins that produce side-effects include database operations, e.g., **assert** and **retract**, I/O operations, e.g., **read** and **write**, and meta-logical operations, e.g., cut(!). The sequential semantics, when coupled with the observable side-effects, produce a given program's *observable behavior*. To execute a Prolog program in parallel and retain its observable behavior, it is required to retain the ordering of side-effects in the program. In addition, there is another class of predicates, whose execution is affected by *assert* and *retract*. We call them *dynamic* predicates. They also have to obey the sequential orderings. This kind of predicates should be treated as side-effect built-ins.

In order to keep the sequential semantics of Prolog, we have to execute the side-effect built-ins sequentially, which is obviously in conflict with exploitation of parallelism. Little work has been done on how to alleviate loss of parallelism while handling side-effect problem. In addition to loss of parallelism, there is recomputation problem in AND/OR parallel execution models/systems, which results from the exploitation of AND-parallelism. For example, in [8], to achieve the same side-effect behaviors as those in sequential model, recomputation of AND-parallel goals is adopted. While it is a simple solution for side-effect problem in AND/OR parallel execution models, another problem arises: too much redundant recomputation, especially when there are speculative branches in AND parallel goals. A detailed analysis will be given in Section 3.

To decrease the recomputations and the loss of parallelism, we propose a Selective Recomputation approach to the side-effect problem with minimum recomputation and maximum parallelism.

The rest of the paper is organized as follows: Section 2 introduces OR-forest model; Section 3 analyses the recomputation approach in *Composition Tree*; Section 4 discusses the orderings of side-effect built-ins; Section 5 gives the *Selective Recomputation(SR)* approach in detail; and Section 6 compares the SR approach with related work.

2   OR-forest

The OR-forest model is an AND/OR parallel execution model that exploits both IAP and ORP. The following is a brief description of the OR-forest model [19].

Consider a goal **G** labeling a node of an OR-tree. If the subgoals in **G** are interdependent (sharing some variables), we describe the execution of **G** in the same way as in the OR-tree, and the node is called *normal node*. However, if **G** contains **n** independent (without sharing any variable) groups of subgoals $g_1, g_2, ..., g_n$, we describe the execution of **G** in a different way:

- **n** separate child trees are derived, with the root nodes of the derived child trees labeled by $g_1, g_2, ..., g_n$, respectively.
- The creation of successors of the node (called **seed node**) labeled by G will depend on the combination of solutions to those independent groups of subgoals.

In this way, a tree may derive some separate child trees and a derived child tree in turn may create new child trees, so a collection of OR-trees can be derived in the course of executing a program. This collection of OR-trees is called an OR-forest. To illustrate this, we describe the execution of the following example program with an initial goal h(X,Y) by the OR-forest method in Fig. 1.

```
h(X,Y) :- p(X), q(Y).
p(1).   p(2).   ...   p(m).
q(1).   q(2).   ...   q(m).   ...   q(n).
```

From the OR-forest in Fig. 1, we observe:

1. OR-parallelism is described by multiple branches and each branch of a tree represents an independent way of solving the goal labeling the root node of the tree.
2. AND-parallelism is described by multiple derived child trees.
3. Redundancy is avoided because the execution of each independent subgoal is described by one separate tree.

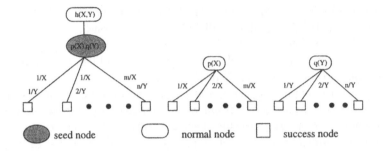

Fig. 1. The OR-forest description of the search space of an example program

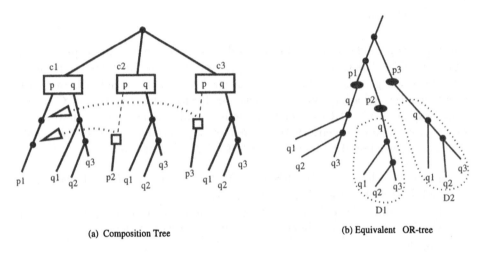

(a) Composition Tree

(b) Equivalent OR-tree

Fig. 2. Composition Tree and its equivalent OR-tree

3 Recomputation in Composition Tree

After the OR-forest [19] was proposed, other AND/OR parallel execution models, e.g., ACE [7], were proposed based on *Composition Tree*. They are variants of solution combination based models, which were proposed in order to solve the side-effects problem while executing Prolog in AND/OR parallel. The *Composition Tree* essentially uses the idea of recomputing independent goals of a parallel conjunction, so that the sequential behavior of side-effects can be achieved (the recomputation problem will be explained in detail in next section). Consider the conjunction p, q, The *Composition Tree* description for which is shown in Fig. 2(a). With recomputation, for every alternatives of p, the goal q is computed entirely.

While *Composition Tree* is a simple and pioneer solution for side-effects problem, the redundant computation, resulting from recomputation of entire AND goals, will seriously affect the performance of a large class of programs. Consider above example again. Suppose p has speculative branches [1] (which may end up with a failure), say, $p1$ will succeed, but $p2$ and $p3$ will fail. In this situation, q has still been computed for $p2$ and $p3$ in *Composition Tree* when $p2$ or $p3$ was initially started. The computations are the same as those of the OR-tree in Fig. 2(b). They are even more than the computations in sequential or OR-parallel execution, since $D1$ and $D2$ of the OR-tree will not be executed in the sequential or OR-parallel execution. From the example, we know that, in the *Composition Tree*, the more speculative branches of AND goals, the more redundant computation than sequential or OR-parallel execution.

After a careful analysis, we find above solution has the following disadvantages:

- it does not avoid the redundant computation of independent AND goals and thus loses the essential advantage of redundancy avoidance in solution combination based models,
- it introduces more redundant computation than sequential or OR-parallel execution.

In next section, we will analyze the side-effects ordering in OR-forest in depth, so as to avoid unnecessary recomputation and to simulate the sequential behavior of side-effects in *Selective Recomputation* approach.

4 Side-effects orderings

In this section, we begin with some definitions in the side-effects problem.

Definition 1. Side-effect procedure
The following is a recursive definition:

1. A side-effect built-in is a *side-effect procedure*.
2. A procedure which invokes *side-effect procedures* in its clauses is a *side-effect procedure*.

A procedure which is not a *side-effect procedure* is a *pure procedure*.

Definition 2. Side-effect subgoal and pure subgoal
A subgoal calling a *side-effect procedure* is a *side-effect subgoal*. A subgoal calling a *pure procedure* is a *pure subgoal*.

In OR-forest, the first OR tree is called the *main tree*. The tree that derives child trees is called their *parent tree*. A normal node is called a *side-effect node* if its first subgoal is a *side-effect built-in*. A seed node is called a *side-effect node* if at least one subgoal in its independent groups of subgoals is a *side-effect subgoal*. A *side-effect node* is also called *side-effective*. A node which is not *side-effective* is called a *pure node*.

---

[1] this assumption is quite reasonable for a real program.

The side-effect built-ins are divided into *soft* ones and *hard* ones. The *soft* side-effect built-ins are those which do not affect the following computation. The *hard* side-effect built-ins are those which may affect or decide the following computation.

For example, the *write* is a *soft* side-effect built-in, but *assert, retract, read* and *cut* are *hard* side-effect built-ins.

It is straightforward to describe the orderings of built-ins in merely OR-parallel or merely AND-parallel execution models based on OR-tree or AND-tree respectively. To retain the observable sequential semantics of a program while exploring an OR-tree or AND-tree in parallel, the conservative way is to suspend the execution of a side-effect built-in until it becomes the left-most active branch in the tree. Many systems adopted this simple strategy [9, 2].

The side-effects orderings become more complex when both the IAP and ORP are exploited in the parallel execution models. In the OR-forest model, the OR-branches may be executed in parallel to exploit the OR-parallelism, and the child trees may be explored in parallel to exploit the AND-parallelism. However, if there are side-effects in the OR-forest, the orderings for executing the side-effect built-ins in an OR-tree should be from left to right (top-to-bottom requirement for clauses in a procedure), and the orderings for executing side-effect built-ins between sibling trees should also be from left to right (left-to-right requirement for subgoals in a clause body).

However, if we only keep above order, there are still some problems when exploiting AND-, OR- parallelism in OR-forest. Consider the following program. If the program is executed sequentially, the observable result on the screen should be the number sequence 1,3,5,6,4,5,6,2,3,5,6,4,5,6. the OR-forest for the program is described as in Fig. 3.

```
:-p(X), q(Y), r(Z).
p(X):-X=1,write(X).     p(X):-X=2,write(X).     q(Y):-Y=3,write(Y).
q(Y):-Y=4,write(Y).     r(Z):-Z=5,write(Z).     r(Z):-Z=6,write(Z).
```

According to above order, the observable result will be 1,2,3,4,5,6, by first executing the child tree labeled by $p(X)$, then $q(Y)$, and then $r(Z)$. This is different from the sequential result. So we have to adopt a new rule of orderings: when the first solution is found in the first child tree, the privilege for executing the side-effect built-ins should be passed to the next sibling tree, and so does the next sibling tree; if a child tree has no next sibling tree(the last one), it has the privilege to execute the side-effects until every solution is found, then it passes the privilege to its previous sibling tree. In terms of the new rule, we can get the result 1,3,5,6,4,2. The orderings are consistent with the sequential ones except several numbers are omitted. It seems we can never get the exact sequential result unless recomputation of the side-effect built-ins is adopted. To keep the sequential semantics, the recomputation of side-effect built-ins should not be ruled out. Therefore, if child trees are recomputed for multiple times according to the number of solutions in previous sibling trees, the sequential result will be achieved. The idea is used in [8]. However, the recomputation in [8] is even

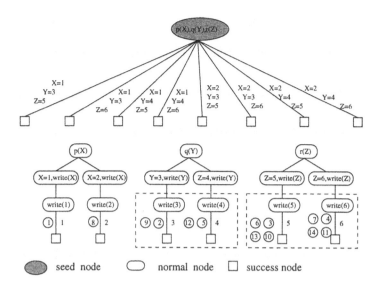

Fig. 3. Side-effects Orderings in OR-forest

more than that in sequential or OR-parallel execution as discussed in previous section.

As a matter of fact, the necessary recomputed parts in a tree are the subtrees, at whose root nodes the side-effect built-ins are executed, instead of the entire tree. If we only selectively recompute from the nodes where the side-effect built-ins are executed, we can get the same result as the sequential execution.

For example, combining the selective recomputation (only recompute the *writes*) with above new rule, we can get the result 1,3,5,6,4,5,6,2,3,5,6,4,5,6 in OR-forest according to the execution order indicated by circled sequence numbers(see Fig. 3). The recomputed parts are those in dashed rectangles.

From above discussion, we know that, to achieve the sequential orderings of side-effects, we should first execute the left-most side-effect built-ins in the first child tree until the left-most solution is found in the tree. Then the left-most side-effect built-ins in the second child tree are executed until the left-most solution is found. After all the child trees find their left-most solutions, none of them can execute side-effect built-ins until the side-effect built-ins in the first successor branch of the seed node are executed. Therefore, the privilege of executing the side-effect built-ins is passed among child trees and successor branches. The passing of privilege can be managed, according to the orderings in sequential execution, by the *seed node*.

In next section, we propose the *SR* approach, which selectively recompute side-effect parts of a child tree instead of the entire child tree as in [8]. It can solve the side-effect problem in OR-forest with minimum recomputation and maximum parallelism.

5 Side-effects handling with Selective Recomputation

For the convenience, we first informally define some terminology.

Definition 3. Parent process and child process
The process working on a seed node in the *parent tree* is called the *parent process* of the processes working on the *child trees* of the seed node. The processes working on the *child trees* are called its *child processes*.

Definition 4. Active branch
An *active branch* is a branch whose execution has not been finished (may be suspended).

5.1 Side-effect execution permit token

To facilitate the maintenance of side-effect orderings, we invent a token, called *side-effect execution permit*, to pass the privilege of executing side-effects around the OR-forest. The rules for passing the token are discussed as below.

Initially, the token is given to the left-most active branch in the *main tree*.

1. When the branch holding the token fails, it passes the token to the left-most active branch in its tree.
2. When the branch holding the token succeeds in the main tree, it passes the token to the left-most active branch in the main tree.
3. When the branch holding the token succeeds in a child tree, it passes the token to the corresponding *seed node* in its *parent tree*.
4. When a *seed node* receives the token, it passes the token to its left-most active successor branch. If the *seed node* has no active successor branch, it passes the token to the left-most active branch in one of its child trees, from which it is waiting for solution to create the next successor branch using the *solution combining algorithm* described later.

Actually, the token is passed in the OR-forest in accordance with the execution order in sequential Prolog.

In above description, to retrieve the left-most active branch in a tree, we can keep some pointers, e.g., *left sibling node*, *right sibling node*, in a *choice point* of WAM [22], as in Aurora [3]. This kind of implementation techniques is very mature in OR-parallel logic programming systems [9, 3]. We will not discuss those implementation techniques, which are beyond the scope of this paper.

Definition 5. left-to-right position
The *left-to-right position* of a node is an order decided by the depth-first search sequence in a tree. The *left-to-right position* of a solution is the same as that of its success node. The *left-to-right position* of a process is also the same as that of the node it is currently expanding.

For example, if node A is reached earlier than node B by the depth-first search, then node A's *left-to-right position* is in front of node B's *left-to-right position*.

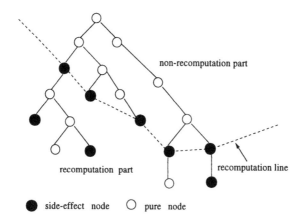

non-recomputation part

recomputation part

recomputation line

● side-effect node   ○ pure node

Fig. 4. Recomputation and non-recomputation part in a OR tree

Definition 6. Recomputation part, non-recomputation part, and recomputation line

An OR tree can be divided by the first appearing side-effect nodes in its branches. The pure part without any side-effect node is called the *non-recomputation part*; the rest of the tree is called the *recomputation part*. The line of side-effect nodes separating the two parts is called *recomputation line*.

For example, in Fig. 4, the OR tree is divided into two parts by the side-effect nodes first appearing in its branches: the *recomputation part* and the *non-recomputation part*. These first appearing side-effect nodes form the *recomputation line*. The behavior of processes working in *non-recomputation part* is different from that of processes working in *recomputation part* when they execute side-effect built-ins. So a process has to know whether it is currently working in *recomputation part* or *non-recomputation part*. There is a flag in a process, indicating if it is in the *recomputation part* or not. Initially, the flag is set to indicate the process is in the *non-recomputation part*. When the first side-effect built-in is to be executed, the flag is set to indicate the process is in *recomputation part*. At this moment, the process is on the *recomputation line*.

When a process reaches an unexpanded normal node, it executes the **Normal Node Function** which is illustrated in Fig. 5. When a process reaches a seed node, it executes the **Seed Node Function** which is illustrated in Fig. 6.

To fulfill the seed node function, some data structures are introduced.

- **number of child trees:** the total number of child trees is recorded in NCT. Each child tree has a sequence number according to its root goal's order in the seed node.
- **solution list:** the list is composed of solutions and *vacant* positions. Each child tree has a solution list in its seed node. If there are possible solutions in some branches in the child tree, *vacant* positions are reserved for them in the list according to their *left-to-right positions* in the tree. The SL_i is used to point to the head of the list of ith child tree. The ES_i points to the

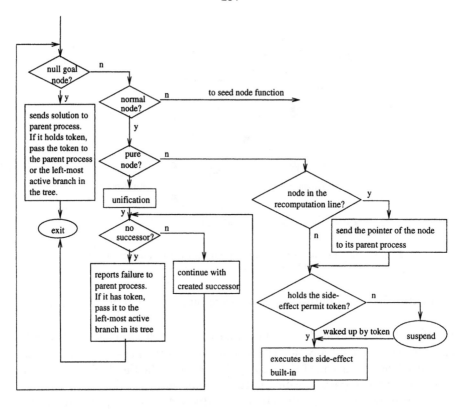

Fig. 5. The normal node function

expected solution position in the list. The list is updated by the seed node when a solution or failure message is received.

- **recomputation line list:** when the seed node is *side-effective*, the recomputation line lists are used for the side-effective child trees. The list is composed of node pointers. When a child tree need to be selectively recomputed, its recomputation line list is used to reconstruct its new solution list and to make the nodes unexpanded on the recomputation line so that the recomputation can start from the recomputation line.

While a process executes the **Seed Node Function**, it may suspend and get the following messages: *side-effect execution permit token, recomputation node pointer, solution from child processes*, and *failure message*. Fig. 6 illustrates the corresponding behaviors for these messages.

The **Token Passing Algorithm** of a seed node can be described as: If there are active successor branches, the token is passed to the left-most active successor branch; otherwise, the token is given to the left-most active branch of the child tree with sequence number CT, whose next left-most solution is expected to compose the next successor branch of the seed node.

The **Solution Combining Algorithm** is described as below in a program-like way.

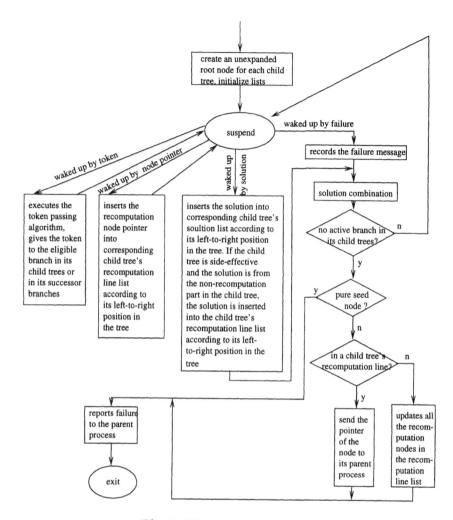

Fig. 6. The seed node function

ESi: points to expected solution position;
SLi: points to the head of solution list;
NCT: the total number of child trees;
CT: the least sequence number of child trees whose solution is
     expected to compose the next successor branch;
R: the least sequence number of recomputation line lists which
     need to be recomputed;

```
for(i=1;i<=NCT;i++) if (ESi == vacant-position) then {
                                           CT = i;  return;}
```

```
j = NCT; R = NCT + 1;
while(1){
    combine solutions ESi(1<=i<=NCT); create an unexpanded node
    for the successor branch;
    ESj = ESj->next;
    while(ESj == end-of-list){
     if(j'th child tree is side-effective)
        then reconstruct the solution list;
     ESj = SLj; R = j; j = j - 1;
     if(j < 1) return;
     ESj = ESj->next;
     }
    for(i=R;i<=NCT;i++){
    make the nodes unexpanded in the i'th recomputation line list
    }
    for(i=j;i<=NCT;i++){
      if (ESi == vacant-position) then { CT = i; return; }
    }
    j = NCT;
}
```

5.2   Execution delay for soft side-effect built-ins

In above approach, the *side-effect procedures* are allowed to be executed in parallel until a *side-effect built-in* becomes the left-most subgoal of a node. There are two benefits: reducing the recomputation and increasing the parallelism. Moreover, to maximize the parallelism, we can delay the execution of *soft* side-effect built-ins, e.g., *write*. Since their execution does not influence their following execution, we can execute their following pure subgoals before they are executed. Their execution can be delayed until **(1)** a *hard* side-effect built-in is to be executed; or **(2)** failure or success occurs; or **(3)** a *seed node* is reached. Thus, every process should keep a *delayed side-effects list* in its state data structure to store the delayed *soft* side-effect built-ins. In this way, the parallelism is increased to the maximum extent, and the selective recomputation is decreased to the minimum extent. For example, consider the following program.

```
h(X, Y) :- p(X), q(Y).
p(X):-write(X),pure_task1(X).    q(Y):-write(Y),pure_task2(Y).
```

If we don't delay the execution of *write*, according to above ordering algorithm, the execution is actually sequential, following the execution order: $write(X)$, $pure\_task1(X)$, $write(Y)$, $pure\_task2(Y)$. And suppose $p(X)$ has N solutions, $write(Y)$ and $pure\_task2(Y)$ have to be recomputed for $N-1$ times. If the execution of *write* is delayed, the $pure\_task1(X)$ and $pure\_task2(Y)$ can be executed in parallel. After their execution, the $write(X)$ and $write(Y)$ are executed sequentially. The execution delay of *soft* side-effect built-ins has the same effect as that of transforming above program into the following one. But since the delay is implemented at run-time, it is more powerful than static transformation.

```
h(X, Y) :- p(X), q(Y).
p(X):-pure_task1(X),write(X).      q(Y):-pure_task2(Y),write(Y).
```

Moreover, if $p(X)$ has N solutions, only $write(Y)$ has to be recomputed for $N-1$ times, and the recomputation of $pure\_task2(Y)$ has been reduced. This reduction is very significant when execution of $pure\_task2$ is very time-consuming.

6 Comparison of related work

From above discussion, the SR can avoid unnecessary recomputation to the maximum extent, and because *side-effect procedures* are allowed to be executed in parallel until a *hard side-effect built-in* becomes the left-most subgoal of a node, it can exploit the parallelism to the maximum extent under the side-effect requirements. There is no extra overhead for the selective recomputation since making a node unexpanded only needs to update the state of the node. To explain the difference between the SR and the recomputation scheme in [8], we give the following example.

```
h(X, Y) :- p(X), q(Y).
p(X):-pure_task11(X),se1(X),pure_task12(X).
p(X):-pure_task21(X),se2(X),pure_task22(X).
q(Y):-pure_task31(Y),se3(Y),pure_task32(Y).
q(Y):-pure_task41(Y),se4(Y),pure_task42(Y).
```

In the example, $p(X)$ and $q(Y)$ can be executed in parallel, $p(X)$ has M branches but only N solutions ($M > N$), and $se1$, $se2$, $se3$, $se4$ are side-effect built-ins. First, we assume $se1$, $se2$, $se3$, $se4$ are *hard* side-effect built-ins. In [8], q(Y) has to be computed for M times. So the $pure\_task31(Y)$, $se3$, $pure\_task32(Y)$, $pure\_task41(Y)$, $se4$, $pure\_task42(Y)$ have to be computed for M times. But in the SR approach, we only compute $se3$, $pure\_task32(Y)$, $se4$, $pure\_task42(Y)$ for N times, instead of the entire $q(Y)$. Usually there are many speculative branches in $p(X)$ in a serious program, so M is much greater than N. Therefore, the recomputation in [8] is usually much more than that in the SR approach.

If we assume $se1$, $se2$, $se3$, $se4$ are *soft* side-effect built-ins. In [8] the recomputation is the same as that in the first case. And because $se1$, $se2$, $se3$, $se4$ have to be executed sequentially, only $pure\_task11(X)$, $pure\_task21(X)$, $pure\_task31(Y)$, $pure\_task41(Y)$ can be executed in parallel. However, because of the delay of *soft* side-effect built-ins, the SR can execute
$(pure\_task11(X),pure\_task12(X))$, $(pure\_task21(X),pure\_task22(X))$,
$(pure\_task31(Y),pure\_task32(Y))$, $(pure\_task41(Y),pure\_task42(Y))$,
in parallel and thus increases the parallelism, and only $se3$ and $se4$ should be recomputed for $N-1$ times. If the pure tasks are time-consuming in above program, the reduction of recomputation and the increase of parallelism in the SR are significant.

Since the above program template is common in real applications, the SR is a useful and practical approach for handling side-effects in AND/OR parallel execution models/systems.

Actually, the SR approach is a flexible and general form of the entire recomputation scheme in [8]. For the worst case, if the *recomputation line* is set to the root node, the SR is degenerated into the scheme in [8].

7 Conclusions

In this paper, we analyzed the side-effect problem in AND/OR parallel execution of logic programs. We have discussed the intricate orderings of side-effect built-ins and recomputation in AND/OR parallel execution models. Based on the discussion, we proposed a SR approach for handling side-effects in the OR-forest model, which only selectively recomputes the side-effect parts in a OR tree instead of the entire OR tree. Compared with other related work, this approach can solve the side-effect problem with minimum recomputation and maximum parallelism. The idea of SR can be adopted to improve other AND/OR parallel execution models/systems [16, 6] as well. The treatment of the special side-effect built-in, *cut*, is not discussed in the paper because of limited space. The detailed discussion for its implementation under the SR approach will be presented in a later paper.

Acknowledgments

The authors would like to thank members of Knowledge Representation and Reasoning Unit, especially Michael Maher and Krishna Rao for their constructive suggestions to this work. The research is supported by an ARC(Australian Research Council) large grant(A49601731), an ARC small grant and a NCGSS grant by Griffith University.

References

1. K.A.M. Ali, Roland Karlsson: "The MUSE Approach to Or-Parallel Prolog," *International Journal of Parallel Programming,* 19(2):129-162, April 1990.
2. A. Calderwood, P. Szeredi: "Scheduling OR-parallelism in Aurora–the Manchester scheduler," *In Proc. of the Sixth International Conference on Logic Programming,* MIT Press, pp419-435, June 1989.
3. Mats Carlsson: "Design and Implementation of an OR-Parallel Prolog Engine," *Ph.D. Thesis,* The Royal Institute of Technology, Stockholm, 1990.
4. D. DeGroot: "Restricted AND-Parallelism and Side-effects," *In International Symposium on Logic Programming,* San Francisco, 1987, pp80-89.
5. Y. Gao, et al: "Intelligent Scheduling AND- and OR-parallelism in the Parallel Logic Programming System RAP/LOP-PIM," *In Proc. of the 20th Annual Inter. Conf. on Parallel Processing (ICPP'91),* St. Charles, IL, USA, Aug. 1991.

6. G. Gupta, et al: "IDIOM: Integrating Dependent and-, Independent and-, and Or-parallelism," *In 1991 International Logic Programming Symposium*, pp152-166, MIT Press, Oct. 1991.

7. G. Gupta, M. Hermenegildo: "ACE: And/Or-parallel Copying-based Execution of Logic Programs," *In Proc. ICLP91 Workshop on Parallel Execution of Logic Programs*, Lecture Notes in Computer Science 569, Springer Verlag, 1991.

8. G. Gupta, V. Santos Costa: "Cut and Side-Effects in And-Or Parallel Prolog," *In Proc. 4th IEEE Symposium on Parallel and Distributed Processing*, Arlington, 1992.

9. Bogumil Hausman: "Pruning and Speculative Work in OR-Parallel Prolog," *Ph.D. Thesis*, The Royal Institute of Technology, Stockholm, 1990.

10. M. Hermenegildo, K. Greene: "The &-prolog System: Exploiting Independent And-Parallelism," *New Generation Computing*, 9(3,4):233-257, 1991.

11. Zhiyi Hwang, Shouren Hu: "A Compiling Approach for Exploiting AND-parallelism in Parallel Logic Programming Systems," *In Proc. of Parallel Architectures and Languages Europe*, ,pp335-345, June 1989.

12. Zhiyi Hwang, Chengzheng Sun, et al: "Reduction of Code Space in Parallel Logic Programming Systems," *In Proc. of Parallel Architectures and Languages Europe*, ,pp454-470, June 1991.

13. Ewing Lusk, D.H.D. Warren, S. Haridi, et al: "The Aurora or-parallel Prolog system," *New Generation Computing*, 7(2,3):243-271, 1990.

14. K. Muthukumar and M. Hermenegildo: "Complete and Efficient Methods for Supporting Side-Effects in Independent/Restricted And-parallelism," *In 1989 International Conference on Logic Programming*, MIT Press, June 1989.

15. G.H. Pollard: "Parallel Execution of Horn Clause Programs," *Ph.D. Thesis*, Dept. of Computing, Imperial College, 1981.

16. E. Pontelli, G. Gupta, M. Hermenegildo: "&ACE: A High-Performance Parallel Prolog System," *In International Parallel Processing Symposium*, IEEE Computer Society, 1995.

17. V. Santos Costa, D.H.D. Warren, R. Yang: "Andorra-I: A parallel Prolog system that transparently exploits both and- and or-parallelism," *In Proc. of the Third ACM SIGPLAN Symposium on Principles and Practice of Parallel Programming*, ACM Press, April 1991.

18. K. Shen: "Initial Results from the Parallel Implementation of DASWAM," *In Proc. of Joint International Symposium of Logic Programming*, pp513-527, Sep. 1996.

19. Chengzheng Sun, Yungui Ci: "The OR-forest Description for the Execution of Logic Programs," *In Proc. of Third International Conference on Logic Programming*, pp457-466, 1986.

20. Chengzheng Sun, Yungui Ci: "The Sharing of Environment in AND-OR-parallel Execution of Logic Programs," *In Proc. of 14th International Symposium on Computer Architecture*, pp137-144, 1987.

21. Chengzheng Sun, Yungui Ci: "The OR-forest-based parallel execution model of logic programs," *Future Generation Computer Systems*, North-Holland, Volume 6, Number 1, (June 1990), pp25-34.

22. D.H.D. Warren: "An Abstract Prolog Instruction Set," *Technical Note 309*, SRI International, 1983.

Tracing Lazy Functional Computations
Using Redex Trails

Jan Sparud and Colin Runciman

Department of Computer Science, University of York,
Heslington, York, YO1 5DD, UK
(e-mail: {sparud,colin}@cs.york.ac.uk)

Abstract. We describe the design and implementation of a system for
tracing computations in a lazy functional language. The basis of our
tracing method is a program transformation carried out by the compiler: transformed programs compute the same values as the original,
but embedded in functional data structures that also include *redex trails*
showing how the values were obtained. A special-purpose display program enables detailed but selective exploration of the redex trails, with
cross-links to the source program.

Keywords: debugging, graph reduction, Haskell, program transformation.

1 Introduction

1.1 Why trace functional computations?

Functional programming languages have many advantages over the conventional
alternative of procedural languages. For example, program construction is more
rapid, more modular and less error-prone. Programs themselves are more concise.

Yet functional programming systems are not very widely used. There are
various reasons for this, but one that crops up time and again is the *lack of tracing
facilities*. Yes, there is less scope for making mistakes in a functional language;
but programmers do still make them! And when their programs go wrong they
need to trace the cause. Unfortunately, implementors of functional languages
are hard-pressed to provide equivalents of the 'debugging tools' routinely used
to investigate faults in procedural programs. Tracing evaluation by normal order
graph reduction is more subtle than following a sequence of commands already
explicit at source level.

There have been various attempts to tackle the problem of tracing lazy functional programs. We discuss some of them in §6. But so far as we know there is
as yet no really effective solution — a state of affairs we'd like to change.

1.2 How? Some design goals and assumptions

Functional language We concentrate on the tracing problem for purely functional languages such as Haskell. Despite the absence of side-effects, lazy evaluation and higher-order functions in languages like Haskell make the problem difficult: there is a big gap between high-level declarative programs and the low-level sequences of events in their computations.

Graph reduction We assume an implementation based on graph-reduction. In essence, the objective of computation is to evaluate an expression represented by a graph. This is achieved by repeatedly replacing one subgraph by another, where the reduction rules used to define replacements are derived from the equations given in the program. At each reduction step, a *redex* matching the left hand side of an equation is replaced by a the corresponding instance of the right hand side. Computation by graph reduction is made efficient by compilation to code for a G-machine, or similar.

Backward traces We need to provide backward traces from results or from run-time errors, because the most pressing need for traces arises in the context of an unexpected output or failure.

Redex trails We use the idea of a *redex trail* to provide the overall framework for answering the question 'How has this value/failure come about?'. At each reduction, parts of the redex no longer attached to the main graph are normally discarded. If we instead make a link from each newly created node of the graph to its *parent redex*, the computation builds its own trail as reduction proceeds.

Non-invasive traces The transformation to introduce redex trails should not change the course of the underlying computation in any way. For example, unevaluated expressions should remain unevaluated.

Complete traces Until we have a very strong reason to discard parts of the information in redex trails, and a clear argument which parts should go, we want to construct traces in full. There must be a representation of every reduction step for definitions and expressions of every kind.

Selective display A full trace of even a modest computation contains a great deal of information — too much for the programmer to absorb in its entirety. Programmers need fine control over what trace information is actually displayed to them, down to the level of interactive link-by-link examination of the trails leading from a run-time fault or selected fragment of output.

Traces linked to source However good the tracing system, source programs are likely to remain the primary reference for programmers. Not only should expressions in traces be displayed just as they might be written in a source program; trace text should be also be linked directly to source text.

A portable implementation Although a prototype tracer must have some specific host implementation (ours will be the Haskell compiler nhc [Röj95]), we aim to produce a portable tracing scheme that could be adopted in other implementations of a functional language. For this reason, we shall prefer to use source-to-source transformation rather than to modify the run-time system.

An efficient implementation Finally, the implementation must be efficient — or at least, not so inefficient that using the tracer is infeasible or unattractive. If execution slows by no more than a factor of ten, we can hope that the value of tracing information will make the speed tolerable; but factors of a hundred or a thousand are unlikely to be acceptable. Also, memory requirements must be such that the tracer can be used on an ordinary workstation.

1.3 Details that follow

§2 explains what we mean by a redex trail, and shows how trails can be represented as functional data structures. §3 gives rules for transforming a program so that all values it computes are wrapped in a construction including a redex trail; it also explains briefly how we implement these rules in the nhc compiler. §4 explains the design of the interactive display program we use to examine redex trails. §5 evaluates aspects of the trace system we have built, including some performance figures. §6 discusses related work on other tracing systems for functional programs. §7 concludes and also gives some of our plans for future work.

2 The design of a trace structure

To appreciate what we mean by a redex trail consider the following example of a simple program testing the validity of a date.

```
daysIn Jan = 31
daysIn Feb = 28
    ...
daysIn Dec = 31
valid (Date d m) = daysIn m >= d
date = Date 31 Feb
main = valid date
```

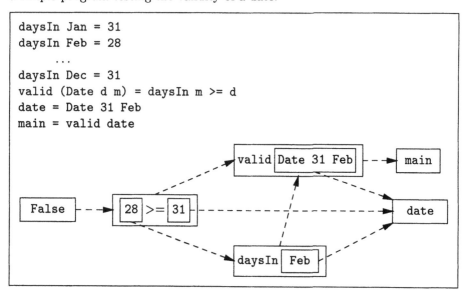

The diagram shows the complete redex trail from the value `False` of the main expression. The immediate parent redex (whose reduction caused the creation of this instance of `False`) was `28 >= 31`. The parent redex of this application of `>=` was `valid (Date 31 Feb)`, but the parent redex of the left operand `28` was `daysIn Feb` and that of the right operand `31` was `date`. And so on. There is a link from every part of every expression to its parent redex.

The idea is to construct such a trace giving comprehensive information about a functional computation. The trace should be built as the computation proceeds. Once the computation is over the trace is just a static data structure.

Such redex trails can be represented as functional data structures of type:

```
data Trace = Ap Trace [Trace] | Nm Trace Name | Root
```

An application is represented by `Ap` t_{ap} `[`t_f, t_{x_1}, ..., t_{x_n}`]`, where t_{ap} is the trace for the application itself, t_f is the trace of the function part of the application, and $t_{x_1} \ldots t_{x_n}$ are the traces of the arguments. A name (a function, variable, constructor or literal) is represented by `Nm` t_{nm} *name* where t_{nm} is the trace of the name and *name* is a textual representation of the name. The application and name nodes should also have *source code references*, but since we are only interested in the structure of the trace at this stage, we have omitted them here. `Root` is the null trace attached to top-level names.

3 Creating traces

In this section we define transformations to derive a self-tracing version of any given program. We will introduce a number of combinators that actually perform the trace creation, but first we will describe how the *types* of a program will change under transformation.

3.1 Type transformation rules

Every value in the program will be wrapped in the R datatype, defined as:

```
data R a = R a Trace
```

The intuition is that every value in the original program should have a wrapped value in the transformed program containing the original value and a trace for that value.

Figure 1 gives the rules determining how types are transformed. Motivation and examples follow.

Traces for structured data values For a structured data value, we want a trace not only for the outermost construction but also for all components. The $\mathcal{D}$ scheme is responsible for transforming datatypes into this form. We don't give the definition of the $\mathcal{D}$ scheme, but here is an example of the transformation of

$$\mathcal{R}[\![t]\!] \Rightarrow \text{R}\ (\mathcal{T}[\![t]\!])$$

$$\mathcal{T}[\![tcon\ t_1 \ldots t_n]\!] \Rightarrow tcon\ \mathcal{T}[\![t_1]\!] \ldots \mathcal{T}[\![t_n]\!]\ (n \geq 0,\ tcon \neq '\!\rightarrow')$$
$$\mathcal{T}[\![t_1 \rightarrow t_2]\!] \Rightarrow \text{Trace} \rightarrow \mathcal{R}[\![t_1]\!] \rightarrow \mathcal{R}[\![t_2]\!]$$
$$\mathcal{T}[\![\alpha]\!] \Rightarrow \alpha$$

Fig. 1. Type rules for transformed expressions.

a simple tree datatype:

$\mathcal{D}[\![$data Tree a = Node (Tree a) Int (Tree a) | Leaf a$]\!]$
$\Rightarrow$
data Tree a = Node $\mathcal{R}[\![$Tree a$]\!]$ $\mathcal{R}[\![$Int$]\!]$ $\mathcal{R}[\![$Tree a$]\!]$ | Leaf $\mathcal{R}[\![$a$]\!]$
$\Rightarrow$
data Tree a = Node (R (Tree a)) (R Int) (R (Tree a)) | Leaf (R a)

Traces for values of function type Perhaps a value of function type $\alpha \rightarrow \beta$ can be treated as a structured value with constructor $\rightarrow$ and components α and β? Then the type $\alpha \rightarrow \beta$ would be transformed into R $(\mathcal{R}[\![\alpha]\!]\rightarrow\mathcal{R}[\![\beta]\!])$. Is this adequate? No! A function of type $\alpha \rightarrow \beta$ has a guarantee to fulfill: given an argument of type α it must return a value of type β. But transformed functions have a further obligation; they must also return a *trace* for that value of type β. A function of type $\mathcal{R}[\![\alpha]\!]\rightarrow\mathcal{R}[\![\beta]\!]$ *cannot* fulfill that obligation, since when the function is applied it does not know the current trace (or evaluation context) so it cannot build a full trace for the return value. Transformed functions need the trace of the application site as an extra argument. As an example, here is how the type of the standard *map* function is transformed:

$\mathcal{R}[\![\ (a\rightarrow b) \rightarrow [a] \rightarrow [b]\ ]\!]$
$\Rightarrow$
R (Trace $\rightarrow \mathcal{R}[\![a\rightarrow b]\!]\rightarrow \mathcal{R}[\![\ [a] \rightarrow [b]\ ]\!])$
$\Rightarrow$
R (Trace $\rightarrow$ R (Trace $\rightarrow$ R a$\rightarrow$ R b) $\rightarrow$ R (Trace $\rightarrow$ R [a] $\rightarrow$ R [b]))

Tracing *partial applications* will only be possible if a transformed function returns an R-value for each argument it is applied to. Note that this requirement is indeed fulfilled.

3.2 Creating traces for expressions

The trace for an expression depends on the *evaluation context* in which it is computed. The evaluation context of an expression is simply the trace of the redex in which the expression occurs. Given an evaluation context t, we will now define the transformation scheme for expressions, $\mathcal{E}[\![e]\!]_t$.

Tracing identifiers Identifiers can be either let-bound or λ-bound. Identifiers in patterns are λ-bound, and they already have traces, so the transformation of such identifiers is the identity transformation. Definitions of let-bound identifiers are transformed to expect a trace as argument; given a trace they produce a Nm node for this particular instance of the identifier.

$$
\begin{aligned}
\mathcal{E}[\![ident_\lambda]\!]_t &\Rightarrow ident \\
\mathcal{E}[\![ident_{let}]\!]_t &\Rightarrow ident\ t
\end{aligned}
$$

Fig. 2. Transforming identifiers.

Tracing constructed values Figure 3 shows the transformation rules for constructed values. The trace for a constructed value with no components is just the Nm node of the constructor. If the constructed value has components, its trace is an Ap node containing traces for the constructor and for each component.

$$
\mathcal{E}[\![conid\ e_1\ e_2\ \ldots\ e_n]\!]_t \Rightarrow con_n\ t\ \mathcal{N}[\![conid]\!]\ conid\ \mathcal{E}[\![e_1]\!]_t\ \mathcal{E}[\![e_2]\!]_t\ \ldots\ \mathcal{E}[\![e_n]\!]_t
$$

```
con0 t nm conid = R conid (Nm t nm)
conn t nm conid e1@(R _ te1) e2@(R _ te2) ...en@(R _ ten) =
     R (conid e1 e2 ... en) (Ap t [Nm t nm, te1, te2, ..., ten])
```

Fig. 3. Transforming constructed values.

Tracing function applications Figure 4 shows the rule for transforming function applications to make them create traces as well as results. The auxiliary function vap_n builds the trace node and then applies the function to one of the arguments, leaving it to another auxiliary function ap_n to apply it to the rest of the arguments. (Functions need to take arguments one at a time, so that partial applications have traces).

Case expressions are transformed in much the same way as function applications, with case as the function name and the scrutinised expression as the argument.

$$\mathcal{E}[\![f\ e_1\ e_2\ \dots\ e_n]\!]_t \Rightarrow \mathtt{vap}_n\ t\ \mathcal{E}[\![f]\!]_t\ \mathcal{E}[\![e_1]\!]_t\ \mathcal{E}[\![e_2]\!]_t\ \dots\ \mathcal{E}[\![e_n]\!]_t$$

```
vapn  t  (R f tf)  e1@(R _ te1)  e2@(R _ te2)  ...  en@(R _ ten)  =
         apn-1  t1  (f t1 e1)  e2  ...  en
         where t1 = Ap t [tf, te1, te2, ..., ten]

apn  t  (R f tf)  e1@(R _ te1)  e2@(R _ te2)  ...  en@(R _ ten)  =
         apn-1  t  (f t e1)  e2  ...  en
ap0  t  e = e
```

Fig. 4. Transforming function applications.

As a simple example application of these rules, consider the transformation of the expression f True $(g\ x)$ in the evaluation context t. Assume that f and g are *let*-bound functions and x is a λ-bound variable.

$$\mathcal{E}[\![\mathtt{f}\ \mathtt{True}\ (\mathtt{g}\ \mathtt{x})]\!]_t$$
$$\Rightarrow$$
$$\mathtt{vap}_2\ t\ \mathcal{E}[\![\mathtt{f}]\!]_t\ \mathcal{E}[\![\mathtt{True}]\!]_t\ \mathcal{E}[\![\mathtt{g}\ \mathtt{x}]\!]_t$$
$$\Rightarrow$$
$$\mathtt{vap}_2\ t\ (\mathtt{f}\ t)\ (\mathtt{con}_0\ t\ \text{"True"}\ \mathtt{True})\ (\mathtt{vap}_1\ t\ (\mathtt{g}\ t)\ \mathtt{x})$$

Tracing let-expressions The transformation rule for let-expressions is shown in Figure 5. It uses the $\mathcal{F}$ scheme (defined in §3.3) to transform the local definitions.

$$\mathcal{E}[\![\mathtt{let}\ \{d_1;\ d_2;\ \dots;\ d_n\}\ \mathtt{in}\ e]\!]_t \Rightarrow \mathtt{let}\ \{\mathcal{F}[\![d_1]\!];\ \mathcal{F}[\![d_2]\!];\ \dots;\ \mathcal{F}[\![d_n]\!]\}\ \mathtt{in}\ \mathcal{E}[\![e]\!]_t$$

Fig. 5. Transforming let-expressions.

Tracing other types of expressions Case expressions are transformed in much the same way as function applications, with **case** as the function name and the scrutinised expression as the argument. This is useful when browsing the trace: one can see in the source code which branch was used in a case expression.

Lambda expressions are treated as functions with the function name \. This works surprisingly well, since source links from the trace make it easy to examine the full lambda abstraction, if necessary.

High level syntactic constructs such as list comprehensions and sequence generators are currently traced as if replaced by their standard translations using list-processing functions.

3.3 Transforming function definitions to create traces

Figure 6 shows the transformation scheme $\mathcal{F}$ for function definitions. A traced function accepts a trace as its argument (see Figure 2) and returns an R-value containing a translated version of the function and a trace for the function identifier. The translated function takes one argument (and application-site trace) at a time, and for each one produces a new R-value, representing the partially applied function. We use an auxiliary function fun_n to build the trace node for the identifier and to accept arguments one at a time. The translated function f itself is not called until enough arguments are available for a full (saturated) application.

The $\mathcal{P}$ transformation scheme transforms patterns. Currently we only have limited support for using guards. The computation of guards of a function are traced, but as soon as one of them is true and the corresponding function body is evaluated, the traces of the guards are discarded.

$$\mathcal{F}[\![f \ p_1 \ \ldots \ p_n = e]\!] \quad \Rightarrow f = \text{fun}_n \ f' \ \mathcal{N}[\![f]\!] \text{ where } f' \ t \ \mathcal{P}[\![p_1]\!] \ \ldots \ \mathcal{P}[\![p_n]\!] = \mathcal{E}[\![e]\!]_t$$

$$
\begin{array}{ll}
\mathcal{P}[\![\_]\!] & \Rightarrow \_ \\
\mathcal{P}[\![ident]\!] & \Rightarrow ident \\
\mathcal{P}[\![conid \ p_1 \ \ldots \ p_n]\!] & \Rightarrow \text{R} \ (conid \ \mathcal{P}[\![p_1]\!] \ \ldots \ \mathcal{P}[\![p_n]\!]) \ \_
\end{array}
$$

```
funn f fs t =
  R (λt1 e1→
    R (λt2 e2→
      ...
        R (λtn en→ f tn e1 ... en)
          tn-1)
      ...
    t1)
  [Nm t fs]
```

Fig. 6. Transformation scheme for function definitions.

We illustrate the $\mathcal{F}$ scheme with an example, in which two simple functions are transformed.

```
f x = g x x True + x
g x y True = x*y
g x y False = 1
    ⇒
f = fun₁ f' "f"
    where f' t x = vap₂ t ((+) t)
                            (vap₃ t (g t) x x (con0 t "True" True)) x
g = fun₃ g' "g"
    where g' t x y (R True _) = vap₂ t ((*) t) x y
          g' t x y (R False _) = con₀ t "1" 1
```

3.4 Two problems and their remedies

Over-saturated applications Trace-construction as we have described it so far works well for both partially and fully saturated applications. But it fails to build correct traces for function applications that *over-saturate* functions (i.e. the function in the application is given more arguments than are shown in the function's definition). In the following example, f 2 3 is an over-saturated application, since f is given two arguments, although by definition f has arity 1.

```
let f x = g x
    g x y = x+y
in  f 2 3
```

Unfortunately, traces for calls made from within an over-saturated function are lost. The reason can be seen in the definition of ap_n. If an application of arity m over-saturates a function of arity n, the functional argument f to ap_{m-n} will represent the result of a saturated call complete with a trace t_f, *which ap ignores!*

Including the trace for the function part in *every* call to an *ap* would be excessive. Suppose we are tracing the function call *f 1 2 3*: the result would be a trace with separate nodes for each of *f 1 2 3*, *(f 1) 2 3*, and *((f 1) 2) 3*.

We only want to include the trace of the function part *if* it is the result of a call to a fully saturated function. But how do we know that? Examining the definition of fun_n we see that an unsaturated function is applied to its own trace. When ap_n applies a function, it can check if the trace in the result *is the same* as the one passed to the function as first argument. If the traces are the same, the application is partial; otherwise it is saturated.

It is not enough to test if the trace objects denote equal values, we must check that the trace objects really are one and the same. This sounds simple, but it is not possible in a pure functional language to test equality of *objects*, one can only test equality of *values*. We overcome the problem by introducing an impure primitive for *pointer equality* which we call **sameAs** — it is the *only* impure function we need at run-time. The modified version of ap_n is presented in Figure 7.

Unevaluated applications When the computation has finished, exploration of the final trace can start, either from a faulting expression or some part of

```
apₙ t (R f t_f) e₁@(R _ t_e₁) e₂@(R _ t_e₂) ... eₙ@(R _ t_eₙ) =
    if t 'sameAs' t_f then
        apₙ₋₁ t (f t e₁) e₂ ... eₙ
    else
        let t' = Ap t [t_f, t_e₁, t_e₂, ..., t_eₙ]
        in apₙ₋₁ t' (f t' e₁) e₂ ... eₙ
ap₀ t e = e
```

Fig. 7. The modified version of ap_n.

the output. But what if we are interested in some saturated but unevaluated function application?

There is a conflict here between needing extra evaluation to obtain a trace, and wishing to avoid the extra evaluation to preserve the usual behaviour. If we evaluate the application to obtain the trace, the computation may diverge, giving us different behaviour for traced computated than for non-traced computations, which is clearly not acceptable.

We had a similar problem with partially applied functions, which we solved by forcing functions to return a new function and a trace for each argument. But when the function is fully saturated, the result may or may not be evaluated.

We solve this problem by introducing a new constructor Sat in the Trace datatype. A Sat node is introduced when a function application becomes fully saturated, and contains two parts: the trace of the fully saturated function call, and the trace of the result of the function call, which may be unevaluated. When the display program encounters a Sat node in the trace, it checks whether the result is evaluated. If so, the trace of that result is used; if not, the saturated function call and its trace is used instead. Note that Sat can be seen as an exceptional *forward* pointer in the trace, and that it is only useful as long as the result part is unevaluated. The revised definition of fun_n is given in Figure 8.

```
funₙ f fs t =
    R (λt₁ e₁→
        R (λt₂ e₂→
            ...
                R (λtₙ eₙ→ let R r t' = f tₙ e₁ ... eₙ in R r (Sat tₙ t'))
                tₙ₋₁)
            ...
        t₁)
    [Nm t fs]
```

Fig. 8. The new definition of fun_n used in the function definition transformation.

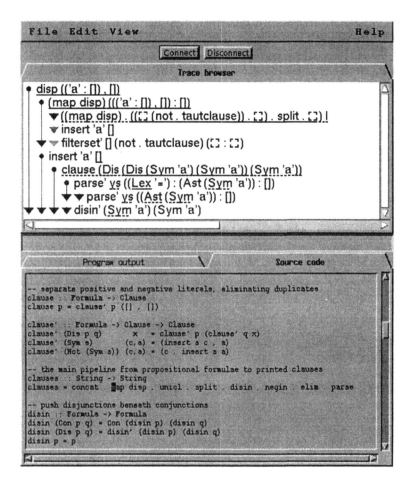

Fig. 9. A session snapshot of the interactive trace display program.

4 Displaying trace information

In this section we describe the interactive display component of our tracer. Information is presented to the user in three panels: (1) redex trails; (2) program sources; (3) program output[1] (see Figure 9 for an example). Though the user is free to browse any of these panels by scrolling, links to and from the redex trails provide the most important form of access. The programmer has access by mouse-click from any identifier in the trace display to both the corresponding definition and the relevant applied occurrence of the identifier in the source program.

---

[1] The current tracer restricts I/O in the traced program to a single textual input and a single textual output.

The number of nodes in a full trace exceeds the number of reductions in the traced computation, so typical traces are large structures containing a great deal of information. How much of this information can sensibly be presented is limited by both the *capacity of the user* and the *capacity of the screen* used for display.

4.1   How the user controls the display

At the start of a tracing session the redex-trail panel may contain an undefined function application detected and reported as a run-time error. If there was no such error the panel is initially empty; by selecting some fragment of text from the output panel, the user requests an initial display of the parent redex for that text.

The user now acts as a source of demand, controlling the extent of 'display by need'. Clicking over an already-displayed subexpression in a trace node requests the display of its parent redex. Moving the mouse to a different part of the display not only changes the currently selected expression; it also causes highlighting of three classes of *related expressions*. If E is the currently selected expression:

- all *shared occurrences* of E currently on display are highlighted in the same colour as E itself;
- all *expressions with the same parent redex* as E are highlighted in a different colour;
- if the *parent redex* of E is already on display, it is highlighted using a third colour.

4.2   Making the most of screen space

Screen-space is an all-too-scarce resource when displaying a complex structure. We have used a combination of techniques to reduce the amount of display space needed to show part of a trace.

Displaying expressions on one line   Even a single expression may be large, yet the user must be able to view the relationships between several of them. We therefore confine each expression to a single line of the display. To make this possible:

- for all expressions, details below a specified depth in the parse-tree are suppressed by default – clicking on a place-holder for any unprinted subexpression requests more detail if needed;
- when tracing to discover the cause of a fault, subexpressions that are *never evaluated* can be suppressed with a distinguished marker – their details *cannot be relevant*;
- to make space for extra detail in one part of an expression the user can click on other parts to collapse them to place-holders;
- when all else fails, horizontal scrolling is available!

Display by need revisited We have already described how parent redexes are displayed only as and when the user demands them. Continuing the analogy with a lazy evaluator:

- it is important to have shared references to a common parent redex rather than displaying it several times — hence the colour-coded information about shared, or already-displayed, parent redexes as the mouse-cursor traverses the display;
- also, re-clicking on a subexpression with a currently displayed parent redex removes the parent (and any displayed parents of its subexpressions, recursively) from the display.
- when all else fails, vertical scrolling is available!

5 Evaluation

Although our tracing system is still being refined, in this section we offer some observations and measurements by way of a preliminary evaluation. We address the following questions:

- What class of functional programs can the tracing system deal with?
- How much extra time and space does its use require?
- To what extent is the tracing scheme portable to other implementations, or even to other functional languages?
- How well does the tracer achieve its purpose as a useful tool for understanding (possibly faulty) functional computations?

5.1 Class of traceable programs

Our current implementation of the tracer is by extension of the nhc13 compiler. Programs to be traced can make use of a very large subset of Haskell 1.3, including type and constructor classes. We have traced a variety of programs, not all of them written by ourselves. The largest programs extend to several modules and some 2000 lines, yet few changes were needed to the original sources.

The most significant of the necessary changes restrict the I/O components of programs to a single output only. We are unsure as yet how best to trace I/O more comprehensively.

Some other things are not yet handled as we eventually intend. For example, comprehensions are currently traced as if replaced by their standard translations into compound applications of list-processing functions; we'd prefer something closer to the source program. Guard expressions are faithfully evaluated, but unless a fault occurs during a guard computation the redex trail for the Boolean value is not currently incorporated in the final trace; we'd like to make this information available to the programmer. We see no fundamental difficulties here; it's just a matter of a bit more work attending to details.

Table 1. The compile-time costs of generating redex trails. Only the `cichelli` program has more than one module.

	compilation time (s)		size of object code (kb)	
	normal	tracing	normal	tracing
cichelli	18.79	50.58	51.21	170.25
clausify	8.32	20.06	39.26	104.17
primes	6.51	14.39	13.15	37.33

Table 2. The run-time costs of generating redex-trails. Garbage-collection time is not included because it varies with heap size.

	reduction time (s)		max live heap (b)		number of
	normal	tracing	normal	tracing	reductions
cichelli	1.05	21.47	34 k	13 M	354 636
clausify	2.05	73.32	7 k	28 M	1 405 539
primes	5.09	33.50	60 k	54 M	520 073

5.2   Time and space costs

Using the tracer incurs extra costs both at compile-time and at run-time. We give here some figures for the construction of *complete* redex trails. We take three example programs: `cichelli` uses a brute-force search to construct a perfect hash function for a set of 16 keywords; `clausify` simplifies a given proposition to clausal form; `primes` generates the first 2,500 primes using a wheel-sieve. All three programs are included in the NoFib benchmark suite [Par93].

Table 1 shows the added costs apparent at *compile-time*. Much the same results are obtained for all three examples: both compile-time and the size of resulting object-code increase by a factor of two or three when we apply the program transformation to build redex trails.

Table 2 illustrates the *run-time* costs of generating redex trails; figures for the traced computations include the costs of evaluating both the result and the trace in full. Recording the details of the parent redex for every subexpression in every instance of every function body is not cheap! A trace-constructing computation takes 6–36 times longer than a normal one. The trace structure itself occupies from 20–100 bytes per application: so to construct traces with a million recorded reductions we need plenty of memory on our workstations! The wide variations in the performance figures for the different programs are accounted for by factors such as the arity of functions involved.

A final aspect of performance is less easily measured. The interactive trace-display program must respond rapidly to the user's requests. For all the examples we have tried to date, response-time has never been a problem.

5.3 Portability

Our current tracing system is implemented in a version of Röjemo's nhc compiler [Röj95]. The transformation to introduce trace values is performed on an intermediate representation of programs internal to nhc, and nhc's run-time system has been modified to support traced computations.

However, our tracing scheme is not closely tied to this one compiler. The results of the program transformation could be expressed in source form and supplied to a different Haskell compiler. Only one special primitive is needed at run-time: sameAs tests whether two traces are the same in a referentially opaque sense as explained in section §3.4. There are just two other additions to the run-time system: one retains access to output; the other provides a link to the display program.

We see no reason why our tracing scheme could not be applied to other lazy functional languages.

5.4 Will it solve 'The Tracing Problem'?

This is both the most important and the most difficult question to answer satisfactorily. A tracer might cope efficiently with a full range of programs and port easily to new compilers, yet fail the acid test: do programmers use it in practice to solve their problems?

At this stage, apart from our own experience trying out the tracer, we have only the results from an extended student exercise with an earlier prototype. Providing direct links between the trace and the source program turns out to be even more important than we expected; as do the links to textual input and output. But from these early trials we are quietly optimistic.

Currently we cannot handle non-terminating programs, unless a *black hole* [Jon92] is detected. A possible solution to this problem is to let the user interrupt the computation (e.g. by pressing control-C), and start browsing from the trace of the interrupted application, which must form a part of the cycle that caused the program to loop.

We would welcome enquiries from readers who teach functional programming and would be interested in 'class-testing' a suitable version of the tracer.

6 Related work

Some previous systems for tracing functional programs systems have been based on monitoring the *series of events* in a computation [KHC91], perhaps with the ability to examine events immediately preceding or following a suspected fault [TA90]. This approach is viable for a strict functional language with eager evaluation but breaks down for non-strict languages with a lazy evaluation strategy. In a Haskell computation closures for function applications can lie dormant for many reductions. If no equation matches when a closure comes to be evaluated it may be irrelevant to ask 'What happened just before this?' because preceding events may have nothing to do with the faulty closure. Simple traces of event sequences have been tried for lazy languages, but found wanting.

Our tracing based on *redex trails* has in common with Nilsson and Fritzson's system [NF94] the construction of a computational history tracing the origin of expressions back through ancestral redexes. However, the structure of their computational history is rather different. A node in their trace tree contains a saturated function application, along with its result and a list of histories for the function applications evaluated in the body of the saturated function. They also suggest using the algorithmic debugging technique [Sha82], which is a method of navigating in the trace by answering questions about the equivalence of (possibly complex) expressions. Naish and Barbour [NB95] use a source-to-source transformation to produce a computational history (which they call an evaluation tree) similar to Nilsson's and Fritzson's for a simple lazy functional language. Nilsson and Sparud [Spa96,NS97] further explores the creation and browsing of such evaluation trees, and address the problem of high memory consumption by constructing the history incrementally.

Hazan and Morgan [HM93] suggests a tracing technique that could be seen as a simplified abstraction of ours. Their *distinguished paths* are like our redex trails but contain *only function names from fully saturated applications*. For example, if main needs the value of f 1, and f needs the value of head [] the consequent run-time fault will be assigned the distinguished path main → f → head.

7 Conclusions and Future Work

So what have we achieved? We have developed a new scheme for constructing a complete trace of a lazy functional computation, based on redex trails. We have expressed this scheme in rules for program transformation, and we have implemented it in a Haskell compiler: the trace is itself represented as a functional data structure and the compiler transforms programs so that they build traces of their own execution. We have also developed a display program that allows the interactive exploration of redex trails, fully linked to the source program.

Previous attempts at similar schemes have often put severe limits on the language used to express traced programs, or on the amount of detail recorded in traces. We aim to build fully-detailed traces for full Haskell computations. Though our present tracer handles most of Haskell, we are keen to lift some of the current restrictions on I/O; special forms such as comprehensions and guards also need more attention as explained in §5.

The usefulness of such a tracer for functional programmers at large critically depends on its performance and capacity. Our ultimate goal is a tracer that can be applied to large computations – such as a functional language compiler. Though applications to date have been modest, as illustrated in §5 they do include fully-traced computations of over a million reductions, derived from multi-module programs several pages in length.

However, the speed penalty of tracing is still too high. We hope to reduce it so that in the *worst case* slow-down is no more than a factor of ten. There is certainly scope for speeding up the trace-constructing machinery — for example, by moving key auxiliary functions into the run-time system.

Space costs are even more critical. The important observation here is that even the most enquiring programmer cannot really want to follow a trail through hundreds of thousands of expressions! Rather they will be interested in just a few selected paths, though there is no way of knowing in advance just which paths these will be. We have just begun work on *trace-pruning* techniques that should substantially reduce the cost of building and storing traces, by confining them to *partial* redex trails. For example, we can bound the length of ancestral paths, truncating longer trails at each garbage collection: even bounding the length to zero there is often a useful trail from an error, since trails are still constructed between collections. Another approach is to discard details of computation inside specified modules: some early results here are very promising — for the `primes` computation, the peak amount of memory needed shrinks by a factor of 50 when we eliminate traces inside the prelude. We also have another line of attack on the space problem: we plan to write trace structures to file in a *compressed binary format* [WR97]. Storing traces in files also has the advantage that the trace of a lengthy run can be re-examined many times without re-incurring the cost of the trace-building computation.

Building a fast and space-efficient tracing system is only one side of the problem. Once the above refinements are made, we are keen to put the tracer to the test in the hands of other users. We'd like to run a series of controlled experiments measuring the speed and accuracy with which users of the tracer can find faults in programs. Only by such experiments and the outcomes of wider use can we hope to confirm that constructing and examining redex trails can be an effective part of functional programming.

Acknowledgements

Niklas Röjemo built the nhc compiler that we have adapted for our experiments in tracing. Anonymous PLILP referees provided helpful comments, questions and suggestions. Our work is funded by the Engineering and Physical Sciences Research Council.

References

[HM93]   Jonathan E. Hazan and Richard G. Morgan. The location of errors in functional programs. In Peter Fritzson, editor, *Automated and Algorithmic Debugging*, volume 749 of *Lecture Notes in Computer Science*, pages 135–152, Linköping, Sweden, May 1993.

[Jon92]   Richard Jones. Tail recursion without space leaks. *Journal of Functional Programming*, 2(1):73–79, January 1992.

[KHC91] A. Kishon, P. Hudak, and C. Consel. Monitoring semantics: a formal framework for specifying, implementing and reasoning about execution monitors. In *ACM Conference on Programming Language Design and Implementation (PLDI'91)*, pages 338–52, June 1991.

[NB95]   Lee Naish and Tim Barbour. Towards a portable lazy functional declarative debugger. Technical Report 95/27, Department of Computer Science, University of Melbourne, Australia, 1995.

[NF94]   H. Nilsson and P. Fritzson. Algorithmic debugging for lazy functional languages. *Journal of Functional Programming*, 4(3), 1994.

[NS97]   Henrik Nilsson and Jan Sparud. The evaluation dependence tree as a basis for lazy functional debugging. *Journal of Automated Software Engineering*, 4(2):152–205, April 1997.

[Par93] W. Partain. The **nofib** benchmark suite of Haskell programs. In J. Launchbury and P. Sansom, editors, *Proc. 1992 Glasgow Workshop on Functional Programming*, pages 195–202. Springer Verlag, Workshops in Computing, 1993.

[Röj95] N. Röjemo. Highlights from nhc – a space efficient haskell compiler. In *Proc. 7th Intl. Conf. on Functional Programming Languages and Computer Architecture (FPCA '95)*, pages 282–292, La Jolla, June 1995. ACM Press.

[Sha82] Ehud Y. Shapiro. *Algorithmic Program Debugging*. MIT Press, May 1982.

[Spa96] Jan Sparud. A transformational approach to debugging lazy functional programs. Licentiate Thesis, Department of Computing Science, Chalmers University of Technology, S-412 96, Göteborg, Sweden, February 1996.

[TA90]   A. P. Tolmach and A. W. Appel. Debugging Standard ML without reverse engineering. In *Proc. ACM conf. on Lisp and functional programming*. ACM Press, 1990.

[WR97]   M. Wallace and C. Runciman. Heap compression and binary I/O in Haskell. In *Proc. 2nd ACM SIGPLAN Workshop on Haskell*, Amsterdam, June 1997.

Functional Programming and Geometry

Guy Cousineau

Laboratoire d'Informatique, Ecole Nornale Supérieure
45 rue d'Ulm, 75251 PARIS CEDEX 05
Guy.Cousineau@ens.fr

Abstract. This paper is based on an experience in teaching functional programming to mathematics students. This experience had two objectives. The first one was to help the student assimilate some mathematical concepts by putting them to practical use in programs. The second one was to give them a good start in programming by emphasizing the fact that abstraction, which is so useful in mathematics, is equally useful in programming and allows for more powerful and more easily extensible programs. The mathematical domain used here is geometry and more precisely geometrical transformations, and their group structure. The programming projects are oriented towards 2D tilings, both Euclidean and hyperbolic.

keywords: education, functional programming, modularity, types, computer geometry, tilings.

1 Introduction

It is commonplace to point out the strong analogy between the design of programs and the design of proofs. In both cases for instance, structuring plays a prominent part and the decomposition of a program into components such as modules, functions or procedures is clearly akin to the decomposition of a proof into suitable lemmas. Also, the aesthetic qualities of a nice program can provide the same kind of intellectual pleasure as a nice proof. Indeed, this is much more than an analogy since, through the so-called Curry-Howard isomorphism, programs and proofs can be both identified to terms with constructive types in the lambda-calculus. However, this deep correspondence between programs and proofs can only be understood by those familiar with completely formalized proofs which are not current practice in mathematics and is not easy to explain to students which are beginners both in mathematics and computer science. Therefore, if the analogy between programs and proofs should be exploited in education, it should be enlighted by simpler means. This paper tries to show that geometry is a field where it is possible to use mathematical concepts to better explain what programming is about and also to use programming as a constructive approach to mathematical concepts.

A first basic basic similarity between mathematics and programming is the importance of notation. It is impossible to do good mathematics without good notations and the counterpart in computer science is that it is impossible to do good programming without good programming languages. Unfortunately, this is not a common belief. But nevertheless, this is exactly why declarative languages are better for education than imperative ones. They enable to reflect the concepts used in a program in a more straighforward way just as mathematical notations are meant to reflect mathematical thinking. Also, we advocate types as an essential part of notation in programming. Types enable us to name collections of objects that play an important part in a given application. For instance, since the notion of isometry is important in geometry, there should be a corresponding type in geometrical programs and the fact that a program is able to characterize the value returned by a function as being an isometry is important in providing evidence that the computer actually performs geometric computations. Moreover types, and more specifically abstract types and also generic or polymorphic types are a key to abstraction which is clearly the essence of program organization.

This paper is based on my experience in teaching programing both at University Denis Diderot and Ecole Normale Supérieure in Paris. In particular, at University Denis Diderot, I give a programming course to first year students with two aims. The first one is to lead them to a substantial programming project and the second one is to give them some opportunity to better assimilate their mathematics curriculum through concrete manipulation of mathematical concepts. In that purpose, I chose to base the project on plane tilings, a subject which makes use of some linear algebra through the use of matrices for isometries and introduces the notion of group through the symmetry group of tilings. With more advanced students, it is possible to extend such a project to hyperbolic geometry using complex numbers and conformal transformations and to get deeper into group theory by using canonical presentations of symmetry groups.

I have used both PASCAL and CAML for these projects but of course, the latter appears more adequate with respect to the aims mentionned before. I will use CAML in the following.

2 Euclidean geometry

Modern presentations of Euclidean geometry, since Hilbert, rely on the notions of metric spaces and isometries. An isometry is one-to-one correspondence between points that preserves distances. As a consequence, they transform straight lines into straight lines. The only isometries are the identity, the translations, the rotations, the reflections (according to an axis which is a straight line) and the glide reflections which are are compositions of a reflection and a translation parallel to its axis. Moreover, it is easy to show that any isometry can be obtained as the composition of at most three reflections.

When points are represented using Cartesian coordinates, the most efficient way to represent isometries is by matrices of the form

$$\begin{pmatrix} m_{11} & m_{12} & m_{13} \\ m_{21} & m_{22} & m_{23} \\ 0 & 0 & 1 \end{pmatrix}$$

which operates on vectors

$$\begin{pmatrix} x \\ y \\ 1 \end{pmatrix}$$

representing the point with coordinates (x,y).

These matrices allow for more transformations than just isometries. In fact, they include all affine transformations and are used as such in the POSTSCRIPT language for instance. We shall introduce a type transformation for such matrices and later define a type isometry as an abstract type using the type transformation as its representation.

Since only six numbers are necessary to represent the transformations, we can use for instance a record type with six fields.

type transformation = $\{m_{11}$: float; m_{12}: float; m_{13}: float;
$\qquad\qquad\qquad\qquad m_{21}$: float; m_{22}: float; m_{23}: float$\}$;;

Points will also be represented by a record type

type point = $\{$xc: float; yc: float$\}$;;

The application of a transformation to a point is

let apply_transformation $\{m_{11}{=}a; m_{12}{=}b; m_{13}{=}c; m_{21}{=}d; m_{22}{=}e; m_{23}{=}f\}$
$\qquad\qquad\qquad\qquad \{$xc=x; yc=y$\}$
= $\{$xc = a∗x+b∗y+c ; yc = d∗x+e∗y+f$\}$;;

and the compositions of transformations is

let compose_transformations
$\quad \{m_{11}{=}a; m_{12}{=}b; m_{13}{=}c; m_{21}{=}d; m_{22}{=}e; m_{23}{=}f\}$
$\quad \{m_{11}{=}a'; m_{12}{=}b'; m_{13}{=}c'; m_{21}{=}d'; m_{22}{=}e'; m_{23}{=}f'\}$
=
$\quad \{m_{11}{=}a{∗}.a' +. b{∗}.d'; m_{12}{=}a{∗}.b' +. b{∗}.e'; m_{13}{=}a{∗}.c' +. b{∗}.f' +. c;$
$\quad m_{21}{=}d{∗}.a' +. e{∗}.d'; m_{22}{=}d{∗}.b' +. e{∗}.e'; m_{23}{=}d{∗}.c' +. e{∗}.f' +. f\}$;;

Now, the various isometries can be first introduced as functions which build transformations. For instance,

let translation (dx,dy) =
$\quad \{m_{11}{=}1.; m_{12}{=}0.; m_{13}{=}dx; m_{21}{=}0.; m_{22}{=}1.; m_{23}{=}dy\}$;;

let origin_rotation alpha =
$\quad \{m_{11}{=}\cos$ alpha ; $m_{12}{=} {-}.(\sin$ alpha$); m_{13} = 0.0$;
$\quad m_{21}{=}\sin$ alpha ; $m_{22}{=}\cos$ alpha ; $m_{23} = 0.0\}$;;

let rotation $\{$xc=x;yc=y$\}$ alpha =
$\quad$ compose_transformations (translation(x,y))
$\quad\quad$ (compose_transformations (origin_rotation alpha)
$\quad\quad\quad$ (translation$({-}.$x,${-}.$y$)))$;;

Finally, the notion of isometry will be built into an abstract type using the CAML module system which will provide the following type and functions

```
type isometry;;
identity : isometry
translation : float * float → isometry
rotation : point → float → isometry
reflection : point → point → isometry
apply_isometry : isometry → point → point
compose_isometries : isometry → isometry → isometry
```

This abstract type gives exactly what we need to put the notion of isometry to practical use. Of course, it would be nicer if that type contained logical information saying that indeed, isometries preserve distances. Here isometry is just a name. But still, the logical information is built into the functions provided with that type and we can safely associate it with the mathematical notion of isometry.

3 Hyperbolic geometry

At the axiomatic level, hyperbolic geometry [2] is obtained from Euclidean geometry by replacing the fifth postulate which says

- For some point A and some line r, not trough A, there is not more than one line through A not meeting r.

  by the following counterpart

- For some point A and some line r, not trough A, there is more than one line through A not meeting r.

It is possible to construct several models of hyperbolic geometry inside Euclidean geometry. One of them is the Poincaré disk model where hyperbolic points are points of the Euclidean plane whose distance to the origin is strictly less than 1 (the open unit disk). Hyperbolic lines are circle arcs which are orthogonal to the unit circle including diameters of the unit circle which are assimilated to circle arcs whose center is at infinity.

Through a point A there is an infinity of lines that do not intersect a given line r and exactly two "parallel" to "r" which meet r on the unit circle. Figure 1 shows the three possible relations between two lines.

In the Poincaré model, it is possible to define a notion of distance and isometries as transformations which preserve this notion of distance. The part played by reflections in Euclidean geometry is played here by inversions. An inversion with respect to a circle with center C and radius r transforms any point M into a point M' colinear with C and M and satisfying the relation $CM.CM' = r^2$. An inversion transforms the interior of the circle into its exterior and vice-versa.

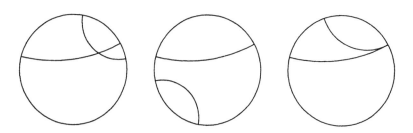

Fig. 1. Intersecting, non-intersecting and parallel lines

Points on the circle remain invariant. Figure 2 compares the effect of an inversion with the effect of an ordinary reflection which is nothing but an inversion with respect to a circle whose center is at infinity i.e. a straight line.

Inversions are easily described using complex numbers. We shall thefore assimilate points with complex numbers and represent hyperbolic points by complex numbers with modulus strictly less than one.

Fig. 2. A reflection and an inversion of the same picture

The inversion with respect to a circle with center c and radius r is the function which transforms any complex z into a complex z' defined by

$$z' - c = \frac{r^2}{\bar{z} - \bar{c}}$$

where $\bar{z}$ and $\bar{z}$ are the conjugates of z and c.

Inversions are thus special cases of (negative) homographies i.e. functions of the form

$$z' = \frac{a\bar{z} + b}{c\bar{z} + d}$$

Positive homographies are functions

$$z' = \frac{az + b}{cz + d}$$

and compositions of homographies respect the rule of signs. So for instance, hyperbolic rotations, which are obtained as the composition of two inversions according to intersecting lines, are positive homographies.

Homographies are exactly the conformal transformations i.e. transformations with preserves angles (or circles). in the Euclidean plane[1]. Hyperbolic isometries in the Poincaré model are a strict subset of conformal transformations. So we are exactly in the same situation as in Euclidean geometry. We can first define a type homography and then use it to define an abstract type isometry.

```
type homo = {ha:complex;hb:complex;hc:complex;hd:complex}
and homography = Positive of homo | Negative of homo ;;
```

The application of an homography to a complex number is for instance

```
let apply_homography h z =
  let a_h {ha=a;hb=b;hc=c;hd=d} z =
  div_cx (add_cx (mult_cx a z) b) (add_cx (mult_cx c z) d)
  in match h with Positive hom → a_h hom z
             | Negative hom → a_h hom (conjugate z);;
```

and the inversion with respect to the circle with center c and radius r is

```
let inversion c r =
  Negative {ha=c; hb=sub_cx (cx_of_float (r*.r)) (mult_cx c (conjugate c));
           hc=(cx_of_float 1.); hd= uminus_cx (conjugate c)};;
```

Finally, the notion of hyperbolic isometry will be built into an abstract type providing the following type and functions

```
type isometry;;
identity : isometry
rotation : complex → float → isometry
inversion : complex → float → isometry
apply_isometry : isometry → complex → complex
compose_isometries : isometry → isometry → isometry
```

4 Tilings

Tilings provide nice illustrations for a course in geometry and they have a strong appeal for programming students like all applications involving graphics.

---

[1] provided they satisfy $ad - bc \neq 0$.

A tiling is a regular filling of a surface with non-overlapping copies of a given pattern. Tilings have been first studied in a scientic context by cristallographers since cristals are precisely regular fillings of the 3-dimension space. They have been used previously by artists of various civilizations for decorative purposes and, in the most impresive way by the arabian civilization. In modern times, the Dutch artist M.C.Escher has produced popular tilings with animal and human patterns.

Tilings are classified according to their symmetry group, that is the isometry group that leaves them invariant. It can be shown that, if we restrict ourselves to periodic tilings (tilings that are invariant through two independent translations), then there are exactly 17 different symmetry groups i.e. 17 essentially different way of tiling the plane.

Each possible symmetry group can be defined by various sets of generators. Given a set of generators, the whole group can be obtained by composing these generators in all possible ways. Therefore, a tiling can be defined by two pieces of data:

– A pattern that will be used to fill the plane.
– A finite set of isometries which will serve as generators for the symmetry group of the tiling.

Then it can be computed by generating a suitable subset of the symmetry group and applying all transformations in this subset to the pattern to obtain its different copies.

Of course, the possible patterns strongly depends on the considered symmetry group and it should be produced with the aid of the generators. We shall not tackle this problem here. The patterns shown here are kangaroos such as the one on figure 3.

Fig. 3. A kangaroo

4.1 Representing patterns

We assume that we have a type picture for objects that can be visualized. This type should be provided by a graphics library. We should use this type to produce the image of the tiling which will be obtained by composing the various images of the basic pattern. For that purpose, we also assume that the graphics library provides a function group_pictures of type picture list → picture which enable use to produce a new picture by grouping a list of already defined pictures.

Now, what should be the type of a pattern? It is not a good choice to represent directly patterns by values of type picture because it is not clear that we would be able to apply isometries to pictures. It might be the case that a graphics library knows about Euclidean isometries but it is certainly not so for hyperbolic ones. Moreover, we might want to perform other operations to pattern that just applying geometrical transformations to them. We might want to change their color or modify some other aspect.

Therefore, we shall represent patterns as functions that produce pictures. For instance, if we are only interested in applying isometries to patterns, we might represent them as functions of type isometry → picture. Or, if we are also interested in varying colors, we might represent them as functions of type isometry * color → picture.

For instance, the pattern in figure ?? will be used in a tiling whose symmetry group contains a glide reflection with respect to a vertical axis. It will be represented as a function kang : isometry * color → picture and if glide is the aforementioned glide reflection, the figure 4 is obtained simply by writing:

group_pictures [kang (identity,gray 0.2); kang (glide,gray 0.5)];;

Fig. 4. A kangaroo and its image by a glide reflection

Tiling images are obtained from a pattern and a list of isometries. If we are not interested in varying colors, we could use the function

```
let make_tiling pattern isos =
  group_pictures (map (fun t → pattern t) isos);;
```

make_tiling : (isometry → picture) → isometry list → picture

4.2 Generating an isometry list

Now we turn to the generation of a suitable isometry list from a list of generators. This is indeed an instance of a very general process. Given a binary operation (here isometry composition) , a neutral element for that operation (here the identity isometry), and a list of elements used as generators, we want to obtain all possible products of generators. If we were using a lazy functional language, we could directly compute the infinite list of all possible products. Since we use CAML which is strict, we generate in fact all possible products of at most n generators where n is a parameter of the generating process.

As already said, this generating process is very generic. We could use the same to create the list of all multiples of a list of integers for instance using multiplication as the binary operation. It is fortunate that polymorphic type systems permit to express this process in the most abstract way. If we use PASCAL instead of CAML, we lose some opportunity to make the students feel how general this process is.

One more thing: we need to generate the isometry list in a non redundant way. This is important because otherwise, the resulting list would be too big. Therefore, the generation process should be parameterized by an equality relation. We shall use a union operation which is parameterized by an equality relation.

First, we introduce a function to perform the product of two lists according to a given binary operation:

```
let product f eq l₁ l₂ =
  let rec prod l l' =
    match l with
      [ ] → l'
    | (x::l) → union eq (map (f x) l₂) (prod l l')
  in prod l₁ [ ];;
```

product : $(\alpha \to \beta \to \gamma) \to (\gamma \to \gamma \to \text{bool}) \to \alpha$ list $\to \beta$ list $\to \gamma$ list

Then, we define a generating function by iterating the product

```
let generate f e eq l n =
  let rec gen n l₁ l₂ =
    if n=0 then l₂
    else let l₃ = product f eq l l₁
         in gen (n−1) l₃ (union eq l₃ l₂)
  in gen n [e] [e];;
```

generate : $(\alpha \to \beta \to \beta) \to \beta \to (\beta \to \beta \to \text{bool}) \to \alpha$ list $\to$ int $\to \beta$ list

Asssuming that eq_iso is an equality fonction on isometries, we obtain a generating function for an symmetry group by applying **generate** to the isometry composition, the isometry identity and this equality function

```
let generate_symmetry_group =
  generate compose_isometries identity eq_iso;;

generate_symmetry_group : isometry list → int → isometry list
```

Fig. 5. A kangaroo tiling

For instance, the tiling in figure 5 can be generated using two isometries, a glide reflection along a vertical axis and an horizontal translation. We shall assume they are defined as values

```
glide : isometry
trans : isometry
```

A monochrome tiling similar to that of figure 5 can be obtained by writing

```
let isos = generate_symmetry_group [glide;trans] n
in make_tiling kang isos;;
```

4.3 Dealing with colors

In order to obtain a colored tiling, we have to use a permutation group on a finite liste of colors which operates together with the transformation group. We assume that we have the following type and functions

type permutation;;

compose_permutations : permutation → permutation → permutation
permutation_identity : permutation

and that our pattern has type

kang : isometry * permutation → picture

We just have to use the slightly modified generating function

```
let generate_symmetry_color_group =
  generate
    (fun (tr₁,perm₁) (tr₂,perm₂)
        → (compose_isometries tr₁ tr₂, compose_permutations perm₁ perm₂))
    (identity , permutation identity)
    (fun (tr₁,_) (tr₂,_) → eq_iso tr₁ tr₂);;
```

generate_symmetry_color_group : (isometry * permutation) list
                                → int → (isometry * permutation) list

4.4 Hyperbolic tilings

There is very little to say about hyperbolic tilings since they are generated exactly in the same way. This is indeed a nice lesson for the students:

- First, they discover that there exist other geometries than the one they are used to.
- Then, they discover that, by reasoning at a sufficiently abstract level (geometric transformations) this new geometry can share many conceptual tools with the classical one.
- Finally, they understand that, if the parametricity of their programs reflects the parametricity of mathematical reasonning, then they can easily adapt their programs to new and apparently much more difficult applications.

In fact, there are differences between hyperbolic tilings and Euclidean tilings. This difference lies is the symmetry groups of tilings. For instance, the famous engraving by M.C.Escher, Circle Limit III, which is imitated in figure 6, involves a symmetry group with 3 rotations of order 3,3,4 which is impossible in the Euclidean world. However, the generating process remains exactly the same. Figure 7 uses the same group with a different pattern.

4.5 Symmetry groups and the word problem

It is possible to build on the introduction of symmetry groups to go deeper into the study of these groups. A priori, this concerns more mathematics than computer science but it is related to term rewriting systems which are clearly important at least in theoretical computer science.

Fig. 6. An imitation of Circle Limit III by Escher

When symmetry groups are generated, we are forced to introduce an equality relation on isometries in order to generate them in a non-redundant way. This equality relation is necessarily ad-hoc since isometries are represented using floating point numbers. Moreover, if the union operation is to be implemented in an efficient way, then we need an order relation on isometries and this is problematic. Therefore, it is a much cleaner approach to use a formal presentation of symmetry groups with formal generators and relations and to define the equality via an algorithm solving the word problem in the group.

It turns out that the word problem for symmetry groups of tilings has been solved first by Coxeter and Mauser [3] and then by Lechenadec [4] using term rewriting systems and the Knuth-Bendix algorithm. Lechenadec obtained canonical term rewriting systems for the various symmetry groups and therefore equality can be defined as identity of normal forms in his system.

It is possible to use these canonical systems for an efficient generation algorithm. We do not have to do any rewriting to normal form. All we have to do is dropping all elements that are not in normal form during the generation process.

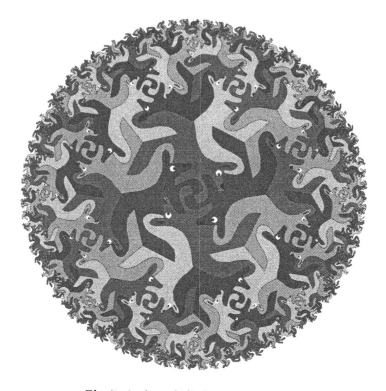

Fig. 7. An hyperbolic kangaroo tiling

5 Conclusion

I hope I have provided some evidence that geometry and more specifically the study of geometrical transformations and tilings is a field where the pleasure of doing mathematics can be combined with the pleasure of programming. When used in education, such applications should at least convince the students that the two activities have some similarities and that each can benefit from the other.

I have tried to emphasize the fact that geometry provides a good opportunity to show the students that a good organization of types, reflecting the organization of involved concepts and, above all, good abstraction facilities are keys to powerful programs.

It is my opinion that, though it is not impossible to follow such an approach with an imperative language, it is more rewarding with a functional one or maybe, more generally, a declarative one.

References

1. G. Cousineau and M. Mauny. *Approche fonctionnelle de la programmation*. Edi-science, 1995. English version to be published by Cambridge University Press in september 97.

2. H.S.M. Coxeter. *Introduction to geometry*. John Wiley and sons, 1980.

3. H.S.M. Coxeter and W.O.J. Mauser. Generators and relations for discrete groups. *Ergenisse der Mathematik und ihrer Grenzgebiete*, 14, 1965.

4. Ph. Lechenadec. *Canonical forms in finitely presented algebras*. Pitman, 1986.

Where Do I Begin? A Problem Solving Approach in Teaching Functional Programming

Simon Thompson

Computing Laboratory
University of Kent at Canterbury
S.J.Thompson@ukc.ac.uk

Abstract. This paper introduces a problem solving method for teaching functional programming, based on Polya's *How To Solve It*, an introductory investigation of mathematical method. We first present the language independent version, and then show in particular how it applies to the development of programs in Haskell. The method is illustrated by a sequence of examples and a larger case study.

Keywords. Functional programming, Haskell, palindrome recognition, Polya, problem solving.

1 Introduction

Many students take easily to functional programming, whilst others experience difficulties of one sort or another. The work reported here is the result of attempts to advise students on how to use problem solving ideas to help them design and develop programs.

Some students come to a computer science degree with considerable experience of programming in an imperative language such as Pascal or C. For these students, a functional approach forces them to look afresh at the process of programming; it is no longer possible to construct programs 'from the middle out'; instead design has to be confronted from the start. Other students come to a CS programme with no prior programming experience, and so with no 'baggage' which might encumber them. Many of these students prefer a functional approach to the imperative, but lacking the background of the experienced students need encouragement and advice about how to build programs.[1]

In this paper we report on how we try to answer our students' question '*Where do I begin?*' by talking explicitly about problem solving and what it means in programming. Beyond enabling students to program more effectively a problem solving approach has a number of other important consequences. The approach is not only beneficial in a functional programming context, as we are able to use the approach across our introductory curriculum, as reported in [1], reinforcing ideas in a disparate set of courses including imperative programming and systems analysis. It is also striking that the cycle of problem solving is very

---

[1] Further reports on instructors' experience of teaching functional programming were given at the recent Workshop in the UK [6].

close to the 'understand, plan, write and review' scheme which is recommended to students experiencing difficulties in writing essays, emphasising the fact that problem solving ability is a transferable skill.

In this paper we first review our general problem solving strategy, modelled on Polya's epoch-making *How To Solve It*, [5], which brought these ideas to prominence in mathematics some fifty years ago. This material is largely language-independent. We then go on to explore how to take these ideas into the functional domain by describing '*How to program it in Haskell*'. After looking at a sequence of examples we examine the case study of palindrome recognition, and the lessons to be learned from this example. We conclude by reviewing the future role of problem solving in functional programming and across the computer science curriculum, since the material on problem solving can also be seen as the first stage in learning software engineering, 'in the small' as it were; more details are given in [1].

I am very grateful to David Barnes and Sally Fincher with whom the cross-curricular ideas were developed, and to Jan Sellers of the Rutherford Study Centre at the University of Kent who provided support for workshops in problem solving, as well as pointing out the overlap with essay writing techniques. The Alumni Fund of the University of Kent provided funding for Jan to work with us. Finally I would like to acknowledge all the colleagues at UKC with whom I have taught functional programming, and from whom I have learned an immense amount.

2 How To Program It

Polya's *How To Solve It*, [5], contains a wealth of material about how to approach mathematical problems of various kinds. This ranges from specific hints which can be used in particular circumstances to general methodological ideas. The latter are summarised in a two-page table giving a four-stage process (or more strictly a cycle) for solving problems. In helping students to program, we have specified a similar summary of method – *How To Program It* – which is presented in Figures 1 and 2. The stages of our cycle are: understanding the problem; designing the program; writing the program and finally looking back (or 'reflection').

The table is largely self-explanatory, so we will not paraphrase it here; instead we will make some comments about its structure and how it has been used.

How To Program It has been written in a language-independent way (at least as much as the terminology of modern computing allows). In Section 3 we look at how it can be specialised for the lazy functional programming language Haskell, [4, 7]. Plainly it can also be used with other programming languages, and at the University of Kent we have used it in teaching Modula-3, [1], for instance.

Our approach emphasizes that a novice can make substantial progress in completing a programming task *before* beginning to write any program code. This is very important in demystifying the programming process for those who find it difficult. As the title of this paper suggests, getting started in the task

UNDERSTANDING THE PROBLEM

First understand the problem.

Name the program or function.

What is its type?

What are the inputs (or arguments)? What are the outputs (or results)? What is the specification of the problem?

Can the specification be satisfied? Is it insufficient? or redundant? or contradictory? What special conditions are there on the inputs and outputs?

Does the problem break into parts? It can help to draw diagrams and to write things down in pseudo-code or plain English.

DESIGNING THE PROGRAM

In designing the program you need to think about the connections between the input and the output.

If there is no immediate connection, you might have to think of auxiliary problems which would help in the solution.

You want to give yourself some sort of plan of how to write the program.

Have you seen the problem before? In a slightly different form?

Do you know a related problem? Do you know any programs or functions which could be useful?

Look at the specification. Try to find a familiar problem with the same or similar specification.

Here is a problem related to yours and solved before. Could you use it? Could you use its results? Could you use its methods? Should you introduce some auxiliary parts to the program?

If you cannot solve the proposed problem try to solve a related one. Can you imagine a more accessible related one? A more general one? A more specific one? An analogous problem?

Can you solve part of the problem? Can you get something useful from the inputs? Can you think of information which would help you to calculate the outputs? How could you change the inputs/outputs so that they were *closer* to each other?

Did you use all the inputs? Did you use the special conditions on the inputs? Have you taken into account all that the specification requires?

Fig. 1. How To Program It, Part I

WRITING YOUR PROGRAM

Writing the program means taking your design into a particular programming language.

In writing your program, make sure that you check each step of the design. Can you see clearly that each step does what it should?

You can write the program in stages. Think about the different cases into which the problem divides; in particular think about the different cases for the inputs. You can also think about computing parts of the result separately, and how to put the parts together to get the final results.

Think about how you can build programs in the language. How do you deal with different cases? With doing things in sequence? With doing things repeatedly or recursively?

You can think of solving the problem by solving it for a smaller input and using the result to get your result; this is recursion.

You also need to know the programs you have already written, and the functions built into the language or library.

Your design may call on you to solve a more general or more specific problem. Write the solutions to these; they may guide how you write the solution itself, or may indeed be used in that solution.

You should also draw on other programs you have written. Can they be used? Can they be modified? Can they guide how to build the solution?

LOOKING BACK

Examine your solution: how can it be improved?

Can you test that the program works, on a variety of arguments?

Can you think of how you might write the program differently if you had to start again?

Can you see how you might use the program or its method to build another program?

Fig. 2. How To Program It, Part II

---

can be a block for many students. For example, in the first stage of the process a student will have to clarify the problem in two complementary ways. First, the informal statement has to be clarified, and perhaps restated, giving a clear informal goal. Secondly, this should mean that the student is able to write down the name of a program or function and more importantly give a type to this artifact at this stage. While this may seem a small step, it means that misconceptions can be spotted at an early stage, and avoid a student going off in a mistaken direction.

The last observation is an example of a general point. Although we have made reflection (or 'looking back') the final stage of the process, it should permeate the whole process. At the first stage, once a type for a function has been given, it is sensible to reflect on this choice: giving some typical inputs and corresponding outputs, does the type specified actually reflect the problem? This means that a student is forced to check both their understanding of the problem and of the types of the target language.

At the design stage, students are encouraged to think about the context of the problem, and the ways in which this can help the solution of the problem itself. We emphasise that programs can be re-used either by calling them or by modifying their definitions, as well as the ideas of specialisation and generalisation. Generalisation is particularly apt in the modern functional context, in which polymorphism and higher-order functions allow libraries of general functions to be written with little overhead (in contrast to the C++ Standard Template Library, say).

Implementation ideas can be discussed in a more concrete way in the context of a particular language. The ideas of this section are next discussed in the context of Haskell by means of a succession of examples in Section 3 and by a lengthier case study in Section 4. Note that the design stage of the case study is essentially language independent.

Students are encouraged to reflect on what they have achieved throughout the problem solving cycle. As well as testing their finished programs, pencil and paper evaluation of Haskell programs is particularly effective, and we expect students to use this as a way of discovering how their programs work.

3   Programming it in Haskell

As we saw in the previous section, it is more difficult to give useful language-independent advice about how to write programs than it is about how to design them. It is also easier to understand the generalities of *How To Program It* in the context of particular examples. We therefore provide students with particular language-specific advice in tabular form. These tables allow us to

- give examples to illustrate the design and programming stages of the process, and
- discuss the programming process in a much more specific way.

The full text of *Programming it in Haskell* is available on the World Wide Web, [9]. Rather than reproduce it here, in the rest of this section we look at some of the examples and the points in the process which they illustrate.

Problem: find the maximum of three integers

A first example is to find the maximum of three integers. In our discussion we link various points in the exposition to the four stages of *How To Program It*.

Understanding the problem Even in a problem of this simplicity there can be some discussion of the specification: what is to be done in the case when two (or three) of the integers are maximal? This is usually resolved by saying that the common value should be returned, but the important learning point here is that the discussion takes place. Also one can state the name and type, beginning the solution:

```
maxThree :: Int -> Int -> Int -> Int
```

Designing and writing the program More interesting points can be made in the design stage. Given a function `max` to find the maximum of two integers,

```
max :: Int -> Int -> Int
max a b
  | a>=b       = a
  | otherwise  = b
```

this can be used in two ways. It can form a model for the solution of the problem:

```
maxThree a b c
  | a>=b && a>=c   = a
  |    ....
```

or it can itself be used in a solution

```
maxThree a b c = max (max a b) c
```

It is almost universally the case that novices produce the first solution rather than the second, so this provides a useful first lesson in the existence of design choices, guided by the resources available (in this case the function `max`). Although it is difficult to interpret exactly why this is the case, it can be taken as an indication that novice students find it more natural to tackle a problem in a single step, rather than stepping back from the problem and looking at it more strategically. This lends support to introducing these problem solving ideas explicitly, rather than hoping that they will be absorbed 'osmotically'.

We also point out that given `maxThree` it is straightforward to generalise to cases of finding the minimum of three numbers, the maximum of four, and so on.

Looking back Finally, this is a non-trivial example for program testing. A not uncommon student error here is to make the inequalities strict, thus

```
maxThreeErr a b c
  | a>b && a>c    = a
  | b>c && b>a    = b
  | otherwise     = c
```

This provides a discussion point in how test data are chosen; the vast majority of student test data sets do not reveal the error. A systematic approach should produce the data which indicate the error – a and b jointly maximal – and indeed the cause of error links back to the initial clarification of the specification.

Problem: add the positive numbers in a list

We use this example to show how to break down the process of *designing* and *writing* a program – stages two and three of our four-step process – into a number of simpler steps. The function we require is

```
addPos :: [Int] -> Int
```

We first consider the design of the equations which describe the function. A paradigm here if we are to define the function from scratch is *primitive recursion* (or structural recursion) over the list argument. In doing this we adopt the general scheme

```
addPos []    = ...
addPos (a:x) = ... addPos x ...
```

in which we have do define the value at [] outright and the value at (a:x) from the value at x. Completing the first equation gives

```
addPos []    = 0
```

The (a:x) case requires more thought. Guidance can often come from looking at examples. Here we take lists

```
[-4,3,2,-1]
[2,3,2,-1]
```

which respectively give sums 0 and 6. In the first case the head does not contribute to the sum; in the second it does. This suggests the case analysis

```
addPos (a:x)
  | a>0       = ...
  | otherwise = ...
```

from which point in development the answer can be seen. The point of this example is less to develop the particular function than to illustrate how the process works.

The example is also enlightening for the other design possibilities it offers by way of *looking back* at the problem. In particularly when students are acquainted with `filter` and `foldr` the explicit definition

```
addPos = foldr (+) 0 . filter (>0)
```

is possible. The definition here reflects very clearly its top-down design.

Further examples

Other examples we have used include

Maximum of a list This is similar to `addPos`, but revisits the questions raised by the `maxThree` example. In particular, will the `max` function be used in the definition?

Counting how many times a maximum occurs among three numbers
This gives a reasonable example in which local definitions (in a `where` clause) naturally structure a definition with a number of parts.

Deciding whether one list is a sublist of another This example naturally gives rise to an auxiliary function during its development.

Summing integers up to n This can give rise to the generalisation of summing numbers from `m` to `n`.

The discussions thus far have been about algorithms; there is a wealth of material which addresses data and object design, the former of which we address in [9].

4 Case study: palindromes

The problem is to recognise palindromes, such as

`"Madam I'm Adam"`

It is chosen as an example since even for a more confident student it requires some thought before implementation can begin. Once the specification is clarified it presents a non-trivial design space in which we can illustrate how choices between alternative designs can take place. Indeed, it is a useful example for small-group work since it is likely that different groups will produce substantially different initial design ideas. It is also an example in which a variety of standard functions can be used.

We address the main ideas in this section; further details are available on the World Wide Web [8].

Understanding the problem

The problem is stated in a deliberately vague way. A palindrome can be identified as a string which is the same read forwards or backwards, so long as

(1) we disregard the punctuation (punctuation marks and spaces) in the string;
(2) we disregard the case (upper or lower: that is capital or small) of the letters in the string.

Requirement (2) is plainly unambiguous, whilst (1) will need to be revisited at the implementation stage.

Overall design

The palindrome example lends itself to a wide choice of designs. The **simpler problem** in which there is no punctuation and all letters in lower case can be helpful in two ways. It can either form a *guide* about how to write the full solution, or be *used* as a part of that solution. The choice here provides a useful discussion point.

Design: the simpler problem

Possible designs which can emerge here may be classified in two different ways.

- Is the string handled as a single entity, or split into two parts?
- Is comparison made between strings, or between individual characters?

These choices generate these outline designs:

- The string is reversed and compared with itself;
- the string is split, one part reversed and the result compared with the other part;
- the first and last characters are compared, and if equal are removed and an iteration or a recursion is performed;
- the string is split, one part reversed and the strings are then compared one character at a time.

Again, it is important for students to be able both to see the possibilities available, and to discuss their relative merits (in the context of the implementation language). Naturally, too, there needs to be a comparison of the different ways in which the string is represented.

Design: the full problem

Assuming we are to use the solution to the simpler problem in solving the full problem, we reach our goal by writing a function which removes punctuation and changes all upper case letters to lower case. Here again we can see an opportunity to split the task in two, and also to discuss the order in which the two operations are performed: do we remove punctuation before or after converting letters to lower case? This allows a discussion of relative efficiency.

Writing the program

At this point we need to revisit the specification and to make plain what is meant by punctuation. This is not clear from the example given in the specification, and we can choose either to be proscriptive and disallow everything but letters and digits, or to be permissive and to say that punctuation consists of a particular set of characters.

There are more specific implementation decisions to be taken here; these reinforce the discussions in Section 3. In particular there is substantial scope for using built-in or library functions.

We give a full implementation of the palindrome recognition problem in Figure 3.

```
palin :: String -> Bool

palin st = simplePalin (disregard st)

simplePalin :: String -> Bool

simplePalin st = (rev st == st)

rev :: String -> String

rev []     = []
rev (a:st) = rev st ++ [a]

disregard :: String -> String

disregard st = change (remove st)

remove :: String -> String
change :: String -> String

remove [] = []
remove (a:st)
  | notPunct a  = a : remove st
  | otherwise   =     remove st

notPunct ch = isAlpha ch || isDigit ch

change [] = []
change (a:st) = convert a : change st

convert :: Char -> Char

convert ch
  | isCap ch      = toEnum (fromEnum ch + offset)
  | otherwise     = ch
    where
    offset = fromEnum 'a' - fromEnum 'A'

isCap :: Char -> Bool

isCap ch = 'A' <= ch && ch <= 'Z'
```

Fig. 3. Recognising palindromes in Haskell

Looking back

Using the approach suggested here, students see that the solution which they have chosen represents one branch in a tree of choices. Their solution can be evaluated against other possibilities, including those written by other students. There is also ample scope for discussion of testing in this problem.

For instance, the solution given in Figure 3 can give rise to numerous discussion points.

- No higher order functions are used in the solution; we would expect to revisit the example after covering HOFs to reveal that `change` is `map convert` and that `remove` is `filter notPunct`.
- In a similar way we would expect to revisit the solution and discuss incorporating function-level definitions such as

  ```
  palin = simplePalin . disregard
  ```

  This would also apply to `disregard` itself.
- Some library functions have been used; digits and letters are recognised by `isDigit` and `isAlpha`.
- An alternative definition of `disregard` is given by

  ```
  disregard st = remove (change st)
  ```

  and other solutions are provided by implementing the two operations in a single function definition, rather than as a composition of two separate pieces of functionality.
- We have chosen the proscriptive definition of punctuation, considering only letters and digits to be significant.

5 Conclusion

In this paper we have given an explicit problem solving method for beginning (functional) programmers, motivated by the desire to equip them with tools to enable them to write complex programs in a disciplined way. The method also gives weaker students the confidence to proceed by showing them the ways in which a seemingly intractable problem can be broken down into simpler parts which can be solved separately. As well as providing a general method we think it crucial to illustrate the method by examples and case studies – this latter approach is not new, see [2] for a very effective account of using case studies in teaching Pascal.

To conclude, it is worth noting that numerous investigations into mathematical method were stimulated by Polya's work. Most prominent are Lakatos' investigations of the roles of proof and counterexample, [3], which we believe have useful parallels for teachers and students of computer science. We intend to develop this correspondence further in the future.

References

1. David Barnes, Sally Fincher, and Simon Thompson. Introductory problem solving in computer science. In *CTC97, Dublin*, 1997.
2. Michael Clancy and Marcia Linn. *Designing Pascal Solutions: Case studies using data structures*. Computer Science Press, W. H. Freeman and Co., 1996.
3. Imre Lakatos. *Proofs and Refuations: The Logic of Mathematical Discovery*. Cambridge University Press, 1976. Edited by John Worrall and Elie Zahar.
4. John Peterson and Kevin Hammond, editors. *Report on the Programming Language Haskell, Version 1.3*.
   http://haskell.cs.yale.edu/haskell-report/haskell-report.html, 1996.
5. G. Polya. *How To Solve It*. Princeton University Press, second edition, 1957.
6. Teaching functional programming: Opportunities & difficulties.
   http://www.ukc.ac.uk/CSDN/conference/96/Report.html, September 1996.
7. Simon Thompson. *Haskell: The Craft of Functional Programming*. Addison-Wesley, 1996.
8. Simon Thompson. Problem solving: recognising palindromes.
   http://www.ukc.ac.uk/computer_science/Haskell_craft/palindrome.html, 1996.
9. Simon Thompson. Programming it in Haskell.
   http://www.ukc.ac.uk/computer_science/Haskell_craft/ProgInHaskell.html, 1996.

Teaching Functional and Logic Programming with a Single Computation Model

Michael Hanus

Informatik II, RWTH Aachen, D-52056 Aachen, Germany
hanus@informatik.rwth-aachen.de

Abstract. Functional and logic programming are often taught in different courses so that students often do not understand the relationships between these declarative programming paradigms. This is mainly due to the different underlying computation models—deterministic reduction and lazy evaluation in functional languages, and non-deterministic search in logic languages. We show in this paper that this need not be the case. Taking into account recent developments in the integration of functional and logic programming, it is possible to teach the ideas of modern functional languages like Haskell and logic programming on the basis of a single computation model. From this point of view, logic programming is considered as an extension of functional programming where ground expressions are extended to contain also free variables. We describe this computation model, the structure of a course based on it, and draw some conclusions from the experiences with such a course.

Keywords: Functional logic languages, lazy evaluation, narrowing, residuation, integration of paradigms

1   Introduction

Declarative programming is motivated by the fact that a higher programming level using powerful abstraction facilities leads to reliable and maintainable software. Thus, declarative programming languages are based on mathematical formalisms and completely abstract from many details of the concrete hardware and the implementation of the programs on this hardware. Since declarative programs strongly correspond to formulae of mathematical calculi, they simplify the reasoning (e.g., verification w.r.t. non-executable specifications), provide freedom in the implementation (e.g., use of parallel architectures), and reduce the program development time in comparison to classical imperative languages.

Unfortunately, declarative programming is currently split into two main fields based on different formalisms, namely functional programming (lambda calculus) and logic programming (predicate logic). As a consequence, functional and logic programming are usually taught in different courses so that students often do not understand the relationships between these declarative programming paradigms. This is mainly due to the different underlying computation models—deterministic reduction and lazy evaluation in functional languages, and non-deterministic search in logic languages. On the other hand, functional and logic languages have a common kernel and can be seen as different facets of a single idea. For instance, the use of algebraic data types instead of pointer structures, and the definition of local comprehensible cases by pattern matching and local definitions instead of complex procedures are emphasized in functional as well as logic programming. However, these commonalities are often hidden by the differences in the computation models and the application areas of these languages. The advantages of logic languages are in areas where computing with partial information and non-deterministic search is important (data bases, knowledge-based systems, optimization problems), where functional languages emphasize the improved abstraction and structuring facilities using referential transparency, higher-order functions and lazy evaluation. If students attend one course on functional programming and another course on logic programming, they know programming in the single languages, but it is often not clear for them that these are different facets of a common idea. As a result, they may not know how to choose the best of both worlds in order to solve a particular application problem.

In this paper we show how to overcome this problem. Our approach is the choice of a single language, an integrated functional logic language, for teaching functional and logic programming. We show that it is possible to teach the ideas of modern functional languages like Haskell and logic programming on the basis of a single language, provided that recent developments in the integration of functional and logic programming are taken into account. For this purpose we use the multi-paradigm language Curry [9, 11] which amalgamates functional, logic, and concurrent computation techniques. Since Curry subsumes many aspects of modern lazy functional languages like Haskell, it can be used to teach functional programming techniques without any reference to logic programming. Logic programming can be introduced at a later point as an extension of functional programming where ground expressions are extended to contain also free variables. The requirement to compute values for such free variables leads naturally to the introduction of non-determinism and search techniques. Curry's operational semantics is based on a single computation model, described in [9], which combines lazy reduction of expressions with a possibly non-deterministic binding of free variables occurring in expressions. Thus, pure functional programming, pure logic programming, and concurrent (logic) programming are obtained as particular restrictions of this model. Moreover, due to the use of an integrated functional logic language, we can choose the best of the two worlds in application programs. For instance, input/output (implemented in logic languages by side effects) can be handled with the monadic I/O concept [18] in a declarative way. Similarly, many other impure features of Prolog (e.g., arithmetic, cut) can be avoided by the use of functions.

In the next section, we introduce some basic notions and motivate the basic computation model of Curry. Some features of Curry are discussed in Section 3. Section 4 describes a course on declarative programming based on Curry's computational model. Section 5 contains our conclusions.

2   A Unified Model for Declarative Programming

This section introduces some basic notions of term rewriting [7] and functional logic programming [8] and recalls the computation model of Curry. In contrast to [9], we provide a more didactically oriented motivation of this computation model.

As mentioned above, a common idea of functional as well as logic programming is the use of algebraic data types instead of pointer structures (e.g., list terms instead of linked lists). Thus, the computational domain of declarative languages is a set of *terms* constructed from constants and data constructors. *Functions* (or *predicates* in logic programming, but we consider predicates as Boolean functions for the sake of simplicity) operate on terms and map terms to terms.

Formally, we consider a *signature* partitioned into a set C of *constructors* and a set $\mathcal{F}$ of (defined) *functions* or *operations*.[1] We write $c/n \in C$ and $f/n \in \mathcal{F}$ for n-ary constructor and function symbols, respectively. A constructor c with arity 0 is also called a *constant*.[2]

We denote by $\mathcal{X}$ a set of variables (with elements x, y). An *expression* (*data term*) is a *variable* $x \in \mathcal{X}$ or an application $\varphi(e_1, \ldots, e_n)$ where $\varphi/n \in C \cup \mathcal{F}$ ($\varphi/n \in C$) and $e_1, \ldots, e_n$ are expressions (data terms).[3] We denote by $\mathcal{T}(C \cup \mathcal{F}, \mathcal{X})$ and $\mathcal{T}(C, \mathcal{X})$ the set of all expressions and data terms, respectively. $\mathcal{V}ar(e)$ denotes the set of variables occurring in an expression e. An expression e is called *ground* if $\mathcal{V}ar(e) = \emptyset$. A *pattern* is an expression of the form $f(t_1, \ldots, t_n)$ where each variable occurs only once, $f/n \in \mathcal{F}$, and $t_1, \ldots, t_n \in \mathcal{T}(C, \mathcal{X})$. A *head normal form* is a variable or an expression of the form $c(e_1, \ldots, e_n)$ with $c/n \in C$.

A *position* p is a sequence of positive integers identifying a subexpression. $e|_p$ denotes the *subterm* or *subexpression* of e at position p, and $e[e']_p$ denotes the result of *replacing the subterm* $e|_p$ by the expression e' (see [7] for details).

A *substitution* is a mapping $\mathcal{X} \to \mathcal{T}(C \cup \mathcal{F}, \mathcal{X})$, where id denotes the identity substitution. Substitutions are extended to morphisms on expressions by $\sigma(\varphi(e_1, \ldots, e_n)) = \varphi(\sigma(e_1), \ldots, \sigma(e_n))$ for every expression $\varphi(e_1, \ldots, e_n)$. A substitution σ is called a *unifier* of two expressions e_1 and e_2 if $\sigma(e_1) = \sigma(e_2)$.

A *(declarative) program* $\mathcal{P}$ is a set of *rules* $l = r$ where l is a pattern and $\mathcal{V}ar(r) \subseteq \mathcal{V}ar(l)$. l and r are called left-hand side and right-hand side, respectively.[4] A rule is called a *variant* of another rule if it is obtained by a unique replacement of variables by other variables. In order to ensure well-definedness of functions, we require that $\mathcal{P}$ contains only trivial overlaps, i.e., if $l_1 = r_1$ and $l_2 = r_2$ are variants of rewrite rules and σ is a unifier for l_1 and l_2, then $\sigma(r_1) = \sigma(r_2)$ (*weak orthogonality*).

Example 1. If natural numbers are data terms built from the constructors 0 and s, we define the addition and the predicate "less than or equal to" as follows:

$$
\begin{aligned}
0 + y &= y \\
s(x) + y &= s(x+y)
\end{aligned}
\qquad\qquad
\begin{aligned}
0 \leqslant x &= \text{true} \\
s(x) \leqslant 0 &= \text{false} \\
s(x) \leqslant s(y) &= x \leqslant y
\end{aligned}
$$

---

[1] We omit the types of the constructors and functions in this section since they are not relevant for the computation model. Note, however, that Curry is typed language with a Hindley/Milner-like polymorphic type system (see Section 3).

[2] Note that elementary built-in types like truth values (true, false), integers, or characters can also be considered as sets with (infinitely) many constants.

[3] We do not consider partial applications in this part since it is not relevant for the computation model. Such higher-order features are discussed in Section 3.

[4] For the sake of simplicity, we consider only unconditional rewrite rules in the main part of this paper. An extension to conditional rules is described in Section 3.

Since the left-hand sides are pairwise non-overlapping, the functions are well defined. □

From a functional point of view, we are interested in computing *values* of expressions, where a value does not contain function symbols (i.e., it is a data term) and should be equivalent (w.r.t. the program rules) to the initial expression. The computation of a value can be done by applying rules from left to right. For instance, we can compute the value of s(s(0))+s(0) by applying the rules for addition to this expression:

$$\mathtt{s(s(0))+s(0)} \rightarrow \mathtt{s(s(0)+s(0))} \rightarrow \mathtt{s(s(0+s(0)))} \rightarrow \mathtt{s(s(s(0)))}$$

Formally, a *reduction step* is an application of a rule $l=r$ to the subterm (*redex*) $t|_p$, i.e., $t \rightarrow s$ if $s = t[\sigma(r)]_p$ for some substitution σ with $\sigma(l) = t|_p$ (i.e., the left-hand side l of the selected rule must *match* the subterm $t|_p$).

In contrast to imperative languages, where the algorithmic control is explicitly contained in the programs by the use of various control structures, declarative languages abstract from the control issue since a program consists of rules and does not contain explicit information about the order to apply the rules. This makes the reasoning about declarative programs easier (program analysis, transformation, or verification) and provides more freedom for the implementor (e.g., transforming call-by-need into call-by-value, implementation on parallel architectures). On the other hand, a concrete programming language must provide a precise model of computation to the programmer. Thus, we can distinguish between different classes of functional languages. In an *eager functional language*, the selected redex in a reduction step is always an innermost redex, i.e., the redex is a ground pattern, where in *lazy functional languages* the selected redex is an outermost one. Innermost reduction may not compute a value of an expression in the presence of nonterminating rules, i.e., innermost reduction is not normalizing (we call a reduction strategy *normalizing* iff it always computes a value of an expression if it exists). Thus, we consider in the following outermost reduction, since it allows the computation with infinite data structures and provides more modularity by separating control aspects [13].

A subtle point in the definition of a lazy evaluation strategy is the selection of the "right" outermost redex. For instance, consider the rules of Example 1 together with the rule f = f. Then the expression 0+0≤f has two outermost redexes, namely 0+0 and f. If we select the first one, we compute the value true after one further outermost reduction step. However, if we select the redex f, we run into an infinite reduction sequence instead of computing the value. Thus, it is important to know which outermost redex is selected. Most lazy functional languages choose the leftmost outermost redex which is implemented by translating pattern matching into case expressions [23]. On the other hand, this may not be the best possible choice since leftmost outermost reduction is in general not normalizing (e.g., take the last example but swap the arguments of ≤ in the rules and the initial expression). It is well known that we can obtain a normalizing reduction strategy by reducing in each step a needed redex [12]. Although the computation of a needed redex is undecidable in general, there are relevant subclasses of programs where needed redexes can be effectively computed. For instance, if functions are inductively defined on the structure of data terms (so-called *inductively sequential functions* [3]), a needed redex can be simply computed by pattern matching. This is the basis of our computation model.

For this purpose, we organize all rules of a function in a hierarchical structure called definitional tree [3].[5] $\mathcal{T}$ is a *definitional tree with pattern* π iff the depth of $\mathcal{T}$ is finite and one of the following cases holds:

$\mathcal{T} = rule(l = r)$, where $l = r$ is a variant of a program rule such that $l = \pi$.

$\mathcal{T} = branch(\pi, p, \mathcal{T}_1, \ldots, \mathcal{T}_k)$, where p is a position of a variable in π, $c_1, \ldots, c_k$ are different constructors ($k > 0$), and, for all $i = 1, \ldots, k$, $\mathcal{T}_i$ is a definitional tree with pattern $\pi[c_i(x_1, \ldots, x_n)]_p$, where n is the arity of c_i and $x_1, \ldots, x_n$ are new variables.

A *definitional tree of an n-ary function* f is a definitional tree $\mathcal{T}$ with pattern $f(x_1, \ldots, x_n)$, where $x_1, \ldots, x_n$ are distinct variables, such that for each rule $l = r$ with $l = f(t_1, \ldots, t_n)$ there is a node $rule(l' = r')$ in $\mathcal{T}$ with l variant of l'. In the following, we write $pat(\mathcal{T})$ for the pattern of a definitional tree $\mathcal{T}$, and DT for the set of all definitional trees. A function is called *inductively sequential* iff there exists a definitional tree for it. A program is inductively sequential if all defined functions are inductively sequential.

For instance, the predicate $\leqslant$ defined in Example 1 is inductively sequential, and a definitional tree for $\leqslant$ is (we underline the case variable in the pattern of each *branch* node):

$$branch(\underline{x1} \leqslant x2, 1, rule(0 \leqslant x2 = \text{true}),$$
$$branch(s(x) \leqslant \underline{x2}, 2, \; rule(s(x) \leqslant 0 \quad = \text{false}),$$
$$rule(s(x) \leqslant s(y) = x \leqslant y \;)))$$

Intuitively, a definitional tree of a function specifies the strategy to evaluate a call to this function. If the tree is a *rule* node, we apply the rule. If it is a *branch* node, it is necessary to evaluate the subterm at the specified position (the so-called *needed* subterm) to head normal form in order to commit to one of the branches. Thus, in order to evaluate the expression 0+0⩽f w.r.t. the previous definitional tree, the top branch node requires that the first subterm 0+0 must be evaluated to head normal form (in this case: 0) in order to commit to the first branch.

Such a reduction strategy has the following advantages:

1. The strategy is normalizing, i.e., it always computes a value if it exists [3].
2. The strategy is independent on the order of rules. Note that pattern matching in traditional lazy functional languages implemented by case expressions is independent on the order of rules only for *uniform* programs [23] which is a strict subclass of inductively sequential programs.[6]

---

[5] We could also introduce our strategy by compiling all rules of a function into a case expression [23]. However, the use of definitional trees has the advantage that the structure of rules is not destroyed and the trees can be easily extended to more general classes of programs which become relevant later.

[6] *Uniform functions* are those functions where a definitional tree with a strict left-to-right order in the positions of the branches exists.

3. The definitional trees can be automatically generated from the left-hand sides of the rules [9] (similarly to the compilation of pattern matching into case expressions), i.e., there is no need for the programmer to explicitly specify the trees.

4. There is a strong equivalence between reduction with definitional trees and reduction with case expressions since definitional trees can be simply translated into case expressions [10]. However, reduction with definitional trees can be easily extended to more general strategies, as can be seen in the following.

Inductively sequential functions have the property that there is a single argument in the left-hand sides which distinguishes the different rules. In particular, functions defined by rules with overlapping left-hand sides, like the "parallel-or"

```
true ∨ x       = true
    x ∨ true   = true
false ∨ false = false
```

are not inductively sequential. However, it is fairly easy to extend definitional trees to cover also such functions. For this purpose, we introduce a further kind of nodes: a definitional tree $\mathcal{T}$ with pattern π can also have the form $or(\mathcal{T}_1, \mathcal{T}_2)$ where $\mathcal{T}_1$ and $\mathcal{T}_2$ are definitional trees with pattern π.[7] It is easy to see that a definitional tree with or nodes can be constructed for each defined function (see [9] for a concrete algorithm). For instance, a definitional tree for the parallel-or is

$$or(branch(\underline{x1} \vee x2, 1, rule(\texttt{true} \vee \texttt{x2} = \texttt{true}),$$
$$branch(\texttt{false} \vee \underline{x2}, 2, rule(\texttt{false} \vee \texttt{false} = \texttt{false}))),$$
$$branch(x1 \vee \underline{x2}, 2, rule(\texttt{x1} \vee \texttt{true} = \texttt{true})))$$

The corresponding extension of the reduction strategy is a more subtle point. One possibility is the parallel reduction of the redexes determined by the different or branches of the tree. This is a deterministic and normalizing reduction strategy [3, 19] but requires some effort in the implementation. Since our computation model must include some kind of non-determinism in order to cover logic programming languages, we take a simpler strategy which non-deterministically computes all alternatives for or nodes, i.e., the evaluation strategy maps expressions into sets of expressions (see Appendix A for the precise formal definition). The solution taken in most lazy functional languages, i.e., the processing of overlapping rules in sequential order, is not considered since it destroys the equational reading of rules (i.e., modularity is lost since the rules cannot be understood independently).

Up to now, we have only considered functional computations where ground expressions are reduced to some value. In logic languages, the initial expression (usually an expression of Boolean type, called a *goal*) may contain free variables. A logic programming system should find values for these variables such that the goal is reducible to **true**. Fortunately, it requires only a slight extension of the reduction strategy introduced so far to cover non-ground expressions and variable instantiation (which also shows that the difference between functional and logic programming is not so large). Remember that there exists no reduction step if

---

[7] For the sake of simplicity, we consider only binary or nodes. The extension to more than two subtrees is straightforward.

a needed subterm is a free variable. Since the value of this variable is needed in order to proceed the computation, we non-deterministically bind the variable to the constructor required in the subtrees. For instance, if the function f is defined by the rules

    f(a) = c
    f(b) = d

(where a, b, c, d are constants), then the expression f(x) with the free variable x is evaluated to c or d if x is bound to a or b, respectively.

Unfortunately, one of the most important aspects, namely the instantiation of free variables, is not explicitly shown by the computation of values. Thus, we have to change our computational domain. Due to the presence of free variables in expressions, an expression may be reduced to different values by binding the free variables to different terms. In functional programming, one is interested in the computed *value*, whereas logic programming has the interest in the different bindings (*answers*). Thus, we define for our integrated framework an *answer expression* as a pair $\sigma \,[]\, e$ consisting of a substitution σ (the answer computed so far) and an expression e. An answer expression $\sigma \,[]\, e$ is *solved* if e is a data term. We sometimes omit the identity substitution in answer expressions, i.e., we write e instead of $id \,[]\, e$ if it is clear from the context.

Since more than one answer may exist for expressions containing free variables, in general, initial expressions are reduced to disjunctions of answer expressions. Thus, a *disjunctive expression* is a (multi-)set of answer expressions $\{\sigma_1 \,[]\, e_1, \ldots, \sigma_n \,[]\, e_n\}$. The set of all disjunctive expressions is denoted by $\mathcal{D}$, which is the *computational domain* of Curry.

For instance, if we consider the previous example, the evaluation of f(x) together with the different bindings for x is reflected by the following non-deterministic computation step:

$$f(x) \;\rightarrow\; \{\{x \mapsto a\} \,[]\, c \,,\; \{x \mapsto b\} \,[]\, d\}$$

For the sake of readability, we write the latter disjunctive expression in the form {x=a}c | {x=b}d. Similarly, the expression f(b) is reduced to d (which abbreviates a disjunctive expression with one element and the identity substitution).

A single *computation step* performs a reduction in exactly one expression of a disjunction (e.g., in the leftmost unsolved expression). This expression is reduced (with a possible variable instantiation) according to our strategy described so far. If the program is inductively sequential, i.e., the definitional trees do not contain *or* nodes, then this strategy is equivalent to the *needed narrowing* strategy [4]. Needed narrowing enjoys several optimality properties: every reduction step is needed, i.e., necessary to compute the final result, it computes the shorted possible derivations (if common subterms are shared) and a minimal set of solutions, and it is fully deterministic on ground expressions, i.e., in the functional programming case. If some definitional trees contain *or* nodes, optimality is lost (however, it is still optimal on the inductively sequential parts of the program), but the resulting strategy is sound and complete in the sense of functional and logic programming, i.e., all values and answers are computed [5].

The strategy described so far covers functional logic languages with a sound and complete operational semantics (i.e., based on narrowing [8]). However, it is still too restrictive for a general course on modern declarative languages due to the following reasons:

1. Narrowing and guessing of free variables should not be applied to all functions, since some functions (defined on recursive data structures) may not terminate if particular arguments are unknown.
2. The computation model requires the explicit definition of all functions by program rules. It is not clear how to connect primitive (external, predefined) functions where the rules are not explicitly given, like arithmetic, I/O etc.
3. Modern logic languages provide flexible selection rules (concurrent computations based on the synchronization on free variables).

All these features can be easily supported by allowing the delay of function calls if a particular argument is not instantiated. Thus, we allow the suspension of a function call if the value of some needed argument is unknown. For this purpose we extend the definition of *branch* nodes by an additional flag, i.e. a *branch* node has the form $branch(\pi, p, r, \mathcal{T}_1, \ldots, \mathcal{T}_k)$ with $r \in \{rigid, flex\}$. A *flex* annotation is treated as before, but a *rigid* annotation specifies that the evaluation of the function call is delayed if the branch argument is a free variable.

Since function calls may suspend, we need a mechanism to specify concurrent computations. For this purpose, we introduce a final extension of definitional trees: a definitional tree $\mathcal{T}$ with pattern π can also have the form $and(\mathcal{T}_1, \mathcal{T}_2)$ where the definitional trees $\mathcal{T}_1$ and $\mathcal{T}_2$ have the same pattern π and contain the same set of rules. An *and* node specifies the necessity to evaluate more than one argument position. The corresponding operational behavior is to try to evaluate one of these arguments. If this is not possible since the function calls in this argument are delayed, we proceed by trying to evaluate the other argument. This generalizes concurrent computation models for residuating logic programs [1, 21] to functional logic programs. For instance, the *concurrent conjunction* $\wedge$ of constraints[8] is defined by the single rule

$$\texttt{valid} \wedge \texttt{valid} = \texttt{valid} \qquad (R_\wedge)$$

together with the definitional tree

$$and(branch(\underline{x1} \wedge x2, 1, rigid, branch(\texttt{valid} \wedge \underline{x2}, 2, rigid, rule(R_\wedge))),$$
$$branch(x1 \wedge \underline{x2}, 2, rigid, branch(\underline{x1} \wedge \texttt{valid}, 1, rigid, rule(R_\wedge))))$$

Due to the *and* node in this tree, an expression of the form $e_1 \wedge e_2$ is evaluated by an attempt to evaluate e_1. If the evaluation of e_1 suspends, an evaluation step is applied to e_2. If a variable responsible to the suspension of e_1 was bound during the last step, the left expression will be evaluated in the subsequent step. Thus, we obtain a concurrent behavior with an interleaving semantics.

The complete specification of this computation model is summarized in Appendix A.

---

[8] The auxiliary constructor `valid` denotes the result value of a solved constraint. In terms of our computation model, the equational constraint (cf. Section 3) `s(x)=s(s(0))` is reduced to the answer expression `{x=s(0)}valid`.

3 Curry: A Multi-Paradigm Declarative Language

Curry [9, 11] is a multi-paradigm declarative language aiming to integrate functional, logic, and concurrent programming paradigms. Curry's operational semantics is based on the computation model motivated and explained in the previous section. The operational behavior of each function is specified by its definitional tree which is automatically generated from the left-hand sides of the rewrite rules using a left-to-right pattern matching algorithm [9]. Non-Boolean functions are annotated with *rigid* branches, and predicates are annotated with *flex* branches (there are compiler pragmas to override these defaults; moreover, definitional trees can also be explicitly provided similarly to type annotations). This has the consequence that the operational behavior is nearly identical to lazy functional languages if the logic programming features are not used, and identical to logic programming if only predicates are defined. Thus, Curry is ideal to teach the concepts of functional and logic programming languages in a single course.

Beyond this computation model, Curry provides a parametrically polymorphic type system (the current implementation has a type inference algorithm for a Hindley/Milner-like type system; the extension to Haskell-like type classes is planned for a future version), modules, monadic I/O [18] etc. Basic arithmetic is provided by considering integer values, like "42" or "-10", as constants, and the usual operations on integers as primitive functions with *rigid* arguments, i.e., they are delayed until all arguments are known constants. For instance, the expression 3+5 is reduced to 8, whereas x+y is delayed until x and y are bound by some other part of the program. Thus, they can act as passive constraints [2] providing for better constraint solvers than in pure logic programming [22] (e.g., by transforming "generate-and-test" into "test-and-generate"). Conceptually, primitive functions can be considered as defined by an infinite set of rules which provides a declarative reading for such functions [6]. In a similar way, any other external (side-effect free!) function can be connected to Curry.

Since functional logic languages are often used to solve equations between expressions containing defined functions, the notion of *equality* needs particular attention. It is well known (e.g., [16]) that the mathematical notion of equality (i.e., least congruence relation containing all instances of program rules) is not reasonable in the presence of nonterminating functions. In this context, the only sensible notion of equality, which is also used in functional languages, is *strict equality*, i.e., an *equational constraint* $e_1=e_2$ is satisfied if both sides e_1 and e_2 are reducible to a same data term. Operationally, an equational constraint $e_1=e_2$ is solved by evaluating e_1 and e_2 to unifiable data terms. Thus, an equation $e_1=e_2$ without occurrences of defined functions has the same meaning (unification) as in Prolog. The basic kernel of Curry only provides strict equations $e_1=e_2$ between expressions as constraints. Since it is conceptually fairly easy to add other constraint structures, future extensions of Curry will provide richer constraint systems to support constraint logic programming applications.

Conditional rules, in particular with *extra variables* (i.e., variables not occurring in the left-hand side) in conditions, are one of the essential features to provide the full power of logic programming. Although the basic computation model only supports unconditional rules, it can be easily extended to conditional rules following the approach taken in Babel [16]: consider a conditional rule[9] "$l \mid \{c\} = r$" (where the constraint c is the condition) as syntactic sugar for the rule $l = (c \Rightarrow r)$, where the right-hand side is a *guarded expression*. The operational meaning of a guarded expression "$c \Rightarrow r$" is defined by the predefined rule

$$(\text{valid} \Rightarrow \text{x}) = \text{x} \ .$$

Thus, a guarded expression is evaluated by solving its guard. If this is successful, the guarded expression is replaced by the right-hand side r of the conditional rule.

Higher-order functions have been shown to be very useful to structure programs and write reusable software [13]. Although the basic computation model includes only first-order functions, higher-order features can be implemented by providing a (first-order) definition of the application function (as shown by Warren [24] for logic programming). Curry supports the higher-order features of current functional languages (partial function applications, lambda abstractions) by this technique, where the rules for the application function are implicitly defined. In particular, function application is *rigid* in the first argument, i.e., an application is delayed until the function to be applied is known (this avoids the expensive and operationally complex synthesis of functions by higher-order unification).

Further features of Curry include a committed choice construct, the encapsulation of search to get more control over the non-deterministic evaluation and to encapsulate non-deterministic computations between monadic I/O actions, and an interface to other constraint solvers. Since these features are not yet implemented, they have not been used in the course on declarative programming.

4 A Course on Declarative Programming

We have shown in Section 2 that the computation model of Curry comprises the models of functional as well as logic programming. Actually, one can obtain the computation models of a number of different declarative programming languages by particular restrictions on definitional trees (see [9] for details). Thus, from our point of view, it is the best available choice to teach functional and logic programming in a seamless way. In the following, we present the structure of a sample course based on this model. This course is not intended for beginners (since we do not discuss imperative or object-oriented programming techniques) but ideal for 2nd year or more advanced students.

"How to start?" is surely an important question for every course. To teach functional and logic programming concepts from the beginning is problematic from a didactic point of view. Thus, one has the alternative to start with functional programming and extend it with logic programming concepts, or vice versa. We take the first alternative since it may be easier to understand deterministic programming concepts than non-deterministic ones. Therefore, we start with functional programming and consider later logic programming as an extension of functional programming where ground expressions are extended to contain free variables and

---

[9] Constraints are enclosed in curly brackets. A Haskell-like guarded rule "$l \mid b = r$", where b is a Boolean expression, is considered as syntactic sugar for "$l \mid \{b=\text{true}\} = r$".

conditional rules may also contain extra variables. Thus, the course has the following structure:

Introduction: General ideas of declarative programming; referential transparency and substitution principle from mathematics (replacing equals by equals); problems of low-level control structures, side effects, and memory management in imperative languages.

Functional programming: Throughout this section, we compute only values, i.e., we do not use free variables in initial expressions or extra variables in conditions. For this kind of programs, free variables do not occur in computed expressions. The substitutions in the answer expressions are always the identity and, therefore, they are omitted. Moreover, function calls will never be delayed. Thus, the computational behavior of Curry is identical to a lazy functional language like Haskell (if function definitions are uniform, see below).

Basics: Function definitions; computing by reduction; strict vs. non-strict languages; if-then-else vs. conditional rules vs. pattern matching.

Here we use only elementary built-in data types like integers or Booleans, and Curry has a clear advantage over traditional narrowing-based functional logic languages, since Curry supports these built-in data types in a straightforward way (cf. Section 3).

Data types: Basic types; list and tuple types; function types; user-defined algebraic data types.

Since Curry has a Hindley-Milner-like type system and higher-order functions, all these topics can be treated as in modern functional languages.

Pattern matching: Patterns; influence of patterns to evaluation; compilation of pattern matching into case expressions; uniform definitions.

Linearity of patterns is a natural requirement. Therefore, students learn to program with linear patterns and put possible equalities in the condition part so that the left-linearity requirement of rules does not cause any difficulties also in the following logic programming part (note that left-linearity is a restriction from a logic programming point of view).

The translation of uniform definitions (cf. Footnote 6) into case expressions is straightforward. The most important problems in this section are non-uniform rules with overlapping left-hand sides. Since they are treated sequentially in traditional pattern matching compilers [23], the produced code is awkward. Moreover, the students partially got the impression that the declarative reading of programs is destroyed by this kind of sequential pattern matching. A parallel outermost reduction strategy (which could be provided by definitional trees but is not yet implemented) seems to be a better choice. Generally, one should better use if-then-else or negated conditions for programs based on sequential pattern matching and leave the optimizations (for instance, avoid repeated evaluations of identical conditions) to the compiler.

Higher-order functions: Generic functions; currying; control structures.

Since Curry provides the usual higher-order features from functional programming (cf. Section 3), this section can be taught like in traditional functional programming courses.

Type systems and type inference: Parametric   polymorphism;   type schemes; type inference.

Since Curry has currently only a Hindley/Milner-like type system, type classes and overloading are not discussed.

Lazy evaluation: Lazy reduction; head normal form; strictness; infinite data structures; stream-oriented programming.

As shown in Section 2, Curry's computation model is identical to lazy reduction if free variables do not occur. Thus, everything is identical to traditional functional programming.

Foundations: Reduction systems; lambda calculus; term rewriting.

This section formally defines important notions like confluence, normalization, critical pairs, orthogonality, or reduction strategies. Definitional trees (without *or* and *and* nodes) are introduced to define an efficient normalizing reduction strategy for inductively sequential programs. This is also the basis to explain the instantiation of variables in the next section.

Computing with partial information: Logic programming: Since Curry supports the (non-deterministic) computation with free variables, it is not necessary to switch to another language with apparently different concepts like Prolog. If free variables are bound, the substitutions in the answer expressions are no longer identity substitutions and, therefore, they are also shown to the user. Thus, it becomes clear in a natural way that in logic programming also the answer part is relevant.

Motivation: We start with a traditional deductive data base example (family relationships) to show the advantages of free variables in initial expressions. Since the same language is used, it is also clear that the concepts are similar. Due to the necessary instantiation of free variables, it becomes obvious that non-deterministic computations must be performed. After this elementary example, the advantages of extra variables in conditions and partial data structures (stepwise accumulation of information) are shown.

Computation with free variables: The idea of narrowing, soundness and completeness of narrowing, and the problems of (strict) equality are discussed. The important notion of unification can be reused from the section on type inference.

Logic programming: Logic programming is introduced as a special case of this general framework where only relations are allowed and all definitions have a flat structure (conditions in rules are conjunction of predicates). Resolution is defined as a special case of narrowing. Backtracking and logic programming techniques (e.g., generate-and-test) are introduced. All this can be done within the language Curry. The linearity of patterns is not a serious problem since non-linear patterns can be translated into linear ones by adding equations between variables in the condition part.

Narrowing strategies: The improvement of simple narrowing by introducing strategies is discussed. This leads to the needed narrowing strategy [4] which is optimal on inductively sequential programs and the basis of Curry's operational semantics. The problem of overlapping rules is discussed by introducing *or* nodes in definitional trees together with some optimizations for narrowing with *or* nodes (dynamic cut [15], parallel narrowing [5]). Now it becomes clear why a sequential implementation of overlapping rules cannot be taken since otherwise the binding of variables caused by the application of rules becomes unsound.

Residuation and concurrent programming: As motivated at the end of Section 2, the non-deterministic evaluation of partially instantiated function calls by narrowing should be avoided in some cases. Thus, the possible delayed evaluation of function calls by the residuation principle [1] is introduced and provides the opportunity to explain the treatment of primitive functions (like arithmetic, see Section 3). Moreover, concurrent programming techniques can be explained, e.g., concurrent objects can be modeled as processes with a stream of messages as input [20]. Since a function can delay if the input stream is not sufficiently instantiated, multiple agents can be simply implemented.

Curry's programming model: The computation model of Curry (cf. Section 2) is presented. A survey on other computation models for pure (lazy) functional, pure (concurrent) logic, narrowing- and residuation-based functional logic languages is given as restrictions of Curry's computation model. Different notions of equality (equality as constraint solving vs. equality as a test), the computation with higher-order functions and the evaluation of conditional rules are discussed.

Extensions: Since we introduced functional and logic programming with a single language, we can choose the best features of both paradigms for extensions which are necessary for application programs. For instance, *input/output* can be handled using the monadic I/O approach of functional languages [18], whereas optimization problems can be treated in the logic programming paradigm by adding particular constraint structures [14] (note that Curry's computation model can be easily extended to more general constraint structures by replacing the substitution part in answer expressions by constraints).

5   Conclusions

Functional and logic programming are often considered as separate programming paradigms and taught in different courses so that the common idea of declarative programming is sometimes lost. We have shown in this paper that this need not be the case if a single declarative language based on a unified computation model is taken into account. From this point of view, the difference between functional and logic programming is the difference between computation with full and partial information which also shows up in a difference in the (non-)determinism of programs. Most of the other ideas, like algebraic data structures, pattern matching, or local definitions, are similar in both paradigms. Thus, we developed a single course on declarative programming based on the computation model of the multi-paradigm language Curry. We taught such a course to advanced students in the 3rd/4th year which was very similar to that described in Section 4 (the minor differences were due to the fact that the full implementation of Curry was not yet available). Our experience with this course, also in comparison to previous courses on functional or logic programming, is quite motivating since we could concentrate on the best concepts and avoid other problematic topics. For instance, the description of the "cut" operator of Prolog could be completely avoided, since the pruning of the search space can be obtained by using functions instead of predicates or an explicit use of "if-then-else". Moreover, an integrated functional logic language leads to a natural amalgamation of programming techniques, e.g., conditions in function rules could be solved by a non-deterministic search in the presence of extra variables, or higher-order programming techniques can be more often applied in logic programming by partial applications of predicates to arguments [17].

Of course, we cannot address all topics discussed in traditional courses on functional or logic programming. For instance, meta-programming techniques, which are useful to implement new or modify existing computation models, are not yet considered. Another important topic in logic programming is the treatment of negative information by the "negation-as-failure" rule. Some basic applications of this rule (e.g., to check the disequality of data terms) can be treated in Curry by strict equality. However, more advanced applications require a better treatment of negative information. Such extensions are topics for future work.

References

1. H. Aït-Kaci, P. Lincoln, and R. Nasr. Le Fun: Logic, equations, and Functions. In *Proc. 4th IEEE Internat. Symposium on Logic Programming*, pp. 17–23, 1987.
2. H. Aït-Kaci and A. Podelski. Functions as Passive Constraints in LIFE. *ACM Transactions on Programming Languages and Systems*, Vol. 16, No. 4, pp. 1279–1318, 1994.
3. S. Antoy. Definitional Trees. In *Proc. of the 3rd International Conference on Algebraic and Logic Programming*, pp. 143–157. Springer LNCS 632, 1992.
4. S. Antoy, R. Echahed, and M. Hanus. A Needed Narrowing Strategy. In *Proc. 21st ACM Symposium on Principles of Programming Languages*, pp. 268–279, Portland, 1994.
5. S. Antoy, R. Echahed, and M. Hanus. Parallel Evaluation Strategies for Functional Logic Languages. In *Proc. of the Fourteenth International Conference on Logic Programming (ICLP'97)*. MIT Press (to appear), 1997.
6. S. Bonnier and J. Maluszynski. Towards a Clean Amalgamation of Logic Programs with External Procedures. In *Proc. 5th Conference on Logic Programming & 5th Symposium on Logic Programming (Seattle)*, pp. 311–326. MIT Press, 1988.
7. N. Dershowitz and J.-P. Jouannaud. Rewrite Systems. In J. van Leeuwen, editor, *Handbook of Theoretical Computer Science, Vol. B*, pp. 243–320. Elsevier, 1990.
8. M. Hanus. The Integration of Functions into Logic Programming: From Theory to Practice. *Journal of Logic Programming*, Vol. 19&20, pp. 583–628, 1994.
9. M. Hanus. A Unified Computation Model for Functional and Logic Programming. In *Proc. of the 24th ACM Symposium on Principles of Programming Languages (Paris)*, pp. 80–93, 1997.
10. M. Hanus and C. Prehofer. Higher-Order Narrowing with Definitional Trees. In *Proc. Seventh International Conference on Rewriting Techniques and Applications (RTA'96)*, pp. 138–152. Springer LNCS 1103, 1996.
11. M. Hanus (ed.). Curry: An Integrated Functional Logic Language. Available at http://www-i2.informatik.rwth-aachen.de/~hanus/curry, 1997.

12. G. Huet and J.-J. Lévy. Computations in Orthogonal Rewriting Systems. In J.-L. Lassez and G. Plotkin, editors, *Computational Logic: Essays in Honor of Alan Robinson*, pp. 395–443. MIT Press, 1991.

13. J. Hughes. Why Functional Programming Matters. In D.A. Turner, editor, *Research Topcis in Functional Programming*, pp. 17–42. Addison Wesley, 1990.

14. J. Jaffar and M.J. Maher. Constraint Logic Programming: A Survey. *Journal of Logic Programming*, Vol. 19&20, pp. 503–581, 1994.

15. R. Loogen and S. Winkler. Dynamic Detection of Determinism in Functional Logic Languages. *Theoretical Computer Science 142*, pp. 59–87, 1995.

16. J.J. Moreno-Navarro and M. Rodríguez-Artalejo. Logic Programming with Functions and Predicates: The Language BABEL. *Journal of Logic Programming*, Vol. 12, pp. 191–223, 1992.

17. L. Naish. Higher-order logic programming in Prolog. In *Proc. JICSLP'96 Workshop on Multi-Paradigm Logic Programming*, pp. 167–176. TU Berlin, Technical Report No. 96-28, 1996.

18. S.L. Peyton Jones and P. Wadler. Imperative Functional Programming. In *Proc. 20th Symposium on Principles of Programming Languages (POPL'93)*, pp. 71–84, 1993.

19. R.C. Sekar and I.V. Ramakrishnan. Programming in Equational Logic: Beyond Strong Sequentiality. *Information and Computation*, Vol. 104, No. 1, pp. 78–109, 1993.

20. E. Shapiro and A. Takeuchi. Object Oriented Programming in Concurrent Prolog. In E. Shapiro, editor, *Concurrent Prolog: Collected Papers*, volume 2, pp. 251–273. MIT Press, 1987.

21. G. Smolka. The Oz Programming Model. In J. van Leeuwen, editor, *Computer Science Today: Recent Trends and Developments*, pp. 324–343. Springer LNCS 1000, 1995.

22. P. Van Hentenryck. *Constraint Satisfaction in Logic Programming*. MIT Press, 1989.

23. P. Wadler. Efficient Compilation of Pattern-Matching. In S.L. Peyton Jones, editor, *The Implementation of Functional Programming Languages*, pp. 78–103. Prentice Hall, 1987.

24. D.H.D. Warren. Higher-order extensions to PROLOG: are they needed? In *Machine Intelligence 10*, pp. 441–454, 1982.

A Operational Semantics of Curry

The operational semantics of Curry is specified using the functions

$$cse : \mathcal{T}(\mathcal{C} \cup \mathcal{F}, \mathcal{X}) \rightarrow \mathcal{D} \cup \{\bot\}$$
$$cs \ : \mathcal{T}(\mathcal{C} \cup \mathcal{F}, \mathcal{X}) \times DT \rightarrow \mathcal{D} \cup \{\bot\}$$

(remember that $\mathcal{D}$ denotes the set of all disjunctions of answer expressions). The function *cse* performs a single computation step on an expression e. It computes a disjunction of answer expressions or the special constant $\bot$ indicating that no computation step is possible in e. As shown in Figure 1, *cse* attempts to apply a reduction step to the leftmost outermost function symbol in e by the use of *cs*, which is called with the appropriate subterm and a definitional tree with fresh variables for the leftmost outermost function symbol. *cs* is defined by a case distinction on the definitional tree. If it is a *rule* node, we apply this rule. If the definitional tree is an *and* node, we try to evaluate the first branch and, if this is not possible due to the suspension of all function calls, the second branch is

---

Computation step for a single (unsolved) expression:

$cse(x) \qquad\qquad = \bot \qquad\qquad\qquad\qquad$ for all variables x

$cse(f(e_1,\ldots,e_n)) = cs(f(e_1,\ldots,e_n),\mathcal{T}) \quad$ if $\mathcal{T}$ is a fresh definitional tree for f

$cse(c(e_1,\ldots,e_n))$

$$= \begin{cases} replace(c(e_1,\ldots,e_n),k,cse(e_k)) & \text{if } cse(e_1) = \cdots = cse(e_{k-1}) = \bot \neq cse(e_k) \\ \bot & \text{if } cse(e_i) = \bot, i = 1,\ldots,n \end{cases}$$

Computation step for an operation-rooted expression e:

$cs(e, rule(l = r)) \ = \{id \,[]\, \sigma(r)\} \qquad\qquad$ if σ is a substitution with $\sigma(l) = e$

$$cs(e, and(\mathcal{T}_1, \mathcal{T}_2)) = \begin{cases} cs(e, \mathcal{T}_1) & \text{if } cs(e, \mathcal{T}_1) \neq \bot \\ cs(e, \mathcal{T}_2) & \text{otherwise} \end{cases}$$

$$cs(e, or(\mathcal{T}_1, \mathcal{T}_2)) \ = \begin{cases} cs(e, \mathcal{T}_1) \cup cs(e, \mathcal{T}_2) & \text{if } cs(e, \mathcal{T}_1) \neq \bot \neq cs(e, \mathcal{T}_2) \\ \bot & \text{otherwise} \end{cases}$$

$cs(e, branch(\pi, p, r, \mathcal{T}_1, \ldots, \mathcal{T}_k))$

$$= \begin{cases} cs(e, \mathcal{T}_i) & \text{if } e|_p = c(e_1,\ldots,e_n) \text{ and } pat(\mathcal{T}_i)|_p = c(x_1,\ldots,x_n) \\ \varnothing & \text{if } e|_p = c(\cdots) \text{ and } pat(\mathcal{T}_i)|_p \neq c(\cdots), i = 1,\ldots,k \\ \bot & \text{if } e|_p = x \text{ and } r = rigid \\ \bigcup_{i=1}^{k}\{\sigma_i \,[]\, \sigma_i(e)\} & \text{if } e|_p = x, r = flex, \text{ and } \sigma_i = \{x \mapsto pat(\mathcal{T}_i)|_p\} \\ replace(e, p, cse(e|_p)) & \text{if } e|_p = f(e_1,\ldots,e_n) \end{cases}$$

Derivation step for a disjunctive expression:

$\{\sigma \,[]\, e\} \cup D \ \to \ \{\sigma_1 \circ \sigma \,[]\, e_1, \ldots, \sigma_n \circ \sigma \,[]\, e_n\} \cup D$

if $\sigma \,[]\, e$ is unsolved and $cse(e) = \{\sigma_1 \,[]\, e_1, \ldots, \sigma_n \,[]\, e_n\}$

Fig. 1. Operational semantics of Curry

tried (this simple sequential strategy for concurrent computations could also be replaced by a more sophisticated strategy with a fair selection of threads). An *or* node produces a disjunction. The most interesting case is a *branch* node. Here we have to branch on the value of the top-level symbol at the selected position. If the symbol is a constructor, we proceed with the appropriate definitional subtree, if possible. If it is a function symbol, we proceed by evaluating this subexpression. If it is a variable, we either suspend (if the branch is *rigid*) or instantiate the variable to the different constructors. The auxiliary function *replace* puts a possibly disjunctive expression into a subterm:

$$replace(e, p, d) = \begin{cases} \{\sigma_1 \,[]\, \sigma_1(e)[e_1]_p, \ldots, \sigma_n \,[]\, \sigma_n(e)[e_n]_p\} & \text{if } d = \{\sigma_1 \,[]\, e_1, \ldots, \sigma_n \,[]\, e_n\} \\ \bot & \text{if } d = \bot \end{cases}$$

The overall computation strategy transforms disjunctive expressions. It takes a disjunct $\sigma \,[]\, e$ not in solved form and computes $cse(e)$. If $cse(e) = \bot$, then the computation of this expression *flounders* (i.e., this expression is not solvable). If $cse(e)$ is a disjunctive expression, we substitute it for $\sigma \,[]\, e$ composed with the old answer substitution.

Logic Implemented Functionally

Norbert Eisinger, Tim Geisler, and Sven Panne

Institut für Informatik, Universität München,
Oettingenstr. 67, D-80538 München, Germany

Abstract. We describe a course intended to introduce second-year undergraduates to medium-scale programming. The project of the course is to implement a nonconventional logic programming language using a functional implementation language. This exercise reinforces two declarative paradigms and puts the students in experimental touch with a wide range of standard computer science concepts. Declarativity is decisive in making this wide range possible.

Keywords. programming course, functional programming, disjunctive logic programming, model generation

1 Introduction

The undergraduate curriculum at our department contains a practical programming course, the major purpose of which is to let the students experience medium-scale programming in their second undergraduate year. Both, the problem to be implemented and the implementation language can be chosen to the taste of the organizers, taking into account what the students learned during their first year.

For our instance of the course, we chose the problem to implement a non-conventional logic programming language using a functional language. The implementation language was Scheme, which had been the first language for the majority of our students. The inference engine for the logic programming language was nonconventional in that it was not restricted to the Horn case and it allowed the derivation of models for a specification.

The implementation of scanner, parser, and inference engine introduced students to a wealth of computer science concepts in an experimental way, emphasizing two declarative paradigms at the same time. The logic programming paradigm was covered both by implementing a logic programming language, which touched upon topics from foundations of logic programming [16], disjunctive logic programming [17], deductive databases [4,2], partial evaluation [7], and others, and by using the implemented system for a wide range of applications from simple theorem proving problems [27,24] to model-based diagnosis [12]. The functional paradigm was covered by implementing in a functional language using a purely functional style and typical programming techniques [8].

The next four sections of this paper describe the curriculum, the problem setting, our audience, and the didactic goals of the course in more detail. The subsequent core section then presents the actual course description. Finally we report about our experiences and consequences.

2 The Undergraduate Computer Science Curriculum at Universität München

The undergraduate curriculum covers a period of normally 4 semesters, that is 2 years. Computer science undergraduates are supposed to take the following courses, apart from mathematics courses and courses for their minor fields.

semester	course	contents
1	*Computer Science I*	introduction to programming
2	*Computer Science II*	algorithms and data structures
3	*Computer Science III*	machine-oriented progr., op. systems
	Technical Fundamentals	digital circuits, Boolean algebra
	Programming Lab	a larger programming project
4	*Computer Science IV*	theoretical foundations
	Seminar	selected computer science topics

In this paper we discuss the *Programming Lab* scheduled for the 3rd semester. Its purpose is to let the students work on some medium-scale, pre-structured programming project, thus consolidating, reinforcing and extending skills they acquired during the first two semesters. The *Programming Lab* is the first (and often the only) experience of undergraduate students with programming beyond small scale, and it can therefore be quite influential in forming their programming habits.

Actually, there are alternatives to the *Programming Lab* not listed in the table above, but more than 50% of each age-class typically choose this course.

One of the difficulties in designing such a practical programming course is that in spite of the seemingly well-defined curriculum the participants have rather heterogeneous backgrounds.

This is due to two idiosyncrasies of the German academic system. First, professors are not subject to any directives concerning the contents of their teaching. As the staff take turns giving the undergraduate courses, the contents usually vary. In particular, the programming languages and even the programming paradigms used in *Computer Science I* and *Computer Science II* may be different every year. Second, students are rather free when to attend which course and when to take which examination, as long as they complete all achievement tests before a certain time limit. Many students postpone or repeat courses.

Hence a course scheduled for the 3rd semester is usually attended by a majority of 3rd-semester students, but also by a substantial percentage of 5th-semester and higher-semester students who were molded on different paradigms.

An instance of the *Programming Lab* is offered every year. Instances given by different lecturers usually differ significantly, but when it is the same person's turn again, an instance may be repeated with little or no change.

3 The Problem Setting

For our instance of the *Programming Lab* we defined the following project. The students have to implement a declarative logic programming language, complete with scanner, parser, and a nonconventional inference engine. The system to be implemented takes as input a text representing a specification, and produces as output a representation of the models of the specification. Moreover, a number of application problems are to be formalized as specifications and solved using the implemented system.

The inference engine is based on the model generation approach [18], more specifically on the technique of positive unit hyper-resolution tableaux, or PUHR tableaux for short [3]. Apart from being able to detect the unsatisfiability of a specification, it can also derive models of a satisfiable specification. This ability transcends the power of SLD-resolution and its variants.

A *specification* is a finite set of rules. Rules are clauses in implication form $A_1 \wedge \cdots \wedge A_n \longrightarrow B_1 \vee \cdots \vee B_m$ with atomic formulae A_i and B_j. We call the conjunction $A_1 \wedge \cdots \wedge A_n$ the *body* and the disjunction $B_1 \vee \cdots \vee B_m$ the *head* of the rule. An empty body can be understood as *true*, and a rule with an empty body corresponds to a fact. An empty head can be understood as *false*, and a rule with an empty head corresponds to an integrity constraint. A *non-Horn* rule, that is a rule with more than one atomic formula in its head, gives rise to alternative solutions. Thus, the specification language is of higher expressive power than the Horn fragment of first-order predicate logic that is usually used in logic programming.

As an example consider the specification in Fig. 1. We use Prolog's lexical convention that variable names start with capital letters and other identifiers with lower case letters.

```
learning(Person) ⟶ successful(Person).
student(Person) ∧ at(Person,uni) ⟶ playing(Person) ∨ learning(Person).
lecturer(Person) ∧ at(Person,uni) ⟶ teaching(Person) ∨ researching(Person).
computerscientist(Person) ∧ playing(Person) ⟶ .
⟶ student(worf).
⟶ computerscientist(worf).
⟶ at(worf,uni).
```

Fig. 1. Sample specification.

Interpretations (more precisely, Herbrand interpretations) are represented by the set of ground atomic formulae they satisfy. The following interpretation is a model of the specification:

```
student(worf)
computerscientist(worf)
at(worf,uni)
learning(worf)
successful(worf)
```

Declaratively, this means that the model satisfies each ground instance of each rule in the specification. An interpretation satisfies a ground rule iff it does not violate it. An interpretation violates a ground rule iff it contains all atomic formulae from the body but none from the head of the rule.

Operationally, models are obtained by a forward reasoning process, which iterates an adapted version of the *immediate consequence operator* $T_P(I)$ defined for Horn clause programs [16], until it reaches a fixpoint. The process is illustrated in Fig. 2.

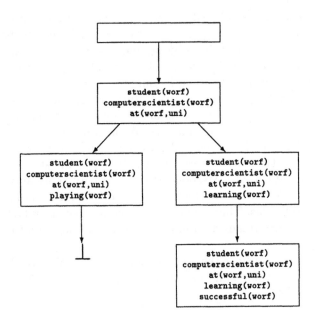

Fig. 2. Development of interpretations for the sample specification.

The inference engine starts with the empty interpretation, which violates the three rules with empty body. In order to satisfy them, the interpretation is extended by their heads.

At this stage the interpretation violates the instance of the second rule `student(worf)` $\wedge$ `at(worf,uni)` $\longrightarrow$ `playing(worf)` $\vee$ `learning(worf)`. In order to satisfy it, the interpretation must be extended by the disjunction `playing(worf)` $\vee$ `learning(worf)`. In order to satisfy a disjunction, the interpretation can be extended by either of the atomic formulae in the disjunction, thus defining separate branches of the search space. (Further branches inserting several of them simultaneously would be redundant.)

In the first branch, the extended interpretation violates the rule with empty head (which states, perhaps contrary to reality, that computer scientists just don't play). If an interpretation violates a rule with an empty head, so does any extension of the interpretation. Thus the current interpretation cannot lead to a model and the branch is *closed*.

In the other branch, the interpretation violates the first rule and is therefore extended by `successful(worf)`. Now all rules are satisfied and the current interpretation is a model of the specification.

This specification happens to have exactly one model. With the additional rule `successful(worf)` $\longrightarrow$ in the specification, the second branch would also be closed, and the specification would be unsatisfiable. If we replaced the rule $\longrightarrow$`student(worf)` by the rule $\longrightarrow$`lecturer(worf)`, the inference engine would derive two models:

lecturer(worf)
computerscientist(worf)
at(worf,uni)
teaching(worf)

lecturer(worf)
computerscientist(worf)
at(worf,uni)
researching(worf)

In this way the inference engine works properly, provided that the specifications are *range-restricted*: each variable in the head of a rule also occurs in its body. For more details and theoretical results about PUHR tableaux see [18,3].

The participants of the *Programming Lab* did not have to read any literature about PUHR tableaux. They were given an introduction that was even more informal than this section, just for a general idea of the expected behavior of their inference engine. Forward reasoning appears to be sufficiently intuitive for this approach. We supplied additional information as needed during the course.

4 Our Audience

We had about 40 participants in our instance of the *Programming Lab*. The 3rd-semester students had attended *Computer Science I* based on Scheme and the Abelson/Sussman textbook [1] and *Computer Science II* based on Modula-2 and Wirth's textbook [26] on algorithms and data structures. Parallel to the *Programming Lab*, they got an insight into the structure of compilers from *Computer Science III* and an idea of (propositional) logic from *Technical Fundamentals* and some math courses. The higher-semester participants all knew Modula-2, and some of them also ML.

Thus, most of the students were familiar with the Abelson/Sussman philosophy of *learning by implementing*. Our own experience with this philosophy was very encouraging, so we tried to adhere to it in the *Programming Lab* as well.

5 Didactic Goals of the Course

The overall didactic goals of the *Programming Lab* are as follows:

- consolidation of what students learned during their first two semesters;
- exposing them to computer science concepts that may be new to them;
- experience of medium-scale programming.

As to consolidation, a number of techniques used in the *Programming Lab*, for instance higher-order functions and continuation-passing, reinforced skills the majority of participants had acquired in *Computer Science I*, while others, such as lazy list processing by streams and syntactic abstraction by macros [8], filled gaps omitted by previous courses.

As to exposing the students to concepts they did not know yet, we were rather ambitious.

Foremost, the project introduced another declarative paradigm, logic programming. The students practiced this paradigm both by implementing a logic programming language and by applying it to a wide range of examples. These examples were essential to ensure the acceptance of the new paradigm. They also provided an insight into some important application areas of logic. Several of them were selected from the TPTP benchmark collection [24].

Further, quite a lot of standard computer science concepts appeared in the project. From compiler construction, there were syntax definition, finite automata and the attainment of their determinism, scanner, recursive-descent parsing, abstract syntax trees, etc. From logic programming and automated deduction, there were propositional and first-order syntax and semantics, matching and unification, immediate consequence operator $T_P(I)$, fixpoint, (un)satisfiability, model, refutation, formalization techniques, etc. From deductive databases, there were range-restriction, materialization, incremental forward reasoning by Δ-iteration, integrity constraints, etc. From functional programming techniques, there were higher-order functions, currying, continuation passing, delayed evaluation, implementation techniques for automata, efficient functional data structures, etc. Our purpose was to let the students work with such concepts to the extent required by their task, but not to emphasize the theoretical background. We expect that they benefit from the *Programming Lab* experience when they fully learn this background in later graduate courses taught by our group, such as Higher-Level Programming Languages, Compiler Construction, Logic Programming Techniques, Theory of Logic Programming, Automated Deduction, Deductive Databases, or Knowledge-Based Systems.

Finally, the students were also put in touch with a number of advanced topics, such as model generation, generation of minimal models, incremental and partial evaluation. Here our intention was to prepare the ground for training young talents in our own fields of interest.

As to medium-scale programming, the project was of nontrivial size and required careful structuring and distribution of the work load. We predefined most of the structure, such that the students could get to know the structuring techniques by filling in appropriate gaps. The students were grouped into teams of three, and each team had to implement the same assignments. Students in a team were expected to experience and solve typical communication and coordination problems. We made sure that at least one member of each team knew Scheme and that the team members complemented each other's background as far as possible, hoping thus to help the higher-semester students catch up on the functional paradigm more easily. We also encouraged the use of version control systems and similar tools supporting group work.

6 Course Description

6.1 Organization of the Course

The participants in our instance of the *Programming Lab* are expected to have a working knowledge of the functional programming language Scheme including techniques for data abstraction and the usage of higher-order functions.

Recommended references for questions on Scheme are the Abelson/Sussman textbook [1] and the Scheme report [6]. Unfortunately, no existing textbook covers all the course material. Therefore, we used detailed slides, which were also accessible to and printable by the students via the World Wide Web.

The course runs for 14 weeks, partitioned into seven two-week blocks. Each block starts with a three hour lecture that presents new material and the assignments for the next two weeks.

Assessments are based on sessions led by a teaching assistant at the end of each block, where students present, explain and demonstrate their solutions. We did not plan additional examinations, although this would be possible.

The total time to be spent by a student for this *Programming Lab* is estimated at about eight hours per week.

We used the public domain Scheme implementation Scheme48 rather than MIT Scheme, which had been used in *Computer Science I*, because it is much smaller, more portable and easier for the students to install at home.

6.2 Material Partitioned into Seven Blocks

Each block defines implementation assignments and/or application assignments that have to be solved by the students within two weeks. The application assignments become more interesting and more numerous as the power of the inference engine increases in later blocks. The implementation assignments are normally based on a program frame with gaps to be filled by the students and sometimes provide signatures of functions to be implemented. Wherever suitable, they come with appropriate test-beds.

This has several advantages. The program frames establish a certain programming style by setting an example. In many cases, the students can obtain their solutions by analogy once they have understood the program frame. The program frames also define the interfaces and thus ensure the interchangeability of different solutions, including our own. This is important to have reentry points in case a team simply cannot come up with a working solution for an assignment.

Block 1: Sequences of Characters

Presentation

- Scheme warmup by introducing additional language constructs.
- Syntactic abstraction with macros.
- Streams (lazy lists).

Implementation Assignments

– Abstract datatype for sequences of characters.
– Conversion of files or strings to sequences of characters.

Didactic Considerations On the one hand, the students know just the Scheme core language. On the other hand, the students are used to a syntactically rich language, Modula-2. The introduction of the corresponding basic Scheme datatypes, records (as proposed in [8]), input and output with files, and additional control structures like **case** helps to refresh the knowledge of Scheme, to comply with the student's desire for a more convenient language, and to increase the acceptance of Scheme.

The stream framework is well suited to structure large parts of the system to implement: A stream of characters is transformed via many intermediate transformations to a stream of models. Therefore, streams (or lazy lists) are introduced, as well as syntactic abstraction with macros, which is needed to build some Scheme special forms constructing streams.

To facilitate testing, both input from a string and input from a file has to be provided in interface functions.

Block 2: Lexical Analysis

Presentation

– Abstraction and classification of character sequences as tokens.
– Semi-systematic construction of a finite automaton recognizing tokens from an EBNF defining tokens.
– Implementation of finite automata in Scheme.

Implementation Assignments

– Development of EBNF and automaton for tokens needed for the specification language (paperwork).
– Conversion of sequences of characters into sequences of tokens.

Didactic Considerations The major utility of the scanning phase, namely abstraction that leads to a simplification of the subsequent parsing phase, can be illustrated with an ill-formed specification including comments.

The whole development from an EBNF specifying tokens to a functional implementation of a deterministic finite automaton is presented stepwise using a simple example grammar that specifies phone numbers. This should enable the students to solve their assignment by analogy.

The syntax of specifications is rich enough to give an idea of attributes and the computation of attribute values.

The implementation technique for hand-coded scanners (adopted from [8]) is straightforward: States are represented as functions and transitions as function calls. For a language with tail-recursion optimization like Scheme, this is just another, but much cleaner, notation for a 'goto' to a state [23].

Furthermore, the functional implementation of a scanner provides the opportunity to teach the usage of higher-order functions as building blocks.

Block 3: Syntactic Analysis

Presentation

- Extraction of structure from token sequences.
- Semi-systematic construction of a parser.

Implementation Assignment

- Conversion of sequences of tokens into abstract syntax trees, that is, development of a parser for specifications.

Didactic Considerations Again, the whole development from a sequence of tokens to an abstract syntax tree is presented stepwise using a simple example grammar. This grammar specifies a tiny command language with a sequencing and an iteration construct and a single primitive print command.

The implementation technique is similar to that used in lexical analysis, with the only difference that the parser can call itself recursively. Note that with partial evaluation of the higher-order functions the parser can be transformed into a standard recursive-descent parser [8].

The first version of the inference engine developed in the next block can handle only a subset of the specification language. Later blocks will successively extend the power of the inference engine to larger subsets. It would be possible to define scanner and parser only for the initial subset of the language and to extend them in parallel with the inference engine. We did not choose this option, because it would result in a much higher workload for the students. A step-by-step extension of scanner and parser would (painfully) open their eyes to modular design, though.

Block 4: Ground Horn Clauses

Presentation

- Review of syntax, semantics, and pragmatics for specifications without variables and without disjunctions.
- Functioning of the inference engine.
- Result of the inference engine: either failure or a model.

Implementation Assignments

- Equality on abstract syntax.
- Abstract datatype for interpretations.
- Inference engine.

Application Assignment

- Missionaries and cannibals (see [27] for a description).

Didactic Considerations The inference engine for the ground Horn case is rather simple. Syntactic equality can be used instead of matching or unification, and no provisions for more than one model are required. Yet, the inference engine for this restricted case uses the same principle of fixpoint iteration as more general cases and can be implemented by the same continuation passing technique. Its stepwise generalization is possible by local modifications of the implementation and can be assigned to later blocks.

The representation of interpretations may be simply a list of ground atomic formulae. But data abstraction is important, because efficiency problems in later blocks are likely to call for more sophisticated representations.

The missionaries and cannibals problem can be formalized as a ground Horn specification, though somewhat awkwardly with a lot of copy and paste. This provides a splendid motivation for the introduction of variables in the next block. Another motivation is that formalizations without variables do not allow the extraction of the sequence of actions solving the problem.

Block 5: Horn Clauses with Variables

Presentation

- Motivation for using variables: More compact specifications and the possibility of infinite structures.
- New concepts and terminology needed for variables.
- Modifications of the inference engine for variables.

Implementation Assignments

- Abstract datatypes for bindings and substitutions.
- Matching.
- Retrieval of matching formulae.
- Test for range-restrictedness of rules.
- Extension of the inference engine.

Application Assignments

- Simplifying the missionaries and cannibals example by using variables.
- Simple logical puzzle (persons criticizing each other).
- Queries to a simple deductive database about geography.

Didactic Considerations There are two possible paths from an inference engine for ground Horn clauses to an inference engine for general clauses: The first path introduces variables first and disjunctive heads afterwards, the second path reverses the order. In our opinion, the first path allows more interesting applications and makes the pragmatics of programming in logic more elaborate.

In order to implement variables, the concept of bindings and substitutions (which is known from *Computer Science I* as environments) is introduced.

The continuation-passing technique introduced in the previous block can excellently be used to implement matching of an atomic formula with variables against a ground formula, resulting in either a substitution or a failure. The combination of substitutions can be implemented just as easily. The continuation-passing technique avoids the introduction of dummy elements for failure and duplicate tests for failure.

The abstract datatype for interpretations is extended by an operation for the retrieval of matching formulae instead of the simple member test.

The PUHR calculus is only correct for range-restricted rules. Similarly to the variable declaration/usage problem in compiler construction, this property is impossible to handle in the syntactic analysis phase based on context-free grammars. Therefore, a separate phase testing rules for range-restrictedness is necessary to ensure correct input to the inference engine.

Logical puzzles are well suited to exercise the pragmatics of logic: When to use terms and when predicates? They are instructive for this kind of course because they usually exhibit complex problems in a compact form and because their understanding requires no special background knowledge about an application domain. And if they are fun, all the better.

The deductive database example introduces the logical analogon to the operations *join*, *select*, and *project* from relational database theory. Beyond that, the response times with larger databases are a good motivation for more efficient data representation and the incremental inference engine introduced in block 7.

Block 6: Fairness, Built-In Predicates

Presentation

- Fairness is necessary for refutational completeness.
- Implementation of a fair inference engine with a queue of derived rule heads, efficient functional implementation of queues [13].
- Application: Theorem proving in group theory.
- Built-in predicates increase efficiency and prevent the generation of infinite models.
- Integration of built-in predicates into the inference engine.

Implementation Assignments

- Functional queues.
- Fair inference engine.
- Built-in predicates.

Application Assignments

- Theorem proving in group theory.
- Mathematical puzzle (pouring buckets), using built-in arithmetic predicates.
- Missionaries and cannibals, using built-in arithmetic predicates and representing the path of the boat.

Didactic Considerations Two independent themes, fairness and built-in predicates, are covered by this block. They have to be scheduled after the introduction of variables, and might be scheduled after block 7.

Fairness (i.e., no applicable rule instance may be delayed infinitely long) is an important concept occuring not only in automated reasoning, but nearly in all fields of computer science. In addition to that, the simple implementation technique for ensuring fairness in the inference engine, queues, gives the possibility to touch the topics of functional data structures and amortized complexity of algorithms.

A fair inference engine opens up a wide range of theorem proving applications. Simple theorems from group theory, with which the students are familiar from their mathematics courses, are formulated in such a way that they can be directly translated into rules in implication form. With that, students learn theorem proving techniques like refutation proofs, the extraction of proofs from traces, and formalization techniques for algebraic laws (e.g., the formalization of associativity) without requiring much theoretical background such as clausal normal form or Herbrand's theorem.

Built-in predicates for arithmetic in our logic language reflect the omnipresence of built-ins in programming languages and built-in theories in automated reasoning. Efficiency and more natural formalizations of applications are good motivations for introducing them. The integration of built-in predicates into the inference engine is straightforward. Furthermore, their implementation gives the possibility to touch the topic of constraint reasoning.

The missionaries and cannibals example links the two topics: With fairness, the path of the boat can be collected in an additional argument and thus a solution of the problem can be extracted. With arithmetic, some of the example's parameters can be changed more easily.

Block 7: Incrementality, General Clauses with Disjunctions

Presentation

- Avoiding redundant work with an incremental inference engine.
- Rules with disjunctive heads.
- Modifications of the inference engine.
- Result of the inference engine: A stream of models.
- Application: Model-based diagnosis of digital circuits.
- Application: Multiplication tables of quasigroups.

Implementation Assignments

- Incremental inference engine.
- Inference engine for rules with disjunctive heads.
- Minimal models.

Application Assignments

- Modeling and diagnosis of some digital circuits.
- Formalization of some quasigroup problems.
- Logical puzzle (from a current newspaper).
- Theorem proving in number theory.

Didactic Considerations Again, two independent extensions to the inference engine are discussed in this block: Incrementality and rules with disjunctive heads.

The inference engine implemented in previous blocks suffers from an efficiency problem: In every iteration, all applicable rule instances have to be recomputed. This can be avoided by an incremental algorithm, which is known from deductive databases as Δ-*iteration*: Compute only the rule instances that became applicable due to the atomic formula added to the interpretation most recently. Surprisingly, this technique can be implemented straightforward and efficiently: Instead of using the original rules to determine the next applicable rule instance, use the rules obtained by combining the added atomic formula with the original rules in all possible ways. This *partial evaluation* typically results in a much smaller set of rules.

Up to now, the inference engine either failed or returned just one model, which was implemented with a continuation-passing technique. For rules with disjunctive heads, more than one model may be returned. A stream-based implementation of this behavior, as proposed in [14,25,1], is more suitable and more easy to understand than a solution based on the continuation-passing technique. By transforming the old inference engine to a stream-based implementation, the students learn that these two organizational principles are just two different points of view. Furthermore, the students again practice the stream paradigm and become acquainted with the virtues of delayed (or lazy) evaluation.

Model-based diagnosis [12] of digital circuits seems to be the most realistic application. As an example known from *Technical Fundamentals*, the formalization of the correct and incorrect behavior of a simple half-adder circuit is presented. As an assignment, the students have to formalize a full-adder circuit. With this example, a clever formalization can make evident the compositionality of a declarative language like logic. To implement a usable interface for this diagnosis application, the parser has to be reused. The concept of minimal diagnoses gives a motivation to implement the extraction of minimal models from the stream of computed models. For this, the procedure described by [3] would fit even better into the stream-based implementation.

The quasigroup problems can help to demonstrate the possibilities of the implemented inference engine—previously open existence problems were solved some years ago with nearly the same techniques [9].

7 Results, Experiences, Consequences

Our instance of the *Programming Lab* confronted the students with many new topics. The logical concepts underlying the inference engine were somewhat demanding for second-year undergraduates. On top of that, our decision to distinguish surface syntax from abstract syntax, unlike Abelson/Sussman's logic programming section 4.4 in [1], dragged in a host of concepts related to scanning and parsing.

Indeed the students confirmed that sometimes they needed more effort to understand the problems than to implement them. However, they did master the concepts, and on hindsight they found the course interesting exactly for this reason. A contributing factor to this judgment may have been that our time planning turned out to be adequate to let them grasp what they needed. We have not got enough feedback yet whether the students benefit from this *Programming Lab* in their graduate courses, nonetheless we think so.

If we have to give the course again, we will probably not change the amount of new material, especially as we now have available new tools that facilitate some presentations [15]. If desired, the material can be reduced by omitting surface syntax altogether or by employing scanner and parser generators [21]. It can be extended by allowing more complex surface syntax, for example operator precedences or general first-order formulae that have to be Skolemized and transformed to conjunctive normal form and perhaps to a range-restricted form.

We feel most confident about making the logic programming paradigm the general theme of the course. It complements the functional paradigm many students get to know early in their education, and together the two declarative paradigms might better counterbalance the strong imperative bias most students entertain nevertheless. However, we do favor a clear distinction between the two paradigms. In addition to that, our ulterior motive is to attract students to our own research interests. This motive could persuade us to include even more specialized topics, such as compilation approaches to the inference engine [22] or efficient representations for sets of terms [11].

Our choice of the implementation language is more debatable. We wanted it to be declarative, and we wanted it to be different from the paradigm to be implemented, for the following reasons.

Since the project requires lots of dynamic data structures, any language that burdens the programmer with memory management problems would be difficult to use. One of our teams attempted a reimplementation in C in order to speed up the inference engine. They failed because of the overwhelming low-level details. This consideration rules out most imperative programming languages (Java or, better yet, Pizza [20] might be an option, though).

We were able to cover such a considerable amount of material, mainly because we could rely on the support of a high-level declarative language, although our pre-structuring certainly helped, too. The students' 'harder to understand than to implement' reaction also means 'easier to implement than to understand' and thus corroborates the claim by other authors [19] that more material and more difficult material can be covered with declarative languages than with imperative languages.

So if it is to be a declarative language, why not implement in a logic programming language, say Prolog? It provides unification, a representation for terms, backtracking, and many other amenities. In fact, an inference engine of the kind we have in mind can be implemented in Prolog in a remarkably concise, simple, and elegant way [18]. However, the point of the *Programming Lab* is to teach students medium-scale programming. With Prolog the danger would have been too high that they simply reuse what the implementation language provides without learning *how* it can be implemented.

What we want, then, is a declarative language, but not a logic programming language. This suggests a functional implementation language.

Among the functional languages, Haskell would have had a number of advantages over Scheme. Being strongly typed, it would have prevented many programming errors at compile time. Its module system would have supported the structuring of the program, whereas Scheme was in this respect a step back from Modula-2, which most students knew well. Abstract data types would have been available without further ado. Streams and other lazy data structures would have been straightforward. Moreover, we noticed that the signatures of Scheme functions we gave to the students were often appropriate for our intended solution only, but became counterintuitive and difficult to handle as students came up with different algorithms (e.g., different nestings of iterations). This inhibition of student creativity could have been avoided by curried definitions of the interfaces, which would have been the natural form with Haskell. After the course, we experimented with a Haskell reimplementation [10] that might be the basis for the next time.

This time we chose Scheme mainly because the students already knew it, and experiences by other lecturers with a previous instance of the *Programming Lab*, where students had to learn C++ and InterViews, strongly discouraged us from introducing a new language. It is not trivial for second-year undergraduates to learn a new programming language. Had we introduced Haskell in this course, too many resources would have had to be allocated for technical teething problems with the language. The same, by the way, would have been true about Prolog.

Even with Scheme, we were not entirely spared such problems. The minority of students whose background was exclusively imperative had enormous trouble adapting to the functional style. With uncanny sureness, they discovered set! and the do construct straightaway, and then wrote C programs in syntactic disguise. As Clack and Myers [5] observe: once students have learned imperative programming, they find it difficult to escape its grasp. Our experience suggests to require an introduction to functional programming as a mandatory prerequisite. The *Programming Lab* cannot really make up for its lack.

Some minor difficulties were caused by the heterogeneous background of students. The good students complained that the program frames we gave them with the assignments kept them on too tight reins. The weaker students found some of those frames too higher-order for comfort. We tried to keep the balance, but may have to adjust some assignments next time.

Many students prefered to do part of the work on their own computers at home. Therefore the use of version control systems and similar tools became more problematic than we expected. This experience may well be typical for any course emphasizing programming.

The one message every participant got out of this *Programming Lab* is that it pays to spend effort on algorithmic improvements rather than $O(1)$ optimizations. There are ample opportunities to make the inference engine prohibitively inefficient, and the students hardly missed any. They experimented with alternative modifications of their code, and observing the effect on the performance was often an unexpected, but in any case a valuable experience to them, regardless of the fact that it would have been the same in any paradigm.

8 Conclusion

In this paper we described a course that reinforces two declarative paradigms, one through implementing and applying a logic programming language, the other through using a functional implementation language.

The primary concern of the course is programming. Declarativity makes it possible, however, to design the course such that it puts the students in experimental touch with a multitude of computer science concepts.

We hope that this paper helps to reproduce the course in other contexts. It is not necessary to cover as wide a range of topics as we did—we were in the lucky position to benefit from a diversity of backgrounds among our staff. Anyone interested in giving a similar course is welcome to contact the authors.

Acknowledgments

We thank all of our colleagues for many useful discussions. Slim Abdennadher and Mathias Kettner helped in preparing and giving the course. François Bry, Thom Frühwirth, and Ingrid Walter read a preliminary draft of this paper and gave us useful comments for its improvement.

References

1. H. Abelson, G. J. Sussman, and J. Sussman. *Structure and Interpretation of Computer Programs.* MIT Press, 1985.
2. F. Bry, R. Manthey, and H. Schütz. Deduktive Datenbanken. *KI – Künstliche Intelligenz – Forschung, Entwicklung, Erfahrungen,* 3:17–23, 1996. In German.
3. F. Bry and A. Yahya. Minimal model generation with positive unit hyper-resolution tableaux. In *Proceedings of the 5th Workshop on Theorem Proving with Tableaux and Related Methods,* number 1071 in Lecture Notes in Artificial Intelligence, pages 143–159. Springer-Verlag, 1996.

4. S. Ceri, G. Gottlob, and L. Tanca. *Logic Programming and Databases.* Springer-Verlag, 1990.
5. C. Clack and C. Myers. The dys-functional student. In *Proceedings of the First International Symposium on Functional Languages in Education, FPLE '95*, number 1022 in Lecture Notes in Computer Science, pages 289–309. Springer-Verlag, 1995.
6. W. Clinger and J. Rees. Revised[4] report on the algorithmic language Scheme. *ACM Lisp Pointers IV*, July–Sept. 1991.
7. O. Danvy, editor. *Partial evaluation.* Number 1110 in Lecture Notes in Computer Science. Springer-Verlag, 1996.
8. D. P. Friedman, M. Wand, and C. T. Haynes. *Essentials of Programming Languages.* MIT Press, 1992.
9. M. Fujita, J. Slaney, and F. Bennett. Automatic generation of some results in finite algebra. In *Proceedings of the 13th International Joint Conference on Artificial Intelligence, IJCAI 93*, pages 52–57. Morgan Kaufmann, 1993.
10. T. Geisler, S. Panne, and H. Schütz. Satchmo: The compiling and functional variants. *Journal of Automated Reasoning*, 18(2):227–236, 1997.
11. P. Graf. *Term Indexing.* Number 1053 in Lecture Notes in Artificial Intelligence. Springer-Verlag, 1996.
12. W. Hamscher, editor. *Readings in model-based diagnosis.* Morgan Kaufmann, 1992.
13. R. R. Hoogerwoord. A symmetric set of efficient list operations. *Journal of Functional Programming*, 2(4):505–513, 1992.
14. K. M. Kahn and M. Carlsson. How to implement Prolog on a LISP machine. In J. A. Campbell, editor, *Implementations of PROLOG*, pages 117–134. Ellis Horwood, 1984.
15. M. Kettner and N. Eisinger. The tableau browser SNARKS—system description. In W. McCune, editor, *Proceedings of the 14th International Conference on Automated Deduction, CADE-14*, number 1249 in Lecture Notes in Artificial Intelligence. Springer-Verlag, 1997.
16. J. W. Lloyd. *Foundations of Logic Programming.* Springer-Verlag, 1984.
17. J. Lobo, J. Minker, and A. Rajasekar. *Foundations of Disjunctive Logic Programming.* MIT Press, 1992.
18. R. Manthey and F. Bry. SATCHMO: A theorem prover implemented in Prolog. In E. Lusk and R. Overbeek, editors, *Proceedings of the 9th International Conference on Automated Deduction, CADE-9*, number 310 in Lecture Notes in Computer Science, pages 415–434. Springer-Verlag, 1988.
19. M. Núñez, P. Palao, and R. Peña. A second year course on data structures based on functional programming. In *Proceedings of the First International Symposium on Functional Languages in Education, FPLE '95*, number 1022 in Lecture Notes in Computer Science, pages 65–84. Springer-Verlag, 1995.
20. M. Odersky and P. Wadler. Pizza into Java: Translating theory into practice. In *24th ACM SIGPLAN-SIGACT Symposium on Principles of Programming Languages*, pages 146–159. ACM Press, 1997.
21. S. Panne. EAGLE — Ein Generator für erweiterte attribuierte LR(1)-Grammatiken. Diplomarbeit, Universität Erlangen-Nürnberg, IMMD8, December 1994. In German.
22. H. Schütz and T. Geisler. Efficient model generation through compilation. In M. McRobbie and J. Slaney, editors, *Proceedings of the 13th International Conference on Automated Deduction, CADE-13*, number 1104 in Lecture Notes in Artificial Intelligence, pages 433–447. Springer-Verlag, 1996.

23. G. L. Steele Jr. Debunking the "expensive procedure call" myth or, Procedure call implementations considered harmful or, Lambda: The ultimative goto. AI Memo 443, Massachusetts Institute of Technology, Artificial Intelligence Laboratory, 1977.

24. G. Sutcliffe, C. B. Suttner, and T. Yemenis. The TPTP problem library. In A. Bundy, editor, *Proceedings of the 12th International Conference on Automated Deduction, CADE-12*, number 814 in Lecture Notes in Artificial Intelligence, pages 252–266. Springer-Verlag, 1994.

25. P. Wadler. How to replace failure by a list of successes. In *Proceedings of the 1985 Conference on Functional Programming Languages and Computer Architecture*, number 201 in Lecture Notes in Computer Science, pages 113–128. Springer-Verlag, 1985.

26. N. Wirth. *Algorithmen und Datenstrukturen mit Modula-2*. Teubner, 1986. In German.

27. L. A. Wos, R. Overbeek, E. Lusk, and J. Boyle. *Automated Reasoning*. McGraw-Hill, 2nd edition, 1992.

DrScheme: A Pedagogic Programming Environment for Scheme

Robert Bruce Findler, Cormac Flanagan, Matthew Flatt,
Shriram Krishnamurthi, and Matthias Felleisen

Department of Computer Science
Rice University
Houston, Texas 77005-1892

Abstract. Teaching introductory computing courses with Scheme elevates the intellectual level of the course and thus makes the subject more appealing to students with scientific interests. Unfortunately, the poor quality of the available programming environments negates many of the pedagogic advantages. To overcome this problem, we have developed DrScheme, a comprehensive programming environment for Scheme. It fully integrates a graphics-enriched editor, a multi-lingual parser that can process a hierarchy of syntactically restrictive variants of Scheme, a functional read-eval-print loop, and an algebraically sensible printer. The environment catches the typical syntactic mistakes of beginners and pinpoints the exact source location of run-time exceptions.

DrScheme also provides an algebraic stepper, a syntax checker and a static debugger. The first reduces Scheme programs, including programs with assignment and control effects, to values (and effects). The tool is useful for explaining the semantics of linguistic facilities and for studying the behavior of small programs. The syntax checker annotates programs with font and color changes based on the syntactic structure of the program. It also draws arrows on demand that point from bound to binding occurrences of identifiers. The static debugger, roughly speaking, provides a type inference system with explanatory capabilities. Preliminary experience with the environment shows that Rice University students find it helpful and that they greatly prefer it to shell- or Emacs-based systems.

Keywords. Programming Environments, Scheme, Programming, Pedagogy, Algebraic Evaluation, Static Debugging. Teaching programming to beginning students.

1 Problems with Teaching Scheme

Over the past ten years, Scheme [7] has become the most widely used functional programming language in introductory courses. A United States-wide count in 1995 put Scheme in fourth place with 11%, behind Pascal (35%), Ada (17%), and C/C++ (17%) (when grouped together) [32, 34]. SML [31] is the only other functional language listed, at 2%. Scheme's success is primarily due to Abelson and Sussman's seminal book [1] on their introductory course at MIT. Their course proved that introductory programming courses can expose students to the interesting concepts of computer science instead of listing the syntactic conventions of currently fashionable programming languages.

When Rice University implemented an MIT-style course, the instructors encountered four significant problems with Scheme and its implementations [6, 17, 33, 36]:

1. Since the syntax of standard Scheme is extremely liberal, simple notational mistakes produce inexplicable results or incomprehensible error messages.
2. The available implementations do not pinpoint the source location of runtime errors.
3. The Lisp-style output syntax obscures the pedagogically important connection between program execution and algebraic expression evaluation.
4. The hidden imperative nature of Scheme's read-eval-print loop introduces subtle bugs that easily frustrate students.

In contrast to experienced Scheme programmers who have, often unconsciously, developed work-arounds for these problems, students are confounded by the resulting effects. As a result, some students dismiss the entire mostly-functional approach to programming because they mistake these environmental problems for flaws of the underlying functional methodology.

To address these problems we have built DrScheme, a Scheme environment targeted at beginning students. The environment eliminates all problems mentioned above by integrating program editing and evaluation in a semantically consistent manner. DrScheme also contains three additional tools that facilitate teaching functional programming. The first one is a symbolic stepper. It models the execution of functional and imperative Scheme programs as algebraic reductions of programs to answers and their effects. The second tool is a syntax checker. It annotates programs with font and color changes based on the syntactic structure of the program and permits students to explore the lexical structure of their programs with arrows overlaid on the program text. The third auxiliary tool is a static debugger that infers what set of values an expression may produce and how values flow from expressions into variables. It exposes potential safety violations and, upon demand, explains its reasoning by drawing value flow graphs over the program text.

The second section of this paper discusses the pedagogy of Rice University's introductory course, and motivates many of the fundamental design decisions of DrScheme but it should be skipped on a first reading if the reader is familiar

---

Data Description: A *list of numbers* is either:
1. null (the empty list), or
2. (cons *n lon*) where *n* is a number and *lon* is a list of numbers.
End

(define (*length a-lon*)
  (cond
    [(null? *a-lon*) 0]
    [(cons? *a-lon*) (add1 (*length* (cdr *a-lon*)))]]))

(define (*fahrenheit→celsius d*)
  (* 5/9 (− *d* 32)))

Fig. 1. The design of a function

---

with teaching Scheme. The third section presents DrScheme and explains how it solves the above problems, especially in the context of Rice University's introductory course. The fourth section briefly explains the additional tools. The last three sections discuss related work, present preliminary experiences, and suggest possible uses in the functional programming community.

2 Rice University's Introductory Computing Course

Rice University's introductory course on computing focuses on levels of abstraction and how the algebraic model and the physical model of computation give rise to the field's fundamental concerns. The course consists of three segments. The first segment covers functional program design and algebraic evaluation. The second segment is dedicated to a study of the basic elements of machine organization, machine language, and assembly language. The course ends with an overview of the important questions of computer science and the key elements of a basic computer science curriculum.

The introduction to functional program design uses a subset of Scheme. It emphasizes program design and the connection between functional programming and secondary school algebra. In particular, the course first argues that a program (fragment) is a function that consumes and produces data, and that the design of programs (or fragments) must therefore be driven by an analysis of these sets of data. The course starts out with the design of list-processing functions, without relying on the fact that lists are a built-in type of data. Students quickly learn to describe such data structures rigorously and to derive functions from these descriptions: see figure 1.

Once the program is designed, students study how it works based on the familiar laws of secondary school algebra. Not counting the primitive laws of arithmetic, two laws suffice: (1) the law of function application and (2) the law of substitution of equals by (provably) equals. A good first example is an application of the temperature conversion function from figure 1:

$(fahrenheit{\rightarrow}celsius$ $(/$ 410 10))
$= (fahrenheit{\rightarrow}celsius$ 41)
$= (*$ 5/9 $(-$ 41 32))
$= 5$

Students know this example from their early schooling and can identify with it.

For examples that involve lists, students must be taught the basic laws of list-processing primitives. That is, (cons v l) is a *value* if v is a value and l a list; (car (cons v l)) $= v$ and (cdr (cons v l)) $= l$, for every value v and list l. From there, it is easy to illustrate how the sample program works:

$(length$ (cons 41 (cons 23 null)))
$= (add1$ $(length$ (cdr (cons 41 (cons 23 null)))))
$= (add1$ $(length$ (cons 23 null)))
$= (add1$ (add1 $(length$ (cdr (cons 23 null)))))
$= (add1$ (add1 $(length$ null)))
$= (add1$ (add1 0))
$= 2$

In short, algebraic calculations completely explain program execution without any references to the underlying hardware or the runtime context of the code.

As the course progresses, students learn to deal with more complex forms of data definitions, non-structural recursion, and accumulator-style programs. At the same time, the course gradually introduces new linguistic elements as needed. Specifically, for the first three weeks, students work in a simple functional language that provides only function definitions, conditional expressions, and basic boolean, arithmetical, and list-processing primitives. Then the language is extended with a facility for defining new data constructors, and parallel and recursive local definitions. The final extension covers variable assignment and data mutation. With each extension of the language, the course also introduces a set of appropriate design recipes and rewriting rules that explain the new language features [9, 10, 11].

At the end of the segment on program design, students understand how to construct programs as (collections of) functions and as (object-oriented) history-sensitive procedures. They can evaluate programs by reducing them algebraically to their values and effects, and understand how to use these evaluations to reason about the correctness and complexity of their designs.

3 The Programming Environment

DrScheme runs under Microsoft Windows 95, Windows NT, MacOS, and the X

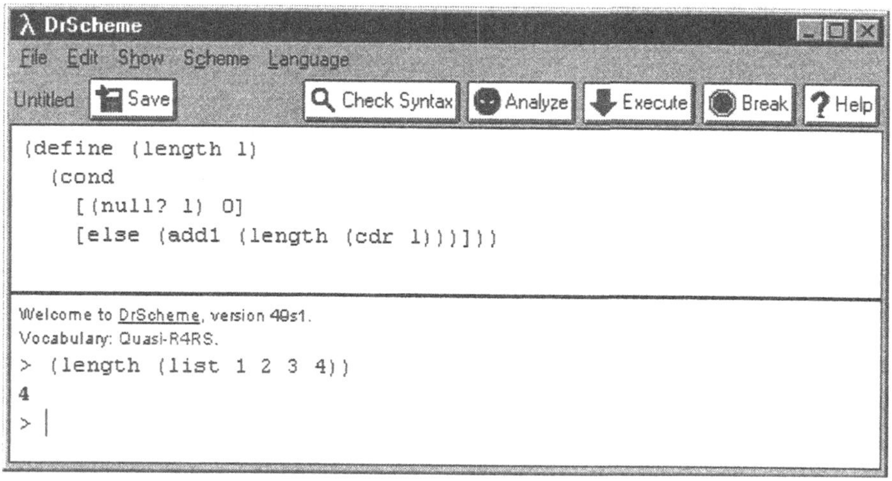

Fig. 2. The DrScheme window (Windows 95/NT version)

Window System. When it starts up, it presents the programmer with a menubar[1] and a window consisting of three pieces: the control panel, the definitions (upper) window, and the interactions (lower) window (see figure 2). The control panel has buttons for important actions, *e.g.*, Save and Help. The definitions window is an editor that contains a sequence of definitions and expressions. The interactions window, which provides the same editing commands as the definitions window, implements a novel read-eval-print loop.

DrScheme's menubar provides five menus: File, Edit, Show, Scheme, and Language. The File and Edit menus contain the standard menu items. In addition, the latter provides the Edit|Insert Image...menu item, which allows the programmer to insert images into the program text. Images are treated as ordinary values, like numbers or symbols.

The Show menu controls the visibility of the sub-windows. The Scheme menu allows programmers to indent, comment, and uncomment regions of text in the definitions window. The Language menu allows the student to choose which sub-languages of Scheme the syntax checker and evaluator accept.

The control panel contains six buttons: Save, Check Syntax, Analyze, Execute, Break and Help. The Save button saves the definitions from the definitions window as a file. Clicking the Check Syntax button ensures that the definitions window contains a correctly formed program, and then annotates the program based on its syntactic and lexical structure (see section 4.2). The Analyze button invokes the static debugger (described in section 4.3) on the contents of the

---

[1] Under Windows and X, the menubar appears at the top of the window; under MacOS, the menubar appears at the top of the screen.

definitions window. The Execute button executes the program in the definitions window. The Break button stops the current computation, and the Help button summons the on-line help facility for DrScheme.

The definitions and interactions windows contain editors that are compatible with typical editors on the various platforms. Under X, the editor has many of the Emacs [35] key bindings. The Windows and MacOS versions have the standard key bindings and menu items for those platforms.

The remainder of this section motivates and describes the new aspects of the core programming environment. In particular, the first subsection describes how DrScheme can gradually support larger and larger subsets of Scheme as students gain more experience with the language and the functional programming philosophy. The second subsection describes how the definitions window and the interactions window (read-eval-print loop) are coordinated. Finally, the third subsection explains how DrScheme reports run-time errors via source locations in the presence of macros. The remaining elements of DrScheme are described in section 4.

3.1 Language Levels

Contrary to oft-stated claims, learning Scheme syntax poses problems for beginning students who are used to conventional algebraic notation. Almost any program with matching parentheses is syntactically valid and therefore has some meaning. For beginning programmers that meaning is often unintended, and as a result they receive inexplicable results or incomprehensible error messages for essentially correct programs.

For example, the author of the program

```
(define (length l)
  (cond
    [(null? l) 0]
    [else 1 + (length (cdr l))]))
```

has lapsed into algebraic syntax in the second clause of the cond-expression. Since the value of a cond-clause is the value of its last expression, this version of *length* always returns 0 as a result, puzzling any programmer, and especially beginning programmers.

Similarly, the program

```
(define (length l)
  (cond
    [null? (l) 0]
    [else (+ 1 (length (cdr l)))]))
```

is syntactically valid. Its author also used algebraic syntax, this time in the first cond-clause. As a result, this version of *length* erroneously treats its argument, *e.g.*, (list 1 2 3), as a function and applies it to no arguments. The resulting error message "apply: (list 1 2 3) not a procedure" is useless to beginners.

While these programs are flawed, their student authors should receive encouragement since the flaws are merely syntactic. They clearly understand the inductive structure of lists and its connection to the structure of recursive programs. Since Scheme's response does not provide any insight into the actual error, the students' learning experience suffers. A good pedagogic programming environment should provide a correct and concise explanations of the students' mistakes.

Students also write programs that use keywords, that they have not yet been taught, as identifiers. It is not the students' fault for using those keywords incorrectly. A programming environment should limit the language to the pieces relevant for each stage of a course rather than leaving the entire language available to trap unwary students.

For example, a student might write:

```
(define (length l start)
  (cond
    [(null? l) start]
    [else (length (cdr l) (add1 begin))]))
```

This program is buggy; it has an unbound identifier **begin**. But, it generates a strange syntax error: "`compile: illegal use of a syntactic form name in: begin`". The student cannot understand that they have uncovered a new part of the programming language.

Eager students also attempt to use features that they have not yet seen in class. For example, they might try to use local definitions before scope is described in class. Many students try to return more than one value from a function by juxtaposing several expressions behind **lambda**. Students with prior experience in C or Pascal might solve a simple functional exercise with imperative features. Again, a good pedagogic programming environment should protect the student from using language features that are inconsistent with the pedagogic goals of a phase of the course.

A natural solution for all of these problems is to stratify the programming language into several levels. Each level should provide enough power to teach a new set of constructs and programming paradigms, and it must not allow irrelevant language features to interfere with the goals of a teaching unit. In short, a pedagogic programming environment must be able to grow along with the students through a course.

DrScheme implements this stratification with four language levels [26]. The student can choose the appropriate language level via the Language|Configure Language... menu item. Choosing Language|Configure Language... opens a window with a choice dialog item that displays the current language level. The choice dialog item mirrors the student's language level. A language consists of several independent settings, which are normally hidden from the student. Clicking on the Show Details button enlarges the dialog, bringing a panel with all of the language settings into view. Figure 3 shows the enlarged dialog.

The description of a language level consist of three parts: input syntax, safety properties, and output syntax. The input syntax is specified through the Case

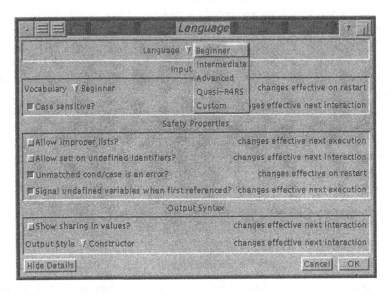

Fig. 3. DrScheme's language configuration dialog box (X version)

Sensitive? check box and a *vocabulary*, a set of syntactic forms. The four pre-defined vocabularies are: *Beginner*, *Intermediate*, *Advanced*, and *Quasi-R⁴RS*. Each vocabulary corresponds to a stage in Rice University's introductory course:

Beginner includes definitions, conditionals and a large class of functional primitives.

Intermediate extends *Beginner* with structure definitions and the local binding constructs: **local**, **let**, **let∗**, and **letrec**.

Advanced adds support for variable assignments, data mutations, as well as implicit and explicit sequencing.

Quasi-R⁴RS subsumes the Scheme language [7, 12, 15].

The first three blocks of the table in figure 4 specify the exact syntactic content of the various language levels. The last block describes other properties of the four language levels.

The safety properties of DrScheme allow the student to choose between conformance with R⁴RS and more sensible error reporting. They can be specified with four check boxes:

- Allow improper lists?,
- Allow set! on undefined identifiers?,
- Unmatched cond/case is an error?, and
- Signal undefined variables when first referenced?.

	Beginner	Intermediate	Advanced	Quasi-R⁴RS
define	√	√	√	√
lambda	√	√	√	√
cond, if	√	√	√	√
quote'd symbols	√	√	√	√
define-struct		√	√	√
local, **let**, **let∗**, **letrec**		√	√	√
delay, *force*		√	√	√
set!			√	√
begin, begin0			√	√
implicit **begin**			√	√
named let, **recur**			√	√
quote'd lists			√	√
quasiquote			√	√
unquote			√	√
call/cc,*let/cc*			√	√
when, unless			√	√
if without **else**			√	√
scheme primitives	√	√	√	√
case sensitive	√	√	√	√
sharing in values			√	
Allow improper lists?				√
Allow **set!** on undefined identifiers				√
Unmatched cond/case is an error?				√

Fig. 4. Language Level Quick Reference

When the Allow improper lists? is unchecked, cons can only be used to construct lists; its second argument must always be either null or a cons cell. The check box Allow set! on undefined identifiers? controls whether set! creates a new name at the top-level or signals an error for unbound identifiers. If Unmatched cond/case is an error? is on, the implicit else clause in cond and case expressions signal a run-time error. If it is off, the implicit else clause returns a dummy value.

The Signal undefined variables when first referenced? check box controls the language's behavior when evaluating potentially circular definitions. Scheme evaluates recursive binding expressions by initializing all identifiers being bound to a special tag value, and then evaluating each definition and rebinding each identifier. If the checkbox is on, an error is signaled when a variable still bound to one of the tag values is evaluated, and if off, errors are only signaled if the initial value flows into a primitive function.

The output syntax is determined by the Show sharing in values? check box and the Printing choice. When the Show sharing in values? is on, all sharing within data structures is displayed in the output. The Printing choice provides three alternatives: constructor style, quasiquote style or R⁴RS style. Under constructor style, the list containing the numbers 1, 2, and 3 prints out as (list 1 2 3). Because it mirrors the input syntax for values, constructor style output is useful for general programs and mandatory for pedagogic programming (see section 4.1). In contrast, quasiquote style is a compromise between the constructor style output and the standard Scheme output style [7]. Like the former, the quasiquote-style output matches quasiquote input syntax. But, by dropping the leading quasiquote, the output can also be used as program text, just like the output of the standard Scheme printer.

3.2 Interactive Evaluation

Many functional languages support the interactive evaluation of expressions via a read-eval-print loop (REPL). Abstractly, a REPL allows students to both construct new programs and evaluate expressions in the context of a program's definitions. A typical REPL implements those operations by prompting the students to input programs fragments. The fragments are then evaluated, and their results are printed.

Interactivity is primarily used for program exploration, the process of evaluating expressions in the context of a program to determine its behavior. Frequent program exploration during development saves large amounts of conventional debugging time. Programmers use interactive environments to test small components of their programs and determine where their programs go wrong. They also patch their programs with the REPL in order to test potential improvements or bug fixes by rebinding names at the top-level.

While interactive REPLs are superior to batch execution for program development, they can introduce confusing bugs into programs. Since they allow ad-hoc program construction, REPLs cause problems for the beginner and experienced programmer alike. For example, a student who practices accumulator-style transformations may try to transform the program

```
(define (length l)            (define (length-helper l n)
  (length-helper l 0))          (cond
                                  [(null? l) n]
                                  [else (length-helper (cdr l) (add1 n))]))
```

into a version that uses local definitions:

```
(define (length l)
  (letrec ([helper (lambda (l n)
                     (cond
                       [(null? l) n]
                       [else (length-helper (cdr l) (add1 n))])])
    (helper l 0)))
```

Unfortunately, the student has forgotten to change one occurrence of *length-helper* to *helper*. Instead of flagging an error when this program is run, the traditional Scheme REPL calls the old version of *length-helper* when *length* is applied to a non-empty list. The new program has a bug, but the confusing REPL semantics hides the bug.

Similar but even more confusing bugs occur when students program with higher-order functions. Consider the program:

(define (*make-adder n*)
  (lambda (*m*)
    (* *m n*)))

(define *add11* (*make-adder* 11))

A student will quickly discover the bug by experimenting with *add11*, replace the primitive * with + and reevaluate the definition of *make-adder*. Unfortunately, the REPL no longer reflects the program, because *add11* still refers to the old value of *make-adder*. Consequently *add11* will still exhibit the bug, confusing the student. The problem is exacerbated when higher-order functions are combined with state.

Experienced functional programmers have learned to avoid this problem by using their REPL in a batch-oriented fashion. They exit, restart and re-load a program file after each change. This action clears the state of the REPL, which eliminates bugs introduced by ghosts of old programs. Unfortunately, manually restarting the environment is both time-consuming and error-prone.

DrScheme provides and enforces this batch-oriented style of interactive program evaluation in a natural way. When the student is ready to test a program, a click on the Execute button submits the program to the interactions window. When the student clicks on Execute, the REPL is set to its initial state and the text from the definitions window is evaluated in the fresh environment. Thus, the REPL namespace exactly reflects the program in the definitions window. Next, the student evaluates test expressions in the REPL. After discovering an error, the student edits the definitions and executes the program again to test the new definitions. In short, after every change to the program, the student starts the program afresh, which eliminates the problems caused by traditional REPLs.

3.3 Error Reporting

A pedagogic programming environment must provide good run-time error reporting; it is crucial to a student's learning experience. The programming environment must catch errors as soon as they occur and provide meaningful explanations for them. The explanations must include the run-time values that caused the errors as well as the source location of the misapplied primitives.

Traditional Scheme programming environments fail in this regard for two reasons. First, with the exception of EdScheme [33], Scheme compilers and interpreters only implement a simplistic read-eval-print loop. If this REPL is executed in a plain command shell, it is impossible to relate errors to source locations in general. The historical solution is to execute the REPL in an Emacs buffer. This

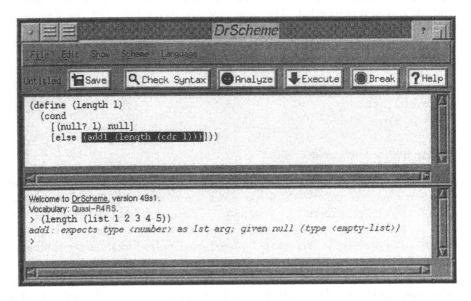

Fig. 5. DrScheme, with a run-time error highlighted (X Motif version)

solution, however, does not truly integrate the REPL and its editing environment, so that the graphical capabilities of modern displays remain unexploited.

Second, Scheme's macro facility [22, 23] tremendously complicates the mapping from a run-time error to its source location [8]. Since Scheme's macro language allows arbitrary mappings on program text during compilation, preserving the original source locations for pieces of program text is difficult. For example, Scheme's **let∗** macro expands to a sequence of nested **let** expressions, and those **let** expressions then expand into **lambda** expressions. Other macros duplicate or delete portions of source text.

DrScheme overcomes all three problems. The underlying Scheme implementation is safe and completely integrated into the editing environment. Furthermore, the front-end of the Scheme implementation maintains a correlation between the original program text and its macro-expanded version [26]. This correlation allows DrScheme to report the source location of run-time errors.

Consider the example in figure 5. The student has written an erroneous version of *length*. When it is applied to (list 1 2 3 4 5), it recurs down the list, and is applied to null. The function then returns null, which flows into the primitive +, generating a run-time error. Then, the run-time error is caught by DrScheme, and the source location of the misapplied primitive is highlighted. With a little effort, any beginning student can now fix the bug.

4 Tools

Thus far we have seen how DrScheme stratifies Scheme into pedagogically useful pieces, improves the read-eval-print loop and provides better error reporting. This section focuses on the additional program understanding tools that DrScheme provides.

4.1 Supporting Reduction Semantics: Printing and The Stepper

As discussed in section 2, Rice University's introductory course emphasizes the connection between program execution and algebraic expression evaluation. Students learn that program evaluation consists of a sequence of reductions that transform an expression to a value in a context of definitions.

Unfortunately, traditional Scheme implementations do not reinforce that connection [37]. They typically use one syntax for values as input and a different syntax for values as output. For example the expression:

(map add1 (list 2 3 4))

evaluates to

(3 4 5)

which gives students the mistaken impression that the original expression has evaluated to an application of 3 to 4 and 5.

DrScheme uses an output syntax for values called constructor syntax that matches their input syntax. Constructor syntax treats the primitives cons,[2] vector, box, *etc.*, as constructors. Thus, when a value is printed the initial constructor shows which subset contains the value.

So, in the the above example, DrScheme prints the value of:

(map add1 (list 2 3 4))

as

(list 3 4 5)

DrScheme's printer produces the same syntax for the values that Scheme's reduction semantics produces.

More importantly, DrScheme also includes a tool that enables students to reduce a program to a value step by step. This symbolic stepper is based on Felleisen and other's work on reduction semantics for Scheme- and ML-like languages [9, 10, 11] and can deal with all the features used in Rice University's course, including the entire functional sub-language, structure definitions, variable assignment, data structure mutation, exceptions, and other control mechanisms.

A student invokes the stepper by choosing Tools|Stepper.[3] By default, the stepper shows every reduction step of a program evaluation. While this is useful

---

[2] list is used as shorthand for consecutive conses ending in null.

[3] The stepper is not available in DrScheme version 49.

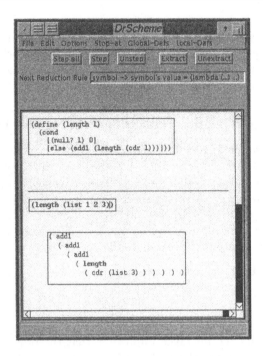

Fig. 6. The stepper (X version)

for a complete novice, a full reduction sequence contains too much information in general. Hence the stepper permits the student to choose which reduction steps are shown or which sub-expressions the stepper is to focus on. At each step, the student can change these controls to view a more detailed reduction sequence.

The stepper window always displays the original program expression and definitions together with the current state of the evaluation as a program (see figure 6). For each step, the stepper explains its action before it proceeds. In the figure, it indicates that it is about to lookup *length* and replace it with its value. If reduction rules for imperative language facilities require memory allocations, they are introduced as global definitions. To focus students' attention, these auxiliary definitions are hidden until mutated. Students may also choose to view them at intermediate stops.

Students use the stepper for two purposes. First, they use it to understand the meaning of new language features as they are introduced in the course. A few sessions with the stepper illustrates the behavior of new language constructs better than any blackboard explanation. Second, students use the stepper to find bugs in small programs. The stepper stops when it encounters a run-time error and permits students to move backwards through the reduction sequence. This usage quickly explains the reasons for bugs and even suggests fixes.

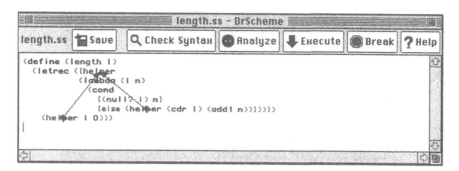

Fig. 7. DrScheme's syntax checker (MacOS version)

4.2 Syntax Checking

Beginning programmers need help understanding the syntactic and lexical structure of their programs. DrScheme provides a syntax checker that annotates the source text of syntactically correct programs based on the syntactic and lexical structure of the program. The syntax checker marks up the source text based on five syntactic categories: primitives, keywords, bound variables, free variables, and constants.

On demand, the syntax checker displays arrows that point from bound identifiers to their binding occurrence, and from binding identifiers to all of the their bound occurrences, see figure 7. Since the checker processes the lexical structure the program, it can also be used to α-rename bound identifiers. If a student checks a syntactically incorrect program, the first incorrect portion of the text is highlighted, and an error message is printed.

4.3 Static Debugging

The most advanced DrScheme tool is MrSpidey, a static debugger [5, 14], which subsumes the syntax checker, but is computationally far more expensive. It analyzes the current program, using a new form of set-based analysis [13, 20], for potential safety violations. That is, the tool infers constraints on the potential value flow in the Scheme program, similar to the equational constraints of a Hindley-Milner type checker, and builds a value flow graph for the program. For each primitive, the static debugger determines whether or not the potential argument values are legal inputs.

Based on the results of the analysis, the static debugger annotates the program with font and color changes. Primitive operations that may be misapplied are highlighted in red, and those that the static debugger can prove are always correctly applied are highlighted in green. In print and on monochrome displays, all primitives are boldfaced, and red primitives are underlined. On demand, the static debugger annotates each program point with:

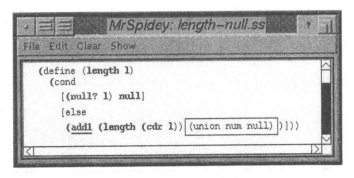

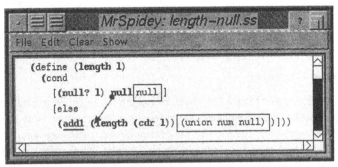

Fig. 8. MrSpidey: The static debugger (X version)

- its inferred value set, and
- arrows describing the inferred flow of values that produced the value set.

Using these mark-ups, a student can browse the invariants that approximate the dynamic behavior of a program to identify which operations are not provably safe. The student can evaluate the coverage of the set of program test cases, and tune the program to improve the accuracy of the generated invariants.

For an illustration, consider the program in the top of figure 8. After the static debugger completes its analysis, it opens a window containing the analyzed program, with each primitive colored either red or green. In this example **add1** is colored red, which indicates that the static debugger cannot prove that the argument will always be a number. The student, using a pop-up menu, can now display the value set of **add1**'s argument. The static debugger responds by inserting a box that contains the value set for the argument to the right of the argument's text as in the top of figure 8. This value set contains null, which is why the static debugger concluded that **add1** may be misapplied. To see how null can flow into the argument of **add1**, the static debugger can also annotate the program with an arrow pointing from the argument of **add1** to the source of null, as in the bottom of figure 8. Since a recursive application of *length* can trigger the flow of null into **add1** (as discussed in section 3.3) the static debugger has given the student the information needed to uncover the bug.

5 Related Work

DrScheme seamlessly integrates a number of ideas that are important for teaching courses with functional languages, especially at the introductory level: well-defined simple sub-languages, a syntax checker with lexical scope analysis, a read-eval-print loop (REPL) with transparent semantics, precise run-time error reporting, an algebraic printer, an algebraic stepper and a full-fledged static debugger. The restriction of the full language to a hierarchy of simplified sub-languages, the syntax checker, the algebraic stepper for full Scheme, the transparent REPL, and the static debugger are novel environment components that no other programming environment provides.

In lieu of source locations for run-time errors, other Scheme implementations provide tracers, stack browsers, and conventional breakpoint-oriented debuggers. In our experience, these tools are too complex to help novice students. Worse, they encourage students with prior experience in Pascal or C++ to fall back into the tinker-until-it-works approach of traditional imperative program construction.

Other functional language environments provide some of the functionality of DrScheme. Specifically, SML/NJ provides a REPL similar to the one described here for the *module* language of SML [3, 19]. Unfortunately this is useless for beginners, who mostly work with the core language. Also, CAML [28], ML-Works [18], and SML/NJ [2] have good source reporting for run-time errors but, due to the unification-based type inference process, report *type errors* of programs at incorrect places and often display incomprehensible messages.

Commercial programming environments [4, 29, 30] for imperative programming languages like C++ incorporate a good portion of the functionality found in DrScheme. Their editors use on-line real-time syntax coloring algorithms, the run-time environments trap segmentation faults and highlight their source location, which is much less useful than catching safety violations but still superior to stand-alone REPLs of Scheme and other functional languages. Indeed, their debuggers serve as primitive REPLs, though with much less flexibility than the REPLs that come with Scheme or SML. None of them, however, provides language levels, full-fledged algebraic printers, steppers, or static debuggers, which we have found to be extremely useful for teaching purposes.

6 User Experiences

All four of the professors who teach the introductory computer science course at Rice University (three of whom are independent of the development group) use DrScheme for the course. DrScheme is used in the course on a weekly basis for both the tutorials and the homework assignments. Also, the programming languages course at Rice uses DrScheme for the weekly programming assignments.

Unfortunately, we do not have any quantitative data for comparing DrScheme to other programming environments, since all sections of the introductory course and the programming languages course use DrScheme. Still, students who know both Emacs-based Scheme environments and DrScheme typically prefer the latter.

We have also received enthusiastic reports from professors and teachers in several countries of North America and Europe who use DrScheme in their classes. Our announcement mailing list consists of nearly one hundred people in academia and industry who use DrScheme and its application suite. We are also aware of several commercial efforts that are incorporating portions of our suite into their products.

Most of the complaints about DrScheme fall into two categories. First, running DrScheme requires at least 24 megabytes of memory on most operating systems and machines. If a machine has less than the required minimum, DrScheme is extremely slow and may even crash. Second, since the development team only uses a small subset of the supported platforms, small platform-dependent errors can go undetected for some time. We expect to eliminate both problems with future research.

7 Conclusion

The poor quality of programming environments for functional languages distracts students from the study of computer science principles. The construction of DrScheme overcomes these problems for Scheme.

Many aspects of DrScheme apply to functional languages other than Scheme. Any functional language becomes more accessible to the beginner in an environment that provides several well-chosen language levels, a functional read-eval-print loop, accurate source highlighting for run-time errors, and a stepping tool that reinforces the algebraic view of computation. In addition, typed languages can benefit from graphical explanations of type errors like those of the static debugger. In general, we hope that DrScheme's success with students and teachers around the world inspires others to build programming environments for functional languages based on pedagogic considerations.

DrScheme is available on the web at http://www.cs.rice.edu/CS/PLT/.

Acknowledgments

We greatly appreciate valuable feedback from R. Cartwright and D.P. Friedman on early drafts of this paper.

References

1. Abelson, H., G. J. Sussman and J. Sussman. *Structure and Interpretation of Computer Programs*. MIT Press, 1985.
2. AT&T Bell Labratories. *Standard ML of New Jersey*, 1993.

3. Blume, M. Standard ML of New Jersey compilation manager. Manual accompanying SML/NJ software, 1995.

4. Borland. *Borland C++*, 1987, 1994.

5. Bourdoncle, F. Abstract debugging of higher-order imperative languages. In *ACM SIGPLAN Conference on Programming Language Design and Implementation*, pages 46–55, 1993.

6. Cadence Research Systems. *Chez* Scheme Reference Manual, 1994.

7. Clinger, W. and J. Rees. The revised[4] report on the algorithmic language Scheme. *ACM Lisp Pointers*, 4(3), July 1991.

8. Dybvig, R. K., R. Hieb and C. Bruggeman. Syntactic abstraction in Scheme. *Lisp and Symbolic Computation*, 5(4):295–326, December 1993.

9. Felleisen, M. An extended λ-calculus for Scheme. In *ACM Symposium on Lisp and Functional Programming*, pages 72–84, 1988.

10. Felleisen, M. On the expressive power of programming languages. *Science of Computer Programming*, 17:35–75, 1991.

11. Felleisen, M. and R. Hieb. The revised report on the syntactic theories of sequential control and state. In *Proceedings of Theoretical Computer Science*, pages 235–271, 1992.

12. Findler, R. B. and M. Flatt. PLT MrEd: Graphical toolbox manual. Technical Report TR97-279, Rice University, 1997.

13. Flanagan, C. and M. Felleisen. Componential set-based analysis. In *ACM SIGPLAN Conference on Programming Language Design and Implementation*, 1997.

14. Flanagan, C., M. Flatt, S. Krishnamurthi, S. Weirich and M. Felleisen. Catching bugs in the web of program invariants. In *ACM SIGPLAN Conference on Programming Language Design and Implementation*, pages 23–32, May 1996.

15. Flatt, M. PLT MzScheme: Language manual. Technical Report TR97-280, Rice University, 1997.

16. Francez, N., S. Goldenberg, R. Y. Pinter, M. Tiomkin and S. Tsur. An environment for logic programming. *SIGPLAN Notices*, 20(7):179–190, July 1985.

17. Hanson, C., The MIT Scheme Team and A Cast of Thousands. *MIT Scheme Reference*, 1993.

18. Harlequin Inc. *MLWorks*, 1996.

19. Harper, R., P. Lee, F. Pfenning and E. Rollins. Incremental recompilation for Standard ML of New Jersey. Technical Report CMU-CS-94-116, Carnegie Mellon University, 1994.

20. Heintze, N. Set based analysis of ML programs. In *ACM Symposium on Lisp and Functional Programming*, 1994.

21. Hsiang, J. and M. Srivas. A Prolog environment. Technical Report 84-074, State University of New York at Stony Brook, Stony Brook, New York, July 1984.

22. Kohlbecker, E. E., D. P. Friedman, M. Felleisen and B. F. Duba. Hygienic macro expansion. In *ACM Symposium on Lisp and Functional Programming*, pages 151–161, 1986.

23. Kohlbecker Jr, E. E. *Syntactic Extensions in the Programming Language Lisp*. PhD thesis, Indiana University, August 1986.

24. Komorowski, H. J. and S. Omori. A model and an implementation of a logic programming environment. *SIGPLAN Notices*, 20(7):191–198, July 1985.

25. Koschmann, T. and M. W. Evens. Bridging the gap between object-oriented and logic programming. *IEEE Software*, 5:36–42, July 1988.

26. Krishnamurthi, S. Zodiac: A framework for building interactive programming tools. Technical Report TR96-262, Rice University, 1996.

27. Lane, A. Turbo Prolog revisited. *BYTE*, 13(10):209–212, October 1988.

28. Leroy, X. *The Objective Caml system, documentation and user's guide*, 1997.

29. Metrowerks. *Code Warrior*, 1993–1996.

30. Microsoft. *Microsoft Developer Studio*, 1995.

31. Milner, R., M. Tofte and R. Harper. *The Definition of Standard ML*. MIT Press, 1990.

32. Reid, R. J. First-course language for computer science majors. *Posting to comp.edu*, October 1995.

33. *EdScheme: A Modern Lisp*, 1991.

34. Schemer's Inc. and Terry Kaufman. Scheme in colleges and high schools. Available on the web.
URL: http://www.schemers.com/schools.html.

35. Stallman, R. *GNU Emacs Manual*. Free Software Foundation Inc., 675 Mass. Ave., Cambridge, MA 02139, 1987.

36. Texas Instruments. *PC Scheme User's Guide & Language Reference Manual— Student Edition*, 1988.

37. Wadler, P. A critique of Abelson and Sussman, or, why calculating is better than scheming. *SIGPLAN Notices*, 22(3), March 1987.

An Editor for Helping Novices to Learn Standard ML

Jon Whittle[1] and Alan Bundy[1] and Helen Lowe[2]*

[1] Dept. of Artificial Intelligence, University of Edinburgh
80 South Bridge, Edinburgh EH1 1HN, UK.
[2] Dept. of Computer Studies, Napier University
Craiglockhart, 219 Colinton Road, Edinburgh
EH14 1DJ, UK.
Email: jonathw@dai.ed.ac.uk

Abstract. This paper describes a novel editor intended as an aid in the learning of the functional programming language Standard ML. A common technique used by novices is programming by analogy whereby students refer to similar programs that they have written before or have seen in the course literature and use these programs as a basis to write a new program. We present a novel editor for ML which supports programming by analogy by providing a collection of editing commands that transform old programs into new ones. Each command makes changes to an isolated part of the program. These changes are propagated to the rest of the program using analogical techniques. We observed a group of novice ML students to determine the most common programming errors in learning ML and restrict our editor such that it is impossible to commit these errors. In this way, students encounter fewer bugs and so their rate of learning increases. Our editor, $CYNTHIA$, has been implemented and is due to be tested on students of ML from September, 1997.

Keywords: Programming Language Learning, Learning Environments, Analogy

1 Introduction

Functional programming languages such as LISP, ML and Haskell are increasingly being used in academe and industry. Many universities now teach functional languages as a key part of their software engineering programme. However, the teaching of such languages presents problems. Functional languages involve abstract concepts such as recursion which are difficult to learn ([1]). Many experiments have been carried out that suggest that students overcome these difficulties by using analogy in the early stages of programming [16, 18]. Given a program to write, novices refer to similar programs they have written before or seen in the course literature. They then use the old program as a basis to construct the new one. We have conducted our own informal experiment with a group of 30

* The first author was supported by an EPSRC studentship. The second and third authors are supported by EPSRC grant GL/L/11724

novice ML students which involved observations of the students over the course of a semester and in-depth interviews with two of the students. This provided additional evidence of programming by analogy [19].

ML is a typed, functional language incorporating extensive use of pattern matching and recursion. We have implemented a program editor, $CYNTHIA$, for Standard ML that supports programming by analogy. Programs are constructed in $CYNTHIA$ by transforming an existing program from an available library. The user is provided with a collection of editing commands. Each command makes an isolated change to the current program, such as adding an extra argument to a function definition. The effects of this change are then propagated automatically throughout the rest of the program. By applying a sequence of editing commands, previously constructed programs can be easily transformed into new ones. In addition, programs produced using $CYNTHIA$ are guaranteed free of certain kinds of bugs.

To illustrate the idea, consider the task of writing a function, *count*, to count the number of nodes in a binary tree, where the definition of the datatype *tree* is given in ML as:[3]

```
datatype tree = leaf of int | node of tree * tree;
```

Suppose the user recognises that a function, *length*, to count the number of items in an integer list, is similar to the desired function. He[4] can then use *length* as a starting point. Below we give the definition of *length* preceded by its type[5].

```
'a list -> int

fun length nil = 0
|    length (x::xs) = 1 + (length xs);
```

Note that *'a list* is the polymorphic list type. We show how *length* could be edited into *count*. This example is taken from [20].

1. The user may indicate any occurrence of *length* and invoke the RENAME command to change *length* to *count*. $CYNTHIA$ then changes all other occurrences of *length* to *count*:

```
'a list -> int

fun count nil = 0
|    count (x::xs) = 1 + (count xs);
```

2. We want to count nodes in a tree so we need to change the type of the parameter. Suppose the user indicates *nil* and invokes CHANGE TYPE to change the type to *tree*.

---

[3] *int* is the built-in datatype integers.

[4] Throughout this document, I refer to the user by the pronoun 'he' although the user may be male or female.

[5] :: is the ML list operator cons

$CYNTHIA$ propagates this change by changing nil to $(leaf\ n)$ and changing :: to $node$:

```
tree -> int

fun count (leaf n) = 0
|    count (node(xs,ys)) = 1 + (count xs);
```

Note that the program no longer contains x. Instead, a new variable ys of type $tree$ has been introduced. In addition, $(count\ ys)$ is made available for use as a recursive call in the program.

3. It remains to alter the results for each pattern. 0 is easily changed to 1 using CHANGE TERM. If the user then clicks on 1 in the second line, a list of terms appear which include $(count\ ys)$. Selecting this term produces the final program:

```
tree -> int

fun count (leaf n) = 1
|    count (node(xs,ys)) = (count ys) + (count xs);
```

The editing commands available can be divided into two types: low- and high-level commands. Low-level commands make only very small changes to the existing program, such as changing 0 to 1 in (3) above. High-level commands affect the overall structure of the program, e.g. changing the top-level type in (2). $CYNTHIA$ encourages the use of high-level commands first to set up a 'shell' for the definition. Low-level commands can then be used to fill in the details.

We aim our system primarily at novices. However, $CYNTHIA$ is general enough to allow complex, practical programs to be produced. It is unlike many tutoring systems (e.g. [2]) that are restricted to a small number of toy examples. This means the novice has the freedom to experiment and enables continued support once the novice has become more expert.

2 The Design of $CYNTHIA$

We wish $CYNTHIA$ programs to be guaranteed correct in some respects. It is natural, therefore, to base the design around established techniques from logic and proof theory which give us a flexible and powerful way of reasoning about the correctness of programs. [9] identifies the necessary machinery to set up a one-to-one correspondence between functional programs and mathematical proofs in a constructive logic. Note that under this correspondence, recursion in a functional program is dual to mathematical induction in a proof. Hence, changing the recursion scheme corresponds to changing the induction scheme. This idea has been used as the basis for program verification and synthesis. For instance, within the paradigm of program verification, given a program, we can prove it correct by proving the corresponding theorem in the constructive logic.

As an example, given a program to append two integer lists together, we could formulate a theorem[6]

$$\forall x : list(int) \ \forall y : list(int) \ \exists z : list(int) \ (\forall e : int \ e \in z \leftrightarrow e \in x \lor e \in y) \quad (1)$$

This theorem or *specification* states the existence of a list z that contains all elements of x and y and no others. Hence, a possible z is $x @ y$ where @ is the append operator[7]. Suppose we have a proof of this specification in a constructive logic. We can extract a functional program from this proof such that the program is guaranteed to be correct with respect to the specification – i.e. it will compute $x @ y$. This is called the *proofs-as-programs* paradigm. It enables us to construct programs that are correct in some way.

We use a restricted form of this idea where the specification does not describe the full behaviour of the corresponding program but instead states the number and the type of input arguments and the type of the output argument. For example, *append* would have a spec $list(int) \rightarrow list(int) \rightarrow list(int)$. Every program is associated with a corresponding specification and *synthesis proof*. Our proofs are written in the proof editor *Oyster* [8] which is based on a constructive logic known as Martin-Löf's Type Theory[8] [12]. The synthesis proof essentially guarantees the correctness of the program extracted from it (with respect to the specification) . The more detailed the specification, the more we can guarantee about the program. Our simple specifications prove that $CYNTHIA$ programs are syntactically correct, well-typed, well-defined and terminating – see §3.2 for more details.

The design of $CYNTHIA$ is depicted in Figure 1. Note that editing commands directly affect the synthesis proof and only affect the program indirectly. $CYNTHIA$ is equipped with an interface that hides the proof details from the user. As far as the user is aware, he is editing the program directly. In this way, the user requires no knowledge of logic and proof. The user begins with an initial program and a corresponding synthesis proof. These may be incomplete. Editing commands make changes to a particular part of the synthesis proof. This yields a new partial proof which may contain gaps or inconsistencies. To fill in these gaps and resolve inconsistencies, we use an analogical mechanism. This mechanism *replays* the proof steps in the original (source) proof to produce a new (target) proof. During this replay, the changes induced by the editing command are propagated throughout the proof. Once gaps in the target proof have been bridged, a new program is extracted. This program incorporates the user's edits and is guaranteed correct with respect to the weak specification.

Let us explain how the analogy works in a little more detail. A tactic is a combination of a number of inference rules. Tactics can be written that allow

---

[6] $X : T$ means X is of type T

[7] In fact, *append* is just one program that would satisfy the specification. We can write the specification to any level of detail.

[8] The type systems of ML and Martin-Löf, although very similar, are not the same, so some minor translating is done between the two. We chose *Oyster* in which to build our constructive proofs because there is a body of work in synthesising programs in *Oyster*.

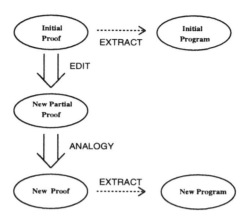

Fig. 1. Editing Programs in $CYNTHIA$

us to apply a frequently used sequence of inference rules in one step. We have implemented a number of tactics that allow us to synthesise ML programs. There are five types of tactics in $CYNTHIA$:

- A tactic for pattern matching.
- Tactics for constructing an ML program fragment. Each ML construct (e.g. if..then..else, case) has a corresponding tactic. Applying the tactic in *Oyster* adds extra branches to the proof tree.
- Result tactics for giving the result of a case in the definition (e.g. giving 0 as the result in the *nil* case of the definition of *length*).
- Tactics for type-checking.
- Tactics for checking termination.

By applying tactics, a synthesis proof is constructed. This synthesis proof is represented as a tree where each node in the tree has slots for the hypotheses, the current goal and a tactic to be applied. In our case, the current goal will be of the form $\vdash T$ where T is the output type of the function being defined. This goal should be interpreted as meaning that an object of type T is required to satisfy the goal.

The analogical mechanism works as follows. When an editing command is invoked, $CYNTHIA$ abstracts away unnecessary information from the proof tree to produce an *abstract rule tree* (ART) which is essentially a tree of tactic applications. If the editing command is applied at a position, P, in the ML program, $CYNTHIA$ calculates the position corresponding to P in the ART and then makes changes in the ART. This may involve adding, removing or modifying tactics. This process yields a new ART which is then replayed by systematically applying the tactics that make it up, hence producing a new synthesis proof. Note that the changes made by the editing commands are propagated during the replay of the ART. There may be tactics that can no longer apply – in this case, a gap is left in the proof tree which is signalled to the user at the corresponding point in the ML program. These gaps must be 'filled in' before the program is accepted. For an example of this, see §4.

Refer to the example in §1. We briefly explain how the analogy works in (2). The user has selected *nil* and indicated a change of type. This induces a change of the type of *length* from `'a list -> int` to `tree -> int`. Hence, the proof tree is abstracted to an ART with a new specification *tree → int*. The ART is now replayed. During this replay, the tactic that implements pattern matching is modified so that the definition is based on a new pattern with constructors *leaf* and *node*. This also changes the induction scheme in the proof hence making the recursive call (*count ys*) available for future use. The two result tactics are replayed without modifications. The new program can be then be extracted from the new proof tree.

In general, constructing proofs by analogy is a difficult task [15]. Because we are restricted to specifications involving a limited amount of detail, the proofs are simpler and so the analogy becomes a viable option in a practical, real-time system such as ours.

3 Increasing the Learning Rate

Over a period of three months we conducted observations of a group of 30 novice ML students from Napier University to ascertain what problems presented themselves when learning ML. The students were observed writing programs during weekly tutorial sessions. In addition to informal observations, their interactions with ML were scripted and analysed. The students completed questionnaires relating their experiences and at the end of the course, two students were interviewed in depth. We describe how ML programs can be built up quickly and easily using $CYNTHIA$. We also point out the problems that the students had with ML and how $CYNTHIA$ can help to overcome them. The students used version 0.93 of New Jersey ML and so our comments refer to this version.

3.1 Program Transformation

To provide the maximum support for programming by analogy, the editing commands in $CYNTHIA$ are structured into low-level commands for making very small changes and high-level commands for changing the overall program structure. Not only does this approach constitute a powerful way of transforming programs but it also encourages the novice to follow a top-down approach to programming – deciding on the high-level structure first and then filling in the details.

Low-Level Commands These are commands that only affect an isolated part of the program. They do not affect the datatype of the function being defined. Nor do they affect the recursion the function is defined by. This means that the analogy needed to produce a new program is fairly straightforward.

The following are the available low-level commands, with a brief description of each:

- ADD CONSTRUCT: add a construct at the current point in the program. The ML constructs currently supported are if..then..else, case, fn, let val and let fun.
- CHANGE TERM: change a sub-expression in a term at the current point in the definition only.

High-Level Commands We now present the high-level commands available. First, we give a list of the commands where the analogy is relatively simple. Then we go into more complicated high-level commands.

- RENAME: change the name of a variable name or function name throughout the definition.
- ADD ARGUMENT: add an additional argument to a function definition.
- ADD COMPONENT: if an argument is a pair, add an extra component to the pair. If the argument is not already a pair, make it into one. For example, consider applying ADD COMPONENT to *nil* in the following program.

```
'a list -> int

fun length nil = 0
|    length (x::xs) = 1 + (length xs);
```
would go to
```
'a list * 'b -> int

fun length (nil,y) = 0
|    length (x::xs,y) = 1 + (length (xs,y));
```
- MOVE ARGUMENTS: swap the positions of two arguments in a definition.

Figure 2 gives an idea of some commands used to transform, *rev* a function for reversing lists, into *delete* for deleting an element from a list. The commands are in upper case. The first step renames the function and adds an extra argument. ADD ARGUMENT is invoked by indicating an occurrence of *rev* and then analogy gives all other occurrences of *rev* an additional argument too. ADD IF..THEN..ELSE places a case-split at the designated position, duplicating whatever is below the current position in the original program. CHANGE TERM is used to edit the result for one of the patterns – e.g. to remove @ in (*delete xs e*) @ [*x*] giving (*delete xs e*).

More complicated high-level commands are for changing the recursion and changing the type of an argument.

Definition by Patterns By *definition by patterns* we mean the common practice as used in ML whereby functions are defined by pattern matching (see *rev* for example in Figure 2). We observed that novices often have difficulty in deciding upon the correct definition by patterns for a function. They are capable in

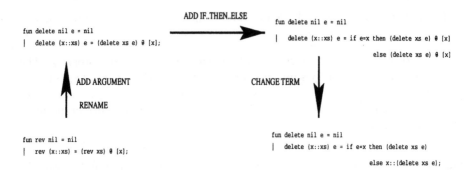

Fig. 2. Low-Level Commands

simple cases where the function has only one argument that is pattern matched against, but become lost when more than one argument is pattern matched or when the pattern used is non-standard. A simple function that pattern matches multiple arguments would be an *nth* function to return the nth element in a list.

We have a command MAKE PATTERN which allows the user to build up non-standard patterns by combining a number of standard ones. We have implemented a version of a technique used in ALF [5]. The user can highlight an object of a certain datatype. The application of the MAKE PATTERN command splits the object into a number of patterns - one for each constructor function used to define the datatype. Hence, MAKE PATTERN on *x:list* below

```
fun f(x,l)=..
```

produces two patterns:

```
fun f(nil,l)=..
|   f(h::t,l)=..
```

Non standard patterns can be defined by applying the command a number of times. Highlighting *t* and applying MAKE PATTERN gives:

```
fun f(nil,l)=..          (1)
|   f(h::nil,l)=..       (2)
|   f(h::h2::t1,l)=..    (3)
```

This can be done for any datatype by using the definition of the type as encoded in ML. Suppose *l* is of type *tree* then we can split *l* in pattern number (2) to give:

```
fun f(nil,l)=..
|   f(h::nil,(leaf x))=..
|   f(h::nil,(node(l1,l2)))=..
|   f(h::h2::t1,l)=..
```

We do not use the same underlying theory as ALF but use the constructive logic already available in our proof system. The result is the same, however.

Recursion Recursion is well-known to be a difficult concept to learn. Novices can have considerable difficulty with even primitive recursion schemes. However, an introductory course will also introduce non-standard schemes involving accumulators, multiple recursion, course-of-values recursion and nested recursion. To help novices to learn non-standard recursions, the commands ADD RECURSIVE CALL and REMOVE RECURSIVE CALL encourage them to think about which recursive calls are needed for the task at hand. $CYNTHIA$ maintains a list of recursive calls that are currently available to the user. When the user is required to enter a term, these recursive calls are among the options presented to the user. He can pick one using the mouse without any need for further typing. The user can change the list of recursive calls by the commands mentioned above. The idea is that the user first decides upon what kind of recursion he should use. He can then use these commands to set up the basic structure within which to use them. Other commands can be used to fill in the details.

As an example of how the commands can be used, consider trying to produce the function zip[9]:

```
fun zip f nil nil = nil
|   zip f nil (i::u) = nil
|   zip f (x::xs) nil = nil
|   zip f (x::xs) (i::u) = f(x,i)::zip f xs u;
```

Figure 3 shows the edits needed to produce zip from rev. The ideal way to proceed is to decide upon the program structure to begin with by applying ADD ARGUMENT twice and then MAKE PATTERN twice. The user then introduces the recursive call (zip f xs u) as necessary[10]. To avoid restricting the user, he is not forced to produce programs in this top-down fashion. The result is generally independent of the order of execution of commands.

Changing Type A major drawback of current learning processes is that novices can ignore datatypes. ML is equipped with a type inference engine which automatically derives (if possible) the type of the top-level function. Although advantageous in that users need not explicitly state the type of each term, novices can ignore types and be unaware of type inconsistencies which may arise. This results in unhelpful error messages from the compiler and confusion. For instance, in the function:

```
fun length nil = nil
|   length (x::xs) = 1 + (length xs);
```

---

[9] A common definition of zip would omit the second and third cases. This is disallowed in $CYNTHIA$ because we restrict to well-defined programs. The current version of $CYNTHIA$ does not support exceptions.

[10] Note that when this recursive call is introduced into the program, the program is checked for termination. In this way, the user is restricted to recursive calls that preserve termination – see §3.2.

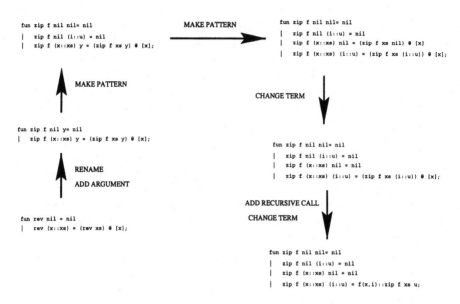

Fig. 3. Writing *zip*

we have an example of a simple but commonly-made error whereby the output type in the first line is list but is an integer in the second. It can often be difficult to pinpoint exactly where the error has occurred.

For this reason, we insist that the user declares the type of a function before anything else. This forces the novice to think about the types hence reducing type errors when writing the rest of the program. Once the top-level type has been given, the types of terms in most other parts of the program are determined and hence need not be given by the user.

During the course of a program the user may realise he has stated the top-level type incorrectly. Or he may want to change the top-level type of an old program to produce a new one. $CYNTHIA$ provides quite advanced facilities for doing this. Changing the output type of a function or changing the type of a non-recursive argument does not present too many problems. It can result in inconsistencies in the proof (ill-typed terms) but this can be dealt with – see §4. The real challenge comes when changing the type of an argument that is pattern matched against since the pattern needs to be changed.

If we wanted to change the type of the first argument in *length* from list to tree, we can invoke CHANGE TYPE to edit *length* into

```
fun length (leaf n) = nil
|    length (node(xs,ys)) = 1 + length xs;
```

In this case, $CYNTHIA$ will also add the recursive call *length ys* to the list available. This could then be used by the user. More complicated examples arise when MAKE PATTERN has been applied more than once. If our original program had been:

```
fun app2 nil 12 = 12
 |   app2 (x::nil) 12 = (x::12)
 |   app2 (x1::x2::xs) 12 = x1::(app2 xs 12);
```

it is not clear what the new pattern should be after a change of type of the first argument to *tree*. $CYNTHIA$ looks for a mapping between the old and new datatype definitions and uses heuristics to select a mapping if necessary[11]. This mapping is then applied to the old pattern definition to produce a new one. A full description of these heuristics is beyond the scope of this paper. The general idea is to map base (step) constructors for the source type to target base (step) constructors. For a datatype, t, we say that a constructor is a base constructor if none of its arguments are of type t. A step constructor has at least one such argument. When mapping individual constructors, we have to map the arguments of the constructors. In this case, we map (non-)recursive arguments to (non-)recursive arguments. An argument is recursive if it is of type t and is non-recursive otherwise. To illustrate, consider the datatype definitions for $list$[12] and *tree*:

```
datatype 'a list = nil | :: of 'a * 'a list;
```

```
datatype tree = leaf of int | node of tree * tree;
```

For these definitions, *nil* is a base constructor, *leaf* is a base-constructor with a single non-recursive argument, :: is a step constructor with one non-recursive and one recursive argument, and *node* is a step constructor with two recursive arguments. The mapping that $CYNTHIA$ selects in this case is $nil \mapsto (leaf\ n)$ and $x :: xs \mapsto node(xs, ys)$, where n, ys are fresh variables. ys is introduced in preference to mapping $x :: xs$ to $node(x, xs)$ because x is not of type *tree*. Applying this mapping to the program *app2* above produces:

```
fun app2 (leaf n) 12 = 12
 |   app2 (node((leaf n),ys)) 12 = (x::12)
 |   app2 (node(node(xs,ys),zs)) 12 = x1::(app2 xs 12);
```

Note that x, $x1$ appear on the RHS of the equalities but not on the LHS. Rather than try to replace these terms with a suitable alternative, we prefer to highlight this fact to the user and let him deal with it. In this way, the user is aware of exactly what effect his change of type has had. If x and $x1$ had been replaced it would be difficult to know what to replace them with. In addition, the user might not notice the change.

3.2 Reducing the Number of Programming Errors

One of the main purposes of our experiment was to identify the kinds of programming errors that novice ML users encounter. Our results suggest that the

---

[11] Although the user may override the heuristics and choose an alternative mapping if necessary.

[12] This is a built-in definition in ML.

learning rate is severly affected by these errors. The most common errors were syntax errors and type errors. C^YNTHIA disallows such errors in its programs. The students found it particularly difficult to pinpoint the source of a type error. Although ML does type checking at compile time and spots type inconsistencies, the system messages provide little or no help in rectifying the problem. C^YNTHIA also incorporates a type checker. The ML type checker is not invoked until compile time. In C^YNTHIA, however, the type checker is called as each new term is entered. Hence, the user receives immediate feedback on whether a term is well-typed. In addition, given the type of the top-level function that the user has already supplied, C^YNTHIA can tell the user what the type of a term should be *before* he enters it. In this way, the number of type errors is reduced considerably. All programs in C^YNTHIA are guaranteed to be well-typed.

A major source of errors in recursive programs is non-termination [4]. An example of a non-terminating function is

```
fun gcd (x:int) y = if x=y then x
                    else gcd (x-y) y;
```

This will not terminate for the call $gcd(2, 3)$. Termination errors are less frequent than type errors but are usually more serious. C^YNTHIA restricts the user to producing terminating programs[13]. Checking the termination of function definitions is undecidable. Hence, C^YNTHIA restricts the user to a decidable subclass known as Walther Recursive functions [14]. It is easy to check if a function definition falls into this class and yet the class is wide enough to be of real use to novice (and indeed more experienced programmers). The class includes most commonly occurring examples of course-of-values, nested and multiple recursions. The idea behind Walther Recursion is that when a definition is made, we attempt to place a bound on the size of the output of the function. The size measure used is based on the size of constructor terms where $w(c(u_1, \ldots, u_n)) = 1 + \sum_{i \in R_c} w(u_i)$ if c is a constructor, and R_c is the set of its recursive arguments. Bounding lemmas derived for previous definitions are then used to show that each recursive call is measure-decreasing, and hence that the definition terminates on all inputs. Walther Recursion is sufficiently wide-ranging to allow the following definition of *msort* modified from the example in [14].

```
fun msort nil = nil
|   msort (x::nil) = x::nil
|   msort (x::h::t) = merge (msort (evenl (x::h::t)))
                            (msort (x::(evenl (h::t))));
```

evenl returns the elements in a list at even positions. *merge* joins two lists by repeatedly taking the smaller of the two heads. Note that this is not the most natural definition of *msort* but is the definition that is easiest to produce using the editing commands in C^YNTHIA. Given the previous bounding lemma,

---

[13] Occasionally, non-terminating programs can be useful. One could envisage, however, a facility for overriding termination restrictions in this small number of cases.

$|evenl\ (z :: zs)| \leq |zs|$ for non-nil inputs, we can derive that both recursive calls decrease the measure.

As mentioned earlier, a common way of defining ML programs is by pattern matching. A source of errors in our analysis was that students wrote programs that were not well-defined – i.e. the pattern for an argument did not exhaustively cover the domain of the datatype with no redundant matches. ML spots such errors at compile time displaying a warning message. Although ML does not consider ill-definedness as an error, it is commonly believed that it is good programming practice to write well-defined programs. Otherwise, there can be serious run-time errors. Students were found to ignore the warnings given by ML because they are not explicitly flagged as errors. We feel, however, that students would make fewer errors if their programs were all well-defined. Hence, in $CYNTHIA$ the editing commands guarantee well-definedness.

In addition to these guarantees, any program defined in $CYNTHIA$ is syntactically correct.

4 The User Interface

We are currently developing a graphical user interface for $CYNTHIA$ written in Tcl/Tk. At present, $CYNTHIA$ supports a functional subset of the core language of Standard ML, and does not yet support exceptions. The user starts off with a library of function definitions to choose from which have been taken from the course notes at Napier University. The user can select one of these functions to transform and can add his own functions to the library.

ML programs are presented to the user in a window and the user may highlight any part of the program by positioning the mouse over it. Clicking on the left mouse button brings up a menu of editing commands that could be applied at this point. After selecting a command, the user is presented with a dialog box for him to enter any necessary parameters for the command. He can either enter these parameters as text or select them from a menu of suitable options. CHANGE TERM can be applied to a subterm of an expression as well as the whole expression. This is possible because when the mouse is moved over a function symbol, the subterm which has that function symbol as top-level functor is highlighted and it is this subterm that is changed. Clicking on the right mouse button when a term is highlighted will display the type of the highlighted expression. This is an invaluable way of providing type feedback to the user during program development. Figure 4 is a screenshot of one stage during the transformation of *length*.

By using a graphical interface, the user is completely unaware of the proof machinery that lies behind $CYNTHIA$. As far as he is aware, he is editing the ML program.

A further development in the interface has been to provide feedback to the user about the next stage of editing. Although the aim is, in general, to produce a valid program at each stage of editing, this is not always possible. Some editing commands will invalidate parts of the program. There are two main ways this

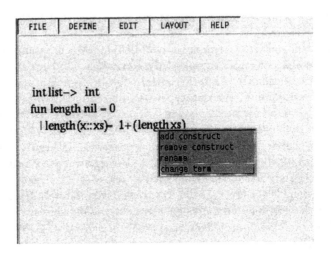

Fig. 4. Graphical user interface to $CYNTHIA$

can happen. We have already given an example of the first – see *app2* in §3.1. If a section, S of a program is deleted and a subsequent part of the program, P depends on S then P can no longer be valid. This is what happened when changing type in *app2* – x and $x1$ were present on the RHS of the equality but not the LHS. The solution we choose to deal with this is to leave such terms in the program but highlight them (by displaying in a different colour) to the user. The user may then inquire why they are highlighted and will be told that unless they change the terms, the program will not be syntactically valid. We prefer this approach to removing the terms because the highlighting process retains as much as possible of the program so that frustrating retyping is not necessary whilst it additionally tells the user exactly which parts of the program must be changed next.

The other situation where this is used is when an editing command causes the program to become ill-typed. In $CYNTHIA$ every term that is entered is type-checked at entry time. If the term is not of the required type, the user will be told and will not be allowed to enter the term. More generally, if an application of the CHANGE TYPE command makes some part of the program ill-typed, $CYNTHIA$ will not only highlight the offending term to alert the user but will also tell the user what the type should be so that when he changes the highlighted term he is told what type the new term should belong to. A simple example of this phenomenon is when changing the output type of a program.

Consider the *length* example again:

```
'a list -> int

fun length nil = 0
 |   length (x::xs) = 1 + (length xs);
```

Suppose the user applies CHANGE TYPE to change *int* to *int list*. Then 0 and
$1 + (length\ xs)$ will no longer be of the same type as the output type. Again,
rather than removing these terms or attempting to change them automatically,
we highlight them to the user by a displaying them in a different colour. The
user then has freedom either to change the terms immediately, or to make some
other sequence of editing commands that will resolve the problem. As soon as
the terms become well-typed, the colouring disappears.

Note that the proofs-as-programs paradigm is a natural way in which to implement this mechanism. No extra checks are needed to highlight terms. Highlighted parts of the program just correspond to proof rules that have failed to
apply. Similarly, highlighting of ill-typedness means that a proof obligation to
prove the well-typedness has failed to be proved and the user is alerted.

We are currently looking into further ways of providing instructive feedback
to the user during program development. One obvious possibility is when using
ADD RECURSIVE CALL. If the user enters a term that means that a program
no longer terminates, rather than just refusing the command application, the
user could be given feedback about why the command cannot be applied, and
perhaps what he should do so that it could be.

5   Related Work

The work closest to our own is the *recursion editor* presented in [4]. In fact, this
was one of the original inspirations. The recursion editor is an editor for writing
terminating programs. Like our system, edits are made by invoking editing commands. $CYNTHIA$'s commands are more general than those in the recursion
editor. In the recursion editor, only a very restricted subset of recursive programs
could be produced. The recursion editor is very sensitive to the order in which
commands are performed. If they are performed in the wrong order, it may be
difficult or impossible to recover. Our proofs-as-programs design overcomes this
by allowing greater flexibility because it keeps track of the dependencies within
the same program and between different programs. Our proof design also allows
us to locate errors in the program easily. [4] makes no consideration of datatypes.

[6] gives an alternative approach to the problem of understanding type errors.
He presents a modification of the unification algorithm used in Hindley-Milner
type inference which allows the decisions that led to a particular type being
inferred to be recorded and fed back to the user. As I have not seen his work in
action, I cannot comment on how useful his explanations are in discovering type
errors. [13] also looks into ways of providing more information to the user about
why particular types have been inferred.

Some work has been done on programming using schemata [10, 7]. This is similar in spirit to our low and high-level commands as the user follows a top-down approach. However, previous attempts are limited to a small range of programs. Our editor is much more general providing a range large enough to be of real practical use. The techniques editor TED [3] features a program transformation perspective but it has no strong theoretical foundations and is therefore much less powerful than $CYNTHIA$.

We do not address the problem of retrieving a previous example – see [17] which indicates that students tend to solve problems in analogy to the most recent problem they have attempted even though this may not be the best starting point. Although we do not address this issue, our system is at least general enough such that a poor choice of base problem should not prevent a correct, albeit sub-optimal, transformation sequence leading to a solution. As yet, the use of metacognitive tools forcing students to think about their problem solving process has not been very effective [17]. Although $CYNTHIA$ encourages students to think about such issues, they retain control to explore unconventional paths.

There exist many editors that guarantee syntactic correctness (e.g. [11]). We are aware of no editor that provides the additional guarantees that we do.

6 Conclusion

This paper has presented an editor for producing correct functional programs. It builds upon ideas in [4]. The editor is intended to be a suitable vehicle for novices to learn the language ML. Its high-level commands provide guidance to the user and the user is prevented from making certain kinds of programming error.

Our work can be seen on a number of levels. First, as an educational aid, it provides support for novices learning a language by reducing the effort needed to produce correct programs but without restricting the user to text book solutions. Second, as a support tool for ML, it is a way to quickly edit existing programs without introducing unnecessary bugs. Third, it is an interesting application of ideas from the field of automated reasoning.

$CYNTHIA$ is due to be tested on ML students at Napier University from September 1997 onwards.

Acknowledgements: We are grateful to Andrew Cumming for help and discussions on the experiment with his ML students. We also thank Paul Brna and Dave Berry for insightful comments on this paper.

References

1. J. R. Anderson, P. Pirolli, and R. Farrel. Learning to program recursive functions. *The Nature of Expertise*, pages 153–183, 1988.

2. S. Bhuiyan, J. Greer, and G. I. McCalla. Supporting the learning of recursive problem solving. *Interactive Learning Environments*, 4(2):115–139, 1994.
3. P. Brna and J. Good. Searching for examples: An evaluation of an intermediate description language for a techniques editor. In P. Vanneste, K. Bertels, B. de Decker, and J-M. Jaques, editors, *Proceedings of the 8th Annual Workshop of the Psychology of Programming Interest Group*, pages 139–152. 1996.
4. A. Bundy, G. Grosse, and P. Brna. A recursive techniques editor for Prolog. *Instructional Science*, 20:135–172, 1991.
5. Th. Coquand. Pattern matching with dependent types. In *Proceedings from the logical framework workshop at Båstad*, June 1992.
6. D. Duggan and F. Bent. Explaining type inference. *Science of Computer Programming*, 27:37–83, 1996.
7. T.S. Gegg-Harrison. Adapting instruction to the student's capabilities. *Journal of AI in Education*, 3:169–181, 1992.
8. C. Horn and A. Smaill. Theorem proving and program synthesis with Oyster. In *Proceedings of the IMA Unified Computation Laboratory*, Stirling, 1990.
9. W. A. Howard. The formulae-as-types notion of construction. In J. P. Seldin and J. R. Hindley, editors, *To H. B. Curry; Essays on Combinatory Logic, Lambda Calculus and Formalism*, pages 479–490. Academic Press, 1980.
10. M. Kirschenbaum, A. Lakhotia, and L.S. Sterling. Skeletons and techniques for Prolog programming. Technical Report Tr-89-170, Case Western Reserve University, 1989.
11. A. Kohne and G. Weber. Struedi: A lisp-structure editor for novice programmers. In *Human-Computer Interaction (INTERACT 87)*, pages 125–129, 1987.
12. Per Martin-Löf. Constructive mathematics and computer programming. In *6th International Congress for Logic, Methodology and Philosophy of Science*, pages 153–175, Hanover, August 1979. Published by North Holland, Amsterdam. 1982.
13. B.J. McAdam. Adding BigTypes to ML. Tech.rep, August 1996. Available at http://www.dcs.ed.ac.uk /home /bjm /summer96 /tech.ps.
14. David McAllester and Kostas Arkoudas. Walther recursion. In *CADE-13*, pages 643–657. Springer Verlag, July 1996.
15. E. Melis and J. Whittle. External analogy in inductive theorem proving. In *Proceedings of KI97, 21st German Conference on Artificial Intelligence*, 1997.
16. P. L. Pirolli and J. R. Anderson. The role of learning from examples in the acquisition of recursive programming. *Canadian Journal of Psychology*, 39:240–272, 1985.
17. G. Weber. Individual selection of examples in an intelligent learning environment. *Journal of AI in Education*, 7(1):3–31, 1996.
18. G. Weber and A. Bögelsack. *Representation of Programming Episodes in the ELM model*. Ablex Publishing Corporation, Norwood, NJ, 1995.
19. J. Whittle. An analysis of errors encountered by novice ML programmers. Tech.rep, University of Edinburgh, 1996. In http: //www.dai.ed.ac.uk/ daidb/ students/ jonathw/ publications.html.
20. J. Whittle, A. Bundy, and H. Lowe. Supporting programming by analogy in the learning of functional programming languages. In *Proceedings of the 8th World Conference on AI in Education*, 1997. Also available from Dept. of Artificial Intelligence, University of Edinburgh.

Introducing the Declarative Dungeon

David De Roure

University of Southampton, Southampton SO17 1BJ, UK

Abstract. We describe an intermediate programming course, based on *Structure and Interpretation of Computer programs* by Abelson and Sussman, into which we have introduced a Multi User Dungeon (MUD) as an extended example. This example has proved beneficial in a number of respects, and over a period of three years the course has been reorganised to fully exploit this. In particular, the approach enables the students to exercise the engineering design principles taught in the course, by participating in the design and construction of a complex software system. It has also proven to be an effective vehicle for explaining many of the concepts in the course.

Keywords. MUD, Scheme, EuLisp, declarative languages

1 Introduction

Structure and Interpretation of Computer Programs [1] was published in 1985 and has achieved a wide following in the teaching and research community; the second edition was published in 1996. Although the choice of the Scheme dialect of Lisp as the language is in some way incidental to the educational goal of the book, it has also become a classic text in Scheme programming.

This paper describes an undergraduate course based firmly on the philosophy of the book. The course has adopted a novel approach in using a Multi-User Dungeon (MUD) as an extended example for teaching the concepts and principles of the book. We have found this to be an effective and popular device. This is certainly not the first time a MUD has been used in teaching *Structure and Interpretation* (MIT have used the '6.001 Adventure Game' as a problem set for some years), but we believe our adoption of a MUD for this syllabus to be more extensive than elsewhere; more than an incidental device to address one topic, our course has become organised around the MUD.

Section 2 describes the background to the introduction of a MUD into our course There is a brief introduction to salient aspects of MUDs in section 3, followed by a description of the MUD we have implemented in section 4. Section 5 describes the ways in which concepts are taught via the MUD, and this is followed by a discussion of teaching experiences in section 6.

2 Course history

After experimenting with *Structure and Interpretation* in an advanced course, in 1988 a new core module was introduced to our Computer Science degree degree, based on chapters 1 to 4 of the book. The format of the course was closely modelled on the 6.001 course at MIT. Part of our programming stream, the primary aim of the course was to examine a variety of programming techniques in a common linguistic framework and hence teach the engineering principles of program design. It is not the first programming course, but acts as a bridge between the small examples of an introductory course and 'programming in the large'. An optional advanced module, which now draws material from [6], permits the students to followup the programming language aspects.

The course evolved over several years, experiencing a 'philosophy-preserving transformation' as we substituted a new Lisp dialect for Scheme. We adopted EuLisp [5], which provides an object system more in line with those used elsewhere in the degree (i.e. C++, and now Java) and an orthogonal module system. Both these features were found to have pedagogical benefit, and we were also able to introduce some material on threads [4].

In 1995 the degree programme was restructured and the time available for the course reduced from 36 to 24 hours. To move topics out of the course would have defeated its object: the main point is that the course integrates a variety of approaches to programming. Furthermore, we wished to address two persistent items of student feedback:

1. Some students felt the course assumed too great a mathematical proficiency. The mathematical demands are perhaps an inevitable consequence of the first part of the book dealing with abstractions of both procedures and data using only numbers as a primitive type. Rather than removing mathematical content, it was felt that more non-numerical examples (other than symbolic differentiation!) would assist these students.
2. Some students felt that the book continued to work with small examples even though we claimed the course was about working with larger software systems than in the introductory course. One can argue that the principles transcend the scale of the examples. In fact the circuit simulator and constraint propagation examples in the book are good demonstrations of larger systems, but we are unable to cover many applications of this scale. This problem is worsened by the reduced teaching time.

In response to these issues, we redesigned the course to consolidate the diverse examples of *Structure and Interpretation* into a single theme as far as possible. The intention was to save time by reducing the number of different examples, to reduce the dependency on mathematical skills by adopting a non-numerical example for as much of the course as we could and to enable a larger system to be created towards the end of the course. The challenge was to maintain the diversity of programming styles within one theme. Our solution was to introduce a new example: the *Multi-User Dungeon*.

3 MUD background

The first MUD was created by Richard Bartle and Roy Trubshaw at the University of Essex in 1979-80 [2]. Since then different kinds of MUDs have evolved, with various implementations. The MUD Frequently Asked Questions defines a MUD thus:

A MUD (Multiple User Dimension, Multiple User Dungeon, or Multiple User Dialogue) is a computer program which users can log into and explore. Each user takes control of a computerized persona (or avatar, incarnation, character). You can walk around, chat with other characters, explore dangerous monster-infested areas, solve puzzles, and even create your very own rooms, descriptions and items.

Not all MUDs involve monster-infested areas, nor the 'combat features' that characterise some. In MUD terminology, the style of MUD discussed here most closely resembles an LPMud (named after the original author, Lars Penso). LP-Muds are programmed in an object-oriented C dialect called LPC. Also related are the object oriented MUDS called MOOs (Xerox holds a good archive of MOO documents, see the reference for [2]), and these have been exploited in an educational context by Bruckman (e.g. [3]).

A user logs into a MUD and then issues commands. Most LPMuds support the following basic command set:

say message Usually aliased to a quotation mark, **say** sends *message* to every character in the same room in the MUD.

look Displays a description of the room.

look at object Displays a description of a particular object.

who Displays a list of every user in the MUD.

In addition, characters can move around from room to room. The available doors are displayed when a character enters or looks in a room.

4 Our MUD

The MUD is constructed throughout the course and the students do not see a full design at the outset. In fact, some parts of the system are a result of class design exercises and have varied from year to year. It is useful here to outline the major components of our MUD before discussing how we use it to cover our syllabus. The MUD is actually a single-user dungeon ('SUD') for most of the course: it contains multiple characters, but only interacts with one human user.

4.1 Class hierarchy and generic functions

This provides the framework for all the other modules, and is a class (sic) design exercise. Typically, there are classes for rooms, characters and items; rooms and characters may be in a 'container' class as they can contain other objects. We use single inheritance. Last year, students introduced elevators, which can be seen as containers that move between predefined rooms. A standard 'protocol' of generic functions is established, including functions which correspond with user commands (e.g. `look-at`) and functions which are called 'behind the scenes' (e.g. the `clock` function, which is called periodically by the system).

4.2 Description

While students are developing their own MUDs, it is necessary to 'boot' the MUDs easily; this contrasts with MUDs which use some kind of persistent object store. Hence the MUD is constructed by a module which describes its topology, the objects within it and their locations. The classes of objects available for use in the MUD are simply the result of importing available modules, and towards the end of the course we are able to share a variety of modules implemented by the students according to the agreed class hierarchy and protocol.

Initially, the room interconnections and initial locations of objects are established 'manually' by calls to the various constructor functions in the MUD description module. Later we use abstractions which simplify creation of the MUD, forming a library of standard topologies which can be used as building blocks.

4.3 Interaction

The 'SUD' is driven by a special read-eval-print loop which enables the user to act on behalf of various characters in the dungeon by naming them, e.g.

```
(Alyssa lookat attic)
(Ben pickup bit)
(Eva say see you later)
(Louis quit)
(Newton drop apple)
(Oliver read bottle)
(Simpson shout doh)
```

Initially, the interaction loop calls the various methods on the appropriate objects, and is not extensible. We later decouple the interaction from the method calls, inserting an event list and scheduler. The interaction just schedules the events, and the main driver loop takes the next event from the event list and executes it.

4.4 Driver

The decoupling of the interaction from the method calls improves the modularity of the system. It also enables events to be scheduled other than by the interaction loop: instead of one method calling another method, it can schedule that call for the future (this has obvious parallels in event driven systems). We introduce one function in particular which causes a 'clock-tick' to occur every 60 units of simulation time:

```
(define clock ()
  (clock-tick! *the-mud*)
  (schedule 60 (lambda () (clock))))
```

The scheduler is supported by the 'event list' module, which permits events to be scheduled a given number of time units in the future, and the next event to be retrieved. It is an effective early exercise in designing and implementing a data structure, with attention to the complexity of update and retrieve operations. This requirement is similar to the 'agenda' implementation for the circuit simulator in *Structure and Interpretation* although it usually yields simpler implementations.

By considering what it means to schedule an event after zero delay, we are able to discuss causality issues. We also discuss the paradigm of 'posting' an event rather than making a function call directly, which is an important consideration for event driven applications.

4.5 Distribution

At the end of the course we are able to provide multiuser access to the MUD using a simple telnet 'multiplexor'. This is a process which accepts multiple incoming telnet connections and relays data from each to the EuLisp listener, which schedules the appropriate events. The multiplexor identifies the character name when the telnet connection is first established, and inserts this in the commands as they are propagated; meanwhile, data from the MUD is directed back to the appropriate user by a similar mechanism. The multiplexor ensures that messages to the MUD are sequentialised, so there are no problems of concurrent access.

It is interesting to consider a distributed implementation of the MUD itself, perhaps with multiple SUDs interacting. Although we have a prototype of such as system, to date we have not used this in the course.

5 Teaching with the MUD

In this section we discuss how various key topics in *Structure and Interpretation* are taught using the MUD.

5.1 Abstraction of procedures and data

We have not changed the way in which we teach the first part of the course: recursion and iteration, complexity and higher order functions are all treated in the traditional manner. This is because many of the students have previously attended an SML course and many of the examples are already familiar to them, so the main purpose of this material is to teach Lisp as a side effect as rapidly as possible. Those students who have not attended an SML course are able to do background work directly from *Structure and Interpretation* and its supporting material.

The MUD material makes frequent reference to this part of the course, so we do have MUD examples with which this material could be taught. This would rely on introducing symbols earlier, more in the line of some other Lisp texts, but it is not clear that these examples would be any more effective than the existing numerical ones.

5.2   Abstraction diagrams

We first use abstraction diagrams as a vehicle for discussing modules. Modules are introduced relatively early in the course; they are orthogonal to classes and can therefore be introduced before discussion of the object system.

From a pragmatic viewpoint, modules provide a convenient mechanism for the weekly exercises: they enable us to provide some existing code to the students in support of an exercise and we can ask the students to create new code in a module of its own. Over the course of several weeks, the students build up the modules that they will later use in the MUD. They can use their own modules, or the 'model answers' that are provided when exercises have been submitted.

We later use abstraction diagrams to discuss data directed programming, and we focus on the dispatch table to discuss data directed dispatch. This table is the key to introducing the object system, where the table entries correspond to methods. It also enables us to demonstrate the orthogonality of modules, because we can group methods into modules in arbitrary ways. Hence we discuss organisation of code. Figure 1 illustrates a simple dispatch table.

	cup	cwk	room
look-at	look-at-cup	look-at-cwk	look-at-room
drop	drop-cup	drop-cwk	
clock	clock-cup	clock-cwk	clock-room

Fig. 1. Dispatch table.

5.3   State

We have replaced the traditional bank account example with an equivalent example which is later used in the MUD. There are many possibilities, and our most successful one has been the cup of coffee. A cup contains a volume of coffee, more coffee can be 'deposited', coffee can be 'withdrawn' by sipping, and when empty the cup provides no more coffee. Unlike a bank account, it is possible to overflow the cup, i.e. there is a ceiling to be checked when increasing the value.

The attraction of this example is that it fits neatly into the MUD metaphor. We can extend it later to demonstrate the passage of time: the coffee temperature falls, and the cup might leak. A cup is an object that can be passed from character to character, left in a room, dropped etc. Finally, there may be some consequence to drinking the coffee.

5.4 Streams

Although streams are not a paradigm used in other courses, we find it useful to introduce a new paradigm here and to consider it alongside the others: streams are particularly thought-provoking. By considering the MUD as a stream processor, the problems of 'purely-functional operating systems' are easy to explain.

The possibility of infinite structures takes on a new fascination within the MUD metaphor. It is possible to deal with infinite streams of objects, and hence infinite sized MUDs, infinite numbers of characters, etc. The endless supply of objects is not the most interesting aspect, but rather the delayed evaluation: a MUD can be constructed lazily, with the rooms being elaborated only when a character enters them. Students enjoy building an infinite list of integers and seeing parts elaborated, but there appears to be something even more compelling about creating an infinite building and seeing parts of that elaborated whilst walking around inside it.

The prime sieve is a traditional streams example and we can demonstrate the sieve principles in the MUD in an interesting way. We use characters to represent prime numbers and move them through a series of rooms. They only leave a room if they cannot be divided by any of the numbers in the room, else they are eliminated. Numbers emerging from the final room are known to be prime relative to the room contents of all rooms. The prime then goes and stands in one of the rooms. Intuitively the rooms are processing in parallel.

5.5 Metalinguistic Abstraction

The MUD is particularly rich in this area. It allows us to discuss the creation of three languages: the interaction language, the MUD description language and the object behaviour language. There is potential for more; e.g. a scripting language to program characters, and an inter-character communication language.

The user interacts via the special read-eval-print loop which translates user commands to function calls (for direct or delayed execution). Most of these commands are looked up in a table; some require processing which deviates from this default behaviour. These can be constructed in the style of an interpreter. By providing an 'alias' mechanism, users can add new commands to the table within the interaction, akin to simple function definition.

The MUD description language is directly analogous to the circuit description language in *Structure and Interpretation*: it describes rooms and their interconnection. Using higher-order functions we can build abstractions of particular MUD constructions. The following sequence of constructions was used in a recent course:

- A 'chain' of rooms with a door at each end;
- A 'circle' of rooms, created by joining the ends of a chain or multiple chains;
- A 'grid' of rooms with doors to north, south, east and west;
- A 'block' of rooms, as above but with doors to top and bottom also.
- A construction which could be embedded on a torus, built by joining the edges of a grid;

- A construction which could be embedded on a sphere, built by joining multiple grids;
- Constructions based on Moebius strips and Klein bottles.

One of the simple construction exercises, the 'treehouse', is presented in appendix A.

The third opportunity for metalinguistic abstraction is the language used to describe the behaviour of objects. This is of course Lisp, but by this stage in the course it is clear that there are some useful linguistic abstractions which can be introduced. In fact we use this as a means of introducing syntactic vs. semantic issues. Firstly we use macros to capture common patterns of code, and we then discuss changing the behaviour of the object system using the meta-object protocol. The example that motivates this is the desire to automate the calls to methods in the superclass when a particular method fails (returns false), as the initial implementation does this explicitly (as in LPC).

5.6 Query language

At the end of the course we are able to 'plug in' the query language from *Structure and Interpretation* so that we can ask questions about the MUD - we derive the facts from the object hierarchy. This is a simple introduction to logic programming ideas; it also introduces a good demonstration of the modularity and multiple paradigms used in the system because the query language actually uses streams in its implementation. There is potential, but not time, for taking this much further.

5.7 Miscellaneous topics

Two ideas which emerged in class discussions are easy to incorporate, interesting to discuss and can introduce relevant concepts. Firstly, the scheduling mechanism can be used to schedule the creation or modification of rooms and their interconnections, hence characters can schedule future actions to change the MUD structure, or the topology of the MUD can evolve automatically over a period of time.

The other example is particularly thought provoking. When a character talks to an object they are essentially sending it a command, and the effect of this is usually isolated to that object. If we let the object execute actions with wider effect, typically by calling parts of the MUD implementation, then it takes on 'magical' qualities.

A simple example is the mobile phone (walkie-talkie, communicator) object with which characters can talk directly to each other regardless of whether or not they are in the same room (in fact, some LPMuds support a **tell** command to achieve this, though it breaks the spatial metaphor). Extending this, we can locate 'computer' objects in various rooms, and the characters can communicate via these with IRC-style commands. Finally, the computers can be running a MUD (either *a* MUD or *the* MUD); e.g. a character can enter a room, sit at a computer, type a command, and this command is executed as part of a separate MUD or indeed as part of the current MUD.

This leads to discussion of modularity and state. If the MUD has been designed well, it is easy to embed an entirely separate MUD (this is directly analogous to the issues of calling `eval` in Lisp: how do the side effects of the evaluation affect the state of the calling program?) It also leads to discussion of reflection, and of the infinite tower where the character finds a computer with a MUD and controls a character which finds a computer with a MUD... etc.

6   Evaluation

We have only qualitative feedback on the adoption of the MUD, together with what can be inferred from comparison with mark distributions for other courses. Our main observations are:

1. We have succeeded in covering the material in a reduced time.
2. We have gained a useful class design exercise which is felt to reinforce the principles of the course in new ways.
3. Teaching staff have found that the course attracts better performance from students who are otherwise felt to be poor performers, and there is no indication that we lose the interest of any students.
4. There are no longer reported problems with mathematical content.
5. There are positive comments about the MUD from students of all abilities; i.e. it is *popular*.

Although the staff involved in assessment feel that there are comparatively fewer poor performers, it is difficult to demonstrate this statistically in the absence of a reliable control. Changes in the mark distribution are not out of line with changes in other courses.

7   Conclusion and future work

Structure and Interpretation is an excellent book and students have always enjoyed the course. We have introduced a new example which has both improved the effectiveness of the course within our degree programme and maintained the popularity of the course.

We are considering extending the MUD to help teach event driven programming and distributed systems, including concurrency and non-determinism (these topics are addressed in the second edition of the book). In previous courses we have successfully used an LPMud to support online tutorials, and we plan to repeat this using the Declarative MUD. We anticipate that the MUD will be sufficiently mature next year to use it to support collaboration between students.

References

1. H. Abelson and G.J. Sussman with Julie Sussman. *Structure and Interpretation of Computer Programs*. MIT Press, 1985. (First edition).
2. Richard Bartle. Interactive multi-user computer games. Technical report, MUSE Ltd., December 1990. Available from parcftp.xerox.com in pub/MOO/papers/mudreport.*.
3. Amy Bruckman. Programming for fun: Muds as a context for collaborative learning. In *National Educational Computing Conference*, June 1994. Available online as ftp://media.mit.edu/pub/asb/papers/necc94.*.
4. D.C. De Roure and R.J. Bradford. EuLisp in Education. *Lisp and Symbolic Computation*, 6(1-2), 1993.
5. J.A. Padget, G. Nuyens, and H. Bretthauer. An Overview of EuLisp. *Lisp and Symbolic Computation*, 6(1-2), 1993.
6. Christian Queinnec. *Lisp in Small Pieces*. Cambridge University Press, 1996.

8 Acknowledgments

David Barron introduced *Structure and Interpretation* to our Computer Science degree course, and thanks are due to Jim Miller for helping us set up the CM203 module in 1988 based entirely on the book. David has taught the course with me again recently and I am very grateful to him and all my academic colleagues who have supported the course, especially Peter Henderson, Hugh Glaser and Eric Cooke; Stephen Adams originally assisted with teaching CM203 and subsequently graduated to 6.001, and I am grateful to him for recent discussions of Problem Set 6 (*'Dulce et decorum est pro computore mori'*). The use of an LPC MUD for teaching was inspired and encouraged by Tim Chown, who built an example MUD for class use and gave me valuable insights. Thanks also to Christian Queinnec for providing additional inspiration and indeed teaching materials. Finally, I am indebted to a series of excellent postgraduate assistants, and ten years of enthusiastic students.

A The treehouse exercise

The exercise was to define a function to assemble the building shown in figure 2. The building has one entrance, and each room has two exits, each of which is the entrance to another such room; the final row of rooms have no exits. (If you consider the first rooms to be corridors, this is a common layout of office buildings.)

Here are two interesting solutions. The first uses a function f which takes zero or more doors as arguments and creates a room, returning a new door to that room. The function tree constructs the building and returns the door which is the entrance to the building.

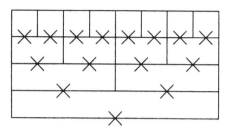

Fig. 2. The treehouse.

```
(defun tree (f depth)
  (if (= depth 0)
      (f)
      (f (tree f (- depth 1))
         (tree f (- depth 1)))))
```

The second is more in the style of the circuit simulator in [1]. Neither the f function nor the **tree** function itself return useful values (i.e. they are executed only for their side effects) but the definition is itself declarative in style. The function **tree** takes the entrance door as an additional argument.

```
(defun tree (f door depth)
  (if (= depth 0)
      (f door)
      (let ((1 (make-door))
            (r (make-door)))
         (f door 1 r)
         (tree f 1 (- depth 1))
         (tree f r (- depth 1)))))
```

A Pragmatic Approach to Compilation of Erlang

Erik Johansson[1], Christer Jonsson[1], Thomas Lindgren[1], Johan Bevemyr[2],
Håkan Millroth[2]

[1] Computing Science Department, Uppsala University
[2] Computer Science Laboratories, Ericsson Telecom AB

We have developed a native code compiler for Erlang [2], a concurrent functional language for embedded soft real-time applications. Measurements show that our system is roughly twice as fast as the best existing Erlang compiler, BEAM [3] on SPARC machines.

Setting. We had two design constraints when writing the compiler. First, Erlang supports code replacement at runtime: running processes may replace their code and continue running. This makes interprocedural optimization awkward, since code replacement invalidates cross-module static analyses and inlining. The current compiler emphasizes intraprocedural optimizations.

Second, code space is often at a premium in an embedded setting. For this reason, we add our compiler as a minimal extension to an existing system, JAM [1], which is built on stack-oriented bytecode emulation. The compiler acts as an *accelerator* for executing JAM bytecode, much as just-in-time Java compilers accelerate the execution of JVM bytecode. The system supports efficient mixed bytecode and native code execution, so that it is possible to trade code size for execution speed.

Compiling to native code. We compile directly into SPARC machine code, since translation into C appears to offer little benefit beyond (potentially) easier retargeting. Since our work is oriented towards low-level compiler optimizations, there is no point in hiding the machine by generating C code.

Techniques and optimizations. Our native compiler translates JAM bytecodes into native code in three steps.

1. Translate stack bytecodes into register based three-address code using Ertl's technique [4]. Some arithmetic primitives are inline expanded in this phase.
2. Perform global optimizations on the code: constant propagation, constant folding, dead code elimination and unreachable code removal.
3. Finally, generate code. Translate the three-address code into SPARC code, perform register allocation (using graph coloring) and fill branch delay slots.

The compiler furthermore optimizes function calls by passing arguments in registers and reduces the 4-word stack frame of JAM into a 1-word frame.

Results. We compared our system with BEAM [3], an Erlang compiler that generates C code (or, optionally, threaded code), and JAM [1], a bytecode interpreter. JAM is the predominant implementation in use today, while BEAM is currently being introduced.

Measuring a range of ten benchmarks of varying sizes on MicroSPARC, HyperSPARC and UltraSPARC workstations we find that, depending on the machine, our system is 1.8-2.1 times faster than BEAM (using geometric means per machine) and 5.9-8.9 times faster than JAM. The benchmarks were fully native compiled for both our system and BEAM.

We find that global optimizations, delay slot filling and passing arguments in registers yield a compound 28% improvement on unoptimized code. Reducing the size of the stack frame, returning the function result in a register and inlining arithmetic primitives provides a further 30-40% improvement.

We compare compile times and compiled code size with BEAM by compiling the entire benchmark suite. We find that our compiler generates 3-5 machine instructions for each JAM byte, yielding a code expansion of 10-20 times, and that BEAM generates code 1.6 times larger than ours, while requiring ten times the compile time (mainly due to invoking the C compiler).

	Compile time (s)	Code size (KB)	Exec. time (ratio)
Our	45	196	1.0
BEAM	464	315	1.8-2.1
JAM	11	9	5.9-8.9

We refer the reader to a companion technical report [5] for more details.

References

1. Armstrong, J.L., Däcker, B.O., Virding, S.R. and Williams, M.C., Implementing a functional language for highly parallel real-time applications, in *Proc. Software Engineering for Telecommunication Switching Systems*, 1992.
2. Armstrong, J.L., Virding, S.R., Wikström, C., and Williams, M.C., *Concurrent Programming in Erlang*. Prentice Hall, second edition, 1996.
3. Hausman, B., Turbo Erlang: Approaching the Speed of C, *Implementations of Logic Programming Systems*, pp. 119–135, Kluwer Academic Publishers, 1994.
4. Ertl, M.A., A New Approach to Forth Native Code Generation, *Proc. EuroForth '92*, pp. 73-78.
5. Johansson, E., Jonsson, C., Lindgren, T., Bevemyr, J., Millroth, H., A pragmatic approach to compilation of Erlang. Technical report 136 (revised, June 1997), Computing Science Department, Uppsala University.

Formal Translations Described by Translation Grammars with $LR(k)$ Input Grammars

Jan Janoušek and Bořivoj Melichar

Department of Computer Science and Engineering
Czech Technical University, Karlovo nám. 13, 121 35, Prague, Czech Republic
e-mail: {janousej|melichar}@cs.felk.cvut.cz

Syntax–directed translations belong to fundamental principles of the compiler construction theory. This paper presents a one-pass formal translator that can be constructed for each translation grammar with an $LR(k)$ input grammar. The formal translator is the conventional LR parser whose operations are extended by actions performing both an output and a temporary storing of output symbols. The temporary storing of some symbols before their appending to the output string is implemented by using one synthesized attribute.

In comparison with the conventional implementation of such translations by evaluating the attributes ([3]), the presented translation technique has these two advantages: First, it decreases the size of memory used. Second, the output string is being created during the parsing process of the input string.

A *context-free translation grammar* is a 5-tuple $TG = (N, T, D, R, S)$, where N, T and D are finite sets of *nonterminal, input* and *output symbols*, respectively. R is a finite set of *rules* $A \to \alpha$, where $A \in N$, $\alpha \in (N \cup T \cup D)^*$; $S \in N$ is the *start symbol*. Relation $\Rightarrow_{rm}$ is called *rightmost derivation*: if $\alpha A \gamma \Rightarrow_{rm} \alpha \beta \gamma$, $A \in N$, α, $\beta \in (N \cup T \cup D)^*$, and $\gamma \in (T \cup D)^*$, then rule $A \to \beta \in R$. The set $NOut$ is defined as $NOut = \{A \in N : A \Rightarrow^*_{rm} w_1 y w_2, y \in D\}$. The *input homomorphism* h_i and the *output homomorphism* h_o from $(N \cup T \cup D)^*$ to $(N \cup T \cup D)^*$ are defined as follows: $h_i(a) = a$ for $a \in (N \cup T)$, or ε for $a \in D$; $h_o(a) = \varepsilon$ for $a \in T$, or a for $a \in (N \cup D)$. The *formal translation* defined by a translation grammar TG is the set $Z(TG) = \{(h_i(w), h_o(w)) : S \Rightarrow^*_{rm} w, w \in (T \cup D)^*\}$. Given an input string $x \in T^*$, the LR parser, which is implemented by deterministic pushdown automaton, performs a sequence of *shift* and *reduce* operations and follows the rightmost derivation $S \Rightarrow^*_{rm} w$, where $h_i(w) = x$, in reverse ([1]). An *attributed translation grammar* $ATG = (TG, AD, F)$, where TG is the underlying translation grammar, AD is a description of attributes and F is a finite set of attribute rules, represents a formalism for specifying the semantics ([2]).

A formal translator is described in two tables TPT and TGT:
- A translation parsing table TPT is a collection of rows. Its columns are for all elements of the set T^{*k}. Its values are either $shift(z_0, X_1.s, z_1, \ldots, X_m.s, z_m)$, $reduce\ i[\Psi](z_0, X_1.s, z_1, \ldots, X_m.s, z_m)$, *error*, or *accept*, where $X_1, \ldots, X_m \in NOut$, $z_0, z_1, \ldots, z_m \in D^*$, $m \geq 0$, $\Psi \in \{\bot, A.s : A \in NOut\}$.
- A translation goto table TGT has the same rows as the table TPT. Its columns are for all elements from the set $(N \cup T)$. Its values are either M_i (for columns $a \in T$) , $M_i(z_0, X_1.s, z_1, \ldots, X_m.s, z_m)$ (for col. $A \in N$) or *error*, where M_i is the name of a row of TPT, $X_1, \ldots, X_m \in NOut$, $z_0, z_1, \ldots, z_m \in D^*$, $m \geq 0$.

Example: Consider an attributed translation grammar $ATG = (TG, AD, F)$, where $TG = (\{S, A, B\}, \{a, b\}, D, R, S)$, $D = \{x, y, w, z\}$, $AD = (\{s\}, \emptyset, \{s\}$, $TYPE(s) = D^*)$, R and F are given by these grammar and attribute rules:

(1)	S	$\rightarrow A$	$S.s = A.s$
(2)	S	$\rightarrow B$	$S.s = B.s$
(3)	A^0	$\rightarrow xaA^1$	$A^0.s = concat('x', A^1.s)$
(4)	A	$\rightarrow y$	$A.s = 'y'$
(5)	B^0	$\rightarrow aB^1w$	$B^0.s = concat(B^1.s, 'w')$
(6)	B	$\rightarrow zb$	$B.s = 'z'$

$Z(TG) = \{(a^n, x^ny), (a^nb, zw^n) : n \geq 0\}$. The following table includes both TPT and TGT tables that describe the formal translator constructed for ATG.

	a	b	ε	S	A	B	a	b
#	shift(ε)	shift('z')	reduce $4[\bot]$('y')	$S(\varepsilon)$	$A_1(\varepsilon)$	$B_1(\varepsilon)$	a_1	b
S			accept					
A_1			reduce $1[\bot](\varepsilon)$					
A_2			reduce $3[\bot](\varepsilon)$					
A_3			reduce $3[A.s](\varepsilon)$					
B_1			reduce $2[\bot](\varepsilon)$					
B_2			reduce $5[\bot]$('w')					
a_1	shift(ε)	shift('z')	reduce $4[A.s](\varepsilon)$		$A_2('x', A.s)$	$B_2(\varepsilon)$	a_2	b
a_2	shift(ε)	shift('z')	reduce $4[A.s](\varepsilon)$		$A_3(\varepsilon)$	$B_2(\varepsilon)$	a_2	b
b			reduce $6[\bot](\varepsilon)$					

A configuration of the formal translator is a triple (α, x, y), where α is the contents of the LR parser pushdown store, x is the unused part of the input string, and y is the created part of the output string.

The formal translator described above performs the following sequences of moves for pairs $(aaa, xxxy)$ and $(aaab, zwww) \in Z(TG)$:

(# | ,aaa ,ε)	$\vdash$ (#a_1 | ,aa ,ε)	$\vdash$ (#a_1a_2 | ,a ,ε) $\vdash$

$(\#a_1a_2a_2, \varepsilon, \varepsilon) \vdash (\#a_1a_2a_2A_3(y), \varepsilon, \varepsilon) \vdash (\#a_1a_2A_3(xy), \varepsilon, \varepsilon) \vdash$

$(\#a_1A_2, \varepsilon, xxxy) \vdash (\#A_1, \varepsilon, xxxy) \vdash$

$(\#S, \varepsilon, xxxy) \vdash$ accept

$(\#, aaab, \varepsilon) \vdash (\#a_1, aab, \varepsilon) \vdash (\#a_1a_2, ab, \varepsilon) \vdash$

$(\#a_1a_2a_2, b, \varepsilon) \vdash (\#a_1a_2a_2b, \varepsilon, z) \vdash (\#a_1a_2a_2B_2, \varepsilon, z) \vdash$

$(\#a_1a_2B_2, \varepsilon, zw) \vdash (\#a_1B_2, \varepsilon, zww) \vdash$

$(\#B_1, \varepsilon, zwww) \vdash (\#S, \varepsilon, zwww) \vdash$ accept

References

[1] Aho, A.V., Ullman, J.D. *The Theory of Parsing, Translation and Compiling.* Vol.1: Parsing, Vol.2: Compiling. New York. Prentice–Hall, 1971, 2.

[2] Alblas, H., Melichar, B. (Eds.) *Attribute Grammars, Applications and Systems.* Lecture Notes in Computer Science, vol 545, Springer–Verlag, Berlin, 1991.

[3] Aho, A.V., Sethi, R., Ullman, J.D. *Compilers – Principles, Techniques and Tools.* Addison–Wesley, Reading, Mass., 1986.

Automatic Run-Time Code Generation in Object-Oriented Languages

Nobuhisa Fujinami

Sony Computer Science Laboratory Inc.

1 Introduction

Run-time code generation improves programs by generating machine code specific to values that are unknown until run time. it is becoming a mature technique, but in the existing systems, the programmer must rewrite the source code to initiate run-time code generation, to invoke the generated machine code, and to maintain consistency between the embedded values in the code and the actual values.

This paper shows that object-oriented languages provide useful information for run-time code generation. It also proposes a system for automatic run-time code generation, code invocation, and management. This is an extention of the already proposed automatic run-time code generation system [Fuj95].

The goals of the run-time code generation system proposed in this paper are automation and efficiency. The programmer is freed from annotating programs and from providing suitable parameters to the system to preserve consistency. The output run-time code generator and the code it generates are both optimized.

2 Run-time Code Generation in Object-Oriented Languages

The machine code generated at run time is optimized to values that are unknown until run time, e.g. intermediate results of computation and the user's inputs. If programs operating on these values are written in object-oriented languages, it is natural to define objects with instance variables that represent the values known at run time.

The benefits of focusing on instance variables of objects are as follows:

Automatic code generation/invalidation: Using the definition of the object, all the assignments to non-public instance variables (e.g. `private` data members in C++) can be known. Values of these variables can be embedded consistently into generated machine code.

Automatic management of generated code: Management of generated code can be left to the object construction/destruction mechanism of object-oriented languages. Generated code can be viewed as a part of the object.

These benefits achieves the first goal. Methods that use "known" instance variables are replaced with machine code routines generated at run time. The values of the "known" instance variables are embedded into the routines with optimizations specific to the values.

3 Implementation

The proposed system is implemented as a preprocessor of a C++ compiler. Keyword `runtime` before a declaration of a member function indicates the use

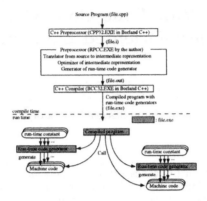

Fig. 1. Organization of the implemented system

of run-time code generation. The system assumes all the **private**, **protected**, or **const** data members used but not changed in that member function to be run-time constants.

Figure 1 shows an overall organization of the implementation of the system. The upper half illustrates the compilation, and the lower half illustrates the program execution. Source program and its intermediate representation are manipulated only at this compile time.

The output code generators not only are specialized to methods but also have embedded specialized optimization routines, such as global run-time constant propagators, full loop unrollers, or dynamic method dispatch determiners specific to the program. This achieves the second goal.

4 Evaluation

Program	execution time (normal / optimized)	ratio
Ray tracer	42.6 / 30.4 sec	1.40
Puzzle solver	72.3 / 36.9 sec	1.96

Table 1. Evaluation results

The evaluation is done using Borland C++ Version 5.0J compiler for Microsoft Windows 95 Operating System running on NEC PC-9821St15/L16 (Pentium Pro 150MHz, 48MBytes). The compiler options are `-6 -O2 -OS -vi`.

Table 1 shows the results. The first program is a ray tracer. The second program is a box-packing puzzle solver. In both cases, the optimized programs run faster than the normal ones.

The cost for code generation is 625 microseconds per 7638 bytes of generated instructions, or about 12 machine cycles per bytes, in the case of the ray tracer.

5 Conclusion

This paper proposed an automatic run-time code generation, code invocation, and management system for object-oriented languages such as C++. The implementation and the evaluation results show that an object-oriented language allows run-time code generation from a simple analysis of source programs.

References

[Fuj95] Nobuhisa Fujinami. Run-Time Optimization in Object-Oriented Languages. In *Proceedings of 12th Conference of Japan Society for Software Science and Technology*, September 1995. In Japanese. Received Takahashi Award.

Author Index

Lecture Notes in Computer Science

For information about Vols. 1–1211

please contact your bookseller or Springer-Verlag